Get the eBook FREE!

(PDF, ePub, Kindle, and liveBook all included)

We believe that once you buy a book from us, you should be able to read it in any format we have available. To get electronic versions of this book at no additional cost to you, purchase and then register this book at the Manning website.

Go to https://www.manning.com/freebook and follow the instructions to complete your pBook registration.

That's it!
Thanks from Manning!

Deep Learning
with PyTorch

ELI STEVENS, LUCA ANTIGA,
AND THOMAS VIEHMANN
FOREWORD BY SOUMITH CHINTALA

MANNING
SHELTER ISLAND

For online information and ordering of this and other Manning books, please visit
www.manning.com. The publisher offers discounts on this book when ordered in quantity.
For more information, please contact

    Special Sales Department
    Manning Publications Co.
    20 Baldwin Road
    PO Box 761
    Shelter Island, NY 11964
    Email: orders@manning.com

Manning Publications Co.
20 Baldwin Road
PO Box 761
Shelter Island, NY 11964

Development editor:	Frances Lefkowitz
Technical development editor:	Arthur Zubarev
Review editor:	Ivan Martinović
Production editor:	Deirdre Hiam
Copyeditor:	Tiffany Taylor
Proofreader:	Katie Tennant
Technical proofreader:	Kostas Passadis
Typesetter:	Gordan Salinovic
Cover designer:	Marija Tudor

ISBN 9781617295263
Printed in the United States of America

To my wife (this book would not have happened without her invaluable support and partnership),
my parents (I would not have happened without them),
and my children (this book would have happened a lot sooner but for them).

Thank you for being my home, my foundation, and my joy.
                                                            —Eli Stevens

Same :-) But, really, this is for you, Alice and Luigi.
                                                            —Luca Antiga

To Eva, Rebekka, Jonathan, and David.
                                                            —Thomas Viehmann

contents

foreword

When we started the PyTorch project in mid-2016, we were a band of open source hackers who met online and wanted to write better deep learning software. Two of the three authors of this book, Luca Antiga and Thomas Viehmann, were instrumental in developing PyTorch and making it the success that it is today.

Our goal with PyTorch was to build the most flexible framework possible to express deep learning algorithms. We executed with focus and had a relatively short development time to build a polished product for the developer market. This wouldn't have been possible if we hadn't been standing on the shoulders of giants. PyTorch derives a significant part of its codebase from the Torch7 project started in 2007 by Ronan Collobert and others, which has roots in the Lush programming language pioneered by Yann LeCun and Leon Bottou. This rich history helped us focus on what needed to change, rather than conceptually starting from scratch.

It is hard to attribute the success of PyTorch to a single factor. The project offers a good user experience and enhanced debuggability and flexibility, ultimately making users more productive. The huge adoption of PyTorch has resulted in a beautiful ecosystem of software and research built on top of it, making PyTorch even richer in its experience.

Several courses and university curricula, as well as a huge number of online blogs and tutorials, have been offered to make PyTorch easier to learn. However, we have seen very few books. In 2017, when someone asked me, "When is the PyTorch book going to be written?" I responded, "If it gets written now, I can guarantee that it will be outdated by the time it is completed."

With the publication of *Deep Learning with PyTorch*, we finally have a definitive treatise on PyTorch. It covers the basics and abstractions in great detail, tearing apart the underpinnings of data structures like tensors and neural networks and making sure you understand their implementation. Additionally, it covers advanced subjects such as JIT and deployment to production (an aspect of PyTorch that no other book currently covers).

Additionally, the book covers applications, taking you through the steps of using neural networks to help solve a complex and important medical problem. With Luca's deep expertise in bioengineering and medical imaging, Eli's practical experience creating software for medical devices and detection, and Thomas's background as a PyTorch core developer, this journey is treated carefully, as it should be.

All in all, I hope this book becomes your "extended" reference document and an important part of your library or workshop.

SOUMITH CHINTALA
COCREATOR OF PYTORCH

preface

As kids in the 1980s, taking our first steps on our Commodore VIC 20 (Eli), the Sinclair Spectrum 48K (Luca), and the Commodore C16 (Thomas), we saw the dawn of personal computers, learned to code and write algorithms on ever-faster machines, and often dreamed about where computers would take us. We also were painfully aware of the gap between what computers did in movies and what they could do in real life, collectively rolling our eyes when the main character in a spy movie said, "Computer, enhance."

Later on, during our professional lives, two of us, Eli and Luca, independently challenged ourselves with medical image analysis, facing the same kind of struggle when writing algorithms that could handle the natural variability of the human body. There was a lot of heuristics involved when choosing the best mix of algorithms that could make things work and save the day. Thomas studied neural nets and pattern recognition at the turn of the century but went on to get a PhD in mathematics doing modeling.

When deep learning came about at the beginning of the 2010s, making its initial appearance in computer vision, it started being applied to medical image analysis tasks like the identification of structures or lesions on medical images. It was at that time, in the first half of the decade, that deep learning appeared on our individual radars. It took a bit to realize that deep learning represented a whole new way of writing software: a new class of multipurpose algorithms that could learn how to solve complicated tasks through the observation of data.

To our kids-of-the-80s minds, the horizon of what computers could do expanded overnight, limited not by the brains of the best programmers, but by the data, the neural network architecture, and the training process. The next step was getting our hands dirty. Luca choose Torch 7 (http://torch.ch), a venerable precursor to PyTorch; it's nimble, lightweight, and fast, with approachable source code written in Lua and plain C, a supportive community, and a long history behind it. For Luca, it was love at first sight. The only real drawback with Torch 7 was being detached from the ever-growing Python data science ecosystem that the other frameworks could draw from. Eli had been interested in AI since college,[1] but his career pointed him in other directions, and he found other, earlier deep learning frameworks a bit too laborious to get enthusiastic about using them for a hobby project.

So we all got really excited when the first PyTorch release was made public on January 18, 2017. Luca started contributing to the core, and Eli was part of the community very early on, submitting the odd bug fix, feature, or documentation update. Thomas contributed a ton of features and bug fixes to PyTorch and eventually became one of the independent core contributors. There was the feeling that something big was starting up, at the right level of complexity and with a minimal amount of cognitive overhead. The lean design lessons learned from the Torch 7 days were being carried over, but this time with a modern set of features like automatic differentiation, dynamic computation graphs, and NumPy integration.

Given our involvement and enthusiasm, and after organizing a couple of PyTorch workshops, writing a book felt like a natural next step. The goal was to write a book that would have been appealing to our former selves getting started just a few years back.

Predictably, we started with grandiose ideas: teach the basics, walk through end-to-end projects, and demonstrate the latest and greatest models in PyTorch. We soon realized that would take a lot more than a single book, so we decided to focus on our initial mission: devote time and depth to cover the key concepts underlying PyTorch, assuming little or no prior knowledge of deep learning, and get to the point where we could walk our readers through a complete project. For the latter, we went back to our roots and chose to demonstrate a medical image analysis challenge.

---

[1] Back when "deep" neural networks meant *three* hidden layers!

acknowledgments

We are deeply indebted to the PyTorch team. It is through their collective effort that PyTorch grew organically from a summer internship project to a world-class deep learning tool. We would like to mention Soumith Chintala and Adam Paszke, who, in addition to their technical excellence, worked actively toward adopting a "community first" approach to managing the project. The level of health and inclusiveness in the PyTorch community is a testament to their actions.

Speaking of community, PyTorch would not be what it is if not for the relentless work of individuals helping early adopters and experts alike on the discussion forum. Of all the honorable contributors, Piotr Bialecki deserves our particular badge of gratitude. Speaking of the book, a particular shout-out goes to Joe Spisak, who believed in the value that this book could bring to the community, and also Jeff Smith, who did an incredible amount of work to bring that value to fruition. Bruce Lin's work to excerpt part 1 of this text and provide it to the PyTorch community free of charge is also hugely appreciated.

We would like to thank the team at Manning for guiding us through this journey, always aware of the delicate balance between family, job, and writing in our respective lives. Thanks to Erin Twohey for reaching out and asking if we'd be interested in writing a book, and thanks to Michael Stephens for tricking us into saying yes. We *told* you we had no time! Brian Hanafee went above and beyond a reviewer's duty. Arthur Zubarev and Kostas Passadis gave great feedback, and Jennifer Houle had to deal with our wacky art style. Our copyeditor, Tiffany Taylor, has an impressive eye for detail; any mistakes are ours and ours alone. We would also like to thank our project editor,

Deirdre Hiam, our proofreader, Katie Tennant, and our review editor, Ivan Martinović. There are also a host of people working behind the scenes, glimpsed only on the CC list of status update threads, and all necessary to bring this book to print. Thank you to every name we've left off this list! The anonymous reviewers who gave their honest feedback helped make this book what it is.

Frances Lefkowitz, our tireless editor, deserves a medal and a week on a tropical island after dragging this book over the finish line. Thank you for all you've done and for the grace with which you did it.

We would also like to thank our reviewers, who have helped to improve our book in many ways: Aleksandr Erofeev, Audrey Carstensen, Bachir Chihani, Carlos Andres Mariscal, Dale Neal, Daniel Berecz, Doniyor Ulmasov, Ezra Stevens, Godfred Asamoah, Helen Mary Labao Barrameda, Hilde Van Gysel, Jason Leonard, Jeff Coggshall, Kostas Passadis, Linnsey Nil, Mathieu Zhang, Michael Constant, Miguel Montalvo, Orlando Alejo Méndez Morales, Philippe Van Bergen, Reece Stevens, Srinivas K. Raman, and Yujan Shrestha.

To our friends and family, wondering what rock we've been hiding under these past two years: Hi! We missed you! Let's have dinner sometime.

about this book

This book has the aim of providing the foundations of deep learning with PyTorch and showing them in action in a real-life project. We strive to provide the key concepts underlying deep learning and show how PyTorch puts them in the hands of practitioners. In the book, we try to provide intuition that will support further exploration, and in doing so we selectively delve into details to show what is going on behind the curtain.

Deep Learning with PyTorch doesn't try to be a reference book; rather, it's a conceptual companion that will allow you to independently explore more advanced material online. As such, we focus on a subset of the features offered by PyTorch. The most notable absence is recurrent neural networks, but the same is true for other parts of the PyTorch API.

Who should read this book

This book is meant for developers who are or aim to become deep learning practitioners and who want to get acquainted with PyTorch. We imagine our typical reader to be a computer scientist, data scientist, or software engineer, or an undergraduate-or-later student in a related program. Since we don't assume prior knowledge of deep learning, some parts in the first half of the book may be a repetition of concepts that are already known to experienced practitioners. For those readers, we hope the exposition will provide a slightly different angle to known topics.

We expect readers to have basic knowledge of imperative and object-oriented programming. Since the book uses Python, you should be familiar with the syntax and operating environment. Knowing how to install Python packages and run scripts on your platform of choice is a prerequisite. Readers coming from C++, Java, JavaScript, Ruby, or other such languages should have an easy time picking it up but will need to do some catch-up outside this book. Similarly, being familiar with NumPy will be useful, if not strictly required. We also expect familiarity with some basic linear algebra, such as knowing what matrices and vectors are and what a dot product is.

How this book is organized: A roadmap

Deep Learning with PyTorch is organized in three distinct parts. Part 1 covers the foundations, while part 2 walks you through an end-to-end project, building on the basic concepts introduced in part 1 and adding more advanced ones. The short part 3 rounds off the book with a tour of what PyTorch offers for deployment. You will likely notice different voices and graphical styles among the parts. Although the book is a result of endless hours of collaborative planning, discussion, and editing, the act of writing and authoring graphics was split among the parts: Luca was primarily in charge of part 1 and Eli of part 2.[2] When Thomas came along, he tried to blend the style in part 3 and various sections here and there with the writing in parts 1 and 2. Rather than finding a minimum common denominator, we decided to preserve the original voices that characterized the parts.

Following is a breakdown of each part into chapters and a brief description of each.

PART 1

In part 1, we take our first steps with PyTorch, building the fundamental skills needed to understand PyTorch projects out there in the wild as well as starting to build our own. We'll cover the PyTorch API and some behind-the-scenes features that make PyTorch the library it is, and work on training an initial classification model. By the end of part 1, we'll be ready to tackle a real-world project.

Chapter 1 introduces PyTorch as a library and its place in the deep learning revolution, and touches on what sets PyTorch apart from other deep learning frameworks.

Chapter 2 shows PyTorch in action by running examples of pretrained networks; it demonstrates how to download and run models in PyTorch Hub.

Chapter 3 introduces the basic building block of PyTorch—the tensor—showing its API and going behind the scenes with some implementation details.

Chapter 4 demonstrates how different kinds of data can be represented as tensors and how deep learning models expects tensors to be shaped.

Chapter 5 walks through the mechanics of learning through gradient descent and how PyTorch enables it with automatic differentiation.

Chapter 6 shows the process of building and training a neural network for regression in PyTorch using the `nn` and `optim` modules.

Chapter 7 builds on the previous chapter to create a fully connected model for image classification and expand the knowledge of the PyTorch API.

Chapter 8 introduces convolutional neural networks and touches on more advanced concepts for building neural network models and their PyTorch implementation.

---

[2] A smattering of Eli's and Thomas's art appears in other parts; don't be shocked if the style changes mid-chapter!

PART 2

In part 2, each chapter moves us closer to a comprehensive solution to automatic detection of lung cancer. We'll use this difficult problem as motivation to demonstrate the real-world approaches needed to solve large-scale problems like cancer screening. It is a large project with a focus on clean engineering, troubleshooting, and problem solving.

Chapter 9 describes the end-to-end strategy we'll use for lung tumor classification, starting from computed tomography (CT) imaging.

Chapter 10 loads the human annotation data along with the images from CT scans and converts the relevant information into tensors, using standard PyTorch APIs.

Chapter 11 introduces a first classification model that consumes the training data introduced in chapter 10. We train the model and collect basic performance metrics. We also introduce using TensorBoard to monitor training.

Chapter 12 explores and implements standard performance metrics and uses those metrics to identify weaknesses in the training done previously. We then mitigate those flaws with an improved training set that uses data balancing and augmentation.

Chapter 13 describes segmentation, a pixel-to-pixel model architecture that we use to produce a heatmap of possible nodule locations that covers the entire CT scan. This heatmap can be used to find nodules on CT scans for which we do not have human-annotated data.

Chapter 14 implements the final end-to-end project: diagnosis of cancer patients using our new segmentation model followed by classification.

PART 3

Part 3 is a single chapter on deployment. Chapter 15 provides an overview of how to deploy PyTorch models to a simple web service, embed them in a C++ program, or bring them to a mobile phone.

About the code

All of the code in this book was written for Python 3.6 or later. The code for the book is available for download from Manning's website (www.manning.com/books/deep-learning-with-pytorch) and on GitHub (https://github.com/deep-learning-with-pytorch/dlwpt-code). Version 3.6.8 was current at the time of writing and is what we used to test the examples in this book. For example:

```
$ python
Python 3.6.8 (default, Jan 14 2019, 11:02:34)
[GCC 8.0.1 20180414 on linux
Type "help", "copyright", "credits" or "license" for more information.
>>>
```

Command lines intended to be entered at a Bash prompt start with $ (for example, the $ python line in this example). Fixed-width inline code looks like self.

Code blocks that begin with >>> are transcripts of a session at the Python interactive prompt. The >>> characters are not meant to be considered input; text lines that do not start with >>> or ... are output. In some cases, an extra blank line is inserted before the >>> to improve readability in print. These blank lines are not included when you actually enter the text at the interactive prompt:

```
>>> print("Hello, world!")
Hello, world!

>>> print("Until next time...")
Until next time...
```

This blank line would not be present during an actual interactive session.

We also make heavy use of Jupyter Notebooks, as described in chapter 1, in section 1.5.1. Code from a notebook that we provide as part of the official GitHub repository looks like this:

```
# In[1]:
print("Hello, world!")

# Out[1]:
Hello, world!

# In[2]:
print("Until next time...")

# Out[2]:
Until next time...
```

Almost all of our example notebooks contain the following boilerplate in the first cell (some lines may be missing in early chapters), which we skip including in the book after this point:

```
# In[1]:
%matplotlib inline
from matplotlib import pyplot as plt
import numpy as np

import torch
import torch.nn as nn
import torch.nn.functional as F
import torch.optim as optim

torch.set_printoptions(edgeitems=2)
torch.manual_seed(123)
```

Otherwise, code blocks are partial or entire sections of .py source files.

Listing 15.1   main.py:5, def main

```
def main():
    print("Hello, world!")

if __name__ == '__main__':
    main()
```

Many of the code samples in the book are presented with two-space indents. Due to the limitations of print, code listings are limited to 80-character lines, which can be impractical for heavily indented sections of code. The use of two-space indents helps to mitigate the excessive line wrapping that would otherwise be present. All of the code available for download for the book (again, at www.manning.com/books/deep-learning-with-pytorch and https://github.com/deep-learning-with-pytorch/dlwpt-code) uses a consistent four-space indent. Variables named with a _t suffix are tensors stored in CPU memory, _g are tensors in GPU memory, and _a are NumPy arrays.

Hardware and software requirements

Part 1 has been designed to not require any particular computing resources. Any recent computer or online computing resource will be adequate. Similarly, no certain operating system is required. In part 2, we anticipate that completing a full training run for the more advanced examples will require a CUDA-capable GPU. The default parameters used in part 2 assume a GPU with 8 GB of RAM (we suggest an NVIDIA GTX 1070 or better), but the parameters can be adjusted if your hardware has less RAM available. The raw data needed for part 2's cancer-detection project is about 60 GB to download, and you will need a total of 200 GB (at minimum) of free disk space on the system that will be used for training. Luckily, online computing services recently started offering GPU time for free. We discuss computing requirements in more detail in the appropriate sections.

You need Python 3.6 or later; instructions can be found on the Python website (www.python.org/downloads). For PyTorch installation information, see the Get Started guide on the official PyTorch website (https://pytorch.org/get-started/locally). We suggest that Windows users install with Anaconda or Miniconda (https://www.anaconda.com/distribution or https://docs.conda.io/en/latest/miniconda.html). Other operating systems like Linux typically have a wider variety of workable options, with Pip being the most common package manager for Python. We provide a requirements.txt file that Pip can use to install dependencies. Since current Apple laptops do not include GPUs that support CUDA, the precompiled macOS packages for PyTorch are CPU-only. Of course, experienced users are free to install packages in the way that is most compatible with your preferred development environment.

liveBook discussion forum

Purchase of *Deep Learning with PyTorch* includes free access to a private web forum run by Manning Publications where you can make comments about the book, ask technical questions, and receive help from the authors and from other users. To access the forum, go to https://livebook.manning.com/#!/book/deep-learning-with-pytorch/discussion. You can learn more about Manning's forums and the rules of conduct at https://livebook.manning .com/#!/discussion. Manning's commitment to our readers is to provide a venue where a meaningful dialogue between individual readers and between readers and the author can take place. It is not a commitment to any specific amount of participation on the part of the authors, whose contribution to the forum remains voluntary (and unpaid). We suggest you try asking them some challenging questions lest their interest stray! The forum and the archives of previous discussions will be accessible from the publisher's website as long as the book is in print.

Other online resources

Although this book does not assume prior knowledge of deep learning, it is not a foundational introduction to deep learning. We cover the basics, but our focus is on proficiency with the PyTorch library. We encourage interested readers to build up an intuitive understanding of deep learning either before, during, or after reading this book. Toward that end, *Grokking Deep Learning* (www.manning.com/books/grokking-deep-learning) is a great resource for developing a strong mental model and intuition about the mechanism underlying deep neural networks. For a thorough introduction and reference, we direct you to *Deep Learning* by Goodfellow et al. (www.deeplearningbook.org). And of course, Manning Publications has an extensive catalog of deep learning titles (www.manning .com/catalog#section-83) that cover a wide variety of topics in the space. Depending on your interests, many of them will make an excellent next book to read.

about the authors

Eli Stevens has spent the majority of his career working at startups in Silicon Valley, with roles ranging from software engineer (making enterprise networking appliances) to CTO (developing software for radiation oncology). At publication, he is working on machine learning in the self-driving-car industry.

Luca Antiga worked as a researcher in biomedical engineering in the 2000s, and spent the last decade as a cofounder and CTO of an AI engineering company. He has contributed to several open source projects, including the PyTorch core. He recently cofounded a US-based startup focused on infrastructure for data-defined software.

Thomas Viehmann is a machine learning and PyTorch specialty trainer and consultant based in Munich, Germany, and a PyTorch core developer. With a PhD in mathematics, he is not scared by theory, but he is thoroughly practical when applying it to computing challenges.

about the cover illustration

The figure on the cover of *Deep Learning with PyTorch* is captioned "Kabardian." The illustration is taken from a collection of dress costumes from various countries by Jacques Grasset de Saint-Sauveur (1757-1810), titled *Costumes civils actuels de tous les peuples connus*, published in France in 1788. Each illustration is finely drawn and colored by hand. The rich variety of Grasset de Saint-Sauveur's collection reminds us vividly of how culturally apart the world's towns and regions were just 200 years ago. Isolated from each other, people spoke different dialects and languages. In the streets or in the countryside, it was easy to identify where they lived and what their trade or station in life was just by their dress.

The way we dress has changed since then and the diversity by region, so rich at the time, has faded away. It is now hard to tell apart the inhabitants of different continents, let alone different towns, regions, or countries. Perhaps we have traded cultural diversity for a more varied personal life—certainly for a more varied and fast-paced technological life.

At a time when it is hard to tell one computer book from another, Manning celebrates the inventiveness and initiative of the computer business with book covers based on the rich diversity of regional life of two centuries ago, brought back to life by Grasset de Saint-Sauveur's pictures.

Part 1

Core PyTorch

Welcome to the first part of this book. This is where we'll take our first steps with PyTorch, gaining the fundamental skills needed to understand its anatomy and work out the mechanics of a PyTorch project.

In chapter 1, we'll make our first contact with PyTorch, understand what it is and what problems it solves, and how it relates to other deep learning frameworks. Chapter 2 will take us on a tour, giving us a chance to play with models that have been pretrained on fun tasks. Chapter 3 gets a bit more serious and teaches the basic data structure used in PyTorch programs: the tensor. Chapter 4 will take us on another tour, this time across ways to represent data from different domains as PyTorch tensors. Chapter 5 unveils how a program can learn from examples and how PyTorch supports this process. Chapter 6 provides the fundamentals of what a neural network is and how to build a neural network with PyTorch. Chapter 7 tackles a simple image classification problem with a neural network architecture. Finally, chapter 8 shows how the same problem can be cracked in a much smarter way using a convolutional neural network.

By the end of part 1, we'll have what it takes to tackle a real-world problem with PyTorch in part 2.

Introducing deep learning and the PyTorch Library

This chapter covers

- How deep learning changes our approach to machine learning
- Understanding why PyTorch is a good fit for deep learning
- Examining a typical deep learning project
- The hardware you'll need to follow along with the examples

The poorly defined term *artificial intelligence* covers a set of disciplines that have been subjected to a tremendous amount of research, scrutiny, confusion, fantastical hype, and sci-fi fearmongering. Reality is, of course, far more sanguine. It would be disingenuous to assert that today's machines are learning to "think" in any human sense of the word. Rather, we've discovered a general class of algorithms that are able to approximate complicated, nonlinear processes very, very effectively, which we can use to automate tasks that were previously limited to humans.

For example, at https://talktotransformer.com, a language model called GPT-2 can generate coherent paragraphs of text one word at a time. When we fed it this very paragraph, it produced the following:

> *Next we're going to feed in a list of phrases from a corpus of email addresses, and see if the program can parse the lists as sentences. Again, this is much more complicated and far more complex than the search at the beginning of this post, but hopefully helps you understand the basics of constructing sentence structures in various programming languages.*

That's remarkably coherent for a machine, even if there isn't a well-defined thesis behind the rambling.

Even more impressively, the ability to perform these formerly human-only tasks is acquired *through examples*, rather than encoded by a human as a set of handcrafted rules. In a way, we're learning that intelligence is a notion we often conflate with self-awareness, and self-awareness is definitely not required to successfully carry out these kinds of tasks. In the end, the question of computer intelligence might not even be important. Edsger W. Dijkstra found that the question of whether machines could think was "about as relevant as the question of whether Submarines Can Swim."[1]

That general class of algorithms we're talking about falls under the AI subcategory of *deep learning*, which deals with training mathematical entities named *deep neural networks* by presenting instructive examples. Deep learning uses large amounts of data to approximate complex functions whose inputs and outputs are far apart, like an input image and, as output, a line of text describing the input; or a written script as input and a natural-sounding voice reciting the script as output; or, even more simply, associating an image of a golden retriever with a flag that tells us "Yes, a golden retriever is present." This kind of capability allows us to create programs with functionality that was, until very recently, exclusively the domain of human beings.

1.1   *The deep learning revolution*

To appreciate the paradigm shift ushered in by this deep learning approach, let's take a step back for a bit of perspective. Until the last decade, the broader class of systems that fell under the label *machine learning* relied heavily on *feature engineering*. Features are transformations on input data that facilitate a downstream algorithm, like a classifier, to produce correct outcomes on new data. Feature engineering consists of coming up with the right transformations so that the downstream algorithm can solve a task. For instance, in order to tell ones from zeros in images of handwritten digits, we would come up with a set of filters to estimate the direction of edges over the image, and then train a classifier to predict the correct digit given a distribution of edge directions. Another useful feature could be the number of enclosed holes, as seen in a zero, an eight, and, particularly, loopy twos.

---

[1]   Edsger W. Dijkstra, "The Threats to Computing Science," http://mng.bz/nPJ5.

Deep learning, on the other hand, deals with finding such representations automatically, from raw data, in order to successfully perform a task. In the ones versus zeros example, filters would be refined during training by iteratively looking at pairs of examples and target labels. This is not to say that feature engineering has no place with deep learning; we often need to inject some form of prior knowledge in a learning system. However, the ability of a neural network to ingest data and extract useful representations on the basis of examples is what makes deep learning so powerful. The focus of deep learning practitioners is not so much on handcrafting those representations, but on operating on a mathematical entity so that it discovers representations from the training data autonomously. Often, these automatically created features are better than those that are handcrafted! As with many disruptive technologies, this fact has led to a change in perspective.

On the left side of figure 1.1, we see a practitioner busy defining engineering features and feeding them to a learning algorithm; the results on the task will be as good as the features the practitioner engineers. On the right, with deep learning, the raw data is fed to an algorithm that extracts hierarchical features automatically, guided by the optimization of its own performance on the task; the results will be as good as the ability of the practitioner to drive the algorithm toward its goal.

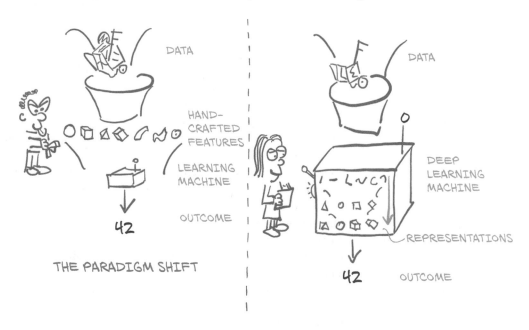

Figure 1.1   Deep learning exchanges the need to handcraft features for an increase in data and computational requirements.

Starting from the right side in figure 1.1, we already get a glimpse of what we need to execute successful deep learning:

- We need a way to ingest whatever data we have at hand.
- We somehow need to define the deep learning machine.
- We must have an automated way, *training*, to obtain useful representations and make the machine produce desired outputs.

This leaves us with taking a closer look at this training thing we keep talking about. During training, we use a *criterion*, a real-valued function of model outputs and reference data, to provide a numerical score for the discrepancy between the desired and actual output of our model (by convention, a lower score is typically better). Training consists of driving the criterion toward lower and lower scores by incrementally modifying our deep learning machine until it achieves low scores, even on data not seen during training.

1.2 *PyTorch for deep learning*

PyTorch is a library for Python programs that facilitates building deep learning projects. It emphasizes flexibility and allows deep learning models to be expressed in idiomatic Python. This approachability and ease of use found early adopters in the research community, and in the years since its first release, it has grown into one of the most prominent deep learning tools across a broad range of applications.

As Python does for programming, PyTorch provides an excellent introduction to deep learning. At the same time, PyTorch has been proven to be fully qualified for use in professional contexts for real-world, high-profile work. We believe that PyTorch's clear syntax, streamlined API, and easy debugging make it an excellent choice for introducing deep learning. We highly recommend studying PyTorch for your first deep learning library. Whether it ought to be the last deep learning library you learn is a decision we leave up to you.

At its core, the deep learning machine in figure 1.1 is a rather complex mathematical function mapping inputs to an output. To facilitate expressing this function, PyTorch provides a core data structure, the *tensor*, which is a multidimensional array that shares many similarities with NumPy arrays. Around that foundation, PyTorch comes with features to perform accelerated mathematical operations on dedicated hardware, which makes it convenient to design neural network architectures and train them on individual machines or parallel computing resources.

This book is intended as a starting point for software engineers, data scientists, and motivated students fluent in Python to become comfortable using PyTorch to build deep learning projects. We want this book to be as accessible and useful as possible, and we expect that you will be able to take the concepts in this book and apply them to other domains. To that end, we use a hands-on approach and encourage you to keep your computer at the ready, so you can play with the examples and take them a step further. By the time we are through with the book, we expect you to be able to take a data source and build out a deep learning project with it, supported by the excellent official documentation.

Although we stress the practical aspects of building deep learning systems with PyTorch, we believe that providing an accessible introduction to a foundational deep learning tool is more than just a way to facilitate the acquisition of new technical skills. It is a step toward equipping a new generation of scientists, engineers, and practitioners from a wide range of disciplines with working knowledge that will be the backbone of many software projects during the decades to come.

In order to get the most out of this book, you will need two things:

- Some experience programming in Python. We're not going to pull any punches on that one; you'll need to be up on Python data types, classes, floating-point numbers, and the like.
- A willingness to dive in and get your hands dirty. We'll be starting from the basics and building up our working knowledge, and it will be much easier for you to learn if you follow along with us.

Deep Learning with PyTorch is organized in three distinct parts. Part 1 covers the foundations, examining in detail the facilities PyTorch offers to put the sketch of deep learning in figure 1.1 into action with code. Part 2 walks you through an end-to-end project involving medical imaging: finding and classifying tumors in CT scans, building on the basic concepts introduced in part 1, and adding more advanced topics. The short part 3 rounds off the book with a tour of what PyTorch offers for deploying deep learning models to production.

Deep learning is a huge space. In this book, we will be covering a tiny part of that space: specifically, using PyTorch for smaller-scope classification and segmentation projects, with image processing of 2D and 3D datasets used for most of the motivating examples. This book focuses on practical PyTorch, with the aim of covering enough ground to allow you to solve real-world machine learning problems, such as in vision, with deep learning or explore new models as they pop up in research literature. Most, if not all, of the latest publications related to deep learning research can be found in the arXiV public preprint repository, hosted at https://arxiv.org.[2]

1.3 Why PyTorch?

As we've said, deep learning allows us to carry out a very wide range of complicated tasks, like machine translation, playing strategy games, or identifying objects in cluttered scenes, by exposing our model to illustrative examples. In order to do so in practice, we need tools that are flexible, so they can be adapted to such a wide range of problems, and efficient, to allow training to occur over large amounts of data in reasonable times; and we need the trained model to perform correctly in the presence of variability in the inputs. Let's take a look at some of the reasons we decided to use PyTorch.

---

[2] We also recommend www.arxiv-sanity.com to help organize research papers of interest.

PyTorch is easy to recommend because of its simplicity. Many researchers and practitioners find it easy to learn, use, extend, and debug. It's Pythonic, and while like any complicated domain it has caveats and best practices, using the library generally feels familiar to developers who have used Python previously.

More concretely, programming the deep learning machine is very natural in PyTorch. PyTorch gives us a data type, the Tensor, to hold numbers, vectors, matrices, or arrays in general. In addition, it provides functions for operating on them. We can program with them incrementally and, if we want, interactively, just like we are used to from Python. If you know NumPy, this will be very familiar.

But PyTorch offers two things that make it particularly relevant for deep learning: first, it provides accelerated computation using graphical processing units (GPUs), often yielding speedups in the range of 50x over doing the same calculation on a CPU. Second, PyTorch provides facilities that support numerical optimization on generic mathematical expressions, which deep learning uses for training. Note that both features are useful for scientific computing in general, not exclusively for deep learning. In fact, we can safely characterize PyTorch as a high-performance library with optimization support for scientific computing in Python.

A design driver for PyTorch is expressivity, allowing a developer to implement complicated models without undue complexity being imposed by the library (it's not a framework!). PyTorch arguably offers one of the most seamless translations of ideas into Python code in the deep learning landscape. For this reason, PyTorch has seen widespread adoption in research, as witnessed by the high citation counts at international conferences.[3]

PyTorch also has a compelling story for the transition from research and development into production. While it was initially focused on research workflows, PyTorch has been equipped with a high-performance C++ runtime that can be used to deploy models for inference without relying on Python, and can be used for designing and training models in C++. It has also grown bindings to other languages and an interface for deploying to mobile devices. These features allow us to take advantage of PyTorch's flexibility and at the same time take our applications where a full Python runtime would be hard to get or would impose expensive overhead.

Of course, claims of ease of use and high performance are trivial to make. We hope that by the time you are in the thick of this book, you'll agree with us that our claims here are well founded.

1.3.1   *The deep learning competitive landscape*

While all analogies are flawed, it seems that the release of PyTorch 0.1 in January 2017 marked the transition from a Cambrian-explosion-like proliferation of deep learning libraries, wrappers, and data-exchange formats into an era of consolidation and unification.

---

[3] At the International Conference on Learning Representations (ICLR) 2019, PyTorch appeared as a citation in 252 papers, up from 87 the previous year and at the same level as TensorFlow, which appeared in 266 papers.

NOTE The deep learning landscape has been moving so quickly lately that by the time you read this in print, it will likely be out of date. If you're unfamiliar with some of the libraries mentioned here, that's fine.

At the time of PyTorch's first beta release:

- Theano and TensorFlow were the premiere low-level libraries, working with a model that had the user define a computational graph and then execute it.
- Lasagne and Keras were high-level wrappers around Theano, with Keras wrapping TensorFlow and CNTK as well.
- Caffe, Chainer, DyNet, Torch (the Lua-based precursor to PyTorch), MXNet, CNTK, DL4J, and others filled various niches in the ecosystem.

In the roughly two years that followed, the landscape changed drastically. The community largely consolidated behind either PyTorch or TensorFlow, with the adoption of other libraries dwindling, except for those filling specific niches. In a nutshell:

- Theano, one of the first deep learning frameworks, has ceased active development.
- TensorFlow:
  - Consumed Keras entirely, promoting it to a first-class API
  - Provided an immediate-execution "eager mode" that is somewhat similar to how PyTorch approaches computation
  - Released TF 2.0 with eager mode by default
- JAX, a library by Google that was developed independently from TensorFlow, has started gaining traction as a NumPy equivalent with GPU, autograd and JIT capabilities.
- PyTorch:
  - Consumed Caffe2 for its backend
  - Replaced most of the low-level code reused from the Lua-based Torch project
  - Added support for ONNX, a vendor-neutral model description and exchange format
  - Added a delayed-execution "graph mode" runtime called *TorchScript*
  - Released version 1.0
  - Replaced CNTK and Chainer as the framework of choice by their respective corporate sponsors

TensorFlow has a robust pipeline to production, an extensive industry-wide community, and massive mindshare. PyTorch has made huge inroads with the research and teaching communities, thanks to its ease of use, and has picked up momentum since, as researchers and graduates train students and move to industry. It has also built up steam in terms of production solutions. Interestingly, with the advent of TorchScript and eager mode, both PyTorch and TensorFlow have seen their feature sets start to converge with the other's, though the presentation of these features and the overall experience is still quite different between the two.

1.4   *An overview of how PyTorch supports deep learning projects*

We have already hinted at a few building blocks in PyTorch. Let's now take some time to formalize a high-level map of the main components that form PyTorch. We can best do this by looking at what a deep learning project needs from PyTorch.

First, PyTorch has the "Py" as in Python, but there's a lot of non-Python code in it. Actually, for performance reasons, most of PyTorch is written in C++ and CUDA (www.geforce.com/hardware/technology/cuda), a C++-like language from NVIDIA that can be compiled to run with massive parallelism on GPUs. There are ways to run PyTorch directly from C++, and we'll look into those in chapter 15. One of the motivations for this capability is to provide a reliable strategy for deploying models in production. However, most of the time we'll interact with PyTorch from Python, building models, training them, and using the trained models to solve actual problems.

Indeed, the Python API is where PyTorch shines in term of usability and integration with the wider Python ecosystem. Let's take a peek at the mental model of what PyTorch is.

As we already touched on, at its core, PyTorch is a library that provides *multidimensional arrays*, or *tensors* in PyTorch parlance (we'll go into details on those in chapter 3), and an extensive library of operations on them, provided by the torch module. Both tensors and the operations on them can be used on the CPU or the GPU. Moving computations from the CPU to the GPU in PyTorch doesn't require more than an additional function call or two. The second core thing that PyTorch provides is the ability of tensors to keep track of the operations performed on them and to analytically compute derivatives of an output of a computation with respect to any of its inputs. This is used for numerical optimization, and it is provided natively by tensors by virtue of dispatching through PyTorch's *autograd* engine under the hood.

By having tensors and the autograd-enabled tensor standard library, PyTorch can be used for physics, rendering, optimization, simulation, modeling, and more—we're very likely to see PyTorch used in creative ways throughout the spectrum of scientific applications. But PyTorch is first and foremost a deep learning library, and as such it provides all the building blocks needed to build neural networks and train them. Figure 1.2 shows a standard setup that loads data, trains a model, and then deploys that model to production.

The core PyTorch modules for building neural networks are located in torch.nn, which provides common neural network layers and other architectural components. Fully connected layers, convolutional layers, activation functions, and loss functions can all be found here (we'll go into more detail about what all that means as we go through the rest of this book). These components can be used to build and initialize the untrained model we see in the center of figure 1.2. In order to train our model, we need a few additional things: a source of training data, an optimizer to adapt the model to the training data, and a way to get the model and data to the hardware that will actually be performing the calculations needed for training the model.

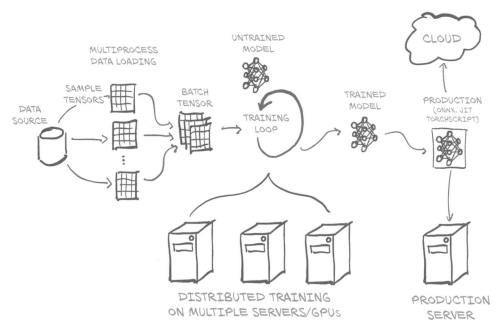

Figure 1.2   Basic, high-level structure of a PyTorch project, with data loading, training, and deployment to production

At left in figure 1.2, we see that quite a bit of data processing is needed before the training data even reaches our model.[4] First we need to physically get the data, most often from some sort of storage as the data source. Then we need to convert each sample from our data into a something PyTorch can actually handle: tensors. This bridge between our custom data (in whatever format it might be) and a standardized PyTorch tensor is the `Dataset` class PyTorch provides in `torch.utils.data`. As this process is wildly different from one problem to the next, we will have to implement this data sourcing ourselves. We will look in detail at how to represent various type of data we might want to work with as tensors in chapter 4.

As data storage is often slow, in particular due to access latency, we want to parallelize data loading. But as the many things Python is well loved for do not include easy, efficient, parallel processing, we will need multiple processes to load our data, in order to assemble them into *batches*: tensors that encompass several samples. This is rather elaborate; but as it is also relatively generic, PyTorch readily provides all that magic in the `DataLoader` class. Its instances can spawn child processes to load data from a dataset in the background so that it's ready and waiting for the training loop as soon as the loop can use it. We will meet and use `Dataset` and `DataLoader` in chapter 7.

---

[4] And that's just the data preparation that is done on the fly, not the preprocessing, which can be a pretty large part in practical projects.

With the mechanism for getting batches of samples in place, we can turn to the training loop itself at the center of figure 1.2. Typically, the training loop is implemented as a standard Python `for` loop. In the simplest case, the model runs the required calculations on the local CPU or a single GPU, and once the training loop has the data, computation can start immediately. Chances are this will be your basic setup, too, and it's the one we'll assume in this book.

At each step in the training loop, we evaluate our model on the samples we got from the data loader. We then compare the outputs of our model to the desired output (the targets) using some *criterion* or *loss function*. Just as it offers the components from which to build our model, PyTorch also has a variety of loss functions at our disposal. They, too, are provided in `torch.nn`. After we have compared our actual outputs to the ideal with the loss functions, we need to push the model a little to move its outputs to better resemble the target. As mentioned earlier, this is where the PyTorch autograd engine comes in; but we also need an *optimizer* doing the updates, and that is what PyTorch offers us in `torch.optim`. We will start looking at training loops with loss functions and optimizers in chapter 5 and then hone our skills in chapters 6 through 8 before embarking on our big project in part 2.

It's increasingly common to use more elaborate hardware like multiple GPUs or multiple machines that contribute their resources to training a large model, as seen in the bottom center of figure 1.2. In those cases, `torch.nn.parallel.Distributed-DataParallel` and the `torch.distributed` submodule can be employed to use the additional hardware.

The training loop might be the most unexciting yet most time-consuming part of a deep learning project. At the end of it, we are rewarded with a model whose parameters have been optimized on our task: the *trained model* depicted to the right of the training loop in the figure. Having a model to solve a task is great, but in order for it to be useful, we must put it where the work is needed. This *deployment* part of the process, depicted on the right in figure 1.2, may involve putting the model on a server or exporting it to load it to a cloud engine, as shown in the figure. Or we might integrate it with a larger application, or run it on a phone.

One particular step of the deployment exercise can be to export the model. As mentioned earlier, PyTorch defaults to an immediate execution model (eager mode). Whenever an instruction involving PyTorch is executed by the Python interpreter, the corresponding operation is immediately carried out by the underlying C++ or CUDA implementation. As more instructions operate on tensors, more operations are executed by the backend implementation.

PyTorch also provides a way to compile models ahead of time through *TorchScript*. Using TorchScript, PyTorch can serialize a model into a set of instructions that can be invoked independently from Python: say, from C++ programs or on mobile devices. We can think about it as a virtual machine with a limited instruction set, specific to tensor operations. This allows us to export our model, either as TorchScript to be used with the PyTorch runtime, or in a standardized format called *ONNX*. These features are at the basis of the production deployment capabilities of PyTorch. We'll cover this in chapter 15.

1.5 Hardware and software requirements

This book will require coding and running tasks that involve heavy numerical computing, such as multiplication of large numbers of matrices. As it turns out, running a pretrained network on new data is within the capabilities of any recent laptop or personal computer. Even taking a pretrained network and retraining a small portion of it to specialize it on a new dataset doesn't necessarily require specialized hardware. You can follow along with everything we do in part 1 of this book using a standard personal computer or laptop.

However, we anticipate that completing a full training run for the more advanced examples in part 2 will require a CUDA-capable GPU. The default parameters used in part 2 assume a GPU with 8 GB of RAM (we suggest an NVIDIA GTX 1070 or better), but those can be adjusted if your hardware has less RAM available. To be clear: such hardware is not mandatory if you're willing to wait, but running on a GPU cuts training time by at least an order of magnitude (and usually it's 40–50x faster). Taken individually, the operations required to compute parameter updates are fast (from fractions of a second to a few seconds) on modern hardware like a typical laptop CPU. The issue is that training involves running these operations over and over, many, many times, incrementally updating the network parameters to minimize the training error.

Moderately large networks can take hours to days to train from scratch on large, real-world datasets on workstations equipped with a good GPU. That time can be reduced by using multiple GPUs on the same machine, and even further on clusters of machines equipped with multiple GPUs. These setups are less prohibitive to access than it sounds, thanks to the offerings of cloud computing providers. DAWNBench (https://dawn.cs.stanford.edu/benchmark/index.html) is an interesting initiative from Stanford University aimed at providing benchmarks on training time and cloud computing costs related to common deep learning tasks on publicly available datasets.

So, if there's a GPU around by the time you reach part 2, then great. Otherwise, we suggest checking out the offerings from the various cloud platforms, many of which offer GPU-enabled Jupyter Notebooks with PyTorch preinstalled, often with a free quota. Google Colaboratory (https://colab.research.google.com) is a great place to start.

The last consideration is the operating system (OS). PyTorch has supported Linux and macOS from its first release, and it gained Windows support in 2018. Since current Apple laptops do not include GPUs that support CUDA, the precompiled macOS packages for PyTorch are CPU-only. Throughout the book, we will try to avoid assuming you are running a particular OS, although some of the scripts in part 2 are shown as if running from a Bash prompt under Linux. Those scripts' command lines should convert to a Windows-compatible form readily. For convenience, code will be listed as if running from a Jupyter Notebook when possible.

For installation information, please see the Get Started guide on the official PyTorch website (https://pytorch.org/get-started/locally). We suggest that Windows users install with Anaconda or Miniconda (https://www.anaconda.com/distribution or https://docs.conda.io/en/latest/miniconda.html). Other operating systems like Linux typically have a wider variety of workable options, with Pip being the most common package manager for Python. We provide a requirements.txt file that pip can use to install dependencies. Of course, experienced users are free to install packages in the way that is most compatible with your preferred development environment.

Part 2 has some nontrivial download bandwidth and disk space requirements as well. The raw data needed for the cancer-detection project in part 2 is about 60 GB to download, and when uncompressed it requires about 120 GB of space. The compressed data can be removed after decompressing it. In addition, due to caching some of the data for performance reasons, another 80 GB will be needed while training. You will need a total of 200 GB (at minimum) of free disk space on the system that will be used for training. While it is possible to use network storage for this, there might be training speed penalties if the network access is slower than local disk. Preferably you will have space on a local SSD to store the data for fast retrieval.

1.5.1 *Using Jupyter Notebooks*

We're going to assume you've installed PyTorch and the other dependencies and have verified that things are working. Earlier we touched on the possibilities for following along with the code in the book. We are going to be making heavy use of Jupyter Notebooks for our example code. A Jupyter Notebook shows itself as a page in the browser through which we can run code interactively. The code is evaluated by a *kernel*, a process running on a server that is ready to receive code to execute and send back the results, which are then rendered inline on the page. A notebook maintains the state of the kernel, like variables defined during the evaluation of code, in memory until it is terminated or restarted. The fundamental unit with which we interact with a notebook is a *cell*: a box on the page where we can type code and have the kernel evaluate it (through the menu item or by pressing Shift-Enter). We can add multiple cells in a notebook, and the new cells will see the variables we created in the earlier cells. The value returned by the last line of a cell will be printed right below the cell after execution, and the same goes for plots. By mixing source code, results of evaluations, and Markdown-formatted text cells, we can generate beautiful interactive documents. You can read everything about Jupyter Notebooks on the project website (https://jupyter.org).

At this point, you need to start the notebook server from the root directory of the code checkout from GitHub. How exactly starting the server looks depends on the details of your OS and how and where you installed Jupyter. If you have questions, feel free to ask on the book's forum.[5] Once started, your default browser will pop up, showing a list of local notebook files.

---

[5] https://forums.manning.com/forums/deep-learning-with-pytorch

NOTE Jupyter Notebooks are a powerful tool for expressing and investigating ideas through code. While we think that they make for a good fit for our use case with this book, they're not for everyone. We would argue that it's important to focus on removing friction and minimizing cognitive overhead, and that's going to be different for everyone. Use what you like during your experimentation with PyTorch.

Full working code for all listings from the book can be found at the book's website (www.manning.com/books/deep-learning-with-pytorch) and in our repository on GitHub (https://github.com/deep-learning-with-pytorch/dlwpt-code).

1.6 Exercises

1 Start Python to get an interactive prompt.
   a What Python version are you using? We hope it is at least 3.6!
   b Can you `import torch`? What version of PyTorch do you get?
   c What is the result of `torch.cuda.is_available()`? Does it match your expectation based on the hardware you're using?
2 Start the Jupyter notebook server.
   a What version of Python is Jupyter using?
   b Is the location of the `torch` library used by Jupyter the same as the one you imported from the interactive prompt?

1.7 Summary

- Deep learning models automatically learn to associate inputs and desired outputs from examples.
- Libraries like PyTorch allow you to build and train neural network models efficiently.
- PyTorch minimizes cognitive overhead while focusing on flexibility and speed. It also defaults to immediate execution for operations.
- TorchScript allows us to precompile models and invoke them not only from Python but also from C++ programs and on mobile devices.
- Since the release of PyTorch in early 2017, the deep learning tooling ecosystem has consolidated significantly.
- PyTorch provides a number of utility libraries to facilitate deep learning projects.

Pretrained networks

This chapter covers

- Running pretrained image-recognition models
- An introduction to GANs and CycleGAN
- Captioning models that can produce text descriptions of images
- Sharing models through Torch Hub

We closed our first chapter promising to unveil amazing things in this chapter, and now it's time to deliver. Computer vision is certainly one of the fields that have been most impacted by the advent of deep learning, for a variety of reasons. The need to classify or interpret the content of natural images existed, very large datasets became available, and new constructs such as convolutional layers were invented and could be run quickly on GPUs with unprecedented accuracy. All of these factors combined with the internet giants' desire to understand pictures taken by millions of users with their mobile devices and managed on said giants' platforms. Quite the perfect storm.

We are going to learn how to use the work of the best researchers in the field by downloading and running very interesting models that have already been trained on open, large-scale datasets. We can think of a pretrained neural network as similar to a program that takes inputs and generates outputs. The behavior of such a program is dictated by the architecture of the neural network and by the examples it saw during training, in terms of desired input-output pairs, or desired properties that the output should satisfy. Using an off-the-shelf model can be a quick way to jump-start a deep learning project, since it draws on expertise from the researchers who designed the model, as well as the computation time that went into training the weights.

In this chapter, we will explore three popular pretrained models: a model that can label an image according to its content, another that can fabricate a new image from a real image, and a model that can describe the content of an image using proper English sentences. We will learn how to load and run these pretrained models in PyTorch, and we will introduce PyTorch Hub, a set of tools through which PyTorch models like the pretrained ones we'll discuss can be easily made available through a uniform interface. Along the way, we'll discuss data sources, define terminology like *label*, and attend a zebra rodeo.

If you're coming to PyTorch from another deep learning framework, and you'd rather jump right into learning the nuts and bolts of PyTorch, you can get away with skipping to the next chapter. The things we'll cover in this chapter are more fun than foundational and are somewhat independent of any given deep learning tool. That's not to say they're not important! But if you've worked with pretrained models in other deep learning frameworks, then you already know how powerful a tool they can be. And if you're already familiar with the generative adversarial network (GAN) game, you don't need us to explain it to you.

We hope you keep reading, though, since this chapter hides some important skills under the fun. Learning how to run a pretrained model using PyTorch is a useful skill—full stop. It's especially useful if the model has been trained on a large dataset. We will need to get accustomed to the mechanics of obtaining and running a neural network on real-world data, and then visualizing and evaluating its outputs, whether we trained it or not.

2.1   *A pretrained network that recognizes the subject of an image*

As our first foray into deep learning, we'll run a state-of-the-art deep neural network that was pretrained on an object-recognition task. There are many pretrained networks that can be accessed through source code repositories. It is common for researchers to publish their source code along with their papers, and often the code comes with weights that were obtained by training a model on a reference dataset. Using one of these models could enable us to, for example, equip our next web service with image-recognition capabilities with very little effort.

The pretrained network we'll explore here was trained on a subset of the ImageNet dataset (http://imagenet.stanford.edu). ImageNet is a very large dataset of over 14 million images maintained by Stanford University. All of the images are labeled with a hierarchy of nouns that come from the WordNet dataset (http://wordnet.princeton.edu), which is in turn a large lexical database of the English language.

The ImageNet dataset, like several other public datasets, has its origin in academic competitions. Competitions have traditionally been some of the main playing fields where researchers at institutions and companies regularly challenge each other. Among others, the ImageNet Large Scale Visual Recognition Challenge (ILSVRC) has gained popularity since its inception in 2010. This particular competition is based on a few tasks, which can vary each year, such as image classification (telling what object categories the image contains), object localization (identifying objects' position in images), object detection (identifying and labeling objects in images), scene classification (classifying a situation in an image), and scene parsing (segmenting an image into regions associated with semantic categories, such as cow, house, cheese, hat). In particular, the image-classification task consists of taking an input image and producing a list of 5 labels out of 1,000 total categories, ranked by confidence, describing the content of the image.

The training set for ILSVRC consists of 1.2 million images labeled with one of 1,000 nouns (for example, "dog"), referred to as the *class* of the image. In this sense, we will use the terms *label* and *class* interchangeably. We can take a peek at images from ImageNet in figure 2.1.

Figure 2.1   A small sample of ImageNet images

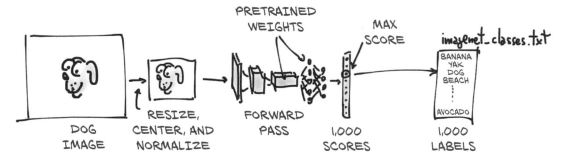

Figure 2.2   The inference process

We are going to end up being able to take our own images and feed them into our pretrained model, as pictured in figure 2.2. This will result in a list of predicted labels for that image, which we can then examine to see what the model thinks our image is. Some images will have predictions that are accurate, and others will not!

The input image will first be preprocessed into an instance of the multidimensional array class `torch.Tensor`. It is an RGB image with height and width, so this tensor will have three dimensions: the three color channels, and two spatial image dimensions of a specific size. (We'll get into the details of what a tensor is in chapter 3, but for now, think of it as being like a vector or matrix of floating-point numbers.) Our model will take that processed input image and pass it into the pretrained network to obtain scores for each class. The highest score corresponds to the most likely class according to the weights. Each class is then mapped one-to-one onto a class label. That output is contained in a `torch.Tensor` with 1,000 elements, each representing the score associated with that class.

Before we can do all that, we'll need to get the network itself, take a peek under the hood to see how it's structured, and learn about how to prepare our data before the model can use it.

2.1.1 Obtaining a pretrained network for image recognition

As discussed, we will now equip ourselves with a network trained on ImageNet. To do so, we'll take a look at the TorchVision project (https://github.com/pytorch/vision), which contains a few of the best-performing neural network architectures for computer vision, such as AlexNet (http://mng.bz/lo6z), ResNet (https://arxiv.org/pdf/1512.03385.pdf), and Inception v3 (https://arxiv.org/pdf/1512.00567.pdf). It also has easy access to datasets like ImageNet and other utilities for getting up to speed with computer vision applications in PyTorch. We'll dive into some of these further along in the book. For now, let's load up and run two networks: first AlexNet, one of the early breakthrough networks for image recognition; and then a residual network, ResNet for short, which won the ImageNet classification, detection, and localization competitions, among others, in 2015. If you didn't get PyTorch up and running in chapter 1, now is a good time to do that.

The predefined models can be found in `torchvision.models` (code/p1ch2/2 _pre_trained_networks.ipynb):

```
# In[1]:
from torchvision import models
```

We can take a look at the actual models:

```
# In[2]:
dir(models)

# Out[2]:
['AlexNet',
 'DenseNet',
 'Inception3',
 'ResNet',
 'SqueezeNet',
 'VGG',
...
 'alexnet',
 'densenet',
 'densenet121',
...
 'resnet',
 'resnet101',
 'resnet152',
...
 ]
```

The capitalized names refer to Python classes that implement a number of popular models. They differ in their architecture—that is, in the arrangement of the operations occurring between the input and the output. The lowercase names are convenience functions that return models instantiated from those classes, sometimes with different parameter sets. For instance, `resnet101` returns an instance of `ResNet` with 101 layers, `resnet18` has 18 layers, and so on. We'll now turn our attention to AlexNet.

2.1.2 *AlexNet*

The AlexNet architecture won the 2012 ILSVRC by a large margin, with a top-5 test error rate (that is, the correct label must be in the top 5 predictions) of 15.4%. By comparison, the second-best submission, which wasn't based on a deep network, trailed at 26.2%. This was a defining moment in the history of computer vision: the moment when the community started to realize the potential of deep learning for vision tasks. That leap was followed by constant improvement, with more modern architectures and training methods getting top-5 error rates as low as 3%.

By today's standards, AlexNet is a rather small network, compared to state-of-the-art models. But in our case, it's perfect for taking a first peek at a neural network that does something and learning how to run a pretrained version of it on a new image.

We can see the structure of AlexNet in figure 2.3. Not that we have all the elements for understanding it now, but we can anticipate a few aspects. First, each block consists of a bunch of multiplications and additions, plus a sprinkle of other functions in the output that we'll discover in chapter 5. We can think of it as a filter—a function that takes one or more images as input and produces other images as output. The way it does so is determined during training, based on the examples it has *seen* and on the desired outputs for those.

ALEXNET

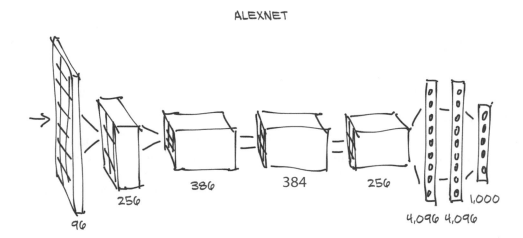

Figure 2.3 The AlexNet architecture

In figure 2.3, input images come in from the left and go through five stacks of filters, each producing a number of output images. After each filter, the images are reduced in size, as annotated. The images produced by the last stack of filters are laid out as a 4,096-element 1D vector and classified to produce 1,000 output probabilities, one for each output class.

In order to run the AlexNet architecture on an input image, we can create an instance of the AlexNet class. This is how it's done:

```
# In[3]:
alexnet = models.AlexNet()
```

At this point, alexnet is an object that can run the AlexNet architecture. It's not essential for us to understand the details of this architecture for now. For the time being, AlexNet is just an opaque object that can be called like a function. By providing alexnet with some precisely sized input data (we'll see shortly what this input data should be), we will run a *forward pass* through the network. That is, the input will run through the first set of neurons, whose outputs will be fed to the next set of neurons, all the way to the final output. Practically speaking, assuming we have an input object of the right type, we can run the forward pass with output = alexnet(input).

But if we did that, we would be feeding data through the whole network to produce … garbage! That's because the network is uninitialized: its weights, the numbers by which inputs are added and multiplied, have not been trained on anything—the network itself is a blank (or rather, *random*) slate. We'd need to either train it from scratch or load weights from prior training, which we'll do now.

To this end, let's go back to the models module. We learned that the uppercase names correspond to classes that implement popular architectures for computer vision. The lowercase names, on the other hand, are functions that instantiate models with predefined numbers of layers and units and optionally download and load pretrained weights into them. Note that there's nothing essential about using one of these functions: they just make it convenient to instantiate the model with a number of layers and units that matches how the pretrained networks were built.

2.1.3   ResNet

Using the resnet101 function, we'll now instantiate a 101-layer convolutional neural network. Just to put things in perspective, before the advent of residual networks in 2015, achieving stable training at such depths was considered extremely hard. Residual networks pulled a trick that made it possible, and by doing so, beat several benchmarks in one sweep that year.

Let's create an instance of the network now. We'll pass an argument that will instruct the function to download the weights of resnet101 trained on the ImageNet dataset, with 1.2 million images and 1,000 categories:

```
# In[4]:
resnet = models.resnet101(pretrained=True)
```

While we're staring at the download progress, we can take a minute to appreciate that resnet101 sports 44.5 million parameters—that's a lot of parameters to optimize automatically!

2.1.4   Ready, set, almost run

OK, what did we just get? Since we're curious, we'll take a peek at what a resnet101 looks like. We can do so by printing the value of the returned model. This gives us a textual representation of the same kind of information we saw in 2.3, providing details about the structure of the network. For now, this will be information overload, but as we progress through the book, we'll increase our ability to understand what this code is telling us:

```
# In[5]:
resnet

# Out[5]:
ResNet(
  (conv1): Conv2d(3, 64, kernel_size=(7, 7), stride=(2, 2), padding=(3, 3),
                  bias=False)
  (bn1): BatchNorm2d(64, eps=1e-05, momentum=0.1, affine=True,
                     track_running_stats=True)
  (relu): ReLU(inplace)
  (maxpool): MaxPool2d(kernel_size=3, stride=2, padding=1, dilation=1,
                       ceil_mode=False)
  (layer1): Sequential(
    (0): Bottleneck(
...
    )
  )
  (avgpool): AvgPool2d(kernel_size=7, stride=1, padding=0)
  (fc): Linear(in_features=2048, out_features=1000, bias=True)
)
```

What we are seeing here is modules, one per line. Note that they have nothing in common with Python modules: they are individual operations, the building blocks of a neural network. They are also called *layers* in other deep learning frameworks.

If we scroll down, we'll see a lot of Bottleneck modules repeating one after the other (101 of them!), containing convolutions and other modules. That's the anatomy of a typical deep neural network for computer vision: a more or less sequential cascade of filters and nonlinear functions, ending with a layer (fc) producing scores for each of the 1,000 output classes (out_features).

The resnet variable can be called like a function, taking as input one or more images and producing an equal number of scores for each of the 1,000 ImageNet classes. Before we can do that, however, we have to preprocess the input images so they are the right size and so that their values (colors) sit roughly in the same numerical range. In order to do that, the torchvision module provides transforms, which allow us to quickly define pipelines of basic preprocessing functions:

```
# In[6]:
from torchvision import transforms
preprocess = transforms.Compose([
        transforms.Resize(256),
        transforms.CenterCrop(224),
        transforms.ToTensor(),
        transforms.Normalize(
            mean=[0.485, 0.456, 0.406],
            std=[0.229, 0.224, 0.225]
        )])
```

In this case, we defined a preprocess function that will scale the input image to 256 × 256, crop the image to 224 × 224 around the center, transform it to a tensor (a PyTorch multidimensional array: in this case, a 3D array with color, height, and width), and normalize its RGB (red, green, blue) components so that they have defined means and standard deviations. These need to match what was presented to the network during training, if we want the network to produce meaningful answers. We'll go into more depth about transforms when we dive into making our own image-recognition models in section 7.1.3.

We can now grab a picture of our favorite dog (say, bobby.jpg from the GitHub repo), preprocess it, and then see what ResNet thinks of it. We can start by loading an image from the local filesystem using Pillow (https://pillow.readthedocs.io/en/stable), an image-manipulation module for Python:

```
# In[7]:
from PIL import Image
img = Image.open("../data/p1ch2/bobby.jpg")
```

If we were following along from a Jupyter Notebook, we would do the following to see the picture inline (it would be shown where the <PIL.JpegImagePlugin… is in the following):

```
# In[8]:
img
# Out[8]:
<PIL.JpegImagePlugin.JpegImageFile image mode=RGB size=1280x720 at
 0x1B1601360B8>
```

Otherwise, we can invoke the show method, which will pop up a window with a viewer, to see the image shown in figure 2.4:

```
>>> img.show()
```

Figure 2.4 Bobby, our very special input image

Next, we can pass the image through our preprocessing pipeline:

```
# In[9]:
img_t = preprocess(img)
```

Then we can reshape, crop, and normalize the input tensor in a way that the network expects. We'll understand more of this in the next two chapters; hold tight for now:

```
# In[10]:
import torch
batch_t = torch.unsqueeze(img_t, 0)
```

We're now ready to run our model.

2.1.5 *Run!*

The process of running a trained model on new data is called *inference* in deep learning circles. In order to do inference, we need to put the network in eval mode:

```
# In[11]:
resnet.eval()
```

```
# Out[11]:
ResNet(
  (conv1): Conv2d(3, 64, kernel_size=(7, 7), stride=(2, 2), padding=(3, 3),
                  bias=False)
  (bn1): BatchNorm2d(64, eps=1e-05, momentum=0.1, affine=True,
                  track_running_stats=True)
  (relu): ReLU(inplace)
  (maxpool): MaxPool2d(kernel_size=3, stride=2, padding=1, dilation=1,
                  ceil_mode=False)
  (layer1): Sequential(
    (0): Bottleneck(
...
    )
  )
  (avgpool): AvgPool2d(kernel_size=7, stride=1, padding=0)
  (fc): Linear(in_features=2048, out_features=1000, bias=True)
)
```

If we forget to do that, some pretrained models, like *batch normalization* and *dropout*, will not produce meaningful answers, just because of the way they work internally. Now that eval has been set, we're ready for inference:

```
# In[12]:
out = resnet(batch_t)
out
```

```
# Out[12]:
tensor([[ -3.4803,  -1.6618,  -2.4515,  -3.2662,  -3.2466,  -1.3611,
          -2.0465,  -2.5112,  -1.3043,  -2.8900,  -1.6862,  -1.3055,
...
           2.8674,  -3.7442,   1.5085,  -3.2500,  -2.4894,  -0.3354,
           0.1286,  -1.1355,   3.3969,   4.4584]])
```

A staggering set of operations involving 44.5 million parameters has just happened, producing a vector of 1,000 scores, one per ImageNet class. That didn't take long, did it?

We now need to find out the label of the class that received the highest score. This will tell us what the model saw in the image. If the label matches how a human would describe the image, that's great! It means everything is working. If not, then either something went wrong during training, or the image is so different from what the model expects that the model can't process it properly, or there's some other similar issue.

To see the list of predicted labels, we will load a text file listing the labels in the same order they were presented to the network during training, and then we will pick out the label at the index that produced the highest score from the network. Almost all models meant for image recognition have output in a form similar to what we're about to work with.

Let's load the file containing the 1,000 labels for the ImageNet dataset classes:

```
# In[13]:
with open('../data/p1ch2/imagenet_classes.txt') as f:
    labels = [line.strip() for line in f.readlines()]
```

At this point, we need to determine the index corresponding to the maximum score in the out tensor we obtained previously. We can do that using the max function in PyTorch, which outputs the maximum value in a tensor as well as the indices where that maximum value occurred:

```
# In[14]:
_, index = torch.max(out, 1)
```

We can now use the index to access the label. Here, index is not a plain Python number, but a one-element, one-dimensional tensor (specifically, tensor([207])), so we need to get the actual numerical value to use as an index into our labels list using index[0]. We also use torch.nn.functional.softmax (http://mng.bz/BYnq) to normalize our outputs to the range [0, 1], and divide by the sum. That gives us something roughly akin to the confidence that the model has in its prediction. In this case, the model is 96% certain that it knows what it's looking at is a golden retriever:

```
# In[15]:
percentage = torch.nn.functional.softmax(out, dim=1)[0] * 100
labels[index[0]], percentage[index[0]].item()

# Out[15]:
('golden retriever', 96.29334259033203)
```

Uh oh, who's a good boy?

Since the model produced scores, we can also find out what the second best, third best, and so on were. To do this, we can use the sort function, which sorts the values in ascending or descending order and also provides the indices of the sorted values in the original array:

```
# In[16]:
_, indices = torch.sort(out, descending=True)
[(labels[idx], percentage[idx].item()) for idx in indices[0][:5]]

# Out[16]:
[('golden retriever', 96.29334259033203),
 ('Labrador retriever', 2.80812406539917),
 ('cocker spaniel, English cocker spaniel, cocker', 0.28267428278923035),
 ('redbone', 0.2086310237646103),
 ('tennis ball', 0.11621569097042084)]
```

We see that the first four are dogs (redbone is a breed; who knew?), after which things start to get funny. The fifth answer, "tennis ball," is probably because there are enough pictures of tennis balls with dogs nearby that the model is essentially saying, "There's a 0.1% chance that I've completely misunderstood what a tennis ball is." This is a great example of the fundamental differences in how humans and neural networks view the world, as well as how easy it is for strange, subtle biases to sneak into our data.

Time to play! We can go ahead and interrogate our network with random images and see what it comes up with. How successful the network will be will largely depend on whether the subjects were well represented in the training set. If we present an image containing a subject outside the training set, it's quite possible that the network will come up with a wrong answer with pretty high confidence. It's useful to experiment and get a feel for how a model reacts to unseen data.

We've just run a network that won an image-classification competition in 2015. It learned to recognize our dog from examples of dogs, together with a ton of other real-world subjects. We'll now see how different architectures can achieve other kinds of tasks, starting with image generation.

2.2 *A pretrained model that fakes it until it makes it*

Let's suppose, for a moment, that we're career criminals who want to move into selling forgeries of "lost" paintings by famous artists. We're criminals, not painters, so as we paint our fake Rembrandts and Picassos, it quickly becomes apparent that they're amateur imitations rather than the real deal. Even if we spend a bunch of time practicing until we get a canvas that *we* can't tell is fake, trying to pass it off at the local art auction house is going to get us kicked out instantly. Even worse, being told "This is clearly fake; get out," doesn't help us improve! We'd have to randomly try a bunch of things, gauge which ones took *slightly* longer to recognize as forgeries, and emphasize those traits on our future attempts, which would take far too long.

Instead, we need to find an art historian of questionable moral standing to inspect our work and tell us exactly what it was that tipped them off that the painting wasn't legit. With that feedback, we can improve our output in clear, directed ways, until our sketchy scholar can no longer tell our paintings from the real thing.

Soon, we'll have our "Botticelli" in the Louvre, and their Benjamins in our pockets. We'll be rich!

While this scenario is a bit farcical, the underlying technology is sound and will likely have a profound impact on the perceived veracity of digital data in the years to come. The entire concept of "photographic evidence" is likely to become entirely suspect, given how easy it will be to automate the production of convincing, yet fake, images and video. The only key ingredient is data. Let's see how this process works.

2.2.1 The GAN game

In the context of deep learning, what we've just described is known as *the GAN game*, where two networks, one acting as the painter and the other as the art historian, compete to outsmart each other at creating and detecting forgeries. GAN stands for *generative adversarial network*, where *generative* means something is being created (in this case, fake masterpieces), *adversarial* means the two networks are competing to outsmart the other, and well, *network* is pretty obvious. These networks are one of the most original outcomes of recent deep learning research.

Remember that our overarching goal is to produce synthetic examples of a class of images that cannot be recognized as fake. When mixed in with legitimate examples, a skilled examiner would have trouble determining which ones are real and which are our forgeries.

The *generator* network takes the role of the painter in our scenario, tasked with producing realistic-looking images, starting from an arbitrary input. The *discriminator* network is the amoral art inspector, needing to tell whether a given image was fabricated by the generator or belongs in a set of real images. This two-network design is atypical for most deep learning architectures but, when used to implement a GAN game, can lead to incredible results.

Figure 2.5 shows a rough picture of what's going on. The end goal for the generator is to fool the discriminator into mixing up real and fake images. The end goal for the discriminator is to find out when it's being tricked, but it also helps inform the generator about the identifiable mistakes in the generated images. At the start, the generator produces confused, three-eyed monsters that look nothing like a Rembrandt portrait. The discriminator is easily able to distinguish the muddled messes from the real paintings. As training progresses, information flows back from the discriminator, and the generator uses it to improve. By the end of training, the generator is able to produce convincing fakes, and the discriminator no longer is able to tell which is which.

Note that "Discriminator wins" or "Generator wins" shouldn't be taken literally—there's no explicit tournament between the two. However, both networks are trained based on the outcome of the other network, which drives the optimization of the parameters of each network.

This technique has proven itself able to lead to generators that produce realistic images from nothing but noise and a conditioning signal, like an attribute (for example, for faces: young, female, glasses on) or another image. In other words, a well-trained generator learns a plausible model for generating images that look real even when examined by humans.

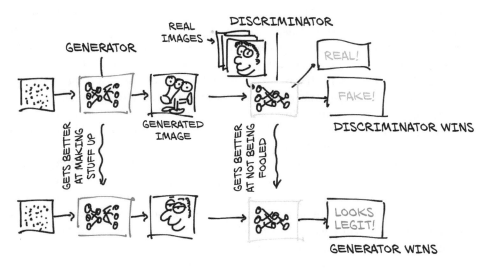

Figure 2.5   Concept of a GAN game

2.2.2   CycleGAN

An interesting evolution of this concept is the CycleGAN. A CycleGAN can turn images of one domain into images of another domain (and back), without the need for us to explicitly provide matching pairs in the training set.

In figure 2.6, we have a CycleGAN workflow for the task of turning a photo of a horse into a zebra, and vice versa. Note that there are two separate generator networks, as well as two distinct discriminators.

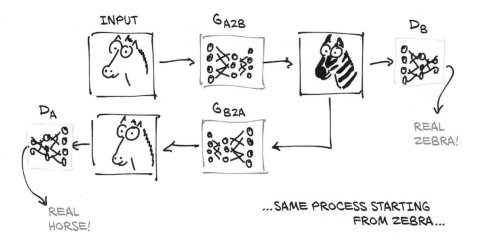

Figure 2.6   A CycleGAN trained to the point that it can fool both discriminator networks

As the figure shows, the first generator learns to produce an image conforming to a target distribution (zebras, in this case) starting from an image belonging to a different distribution (horses), so that the discriminator can't tell if the image produced from a horse photo is actually a genuine picture of a zebra or not. At the same time—and here's where the *Cycle* prefix in the acronym comes in—the resulting fake zebra is sent through a different generator going the other way (zebra to horse, in our case), to be judged by another discriminator on the other side. Creating such a cycle stabilizes the training process considerably, which addresses one of the original issues with GANs.

The fun part is that at this point, we don't need matched horse/zebra pairs as ground truths (good luck getting them to match poses!). It's enough to start from a collection of unrelated horse images and zebra photos for the generators to learn their task, going beyond a purely supervised setting. The implications of this model go even further than this: the generator learns how to selectively change the appearance of objects in the scene without supervision about what's what. There's no signal indicating that manes are manes and legs are legs, but they get translated to something that lines up with the anatomy of the other animal.

2.2.3   *A network that turns horses into zebras*

We can play with this model right now. The CycleGAN network has been trained on a dataset of (unrelated) horse images and zebra images extracted from the ImageNet dataset. The network learns to take an image of one or more horses and turn them all into zebras, leaving the rest of the image as unmodified as possible. While humankind hasn't held its breath over the last few thousand years for a tool that turn horses into zebras, this task showcases the ability of these architectures to model complex real-world processes with distant supervision. While they have their limits, there are hints that in the near future we won't be able to tell real from fake in a live video feed, which opens a can of worms that we'll duly close right now.

Playing with a pretrained CycleGAN will give us the opportunity to take a step closer and look at how a network—a generator, in this case—is implemented. We'll use our old friend ResNet. We'll define a `ResNetGenerator` class offscreen. The code is in the first cell of the 3_cyclegan.ipynb file, but the implementation isn't relevant right now, and it's too complex to follow until we've gotten a lot more PyTorch experience. Right now, we're focused on *what* it can do, rather than *how* it does it. Let's instantiate the class with default parameters (code/p1ch2/3_cyclegan.ipynb):

```
# In[2]:
netG = ResNetGenerator()
```

The netG model has been created, but it contains random weights. We mentioned earlier that we would run a generator model that had been pretrained on the horse2zebra dataset, whose training set contains two sets of 1068 and 1335 images of horses and zebras, respectively. The dataset be found at http://mng.bz/8pKP. The weights of the model have been saved in a .pth file, which is nothing but a `pickle` file of the model's tensor parameters. We can load those into `ResNetGenerator` using the model's `load_state_dict` method:

```
# In[3]:
model_path = '../data/p1ch2/horse2zebra_0.4.0.pth'
model_data = torch.load(model_path)
netG.load_state_dict(model_data)
```

At this point, `netG` has acquired all the knowledge it achieved during training. Note that this is fully equivalent to what happened when we loaded `resnet101` from torch-vision in section 2.1.3; but the `torchvision.resnet101` function hid the loading from us.

Let's put the network in `eval` mode, as we did for `resnet101`:

```
# In[4]:
netG.eval()

# Out[4]:
ResNetGenerator(
  (model): Sequential(
...
  )
)
```

Printing out the model as we did earlier, we can appreciate that it's actually pretty condensed, considering what it does. It takes an image, recognizes one or more horses in it by looking at pixels, and individually modifies the values of those pixels so that what comes out looks like a credible zebra. We won't recognize anything zebra-like in the printout (or in the source code, for that matter): that's because there's nothing zebra-like in there. The network is a scaffold—the juice is in the weights.

We're ready to load a random image of a horse and see what our generator produces. First, we need to import `PIL` and `torchvision`:

```
# In[5]:
from PIL import Image
from torchvision import transforms
```

Then we define a few input transformations to make sure data enters the network with the right shape and size:

```
# In[6]:
preprocess = transforms.Compose([transforms.Resize(256),
                                 transforms.ToTensor()])
```

Let's open a horse file (see figure 2.7):

```
# In[7]:
img = Image.open("../data/p1ch2/horse.jpg")
img
```

Figure 2.7   A man riding a horse. The horse is not having it.

OK, there's a dude on the horse. (Not for long, judging by the picture.) Anyhow, let's pass it through preprocessing and turn it into a properly shaped variable:

```
# In[8]:
img_t = preprocess(img)
batch_t = torch.unsqueeze(img_t, 0)
```

We shouldn't worry about the details right now. The important thing is that we follow from a distance. At this point, batch_t can be sent to our model:

```
# In[9]:
batch_out = netG(batch_t)
```

batch_out is now the output of the generator, which we can convert back to an image:

```
# In[10]:
out_t = (batch_out.data.squeeze() + 1.0) / 2.0
out_img = transforms.ToPILImage()(out_t)
# out_img.save('../data/p1ch2/zebra.jpg')
out_img

# Out[10]:
<PIL.Image.Image image mode=RGB size=316x256 at 0x23B24634F98>
```

Oh, man. Who rides a zebra that way? The resulting image (figure 2.8) is not perfect, but consider that it is a bit unusual for the network to find someone (sort of) riding on top of a horse. It bears repeating that the learning process has not passed through direct supervision, where humans have delineated tens of thousands of horses or manually Photoshopped thousands of zebra stripes. The generator has learned to produce an image that would fool the discriminator into thinking that was a zebra, and there was nothing fishy about the image (clearly the discriminator has never been to a rodeo).

Figure 2.8   A man riding a zebra. The zebra is not having it.

Many other fun generators have been developed using adversarial training or other approaches. Some of them are capable of creating credible human faces of nonexistent individuals; others can translate sketches into real-looking pictures of imaginary landscapes. Generative models are also being explored for producing real-sounding audio, credible text, and enjoyable music. It is likely that these models will be the basis of future tools that support the creative process.

On a serious note, it's hard to overstate the implications of this kind of work. Tools like the one we just downloaded are only going to become higher quality and more ubiquitous. Face-swapping technology, in particular, has gotten considerable media attention. Searching for "deep fakes" will turn up a plethora of example content[1] (though we must note that there is a nontrivial amount of not-safe-for-work content labeled as such; as with everything on the internet, click carefully).

So far, we've had a chance to play with a model that sees into images and a model that generates new images. We'll end our tour with a model that involves one more, fundamental ingredient: natural language.

2.3   *A pretrained network that describes scenes*

In order to get firsthand experience with a model involving natural language, we will use a pretrained image-captioning model, generously provided by Ruotian Luo.[2] It is an implementation of the NeuralTalk2 model by Andrej Karpathy. When presented with a natural image, this kind of model generates a caption in English that describes the scene, as shown in figure 2.9. The model is trained on a large dataset of images

---

[1] A relevant example is described in the Vox article "Jordan Peele's simulated Obama PSA is a double-edged warning against fake news," by Aja Romano; http://mng.bz/dxBz (warning: coarse language).

[2] We maintain a clone of the code at https://github.com/deep-learning-with-pytorch/ImageCaptioning .pytorch.

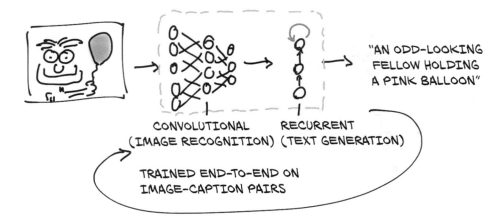

Figure 2.9   Concept of a captioning model

along with a paired sentence description: for example, "A Tabby cat is leaning on a wooden table, with one paw on a laser mouse and the other on a black laptop."[3]

This captioning model has two connected halves. The first half of the model is a network that learns to generate "descriptive" numerical representations of the scene (Tabby cat, laser mouse, paw), which are then taken as input to the second half. That second half is a *recurrent neural network* that generates a coherent sentence by putting those numerical descriptions together. The two halves of the model are trained together on image-caption pairs.

The second half of the model is called *recurrent* because it generates its outputs (individual words) in subsequent forward passes, where the input to each forward pass includes the outputs of the previous forward pass. This generates a dependency of the next word on words that were generated earlier, as we would expect when dealing with sentences or, in general, with sequences.

2.3.1   *NeuralTalk2*

The NeuralTalk2 model can be found at https://github.com/deep-learning-with-pytorch/ImageCaptioning.pytorch. We can place a set of images in the `data` directory and run the following script:

```
python eval.py --model ./data/FC/fc-model.pth
⇨ --infos_path ./data/FC/fc-infos.pkl --image_folder ./data
```

Let's try it with our horse.jpg image. It says, "A person riding a horse on a beach." Quite appropriate.

---

[3] Andrej Karpathy and Li Fei-Fei, "Deep Visual-Semantic Alignments for Generating Image Descriptions," https://cs.stanford.edu/people/karpathy/cvpr2015.pdf.

Now, just for fun, let's see if our CycleGAN can also fool this NeuralTalk2 model. Let's add the zebra.jpg image in the data folder and rerun the model: "A group of zebras are standing in a field." Well, it got the animal right, but it saw more than one zebra in the image. Certainly this is not a pose that the network has ever seen a zebra in, nor has it ever seen a rider on a zebra (with some spurious zebra patterns). In addition, it is very likely that zebras are depicted in groups in the training dataset, so there might be some bias that we could investigate. The captioning network hasn't described the rider, either. Again, it's probably for the same reason: the network wasn't shown a rider on a zebra in the training dataset. In any case, this is an impressive feat: we generated a fake image with an impossible situation, and the captioning network was flexible enough to get the subject right.

We'd like to stress that something like this, which would have been extremely hard to achieve before the advent of deep learning, can be obtained with under a thousand lines of code, with a general-purpose architecture that knows nothing about horses or zebras, and a corpus of images and their descriptions (the MS COCO dataset, in this case). No hardcoded criterion or grammar—everything, including the sentence, emerges from patterns in the data.

The network architecture in this last case was, in a way, more complex than the ones we saw earlier, as it includes two networks. One is recurrent, but it was built out of the same building blocks, all of which are provided by PyTorch.

At the time of this writing, models such as these exist more as applied research or novelty projects, rather than something that has a well-defined, concrete use. The results, while promising, just aren't good enough to use … yet. With time (and additional training data), we should expect this class of models to be able to describe the world to people with vision impairment, transcribe scenes from video, and perform other similar tasks.

2.4 Torch Hub

Pretrained models have been published since the early days of deep learning, but until PyTorch 1.0, there was no way to ensure that users would have a uniform interface to get them. TorchVision was a good example of a clean interface, as we saw earlier in this chapter; but other authors, as we have seen for CycleGAN and NeuralTalk2, chose different designs.

PyTorch 1.0 saw the introduction of Torch Hub, which is a mechanism through which authors can publish a model on GitHub, with or without pretrained weights, and expose it through an interface that PyTorch understands. This makes loading a pretrained model from a third party as easy as loading a TorchVision model.

All it takes for an author to publish a model through the Torch Hub mechanism is to place a file named hubconf.py in the root directory of the GitHub repository. The file has a very simple structure:

Optional list of modules the code depends on

```
dependencies = ['torch', 'math']

def some_entry_fn(*args, **kwargs):
    model = build_some_model(*args, **kwargs)
    return model

def another_entry_fn(*args, **kwargs):
    model = build_another_model(*args, **kwargs)
    return model
```

One or more functions to be exposed to users as entry points for the repository. These functions should initialize models according to the arguments and return them.

In our quest for interesting pretrained models, we can now search for GitHub repositories that include hubconf.py, and we'll know right away that we can load them using the torch.hub module. Let's see how this is done in practice. To do that, we'll go back to TorchVision, because it provides a clean example of how to interact with Torch Hub.

Let's visit https://github.com/pytorch/vision and notice that it contains a hubconf.py file. Great, that checks. The first thing to do is to look in that file to see the entry points for the repo—we'll need to specify them later. In the case of TorchVision, there are two: `resnet18` and `resnet50`. We already know what these do: they return an 18-layer and a 50-layer ResNet model, respectively. We also see that the entry-point functions include a `pretrained` keyword argument. If `True`, the returned models will be initialized with weights learned from ImageNet, as we saw earlier in the chapter.

Now we know the repo, the entry points, and one interesting keyword argument. That's about all we need to load the model using torch.hub, without even cloning the repo. That's right, PyTorch will handle that for us:

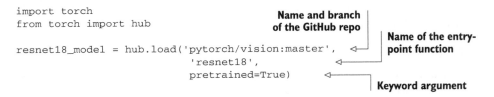

```
import torch
from torch import hub                          Name and branch
                                               of the GitHub repo
                                                                   Name of the entry-
resnet18_model = hub.load('pytorch/vision:master',    point function
                          'resnet18',
                          pretrained=True)
                                                   Keyword argument
```

This manages to download a snapshot of the master branch of the pytorch/vision repo, along with the weights, to a local directory (defaults to .torch/hub in our home directory) and run the `resnet18` entry-point function, which returns the instantiated model. Depending on the environment, Python may complain that there's a module missing, like `PIL`. Torch Hub won't install missing dependencies, but it will report them to us so that we can take action.

At this point, we can invoke the returned model with proper arguments to run a forward pass on it, the same way we did earlier. The nice part is that now every model published through this mechanism will be accessible to us using the same modalities, well beyond vision.

Note that entry points are supposed to return models; but, strictly speaking, they are not forced to. For instance, we could have an entry point for transforming inputs and another one for turning the output probabilities into a text label. Or we could have an entry point for just the model, and another that includes the model along with the pre- and postprocessing steps. By leaving these options open, the PyTorch developers have provided the community with just enough standardization and a lot of flexibility. We'll see what patterns will emerge from this opportunity.

Torch Hub is quite new at the time of writing, and there are only a few models published this way. We can get at them by Googling "github.com hubconf.py." Hopefully the list will grow in the future, as more authors share their models through this channel.

2.5 Conclusion

We hope this was a fun chapter. We took some time to play with models created with PyTorch, which were optimized to carry out specific tasks. In fact, the more enterprising of us could already put one of these models behind a web server and start a business, sharing the profits with the original authors![4] Once we learn how these models are built, we will also be able to use the knowledge we gained here to download a pretrained model and quickly fine-tune it on a slightly different task.

We will also see how building models that deal with different problems on different kinds of data can be done using the same building blocks. One thing that PyTorch does particularly right is providing those building blocks in the form of an essential toolset—PyTorch is not a very large library from an API perspective, especially when compared with other deep learning frameworks.

This book does not focus on going through the complete PyTorch API or reviewing deep learning architectures; rather, we will build hands-on knowledge of these building blocks. This way, you will be able to consume the excellent online documentation and repositories on top of a solid foundation.

Starting with the next chapter, we'll embark on a journey that will enable us to teach our computer skills like those described in this chapter from scratch, using PyTorch. We'll also learn that starting from a pretrained network and fine-tuning it on new data, without starting from scratch, is an effective way to solve problems when the data points we have are not particularly numerous. This is one further reason pretrained networks are an important tool for deep learning practitioners to have. Time to learn about the first fundamental building block: tensors.

---

[4] Contact the publisher for franchise opportunities!

2.6   *Exercises*

1   Feed the image of the golden retriever into the horse-to-zebra model.

   a   What do you need to do to the image to prepare it?

   b   What does the output look like?

2   Search GitHub for projects that provide a hubconf.py file.

   a   How many repositories are returned?

   b   Find an interesting-looking project with a hubconf.py. Can you understand the purpose of the project from the documentation?

   c   Bookmark the project, and come back after you've finished this book. Can you understand the implementation?

2.7   *Summary*

- A pretrained network is a model that has already been trained on a dataset. Such networks can typically produce useful results immediately after loading the network parameters.

- By knowing how to use a pretrained model, we can integrate a neural network into a project without having to design or train it.

- AlexNet and ResNet are two deep convolutional networks that set new benchmarks for image recognition in the years they were released.

- Generative adversarial networks (GANs) have two parts—the generator and the discriminator—that work together to produce output indistinguishable from authentic items.

- CycleGAN uses an architecture that supports converting back and forth between two different classes of images.

- NeuralTalk2 uses a hybrid model architecture to consume an image and produce a text description of the image.

- Torch Hub is a standardized way to load models and weights from any project with an appropriate hubconf.py file.

It starts with a tensor

In the previous chapter, we took a tour of some of the many applications that deep learning enables. They invariably consisted of taking data in some form, like images or text, and producing data in another form, like labels, numbers, or more images or text. Viewed from this angle, deep learning really consists of building a system that can transform data from one representation to another. This transformation is driven by extracting commonalities from a series of examples that demonstrate the desired mapping. For example, the system might note the general shape of a dog and the typical colors of a golden retriever. By combining the two image properties, the system can correctly map images with a given shape and color to the golden retriever label, instead of a black lab (or a tawny tomcat, for that matter). The resulting system can consume broad swaths of similar inputs and produce meaningful output for those inputs.

The process begins by converting our input into floating-point numbers. We will cover converting image pixels to numbers, as we see in the first step of figure 3.1, in chapter 4 (along with many other types of data). But before we can get to that, in this chapter, we learn how to deal with all the floating-point numbers in PyTorch by using tensors.

3.1   *The world as floating-point numbers*

Since floating-point numbers are the way a network deals with information, we need a way to encode real-world data of the kind we want to process into something digestible by a network and then decode the output back to something we can understand and use for our purpose.

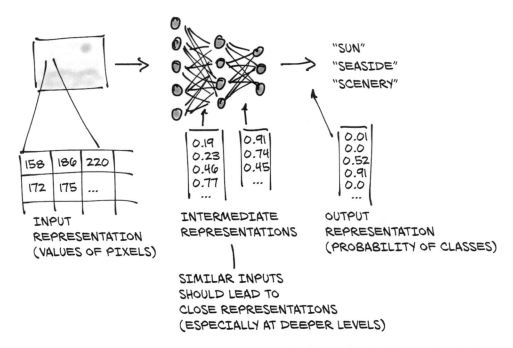

Figure 3.1   A deep neural network learns how to transform an input representation to an output representation. (Note: The numbers of neurons and outputs are not to scale.)

A deep neural network typically learns the transformation from one form of data to another in stages, which means the partially transformed data between each stage can be thought of as a sequence of intermediate representations. For image recognition, early representations can be things such as edge detection or certain textures like fur. Deeper representations can capture more complex structures like ears, noses, or eyes.

In general, such intermediate representations are collections of floating-point numbers that characterize the input and capture the data's structure in a way that is instrumental for describing how inputs are mapped to the outputs of the neural network. Such characterization is specific to the task at hand and is learned from relevant examples. These collections of floating-point numbers and their manipulation are at the heart of modern AI—we will see several examples of this throughout the book.

It's important to keep in mind that these intermediate representations (like those shown in the second step of figure 3.1) are the results of combining the input with the weights of the previous layer of neurons. Each intermediate representation is unique to the inputs that preceeded it.

Before we can begin the process of converting our data to floating-point input, we must first have a solid understanding of how PyTorch handles and stores data—as input, as intermediate representations, and as output. This chapter will be devoted to precisely that.

To this end, PyTorch introduces a fundamental data structure: the *tensor*. We already bumped into tensors in chapter 2, when we ran inference on pretrained networks. For those who come from mathematics, physics, or engineering, the term *tensor* comes bundled with the notion of spaces, reference systems, and transformations between them. For better or worse, those notions do not apply here. In the context of deep learning, tensors refer to the generalization of vectors and matrices to an arbitrary number of dimensions, as we can see in figure 3.2. Another name for the same concept is *multidimensional array*. The dimensionality of a tensor coincides with the number of indexes used to refer to scalar values within the tensor.

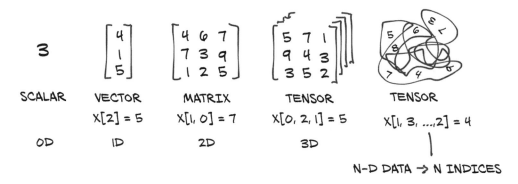

Figure 3.2 Tensors are the building blocks for representing data in PyTorch.

PyTorch is not the only library that deals with multidimensional arrays. NumPy is by far the most popular multidimensional array library, to the point that it has now arguably become the *lingua franca* of data science. PyTorch features seamless interoperability with NumPy, which brings with it first-class integration with the rest of the scientific libraries in Python, such as SciPy (www.scipy.org), Scikit-learn (https://scikit-learn.org), and Pandas (https://pandas.pydata.org).

Compared to NumPy arrays, PyTorch tensors have a few superpowers, such as the ability to perform very fast operations on graphical processing units (GPUs), distribute operations on multiple devices or machines, and keep track of the graph of computations that created them. These are all important features when implementing a modern deep learning library.

We'll start this chapter by introducing PyTorch tensors, covering the basics in order to set things in motion for our work in the rest of the book. First and foremost, we'll learn how to manipulate tensors using the PyTorch tensor library. This includes things like how the data is stored in memory, how certain operations can be performed on arbitrarily large tensors in constant time, and the aforementioned NumPy interoperability and GPU acceleration. Understanding the capabilities and API of tensors is important if they're to become go-to tools in our programming toolbox. In the next chapter, we'll put this knowledge to good use and learn how to represent several different kinds of data in a way that enables learning with neural networks.

3.2   *Tensors: Multidimensional arrays*

We have already learned that tensors are the fundamental data structure in PyTorch. A tensor is an array: that is, a data structure that stores a collection of numbers that are accessible individually using an index, and that can be indexed with multiple indices.

3.2.1   *From Python lists to PyTorch tensors*

Let's see `list` indexing in action so we can compare it to tensor indexing. Take a list of three numbers in Python (.code/p1ch3/1_tensors.ipynb):

```
# In[1]:
a = [1.0, 2.0, 1.0]
```

We can access the first element of the list using the corresponding zero-based index:

```
# In[2]:
a[0]

# Out[2]:
1.0

# In[3]:
a[2] = 3.0
a

# Out[3]:
[1.0, 2.0, 3.0]
```

It is not unusual for simple Python programs dealing with vectors of numbers, such as the coordinates of a 2D line, to use Python lists to store the vectors. As we will see in the following chapter, using the more efficient tensor data structure, many types of data—from images to time series, and even sentences—can be represented. By defining operations over tensors, some of which we'll explore in this chapter, we can slice and manipulate data expressively and efficiently at the same time, even from a high-level (and not particularly fast) language such as Python.

3.2.2 Constructing our first tensors

Let's construct our first PyTorch tensor and see what it looks like. It won't be a particularly meaningful tensor for now, just three ones in a column:

```
# In[4]:
import torch         ◄────┐   Imports the torch module
a = torch.ones(3)    ◄──┐
a                       │   Creates a one-dimensional
                        │   tensor of size 3 filled with 1s
# Out[4]:
tensor([1., 1., 1.])

# In[5]:
a[1]

# Out[5]:
tensor(1.)

# In[6]:
float(a[1])

# Out[6]:
1.0

# In[7]:
a[2] = 2.0
a

# Out[7]:
tensor([1., 1., 2.])
```

After importing the `torch` module, we call a function that creates a (one-dimensional) tensor of size 3 filled with the value `1.0`. We can access an element using its zero-based index or assign a new value to it. Although on the surface this example doesn't differ much from a list of number objects, under the hood things are completely different.

3.2.3 The essence of tensors

Python lists or tuples of numbers are collections of Python objects that are individually allocated in memory, as shown on the left in figure 3.3. PyTorch tensors or NumPy arrays, on the other hand, are views over (typically) contiguous memory blocks containing *unboxed* C numeric types rather than Python objects. Each element is a 32-bit (4-byte) `float` in this case, as we can see on the right side of figure 3.3. This means storing a 1D tensor of 1,000,000 float numbers will require exactly 4,000,000 contiguous bytes, plus a small overhead for the metadata (such as dimensions and numeric type).

Say we have a list of coordinates we'd like to use to represent a geometrical object: perhaps a 2D triangle with vertices at coordinates (4, 1), (5, 3), and (2, 1). The example is not particularly pertinent to deep learning, but it's easy to follow. Instead of having coordinates as numbers in a Python list, as we did earlier, we can use a

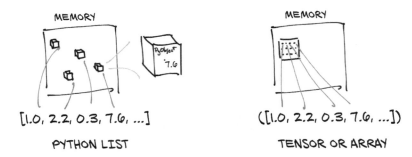

Figure 3.3   Python object (boxed) numeric values versus tensor (unboxed array) numeric values

one-dimensional tensor by storing *Xs* in the even indices and *Ys* in the odd indices, like this:

```
# In[8]:
points = torch.zeros(6)
points[0] = 4.0
points[1] = 1.0
points[2] = 5.0
points[3] = 3.0
points[4] = 2.0
points[5] = 1.0
```

Using .zeros is just a way to get an appropriately sized array.

We overwrite those zeros with the values we actually want.

We can also pass a Python list to the constructor, to the same effect:

```
# In[9]:
points = torch.tensor([4.0, 1.0, 5.0, 3.0, 2.0, 1.0])
points
```

```
# Out[9]:
tensor([4., 1., 5., 3., 2., 1.])
```

To get the coordinates of the first point, we do the following:

```
# In[10]:
float(points[0]), float(points[1])
```

```
# Out[10]:
(4.0, 1.0)
```

This is OK, although it would be practical to have the first index refer to individual 2D points rather than point coordinates. For this, we can use a 2D tensor:

```
# In[11]:
points = torch.tensor([[4.0, 1.0], [5.0, 3.0], [2.0, 1.0]])
points
```

```
# Out[11]:
tensor([[4., 1.],
        [5., 3.],
        [2., 1.]])
```

Here, we pass a list of lists to the constructor. We can ask the tensor about its shape:

```
# In[12]:
points.shape
```

```
# Out[12]:
torch.Size([3, 2])
```

This informs us about the size of the tensor along each dimension. We could also use zeros or ones to initialize the tensor, providing the size as a tuple:

```
# In[13]:
points = torch.zeros(3, 2)
points
```

```
# Out[13]:
tensor([[0., 0.],
        [0., 0.],
        [0., 0.]])
```

Now we can access an individual element in the tensor using two indices:

```
# In[14]:
points = torch.tensor([[4.0, 1.0], [5.0, 3.0], [2.0, 1.0]])
points
```

```
# Out[14]:
tensor([[4., 1.],
        [5., 3.],
        [2., 1.]])
```

```
# In[15]:
points[0, 1]
```

```
# Out[15]:
tensor(1.)
```

This returns the *Y*-coordinate of the zeroth point in our dataset. We can also access the first element in the tensor as we did before to get the 2D coordinates of the first point:

```
# In[16]:
points[0]
```

```
# Out[16]:
tensor([4., 1.])
```

The output is another tensor that presents a different *view* of the same underlying data. The new tensor is a 1D tensor of size 2, referencing the values of the first row in the `points` tensor. Does this mean a new chunk of memory was allocated, values were copied into it, and the new memory was returned wrapped in a new tensor object? No, because that would be very inefficient, especially if we had millions of points. We'll revisit how tensors are stored later in this chapter when we cover views of tensors in section 3.7.

3.3   Indexing tensors

What if we need to obtain a tensor containing all points but the first? That's easy using range indexing notation, which also applies to standard Python lists. Here's a reminder:

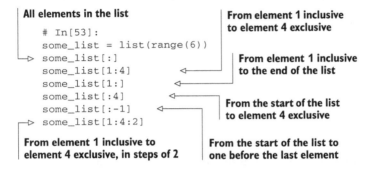

To achieve our goal, we can use the same notation for PyTorch tensors, with the added benefit that, just as in NumPy and other Python scientific libraries, we can use range indexing for each of the tensor's dimensions:

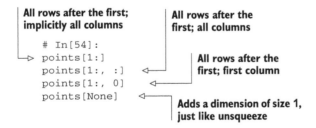

In addition to using ranges, PyTorch features a powerful form of indexing, called *advanced indexing*, which we will look at in the next chapter.

3.4   Named tensors

The dimensions (or axes) of our tensors usually index something like pixel locations or color channels. This means when we want to index into a tensor, we need to remember the ordering of the dimensions and write our indexing accordingly. As data is transformed through multiple tensors, keeping track of which dimension contains what data can be error-prone.

To make things concrete, imagine that we have a 3D tensor like `img_t` from section 2.1.4 (we will use dummy data for simplicity here), and we want to convert it to grayscale. We looked up typical weights for the colors to derive a single brightness value:[1]

```
# In[2]:
img_t = torch.randn(3, 5, 5) # shape [channels, rows, columns]
weights = torch.tensor([0.2126, 0.7152, 0.0722])
```

We also often want our code to generalize—for example, from grayscale images represented as 2D tensors with height and width dimensions to color images adding a third channel dimension (as in RGB), or from a single image to a batch of images. In section 2.1.4, we introduced an additional batch dimension in `batch_t`; here we pretend to have a batch of 2:

```
# In[3]:
batch_t = torch.randn(2, 3, 5, 5) # shape [batch, channels, rows, columns]
```

So sometimes the RGB channels are in dimension 0, and sometimes they are in dimension 1. But we can generalize by counting from the end: they are always in dimension −3, the third from the end. The lazy, unweighted mean can thus be written as follows:

```
# In[4]:
img_gray_naive = img_t.mean(-3)
batch_gray_naive = batch_t.mean(-3)
img_gray_naive.shape, batch_gray_naive.shape

# Out[4]:
(torch.Size([5, 5]), torch.Size([2, 5, 5]))
```

But now we have the weight, too. PyTorch will allow us to multiply things that are the same shape, as well as shapes where one operand is of size 1 in a given dimension. It also appends leading dimensions of size 1 automatically. This is a feature called *broadcasting*. `batch_t` of shape (2, 3, 5, 5) is multiplied by `unsqueezed_weights` of shape (3, 1, 1), resulting in a tensor of shape (2, 3, 5, 5), from which we can then sum the third dimension from the end (the three channels):

```
# In[5]:
unsqueezed_weights = weights.unsqueeze(-1).unsqueeze_(-1)
img_weights = (img_t * unsqueezed_weights)
batch_weights = (batch_t * unsqueezed_weights)
img_gray_weighted = img_weights.sum(-3)
batch_gray_weighted = batch_weights.sum(-3)
batch_weights.shape, batch_t.shape, unsqueezed_weights.shape

# Out[5]:
(torch.Size([2, 3, 5, 5]), torch.Size([2, 3, 5, 5]), torch.Size([3, 1, 1]))
```

---

[1] As perception is not trivial to norm, people have come up with many weights. For example, see https://en.wikipedia.org/wiki/Luma_(video).

Because this gets messy quickly—and for the sake of efficiency—the PyTorch function einsum (adapted from NumPy) specifies an indexing mini-language[2] giving index names to dimensions for sums of such products. As often in Python, broadcasting—a form of summarizing unnamed things—is done using three dots '...'; but don't worry too much about einsum, because we will not use it in the following:

```
# In[6]:
img_gray_weighted_fancy = torch.einsum('...chw,c->...hw', img_t, weights)
batch_gray_weighted_fancy = torch.einsum('...chw,c->...hw', batch_t, weights)
batch_gray_weighted_fancy.shape

# Out[6]:
torch.Size([2, 5, 5])
```

As we can see, there is quite a lot of bookkeeping involved. This is error-prone, especially when the locations where tensors are created and used are far apart in our code. This has caught the eye of practitioners, and so it has been suggested[3] that the dimension be given a name instead.

PyTorch 1.3 added *named tensors* as an experimental feature (see https://pytorch .org/tutorials/intermediate/named_tensor_tutorial.html and https://pytorch.org/ docs/stable/named_tensor.html). Tensor factory functions such as tensor and rand take a names argument. The names should be a sequence of strings:

```
# In[7]:
weights_named = torch.tensor([0.2126, 0.7152, 0.0722], names=['channels'])
weights_named

# Out[7]:
tensor([0.2126, 0.7152, 0.0722], names=('channels',))
```

When we already have a tensor and want to add names (but not change existing ones), we can call the method refine_names on it. Similar to indexing, the ellipsis (...) allows you to leave out any number of dimensions. With the rename sibling method, you can also overwrite or drop (by passing in None) existing names:

```
# In[8]:
img_named =  img_t.refine_names(..., 'channels', 'rows', 'columns')
batch_named = batch_t.refine_names(..., 'channels', 'rows', 'columns')
print("img named:", img_named.shape, img_named.names)
print("batch named:", batch_named.shape, batch_named.names)

# Out[8]:
img named: torch.Size([3, 5, 5]) ('channels', 'rows', 'columns')
batch named: torch.Size([2, 3, 5, 5]) (None, 'channels', 'rows', 'columns')
```

---

[2] Tim Rocktäschel's blog post "Einsum is All You Need—Einstein Summation in Deep Learning" (https:// rockt.github.io/2018/04/30/einsum) gives a good overview.

[3] See Sasha Rush, "Tensor Considered Harmful," Harvardnlp, http://nlp.seas.harvard.edu/NamedTensor.

For operations with two inputs, in addition to the usual dimension checks—whether sizes are the same, or if one is 1 and can be broadcast to the other—PyTorch will now check the names for us. So far, it does not automatically align dimensions, so we need to do this explicitly. The method `align_as` returns a tensor with missing dimensions added and existing ones permuted to the right order:

```
# In[9]:
weights_aligned = weights_named.align_as(img_named)
weights_aligned.shape, weights_aligned.names

# Out[9]:
(torch.Size([3, 1, 1]), ('channels', 'rows', 'columns'))
```

Functions accepting dimension arguments, like sum, also take named dimensions:

```
# In[10]:
gray_named = (img_named * weights_aligned).sum('channels')
gray_named.shape, gray_named.names

# Out[10]:
(torch.Size([5, 5]), ('rows', 'columns'))
```

If we try to combine dimensions with different names, we get an error:

```
gray_named = (img_named[..., :3] * weights_named).sum('channels')

RuntimeError: Error when
  attempting to broadcast dims ['channels', 'rows',
    'columns'] and dims ['channels']: dim 'columns' and dim 'channels'
    are at the same position from the right but do not match.
```

If we want to use tensors outside functions that operate on named tensors, we need to drop the names by renaming them to None. The following gets us back into the world of unnamed dimensions:

```
# In[12]:
gray_plain = gray_named.rename(None)
gray_plain.shape, gray_plain.names

# Out[12]:
(torch.Size([5, 5]), (None, None))
```

Given the experimental nature of this feature at the time of writing, and to avoid mucking around with indexing and alignment, we will stick to unnamed in the remainder of the book. Named tensors have the potential to eliminate many sources of alignment errors, which—if the PyTorch forum is any indication—can be a source of headaches. It will be interesting to see how widely they will be adopted.

3.5   *Tensor element types*

So far, we have covered the basics of how tensors work, but we have not yet touched on what kinds of numeric types we can store in a Tensor. As we hinted at in section 3.2, using the standard Python numeric types can be suboptimal for several reasons:

- *Numbers in Python are objects.* Whereas a floating-point number might require only, for instance, 32 bits to be represented on a computer, Python will convert it into a full-fledged Python object with reference counting, and so on. This operation, called *boxing*, is not a problem if we need to store a small number of numbers, but allocating millions gets very inefficient.
- *Lists in Python are meant for sequential collections of objects.* There are no operations defined for, say, efficiently taking the dot product of two vectors, or summing vectors together. Also, Python lists have no way of optimizing the layout of their contents in memory, as they are indexable collections of pointers to Python objects (of any kind, not just numbers). Finally, Python lists are one-dimensional, and although we can create lists of lists, this is again very inefficient.
- *The Python interpreter is slow compared to optimized, compiled code.* Performing mathematical operations on large collections of numerical data can be much faster using optimized code written in a compiled, low-level language like C.

For these reasons, data science libraries rely on NumPy or introduce dedicated data structures like PyTorch tensors, which provide efficient low-level implementations of numerical data structures and related operations on them, wrapped in a convenient high-level API. To enable this, the objects within a tensor must all be numbers of the same type, and PyTorch must keep track of this numeric type.

3.5.1   *Specifying the numeric type with dtype*

The dtype argument to tensor constructors (that is, functions like tensor, zeros, and ones) specifies the numerical data (d) type that will be contained in the tensor. The data type specifies the possible values the tensor can hold (integers versus floating-point numbers) and the number of bytes per value.[4] The dtype argument is deliberately similar to the standard NumPy argument of the same name. Here's a list of the possible values for the dtype argument:

- torch.float32 or torch.float: 32-bit floating-point
- torch.float64 or torch.double: 64-bit, double-precision floating-point
- torch.float16 or torch.half: 16-bit, half-precision floating-point
- torch.int8: signed 8-bit integers
- torch.uint8: unsigned 8-bit integers
- torch.int16 or torch.short: signed 16-bit integers
- torch.int32 or torch.int: signed 32-bit integers
- torch.int64 or torch.long: signed 64-bit integers
- torch.bool: Boolean

---

[4] And signed-ness, in the case of uint8.

The default data type for tensors is 32-bit floating-point.

3.5.2 *A dtype for every occasion*

As we will see in future chapters, computations happening in neural networks are typically executed with 32-bit floating-point precision. Higher precision, like 64-bit, will not buy improvements in the accuracy of a model and will require more memory and computing time. The 16-bit floating-point, half-precision data type is not present natively in standard CPUs, but it is offered on modern GPUs. It is possible to switch to half-precision to decrease the footprint of a neural network model if needed, with a minor impact on accuracy.

Tensors can be used as indexes in other tensors. In this case, PyTorch expects indexing tensors to have a 64-bit integer data type. Creating a tensor with integers as arguments, such as using `torch.tensor([2, 2])`, will create a 64-bit integer tensor by default. As such, we'll spend most of our time dealing with `float32` and `int64`.

Finally, predicates on tensors, such as `points > 1.0`, produce `bool` tensors indicating whether each individual element satisfies the condition. These are the numeric types in a nutshell.

3.5.3 *Managing a tensor's dtype attribute*

In order to allocate a tensor of the right numeric type, we can specify the proper `dtype` as an argument to the constructor. For example:

```
# In[47]:
double_points = torch.ones(10, 2, dtype=torch.double)
short_points = torch.tensor([[1, 2], [3, 4]], dtype=torch.short)
```

We can find out about the `dtype` for a tensor by accessing the corresponding attribute:

```
# In[48]:
short_points.dtype

# Out[48]:
torch.int16
```

We can also cast the output of a tensor creation function to the right type using the corresponding casting method, such as

```
# In[49]:
double_points = torch.zeros(10, 2).double()
short_points = torch.ones(10, 2).short()
```

or the more convenient `to` method:

```
# In[50]:
double_points = torch.zeros(10, 2).to(torch.double)
short_points = torch.ones(10, 2).to(dtype=torch.short)
```

Under the hood, to checks whether the conversion is necessary and, if so, does it. The dtype-named casting methods like float are shorthands for to, but the to method can take additional arguments that we'll discuss in section 3.9.

When mixing input types in operations, the inputs are converted to the larger type automatically. Thus, if we want 32-bit computation, we need to make sure all our inputs are (at most) 32-bit:

```
# In[51]:
points_64 = torch.rand(5, dtype=torch.double)   ◁───  rand initializes the tensor elements to
points_short = points_64.to(torch.short)              random numbers between 0 and 1.
points_64 * points_short   # works from PyTorch 1.3 onwards

# Out[51]:
tensor([0., 0., 0., 0., 0.], dtype=torch.float64)
```

3.6 *The tensor API*

At this point, we know what PyTorch tensors are and how they work under the hood. Before we wrap up, it is worth taking a look at the tensor operations that PyTorch offers. It would be of little use to list them all here. Instead, we're going to get a general feel for the API and establish a few directions on where to find things in the online documentation at http://pytorch.org/docs.

First, the vast majority of operations on and between tensors are available in the torch module and can also be called as methods of a tensor object. For instance, the transpose function we encountered earlier can be used from the torch module

```
# In[71]:
a = torch.ones(3, 2)
a_t = torch.transpose(a, 0, 1)

a.shape, a_t.shape

# Out[71]:
(torch.Size([3, 2]), torch.Size([2, 3]))
```

or as a method of the a tensor:

```
# In[72]:
a = torch.ones(3, 2)
a_t = a.transpose(0, 1)

a.shape, a_t.shape

# Out[72]:
(torch.Size([3, 2]), torch.Size([2, 3]))
```

There is no difference between the two forms; they can be used interchangeably.

We mentioned the online docs earlier (http://pytorch.org/docs). They are exhaustive and well organized, with the tensor operations divided into groups:

- *Creation ops*—Functions for constructing a tensor, like `ones` and `from_numpy`
- *Indexing, slicing, joining, mutating ops*—Functions for changing the shape, stride, or content of a tensor, like `transpose`
- *Math ops*—Functions for manipulating the content of the tensor through computations
  - *Pointwise ops*—Functions for obtaining a new tensor by applying a function to each element independently, like `abs` and `cos`
  - *Reduction ops*—Functions for computing aggregate values by iterating through tensors, like `mean`, `std`, and `norm`
  - *Comparison ops*—Functions for evaluating numerical predicates over tensors, like `equal` and `max`
  - *Spectral ops*—Functions for transforming in and operating in the frequency domain, like `stft` and `hamming_window`
  - *Other operations*—Special functions operating on vectors, like `cross`, or matrices, like `trace`
  - *BLAS and LAPACK operations*—Functions following the Basic Linear Algebra Subprograms (BLAS) specification for scalar, vector-vector, matrix-vector, and matrix-matrix operations
- *Random sampling*—Functions for generating values by drawing randomly from probability distributions, like `randn` and `normal`
- *Serialization*—Functions for saving and loading tensors, like `load` and `save`
- *Parallelism*—Functions for controlling the number of threads for parallel CPU execution, like `set_num_threads`

Take some time to play with the general tensor API. This chapter has provided all the prerequisites to enable this kind of interactive exploration. We will also encounter several of the tensor operations as we proceed with the book, starting in the next chapter.

3.7 *Tensors: Scenic views of storage*

It is time for us to look a bit closer at the implementation under the hood. Values in tensors are allocated in contiguous chunks of memory managed by `torch.Storage` instances. A storage is a one-dimensional array of numerical data: that is, a contiguous block of memory containing numbers of a given type, such as `float` (32 bits representing a floating-point number) or `int64` (64 bits representing an integer). A PyTorch `Tensor` instance is a view of such a `Storage` instance that is capable of indexing into that storage using an offset and per-dimension strides.[5]

Multiple tensors can index the same storage even if they index into the data differently. We can see an example of this in figure 3.4. In fact, when we requested `points[0]` in section 3.2, what we got back is another tensor that indexes the same

---

[5] `Storage` may not be directly accessible in future PyTorch releases, but what we show here still provides a good mental picture of how tensors work under the hood.

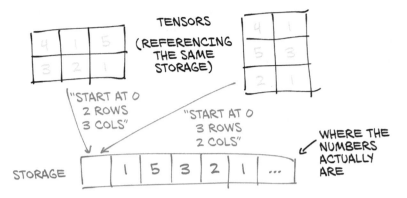

Figure 3.4 Tensors are views of a Storage instance.

storage as the `points` tensor—just not all of it, and with different dimensionality (1D versus 2D). The underlying memory is allocated only once, however, so creating alternate tensor-views of the data can be done quickly regardless of the size of the data managed by the `Storage` instance.

3.7.1 *Indexing into storage*

Let's see how indexing into the storage works in practice with our 2D points. The storage for a given tensor is accessible using the `.storage` property:

```
# In[17]:
points = torch.tensor([[4.0, 1.0], [5.0, 3.0], [2.0, 1.0]])
points.storage()
```

```
# Out[17]:
 4.0
 1.0
 5.0
 3.0
 2.0
 1.0
[torch.FloatStorage of size 6]
```

Even though the tensor reports itself as having three rows and two columns, the storage under the hood is a contiguous array of size 6. In this sense, the tensor just knows how to translate a pair of indices into a location in the storage.

We can also index into a storage manually. For instance:

```
# In[18]:
points_storage = points.storage()
points_storage[0]
```

```
# Out[18]:
4.0
```

```
# In[19]:
points.storage()[1]

# Out[19]:
1.0
```

We can't index a storage of a 2D tensor using two indices. The layout of a storage is always one-dimensional, regardless of the dimensionality of any and all tensors that might refer to it.

At this point, it shouldn't come as a surprise that changing the value of a storage leads to changing the content of its referring tensor:

```
# In[20]:
points = torch.tensor([[4.0, 1.0], [5.0, 3.0], [2.0, 1.0]])
points_storage = points.storage()
points_storage[0] = 2.0
points

# Out[20]:
tensor([[2., 1.],
        [5., 3.],
        [2., 1.]])
```

3.7.2 *Modifying stored values: In-place operations*

In addition to the operations on tensors introduced in the previous section, a small number of operations exist only as methods of the Tensor object. They are recognizable from a trailing underscore in their name, like zero_, which indicates that the method operates *in place* by modifying the input instead of creating a new output tensor and returning it. For instance, the zero_ method zeros out all the elements of the input. Any method *without* the trailing underscore leaves the source tensor unchanged and instead returns a new tensor:

```
# In[73]:
a = torch.ones(3, 2)

# In[74]:
a.zero_()
a

# Out[74]:
tensor([[0., 0.],
        [0., 0.],
        [0., 0.]])
```

3.8 *Tensor metadata: Size, offset, and stride*

In order to index into a storage, tensors rely on a few pieces of information that, together with their storage, unequivocally define them: size, offset, and stride. How these interact is shown in figure 3.5. The size (or shape, in NumPy parlance) is a tuple

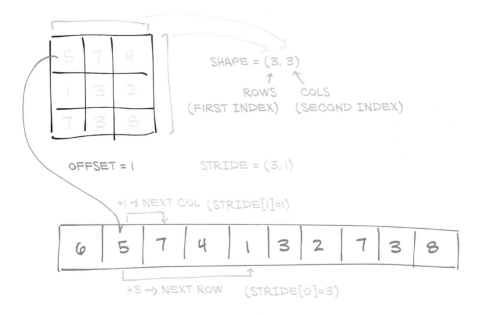

Figure 3.5 Relationship between a tensor's offset, size, and stride. Here the tensor is a view of a larger storage, like one that might have been allocated when creating a larger tensor.

indicating how many elements across each dimension the tensor represents. The storage offset is the index in the storage corresponding to the first element in the tensor. The stride is the number of elements in the storage that need to be skipped over to obtain the next element along each dimension.

3.8.1 *Views of another tensor's storage*

We can get the second point in the tensor by providing the corresponding index:

```
# In[21]:
points = torch.tensor([[4.0, 1.0], [5.0, 3.0], [2.0, 1.0]])
second_point = points[1]
second_point.storage_offset()

# Out[21]:
2

# In[22]:
second_point.size()

# Out[22]:
torch.Size([2])
```

The resulting tensor has offset 2 in the storage (since we need to skip the first point, which has two items), and the size is an instance of the `Size` class containing one

TIP To help build a solid understanding of the mechanics of tensors, it may be a good idea to grab a pencil and a piece of paper and scribble diagrams like the one in figure 3.5 as we step through the code in this section.

We can easily verify that the two tensors share the same storage

```
# In[32]:
id(points.storage()) == id(points_t.storage())
```

```
# Out[32]:
True
```

and that they differ only in shape and stride:

```
# In[33]:
points.stride()
```

```
# Out[33]:
(2, 1)
# In[34]:
points_t.stride()
```

```
# Out[34]:
(1, 2)
```

This tells us that increasing the first index by one in `points`—for example, going from `points[0,0]` to `points[1,0]`—will skip along the storage by two elements, while increasing the second index—from `points[0,0]` to `points[0,1]`—will skip along the storage by one. In other words, the storage holds the elements in the tensor sequentially row by row.

We can transpose `points` into `points_t`, as shown in figure 3.6. We change the order of the elements in the stride. After that, increasing the row (the first index of the tensor) will skip along the storage by one, just like when we were moving along columns in `points`. This is the very definition of transposing. No new memory is allocated: transposing is obtained only by creating a new `Tensor` instance with different stride ordering than the original.

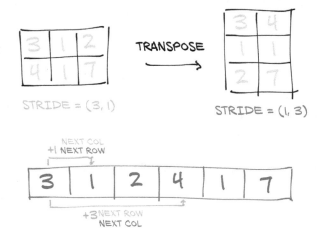

Figure 3.6 Transpose operation applied to a tensor

3.8.3   *Transposing in higher dimensions*

Transposing in PyTorch is not limited to matrices. We can transpose a multidimensional array by specifying the two dimensions along which transposing (flipping shape and stride) should occur:

```
# In[35]:
some_t = torch.ones(3, 4, 5)
transpose_t = some_t.transpose(0, 2)
some_t.shape

# Out[35]:
torch.Size([3, 4, 5])

# In[36]:
transpose_t.shape

# Out[36]:
torch.Size([5, 4, 3])

# In[37]:
some_t.stride()

# Out[37]:
(20, 5, 1)

# In[38]:
transpose_t.stride()

# Out[38]:
(1, 5, 20)
```

A tensor whose values are laid out in the storage starting from the rightmost dimension onward (that is, moving along rows for a 2D tensor) is defined as contiguous. Contiguous tensors are convenient because we can visit them efficiently in order without jumping around in the storage (improving data locality improves performance because of the way memory access works on modern CPUs). This advantage of course depends on the way algorithms visit.

3.8.4   *Contiguous tensors*

Some tensor operations in PyTorch only work on contiguous tensors, such as view, which we'll encounter in the next chapter. In that case, PyTorch will throw an informative exception and require us to call contiguous explicitly. It's worth noting that calling contiguous will do nothing (and will not hurt performance) if the tensor is already contiguous.

In our case, points is contiguous, while its transpose is not:

```
# In[39]:
points.is_contiguous()
```

```
# Out[39]:
True

# In[40]:
points_t.is_contiguous()

# Out[40]:
False
```

We can obtain a new contiguous tensor from a non-contiguous one using the `contiguous` method. The content of the tensor will be the same, but the stride will change, as will the storage:

```
# In[41]:
points = torch.tensor([[4.0, 1.0], [5.0, 3.0], [2.0, 1.0]])
points_t = points.t()
points_t

# Out[41]:
tensor([[4., 5., 2.],
        [1., 3., 1.]])

# In[42]:
points_t.storage()

# Out[42]:
 4.0
 1.0
 5.0
 3.0
 2.0
 1.0
[torch.FloatStorage of size 6]

# In[43]:
points_t.stride()

# Out[43]:
(1, 2)

# In[44]:
points_t_cont = points_t.contiguous()
points_t_cont

# Out[44]:
tensor([[4., 5., 2.],
        [1., 3., 1.]])

# In[45]:
points_t_cont.stride()

# Out[45]:
(3, 1)
```

```
# In[46]:
points_t_cont.storage()

# Out[46]:
 4.0
 5.0
 2.0
 1.0
 3.0
 1.0
[torch.FloatStorage of size 6]
```

Notice that the storage has been reshuffled in order for elements to be laid out row-by-row in the new storage. The stride has been changed to reflect the new layout.

As a refresher, figure 3.7 shows our diagram again. Hopefully it will all make sense now that we've taken a good look at how tensors are built.

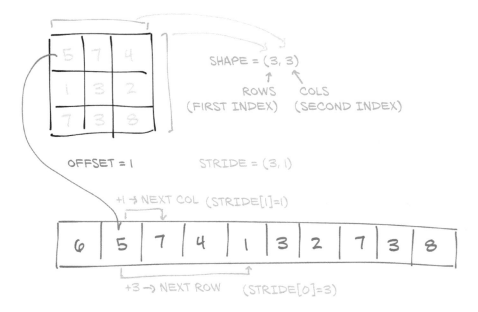

Figure 3.7 Relationship between a tensor's offset, size, and stride. Here the tensor is a view of a larger storage, like one that might have been allocated when creating a larger tensor.

3.9   *Moving tensors to the GPU*

So far in this chapter, when we've talked about storage, we've meant memory on the CPU. PyTorch tensors also can be stored on a different kind of processor: a graphics processing unit (GPU). Every PyTorch tensor can be transferred to (one of) the GPU(s) in order to perform massively parallel, fast computations. All operations that will be performed on the tensor will be carried out using GPU-specific routines that come with PyTorch.

> **PyTorch support for various GPUs**
>
> As of mid-2019, the main PyTorch releases only have acceleration on GPUs that have support for CUDA. PyTorch can run on AMD's ROCm (https://rocm.github.io), and the master repository provides support, but so far, you need to compile it yourself. (Before the regular build process, you need to run `tools/amd_build/build_amd.py` to translate the GPU code.) Support for Google's tensor processing units (TPUs) is a work in progress (https://github.com/pytorch/xla), with the current proof of concept available to the public in Google Colab: https://colab.research.google.com. Implementation of data structures and kernels on other GPU technologies, such as OpenCL, are not planned at the time of this writing.

3.9.1 Managing a tensor's device attribute

In addition to `dtype`, a PyTorch `Tensor` also has the notion of `device`, which is where on the computer the tensor data is placed. Here is how we can create a tensor on the GPU by specifying the corresponding argument to the constructor:

```
# In[64]:
points_gpu = torch.tensor([[4.0, 1.0], [5.0, 3.0], [2.0, 1.0]], device='cuda')
```

We could instead copy a tensor created on the CPU onto the GPU using the `to` method:

```
# In[65]:
points_gpu = points.to(device='cuda')
```

Doing so returns a new tensor that has the same numerical data, but stored in the RAM of the GPU, rather than in regular system RAM. Now that the data is stored locally on the GPU, we'll start to see the speedups mentioned earlier when performing mathematical operations on the tensor. In almost all cases, CPU- and GPU-based tensors expose the same user-facing API, making it much easier to write code that is agnostic to where, exactly, the heavy number crunching is running.

If our machine has more than one GPU, we can also decide on which GPU we allocate the tensor by passing a zero-based integer identifying the GPU on the machine, such as

```
# In[66]:
points_gpu = points.to(device='cuda:0')
```

At this point, any operation performed on the tensor, such as multiplying all elements by a constant, is carried out on the GPU:

```
# In[67]:
points = 2 * points                              ◁──────┐   Multiplication performed on the CPU
points_gpu = 2 * points.to(device='cuda')        ◁──────┘   Multiplication performed on the GPU
```

Note that the points_gpu tensor is not brought back to the CPU once the result has been computed. Here's what happened in this line:

1 The points tensor is copied to the GPU.
2 A new tensor is allocated on the GPU and used to store the result of the multiplication.
3 A handle to that GPU tensor is returned.

Therefore, if we also add a constant to the result

```
# In[68]:
points_gpu = points_gpu + 4
```

the addition is still performed on the GPU, and no information flows to the CPU (unless we print or access the resulting tensor). In order to move the tensor back to the CPU, we need to provide a cpu argument to the to method, such as

```
# In[69]:
points_cpu = points_gpu.to(device='cpu')
```

We can also use the shorthand methods cpu and cuda instead of the to method to achieve the same goal:

```
# In[70]:
points_gpu = points.cuda()      ◁—— Defaults to GPU index 0
points_gpu = points.cuda(0)
points_cpu = points_gpu.cpu()
```

It's also worth mentioning that by using the to method, we can change the placement and the data type simultaneously by providing both device and dtype as arguments.

3.10 *NumPy interoperability*

We've mentioned NumPy here and there. While we do not consider NumPy a prerequisite for reading this book, we strongly encourage you to become familiar with NumPy due to its ubiquity in the Python data science ecosystem. PyTorch tensors can be converted to NumPy arrays and vice versa very efficiently. By doing so, we can take advantage of the huge swath of functionality in the wider Python ecosystem that has built up around the NumPy array type. This zero-copy interoperability with NumPy arrays is due to the storage system working with the Python buffer protocol (https://docs.python.org/3/c-api/buffer.html).

To get a NumPy array out of our points tensor, we just call

```
# In[55]:
points = torch.ones(3, 4)
points_np = points.numpy()
points_np

# Out[55]:
```

```
array([[1., 1., 1., 1.],
       [1., 1., 1., 1.],
       [1., 1., 1., 1.]], dtype=float32)
```

which will return a NumPy multidimensional array of the right size, shape, and numerical type. Interestingly, the returned array shares the same underlying buffer with the tensor storage. This means the `numpy` method can be effectively executed at basically no cost, as long as the data sits in CPU RAM. It also means modifying the NumPy array will lead to a change in the originating tensor. If the tensor is allocated on the GPU, PyTorch will make a copy of the content of the tensor into a NumPy array allocated on the CPU.

Conversely, we can obtain a PyTorch tensor from a NumPy array this way

```
# In[56]:
points = torch.from_numpy(points_np)
```

which will use the same buffer-sharing strategy we just described.

> **NOTE** While the default numeric type in PyTorch is 32-bit floating-point, for NumPy it is 64-bit. As discussed in section 3.5.2, we usually want to use 32-bit floating-points, so we need to make sure we have tensors of dtype `torch.float` after converting.

3.11 *Generalized tensors are tensors, too*

For the purposes of this book, and for the vast majority of applications in general, tensors are multidimensional arrays, just as we've seen in this chapter. If we risk a peek under the hood of PyTorch, there is a twist: how the data is stored under the hood is separate from the tensor API we discussed in section 3.6. Any implementation that meets the contract of that API can be considered a tensor!

PyTorch will cause the right computation functions to be called regardless of whether our tensor is on the CPU or the GPU. This is accomplished through a *dispatching* mechanism, and that mechanism can cater to other tensor types by hooking up the user-facing API to the right backend functions. Sure enough, there are other kinds of tensors: some are specific to certain classes of hardware devices (like Google TPUs), and others have data-representation strategies that differ from the dense array style we've seen so far. For example, sparse tensors store only nonzero entries, along with index information. The PyTorch dispatcher on the left in figure 3.8 is designed to be extensible; the subsequent switching done to accommodate the various numeric types of figure 3.8 shown on the right is a fixed aspect of the implementation coded into each backend.

We will meet *quantized* tensors in chapter 15, which are implemented as another type of tensor with a specialized computational backend. Sometimes the usual tensors we use are called *dense* or *strided* to differentiate them from tensors using other memory layouts.

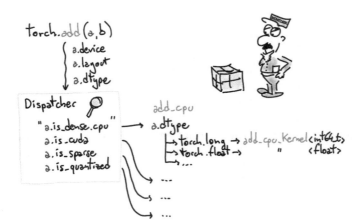

Figure 3.8   The dispatcher in PyTorch is one of its key infrastructure bits.

As with many things, the number of kinds of tensors has grown as PyTorch supports a broader range of hardware and applications. We can expect new kinds to continue to arise as people explore new ways to express and perform computations with PyTorch.

3.12   *Serializing tensors*

Creating a tensor on the fly is all well and good, but if the data inside is valuable, we will want to save it to a file and load it back at some point. After all, we don't want to have to retrain a model from scratch every time we start running our program! PyTorch uses `pickle` under the hood to serialize the tensor object, plus dedicated serialization code for the storage. Here's how we can save our `points` tensor to an ourpoints.t file:

```
# In[57]:
torch.save(points, '../data/p1ch3/ourpoints.t')
```

As an alternative, we can pass a file descriptor in lieu of the filename:

```
# In[58]:
with open('../data/p1ch3/ourpoints.t','wb') as f:
   torch.save(points, f)
```

Loading our points back is similarly a one-liner

```
# In[59]:
points = torch.load('../data/p1ch3/ourpoints.t')
```

or, equivalently,

```
# In[60]:
with open('../data/p1ch3/ourpoints.t','rb') as f:
   points = torch.load(f)
```

While we can quickly save tensors this way if we only want to load them with PyTorch, the file format itself is not interoperable: we can't read the tensor with software other than PyTorch. Depending on the use case, this may or may not be a limitation, but we should learn how to save tensors interoperably for those times when it is. We'll look next at how to do so.

3.12.1 *Serializing to HDF5 with h5py*

Every use case is unique, but we suspect needing to save tensors interoperably will be more common when introducing PyTorch into existing systems that already rely on different libraries. New projects probably won't need to do this as often.

For those cases when you need to, however, you can use the HDF5 format and library (www.hdfgroup.org/solutions/hdf5). HDF5 is a portable, widely supported format for representing serialized multidimensional arrays, organized in a nested key-value dictionary. Python supports HDF5 through the h5py library (www.h5py.org), which accepts and returns data in the form of NumPy arrays.

We can install h5py using

```
$ conda install h5py
```

At this point, we can save our `points` tensor by converting it to a NumPy array (at no cost, as we noted earlier) and passing it to the `create_dataset` function:

```
# In[61]:
import h5py

f = h5py.File('../data/p1ch3/ourpoints.hdf5', 'w')
dset = f.create_dataset('coords', data=points.numpy())
f.close()
```

Here `'coords'` is a key into the HDF5 file. We can have other keys—even nested ones. One of the interesting things in HDF5 is that we can index the dataset while on disk and access only the elements we're interested in. Let's suppose we want to load just the last two points in our dataset:

```
# In[62]:
f = h5py.File('../data/p1ch3/ourpoints.hdf5', 'r')
dset = f['coords']
last_points = dset[-2:]
```

The data is not loaded when the file is opened or the dataset is required. Rather, the data stays on disk until we request the second and last rows in the dataset. At that point, h5py accesses those two columns and returns a NumPy array-like object encapsulating that region in that dataset that behaves like a NumPy array and has the same API.

Owing to this fact, we can pass the returned object to the `torch.from_numpy` function to obtain a tensor directly. Note that in this case, the data is copied over to the tensor's storage:

```
# In[63]:
last_points = torch.from_numpy(dset[-2:])
f.close()
```

Once we're finished loading data, we close the file. Closing the HDFS file invalidates the datasets, and trying to access `dset` afterward will give an exception. As long as we stick to the order shown here, we are fine and can now work with the `last_points` tensor.

3.13   *Conclusion*

Now we have covered everything we need to get started with representing everything in floats. We'll cover other aspects of tensors—such as creating views of tensors; indexing tensors with other tensors; and broadcasting, which simplifies performing element-wise operations between tensors of different sizes or shapes—as needed along the way.

In chapter 4, we will learn how to represent real-world data in PyTorch. We will start with simple tabular data and move on to something more elaborate. In the process, we will get to know more about tensors.

3.14   *Exercises*

1   Create a tensor a from `list(range(9))`. Predict and then check the size, offset, and stride.
   a   Create a new tensor using `b = a.view(3, 3)`. What does `view` do? Check that a and b share the same storage.
   b   Create a tensor `c = b[1:,1:]`. Predict and then check the size, offset, and stride.
2   Pick a mathematical operation like cosine or square root. Can you find a corresponding function in the `torch` library?
   a   Apply the function element-wise to a. Why does it return an error?
   b   What operation is required to make the function work?
   c   Is there a version of your function that operates in place?

3.15   *Summary*

- Neural networks transform floating-point representations into other floating-point representations. The starting and ending representations are typically human interpretable, but the intermediate representations are less so.
- These floating-point representations are stored in tensors.
- Tensors are multidimensional arrays; they are the basic data structure in PyTorch.

- PyTorch has a comprehensive standard library for tensor creation, manipulation, and mathematical operations.
- Tensors can be serialized to disk and loaded back.
- All tensor operations in PyTorch can execute on the CPU as well as on the GPU, with no change in the code.
- PyTorch uses a trailing underscore to indicate that a function operates in place on a tensor (for example, `Tensor.sqrt_`).

Real-world data representation using tensors

This chapter covers

- Representing real-world data as PyTorch tensors
- Working with a range of data types
- Loading data from a file
- Converting data to tensors
- Shaping tensors so they can be used as inputs for neural network models

In the previous chapter, we learned that tensors are the building blocks for data in PyTorch. Neural networks take tensors as input and produce tensors as outputs. In fact, all operations within a neural network and during optimization are operations between tensors, and all parameters (for example, weights and biases) in a neural network are tensors. Having a good sense of how to perform operations on tensors and index them effectively is central to using tools like PyTorch successfully. Now that you know the basics of tensors, your dexterity with them will grow as you make your way through the book.

Here's a question that we can already address: how do we take a piece of data, a video, or a line of text, and represent it with a tensor in a way that is appropriate for training a deep learning model? This is what we'll learn in this chapter. We'll cover different types of data with a focus on the types relevant to this book and show how to represent that data as tensors. Then we'll learn how to load the data from the most common on-disk formats and get a feel for those data types' structure so we can see how to prepare them for training a neural network. Often, our raw data won't be perfectly formed for the problem we'd like to solve, so we'll have a chance to practice our tensor-manipulation skills with a few more interesting tensor operations.

Each section in this chapter will describe a data type, and each will come with its own dataset. While we've structured the chapter so that each data type builds on the previous one, feel free to skip around a bit if you're so inclined.

We'll be using a lot of image and volumetric data through the rest of the book, since those are common data types and they reproduce well in book format. We'll also cover tabular data, time series, and text, as those will also be of interest to a number of our readers. Since a picture is worth a thousand words, we'll start with image data. We'll then demonstrate working with a three-dimensional array using medical data that represents patient anatomy as a volume. Next, we'll work with tabular data about wines, just like what we'd find in a spreadsheet. After that, we'll move to *ordered* tabular data, with a time-series dataset from a bike-sharing program. Finally, we'll dip our toes into text data from Jane Austen. Text data retains its ordered aspect but introduces the problem of representing words as arrays of numbers.

In every section, we will stop where a deep learning researcher would start: right before feeding the data to a model. We encourage you to keep these datasets; they will constitute excellent material for when we start learning how to train neural network models in the next chapter.

4.1 Working with images

The introduction of convolutional neural networks revolutionized computer vision (see http://mng.bz/zjMa), and image-based systems have since acquired a whole new set of capabilities. Problems that required complex pipelines of highly tuned algorithmic building blocks are now solvable at unprecedented levels of performance by training end-to-end networks using paired input-and-desired-output examples. In order to participate in this revolution, we need to be able to load an image from common image formats and then transform the data into a tensor representation that has the various parts of the image arranged in the way PyTorch expects.

An image is represented as a collection of scalars arranged in a regular grid with a height and a width (in pixels). We might have a single scalar per grid point (the pixel), which would be represented as a grayscale image; or multiple scalars per grid point, which would typically represent different colors, as we saw in the previous chapter, or different *features* like depth from a depth camera.

Scalars representing values at individual pixels are often encoded using 8-bit integers, as in consumer cameras. In medical, scientific, and industrial applications, it is not unusual to find higher numerical precision, such as 12-bit or 16-bit. This allows a wider range or increased sensitivity in cases where the pixel encodes information about a physical property, like bone density, temperature, or depth.

4.1.1 Adding color channels

We mentioned colors earlier. There are several ways to encode colors into numbers.[1] The most common is RGB, where a color is defined by three numbers representing the intensity of red, green, and blue. We can think of a color channel as a grayscale intensity map of only the color in question, similar to what you'd see if you looked at the scene in question using a pair of pure red sunglasses. Figure 4.1 shows a rainbow, where each of the RGB channels captures a certain portion of the spectrum (the figure is simplified, in that it elides things like the orange and yellow bands being represented as a combination of red and green).

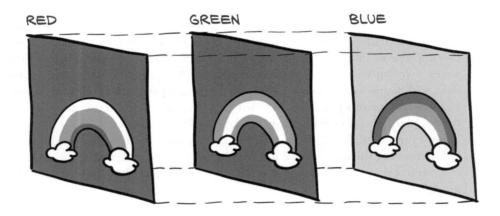

Figure 4.1   A rainbow, broken into red, green, and blue channels

The red band of the rainbow is brightest in the red channel of the image, while the blue channel has both the blue band of the rainbow and the sky as high-intensity. Note also that the white clouds are high-intensity in all three channels.

4.1.2 Loading an image file

Images come in several different file formats, but luckily there are plenty of ways to load images in Python. Let's start by loading a PNG image using the imageio module (code/p1ch4/1_image_dog.ipynb).

---

[1] This is something of an understatement: https://en.wikipedia.org/wiki/Color_model.

Listing 4.1 code/p1ch4/1_image_dog.ipynb

```
# In[2]:
import imageio

img_arr = imageio.imread('../data/p1ch4/image-dog/bobby.jpg')
img_arr.shape

# Out[2]:
(720, 1280, 3)
```

> **NOTE** We'll use `imageio` throughout the chapter because it handles different data types with a uniform API. For many purposes, using TorchVision is a great default choice to deal with image and video data. We go with `imageio` here for somewhat lighter exploration.

At this point, `img` is a NumPy array-like object with three dimensions: two spatial dimensions, width and height; and a third dimension corresponding to the red, green, and blue channels. Any library that outputs a NumPy array will suffice to obtain a PyTorch tensor. The only thing to watch out for is the layout of the dimensions. PyTorch modules dealing with image data require tensors to be laid out as $C \times H \times W$: channels, height, and width, respectively.

4.1.3 *Changing the layout*

We can use the tensor's `permute` method with the old dimensions for each new dimension to get to an appropriate layout. Given an input tensor $H \times W \times C$ as obtained previously, we get a proper layout by having channel 2 first and then channels 0 and 1:

```
# In[3]:
img = torch.from_numpy(img_arr)
out = img.permute(2, 0, 1)
```

We've seen this previously, but note that this operation does not make a copy of the tensor data. Instead, `out` uses the same underlying storage as `img` and only plays with the size and stride information at the tensor level. This is convenient because the operation is very cheap; but just as a heads-up: changing a pixel in `img` will lead to a change in `out`.

Note also that other deep learning frameworks use different layouts. For instance, originally TensorFlow kept the channel dimension last, resulting in an $H \times W \times C$ layout (it now supports multiple layouts). This strategy has pros and cons from a low-level performance standpoint, but for our concerns, it doesn't make a difference as long as we reshape our tensors properly.

So far, we have described a single image. Following the same strategy we've used for earlier data types, to create a dataset of multiple images to use as an input for our neural networks, we store the images in a batch along the first dimension to obtain an $N \times C \times H \times W$ tensor.

As a slightly more efficient alternative to using `stack` to build up the tensor, we can pre-allocate a tensor of appropriate size and fill it with images loaded from a directory, like so:

```
# In[4]:
batch_size = 3
batch = torch.zeros(batch_size, 3, 256, 256, dtype=torch.uint8)
```

This indicates that our batch will consist of three RGB images 256 pixels in height and 256 pixels in width. Notice the type of the tensor: we're expecting each color to be represented as an 8-bit integer, as in most photographic formats from standard consumer cameras. We can now load all PNG images from an input directory and store them in the tensor:

```
# In[5]:
import os

data_dir = '../data/p1ch4/image-cats/'
filenames = [name for name in os.listdir(data_dir)
             if os.path.splitext(name)[-1] == '.png']
for i, filename in enumerate(filenames):
    img_arr = imageio.imread(os.path.join(data_dir, filename))
    img_t = torch.from_numpy(img_arr)
    img_t = img_t.permute(2, 0, 1)
    img_t = img_t[:3]             ◄─┐
    batch[i] = img_t
```

> Here we keep only the first three channels.
> Sometimes images also have an alpha channel
> indicating transparency, but our network only
> wants RGB input.

4.1.4   *Normalizing the data*

We mentioned earlier that neural networks usually work with floating-point tensors as their input. Neural networks exhibit the best training performance when the input data ranges roughly from 0 to 1, or from -1 to 1 (this is an effect of how their building blocks are defined).

So a typical thing we'll want to do is cast a tensor to floating-point and normalize the values of the pixels. Casting to floating-point is easy, but normalization is trickier, as it depends on what range of the input we decide should lie between 0 and 1 (or -1 and 1). One possibility is to just divide the values of the pixels by 255 (the maximum representable number in 8-bit unsigned):

```
# In[6]:
batch = batch.float()
batch /= 255.0
```

Another possibility is to compute the mean and standard deviation of the input data and scale it so that the output has zero mean and unit standard deviation across each channel:

```
# In[7]:
n_channels = batch.shape[1]
for c in range(n_channels):
    mean = torch.mean(batch[:, c])
    std = torch.std(batch[:, c])
    batch[:, c] = (batch[:, c] - mean) / std
```

NOTE Here, we normalize just a single batch of images because we do not know yet how to operate on an entire dataset. In working with images, it is good practice to compute the mean and standard deviation on all the training data in advance and then subtract and divide by these fixed, precomputed quantities. We saw this in the preprocessing for the image classifier in section 2.1.4.

We can perform several other operations on inputs, such as geometric transformations like rotations, scaling, and cropping. These may help with training or may be required to make an arbitrary input conform to the input requirements of a network, like the size of the image. We will stumble on quite a few of these strategies in section 12.6. For now, just remember that you have image-manipulation options available.

4.2 *3D images: Volumetric data*

We've learned how to load and represent 2D images, like the ones we take with a camera. In some contexts, such as medical imaging applications involving, say, CT (computed tomography) scans, we typically deal with sequences of images stacked along the head-to-foot axis, each corresponding to a slice across the human body. In CT scans, the intensity represents the density of the different parts of the body—lungs, fat, water, muscle, and bone, in order of increasing density—mapped from dark to bright when the CT scan is displayed on a clinical workstation. The density at each point is computed from the amount of X-rays reaching a detector after crossing through the body, with some complex math to deconvolve the raw sensor data into the full volume.

CTs have only a single intensity channel, similar to a grayscale image. This means that often, the channel dimension is left out in native data formats; so, similar to the last section, the raw data typically has three dimensions. By stacking individual 2D slices into a 3D tensor, we can build volumetric data representing the 3D anatomy of a subject. Unlike what we saw in figure 4.1, the extra dimension in figure 4.2 represents an offset in physical space, rather than a particular band of the visible spectrum.

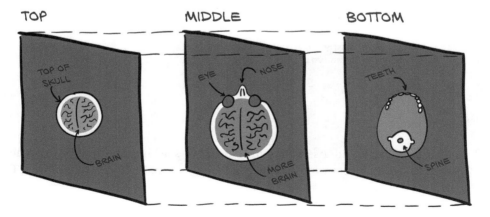

Figure 4.2   Slices of a CT scan, from the top of the head to the jawline

Part 2 of this book will be devoted to tackling a medical imaging problem in the real world, so we won't go into the details of medical-imaging data formats. For now, it suffices to say that there's no fundamental difference between a tensor storing volumetric data versus image data. We just have an extra dimension, *depth*, after the *channel* dimension, leading to a 5D tensor of shape $N \times C \times D \times H \times W$.

4.2.1 *Loading a specialized format*

Let's load a sample CT scan using the `volread` function in the `imageio` module, which takes a directory as an argument and assembles all Digital Imaging and Communications in Medicine (DICOM) files[2] in a series in a NumPy 3D array (code/p1ch4/2_volumetric_ct.ipynb).

Listing 4.2   code/p1ch4/2_volumetric_ct.ipynb

```
# In[2]:
import imageio

dir_path = "../data/p1ch4/volumetric-dicom/2-LUNG 3.0  B70f-04083"
vol_arr = imageio.volread(dir_path, 'DICOM')
vol_arr.shape

# Out[2]:
Reading DICOM (examining files): 1/99 files (1.0%99/99 files (100.0%)
  Found 1 correct series.
Reading DICOM (loading data): 31/99  (31.392/99  (92.999/99  (100.0%)

(99, 512, 512)
```

As was true in section 4.1.3, the layout is different from what PyTorch expects, due to having no channel information. So we'll have to make room for the `channel` dimension using `unsqueeze`:

```
# In[3]:
vol = torch.from_numpy(vol_arr).float()
vol = torch.unsqueeze(vol, 0)

vol.shape

# Out[3]:
torch.Size([1, 99, 512, 512])
```

At this point we could assemble a 5D dataset by stacking multiple volumes along the `batch` direction, just as we did in the previous section. We'll see a lot more CT data in part 2.

---

[2] From the Cancer Imaging Archive's CPTAC-LSCC collection: http://mng.bz/K21K.

4.3 Representing tabular data

The simplest form of data we'll encounter on a machine learning job is sitting in a spreadsheet, CSV file, or database. Whatever the medium, it's a table containing one row per sample (or record), where columns contain one piece of information about our sample.

At first we are going to assume there's no meaning to the order in which samples appear in the table: such a table is a collection of independent samples, unlike a time series, for instance, in which samples are related by a time dimension.

Columns may contain numerical values, like temperatures at specific locations; or labels, like a string expressing an attribute of the sample, like "blue." Therefore, tabular data is typically not homogeneous: different columns don't have the same type. We might have a column showing the weight of apples and another encoding their color in a label.

PyTorch tensors, on the other hand, are homogeneous. Information in PyTorch is typically encoded as a number, typically floating-point (though integer types and Boolean are supported as well). This numeric encoding is deliberate, since neural networks are mathematical entities that take real numbers as inputs and produce real numbers as output through successive application of matrix multiplications and nonlinear functions.

4.3.1 Using a real-world dataset

Our first job as deep learning practitioners is to encode heterogeneous, real-world data into a tensor of floating-point numbers, ready for consumption by a neural network. A large number of tabular datasets are freely available on the internet; see, for instance, https://github.com/caesar0301/awesome-public-datasets. Let's start with something fun: wine! The Wine Quality dataset is a freely available table containing chemical characterizations of samples of *vinho verde*, a wine from north Portugal, together with a sensory quality score. The dataset for white wines can be downloaded here: http://mng.bz/90Ol. For convenience, we also created a copy of the dataset on the Deep Learning with PyTorch Git repository, under data/p1ch4/tabular-wine.

The file contains a comma-separated collection of values organized in 12 columns preceded by a header line containing the column names. The first 11 columns contain values of chemical variables, and the last column contains the sensory quality score from 0 (very bad) to 10 (excellent). These are the column names in the order they appear in the dataset:

```
fixed acidity
volatile acidity
citric acid
residual sugar
chlorides
free sulfur dioxide
total sulfur dioxide
density
```

```
pH
sulphates
alcohol
quality
```

A possible machine learning task on this dataset is predicting the quality score from chemical characterization alone. Don't worry, though; machine learning is not going to kill wine tasting anytime soon. We have to get the training data from somewhere! As we can see in figure 4.3, we're hoping to find a relationship between one of the chemical columns in our data and the quality column. Here, we're expecting to see quality increase as sulfur decreases.

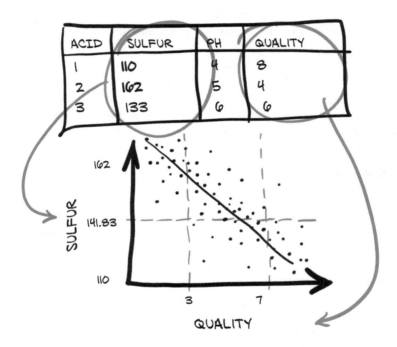

Figure 4.3   The (we hope) relationship between sulfur and quality in wine

4.3.2   *Loading a wine data tensor*

Before we can get to that, however, we need to be able to examine the data in a more usable way than opening the file in a text editor. Let's see how we can load the data using Python and then turn it into a PyTorch tensor. Python offers several options for quickly loading a CSV file. Three popular options are

- The csv module that ships with Python
- NumPy
- Pandas

The third option is the most time- and memory-efficient. However, we'll avoid introducing an additional library in our learning trajectory just because we need to load a file. Since we already introduced NumPy in the previous section, and PyTorch has excellent NumPy interoperability, we'll go with that. Let's load our file and turn the resulting NumPy array into a PyTorch tensor (code/p1ch4/3_tabular_wine.ipynb).

Listing 4.3   code/p1ch4/3_tabular_wine.ipynb

```
# In[2]:
import csv
wine_path = "../data/p1ch4/tabular-wine/winequality-white.csv"
wineq_numpy = np.loadtxt(wine_path, dtype=np.float32, delimiter=";",
                         skiprows=1)
wineq_numpy

# Out[2]:
array([[ 7.  ,  0.27,  0.36, ...,  0.45,  8.8 ,  6.  ],
       [ 6.3 ,  0.3 ,  0.34, ...,  0.49,  9.5 ,  6.  ],
       [ 8.1 ,  0.28,  0.4 , ...,  0.44, 10.1 ,  6.  ],
       ...,
       [ 6.5 ,  0.24,  0.19, ...,  0.46,  9.4 ,  6.  ],
       [ 5.5 ,  0.29,  0.3 , ...,  0.38, 12.8 ,  7.  ],
       [ 6.  ,  0.21,  0.38, ...,  0.32, 11.8 ,  6.  ]], dtype=float32)
```

Here we just prescribe what the type of the 2D array should be (32-bit floating-point), the delimiter used to separate values in each row, and the fact that the first line should not be read since it contains the column names. Let's check that all the data has been read

```
# In[3]:
col_list = next(csv.reader(open(wine_path), delimiter=';'))

wineq_numpy.shape, col_list

# Out[3]:
((4898, 12),
 ['fixed acidity',
  'volatile acidity',
  'citric acid',
  'residual sugar',
  'chlorides',
  'free sulfur dioxide',
  'total sulfur dioxide',
  'density',
  'pH',
  'sulphates',
  'alcohol',
  'quality'])
```

and proceed to convert the NumPy array to a PyTorch tensor:

```
# In[4]:
wineq = torch.from_numpy(wineq_numpy)

wineq.shape, wineq.dtype

# Out[4]:
(torch.Size([4898, 12]), torch.float32)
```

At this point, we have a floating-point `torch.Tensor` containing all the columns, including the last, which refers to the quality score.

Continuous, ordinal, and categorical values

We should be aware of three different kinds of numerical values as we attempt to make sense of our data.[3] The first kind is *continuous* values. These are the most intuitive when represented as numbers. They are strictly ordered, and a difference between various values has a strict meaning. Stating that package A is 2 kilograms heavier than package B, or that package B came from 100 miles farther away than A has a fixed meaning, regardless of whether package A is 3 kilograms or 10, or if B came from 200 miles away or 2,000. If you're counting or measuring something with units, it's probably a continuous value. The literature actually divides continuous values further: in the previous examples, it makes sense to say something is twice as heavy or three times farther away, so those values are said to be on a *ratio scale*. The time of day, on the other hand, does have the notion of difference, but it is not reasonable to claim that 6:00 is twice as late as 3:00; so time of day only offers an *interval scale*.

Next we have *ordinal* values. The strict ordering we have with continuous values remains, but the fixed relationship between values no longer applies. A good example of this is ordering a small, medium, or large drink, with small mapped to the value 1, medium 2, and large 3. The large drink is bigger than the medium, in the same way that 3 is bigger than 2, but it doesn't tell us anything about *how much* bigger. If we were to convert our 1, 2, and 3 to the actual volumes (say, 8, 12, and 24 fluid ounces), then they would switch to being interval values. It's important to remember that we can't "do math" on the values outside of ordering them; trying to average large = 3 and small = 1 does *not* result in a medium drink!

Finally, *categorical* values have neither ordering nor numerical meaning to their values. These are often just enumerations of possibilities assigned arbitrary numbers. Assigning water to 1, coffee to 2, soda to 3, and milk to 4 is a good example. There's no real logic to placing water first and milk last; they simply need distinct values to differentiate them. We could assign coffee to 10 and milk to −3, and there would be no significant change (though assigning values in the range $0..N-1$ will have advantages for one-hot encoding and the embeddings we'll discuss in section 4.5.4.) Because the numerical values bear no meaning, they are said to be on a *nominal scale*.

---

[3]   As a starting point for a more in-depth discussion, refer to https://en.wikipedia.org/wiki/Level_of_measurement.

4.3.3 *Representing scores*

We could treat the score as a continuous variable, keep it as a real number, and perform a regression task, or treat it as a label and try to guess the label from the chemical analysis in a classification task. In both approaches, we will typically remove the score from the tensor of input data and keep it in a separate tensor, so that we can use the score as the ground truth without it being input to our model:

```
# In[5]:
data = wineq[:, :-1]        ◁─┐  Selects all rows and all
data, data.shape              │  columns except the last

# Out[5]:
(tensor([[ 7.00,   0.27,   ...,   0.45,   8.80],
         [ 6.30,   0.30,   ...,   0.49,   9.50],
         ...,
         [ 5.50,   0.29,   ...,   0.38,  12.80],
         [ 6.00,   0.21,   ...,   0.32,  11.80]]), torch.Size([4898, 11]))

# In[6]:
target = wineq[:, -1]       ◁─┐  Selects all rows and
target, target.shape          │  the last column

# Out[6]:
(tensor([6., 6.,   ..., 7., 6.]), torch.Size([4898]))
```

If we want to transform the `target` tensor in a tensor of labels, we have two options, depending on the strategy or what we use the categorical data for. One is simply to treat labels as an integer vector of scores:

```
# In[7]:
target = wineq[:, -1].long()
target

# Out[7]:
tensor([6, 6,   ..., 7, 6])
```

If targets were string labels, like *wine color*, assigning an integer number to each string would let us follow the same approach.

4.3.4 *One-hot encoding*

The other approach is to build a *one-hot encoding* of the scores: that is, encode each of the 10 scores in a vector of 10 elements, with all elements set to 0 but one, at a different index for each score. This way, a score of 1 could be mapped onto the vector $(1,0,0,0,0,0,0,0,0,0)$, a score of 5 onto $(0,0,0,0,1,0,0,0,0,0)$, and so on. Note that the fact that the score corresponds to the index of the nonzero element is purely incidental: we could shuffle the assignment, and nothing would change from a classification standpoint.

There's a marked difference between the two approaches. Keeping wine quality scores in an integer vector of scores induces an ordering on the scores—which might be totally appropriate in this case, since a score of 1 is lower than a score of 4. It also induces some sort of distance between scores: that is, the distance between 1 and 3 is the same as the distance between 2 and 4. If this holds for our quantity, then great. If, on the other hand, scores are purely discrete, like grape variety, one-hot encoding will be a much better fit, as there's no implied ordering or distance. One-hot encoding is also appropriate for quantitative scores when fractional values in between integer scores, like 2.4, make no sense for the application—for when the score is either *this* or *that*.

We can achieve one-hot encoding using the scatter_ method, which fills the tensor with values from a source tensor along the indices provided as arguments:

```
# In[8]:
target_onehot = torch.zeros(target.shape[0], 10)

target_onehot.scatter_(1, target.unsqueeze(1), 1.0)

# Out[8]:
tensor([[0., 0.,   ..., 0., 0.],
        [0., 0.,   ..., 0., 0.],
        ...,
        [0., 0.,   ..., 0., 0.],
        [0., 0.,   ..., 0., 0.]])
```

Let's see what scatter_ does. First, we notice that its name ends with an underscore. As you learned in the previous chapter, this is a convention in PyTorch that indicates the method will not return a new tensor, but will instead modify the tensor in place. The arguments for scatter_ are as follows:

- The dimension along which the following two arguments are specified
- A column tensor indicating the indices of the elements to scatter
- A tensor containing the elements to scatter or a single scalar to scatter (1, in this case)

In other words, the previous invocation reads, "For each row, take the index of the target label (which coincides with the score in our case) and use it as the column index to set the value 1.0." The end result is a tensor encoding categorical information.

The second argument of scatter_, the index tensor, is required to have the same number of dimensions as the tensor we scatter into. Since target_onehot has two dimensions (4,898 × 10), we need to add an extra dummy dimension to target using unsqueeze:

```
# In[9]:
target_unsqueezed = target.unsqueeze(1)
target_unsqueezed

# Out[9]:
tensor([[6],
```

```
       [6],
       ...,
       [7],
       [6]])
```

The call to `unsqueeze` adds a *singleton* dimension, from a 1D tensor of 4,898 elements to a 2D tensor of size (4,898 × 1), without changing its contents—no extra elements are added; we just decided to use an extra index to access the elements. That is, we access the first element of `target` as `target[0]` and the first element of its unsqueezed counterpart as `target_unsqueezed[0,0]`.

PyTorch allows us to use class indices directly as targets while training neural networks. However, if we wanted to use the score as a categorical input to the network, we would have to transform it to a one-hot-encoded tensor.

4.3.5 *When to categorize*

Now we have seen ways to deal with both continuous and categorical data. You may wonder what the deal is with the ordinal case discussed in the earlier sidebar. There is no general recipe for it; most commonly, such data is either treated as categorical (losing the ordering part, and hoping that maybe our model will pick it up during training if we only have a few categories) or continuous (introducing an arbitrary notion of distance). We will do the latter for the weather situation in figure 4.5. We summarize our data mapping in a small flow chart in figure 4.4.

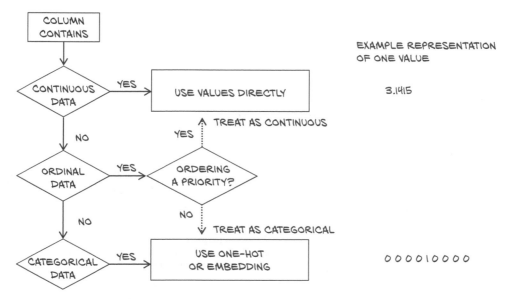

Figure 4.4 How to treat columns with continuous, ordinal, and categorical data

Let's go back to our data tensor, containing the 11 variables associated with the chemical analysis. We can use the functions in the PyTorch Tensor API to manipulate our data in tensor form. Let's first obtain the mean and standard deviations for each column:

```
# In[10]:
data_mean = torch.mean(data, dim=0)
data_mean

# Out[10]:
tensor([6.85e+00, 2.78e-01, 3.34e-01, 6.39e+00, 4.58e-02, 3.53e+01,
        1.38e+02, 9.94e-01, 3.19e+00, 4.90e-01, 1.05e+01])

# In[11]:
data_var = torch.var(data, dim=0)
data_var

# Out[11]:
tensor([7.12e-01, 1.02e-02, 1.46e-02, 2.57e+01, 4.77e-04, 2.89e+02,
        1.81e+03, 8.95e-06, 2.28e-02, 1.30e-02, 1.51e+00])
```

In this case, dim=0 indicates that the reduction is performed along dimension 0. At this point, we can normalize the data by subtracting the mean and dividing by the standard deviation, which helps with the learning process (we'll discuss this in more detail in chapter 5, in section 5.4.4):

```
# In[12]:
data_normalized = (data - data_mean) / torch.sqrt(data_var)
data_normalized

# Out[12]:
tensor([[ 1.72e-01, -8.18e-02,  ...,  -3.49e-01, -1.39e+00],
        [-6.57e-01,  2.16e-01,  ...,   1.35e-03, -8.24e-01],
        ...,
        [-1.61e+00,  1.17e-01,  ...,  -9.63e-01,  1.86e+00],
        [-1.01e+00, -6.77e-01,  ...,  -1.49e+00,  1.04e+00]])
```

4.3.6 *Finding thresholds*

Next, let's start to look at the data with an eye to seeing if there is an easy way to tell good and bad wines apart at a glance. First, we're going to determine which rows in target correspond to a score less than or equal to 3:

> PyTorch also provides comparison functions, here torch.le(target, 3), but using operators seems to be a good standard.

```
# In[13]:
bad_indexes = target <= 3   ◁──┘
bad_indexes.shape, bad_indexes.dtype, bad_indexes.sum()

# Out[13]:
(torch.Size([4898]), torch.bool, tensor(20))
```

Note that only 20 of the bad_indexes entries are set to True! By using a feature in PyTorch called *advanced indexing*, we can use a tensor with data type torch.bool to index the data tensor. This will essentially filter data to be only items (or rows) corresponding to True in the indexing tensor. The bad_indexes tensor has the same shape as target, with values of False or True depending on the outcome of the comparison between our threshold and each element in the original target tensor:

```
# In[14]:
bad_data = data[bad_indexes]
bad_data.shape

# Out[14]:
torch.Size([20, 11])
```

Note that the new bad_data tensor has 20 rows, the same as the number of rows with True in the bad_indexes tensor. It retains all 11 columns. Now we can start to get information about wines grouped into good, middling, and bad categories. Let's take the .mean() of each column:

```
# In[15]:
bad_data = data[target <= 3]
mid_data = data[(target > 3) & (target < 7)]    ◁────  For Boolean NumPy arrays and
good_data = data[target >= 7]                           PyTorch tensors, the & operator
                                                        does a logical "and" operation.
bad_mean = torch.mean(bad_data, dim=0)
mid_mean = torch.mean(mid_data, dim=0)
good_mean = torch.mean(good_data, dim=0)

for i, args in enumerate(zip(col_list, bad_mean, mid_mean, good_mean)):
    print('{:2} {:20} {:6.2f} {:6.2f} {:6.2f}'.format(i, *args))

# Out[15]:
 0 fixed acidity          7.60    6.89    6.73
 1 volatile acidity       0.33    0.28    0.27
 2 citric acid            0.34    0.34    0.33
 3 residual sugar         6.39    6.71    5.26
 4 chlorides              0.05    0.05    0.04
 5 free sulfur dioxide   53.33   35.42   34.55
 6 total sulfur dioxide 170.60  141.83  125.25
 7 density                0.99    0.99    0.99
 8 pH                     3.19    3.18    3.22
 9 sulphates              0.47    0.49    0.50
10 alcohol               10.34   10.26   11.42
```

It looks like we're on to something here: at first glance, the bad wines seem to have higher total sulfur dioxide, among other differences. We could use a threshold on total sulfur dioxide as a crude criterion for discriminating good wines from bad ones. Let's get the indexes where the total sulfur dioxide column is below the midpoint we calculated earlier, like so:

```
# In[16]:
total_sulfur_threshold = 141.83
total_sulfur_data = data[:,6]
predicted_indexes = torch.lt(total_sulfur_data, total_sulfur_threshold)

predicted_indexes.shape, predicted_indexes.dtype, predicted_indexes.sum()

# Out[16]:
(torch.Size([4898]), torch.bool, tensor(2727))
```

This means our threshold implies that just over half of all the wines are going to be high quality. Next, we'll need to get the indexes of the actually good wines:

```
# In[17]:
actual_indexes = target > 5

actual_indexes.shape, actual_indexes.dtype, actual_indexes.sum()

# Out[17]:
(torch.Size([4898]), torch.bool, tensor(3258))
```

Since there are about 500 more actually good wines than our threshold predicted, we already have hard evidence that it's not perfect. Now we need to see how well our predictions line up with the actual rankings. We will perform a logical "and" between our prediction indexes and the actual good indexes (remember that each is just an array of zeros and ones) and use that intersection of wines-in-agreement to determine how well we did:

```
# In[18]:
n_matches = torch.sum(actual_indexes & predicted_indexes).item()
n_predicted = torch.sum(predicted_indexes).item()
n_actual = torch.sum(actual_indexes).item()

n_matches, n_matches / n_predicted, n_matches / n_actual

# Out[18]:
(2018, 0.74000733406674, 0.6193984039287906)
```

We got around 2,000 wines right! Since we predicted 2,700 wines, this gives us a 74% chance that if we predict a wine to be high quality, it actually is. Unfortunately, there are 3,200 good wines, and we only identified 61% of them. Well, we got what we signed up for; that's barely better than random! Of course, this is all very naive: we know for sure that multiple variables contribute to wine quality, and the relationships between the values of these variables and the outcome (which could be the actual score, rather than a binarized version of it) is likely more complicated than a simple threshold on a single value.

Indeed, a simple neural network would overcome all of these limitations, as would a lot of other basic machine learning methods. We'll have the tools to tackle this problem after the next two chapters, once we have learned how to build our first neural network from scratch. We will also revisit how to better grade our results in chapter 12. Let's move on to other data types for now.

4.4 Working with time series

In the previous section, we covered how to represent data organized in a flat table. As we noted, every row in the table was independent from the others; their order did not matter. Or, equivalently, there was no column that encoded information about what rows came earlier and what came later.

Going back to the wine dataset, we could have had a "year" column that allowed us to look at how wine quality evolved year after year. Unfortunately, we don't have such data at hand, but we're working hard on manually collecting the data samples, bottle by bottle. (Stuff for our second edition.) In the meantime, we'll switch to another interesting dataset: data from a Washington, D.C., bike-sharing system reporting the hourly count of rental bikes in 2011–2012 in the Capital Bikeshare system, along with weather and seasonal information (available here: http://mng.bz/jgOx). Our goal will be to take a flat, 2D dataset and transform it into a 3D one, as shown in figure 4.5.

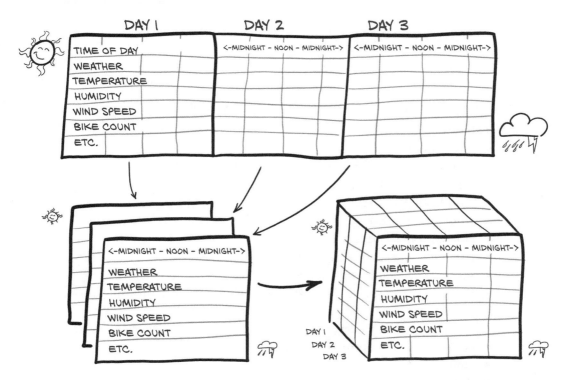

Figure 4.5 Transforming a 1D, multichannel dataset into a 2D, multichannel dataset by separating the date and hour of each sample into separate axes

4.4.1 Adding a time dimension

In the source data, each row is a separate hour of data (figure 4.5 shows a transposed version of this to better fit on the printed page). We want to change the row-per-hour organization so that we have one axis that increases at a rate of one day per index increment, and another axis that represents the hour of the day (independent of the date). The third axis will be our different columns of data (weather, temperature, and so on).

Let's load the data (code/p1ch4/4_time_series_bikes.ipynb).

Listing 4.4   code/p1ch4/4_time_series_bikes.ipynb

```
# In[2]:
bikes_numpy = np.loadtxt(
    "../data/p1ch4/bike-sharing-dataset/hour-fixed.csv",
    dtype=np.float32,
    delimiter=",",
    skiprows=1,
    converters={1: lambda x: float(x[8:10])})          ◁
bikes = torch.from_numpy(bikes_numpy)
bikes
```

Converts date strings to
numbers corresponding to the
day of the month in column 1

```
# Out[2]:
tensor([[1.0000e+00, 1.0000e+00,  ..., 1.3000e+01, 1.6000e+01],
        [2.0000e+00, 1.0000e+00,  ..., 3.2000e+01, 4.0000e+01],
        ...,
        [1.7378e+04, 3.1000e+01,  ..., 4.8000e+01, 6.1000e+01],
        [1.7379e+04, 3.1000e+01,  ..., 3.7000e+01, 4.9000e+01]])
```

For every hour, the dataset reports the following variables:

- Index of record: `instant`
- Day of month: `day`
- Season: `season` (1: spring, 2: summer, 3: fall, 4: winter)
- Year: `yr` (0: 2011, 1: 2012)
- Month: `mnth` (1 to 12)
- Hour: `hr` (0 to 23)
- Holiday status: `holiday`
- Day of the week: `weekday`
- Working day status: `workingday`
- Weather situation: `weathersit` (1: clear, 2:mist, 3: light rain/snow, 4: heavy rain/snow)
- Temperature in °C: `temp`
- Perceived temperature in °C: `atemp`
- Humidity: `hum`
- Wind speed: `windspeed`
- Number of casual users: `casual`
- Number of registered users: `registered`
- Count of rental bikes: `cnt`

In a time series dataset such as this one, rows represent successive time-points: there is a dimension along which they are ordered. Sure, we could treat each row as independent and try to predict the number of circulating bikes based on, say, a particular time of day regardless of what happened earlier. However, the existence of an ordering gives us the opportunity to exploit causal relationships across time. For instance, it allows us to predict bike rides at one time based on the fact that it was raining at an earlier time. For the time being, we're going to focus on learning how to turn our bike-sharing dataset into something that our neural network will be able to ingest in fixed-size chunks.

This neural network model will need to see a number of sequences of values for each different quantity, such as ride count, time of day, temperature, and weather conditions: N parallel sequences of size C. C stands for *channel*, in neural network parlance, and is the same as *column* for 1D data like we have here. The N dimension represents the time axis, here one entry per hour.

4.4.2 *Shaping the data by time period*

We might want to break up the two-year dataset into wider observation periods, like days. This way we'll have N (for *number of samples*) collections of C sequences of length L. In other words, our time series dataset would be a tensor of dimension 3 and shape $N \times C \times L$. The C would remain our 17 channels, while L would be 24: 1 per hour of the day. There's no particular reason why we *must* use chunks of 24 hours, though the general daily rhythm is likely to give us patterns we can exploit for predictions. We could also use $7 \times 24 = 168$ hour blocks to chunk by week instead, if we desired. All of this depends, naturally, on our dataset having the right size—the number of rows must be a multiple of 24 or 168. Also, for this to make sense, we cannot have gaps in the time series.

Let's go back to our bike-sharing dataset. The first column is the index (the global ordering of the data), the second is the date, and the sixth is the time of day. We have everything we need to create a dataset of daily sequences of ride counts and other exogenous variables. Our dataset is already sorted, but if it were not, we could use `torch.sort` on it to order it appropriately.

> **NOTE** The version of the file we're using, hour-fixed.csv, has had some processing done to include rows missing from the original dataset. We presume that the missing hours had zero bike active (they were typically in the early morning hours).

All we have to do to obtain our daily hours dataset is view the same tensor in batches of 24 hours. Let's take a look at the shape and strides of our `bikes` tensor:

```
# In[3]:
bikes.shape, bikes.stride()
```

```
# Out[3]:
(torch.Size([17520, 17]), (17, 1))
```

That's 17,520 hours, 17 columns. Now let's reshape the data to have 3 axes—day, hour, and then our 17 columns:

```
# In[4]:
daily_bikes = bikes.view(-1, 24, bikes.shape[1])
daily_bikes.shape, daily_bikes.stride()

# Out[4]:
(torch.Size([730, 24, 17]), (408, 17, 1))
```

What happened here? First, bikes.shape[1] is 17, the number of columns in the bikes tensor. But the real crux of this code is the call to view, which is really important: it changes the way the tensor looks at the same data as contained in storage.

As you learned in the previous chapter, calling view on a tensor returns a new tensor that changes the number of dimensions and the striding information, without changing the storage. This means we can rearrange our tensor at basically zero cost, because no data will be copied. Our call to view requires us to provide the new shape for the returned tensor. We use -1 as a placeholder for "however many indexes are left, given the other dimensions and the original number of elements."

Remember also from the previous chapter that storage is a contiguous, linear container for numbers (floating-point, in this case). Our bikes tensor will have each row stored one after the other in its corresponding storage. This is confirmed by the output from the call to bikes.stride() earlier.

For daily_bikes, the stride is telling us that advancing by 1 along the hour dimension (the second dimension) requires us to advance by 17 places in the storage (or one set of columns); whereas advancing along the day dimension (the first dimension) requires us to advance by a number of elements equal to the length of a row in the storage times 24 (here, 408, which is 17×24).

We see that the rightmost dimension is the number of columns in the original dataset. Then, in the middle dimension, we have time, split into chunks of 24 sequential hours. In other words, we now have N sequences of L hours in a day, for C channels. To get to our desired $N \times C \times L$ ordering, we need to transpose the tensor:

```
# In[5]:
daily_bikes = daily_bikes.transpose(1, 2)
daily_bikes.shape, daily_bikes.stride()

# Out[5]:
(torch.Size([730, 17, 24]), (408, 1, 17))
```

Now let's apply some of the techniques we learned earlier to this dataset.

4.4.3 *Ready for training*

The "weather situation" variable is ordinal. It has four levels: 1 for good weather, and 4 for, er, really bad. We could treat this variable as categorical, with levels interpreted as labels, or as a continuous variable. If we decided to go with categorical, we would turn the variable into a one-hot-encoded vector and concatenate the columns with the dataset.[4]

In order to make it easier to render our data, we're going to limit ourselves to the first day for a moment. We initialize a zero-filled matrix with a number of rows equal to the number of hours in the day and number of columns equal to the number of weather levels:

```
# In[6]:
first_day = bikes[:24].long()
weather_onehot = torch.zeros(first_day.shape[0], 4)
first_day[:,9]

# Out[6]:
tensor([1, 1, 1, 1, 1, 2, 1, 1, 1, 1, 1, 1, 1, 2, 2, 2, 2, 2, 3, 3, 2, 2,
        2, 2])
```

Then we scatter ones into our matrix according to the corresponding level at each row. Remember the use of unsqueeze to add a singleton dimension as we did in the previous sections:

```
# In[7]:
weather_onehot.scatter_(
    dim=1,
    index=first_day[:,9].unsqueeze(1).long() - 1,    ◁——┐
    value=1.0)
```

Decreases the values by 1 because weather situation ranges from 1 to 4, while indices are 0-based

```
# Out[7]:
tensor([[1., 0., 0., 0.],
        [1., 0., 0., 0.],
        ...,
        [0., 1., 0., 0.],
        [0., 1., 0., 0.]])
```

Our day started with weather "1" and ended with "2," so that seems right.

Last, we concatenate our matrix to our original dataset using the cat function. Let's look at the first of our results:

```
# In[8]:
torch.cat((bikes[:24], weather_onehot), 1)[:1]

# Out[8]:
tensor([[ 1.0000,  1.0000,  1.0000,  0.0000,  1.0000,  0.0000,  0.0000,
          6.0000,  0.0000,  1.0000,  0.2400,  0.2879,  0.8100,  0.0000,
          3.0000, 13.0000, 16.0000,  1.0000,  0.0000,  0.0000,  0.0000]])
```

---

[4] This could also be a case where it is useful to go beyond the main path. Speculatively, we could also try to reflect *like categorical, but with order* more directly by generalizing one-hot encodings to mapping the ith of our four categories here to a vector that has ones in the positions $0...i$ and zeros beyond that. Or—similar to the embeddings we discussed in section 4.5.4—we could take partial sums of embeddings, in which case it might make sense to make those positive. As with many things we encounter in practical work, this could be a place where *trying what works for others* and then experimenting in a systematic fashion is a good idea.

Here we prescribed our original bikes dataset and our one-hot-encoded "weather situation" matrix to be concatenated along the *column* dimension (that is, 1). In other words, the columns of the two datasets are stacked together; or, equivalently, the new one-hot-encoded columns are appended to the original dataset. For cat to succeed, it is required that the tensors have the same size along the other dimensions—the *row* dimension, in this case. Note that our new last four columns are 1, 0, 0, 0, exactly as we would expect with a weather value of 1.

We could have done the same with the reshaped daily_bikes tensor. Remember that it is shaped (B, C, L), where $L = 24$. We first create the zero tensor, with the same B and L, but with the number of additional columns as C:

```
# In[9]:
daily_weather_onehot = torch.zeros(daily_bikes.shape[0], 4,
                                   daily_bikes.shape[2])
daily_weather_onehot.shape

# Out[9]:
torch.Size([730, 4, 24])
```

Then we scatter the one-hot encoding into the tensor in the C dimension. Since this operation is performed in place, only the content of the tensor will change:

```
# In[10]:
daily_weather_onehot.scatter_(
    1, daily_bikes[:,9,:].long().unsqueeze(1) - 1, 1.0)
daily_weather_onehot.shape

# Out[10]:
torch.Size([730, 4, 24])
```

And we concatenate along the C dimension:

```
# In[11]:
daily_bikes = torch.cat((daily_bikes, daily_weather_onehot), dim=1)
```

We mentioned earlier that this is not the only way to treat our "weather situation" variable. Indeed, its labels have an ordinal relationship, so we could pretend they are special values of a continuous variable. We could just transform the variable so that it runs from 0.0 to 1.0:

```
# In[12]:
daily_bikes[:, 9, :] = (daily_bikes[:, 9, :] - 1.0) / 3.0
```

As we mentioned in the previous section, rescaling variables to the [0.0, 1.0] interval or the [-1.0, 1.0] interval is something we'll want to do for all quantitative variables, like temperature (column 10 in our dataset). We'll see why later; for now, let's just say that this is beneficial to the training process.

There are multiple possibilities for rescaling variables. We can either map their range to [0.0, 1.0]

```
# In[13]:
temp = daily_bikes[:, 10, :]
temp_min = torch.min(temp)
temp_max = torch.max(temp)
daily_bikes[:, 10, :] = ((daily_bikes[:, 10, :] - temp_min)
                        / (temp_max - temp_min))
```

or subtract the mean and divide by the standard deviation:

```
# In[14]:
temp = daily_bikes[:, 10, :]
daily_bikes[:, 10, :] = ((daily_bikes[:, 10, :] - torch.mean(temp))
                        / torch.std(temp))
```

In the latter case, our variable will have 0 mean and unitary standard deviation. If our variable were drawn from a Gaussian distribution, 68% of the samples would sit in the [-1.0, 1.0] interval.

Great: we've built another nice dataset, and we've seen how to deal with time series data. For this tour d'horizon, it's important only that we got an idea of how a time series is laid out and how we can wrangle the data in a form that a network will digest.

Other kinds of data look like a time series, in that there is a strict ordering. Top two on the list? Text and audio. We'll take a look at text next, and the "Conclusion" section has links to additional examples for audio.

4.5 *Representing text*

Deep learning has taken the field of natural language processing (NLP) by storm, particularly using models that repeatedly consume a combination of new input and previous model output. These models are called *recurrent neural networks* (RNNs), and they have been applied with great success to text categorization, text generation, and automated translation systems. More recently, a class of networks called *transformers* with a more flexible way to incorporate past information has made a big splash. Previous NLP workloads were characterized by sophisticated multistage pipelines that included rules encoding the grammar of a language.[5] Now, state-of-the-art work trains networks end to end on large corpora starting from scratch, letting those rules emerge from the data. For the last several years, the most-used automated translation systems available as services on the internet have been based on deep learning.

Our goal in this section is to turn text into something a neural network can process: a tensor of numbers, just like our previous cases. If we can do that and later choose the right architecture for our text-processing job, we'll be in the position of doing NLP with PyTorch. We see right away how powerful this all is: we can achieve

---

[5] Nadkarni et al., "Natural language processing: an introduction," JAMIA, http://mng.bz/8pJP. See also https://en.wikipedia.org/wiki/Natural-language_processing.

state-of-the-art performance on a number of tasks in different domains *with the same PyTorch tools*; we just need to cast our problem in the right form. The first part of this job is reshaping the data.

4.5.1   *Converting text to numbers*

There are two particularly intuitive levels at which networks operate on text: at the character level, by processing one character at a time, and at the word level, where individual words are the finest-grained entities to be seen by the network. The technique with which we encode text information into tensor form is the same whether we operate at the character level or the word level. And it's not magic, either. We stumbled upon it earlier: one-hot encoding.

Let's start with a character-level example. First, let's get some text to process. An amazing resource here is Project Gutenberg (www.gutenberg.org), a volunteer effort to digitize and archive cultural work and make it available for free in open formats, including plain text files. If we're aiming at larger-scale corpora, the Wikipedia corpus stands out: it's the complete collection of Wikipedia articles, containing 1.9 billion words and more than 4.4 million articles. Several other corpora can be found at the English Corpora website (www.english-corpora.org).

Let's load Jane Austen's *Pride and Prejudice* from the Project Gutenberg website: www.gutenberg.org/files/1342/1342-0.txt. We'll just save the file and read it in (code/p1ch4/5_text_jane_austen.ipynb).

Listing 4.5   code/p1ch4/5_text_jane_austen.ipynb

```
# In[2]:
with open('../data/p1ch4/jane-austen/1342-0.txt', encoding='utf8') as f:
    text = f.read()
```

4.5.2   *One-hot-encoding characters*

There's one more detail we need to take care of before we proceed: encoding. This is a pretty vast subject, and we will just touch on it. Every written character is represented by a code: a sequence of bits of appropriate length so that each character can be uniquely identified. The simplest such encoding is ASCII (American Standard Code for Information Interchange), which dates back to the 1960s. ASCII encodes 128 characters using 128 integers. For instance, the letter *a* corresponds to binary 1100001 or decimal 97, the letter *b* to binary 1100010 or decimal 98, and so on. The encoding fits 8 bits, which was a big bonus in 1965.

> **NOTE** 128 characters are clearly not enough to account for all the glyphs, accents, ligatures, and so on that are needed to properly represent written text in languages other than English. To this end, a number of encodings have been developed that use a larger number of bits as code for a wider range of characters. That wider range of characters was standardized as Unicode, which maps all known characters to numbers, with the representation

in bits of those numbers provided by a specific encoding. Popular encodings are UTF-8, UTF-16, and UTF-32, in which the numbers are a sequence of 8-, 16-, or 32-bit integers, respectively. Strings in Python 3.x are Unicode strings.

We are going to one-hot encode our characters. It is instrumental to limit the one-hot encoding to a character set that is useful for the text being analyzed. In our case, since we loaded text in English, it is safe to use ASCII and deal with a small encoding. We could also make all of the characters lowercase, to reduce the number of different characters in our encoding. Similarly, we could screen out punctuation, numbers, or other characters that aren't relevant to our expected kinds of text. This may or may not make a practical difference to a neural network, depending on the task at hand.

At this point, we need to parse through the characters in the text and provide a one-hot encoding for each of them. Each character will be represented by a vector of length equal to the number of different characters in the encoding. This vector will contain all zeros except a one at the index corresponding to the location of the character in the encoding.

We first split our text into a list of lines and pick an arbitrary line to focus on:

```
# In[3]:
lines = text.split('\n')
line = lines[200]
line

# Out[3]:
'"Impossible, Mr. Bennet, impossible, when I am not acquainted with him'
```

Let's create a tensor that can hold the total number of one-hot-encoded characters for the whole line:

```
# In[4]:
letter_t = torch.zeros(len(line), 128)    ◁── 128 hardcoded due to
letter_t.shape                                 the limits of ASCII

# Out[4]:
torch.Size([70, 128])
```

Note that `letter_t` holds a one-hot-encoded character per row. Now we just have to set a one on each row in the correct position so that each row represents the correct character. The index where the one has to be set corresponds to the index of the character in the encoding:

```
# In[5]:
for i, letter in enumerate(line.lower().strip()):
    letter_index = ord(letter) if ord(letter) < 128 else 0    ◁──
    letter_t[i][letter_index] = 1
```

The text uses directional double quotes, which are not valid ASCII, so we screen them out here.

4.5.3   *One-hot encoding whole words*

We have one-hot encoded our sentence into a representation that a neural network could digest. Word-level encoding can be done the same way by establishing a vocabulary and one-hot encoding sentences—sequences of words—along the rows of our tensor. Since a vocabulary has many words, this will produce very wide encoded vectors, which may not be practical. We will see in the next section that there is a more efficient way to represent text at the word level, using *embeddings*. For now, let's stick with one-hot encodings and see what happens.

We'll define `clean_words`, which takes text and returns it in lowercase and stripped of punctuation. When we call it on our "Impossible, Mr. Bennet" `line`, we get the following:

```
# In[6]:
def clean_words(input_str):
    punctuation = '.,;:"!?"""_-'
    word_list = input_str.lower().replace('\n',' ').split()
    word_list = [word.strip(punctuation) for word in word_list]
    return word_list

words_in_line = clean_words(line)
line, words_in_line

# Out[6]:
('"Impossible, Mr. Bennet, impossible, when I am not acquainted with him',
 ['impossible',
  'mr',
  'bennet',
  'impossible',
  'when',
  'i',
  'am',
  'not',
  'acquainted',
  'with',
  'him'])
```

Next, let's build a mapping of words to indexes in our encoding:

```
# In[7]:
word_list = sorted(set(clean_words(text)))
word2index_dict = {word: i for (i, word) in enumerate(word_list)}

len(word2index_dict), word2index_dict['impossible']

# Out[7]:
(7261, 3394)
```

Note that `word2index_dict` is now a dictionary with words as keys and an integer as a value. We will use it to efficiently find the index of a word as we one-hot encode it. Let's now focus on our sentence: we break it up into words and one-hot encode it—

that is, we populate a tensor with one one-hot-encoded vector per word. We create an empty vector and assign the one-hot-encoded values of the word in the sentence:

```
# In[8]:
word_t = torch.zeros(len(words_in_line), len(word2index_dict))
for i, word in enumerate(words_in_line):
    word_index = word2index_dict[word]
    word_t[i][word_index] = 1
    print('{:2} {:4} {}'.format(i, word_index, word))

print(word_t.shape)
```

```
# Out[8]:
 0 3394 impossible
 1 4305 mr
 2  813 bennet
 3 3394 impossible
 4 7078 when
 5 3315 i
 6  415 am
 7 4436 not
 8  239 acquainted
 9 7148 with
10 3215 him
torch.Size([11, 7261])
```

At this point, `tensor` represents one sentence of length 11 in an encoding space of size 7,261, the number of words in our dictionary. Figure 4.6 compares the gist of our two options for splitting text (and using the embeddings we'll look at in the next section).

The choice between character-level and word-level encoding leaves us to make a trade-off. In many languages, there are significantly fewer characters than words: representing characters has us representing just a few classes, while representing words requires us to represent a very large number of classes and, in any practical application, deal with words that are not in the dictionary. On the other hand, words convey much more meaning than individual characters, so a representation of words is considerably more informative by itself. Given the stark contrast between these two options, it is perhaps unsurprising that intermediate ways have been sought, found, and applied with great success: for example, the *byte pair encoding* method[6] starts with a dictionary of individual letters but then iteratively adds the most frequently observed pairs to the dictionary until it reaches a prescribed dictionary size. Our example sentence might then be split into tokens like this:[7]

```
?Im|pos|s|ible|,|?Mr|.|?B|en|net|,|?impossible|,|?when|?I|?am|?not|➡
?acquainted|?with|?him
```

---

[6] Most commonly implemented by the subword-nmt and SentencePiece libraries. The conceptual drawback is that the representation of a sequence of characters is no longer unique.

[7] This is from a SentencePiece tokenizer trained on a machine translation dataset.

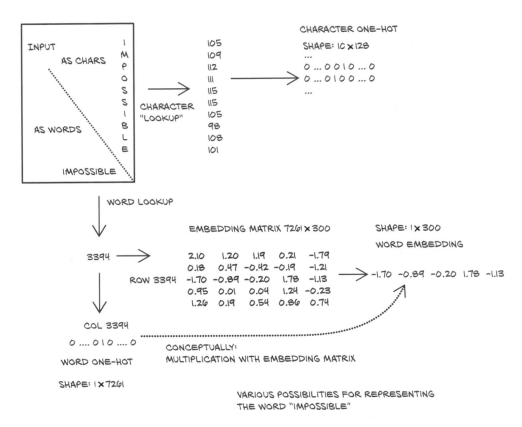

Figure 4.6   Three ways to encode a word

For most things, our mapping is just splitting by words. But the rarer parts—the capitalized *Impossible* and the name *Bennet*—are composed of subunits.

4.5.4   *Text embeddings*

One-hot encoding is a very useful technique for representing categorical data in tensors. However, as we have anticipated, one-hot encoding starts to break down when the number of items to encode is effectively unbound, as with words in a corpus. In just one book, we had over 7,000 items!

We certainly could do some work to deduplicate words, condense alternate spellings, collapse past and future tenses into a single token, and that kind of thing. Still, a general-purpose English-language encoding would be *huge*. Even worse, every time we encountered a new word, we would have to add a new column to the vector, which would mean adding a new set of weights to the model to account for that new vocabulary entry—which would be painful from a training perspective.

How can we compress our encoding down to a more manageable size and put a cap on the size growth? Well, instead of vectors of many zeros and a single one, we can use vectors of floating-point numbers. A vector of, say, 100 floating-point numbers can indeed represent a large number of words. The trick is to find an effective way to map individual words into this 100-dimensional space in a way that facilitates downstream learning. This is called an *embedding*.

In principle, we could simply iterate over our vocabulary and generate a set of 100 random floating-point numbers for each word. This would work, in that we could cram a very large vocabulary into just 100 numbers, but it would forgo any concept of distance between words based on meaning or context. A model using this word embedding would have to deal with very little structure in its input vectors. An ideal solution would be to generate the embedding in such a way that words used in similar contexts mapped to nearby regions of the embedding.

Well, if we were to design a solution to this problem by hand, we might decide to build our embedding space by choosing to map basic nouns and adjectives along the axes. We can generate a 2D space where axes map to nouns—*fruit* (0.0-0.33), *flower* (0.33-0.66), and *dog* (0.66-1.0)—and adjectives—*red* (0.0-0.2), *orange* (0.2-0.4), *yellow* (0.4-0.6), *white* (0.6-0.8), and *brown* (0.8-1.0). Our goal is to take actual fruit, flowers, and dogs and lay them out in the embedding.

As we start embedding words, we can map *apple* to a number in the *fruit* and *red* quadrant. Likewise, we can easily map *tangerine*, *lemon*, *lychee*, and *kiwi* (to round out our list of colorful fruits). Then we can start on flowers, and assign *rose*, *poppy*, *daffodil*, *lily*, and … Hmm. Not many brown flowers out there. Well, *sunflower* can get *flower, yellow*, and *brown*, and then *daisy* can get *flower, white*, and *yellow*. Perhaps we should update *kiwi* to map close to *fruit, brown*, and *green*.[8] For dogs and color, we can embed *redbone* near *red*; uh, *fox* perhaps for *orange*; *golden retriever* for *yellow*, *poodle* for *white*, and … most kinds of dogs are *brown*.

Now our embeddings look like figure 4.7. While doing this manually isn't really feasible for a large corpus, note that although we had an embedding size of 2, we described 15 different words *besides the base 8* and could probably cram in quite a few more if we took the time to be creative about it.

As you've probably already guessed, this kind of work can be automated. By processing a large corpus of organic text, embeddings similar to the one we just discussed can be generated. The main differences are that there are 100 to 1,000 elements in the embedding vector and that axes do not map directly to concepts: rather, conceptually similar words map in neighboring regions of an embedding space whose axes are arbitrary floating-point dimensions.

While the exact algorithms[9] used are a bit out of scope for what we're wanting to focus on here, we'd just like to mention that embeddings are often generated using neural networks, trying to predict a word from nearby words (the context) in a sentence. In this case, we could start from one-hot-encoded words and use a (usually

---

[8] Actually, with our 1D view of color, this is not possible, as *sunflower*'s *yellow* and *brown* will average to *white*— but you get the idea, and it does work better in higher dimensions.

[9] One example is word2vec: https://code.google.com/archive/p/word2vec.

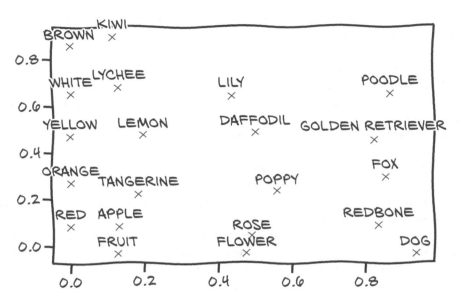

Figure 4.7   Our manual word embeddings

rather shallow) neural network to generate the embedding. Once the embedding was available, we could use it for downstream tasks.

One interesting aspect of the resulting embeddings is that similar words end up not only clustered together, but also having consistent spatial relationships with other words. For example, if we were to take the embedding vector for *apple* and begin to add and subtract the vectors for other words, we could begin to perform analogies like *apple - red - sweet + yellow + sour* and end up with a vector very similar to the one for *lemon*.

More contemporary embedding models—with BERT and GPT-2 making headlines even in mainstream media—are much more elaborate and are context sensitive: that is, the mapping of a word in the vocabulary to a vector is not fixed but depends on the surrounding sentence. Yet they are often used just like the simpler *classic* embeddings we've touched on here.

4.5.5   *Text embeddings as a blueprint*

Embeddings are an essential tool for when a large number of entries in the vocabulary have to be represented by numeric vectors. But we won't be using text and text embeddings in this book, so you might wonder why we introduce them here. We believe that how text is represented and processed can also be seen as an example for dealing with categorical data in general. Embeddings are useful wherever one-hot encoding becomes cumbersome. Indeed, in the form described previously, they are an efficient way of representing one-hot encoding immediately followed by multiplication with the matrix containing the embedding vectors as rows.

In non-text applications, we usually do not have the ability to construct the embeddings beforehand, but we will start with the random numbers we eschewed earlier and consider improving them part of our learning problem. This is a standard technique—so much so that embeddings are a prominent alternative to one-hot encodings for any categorical data. On the flip side, even when we deal with text, improving the prelearned embeddings while solving the problem at hand has become a common practice.[10]

When we are interested in co-occurrences of observations, the word embeddings we saw earlier can serve as a blueprint, too. For example, recommender systems—customers who liked our book also bought …—use the items the customer already interacted with as the context for predicting what else will spark interest. Similarly, processing text is perhaps the most common, well-explored task dealing with sequences; so, for example, when working on tasks with time series, we might look for inspiration in what is done in natural language processing.

4.6 *Conclusion*

We've covered a lot of ground in this chapter. We learned to load the most common types of data and shape them for consumption by a neural network. Of course, there are more data formats in the wild than we could hope to describe in a single volume. Some, like medical histories, are too complex to cover here. Others, like audio and video, were deemed less crucial for the path of this book. If you're interested, however, we provide short examples of audio and video tensor creation in bonus Jupyter Notebooks provided on the book's website (www.manning.com/books/deep-learning-with-pytorch) and in our code repository (https://github.com/deep-learning-with-pytorch/dlwpt-code/tree/master/p1ch4).

Now that we're familiar with tensors and how to store data in them, we can move on to the next step towards the goal of the book: teaching you to train deep neural networks! The next chapter covers the mechanics of learning for simple linear models.

4.7 *Exercises*

1 Take several pictures of red, blue, and green items with your phone or other digital camera (or download some from the internet, if a camera isn't available).

   a Load each image, and convert it to a tensor.

   b For each image tensor, use the .mean() method to get a sense of how bright the image is.

   c Take the mean of each channel of your images. Can you identify the red, green, and blue items from only the channel averages?

---

[10] This goes by the name *fine-tuning*.

2 Select a relatively large file containing Python source code.

    a Build an index of all the words in the source file (feel free to make your tokenization as simple or as complex as you like; we suggest starting with replacing r"[^a-zA-Z0-9_]+" with spaces).

    b Compare your index with the one we made for *Pride and Prejudice*. Which is larger?

    c Create the one-hot encoding for the source code file.

    d What information is lost with this encoding? How does that information compare to what's lost in the *Pride and Prejudice* encoding?

4.8   Summary

- Neural networks require data to be represented as multidimensional numerical tensors, often 32-bit floating-point.
- In general, PyTorch expects data to be laid out along specific dimensions according to the model architecture—for example, convolutional versus recurrent. We can reshape data effectively with the PyTorch tensor API.
- Thanks to how the PyTorch libraries interact with the Python standard library and surrounding ecosystem, loading the most common types of data and converting them to PyTorch tensors is convenient.
- Images can have one or many channels. The most common are the red-green-blue channels of typical digital photos.
- Many images have a per-channel bit depth of 8, though 12 and 16 bits per channel are not uncommon. These bit depths can all be stored in a 32-bit floating-point number without loss of precision.
- Single-channel data formats sometimes omit an explicit channel dimension.
- Volumetric data is similar to 2D image data, with the exception of adding a third dimension (depth).
- Converting spreadsheets to tensors can be very straightforward. Categorical- and ordinal-valued columns should be handled differently from interval-valued columns.
- Text or categorical data can be encoded to a one-hot representation through the use of dictionaries. Very often, embeddings give good, efficient representations.

The mechanics
of learning

This chapter covers
- Understanding how algorithms can learn from data
- Reframing learning as parameter estimation, using differentiation and gradient descent
- Walking through a simple learning algorithm
- How PyTorch supports learning with autograd

With the blooming of machine learning that has occurred over the last decade, the notion of machines that learn from experience has become a mainstream theme in both technical and journalistic circles. Now, how is it exactly that a machine learns? What are the mechanics of this process—or, in words, what is the *algorithm* behind it? From the point of view of an observer, a learning algorithm is presented with input data that is paired with desired outputs. Once learning has occurred, that algorithm will be capable of producing correct outputs when it is fed new data that is *similar enough* to the input data it was trained on. With deep learning, this process works even when the input data and the desired output are *far* from each other: when they come from different domains, like an image and a sentence describing it, as we saw in chapter 2.

5.1   *A timeless lesson in modeling*

Building models that allow us to explain input/output relationships dates back centuries at least. When Johannes Kepler, a German mathematical astronomer (1571–1630), figured out his three laws of planetary motion in the early 1600s, he based them on data collected by his mentor Tycho Brahe during naked-eye observations (yep, seen with the naked eye and written on a piece of paper). Not having Newton's law of gravitation at his disposal (actually, Newton used Kepler's work to figure things out), Kepler extrapolated the simplest possible geometric model that could fit the data. And, by the way, it took him six years of staring at data that didn't make sense to him, together with incremental realizations, to finally formulate these laws.[1] We can see this process in figure 5.1.

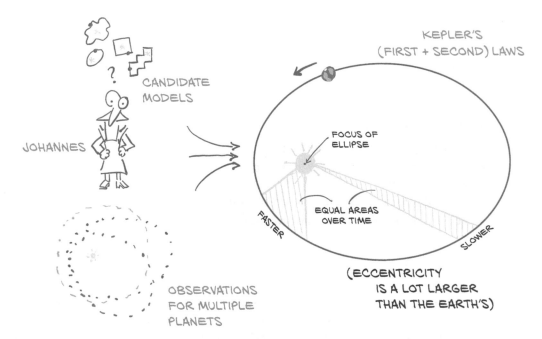

Figure 5.1   Johannes Kepler considers multiple candidate models that might fit the data at hand, settling on an ellipse.

Kepler's first law reads: "The orbit of every planet is an ellipse with the Sun at one of the two *foci*." He didn't know what caused orbits to be ellipses, but given a set of observations for a planet (or a moon of a large planet, like Jupiter), he could estimate the shape (the *eccentricity*) and size (the *semi-latus rectum*) of the ellipse. With those two parameters computed from the data, he could tell where the planet might be during

---

[1] As recounted by physicist Michael Fowler: http://mng.bz/K2Ej.

its journey in the sky. Once he figured out the second law—"A line joining a planet and the Sun sweeps out equal areas during equal intervals of time"—he could also tell *when* a planet would be at a particular point in space, given observations in time.[2]

So, how did Kepler estimate the eccentricity and size of the ellipse without computers, pocket calculators, or even calculus, none of which had been invented yet? We can learn how from Kepler's own recollection, in his book *New Astronomy*, or from how J. V. Field put it in his series of articles, "The origins of proof," (http://mng.bz/9007):

> *Essentially, Kepler had to try different shapes, using a certain number of observations to find the curve, then use the curve to find some more positions, for times when he had observations available, and then check whether these calculated positions agreed with the observed ones.*
>
> —J. V. Field

So let's sum things up. Over six years, Kepler

1 Got lots of good data from his friend Brahe (not without some struggle)
2 Tried to visualize the heck out of it, because he felt there was something fishy going on
3 Chose the simplest possible model that had a chance to fit the data (an ellipse)
4 Split the data so that he could work on part of it and keep an independent set for validation
5 Started with a tentative eccentricity and size for the ellipse and iterated until the model fit the observations
6 Validated his model on the independent observations
7 Looked back in disbelief

There's a data science handbook for you, all the way from 1609. The history of science is literally constructed on these seven steps. And we have learned over the centuries that deviating from them is a recipe for disaster.[3]

This is exactly what we will set out to do in order to *learn* something from data. In fact, in this book there is virtually no difference between saying that we'll *fit* the data or that we'll make an algorithm *learn* from data. The process always involves a function with a number of unknown parameters whose values are estimated from data: in short, a *model*.

We can argue that *learning from data* presumes the underlying model is not engineered to solve a specific problem (as was the ellipse in Kepler's work) and is instead capable of approximating a much wider family of functions. A neural network would have predicted Tycho Brahe's trajectories really well without requiring Kepler's flash of insight to try fitting the data to an ellipse. However, Sir Isaac Newton would have had a much harder time deriving his laws of gravitation from a generic model.

---

[2] Understanding the details of Kepler's laws is not needed to understand this chapter, but you can find more information at https://en.wikipedia.org/wiki/Kepler%27s_laws_of_planetary_motion.

[3] Unless you're a theoretical physicist ;).

In this book, we're interested in models that are not engineered for solving a specific narrow task, but that can be automatically adapted to specialize themselves for any one of many similar tasks using input and output pairs—in other words, general models trained on data relevant to the specific task at hand. In particular, PyTorch is designed to make it easy to create models for which the derivatives of the fitting error, with respect to the parameters, can be expressed analytically. No worries if this last sentence didn't make any sense at all; coming next, we have a full section that hopefully clears it up for you.

This chapter is about how to automate generic function-fitting. After all, this is what we do with deep learning—deep neural networks being the generic functions we're talking about—and PyTorch makes this process as simple and transparent as possible. In order to make sure we get the key concepts right, we'll start with a model that is a lot simpler than a deep neural network. This will allow us to understand the mechanics of learning algorithms from first principles in this chapter, so we can move to more complicated models in chapter 6.

5.2 *Learning is just parameter estimation*

In this section, we'll learn how we can take data, choose a model, and estimate the parameters of the model so that it will give good predictions on new data. To do so, we'll leave the intricacies of planetary motion and divert our attention to the second-hardest problem in physics: calibrating instruments.

Figure 5.2 shows the high-level overview of what we'll implement by the end of the chapter. Given input data and the corresponding desired outputs (ground truth), as well as initial values for the weights, the model is fed input data (forward pass), and a measure of the error is evaluated by comparing the resulting outputs to the ground truth. In order to optimize the parameter of the model—its *weights*—the change in the error following a unit change in weights (that is, the *gradient* of the error with respect to the parameters) is computed using the chain rule for the derivative of a composite function (backward pass). The value of the weights is then updated in the direction that leads to a decrease in the error. The procedure is repeated until the error, evaluated on unseen data, falls below an acceptable level. If what we just said sounds obscure, we've got a whole chapter to clear things up. By the time we're done, all the pieces will fall into place, and this paragraph will make perfect sense.

We're now going to take a problem with a noisy dataset, build a model, and implement a learning algorithm for it. When we start, we'll be doing everything by hand, but by the end of the chapter we'll be letting PyTorch do all the heavy lifting for us. When we finish the chapter, we will have covered many of the essential concepts that underlie training deep neural networks, even if our motivating example is very simple and our model isn't actually a neural network (yet!).

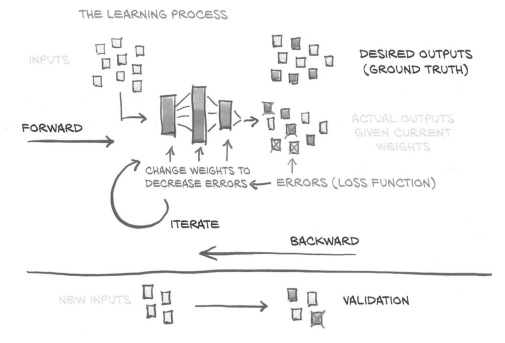

THE LEARNING PROCESS

INPUTS

FORWARD

DESIRED OUTPUTS
(GROUND TRUTH)

ACTUAL OUTPUTS
GIVEN CURRENT
WEIGHTS

CHANGE WEIGHTS TO
DECREASE ERRORS ← ERRORS (LOSS FUNCTION)

ITERATE

BACKWARD

NEW INPUTS

VALIDATION

Figure 5.2 Our mental model of the learning process

5.2.1 A hot problem

We just got back from a trip to some obscure location, and we brought back a fancy, wall-mounted analog thermometer. It looks great, and it's a perfect fit for our living room. Its only flaw is that it doesn't show units. Not to worry, we've got a plan: we'll build a dataset of readings and corresponding temperature values in our favorite units, choose a model, adjust its weights iteratively until a measure of the error is low enough, and finally be able to interpret the new readings in units we understand.[4]

Let's try following the same process Kepler used. Along the way, we'll use a tool he never had available: PyTorch!

5.2.2 Gathering some data

We'll start by making a note of temperature data in good old Celsius[5] and measurements from our new thermometer, and figure things out. After a couple of weeks, here's the data (code/p1ch5/1_parameter_estimation.ipynb):

---

[4] This task—fitting model outputs to continuous values in terms of the types discussed in chapter 4—is called a *regression* problem. In chapter 7 and part 2, we will be concerned with *classification* problems.

[5] The author of this chapter is Italian, so please forgive him for using sensible units.

```
# In[2]:
t_c = [0.5,   14.0, 15.0, 28.0, 11.0,   8.0,   3.0,  -4.0,   6.0, 13.0, 21.0]
t_u = [35.7, 55.9, 58.2, 81.9, 56.3, 48.9, 33.9, 21.8, 48.4, 60.4, 68.4]
t_c = torch.tensor(t_c)
t_u = torch.tensor(t_u)
```

Here, the t_c values are temperatures in Celsius, and the t_u values are our unknown units. We can expect noise in both measurements, coming from the devices themselves and from our approximate readings. For convenience, we've already put the data into tensors; we'll use it in a minute.

5.2.3   *Visualizing the data*

A quick plot of our data in figure 5.3 tells us that it's noisy, but we think there's a pattern here.

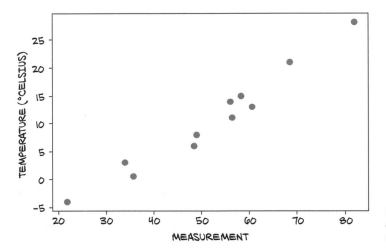

Figure 5.3   **Our unknown data just might follow a linear model.**

> **NOTE** Spoiler alert: we know a linear model is correct because the problem and data have been fabricated, but please bear with us. It's a useful motivating example to build our understanding of what PyTorch is doing under the hood.

5.2.4   *Choosing a linear model as a first try*

In the absence of further knowledge, we assume the simplest possible model for converting between the two sets of measurements, just like Kepler might have done. The two may be linearly related—that is, multiplying t_u by a factor and adding a constant, we may get the temperature in Celsius (up to an error that we omit):

```
t_c = w * t_u + b
```

Is this a reasonable assumption? Probably; we'll see how well the final model performs. We chose to name w and b after *weight* and *bias*, two very common terms for linear scaling and the additive constant—we'll bump into those all the time.[6]

OK, now we need to estimate w and b, the parameters in our model, based on the data we have. We must do it so that temperatures we obtain from running the unknown temperatures t_u through the model are close to temperatures we actually measured in Celsius. If that sounds like fitting a line through a set of measurements, well, yes, because that's exactly what we're doing. We'll go through this simple example using PyTorch and realize that training a neural network will essentially involve changing the model for a slightly more elaborate one, with a few (or a metric ton) more parameters.

Let's flesh it out again: we have a model with some unknown parameters, and we need to estimate those parameters so that the error between predicted outputs and measured values is as low as possible. We notice that we still need to exactly define a measure of the error. Such a measure, which we refer to as the *loss function*, should be high if the error is high and should ideally be as low as possible for a perfect match. Our optimization process should therefore aim at finding w and b so that the loss function is at a minimum.

5.3   *Less loss is what we want*

A *loss function* (or *cost function*) is a function that computes a single numerical value that the learning process will attempt to minimize. The calculation of loss typically involves taking the difference between the desired outputs for some training samples and the outputs actually produced by the model when fed those samples. In our case, that would be the difference between the predicted temperatures t_p output by our model and the actual measurements: t_p - t_c.

We need to make sure the loss function makes the loss positive both when t_p is greater than and when it is less than the true t_c, since the goal is for t_p to match t_c. We have a few choices, the most straightforward being |t_p - t_c| and (t_p - t_c)^2. Based on the mathematical expression we choose, we can emphasize or discount certain errors. Conceptually, a loss function is a way of prioritizing which errors to fix from our training samples, so that our parameter updates result in adjustments to the outputs for the highly weighted samples instead of changes to some other samples' output that had a smaller loss.

Both of the example loss functions have a clear minimum at zero and grow monotonically as the predicted value moves further from the true value in either direction. Because the steepness of the growth also monotonically increases away from the minimum, both of them are said to be *convex*. Since our model is linear, the loss as a function of w and b is also convex.[7] Cases where the loss is a convex function of the model parameters are usually great to deal with because we can find a minimum very efficiently

---

[6] The weight tells us how much a given input influences the output. The bias is what the output would be if all inputs were zero.

[7] Contrast that with the function shown in figure 5.6, which is not convex.

through specialized algorithms. However, we will instead use less powerful but more generally applicable methods in this chapter. We do so because for the deep neural networks we are ultimately interested in, the loss is not a convex function of the inputs.

For our two loss functions $|t\_p - t\_c|$ and $(t\_p - t\_c)^2$, as shown in figure 5.4, we notice that the square of the differences behaves more nicely around the minimum: the derivative of the error-squared loss with respect to t_p is zero when t_p equals t_c. The absolute value, on the other hand, has an undefined derivative right where we'd like to converge. This is less of an issue in practice than it looks like, but we'll stick to the square of differences for the time being.

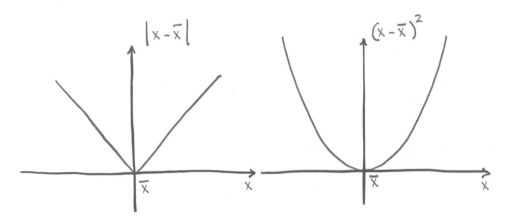

Figure 5.4   Absolute difference versus difference squared

It's worth noting that the square difference also penalizes wildly wrong results more than the absolute difference does. Often, having more slightly wrong results is better than having a few wildly wrong ones, and the squared difference helps prioritize those as desired.

5.3.1   *From problem back to PyTorch*

We've figured out the model and the loss function—we've already got a good part of the high-level picture in figure 5.2 figured out. Now we need to set the learning process in motion and feed it actual data. Also, enough with math notation; let's switch to PyTorch—after all, we came here for the *fun*.

We've already created our data tensors, so now let's write out the model as a Python function:

```
# In[3]:
def model(t_u, w, b):
    return w * t_u + b
```

We're expecting t_u, w, and b to be the input tensor, weight parameter, and bias parameter, respectively. In our model, the parameters will be PyTorch scalars (aka zero-dimensional tensors), and the product operation will use broadcasting to yield the returned tensors. Anyway, time to define our loss:

```
# In[4]:
def loss_fn(t_p, t_c):
    squared_diffs = (t_p - t_c)**2
    return squared_diffs.mean()
```

Note that we are building a tensor of differences, taking their square element-wise, and finally producing a scalar loss function by averaging all of the elements in the resulting tensor. It is a *mean square loss*.

We can now initialize the parameters, invoke the model,

```
# In[5]:
w = torch.ones(())
b = torch.zeros(())

t_p = model(t_u, w, b)
t_p

# Out[5]:
tensor([35.7000, 55.9000, 58.2000, 81.9000, 56.3000, 48.9000, 33.9000,
        21.8000, 48.4000, 60.4000, 68.4000])
```

and check the value of the loss:

```
# In[6]:
loss = loss_fn(t_p, t_c)
loss

# Out[6]:
tensor(1763.8846)
```

We implemented the model and the loss in this section. We've finally reached the meat of the example: how do we estimate w and b such that the loss reaches a minimum? We'll first work things out by hand and then learn how to use PyTorch's superpowers to solve the same problem in a more general, off-the-shelf way.

Broadcasting

We mentioned broadcasting in chapter 3, and we promised to look at it more carefully when we need it. In our example, we have two scalars (zero-dimensional tensors) w and b, and we multiply them with and add them to vectors (one-dimensional tensors) of length *b*.

Usually—and in early versions of PyTorch, too—we can only use element-wise binary operations such as addition, subtraction, multiplication, and division for arguments of the same shape. The entries in matching positions in each of the tensors will be used to calculate the corresponding entry in the result tensor.

(continued)

Broadcasting, which is popular in NumPy and adapted by PyTorch, relaxes this assumption for most binary operations. It uses the following rules to match tensor elements:

- For each index dimension, counted from the back, if one of the operands is size 1 in that dimension, PyTorch will use the single entry along this dimension with each of the entries in the other tensor along this dimension.
- If both sizes are greater than 1, they must be the same, and natural matching is used.
- If one of the tensors has more index dimensions than the other, the entirety of the other tensor will be used for each entry along these dimensions.

This sounds complicated (and it can be error-prone if we don't pay close attention, which is why we have named the tensor dimensions as shown in section 3.4), but usually, we can either write down the tensor dimensions to see what happens or picture what happens by using space dimensions to show the broadcasting, as in the following figure.

Of course, this would all be theory if we didn't have some code examples:

```
# In[7]:
x = torch.ones(())
y = torch.ones(3,1)
z = torch.ones(1,3)
a = torch.ones(2, 1, 1)
print(f"shapes: x: {x.shape}, y: {y.shape}")
```

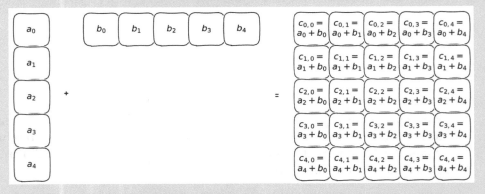

```
print(f"        z: {z.shape}, a: {a.shape}")
print("x * y:", (x * y).shape)
print("y * z:", (y * z).shape)
print("y * z * a:", (y * z * a).shape)

# Out[7]:

shapes: x: torch.Size([]), y: torch.Size([3, 1])
        z: torch.Size([1, 3]), a: torch.Size([2, 1, 1])
x * y: torch.Size([3, 1])

y * z: torch.Size([3, 3])
y * z * a: torch.Size([2, 3, 3])
```

5.4 Down along the gradient

We'll optimize the loss function with respect to the parameters using the *gradient descent* algorithm. In this section, we'll build our intuition for how gradient descent works from first principles, which will help us a lot in the future. As we mentioned, there are ways to solve our example problem more efficiently, but those approaches aren't applicable to most deep learning tasks. Gradient descent is actually a very simple idea, and it scales up surprisingly well to large neural network models with millions of parameters.

Let's start with a mental image, which we conveniently sketched out in figure 5.5. Suppose we are in front of a machine sporting two knobs, labeled w and b. We are allowed to see the value of the loss on a screen, and we are told to minimize that value. Not knowing the effect of the knobs on the loss, we start fiddling with them and decide for each knob which direction makes the loss decrease. We decide to rotate both knobs in their direction of decreasing loss. Suppose we're far from the optimal value: we'd likely see the loss decrease quickly and then slow down as it gets closer to the minimum. We notice that at some point, the loss climbs back up again, so we invert the direction of rotation for one or both knobs. We also learn that when the loss changes slowly, it's a good idea to adjust the knobs

Figure 5.5 A cartoon depiction of the optimization process, where a person with knobs for w and b searches for the direction to turn the knobs that makes the loss decrease

more finely, to avoid reaching the point where the loss goes back up. After a while, eventually, we converge to a minimum.

5.4.1 Decreasing loss

Gradient descent is not that different from the scenario we just described. The idea is to compute the rate of change of the loss with respect to each parameter, and modify each parameter in the direction of decreasing loss. Just like when we were fiddling with the knobs, we can estimate the rate of change by adding a small number to w and b and seeing how much the loss changes in that neighborhood:

```
# In[8]:
delta = 0.1

loss_rate_of_change_w = \
    (loss_fn(model(t_u, w + delta, b), t_c) -
     loss_fn(model(t_u, w - delta, b), t_c)) / (2.0 * delta)
```

This is saying that in the neighborhood of the current values of w and b, a unit increase in w leads to some change in the loss. If the change is negative, then we need to increase w to minimize the loss, whereas if the change is positive, we need to decrease w. By how much? Applying a change to w that is proportional to the rate of change of the loss is a good idea, especially when the loss has several parameters: we apply a change to those that exert a significant change on the loss. It is also wise to change the parameters slowly in general, because the rate of change could be dramatically different at a distance from the neighborhood of the current w value. Therefore, we typically should scale the rate of change by a small factor. This scaling factor has many names; the one we use in machine learning is `learning_rate`:

```
# In[9]:
learning_rate = 1e-2

w = w - learning_rate * loss_rate_of_change_w
```

We can do the same with b:

```
# In[10]:
loss_rate_of_change_b = \
    (loss_fn(model(t_u, w, b + delta), t_c) -
    loss_fn(model(t_u, w, b - delta), t_c)) / (2.0 * delta)

b = b - learning_rate * loss_rate_of_change_b
```

This represents the basic parameter-update step for gradient descent. By reiterating these evaluations (and provided we choose a small enough learning rate), we will converge to an optimal value of the parameters for which the loss computed on the given data is minimal. We'll show the complete iterative process soon, but the way we just computed our rates of change is rather crude and needs an upgrade before we move on. Let's see why and how.

5.4.2   *Getting analytical*

Computing the rate of change by using repeated evaluations of the model and loss in order to probe the behavior of the loss function in the neighborhood of w and b doesn't scale well to models with many parameters. Also, it is not always clear how large the neighborhood should be. We chose `delta` equal to 0.1 in the previous section, but it all depends on the shape of the loss as a function of w and b. If the loss changes too quickly compared to `delta`, we won't have a very good idea of in which direction the loss is decreasing the most.

What if we could make the neighborhood infinitesimally small, as in figure 5.6? That's exactly what happens when we analytically take the derivative of the loss with respect to a parameter. In a model with two or more parameters like the one we're dealing with, we compute the individual derivatives of the loss with respect to each parameter and put them in a vector of derivatives: the *gradient*.

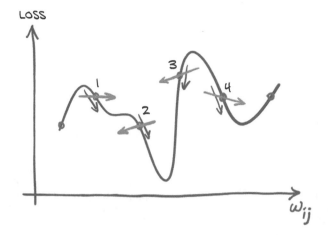

Figure 5.6 Differences in the estimated directions for descent when evaluating them at discrete locations versus analytically

COMPUTING THE DERIVATIVES

In order to compute the derivative of the loss with respect to a parameter, we can apply the chain rule and compute the derivative of the loss with respect to its input (which is the output of the model), times the derivative of the model with respect to the parameter:

```
d loss_fn / d w = (d loss_fn / d t_p) * (d t_p / d w)
```

Recall that our model is a linear function, and our loss is a sum of squares. Let's figure out the expressions for the derivatives. Recalling the expression for the loss:

```
# In[4]:
def loss_fn(t_p, t_c):
    squared_diffs = (t_p - t_c)**2
    return squared_diffs.mean()
```

Remembering that `d x^2 / d x = 2 x`, we get

```
# In[11]:
def dloss_fn(t_p, t_c):
    dsq_diffs = 2 * (t_p - t_c) / t_p.size(0)    ← │ The division is from the
    return dsq_diffs                                 derivative of mean.
```

APPLYING THE DERIVATIVES TO THE MODEL

For the model, recalling that our model is

```
# In[3]:
def model(t_u, w, b):
    return w * t_u + b
```

we get these derivatives:

```
# In[12]:
def dmodel_dw(t_u, w, b):
    return t_u
```

```
# In[13]:
def dmodel_db(t_u, w, b):
    return 1.0
```

DEFINING THE GRADIENT FUNCTION

Putting all of this together, the function returning the gradient of the loss with respect to w and b is

```
# In[14]:
def grad_fn(t_u, t_c, t_p, w, b):
    dloss_dtp = dloss_fn(t_p, t_c)
    dloss_dw = dloss_dtp * dmodel_dw(t_u, w, b)
    dloss_db = dloss_dtp * dmodel_db(t_u, w, b)
    return torch.stack([dloss_dw.sum(), dloss_db.sum()])
```

> The summation is the reverse of the broadcasting we implicitly do when applying the parameters to an entire vector of inputs in the model.

The same idea expressed in mathematical notation is shown in figure 5.7. Again, we're averaging (that is, summing and dividing by a constant) over all the data points to get a single scalar quantity for each partial derivative of the loss.

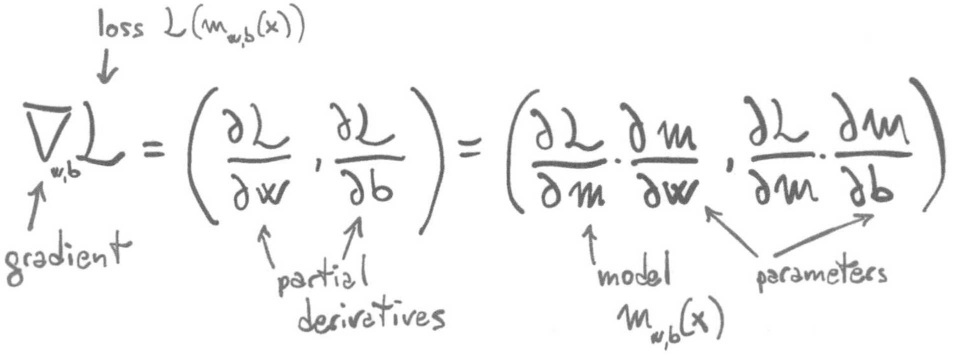

$$\underset{\substack{\uparrow\\ \text{gradient}}}{\nabla_{w,b}\mathcal{L}} = \underset{\substack{\uparrow\uparrow\\ \text{partial}\\ \text{derivatives}}}{\left(\frac{\partial\mathcal{L}}{\partial w}, \frac{\partial\mathcal{L}}{\partial b}\right)} = \left(\frac{\partial\mathcal{L}}{\partial m}\cdot\frac{\partial m}{\partial w}, \frac{\partial\mathcal{L}}{\partial m}\cdot\frac{\partial m}{\partial b}\right)$$

loss $\mathcal{L}(m_{w,b}(x))$

model $m_{w,b}(x)$ parameters

Figure 5.7   The derivative of the loss function with respect to the weights

5.4.3   *Iterating to fit the model*

We now have everything in place to optimize our parameters. Starting from a tentative value for a parameter, we can iteratively apply updates to it for a fixed number of iterations, or until w and b stop changing. There are several stopping criteria; for now, we'll stick to a fixed number of iterations.

THE TRAINING LOOP

Since we're at it, let's introduce another piece of terminology. We call a training iteration during which we update the parameters for all of our training samples an *epoch*.

The complete training loop looks like this (code/p1ch5/1_parameter_estimation .ipynb):

```
# In[15]:
def training_loop(n_epochs, learning_rate, params, t_u, t_c):
    for epoch in range(1, n_epochs + 1):
        w, b = params

        t_p = model(t_u, w, b)                    ⟵ Forward pass
        loss = loss_fn(t_p, t_c)
        grad = grad_fn(t_u, t_c, t_p, w, b)       ⟵ Backward pass

        params = params - learning_rate * grad

        print('Epoch %d, Loss %f' % (epoch, float(loss)))   ⟵┐ This logging line can
                                                             │  be very verbose.
    return params
```

The actual logging logic used for the output in this text is more complicated (see cell 15 in the same notebook: http://mng.bz/pBB8), but the differences are unimportant for understanding the core concepts in this chapter.

Now, let's invoke our training loop:

```
# In[17]:
training_loop(
    n_epochs = 100,
    learning_rate = 1e-2,
    params = torch.tensor([1.0, 0.0]),
    t_u = t_u,
    t_c = t_c)

# Out[17]:
Epoch 1, Loss 1763.884644
    Params: tensor([-44.1730,  -0.8260])
    Grad:   tensor([4517.2969,  82.6000])
Epoch 2, Loss 5802485.500000
    Params: tensor([2568.4014,  45.1637])
    Grad:   tensor([-261257.4219,  -4598.9712])
Epoch 3, Loss 19408035840.000000
    Params: tensor([-148527.7344,  -2616.3933])
    Grad:   tensor([15109614.0000,  266155.7188])
...
Epoch 10, Loss 90901154706620645225508955521810432.000000
    Params: tensor([3.2144e+17, 5.6621e+15])
    Grad:   tensor([-3.2700e+19, -5.7600e+17])
Epoch 11, Loss inf
    Params: tensor([-1.8590e+19, -3.2746e+17])
    Grad:   tensor([1.8912e+21, 3.3313e+19])

tensor([-1.8590e+19, -3.2746e+17])
```

OVERTRAINING

Wait, what happened? Our training process literally blew up, leading to losses becoming inf. This is a clear sign that params is receiving updates that are too large, and their values start oscillating back and forth as each update overshoots and the next overcorrects even more. The optimization process is unstable: it *diverges* instead of converging to a minimum. We want to see smaller and smaller updates to params, not larger, as shown in figure 5.8.

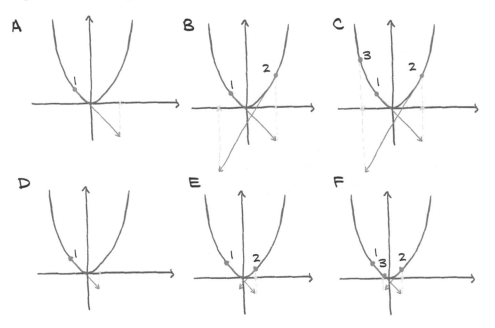

Figure 5.8   Top: Diverging optimization on a convex function (parabola-like) due to large steps. Bottom: Converging optimization with small steps.

How can we limit the magnitude of learning_rate * grad? Well, that looks easy. We could simply choose a smaller learning_rate, and indeed, the learning rate is one of the things we typically change when training does not go as well as we would like.[8] We usually change learning rates by orders of magnitude, so we might try with 1e-3 or 1e-4, which would decrease the magnitude of the updates by orders of magnitude. Let's go with 1e-4 and see how it works out:

```
# In[18]:
training_loop(
    n_epochs = 100,
```

---

[8] The fancy name for this is *hyperparameter tuning*. *Hyperparameter* refers to the fact that we are training the model's parameters, but the hyperparameters control how this training goes. Typically these are more or less set manually. In particular, they cannot be part of the same optimization.

```
          learning_rate = 1e-4,
          params = torch.tensor([1.0, 0.0]),
          t_u = t_u,
          t_c = t_c)

# Out[18]:
Epoch 1, Loss 1763.884644
    Params: tensor([ 0.5483, -0.0083])
    Grad:   tensor([4517.2969,   82.6000])
Epoch 2, Loss 323.090546
    Params: tensor([ 0.3623, -0.0118])
    Grad:   tensor([1859.5493,   35.7843])
Epoch 3, Loss 78.929634
    Params: tensor([ 0.2858, -0.0135])
    Grad:   tensor([765.4667,   16.5122])
...
Epoch 10, Loss 29.105242
    Params: tensor([ 0.2324, -0.0166])
    Grad:   tensor([1.4803, 3.0544])
Epoch 11, Loss 29.104168
    Params: tensor([ 0.2323, -0.0169])
    Grad:   tensor([0.5781, 3.0384])
...
Epoch 99, Loss 29.023582
    Params: tensor([ 0.2327, -0.0435])
    Grad:   tensor([-0.0533,   3.0226])
Epoch 100, Loss 29.022669
    Params: tensor([ 0.2327, -0.0438])
    Grad:   tensor([-0.0532,   3.0226])

tensor([ 0.2327, -0.0438])
```

Nice—the behavior is now stable. But there's another problem: the updates to parameters are very small, so the loss decreases very slowly and eventually stalls. We could obviate this issue by making `learning_rate` adaptive: that is, change according to the magnitude of updates. There are optimization schemes that do that, and we'll see one toward the end of this chapter, in section 5.5.2.

However, there's another potential troublemaker in the update term: the gradient itself. Let's go back and look at `grad` at epoch 1 during optimization.

5.4.4 *Normalizing inputs*

We can see that the first-epoch gradient for the weight is about 50 times larger than the gradient for the bias. This means the weight and bias live in differently scaled spaces. If this is the case, a learning rate that's large enough to meaningfully update one will be so large as to be unstable for the other; and a rate that's appropriate for the other won't be large enough to meaningfully change the first. That means we're not going to be able to update our parameters unless we change something about our formulation of the problem. We could have individual learning rates for each parameter, but for models with many parameters, this would be too much to bother with; it's babysitting of the kind we don't like.

There's a simpler way to keep things in check: changing the inputs so that the gradients aren't quite so different. We can make sure the range of the input doesn't get too far from the range of –1.0 to 1.0, roughly speaking. In our case, we can achieve something close enough to that by simply multiplying t_u by 0.1:

```
# In[19]:
t_un = 0.1 * t_u
```

Here, we denote the normalized version of t_u by appending an n to the variable name. At this point, we can run the training loop on our normalized input:

```
# In[20]:
training_loop(
    n_epochs = 100,
    learning_rate = 1e-2,
    params = torch.tensor([1.0, 0.0]),
    t_u = t_un,                            We've updated t_u to
    t_c = t_c)                             our new, rescaled t_un.
```

```
# Out[20]:
Epoch 1, Loss 80.364342
    Params: tensor([1.7761, 0.1064])
    Grad:   tensor([-77.6140, -10.6400])
Epoch 2, Loss 37.574917
    Params: tensor([2.0848, 0.1303])
    Grad:   tensor([-30.8623,  -2.3864])
Epoch 3, Loss 30.871077
    Params: tensor([2.2094, 0.1217])
    Grad:   tensor([-12.4631,   0.8587])
...
Epoch 10, Loss 29.030487
    Params: tensor([ 2.3232, -0.0710])
    Grad:   tensor([-0.5355,   2.9295])
Epoch 11, Loss 28.941875
    Params: tensor([ 2.3284, -0.1003])
    Grad:   tensor([-0.5240,   2.9264])
...
Epoch 99, Loss 22.214186
    Params: tensor([ 2.7508, -2.4910])
    Grad:   tensor([-0.4453,   2.5208])
Epoch 100, Loss 22.148710
    Params: tensor([ 2.7553, -2.5162])
    Grad:   tensor([-0.4446,   2.5165])

tensor([ 2.7553, -2.5162])
```

Even though we set our learning rate back to 1e-2, parameters don't blow up during iterative updates. Let's take a look at the gradients: they're of similar magnitude, so using a single learning_rate for both parameters works just fine. We could probably do a better job of normalization than a simple rescaling by a factor of 10, but since doing so is good enough for our needs, we're going to stick with that for now.

NOTE The normalization here absolutely helps get the network trained, but you could make an argument that it's not strictly needed to optimize the parameters for this particular problem. That's absolutely true! This problem is small enough that there are numerous ways to beat the parameters into submission. However, for larger, more sophisticated problems, normalization is an easy and effective (if not crucial!) tool to use to improve model convergence.

Let's run the loop for enough iterations to see the changes in params get small. We'll change n_epochs to 5,000:

```
# In[21]:
params = training_loop(
    n_epochs = 5000,
    learning_rate = 1e-2,
    params = torch.tensor([1.0, 0.0]),
    t_u = t_un,
    t_c = t_c,
    print_params = False)

params

# Out[21]:
Epoch 1, Loss 80.364342
Epoch 2, Loss 37.574917
Epoch 3, Loss 30.871077
...
Epoch 10, Loss 29.030487
Epoch 11, Loss 28.941875
...
Epoch 99, Loss 22.214186
Epoch 100, Loss 22.148710
...
Epoch 4000, Loss 2.927680
Epoch 5000, Loss 2.927648

tensor([  5.3671, -17.3012])
```

Good: our loss decreases while we change parameters along the direction of gradient descent. It doesn't go exactly to zero; this could mean there aren't enough iterations to converge to zero, or that the data points don't sit exactly on a line. As we anticipated, our measurements were not perfectly accurate, or there was noise involved in the reading.

But look: the values for w and b look an awful lot like the numbers we need to use to convert Celsius to Fahrenheit (after accounting for our earlier normalization when we multiplied our inputs by 0.1). The exact values would be w=5.5556 and b=-17.7778. Our fancy thermometer was showing temperatures in Fahrenheit the whole time. No big discovery, except that our gradient descent optimization process works!

5.4.5   *Visualizing (again)*

Let's revisit something we did right at the start: plotting our data. Seriously, this is the first thing anyone doing data science should do. Always plot the heck out of the data:

```
# In[22]:
%matplotlib inline
from matplotlib import pyplot as plt

t_p = model(t_un, *params)

fig = plt.figure(dpi=600)
plt.xlabel("Temperature (°Fahrenheit)")
plt.ylabel("Temperature (°Celsius)")
plt.plot(t_u.numpy(), t_p.detach().numpy())
plt.plot(t_u.numpy(), t_c.numpy(), 'o')
```

Remember that we're training on the normalized unknown units. We also use argument unpacking.

But we're plotting the raw unknown values.

We are using a Python trick called *argument unpacking* here: *params means to pass the elements of params as individual arguments. In Python, this is usually done with lists or tuples, but we can also use argument unpacking with PyTorch tensors, which are split along the leading dimension. So here, model(t_un, *params) is equivalent to model(t_un, params[0], params[1]).

This code produces figure 5.9. Our linear model is a good model for the data, it seems. It also seems our measurements are somewhat erratic. We should either call our optometrist for a new pair of glasses or think about returning our fancy thermometer.

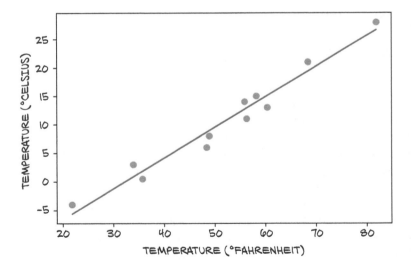

Figure 5.9   The plot of our linear-fit model (solid line) versus our input data (circles)

5.5   *PyTorch's autograd: Backpropagating all things*

In our little adventure, we just saw a simple example of backpropagation: we computed the gradient of a composition of functions—the model and the loss—with respect to their innermost parameters (w and b) by propagating derivatives backward using the *chain rule*. The basic requirement here is that all functions we're dealing with can be differentiated analytically. If this is the case, we can compute the gradient—what we earlier called "the rate of change of the loss"—with respect to the parameters in one sweep.

Even if we have a complicated model with millions of parameters, as long as our model is differentiable, computing the gradient of the loss with respect to the parameters amounts to writing the analytical expression for the derivatives and evaluating them *once*. Granted, writing the analytical expression for the derivatives of a very deep composition of linear and nonlinear functions is not a lot of fun.[9] It isn't particularly quick, either.

5.5.1   *Computing the gradient automatically*

This is when PyTorch tensors come to the rescue, with a PyTorch component called *autograd*. Chapter 3 presented a comprehensive overview of what tensors are and what functions we can call on them. We left out one very interesting aspect, however: PyTorch tensors can remember where they come from, in terms of the operations and parent tensors that originated them, and they can automatically provide the chain of derivatives of such operations with respect to their inputs. This means we won't need to derive our model by hand;[10] given a forward expression, no matter how nested, PyTorch will automatically provide the gradient of that expression with respect to its input parameters.

APPLYING AUTOGRAD

At this point, the best way to proceed is to rewrite our thermometer calibration code, this time using autograd, and see what happens. First, we recall our model and loss function.

Listing 5.1   code/p1ch5/2_autograd.ipynb

```
# In[3]:
def model(t_u, w, b):
    return w * t_u + b

# In[4]:
def loss_fn(t_p, t_c):
    squared_diffs = (t_p - t_c)**2
    return squared_diffs.mean()
```

---

[9]   Or maybe it is; we won't judge how you spend your weekend!

[10]   Bummer! What are we going to do on Saturdays, now?

Let's again initialize a parameters tensor:

```
# In[5]:
params = torch.tensor([1.0, 0.0], requires_grad=True)
```

USING THE GRAD ATTRIBUTE

Notice the `requires_grad=True` argument to the tensor constructor? That argument is telling PyTorch to track the entire family tree of tensors resulting from operations on params. In other words, any tensor that will have params as an ancestor will have access to the chain of functions that were called to get from params to that tensor. In case these functions are differentiable (and most PyTorch tensor operations will be), the value of the derivative will be automatically populated as a grad attribute of the params tensor.

In general, all PyTorch tensors have an attribute named grad. Normally, it's None:

```
# In[6]:
params.grad is None
```

```
# Out[6]:
True
```

All we have to do to populate it is to start with a tensor with `requires_grad` set to True, then call the model and compute the loss, and then call backward on the loss tensor:

```
# In[7]:
loss = loss_fn(model(t_u, *params), t_c)
loss.backward()

params.grad
```

```
# Out[7]:
tensor([4517.2969,    82.6000])
```

At this point, the grad attribute of params contains the derivatives of the loss with respect to each element of params.

When we compute our loss while the parameters w and b require gradients, in addition to performing the actual computation, PyTorch creates the autograd graph with the operations (in black circles) as nodes, as shown in the top row of figure 5.10. When we call loss.backward(), PyTorch traverses this graph in the reverse direction to compute the gradients, as shown by the arrows in the bottom row of the figure.

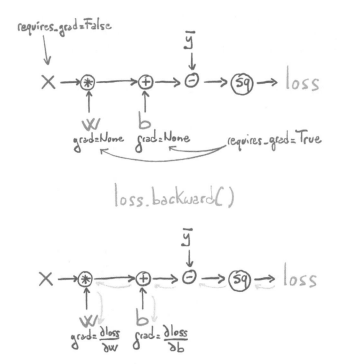

Figure 5.10 The forward graph and backward graph of the model as computed with autograd

ACCUMULATING GRAD FUNCTIONS

We could have any number of tensors with `requires_grad` set to `True` and any composition of functions. In this case, PyTorch would compute the derivatives of the loss throughout the chain of functions (the computation graph) and accumulate their values in the `grad` attribute of those tensors (the leaf nodes of the graph).

Alert! *Big gotcha ahead.* This is something PyTorch newcomers—and a lot of more experienced folks, too—trip up on regularly. We just wrote *accumulate*, not *store*.

> **WARNING** Calling `backward` will lead derivatives to *accumulate* at leaf nodes. We need to *zero the gradient explicitly* after using it for parameter updates.

Let's repeat together: calling `backward` will lead derivatives to *accumulate* at leaf nodes. So if `backward` was called earlier, the loss is evaluated again, `backward` is called again (as in any training loop), and the gradient at each leaf is accumulated (that is, summed) on top of the one computed at the previous iteration, which leads to an incorrect value for the gradient.

In order to prevent this from occurring, we need to *zero the gradient explicitly* at each iteration. We can do this easily using the in-place `zero_` method:

```
# In[8]:
if params.grad is not None:
    params.grad.zero_()
```

NOTE You might be curious why zeroing the gradient is a required step instead of zeroing happening automatically whenever we call `backward`. Doing it this way provides more flexibility and control when working with gradients in complicated models.

Having this reminder drilled into our heads, let's see what our autograd-enabled training code looks like, start to finish:

```
# In[9]:
def training_loop(n_epochs, learning_rate, params, t_u, t_c):
    for epoch in range(1, n_epochs + 1):
        if params.grad is not None:          ◁─┐  This could be done at any point in the
            params.grad.zero_()                │  loop prior to calling loss.backward().

        t_p = model(t_u, *params)
        loss = loss_fn(t_p, t_c)
        loss.backward()
                                                      This is a somewhat cumbersome bit
        with torch.no_grad():             ◁────┐  of code, but as we'll see in the next
            params -= learning_rate * params.grad   section, it's not an issue in practice.

        if epoch % 500 == 0:
            print('Epoch %d, Loss %f' % (epoch, float(loss)))

    return params
```

Note that our code updating `params` is not quite as straightforward as we might have expected. There are two particularities. First, we are encapsulating the update in a no_grad context using the Python `with` statement. This means within the `with` block, the PyTorch autograd mechanism should *look away*:[11] that is, not add edges to the forward graph. In fact, when we are executing this bit of code, the forward graph that PyTorch records is consumed when we call `backward`, leaving us with the `params` leaf node. But now we want to change this leaf node before we start building a fresh forward graph on top of it. While this use case is usually wrapped inside the optimizers we discuss in section 5.5.2, we will take a closer look when we see another common use of no_grad in section 5.5.4.

Second, we update `params` in place. This means we keep the same `params` tensor around but subtract our update from it. When using autograd, we usually avoid in-place updates because PyTorch's autograd engine might need the values we would be modifying for the backward pass. Here, however, we are operating without autograd, and it is beneficial to keep the `params` tensor. Not replacing the parameters by assigning new tensors to their variable name will become crucial when we register our parameters with the optimizer in section 5.5.2.

---

[11] In reality, it will track that something changed params using an in-place operation.

Let's see if it works:

```
# In[10]:
training_loop(
    n_epochs = 5000,
    learning_rate = 1e-2,
    params = torch.tensor([1.0, 0.0], requires_grad=True),
    t_u = t_un,
    t_c = t_c)
```

**Adding
requires_grad=True is key.**

**Again, we're using the
normalized t_un instead of t_u.**

```
# Out[10]:
Epoch 500, Loss 7.860116
Epoch 1000, Loss 3.828538
Epoch 1500, Loss 3.092191
Epoch 2000, Loss 2.957697
Epoch 2500, Loss 2.933134
Epoch 3000, Loss 2.928648
Epoch 3500, Loss 2.927830
Epoch 4000, Loss 2.927679
Epoch 4500, Loss 2.927652
Epoch 5000, Loss 2.927647

tensor([  5.3671, -17.3012], requires_grad=True)
```

The result is the same as we got previously. Good for us! It means that while we are *capable* of computing derivatives by hand, we no longer need to.

5.5.2 *Optimizers a la carte*

In the example code, we used *vanilla* gradient descent for optimization, which worked fine for our simple case. Needless to say, there are several optimization strategies and tricks that can assist convergence, especially when models get complicated.

We'll dive deeper into this topic in later chapters, but now is the right time to introduce the way PyTorch abstracts the optimization strategy away from user code: that is, the training loop we've examined. This saves us from the boilerplate busywork of having to update each and every parameter to our model ourselves. The torch module has an optim submodule where we can find classes implementing different optimization algorithms. Here's an abridged list (code/p1ch5/3_optimizers.ipynb):

```
# In[5]:
import torch.optim as optim

dir(optim)

# Out[5]:
['ASGD',
 'Adadelta',
 'Adagrad',
 'Adam',
 'Adamax',
 'LBFGS',
 'Optimizer',
```

```
'RMSprop',
'Rprop',
'SGD',
'SparseAdam',
...
]
```

Every optimizer constructor takes a list of parameters (aka PyTorch tensors, typically with requires_grad set to True) as the first input. All parameters passed to the optimizer are retained inside the optimizer object so the optimizer can update their values and access their grad attribute, as represented in figure 5.11.

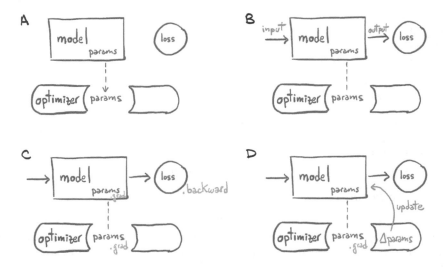

Figure 5.11   (A) Conceptual representation of how an optimizer holds a reference to parameters. (B) After a loss is computed from inputs, (C) a call to .backward leads to .grad being populated on parameters. (D) At that point, the optimizer can access .grad and compute the parameter updates.

Each optimizer exposes two methods: zero_grad and step. zero_grad zeroes the grad attribute of all the parameters passed to the optimizer upon construction. step updates the value of those parameters according to the optimization strategy implemented by the specific optimizer.

USING A GRADIENT DESCENT OPTIMIZER

Let's create params and instantiate a gradient descent optimizer:

```
# In[6]:
params = torch.tensor([1.0, 0.0], requires_grad=True)
learning_rate = 1e-5
optimizer = optim.SGD([params], lr=learning_rate)
```

Here SGD stands for *stochastic gradient descent*. Actually, the optimizer itself is exactly a vanilla gradient descent (as long as the momentum argument is set to 0.0, which is the default). The term *stochastic* comes from the fact that the gradient is typically obtained by averaging over a random subset of all input samples, called a *minibatch*. However, the optimizer does not know if the loss was evaluated on all the samples (vanilla) or a random subset of them (stochastic), so the algorithm is literally the same in the two cases.

Anyway, let's take our fancy new optimizer for a spin:

```
# In[7]:
t_p = model(t_u, *params)
loss = loss_fn(t_p, t_c)
loss.backward()

optimizer.step()

params

# Out[7]:
tensor([ 9.5483e-01, -8.2600e-04], requires_grad=True)
```

The value of params is updated upon calling step without us having to touch it ourselves! What happens is that the optimizer looks into params.grad and updates params, subtracting learning_rate times grad from it, exactly as in our former hand-rolled code.

Ready to stick this code in a training loop? Nope! The big gotcha almost got us— we forgot to zero out the gradients. Had we called the previous code in a loop, gradients would have accumulated in the leaves at every call to backward, and our gradient descent would have been all over the place! Here's the loop-ready code, with the extra zero_grad at the correct spot (right before the call to backward):

```
# In[8]:
params = torch.tensor([1.0, 0.0], requires_grad=True)
learning_rate = 1e-2
optimizer = optim.SGD([params], lr=learning_rate)

t_p = model(t_un, *params)
loss = loss_fn(t_p, t_c)

optimizer.zero_grad()    ◄────┐  As before, the exact placement of
loss.backward()               │  this call is somewhat arbitrary. It
optimizer.step()              │  could be earlier in the loop as well.

params

# Out[8]:
tensor([1.7761, 0.1064], requires_grad=True)
```

Perfect! See how the optim module helps us abstract away the specific optimization scheme? All we have to do is provide a list of params to it (that list can be extremely long, as is needed for very deep neural network models), and we can forget about the details.

Let's update our training loop accordingly:

```
# In[9]:
def training_loop(n_epochs, optimizer, params, t_u, t_c):
    for epoch in range(1, n_epochs + 1):
        t_p = model(t_u, *params)
        loss = loss_fn(t_p, t_c)

        optimizer.zero_grad()
        loss.backward()
        optimizer.step()

        if epoch % 500 == 0:
            print('Epoch %d, Loss %f' % (epoch, float(loss)))

    return params
```

```
# In[10]:
params = torch.tensor([1.0, 0.0], requires_grad=True)
learning_rate = 1e-2
optimizer = optim.SGD([params], lr=learning_rate)       ◁─┐  It's important that both
                                                           │  params are the same object;
training_loop(                                             │  otherwise the optimizer won't
    n_epochs = 5000,                                       │  know what parameters were
    optimizer = optimizer,                                 │  used by the model.
    params = params,                                    ◁─┘
    t_u = t_un,
    t_c = t_c)
```

```
# Out[10]:
Epoch 500, Loss 7.860118
Epoch 1000, Loss 3.828538
Epoch 1500, Loss 3.092191
Epoch 2000, Loss 2.957697
Epoch 2500, Loss 2.933134
Epoch 3000, Loss 2.928648
Epoch 3500, Loss 2.927830
Epoch 4000, Loss 2.927680
Epoch 4500, Loss 2.927651
Epoch 5000, Loss 2.927648

tensor([  5.3671, -17.3012], requires_grad=True)
```

Again, we get the same result as before. Great: this is further confirmation that we know how to descend a gradient by hand!

TESTING OTHER OPTIMIZERS

In order to test more optimizers, all we have to do is instantiate a different optimizer, say Adam, instead of SGD. The rest of the code stays as it is. Pretty handy stuff.

We won't go into much detail about Adam; suffice to say that it is a more sophisticated optimizer in which the learning rate is set adaptively. In addition, it is a lot less sensitive to the scaling of the parameters—so insensitive that we can go back to using the original (non-normalized) input t_u, and even increase the learning rate to 1e-1, and Adam won't even blink:

```
# In[11]:
params = torch.tensor([1.0, 0.0], requires_grad=True)
learning_rate = 1e-1
optimizer = optim.Adam([params], lr=learning_rate)       ◁── New optimizer class

training_loop(
    n_epochs = 2000,
    optimizer = optimizer,
    params = params,
    t_u = t_u,       ◁───┐  We're back to the original
    t_c = t_c)           │  t_u as our input.

# Out[11]:
Epoch 500, Loss 7.612903
Epoch 1000, Loss 3.086700
Epoch 1500, Loss 2.928578
Epoch 2000, Loss 2.927646

tensor([  0.5367, -17.3021], requires_grad=True)
```

The optimizer is not the only flexible part of our training loop. Let's turn our attention to the model. In order to train a neural network on the same data and the same loss, all we would need to change is the model function. It wouldn't make particular sense in this case, since we know that converting Celsius to Fahrenheit amounts to a linear transformation, but we'll do it anyway in chapter 6. We'll see quite soon that neural networks allow us to remove our arbitrary assumptions about the shape of the function we should be approximating. Even so, we'll see how neural networks manage to be trained even when the underlying processes are highly nonlinear (such in the case of describing an image with a sentence, as we saw in chapter 2).

We have touched on a lot of the essential concepts that will enable us to train complicated deep learning models while knowing what's going on under the hood: backpropagation to estimate gradients, autograd, and optimizing weights of models using gradient descent or other optimizers. Really, there isn't a lot more. The rest is mostly filling in the blanks, however extensive they are.

Next up, we're going to offer an aside on how to split our samples, because that sets up a perfect use case for learning how to better control autograd.

5.5.3 *Training, validation, and overfitting*

Johannes Kepler taught us one last thing that we didn't discuss so far, remember? He kept part of the data on the side so that he could validate his models on independent observations. This is a vital thing to do, especially when the model we adopt could potentially approximate functions of any shape, as in the case of neural networks. In other words, a highly adaptable model will tend to use its many parameters to make sure the loss is minimal *at* the data points, but we'll have no guarantee that the model behaves well *away from* or *in between* the data points. After all, that's what we're asking the optimizer to do: minimize the loss *at* the data points. Sure enough, if we had independent data points that we didn't use to evaluate our loss or descend along its negative gradient, we would soon find out that evaluating the loss at those independent data points would yield higher-than-expected loss. We have already mentioned this phenomenon, called *overfitting.*

The first action we can take to combat overfitting is recognizing that it might happen. In order to do so, as Kepler figured out in 1600, we must take a few data points out of our dataset (the *validation set*) and only fit our model on the remaining data points (the *training set*), as shown in figure 5.12. Then, while we're fitting the model, we can evaluate the loss once on the training set and once on the validation set. When we're trying to decide if we've done a good job of fitting our model to the data, we must look at both!

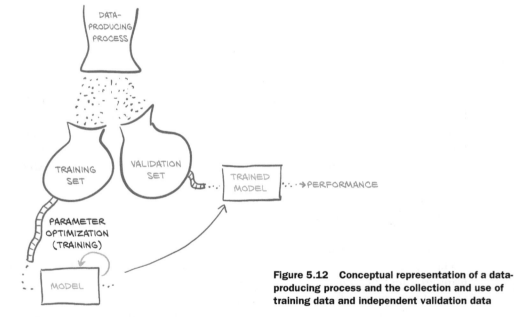

Figure 5.12 Conceptual representation of a data-producing process and the collection and use of training data and independent validation data

EVALUATING THE TRAINING LOSS

The training loss will tell us if our model can fit the training set at all—in other words, if our model has enough *capacity* to process the relevant information in the data. If our mysterious thermometer somehow managed to measure temperatures using a logarithmic scale, our poor linear model would not have had a chance to fit those measurements and provide us with a sensible conversion to Celsius. In that case, our training loss (the loss we were printing in the training loop) would stop decreasing well before approaching zero.

A deep neural network can potentially approximate complicated functions, provided that the number of neurons, and therefore parameters, is high enough. The fewer the number of parameters, the simpler the shape of the function our network will be able to approximate. So, rule 1: if the training loss is not decreasing, chances are the model is too simple for the data. The other possibility is that our data just doesn't contain meaningful information that lets it explain the output: if the nice folks at the shop sell us a barometer instead of a thermometer, we will have little chance of predicting temperature in Celsius from just pressure, even if we use the latest neural network architecture from Quebec (www.umontreal.ca/en/artificialintelligence).

GENERALIZING TO THE VALIDATION SET

What about the validation set? Well, if the loss evaluated in the validation set doesn't decrease along with the training set, it means our model is improving its fit of the samples it is seeing during training, but it is not *generalizing* to samples outside this precise set. As soon as we evaluate the model at new, previously unseen points, the values of the loss function are poor. So, rule 2: if the training loss and the validation loss diverge, we're overfitting.

Let's delve into this phenomenon a little, going back to our thermometer example. We could have decided to fit the data with a more complicated function, like a piecewise polynomial or a really large neural network. It could generate a model meandering its way through the data points, as in figure 5.13, just because it pushes the loss very close to zero. Since the behavior of the function away from the data points does not increase the loss, there's nothing to keep the model in check for inputs away from the training data points.

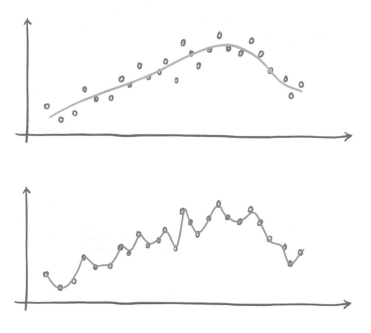

Figure 5.13 Rather extreme example of overfitting

What's the cure, though? Good question. From what we just said, overfitting really looks like a problem of making sure the behavior of the model *in between* data points is sensible for the process we're trying to approximate. First of all, we should make sure we get enough data for the process. If we collected data from a sinusoidal process by sampling it regularly at a low frequency, we would have a hard time fitting a model to it.

Assuming we have enough data points, we should make sure the model that is capable of fitting the training data is as regular as possible in between them. There are several ways to achieve this. One is adding *penalization terms* to the loss function, to make it cheaper for the model to behave more smoothly and change more slowly (up to a point). Another is to add noise to the input samples, to artificially create new data points in between training data samples and force the model to try to fit those, too. There are several other ways, all of them somewhat related to these. But the best favor we can do to ourselves, at least as a first move, is to make our model simpler. From an intuitive standpoint, a simpler model may not fit the training data as perfectly as a more complicated model would, but it will likely behave more regularly in between data points.

We've got some nice trade-offs here. On the one hand, we need the model to have enough capacity for it to fit the training set. On the other, we need the model to avoid overfitting. Therefore, in order to choose the right size for a neural network model in terms of parameters, the process is based on two steps: increase the size until it fits, and then scale it down until it stops overfitting.

We'll see more about this in chapter 12—we'll discover that our life will be a balancing act between fitting and overfitting. For now, let's get back to our example and see how we can split the data into a training set and a validation set. We'll do it by shuffling t_u and t_c the same way and then splitting the resulting shuffled tensors into two parts.

SPLITTING A DATASET

Shuffling the elements of a tensor amounts to finding a permutation of its indices. The randperm function does exactly this:

```
# In[12]:
n_samples = t_u.shape[0]
n_val = int(0.2 * n_samples)

shuffled_indices = torch.randperm(n_samples)

train_indices = shuffled_indices[:-n_val]
val_indices = shuffled_indices[-n_val:]

train_indices, val_indices

# Out[12]:
(tensor([9, 6, 5, 8, 4, 7, 0, 1, 3]), tensor([ 2, 10]))
```

Since these are random, don't be surprised if your values end up different from here on out.

We just got index tensors that we can use to build training and validation sets starting from the data tensors:

```
# In[13]:
train_t_u = t_u[train_indices]
train_t_c = t_c[train_indices]

val_t_u = t_u[val_indices]
val_t_c = t_c[val_indices]

train_t_un = 0.1 * train_t_u
val_t_un = 0.1 * val_t_u
```

Our training loop doesn't really change. We just want to additionally evaluate the validation loss at every epoch, to have a chance to recognize whether we're overfitting:

```
# In[14]:
def training_loop(n_epochs, optimizer, params, train_t_u, val_t_u,
                  train_t_c, val_t_c):
    for epoch in range(1, n_epochs + 1):
        train_t_p = model(train_t_u, *params)              ◄─┐  These two pairs of lines are the
        train_loss = loss_fn(train_t_p, train_t_c)           │  same except for the train_* vs.
                                                             │  val_* inputs.
        val_t_p = model(val_t_u, *params)                  ◄─┘
        val_loss = loss_fn(val_t_p, val_t_c)

        optimizer.zero_grad()          │  Note that there is no val_loss.backward()
        train_loss.backward()        ◄─┤  here, since we don't want to train the
        optimizer.step()               │  model on the validation data.

        if epoch <= 3 or epoch % 500 == 0:
            print(f"Epoch {epoch}, Training loss {train_loss.item():.4f},"
                  f" Validation loss {val_loss.item():.4f}")

    return params
```

```
# In[15]:
params = torch.tensor([1.0, 0.0], requires_grad=True)
learning_rate = 1e-2
optimizer = optim.SGD([params], lr=learning_rate)

training_loop(
    n_epochs = 3000,
    optimizer = optimizer,
    params = params,
    train_t_u = train_t_un,       │  Since we're using SGD again, we're
    val_t_u = val_t_un,           │  back to using normalized inputs.
    train_t_c = train_t_c,
    val_t_c = val_t_c)
```

```
# Out[15]:
Epoch 1, Training loss 66.5811, Validation loss 142.3890
Epoch 2, Training loss 38.8626, Validation loss 64.0434
Epoch 3, Training loss 33.3475, Validation loss 39.4590
Epoch 500, Training loss 7.1454, Validation loss 9.1252
```

```
Epoch 1000, Training loss 3.5940, Validation loss 5.3110
Epoch 1500, Training loss 3.0942, Validation loss 4.1611
Epoch 2000, Training loss 3.0238, Validation loss 3.7693
Epoch 2500, Training loss 3.0139, Validation loss 3.6279
Epoch 3000, Training loss 3.0125, Validation loss 3.5756

tensor([  5.1964, -16.7512], requires_grad=True)
```

Here we are not being entirely fair to our model. The validation set is really small, so the validation loss will only be meaningful up to a point. In any case, we note that the validation loss is higher than our training loss, although not by an order of magnitude. We expect a model to perform better on the training set, since the model parameters are being shaped by the training set. Our main goal is to also see both the training loss *and* the validation loss decreasing. While ideally both losses would be roughly the same value, as long as the validation loss stays reasonably close to the training loss, we know that our model is continuing to learn generalized things about our data. In figure 5.14, case C is ideal, while D is acceptable. In case A, the model isn't learning at all; and in case B, we see overfitting. We'll see more meaningful examples of overfitting in chapter 12.

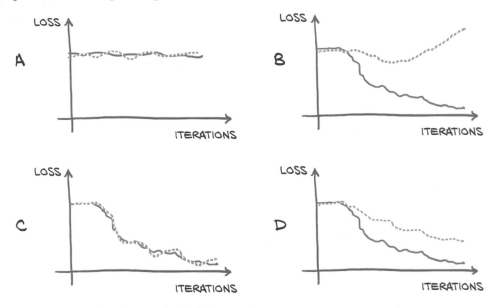

Figure 5.14   Overfitting scenarios when looking at the training (solid line) and validation (dotted line) losses. (A) Training and validation losses do not decrease; the model is not learning due to no information in the data or insufficient capacity of the model. (B) Training loss decreases while validation loss increases: overfitting. (C) Training and validation losses decrease exactly in tandem. Performance may be improved further as the model is not at the limit of overfitting. (D) Training and validation losses have different absolute values but similar trends: overfitting is under control.

5.5.4 Autograd nits and switching it off

From the previous training loop, we can appreciate that we only ever call backward on train_loss. Therefore, errors will only ever backpropagate based on the training set—the validation set is used to provide an independent evaluation of the accuracy of the model's output on data that wasn't used for training.

The curious reader will have an embryo of a question at this point. The model is evaluated twice—once on train_t_u and once on val_t_u—and then backward is called. Won't this confuse autograd? Won't backward be influenced by the values generated during the pass on the validation set?

Luckily for us, this isn't the case. The first line in the training loop evaluates model on train_t_u to produce train_t_p. Then train_loss is evaluated from train_t_p. This creates a computation graph that links train_t_u to train_t_p to train_loss. When model is evaluated again on val_t_u, it produces val_t_p and val_loss. In this case, a separate computation graph will be created that links val_t_u to val_t_p to val_loss. Separate tensors have been run through the same functions, model and loss_fn, generating separate computation graphs, as shown in figure 5.15.

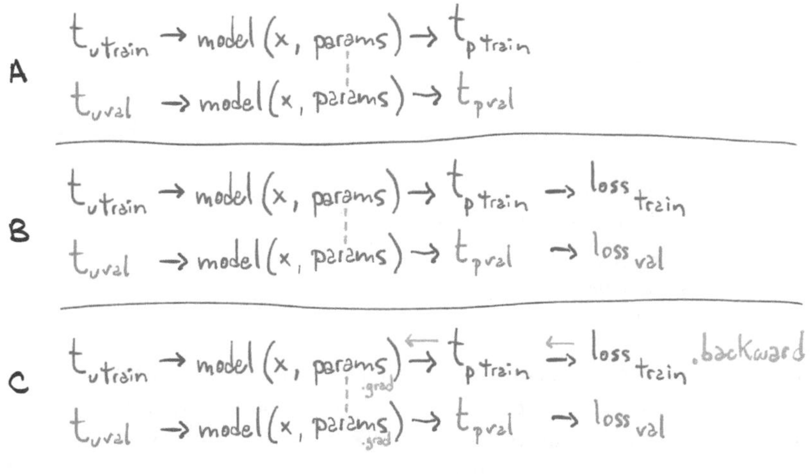

Figure 5.15 Diagram showing how gradients propagate through a graph with two losses when .backward is called on one of them

The only tensors these two graphs have in common are the parameters. When we call backward on train_loss, we run backward on the first graph. In other words, we accumulate the derivatives of train_loss with respect to the parameters based on the computation generated from train_t_u.

If we (incorrectly) called backward on val_loss as well, we would accumulate the derivatives of val_loss with respect to the parameters *on the same leaf nodes*. Remember the zero_grad thing, whereby gradients are accumulated on top of each other every time we call backward unless we zero out the gradients explicitly? Well, here something very similar would happen: calling backward on val_loss would lead to gradients accumulating in the params tensor, on top of those generated during the train_loss.backward() call. In this case, we would effectively train our model on the whole dataset (both training and validation), since the gradient would depend on both. Pretty interesting.

There's another element for discussion here. Since we're not ever calling backward on val_loss, why are we building the graph in the first place? We could in fact just call model and loss_fn as plain functions, without tracking the computation. However optimized, building the autograd graph comes with additional costs that we could totally forgo during the validation pass, especially when the model has millions of parameters.

In order to address this, PyTorch allows us to switch off autograd when we don't need it, using the torch.no_grad context manager.[12] We won't see any meaningful advantage in terms of speed or memory consumption on our small problem. However, for larger models, the differences can add up. We can make sure this works by checking the value of the requires_grad attribute on the val_loss tensor:

```
# In[16]:
def training_loop(n_epochs, optimizer, params, train_t_u, val_t_u,
                  train_t_c, val_t_c):
    for epoch in range(1, n_epochs + 1):
        train_t_p = model(train_t_u, *params)
        train_loss = loss_fn(train_t_p, train_t_c)

        with torch.no_grad():
            val_t_p = model(val_t_u, *params)
            val_loss = loss_fn(val_t_p, val_t_c)
            assert val_loss.requires_grad == False

        optimizer.zero_grad()
        train_loss.backward()
        optimizer.step()
```

Context manager here ⟶ (points to `with torch.no_grad():`)

Checks that our output requires_grad args are forced to False inside this block ⟵ (points to `assert val_loss.requires_grad == False`)

Using the related set_grad_enabled context, we can also condition the code to run with autograd enabled or disabled, according to a Boolean expression—typically indicating whether we are running in training or inference mode. We could, for instance, define a calc_forward function that takes data as input and runs model and loss_fn with or without autograd according to a Boolean train_is argument:

```
# In[17]:
def calc_forward(t_u, t_c, is_train):
    with torch.set_grad_enabled(is_train):
        t_p = model(t_u, *params)
        loss = loss_fn(t_p, t_c)
    return loss
```

---

[12] We should not think that using torch.no_grad necessarily implies that the outputs do not require gradients. There are particular circumstances (involving views, as discussed in section 3.8.1) in which requires_grad is not set to False even when created in a no_grad context. It is best to use the detach function if we need to be sure.

5.6   *Conclusion*

We started this chapter with a big question: how is it that a machine can learn from examples? We spent the rest of the chapter describing the mechanism with which a model can be optimized to fit data. We chose to stick with a simple model in order to see all the moving parts without unneeded complications.

Now that we've had our fill of appetizers, in chapter 6 we'll finally get to the main course: using a neural network to fit our data. We'll work on solving the same thermometer problem, but with the more powerful tools provided by the `torch.nn` module. We'll adopt the same spirit of using this small problem to illustrate the larger uses of PyTorch. The problem doesn't need a neural network to reach a solution, but it will allow us to develop a simpler understanding of what's required to train a neural network.

5.7   *Exercise*

1 Redefine the model to be `w2 * t_u ** 2 + w1 * t_u + b`.
   a What parts of the training loop, and so on, need to change to accommodate this redefinition?
   b What parts are agnostic to swapping out the model?
   c Is the resulting loss higher or lower after training?
   d Is the actual result better or worse?

5.8   *Summary*

- Linear models are the simplest reasonable model to use to fit data.
- Convex optimization techniques can be used for linear models, but they do not generalize to neural networks, so we focus on stochastic gradient descent for parameter estimation.
- Deep learning can be used for generic models that are not engineered for solving a specific task, but instead can be automatically adapted to specialize themselves on the problem at hand.
- Learning algorithms amount to optimizing parameters of models based on observations. A loss function is a measure of the error in carrying out a task, such as the error between predicted outputs and measured values. The goal is to get the loss function as low as possible.
- The rate of change of the loss function with respect to the model parameters can be used to update the same parameters in the direction of decreasing loss.
- The `optim` module in PyTorch provides a collection of ready-to-use optimizers for updating parameters and minimizing loss functions.
- Optimizers use the autograd feature of PyTorch to compute the gradient for each parameter, depending on how that parameter contributes to the final output. This allows users to rely on the dynamic computation graph during complex forward passes.

- Context managers like `with torch.no_grad():` can be used to control auto-grad's behavior.
- Data is often split into separate sets of training samples and validation samples. This lets us evaluate a model on data it was not trained on.
- Overfitting a model happens when the model's performance continues to improve on the training set but degrades on the validation set. This is usually due to the model not generalizing, and instead memorizing the desired outputs for the training set.

Using a neural
network to fit the data

6

This chapter covers

- Nonlinear activation functions as the key difference compared with linear models
- Working with PyTorch's nn module
- Solving a linear-fit problem with a neural network

So far, we've taken a close look at how a linear model can learn and how to make that happen in PyTorch. We've focused on a very simple regression problem that used a linear model with only one input and one output. Such a simple example allowed us to dissect the mechanics of a model that learns, without getting overly distracted by the implementation of the model itself. As we saw in the overview diagram in chapter 5, figure 5.2 (repeated here as figure 6.1), the exact details of a model are not needed to understand the high-level process that trains the model. Backpropagating errors to parameters and then updating those parameters by taking the gradient with respect to the loss is the same no matter what the underlying model is.

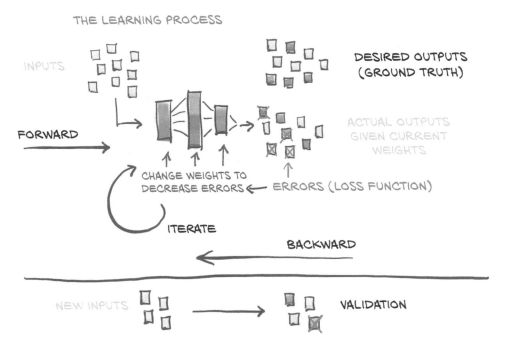

THE LEARNING PROCESS

INPUTS

DESIRED OUTPUTS
(GROUND TRUTH)

FORWARD

ACTUAL OUTPUTS
GIVEN CURRENT
WEIGHTS

CHANGE WEIGHTS TO
DECREASE ERRORS ← ERRORS (LOSS FUNCTION)

ITERATE

BACKWARD

NEW INPUTS ———→ VALIDATION

Figure 6.1   Our mental model of the learning process, as implemented in chapter 5

In this chapter, we will make some changes to our model architecture: we're going to implement a full artificial neural network to solve our temperature-conversion problem. We'll continue using our training loop from the last chapter, along with our Fahrenheit-to-Celsius samples split into training and validation sets. We could start to use a quadratic model: rewriting `model` as a quadratic function of its input (for example, y = a * x**2 + b * x + c). Since such a model would be differentiable, PyTorch would take care of computing gradients, and the training loop would work as usual. That wouldn't be too interesting for us, though, because we would still be fixing the shape of the function.

This is the chapter where we begin to hook together the foundational work we've put in and the PyTorch features you'll be using day in and day out as you work on your projects. You'll gain an understanding of what's going on underneath the porcelain of the PyTorch API, rather than it just being so much black magic. Before we get into the implementation of our new model, though, let's cover what we mean by *artificial neural network*.

6.1   *Artificial neurons*

At the core of deep learning are neural networks: mathematical entities capable of representing complicated functions through a composition of simpler functions. The term *neural network* is obviously suggestive of a link to the way our brain works. As a matter of fact, although the initial models were inspired by neuroscience,[1] modern artificial neural networks bear only a slight resemblance to the mechanisms of neurons in the brain. It seems likely that both artificial and physiological neural networks use vaguely similar mathematical strategies for approximating complicated functions because that family of strategies works very effectively.

NOTE We are going to drop the *artificial* and refer to these constructs as just *neural networks* from here forward.

The basic building block of these complicated functions is the *neuron*, as illustrated in figure 6.2. At its core, it is nothing but a linear transformation of the input (for example, multiplying the input by a number [the *weight*] and adding a constant [the *bias*]) followed by the application of a fixed nonlinear function (referred to as the *activation function*).

Mathematically, we can write this out as $o = f(w * x + b)$, with x as our input, w our weight or scaling factor, and b as our bias or offset. f is our activation function, set to the hyperbolic tangent, or tanh function here. In general, x and, hence, o can be simple scalars, or vector-valued (meaning holding many scalar values); and similarly, w

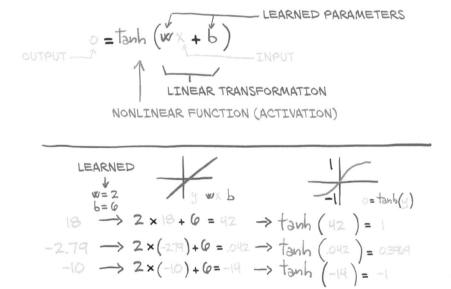

Figure 6.2   An artificial neuron: a linear transformation enclosed in a nonlinear function

[1]   See F. Rosenblatt, "The Perceptron: A Probabilistic Model for Information Storage and Organization in the Brain," *Psychological Review* 65(6), 386–408 (1958), https://pubmed.ncbi.nlm.nih.gov/13602029/.

can be a single scalar or matrix, while b is a scalar or vector (the dimensionality of the inputs and weights must match, however). In the latter case, the previous expression is referred to as a *layer* of neurons, since it represents many neurons via the multidimensional weights and biases.

6.1.1 Composing a multilayer network

A multilayer neural network, as represented in figure 6.3, is made up of a composition of functions like those we just discussed

```
x_1 = f(w_0 * x + b_0)
x_2 = f(w_1 * x_1 + b_1)
...
y = f(w_n * x_n + b_n)
```

where the output of a layer of neurons is used as an input for the following layer. Remember that w_0 here is a matrix, and x is a vector! Using a vector allows w_0 to hold an entire *layer* of neurons, not just a single weight.

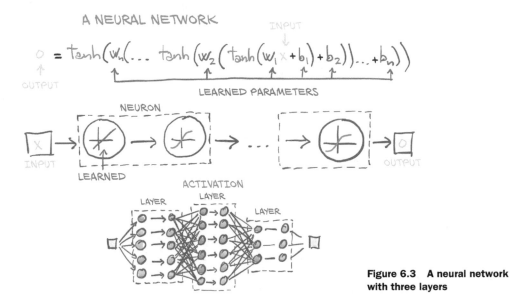

Figure 6.3   A neural network with three layers

6.1.2 Understanding the error function

An important difference between our earlier linear model and what we'll actually be using for deep learning is the shape of the error function. Our linear model and error-squared loss function had a convex error curve with a singular, clearly defined minimum. If we were to use other methods, we could solve for the parameters minimizing the error function automatically and definitively. That means that our parameter updates were attempting to *estimate* that singular correct answer as best they could.

```
                    loss_train += loss.item()

         if epoch == 1 or epoch % 10 == 0:
            print('{} Epoch {}, Training loss {}'.format(
                datetime.datetime.now(), epoch,
                loss_train / len(train_loader)))
```

Sums the losses we saw over the epoch. Recall that it is important to transform the loss to a Python number with .item(), to escape the gradients.

Divides by the length of the training data loader to get the average loss per batch. This is a much more intuitive measure than the sum.

We use the Dataset from chapter 7; wrap it into a DataLoader; instantiate our network, an optimizer, and a loss function as before; and call our training loop.

The substantial changes in our model from the last chapter are that now our model is a custom subclass of nn.Module and that we're using convolutions. Let's run training for 100 epochs while printing the loss. Depending on your hardware, this may take 20 minutes or more to finish!

**The DataLoader batches up the examples of our cifar2 dataset.
Shuffling randomizes the order of the examples from the dataset.**

```
# In[31]:
train_loader = torch.utils.data.DataLoader(cifar2, batch_size=64,
                                            shuffle=True)

model = Net()     #
optimizer = optim.SGD(model.parameters(), lr=1e-2)   #
loss_fn = nn.CrossEntropyLoss()   #

training_loop(
    n_epochs = 100,
    optimizer = optimizer,
    model = model,
    loss_fn = loss_fn,
    train_loader = train_loader,
)
```

Instantiates our network ...

... the stochastic gradient descent optimizer we have been working with ...

Calls the training loop we defined earlier

... and the cross entropy loss we met in 7.10

```
# Out[31]:
2020-01-16 23:07:21.889707 Epoch 1, Training loss 0.5634813266954605
2020-01-16 23:07:37.560610 Epoch 10, Training loss 0.3277610331109375
2020-01-16 23:07:54.966180 Epoch 20, Training loss 0.3035225479086493
2020-01-16 23:08:12.361597 Epoch 30, Training loss 0.28249378549824855
2020-01-16 23:08:29.769820 Epoch 40, Training loss 0.2611226033253275
2020-01-16 23:08:47.185401 Epoch 50, Training loss 0.24105800626574048
2020-01-16 23:09:04.644522 Epoch 60, Training loss 0.21997178820477928
2020-01-16 23:09:22.079625 Epoch 70, Training loss 0.20370126601047578
2020-01-16 23:09:39.593780 Epoch 80, Training loss 0.18939699422401987
2020-01-16 23:09:57.111441 Epoch 90, Training loss 0.17283396527266046
2020-01-16 23:10:14.632351 Epoch 100, Training loss 0.1614033816868712
```

So now we can train our network. But again, our friend the bird watcher will likely not be impressed when we tell her that we trained to very low training loss.

Neural networks do not have that same property of a convex error surface, even when using the same error-squared loss function! There's no single right answer for each parameter we're attempting to approximate. Instead, we are trying to get all of the parameters, when acting *in concert*, to produce a useful output. Since that useful output is only going to *approximate* the truth, there will be some level of imperfection. Where and how imperfections manifest is somewhat arbitrary, and by implication the parameters that control the output (and, hence, the imperfections) are somewhat arbitrary as well. This results in neural network training looking very much like parameter estimation from a mechanical perspective, but we must remember that the theoretical underpinnings are quite different.

A big part of the reason neural networks have non-convex error surfaces is due to the activation function. The ability of an ensemble of neurons to approximate a very wide range of useful functions depends on the combination of the linear and nonlinear behavior inherent to each neuron.

6.1.3 *All we need is activation*

As we have seen, the simplest unit in (deep) neural networks is a linear operation (scaling + offset) followed by an activation function. We already had our linear operation in our latest model—the linear operation *was* the entire model. The activation function plays two important roles:

- In the inner parts of the model, it allows the output function to have different slopes at different values—something a linear function by definition cannot do. By trickily composing these differently sloped parts for many outputs, neural networks can approximate arbitrary functions, as we will see in section 6.1.6.[2]
- At the last layer of the network, it has the role of concentrating the outputs of the preceding linear operation into a given range.

Let's talk about what the second point means. Pretend that we're assigning a "good doggo" score to images. Pictures of retrievers and spaniels should have a high score, while images of airplanes and garbage trucks should have a low score. Bear pictures should have a lowish score, too, although higher than garbage trucks.

The problem is, we have to define a "high score": we've got the entire range of float32 to work with, and that means we can go pretty high. Even if we say "it's a 10-point scale," there's still the issue that sometimes our model is going to produce a score of 11 out of 10. Remember that under the hood, it's all sums of (w*x+b) matrix multiplications, and those won't naturally limit themselves to a specific range of outputs.

---

[2] For an intuitive appreciation of this universal approximation property, you can pick a function from figure 6.5 and then build a building-block function that is almost zero in most parts and positive around $x = 0$ from scaled (including multiplied by negative numbers) and translated copies of the activation function. With scaled, translated, and dilated (squeezed along the X-axis) copies of this building-block function, you can then approximate any (continuous) function. In figure 6.6 the function in the middle row to the right could be such a building block. Michael Nielsen has an interactive demonstration in his online book *Neural Networks and Deep Learning* at http://mng.bz/Mdon.

CAPPING THE OUTPUT RANGE

We want to firmly constrain the output of our linear operation to a specific range so that the consumer of this output doesn't have to handle numerical inputs of puppies at 12/10, bears at –10, and garbage trucks at –1,000.

One possibility is to just cap the output values: anything below 0 is set to 0, and anything above 10 is set to 10. That's a simple activation function called `torch.nn.Hardtanh` (https://pytorch.org/docs/stable/nn.html#hardtanh, but note that the default range is –1 to +1).

COMPRESSING THE OUTPUT RANGE

Another family of functions that work well is `torch.nn.Sigmoid`, which includes `1 / (1 + e ** -x)`, `torch.tanh`, and others that we'll see in a moment. These functions have a curve that asymptotically approaches 0 or –1 as x goes to negative infinity, approaches 1 as x increases, and have a mostly constant slope at $x == 0$. Conceptually, functions shaped this way work well because there's an area in the middle of our linear function's output that our neuron (which, again, is just a linear function followed by an activation) will be sensitive to, while everything else gets lumped next to the boundary values. As we can see in figure 6.4, our garbage truck gets a score of –0.97, while bears and foxes and wolves end up somewhere in the –0.3 to 0.3 range.

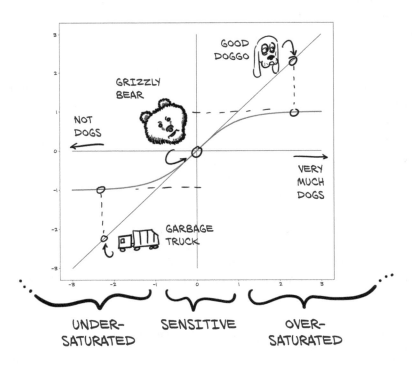

Figure 6.4   Dogs, bears, and garbage trucks being mapped to how dog-like they are via the `tanh` activation function

This results in garbage trucks being flagged as "not dogs," our good dog mapping to "clearly a dog," and our bear ending up somewhere in the middle. In code, we can see the exact values:

```
>>> import math
>>> math.tanh(-2.2)          <—— Garbage truck
-0.9757431300314515
>>> math.tanh(0.1)           <—— Bear
0.09966799462495582
>>> math.tanh(2.5)           <—— Good doggo
0.9866142981514303
```

With the bear in the sensitive range, small changes to the bear will result in a noticeable change to the result. For example, we could switch from a grizzly to a polar bear (which has a vaguely more traditionally canine face) and see a jump up the *Y*-axis as we slide toward the "very much a dog" end of the graph. Conversely, a koala bear would register as less dog-like, and we would see a drop in the activated output. There isn't much we could do to the garbage truck to make it register as dog-like, though: even with drastic changes, we might only see a shift from –0.97 to –0.8 or so.

6.1.4 *More activation functions*

There are quite a few activation functions, some of which are shown in figure 6.5. In the first column, we see the smooth functions Tanh and Softplus, while the second column has "hard" versions of the activation functions to their left: Hardtanh and ReLU. ReLU (for *rectified linear unit*) deserves special note, as it is currently considered

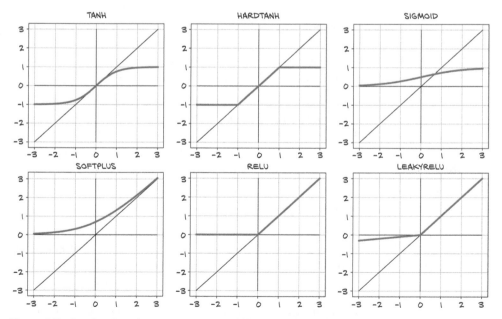

Figure 6.5   A collection of common and not-so-common activation functions

one of the best-performing general activation functions; many state-of-the-art results have used it. The `Sigmoid` activation function, also known as the *logistic function*, was widely used in early deep learning work but has since fallen out of common use except where we explicitly want to move to the 0...1 range: for example, when the output should be a probability. Finally, the `LeakyReLU` function modifies the standard `ReLU` to have a small positive slope, rather than being strictly zero for negative inputs (typically this slope is 0.01, but it's shown here with slope 0.1 for clarity).

6.1.5 *Choosing the best activation function*

Activation functions are curious, because with such a wide variety of proven successful ones (many more than shown in figure 6.5), it's clear that there are few, if any, strict requirements. As such, we're going to discuss some generalities about activation functions that can probably be trivially disproved in the specific. That said, by definition,[3] activation functions

- Are nonlinear. Repeated applications of (w*x+b) without an activation function results in a function of the same (affine linear) form. The nonlinearity allows the overall network to approximate more complex functions.
- Are differentiable, so that gradients can be computed through them. Point discontinuities, as we can see in `Hardtanh` or `ReLU`, are fine.

Without these characteristics, the network either falls back to being a linear model or becomes difficult to train.

The following are true for the functions:

- They have at least one sensitive range, where nontrivial changes to the input result in a corresponding nontrivial change to the output. This is needed for training.
- Many of them have an insensitive (or saturated) range, where changes to the input result in little or no change to the output.

By way of example, the `Hardtanh` function could easily be used to make piecewise-linear approximations of a function by combining the sensitive range with different weights and biases on the input.

Often (but far from universally so), the activation function will have at least one of these:

- A lower bound that is approached (or met) as the input goes to negative infinity
- A similar-but-inverse upper bound for positive infinity

Thinking of what we know about how backpropagation works, we can figure out that the errors will propagate backward through the activation more effectively when the inputs are in the response range, while errors will not greatly affect neurons for which

---

[3] Of course, even these statements aren't *always* true; see Jakob Foerster, "Nonlinear Computation in Deep Linear Networks," OpenAI, 2019, http://mng.bz/gygE.

the input is saturated (since the gradient will be close to zero, due to the flat area around the output).

Put together, all this results in a pretty powerful mechanism: we're saying that in a network built out of linear + activation units, when different inputs are presented to the network, (a) different units will respond in different ranges for the same inputs, and (b) the errors associated with those inputs will primarily affect the neurons operating in the sensitive range, leaving other units more or less unaffected by the learning process. In addition, thanks to the fact that derivatives of the activation with respect to its inputs are often close to 1 in the sensitive range, estimating the parameters of the linear transformation through gradient descent for the units that operate in that range will look a lot like the linear fit we have seen previously.

We are starting to get a deeper intuition for how joining many linear + activation units in parallel and stacking them one after the other leads us to a mathematical object that is capable of approximating complicated functions. Different combinations of units will respond to inputs in different ranges, and those parameters for those units are relatively easy to optimize through gradient descent, since learning will behave a lot like that of a linear function until the output saturates.

6.1.6 *What learning means for a neural network*

Building models out of stacks of linear transformations followed by differentiable activations leads to models that can approximate highly nonlinear processes and whose parameters we can estimate surprisingly well through gradient descent. This remains true even when dealing with models with millions of parameters. What makes using deep neural networks so attractive is that it saves us from worrying too much about the exact function that represents our data—whether it is quadratic, piecewise polynomial, or something else. With a deep neural network model, we have a universal approximator and a method to estimate its parameters. This approximator can be customized to our needs, in terms of model capacity and its ability to model complicated input/output relationships, just by composing simple building blocks. We can see some examples of this in figure 6.6.

The four upper-left graphs show four neurons—A, B, C, and D—each with its own (arbitrarily chosen) weight and bias. Each neuron uses the Tanh activation function with a min of –1 and a max of 1. The varied weights and biases move the center point and change how drastically the transition from min to max happens, but they clearly all have the same general shape. The columns to the right of those show both pairs of neurons added together (A + B and then C + D). Here, we start to see some interesting properties that mimic a single layer of neurons. A + B shows a slight *S* curve, with the extremes approaching 0, but both a positive bump and a negative bump in the middle. Conversely, C + D has only a large positive bump, which peaks at a higher value than our single-neuron max of 1.

In the third row, we begin to compose our neurons as they would be in a two-layer network. Both C(A + B) and D(A + B) have the same positive and negative bumps that A + B shows, but the positive peak is more subtle. The composition of C(A + B) + D(A + B)

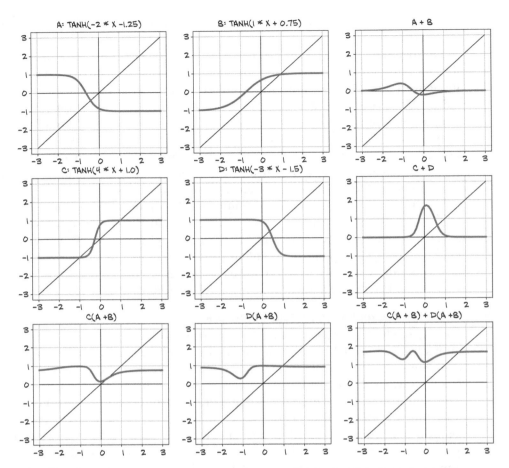

Figure 6.6   Composing multiple linear units and `tanh` activation functions to produce nonlinear outputs

shows a new property: *two* clearly negative bumps, and possibly a very subtle second positive peak as well, to the left of the main area of interest. All this with only four neurons in two layers!

Again, these neurons' parameters were chosen only to have a visually interesting result. Training consists of finding acceptable values for these weights and biases so that the resulting network correctly carries out a task, such as predicting likely temperatures given geographic coordinates and time of the year. By *carrying out a task successfully*, we mean obtaining a correct output on unseen data produced by the same data-generating process used for training data. A successfully trained network, through the values of its weights and biases, will capture the inherent structure of the data in the form of meaningful numerical representations that work correctly for previously unseen data.

Let's take another step in our realization of the mechanics of learning: deep neural networks give us the ability to approximate highly nonlinear phenomena without having an explicit model for them. Instead, starting from a generic, untrained model, we specialize it on a task by providing it with a set of inputs and outputs and a loss function from which to backpropagate. Specializing a generic model to a task using examples is what we refer to as *learning*, because the model wasn't built with that specific task in mind—no rules describing how that task worked were encoded in the model.

For our thermometer example, we assumed that both thermometers measured temperatures linearly. That assumption is where we implicitly encoded a rule for our task: we hardcoded the shape of our input/output function; we couldn't have approximated anything other than data points sitting around a line. As the dimensionality of a problem grows (that is, many inputs to many outputs) and input/output relationships get complicated, assuming a shape for the input/output function is unlikely to work. The job of a physicist or an applied mathematician is often to come up with a functional description of a phenomenon from first principles, so that we can estimate the unknown parameters from measurements and get an accurate model of the world. Deep neural networks, on the other hand, are families of functions that have the ability to approximate a wide range of input/output relationships without necessarily requiring us to come up with an explanatory model of a phenomenon. In a way, we're renouncing an explanation in exchange for the possibility of tackling increasingly complicated problems. In another way, we sometimes lack the ability, information, or computational resources to build an explicit model of what we're presented with, so data-driven methods are our only way forward.

6.2 *The PyTorch nn module*

All this talking about neural networks is probably making you really curious about building one from scratch with PyTorch. Our first step will be to replace our linear model with a neural network unit. This will be a somewhat useless step backward from a correctness perspective, since we've already verified that our calibration only required a linear function, but it will still be instrumental for starting on a sufficiently simple problem and scaling up later.

PyTorch has a whole submodule dedicated to neural networks, called `torch.nn`. It contains the building blocks needed to create all sorts of neural network architectures. Those building blocks are called *modules* in PyTorch parlance (such building blocks are often referred to as *layers* in other frameworks). A PyTorch module is a Python class deriving from the `nn.Module` base class. A module can have one or more `Parameter` instances as attributes, which are tensors whose values are optimized during the training process (think `w` and `b` in our linear model). A module can also have one or more submodules (subclasses of `nn.Module`) as attributes, and it will be able to track their parameters as well.

> **NOTE** The submodules must be top-level *attributes*, not buried inside `list` or `dict` instances! Otherwise, the optimizer will not be able to locate the submodules (and, hence, their parameters). For situations where your model requires a list or dict of submodules, PyTorch provides `nn.ModuleList` and `nn.ModuleDict`.

Unsurprisingly, we can find a subclass of `nn.Module` called `nn.Linear`, which applies an affine transformation to its input (via the parameter attributes `weight` and `bias`) and is equivalent to what we implemented earlier in our thermometer experiments. We'll now start precisely where we left off and convert our previous code to a form that uses nn.

6.2.1 Using __call__ rather than forward

All PyTorch-provided subclasses of `nn.Module` have their `__call__` method defined. This allows us to instantiate an `nn.Linear` and call it as if it was a function, like so (code/p1ch6/1_neural_networks.ipynb):

```
# In[5]:
import torch.nn as nn

linear_model = nn.Linear(1, 1)      ◁─┐  We'll look into the constructor
linear_model(t_un_val)                │  arguments in a moment.

# Out[5]:
tensor([[0.6018],
        [0.2877]], grad_fn=<AddmmBackward>)
```

Calling an instance of `nn.Module` with a set of arguments ends up calling a method named `forward` with the same arguments. The `forward` method is what executes the forward computation, while `__call__` does other rather important chores before and after calling `forward`. So, it is technically possible to call `forward` directly, and it will produce the same output as `__call__`, but this should not be done from user code:

```
y = model(x)          ◁─── Correct!
y = model.forward(x)  ◁─┐
                        │  Silent error. Don't do it!
```

Here's the implementation of `Module._call_` (we left out the bits related to the JIT and made some simplifications for clarity; torch/nn/modules/module.py, line 483, class: Module):

```
def __call__(self, *input, **kwargs):
    for hook in self._forward_pre_hooks.values():
        hook(self, input)

    result = self.forward(*input, **kwargs)

    for hook in self._forward_hooks.values():
        hook_result = hook(self, input, result)
```

```
    # ...

for hook in self._backward_hooks.values():
    # ...

return result
```

As we can see, there are a lot of hooks that won't get called properly if we just use `.forward(…)` directly.

6.2.2 *Returning to the linear model*

Back to our linear model. The constructor to `nn.Linear` accepts three arguments: the number of input features, the number of output features, and whether the linear model includes a bias or not (defaulting to `True`, here):

```
# In[5]:
import torch.nn as nn

linear_model = nn.Linear(1, 1)       ◁───┐  The arguments are input size, output
linear_model(t_un_val)                   └  size, and bias defaulting to True.

# Out[5]:
tensor([[0.6018],
        [0.2877]], grad_fn=<AddmmBackward>)
```

The number of features in our case just refers to the size of the input and the output tensor for the module, so 1 and 1. If we used both temperature and barometric pressure as input, for instance, we would have two features in input and one feature in output. As we will see, for more complex models with several intermediate modules, the number of features will be associated with the capacity of the model.

We have an instance of `nn.Linear` with one input and one output feature. That only requires one weight and one bias:

```
# In[6]:
linear_model.weight

# Out[6]:
Parameter containing:
tensor([[-0.0674]], requires_grad=True)

# In[7]:
linear_model.bias

# Out[7]:
Parameter containing:
tensor([0.7488], requires_grad=True)
```

We can call the module with some input:

```
# In[8]:
x = torch.ones(1)
linear_model(x)

# Out[8]:
tensor([0.6814], grad_fn=<AddBackward0>)
```

Although PyTorch lets us get away with it, we don't actually provide an input with the right dimensionality. We have a model that takes one input and produces one output, but PyTorch nn.Module and its subclasses are designed to do so on multiple samples at the same time. To accommodate multiple samples, modules expect the zeroth dimension of the input to be the number of samples in the *batch*. We encountered this concept in chapter 4, when we learned how to arrange real-world data into tensors.

BATCHING INPUTS

Any module in nn is written to produce outputs for a *batch* of multiple inputs at the same time. Thus, assuming we need to run nn.Linear on 10 samples, we can create an input tensor of size $B \times Nin$, where B is the size of the batch and Nin is the number of input features, and run it once through the model. For example:

```
# In[9]:
x = torch.ones(10, 1)
linear_model(x)

# Out[9]:
tensor([[0.6814],
        [0.6814],
        [0.6814],
        [0.6814],
        [0.6814],
        [0.6814],
        [0.6814],
        [0.6814],
        [0.6814],
        [0.6814]], grad_fn=<AddmmBackward>)
```

Let's dig into what's going on here, with figure 6.7 showing a similar situation with batched image data. Our input is $B \times C \times H \times W$ with a batch size of 3 (say, images of a dog, a bird, and then a car), three channel dimensions (red, green, and blue), and an unspecified number of pixels for height and width. As we can see, the output is a tensor of size $B \times Nout$, where $Nout$ is the number of output features: four, in this case.

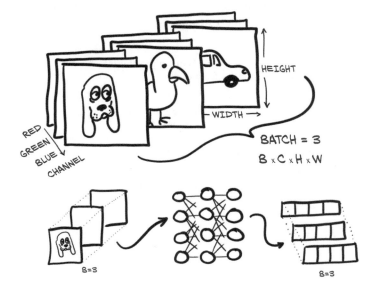

Figure 6.7 Three RGB images batched together and fed into a neural network. The output is a batch of three vectors of size 4.

OPTIMIZING BATCHES

The reason we want to do this batching is multifaceted. One big motivation is to make sure the computation we're asking for is big enough to saturate the computing resources we're using to perform the computation. GPUs in particular are highly parallelized, so a single input on a small model will leave most of the computing units idle. By providing batches of inputs, the calculation can be spread across the otherwise-idle units, which means the batched results come back just as quickly as a single result would. Another benefit is that some advanced models use statistical information from the entire batch, and those statistics get better with larger batch sizes.

Back to our thermometer data, t_u and t_c were two 1D tensors of size B. Thanks to broadcasting, we could write our linear model as w * x + b, where w and b were two scalar parameters. This worked because we had a single input feature: if we had two, we would need to add an extra dimension to turn that 1D tensor into a matrix with samples in the rows and features in the columns.

That's exactly what we need to do to switch to using nn.Linear. We reshape our *B* inputs to *B* × *Nin*, where *Nin* is 1. That is easily done with unsqueeze:

```
# In[2]:
t_c = [0.5, 14.0, 15.0, 28.0, 11.0, 8.0, 3.0, -4.0, 6.0, 13.0, 21.0]
t_u = [35.7, 55.9, 58.2, 81.9, 56.3, 48.9, 33.9, 21.8, 48.4, 60.4, 68.4]
t_c = torch.tensor(t_c).unsqueeze(1)
t_u = torch.tensor(t_u).unsqueeze(1)      │ Adds the extra dimension at axis 1

t_u.shape

# Out[2]:
torch.Size([11, 1])
```

We're done; let's update our training code. First, we replace our handmade model with nn.Linear(1,1), and then we need to pass the linear model parameters to the optimizer:

```
# In[10]:
linear_model = nn.Linear(1, 1)        ◁─┐ This is just a redefinition
optimizer = optim.SGD(                   └ from earlier.
    linear_model.parameters(),  ◁─┐ This method call
    lr=1e-2)                       │ replaces [params].
```

Earlier, it was our responsibility to create parameters and pass them as the first argument to optim.SGD. Now we can use the parameters method to ask any nn.Module for a list of parameters owned by it or any of its submodules:

```
# In[11]:
linear_model.parameters()
```

```
# Out[11]:
<generator object Module.parameters at 0x7f94b4a8a750>
```

```
# In[12]:
list(linear_model.parameters())
```

```
# Out[12]:
[Parameter containing:
 tensor([[0.7398]], requires_grad=True), Parameter containing:
 tensor([0.7974], requires_grad=True)]
```

This call recurses into submodules defined in the module's init constructor and returns a flat list of all parameters encountered, so that we can conveniently pass it to the optimizer constructor as we did previously.

We can already figure out what happens in the training loop. The optimizer is provided with a list of tensors that were defined with requires_grad = True—all Parameters are defined this way by definition, since they need to be optimized by gradient descent. When training_loss.backward() is called, grad is accumulated on the leaf nodes of the graph, which are precisely the parameters that were passed to the optimizer.

At this point, the SGD optimizer has everything it needs. When optimizer.step() is called, it will iterate through each Parameter and change it by an amount proportional to what is stored in its grad attribute. Pretty clean design.

Let's take a look a the training loop now:

```
# In[13]:
def training_loop(n_epochs, optimizer, model, loss_fn, t_u_train, t_u_val,
                  t_c_train, t_c_val):
    for epoch in range(1, n_epochs + 1):
        t_p_train = model(t_u_train)          ◁─┐ The model is now
        loss_train = loss_fn(t_p_train, t_c_train)  │ passed in, instead of
                                                    │ the individual params.
        t_p_val = model(t_u_val)              ◁─┘
```

```
        loss_val = loss_fn(t_p_val, t_c_val)

        optimizer.zero_grad()
        loss_train.backward()        ◁──┐  The loss function is also passed
        optimizer.step()                │  in. We'll use it in a moment.

        if epoch == 1 or epoch % 1000 == 0:
            print(f"Epoch {epoch}, Training loss {loss_train.item():.4f},"
                  f" Validation loss {loss_val.item():.4f}")
```

It hasn't changed practically at all, except that now we don't pass params explicitly to model since the model itself holds its Parameters internally.

There's one last bit that we can leverage from torch.nn: the loss. Indeed, nn comes with several common loss functions, among them nn.MSELoss (MSE stands for Mean Square Error), which is exactly what we defined earlier as our loss_fn. Loss functions in nn are still subclasses of nn.Module, so we will create an instance and call it as a function. In our case, we get rid of the handwritten loss_fn and replace it:

```
# In[15]:
linear_model = nn.Linear(1, 1)
optimizer = optim.SGD(linear_model.parameters(), lr=1e-2)

training_loop(
    n_epochs = 3000,
    optimizer = optimizer,
    model = linear_model,                  │  We are no longer using our hand-
    loss_fn = nn.MSELoss(),        ◁──┘  written loss function from earlier.
    t_u_train = t_un_train,
    t_u_val = t_un_val,
    t_c_train = t_c_train,
    t_c_val = t_c_val)

print()
print(linear_model.weight)
print(linear_model.bias)

# Out[15]:
Epoch 1, Training loss 134.9599, Validation loss 183.1707
Epoch 1000, Training loss 4.8053, Validation loss 4.7307
Epoch 2000, Training loss 3.0285, Validation loss 3.0889
Epoch 3000, Training loss 2.8569, Validation loss 3.9105

Parameter containing:
tensor([[5.4319]], requires_grad=True)
Parameter containing:
tensor([-17.9693], requires_grad=True)
```

Everything else input into our training loop stays the same. Even our results remain the same as before. Of course, getting the same results is expected, as a difference would imply a bug in one of the two implementations.

6.3   *Finally a neural network*

It's been a long journey—there has been a lot to explore for these 20-something lines of code we require to define and train a model. Hopefully by now the magic involved in training has vanished and left room for the mechanics. What we learned so far will allow us to own the code we write instead of merely poking at a black box when things get more complicated.

There's one last step left to take: replacing our linear model with a neural network as our approximating function. We said earlier that using a neural network will not result in a higher-quality model, since the process underlying our calibration problem was fundamentally linear. However, it's good to make the leap from linear to neural network in a controlled environment so we won't feel lost later.

6.3.1   *Replacing the linear model*

We are going to keep everything else fixed, including the loss function, and only redefine `model`. Let's build the simplest possible neural network: a linear module, followed by an activation function, feeding into another linear module. The first linear + activation layer is commonly referred to as a *hidden* layer for historical reasons, since its outputs are not observed directly but fed into the output layer. While the input and output of the model are both of size 1 (they have one input and one output feature), the size of the output of the first linear module is usually larger than 1. Recalling our earlier explanation of the role of activations, this can lead different units to respond to different ranges of the input, which increases the capacity of our model. The last linear layer will take the output of activations and combine them linearly to produce the output value.

There is no standard way to depict neural networks. Figure 6.8 shows two ways that seem to be somewhat prototypical: the left side shows how our network might be depicted in basic introductions, whereas a style similar to that on the right is often used in the more advanced literature and research papers. It is common to make diagram blocks that roughly correspond to the neural network modules PyTorch offers (though sometimes things like the `Tanh` activation layer are not explicitly shown). Note that one somewhat subtle difference between the two is that the graph on the left has the inputs and (intermediate) results in the circles as the main elements. On the right, the computational steps are more prominent.

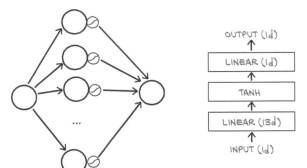

Figure 6.8   **Our simplest neural network in two views. Left: beginner's version. Right: higher-level version.**

nn provides a simple way to concatenate modules through the `nn.Sequential` container:

```
# In[16]:
seq_model = nn.Sequential(
            nn.Linear(1, 13),
            nn.Tanh(),
            nn.Linear(13, 1))
seq_model
```

> We chose 13 arbitrarily. We wanted a number that was a different size from the other tensor shapes we have floating around. ←┘ (on `nn.Linear(1, 13)`)

> This 13 must match the first size, however. ← (on `nn.Linear(13, 1)`)

```
# Out[16]:
Sequential(
  (0): Linear(in_features=1, out_features=13, bias=True)
  (1): Tanh()
  (2): Linear(in_features=13, out_features=1, bias=True)
)
```

The end result is a model that takes the inputs expected by the first module specified as an argument of `nn.Sequential`, passes intermediate outputs to subsequent modules, and produces the output returned by the last module. The model fans out from 1 input feature to 13 hidden features, passes them through a `tanh` activation, and linearly combines the resulting 13 numbers into 1 output feature.

6.3.2 Inspecting the parameters

Calling `model.parameters()` will collect `weight` and `bias` from both the first and second linear modules. It's instructive to inspect the parameters in this case by printing their shapes:

```
# In[17]:
[param.shape for param in seq_model.parameters()]
```

```
# Out[17]:
[torch.Size([13, 1]), torch.Size([13]), torch.Size([1, 13]), torch.Size([1])]
```

These are the tensors that the optimizer will get. Again, after we call `model.backward()`, all parameters are populated with their `grad`, and the optimizer then updates their values accordingly during the `optimizer.step()` call. Not that different from our previous linear model, eh? After all, they're both differentiable models that can be trained using gradient descent.

A few notes on parameters of `nn.Modules`. When inspecting parameters of a model made up of several submodules, it is handy to be able to identify parameters by name. There's a method for that, called `named_parameters`:

```
# In[18]:
for name, param in seq_model.named_parameters():
    print(name, param.shape)
```

```
# Out[18]:
0.weight torch.Size([13, 1])
```

```
0.bias torch.Size([13])
2.weight torch.Size([1, 13])
2.bias torch.Size([1])
```

The name of each module in `Sequential` is just the ordinal with which the module appears in the arguments. Interestingly, `Sequential` also accepts an `OrderedDict`,[4] in which we can name each module passed to `Sequential`:

```
# In[19]:
from collections import OrderedDict

seq_model = nn.Sequential(OrderedDict([
    ('hidden_linear', nn.Linear(1, 8)),
    ('hidden_activation', nn.Tanh()),
    ('output_linear', nn.Linear(8, 1))
]))

seq_model

# Out[19]:
Sequential(
  (hidden_linear): Linear(in_features=1, out_features=8, bias=True)
  (hidden_activation): Tanh()
  (output_linear): Linear(in_features=8, out_features=1, bias=True)
)
```

This allows us to get more explanatory names for submodules:

```
# In[20]:
for name, param in seq_model.named_parameters():
    print(name, param.shape)

# Out[20]:
hidden_linear.weight torch.Size([8, 1])
hidden_linear.bias torch.Size([8])
output_linear.weight torch.Size([1, 8])
output_linear.bias torch.Size([1])
```

This is more descriptive; but it does not give us more flexibility in the flow of data through the network, which remains a purely sequential pass-through—the `nn.Sequential` is very aptly named. We will see how to take full control of the processing of input data by subclassing `nn.Module` ourselves in chapter 8.

We can also access a particular `Parameter` by using submodules as attributes:

```
# In[21]:
seq_model.output_linear.bias

# Out[21]:
Parameter containing:
tensor([-0.0173], requires_grad=True)
```

---

[4] Not all versions of Python specify the iteration order for `dict`, so we're using `OrderedDict` here to ensure the ordering of the layers and emphasize that the order of the layers matters.

This is useful for inspecting parameters or their gradients: for instance, to monitor gradients during training, as we did at the beginning of this chapter. Say we want to print out the gradients of weight of the linear portion of the hidden layer. We can run the training loop for the new neural network model and then look at the resulting gradients after the last epoch:

```
# In[22]:
optimizer = optim.SGD(seq_model.parameters(), lr=1e-3)     ◁──┐  We've dropped the
                                                              learning rate a bit to
training_loop(                                                 help with stability.
    n_epochs = 5000,
    optimizer = optimizer,
    model = seq_model,
    loss_fn = nn.MSELoss(),
    t_u_train = t_un_train,
    t_u_val = t_un_val,
    t_c_train = t_c_train,
    t_c_val = t_c_val)

print('output', seq_model(t_un_val))
print('answer', t_c_val)
print('hidden', seq_model.hidden_linear.weight.grad)

# Out[22]:
Epoch 1, Training loss 182.9724, Validation loss 231.8708
Epoch 1000, Training loss 6.6642, Validation loss 3.7330
Epoch 2000, Training loss 5.1502, Validation loss 0.1406
Epoch 3000, Training loss 2.9653, Validation loss 1.0005
Epoch 4000, Training loss 2.2839, Validation loss 1.6580
Epoch 5000, Training loss 2.1141, Validation loss 2.0215
output tensor([[-1.9930],
        [20.8729]], grad_fn=<AddmmBackward>)
answer tensor([[-4.],
        [21.]])
hidden tensor([[ 0.0272],
        [ 0.0139],
        [ 0.1692],
        [ 0.1735],
        [-0.1697],
        [ 0.1455],
        [-0.0136],
        [-0.0554]])
```

6.3.3 Comparing to the linear model

We can also evaluate the model on all of the data and see how it differs from a line:

```
# In[23]:
from matplotlib import pyplot as plt

t_range = torch.arange(20., 90.).unsqueeze(1)

fig = plt.figure(dpi=600)
```

```
plt.xlabel("Fahrenheit")
plt.ylabel("Celsius")
plt.plot(t_u.numpy(), t_c.numpy(), 'o')
plt.plot(t_range.numpy(), seq_model(0.1 * t_range).detach().numpy(), 'c-')
plt.plot(t_u.numpy(), seq_model(0.1 * t_u).detach().numpy(), 'kx')
```

The result is shown in figure 6.9. We can appreciate that the neural network has a tendency to overfit, as we discussed in chapter 5, since it tries to chase the measurements, including the noisy ones. Even our tiny neural network has too many parameters to fit the few measurements we have. It doesn't do a bad job, though, overall.

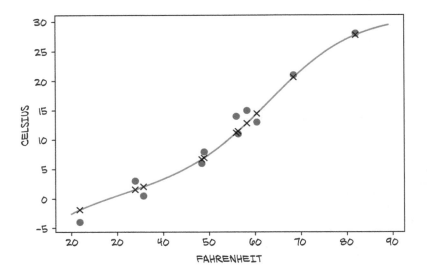

Figure 6.9 The plot of our neural network model, with input data (circles) and model output (Xs). The continuous line shows behavior between samples.

6.4   *Conclusion*

We've covered a lot in chapters 5 and 6, although we have been dealing with a very simple problem. We dissected building differentiable models and training them using gradient descent, first using raw autograd and then relying on nn. By now you should have confidence in your understanding of what's going on behind the scenes. Hopefully this taste of PyTorch has given you an appetite for more!

6.5   *Exercises*

1 Experiment with the number of hidden neurons in our simple neural network model, as well as the learning rate.

   a What changes result in more linear output from the model?

   b Can you get the model to obviously overfit the data?

2 The third-hardest problem in physics is finding a proper wine to celebrate discoveries. Load the wine data from chapter 4, and create a new model with the appropriate number of input parameters.

a How long does it take to train compared to the temperature data we have been using?

b Can you explain what factors contribute to the training times?

c Can you get the loss to decrease while training on this dataset?

d How would you go about graphing this dataset?

6.6 Summary

- Neural networks can be automatically adapted to specialize themselves on the problem at hand.

- Neural networks allow easy access to the analytical derivatives of the loss with respect to any parameter in the model, which makes evolving the parameters very efficient. Thanks to its automated differentiation engine, PyTorch provides such derivatives effortlessly.

- Activation functions around linear transformations make neural networks capable of approximating highly nonlinear functions, at the same time keeping them simple enough to optimize.

- The nn module together with the tensor standard library provide all the building blocks for creating neural networks.

- To recognize overfitting, it's essential to maintain the training set of data points separate from the validation set. There's no one recipe to combat overfitting, but getting more data, or more variability in the data, and resorting to simpler models are good starts.

- Anyone doing data science should be plotting data all the time.

Telling birds
from airplanes:
Learning from images

This chapter covers

- Building a feed-forward neural network
- Loading data using `Datasets` and `DataLoaders`
- Understanding classification loss

The last chapter gave us the opportunity to dive into the inner mechanics of learning through gradient descent, and the facilities that PyTorch offers to build models and optimize them. We did so using a simple regression model of one input and one output, which allowed us to have everything in plain sight but admittedly was only borderline exciting.

In this chapter, we'll keep moving ahead with building our neural network foundations. This time, we'll turn our attention to images. Image recognition is arguably the task that made the world realize the potential of deep learning.

We will approach a simple image recognition problem step by step, building from a simple neural network like the one we defined in the last chapter. This time, instead of a tiny dataset of numbers, we'll use a more extensive dataset of tiny images. Let's download the dataset first and get to work preparing it for use.

7.1 A dataset of tiny images

There is nothing like an intuitive understanding of a subject, and there is nothing to achieve that like working on simple data. One of the most basic datasets for image recognition is the handwritten digit-recognition dataset known as MNIST. Here we will use another dataset that is similarly simple and a bit more fun. It's called CIFAR-10, and, like its sibling CIFAR-100, it has been a computer vision classic for a decade.

CIFAR-10 consists of 60,000 tiny 32 × 32 color (RGB) images, labeled with an integer corresponding to 1 of 10 classes: airplane (0), automobile (1), bird (2), cat (3), deer (4), dog (5), frog (6), horse (7), ship (8), and truck (9).[1] Nowadays, CIFAR-10 is considered too simple for developing or validating new research, but it serves our learning purposes just fine. We will use the torchvision module to automatically download the dataset and load it as a collection of PyTorch tensors. Figure 7.1 gives us a taste of CIFAR-10.

Figure 7.1 Image samples from all CIFAR-10 classes

---

[1] The images were collected and labeled by Krizhevsky, Nair, and Hinton of the Canadian Institute For Advanced Research (CIFAR) and were drawn from a larger collection of unlabeled 32 × 32 color images: the "80 million tiny images dataset" from the Computer Science and Artificial Intelligence Laboratory (CSAIL) at the Massachusetts Institute of Technology.

7.1.1   Downloading CIFAR-10

As we anticipated, let's import torchvision and use the datasets module to download the CIFAR-10 data:

**Instantiates a dataset for the training data;
TorchVision downloads the data if it is not present.**

**With train=False, this gets us a
dataset for the validation data,
again downloading as necessary.**

```
# In[2]:
from torchvision import datasets
data_path = '../data-unversioned/p1ch7/'
cifar10 = datasets.CIFAR10(data_path, train=True, download=True)
cifar10_val = datasets.CIFAR10(data_path, train=False, download=True)
```

The first argument we provide to the CIFAR10 function is the location from which the data will be downloaded; the second specifies whether we're interested in the training set or the validation set; and the third says whether we allow PyTorch to download the data if it is not found in the location specified in the first argument.

Just like CIFAR10, the datasets submodule gives us precanned access to the most popular computer vision datasets, such as MNIST, Fashion-MNIST, CIFAR-100, SVHN, Coco, and Omniglot. In each case, the dataset is returned as a subclass of torch.utils.data.Dataset. We can see that the method-resolution order of our cifar10 instance includes it as a base class:

```
# In[4]:
type(cifar10).__mro__
```

```
# Out[4]:
(torchvision.datasets.cifar.CIFAR10,
 torchvision.datasets.vision.VisionDataset,
 torch.utils.data.dataset.Dataset,
 object)
```

7.1.2   The Dataset class

It's a good time to discover what being a subclass of torch.utils.data.Dataset means in practice. Looking at figure 7.2, we see what PyTorch Dataset is all about. It is an object that is required to implement two methods: __len__ and __getitem__. The former should return the number of items in the dataset; the latter should return the item, consisting of a sample and its corresponding label (an integer index).[2]

In practice, when a Python object is equipped with the __len__ method, we can pass it as an argument to the len Python built-in function:

```
# In[5]:
len(cifar10)
```

```
# Out[5]:
50000
```

---

[2]   For some advanced uses, PyTorch also provides IterableDataset. This can be used in cases like datasets in which random access to the data is prohibitively expensive or does not make sense: for example, because data is generated on the fly.

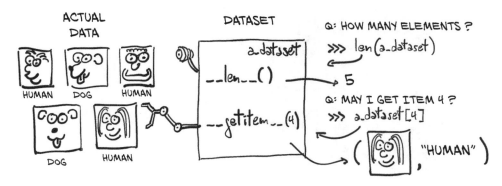

Figure 7.2 Concept of a PyTorch `Dataset` object: it doesn't necessarily hold the data, but it provides uniform access to it through __len__ and __getitem__.

Similarly, since the dataset is equipped with the __getitem__ method, we can use the standard subscript for indexing tuples and lists to access individual items. Here, we get a PIL (Python Imaging Library, the `PIL` package) image with our desired output—an integer with the value 1, corresponding to "automobile":

```
# In[6]:
img, label = cifar10[99]
img, label, class_names[label]

# Out[6]:
(<PIL.Image.Image image mode=RGB size=32x32 at 0x7FB383657390>,
 1,
 'automobile')
```

So, the sample in the `data.CIFAR10` dataset is an instance of an RGB PIL image. We can plot it right away:

```
# In[7]:
plt.imshow(img)
plt.show()
```

This produces the output shown in figure 7.3. It's a red car![3]

---

[3] It doesn't translate well to print; you'll take our word for it, or check it out in the eBook or the Jupyter Notebook.

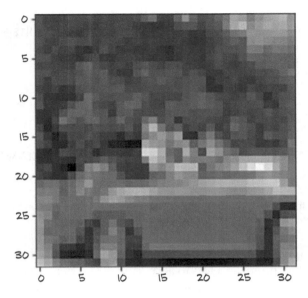

Figure 7.3   The 99th image from the CIFAR-10 dataset: an automobile

7.1.3   *Dataset transforms*

That's all very nice, but we'll likely need a way to convert the PIL image to a PyTorch tensor before we can do anything with it. That's where `torchvision.transforms` comes in. This module defines a set of composable, function-like objects that can be passed as an argument to a `torchvision` dataset such as `datasets.CIFAR10(…)`, and that perform transformations on the data after it is loaded but before it is returned by `__getitem__`. We can see the list of available objects as follows:

```
# In[8]:
from torchvision import transforms
dir(transforms)

# Out[8]:
['CenterCrop',
 'ColorJitter',
 ...
 'Normalize',
 'Pad',
 'RandomAffine',
 ...
 'RandomResizedCrop',
 'RandomRotation',
 'RandomSizedCrop',
 ...
 'TenCrop',
 'ToPILImage',
 'ToTensor',
 ...
]
```

Among those transforms, we can spot `ToTensor`, which turns NumPy arrays and PIL images to tensors. It also takes care to lay out the dimensions of the output tensor as $C \times H \times W$ (channel, height, width; just as we covered in chapter 4).

Let's try out the `ToTensor` transform. Once instantiated, it can be called like a function with the PIL image as the argument, returning a tensor as output:

```
# In[9]:
from torchvision import transforms

to_tensor = transforms.ToTensor()
img_t = to_tensor(img)
img_t.shape

# Out[9]:
torch.Size([3, 32, 32])
```

The image has been turned into a $3 \times 32 \times 32$ tensor and therefore a 3-channel (RGB) 32×32 image. Note that nothing has happened to `label`; it is still an integer.

As we anticipated, we can pass the transform directly as an argument to `dataset`
`.CIFAR10`:

```
# In[10]:
tensor_cifar10 = datasets.CIFAR10(data_path, train=True, download=False,
                       transform=transforms.ToTensor())
```

At this point, accessing an element of the dataset will return a tensor, rather than a PIL image:

```
# In[11]:
img_t, _ = tensor_cifar10[99]
type(img_t)

# Out[11]:
torch.Tensor
```

As expected, the shape has the channel as the first dimension, while the scalar type is `float32`:

```
# In[12]:
img_t.shape, img_t.dtype

# Out[12]:
(torch.Size([3, 32, 32]), torch.float32)
```

Whereas the values in the original PIL image ranged from 0 to 255 (8 bits per channel), the `ToTensor` transform turns the data into a 32-bit floating-point per channel, scaling the values down from 0.0 to 1.0. Let's verify that:

```
# In[13]:
img_t.min(), img_t.max()

# Out[13]:
(tensor(0.), tensor(1.))
```

And let's verify that we're getting the same image out:

```
# In[14]:
plt.imshow(img_t.permute(1, 2, 0))    ◁─┐  Changes the order of the axes from
plt.show()                              │  C × H × W to H × W × C

# Out[14]:
<Figure size 432x288 with 1 Axes>
```

As we can see in figure 7.4, we get the same output as before.

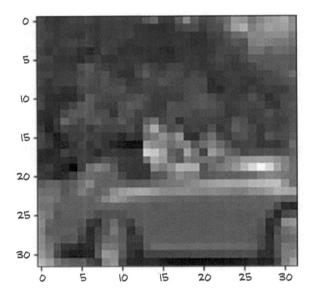

Figure 7.4   We've seen
this one already.

It checks. Note how we have to use `permute` to change the order of the axes from
C × H × W to H × W × C to match what Matplotlib expects.

7.1.4   *Normalizing data*

Transforms are really handy because we can chain them using `transforms.Compose`,
and they can handle normalization and data augmentation transparently, directly in
the data loader. For instance, it's good practice to normalize the dataset so that each
channel has zero mean and unitary standard deviation. We mentioned this in chapter
4, but now, after going through chapter 5, we also have an intuition for why: by choosing
activation functions that are linear around 0 plus or minus 1 (or 2), keeping the data
in the same range means it's more likely that neurons have nonzero gradients and,

hence, will learn sooner. Also, normalizing each channel so that it has the same distribution will ensure that channel information can be mixed and updated through gradient descent using the same learning rate. This is just like the situation in section 5.4.4 when we rescaled the weight to be of the same magnitude as the bias in our temperature-conversion model.

In order to make it so that each channel has zero mean and unitary standard deviation, we can compute the mean value and the standard deviation of each channel across the dataset and apply the following transform: v_n[c] = (v[c] - mean[c]) / stdev[c]. This is what transforms.Normalize does. The values of mean and stdev must be computed offline (they are not computed by the transform). Let's compute them for the CIFAR-10 training set.

Since the CIFAR-10 dataset is small, we'll be able to manipulate it entirely in memory. Let's stack all the tensors returned by the dataset along an extra dimension:

```
# In[15]:
imgs = torch.stack([img_t for img_t, _ in tensor_cifar10], dim=3)
imgs.shape

# Out[15]:
torch.Size([3, 32, 32, 50000])
```

Now we can easily compute the mean per channel:

```
# In[16]:
imgs.view(3, -1).mean(dim=1)          ◀──
```

Recall that view(3, -I) keeps the three channels and merges all the remaining dimensions into one, figuring out the appropriate size. Here our 3 × 32 × 32 image is transformed into a 3 × 1,024 vector, and then the mean is taken over the 1,024 elements of each channel.

```
# Out[16]:
tensor([0.4915, 0.4823, 0.4468])
```

Computing the standard deviation is similar:

```
# In[17]:
imgs.view(3, -1).std(dim=1)

# Out[17]:
tensor([0.2470, 0.2435, 0.2616])
```

With these numbers in our hands, we can initialize the Normalize transform

```
# In[18]:
transforms.Normalize((0.4915, 0.4823, 0.4468), (0.2470, 0.2435, 0.2616))

# Out[18]:
Normalize(mean=(0.4915, 0.4823, 0.4468), std=(0.247, 0.2435, 0.2616))
```

and concatenate it after the ToTensor transform:

```
# In[19]:
transformed_cifar10 = datasets.CIFAR10(
    data_path, train=True, download=False,
```

```
transform=transforms.Compose([
    transforms.ToTensor(),
    transforms.Normalize((0.4915, 0.4823, 0.4468),
                         (0.2470, 0.2435, 0.2616))
]))
```

Note that, at this point, plotting an image drawn from the dataset won't provide us with a faithful representation of the actual image:

```
# In[21]:
img_t, _ = transformed_cifar10[99]

plt.imshow(img_t.permute(1, 2, 0))
plt.show()
```

The renormalized red car we get is shown in figure 7.5. This is because normalization has shifted the RGB levels outside the 0.0 to 1.0 range and changed the overall magnitudes of the channels. All of the data is still there; it's just that Matplotlib renders it as black. We'll keep this in mind for the future.

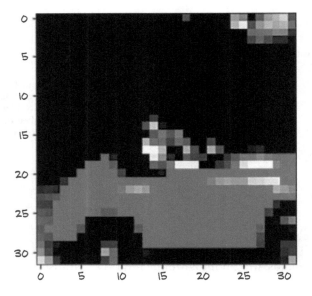

Figure 7.5 Our random CIFAR-10 image after normalization

Still, we have a fancy dataset loaded that contains tens of thousands of images! That's quite convenient, because we were going to need something exactly like it.

7.2 *Distinguishing birds from airplanes*

Jane, our friend at the bird-watching club, has set up a fleet of cameras in the woods south of the airport. The cameras are supposed to save a shot when something enters the frame and upload it to the club's real-time bird-watching blog. The problem is that a lot of planes coming and going from the airport end up triggering the camera,

Figure 7.6 **The problem at hand: we're going to help our friend tell birds from airplanes for her blog, by training a neural network to do the job.**

so Jane spends a lot of time deleting pictures of airplanes from the blog. What she needs is an automated system like that shown in figure 7.6. Instead of manually deleting, she needs a neural network—an AI if we're into fancy marketing speak—to throw away the airplanes right away.

No worries! We'll take care of that, no problem—we just got the perfect dataset for it (what a coincidence, right?). We'll pick out all the birds and airplanes from our CIFAR-10 dataset and build a neural network that can tell birds and airplanes apart.

7.2.1 *Building the dataset*

The first step is to get the data in the right shape. We could create a `Dataset` subclass that only includes birds and airplanes. However, the dataset is small, and we only need indexing and `len` to work on our dataset. It doesn't actually have to be a subclass of `torch.utils.data.dataset.Dataset`! Well, why not take a shortcut and just filter the data in `cifar10` and remap the labels so they are contiguous? Here's how:

```
# In[5]:
label_map = {0: 0, 2: 1}
class_names = ['airplane', 'bird']
cifar2 = [(img, label_map[label])
          for img, label in cifar10
          if label in [0, 2]]
cifar2_val = [(img, label_map[label])
              for img, label in cifar10_val
              if label in [0, 2]]
```

The cifar2 object satisfies the basic requirements for a Dataset—that is, __len__ and __getitem__ are defined—so we're going to use that. We should be aware, however, that this is a clever shortcut and we might wish to implement a proper Dataset if we hit limitations with it.[4]

We have a dataset! Next, we need a model to feed our data to.

7.2.2   *A fully connected model*

We learned how to build a neural network in chapter 5. We know that it's a tensor of features in, a tensor of features out. After all, an image is just a set of numbers laid out in a spatial configuration. OK, we don't know how to handle the spatial configuration part just yet, but in theory if we just take the image pixels and straighten them into a long 1D vector, we could consider those numbers as input features, right? This is what figure 7.7 illustrates.

Let's try that. How many features per sample? Well, 32 × 32 × 3: that is, 3,072 input features per sample. Starting from the model we built in chapter 5, our new model would be an nn.Linear with 3,072 input features and some number of hidden features,

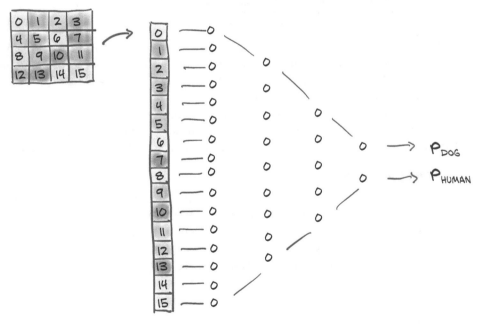

Figure 7.7   Treating our image as a 1D vector of values and training a fully connected classifier on it

---

[4]   Here, we built the new dataset manually and also wanted to remap the classes. In some cases, it may be enough to take a subset of the indices of a given dataset. This can be accomplished using the torch.utils .data.Subset class. Similarly, there is ConcatDataset to join datasets (of compatible items) into a larger one. For iterable datasets, ChainDataset gives a larger, iterable dataset.

followed by an activation, and then another nn.Linear that tapers the network down to an appropriate output number of features (2, for this use case):

```
# In[6]:
import torch.nn as nn

n_out = 2

model = nn.Sequential(
            nn.Linear(
                3072,
                512,
            ),
            nn.Tanh(),
            nn.Linear(
                512,
                n_out,
            )
        )
```

Input features ⟶ 3072

Hidden layer size ⟵ 512 / 512

Output classes ⟶ n_out,

We somewhat arbitrarily pick 512 hidden features. A neural network needs at least one hidden layer (of activations, so two modules) with a nonlinearity in between in order to be able to learn arbitrary functions in the way we discussed in section 6.3—otherwise, it would just be a linear model. The hidden features represent (learned) relations between the inputs encoded through the weight matrix. As such, the model might learn to "compare" vector elements 176 and 208, but it does not a priori focus on them because it is structurally unaware that these are, indeed (row 5, pixel 16) and (row 6, pixel 16), and thus adjacent.

So we have a model. Next we'll discuss what our model output should be.

7.2.3 *Output of a classifier*

In chapter 6, the network produced the predicted temperature (a number with a quantitative meaning) as output. We could do something similar here: make our network output a single scalar value (so n_out = 1), cast the labels to floats (0.0 for airplane and 1.0 for bird), and use those as a target for MSELoss (the average of squared differences in the batch). Doing so, we would cast the problem into a regression problem. However, looking more closely, we are now dealing with something a bit different in nature.[5]

We need to recognize that the output is categorical: it's either a bird or an airplane (or something else if we had all 10 of the original classes). As we learned in chapter 4, when we have to represent a categorical variable, we should switch to a one-hot-encoding representation of that variable, such as [1, 0] for airplane or [0, 1]

---

[5] Using distance on the "probability" vectors would already have been much better than using MSELoss with the class numbers—which, recalling our discussion of types of values in the sidebar "Continuous, ordinal, and categorical values" from chapter 4, does not make sense for categories and does not work at all in practice. Still, MSELoss is not very well suited to classification problems.

for bird (the order is arbitrary). This will still work if we have 10 classes, as in the full CIFAR-10 dataset; we'll just have a vector of length 10.[6]

In the ideal case, the network would output `torch.tensor([1.0, 0.0])` for an airplane and `torch.tensor([0.0, 1.0])` for a bird. Practically speaking, since our classifier will not be perfect, we can expect the network to output something in between. The key realization in this case is that we can interpret our output as probabilities: the first entry is the probability of "airplane," and the second is the probability of "bird."

Casting the problem in terms of probabilities imposes a few extra constraints on the outputs of our network:

- Each element of the output must be in the `[0.0, 1.0]` range (a probability of an outcome cannot be less than 0 or greater than 1).
- The elements of the output must add up to 1.0 (we're certain that one of the two outcomes will occur).

It sounds like a tough constraint to enforce in a differentiable way on a vector of numbers. Yet there's a very smart trick that does exactly that, and it's differentiable: it's called *softmax*.

7.2.4   *Representing the output as probabilities*

Softmax is a function that takes a vector of values and produces another vector of the same dimension, where the values satisfy the constraints we just listed to represent probabilities. The expression for softmax is shown in figure 7.8.

That is, we take the elements of the vector, compute the elementwise exponential, and divide each element by the sum of exponentials. In code, it's something like this:

```
# In[7]:
def softmax(x):
    return torch.exp(x) / torch.exp(x).sum()
```

Let's test it on an input vector:

```
# In[8]:
x = torch.tensor([1.0, 2.0, 3.0])

softmax(x)

# Out[8]:
tensor([0.0900, 0.2447, 0.6652])
```

---

[6] For the special binary classification case, using two values here is redundant, as one is always 1 minus the other. And indeed PyTorch lets us output only a single probability using the `nn.Sigmoid` activation at the end of the model to get a probability and the binary cross-entropy loss function `nn.BCELoss`. There also is an `nn.BCELossWithLogits` merging these two steps.

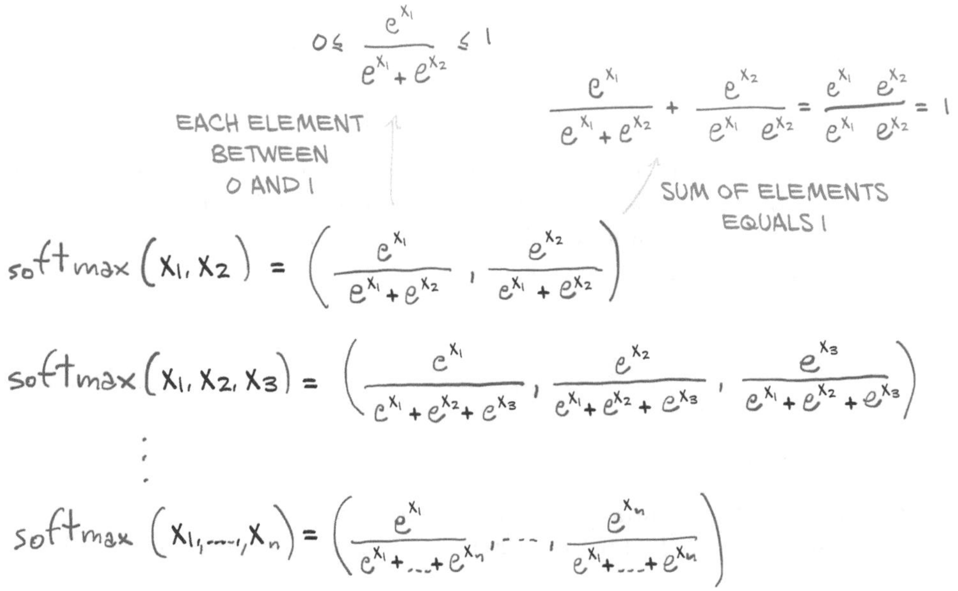

$$0 \leq \frac{e^{x_1}}{e^{x_1} + e^{x_2}} \leq 1$$

EACH ELEMENT
BETWEEN
0 AND 1

$$\frac{e^{x_1}}{e^{x_1} + e^{x_2}} + \frac{e^{x_2}}{e^{x_1} e^{x_2}} = \frac{e^{x_1}}{e^{x_1}} \frac{e^{x_2}}{e^{x_2}} = 1$$

SUM OF ELEMENTS
EQUALS 1

$$\text{softmax}\left(x_1, x_2\right) = \left(\frac{e^{x_1}}{e^{x_1} + e^{x_2}}, \frac{e^{x_2}}{e^{x_1} + e^{x_2}}\right)$$

$$\text{softmax}\left(x_1, x_2, x_3\right) = \left(\frac{e^{x_1}}{e^{x_1} + e^{x_2} + e^{x_3}}, \frac{e^{x_2}}{e^{x_1} + e^{x_2} + e^{x_3}}, \frac{e^{x_3}}{e^{x_1} + e^{x_2} + e^{x_3}}\right)$$

$$\vdots$$

$$\text{softmax}\left(x_1, \ldots, x_n\right) = \left(\frac{e^{x_1}}{e^{x_1} + \ldots + e^{x_n}}, \ldots, \frac{e^{x_n}}{e^{x_1} + \ldots + e^{x_n}}\right)$$

Figure 7.8   Handwritten softmax

As expected, it satisfies the constraints on probability:

```
# In[9]:
softmax(x).sum()

# Out[9]:
tensor(1.)
```

Softmax is a monotone function, in that lower values in the input will correspond to lower values in the output. However, it's not *scale invariant*, in that the ratio between values is not preserved. In fact, the ratio between the first and second elements of the input is 0.5, while the ratio between the elements in the output is 0.3678. This is not a real issue, since the learning process will drive the parameters of the model in a way that values have appropriate ratios.

The nn module makes softmax available as a module. Since, as usual, input tensors may have an additional batch 0th dimension, or have dimensions along which they encode probabilities and others in which they don't, nn.Softmax requires us to specify the dimension along which the softmax function is applied:

```
# In[10]:
softmax = nn.Softmax(dim=1)

x = torch.tensor([[1.0, 2.0, 3.0],
                  [1.0, 2.0, 3.0]])
```

```
softmax(x)

# Out[10]:
tensor([[0.0900, 0.2447, 0.6652],
        [0.0900, 0.2447, 0.6652]])
```

In this case, we have two input vectors in two rows (just like when we work with batches), so we initialize nn.Softmax to operate along dimension 1.

Excellent! We can now add a softmax at the end of our model, and our network will be equipped to produce probabilities:

```
# In[11]:
model = nn.Sequential(
            nn.Linear(3072, 512),
            nn.Tanh(),
            nn.Linear(512, 2),
            nn.Softmax(dim=1))
```

We can actually try running the model before even training it. Let's do it, just to see what comes out. We first build a batch of one image, our bird (figure 7.9):

```
# In[12]:
img, _ = cifar2[0]

plt.imshow(img.permute(1, 2, 0))
plt.show()
```

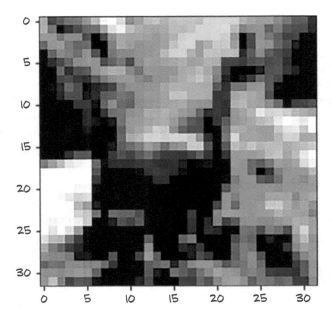

Figure 7.9 A random bird from the CIFAR-10 dataset (after normalization)

Oh, hello there. In order to call the model, we need to make the input have the right dimensions. We recall that our model expects 3,072 features in the input, and that nn works with data organized into batches along the zeroth dimension. So we need to turn our $3 \times 32 \times 32$ image into a 1D tensor and then add an extra dimension in the zeroth position. We learned how to do this in chapter 3:

```
# In[13]:
img_batch = img.view(-1).unsqueeze(0)
```

Now we're ready to invoke our model:

```
# In[14]:
out = model(img_batch)
out

# Out[14]:
tensor([[0.4784, 0.5216]], grad_fn=<SoftmaxBackward>)
```

So, we got probabilities! Well, we know we shouldn't get too excited: the weights and biases of our linear layers have not been trained at all. Their elements are initialized randomly by PyTorch between –1.0 and 1.0. Interestingly, we also see grad_fn for the output, which is the tip of the backward computation graph (it will be used as soon as we need to backpropagate).[7]

In addition, while we know which output probability is supposed to be which (recall our class_names), our network has no indication of that. Is the first entry "airplane" and the second "bird," or the other way around? The network can't even tell that at this point. It's the loss function that associates a meaning with these two numbers, after backpropagation. If the labels are provided as index 0 for "airplane" and index 1 for "bird," then that's the order the outputs will be induced to take. Thus, after training, we will be able to get the label as an index by computing the *argmax* of the output probabilities: that is, the index at which we get the maximum probability. Conveniently, when supplied with a dimension, torch.max returns the maximum element along that dimension as well as the index at which that value occurs. In our case, we need to take the max along the probability vector (not across batches), therefore, dimension 1:

```
# In[15]:
_, index = torch.max(out, dim=1)

index

# Out[15]:
tensor([1])
```

---

[7] While it is, in principle, possible to say that here the model is uncertain (because it assigns 48% and 52% probabilities to the two classes), it will turn out that typical training results in highly overconfident models. Bayesian neural networks can provide some remedy, but they are beyond the scope of this book.

It says the image is a bird. Pure luck. But we have adapted our model output to the classification task at hand by getting it to output probabilities. We also have now run our model against an input image and verified that our plumbing works. Time to get training. As in the previous two chapters, we need a loss to minimize during training.

7.2.5 *A loss for classifying*

We just mentioned that the loss is what gives probabilities meaning. In chapters 5 and 6, we used mean square error (MSE) as our loss. We could still use MSE and make our output probabilities converge to [0.0, 1.0] and [1.0, 0.0]. However, thinking about it, we're not really interested in reproducing these values exactly. Looking back at the argmax operation we used to extract the index of the predicted class, what we're really interested in is that the first probability is higher than the second for airplanes and vice versa for birds. In other words, we want to penalize misclassifications rather than painstakingly penalize everything that doesn't look exactly like a 0.0 or 1.0.

What we need to maximize in this case is the probability associated with the correct class, out[class_index], where out is the output of softmax and class_index is a vector containing 0 for "airplane" and 1 for "bird" for each sample. This quantity—that is, the probability associated with the correct class—is referred to as the *likelihood* (of our model's parameters, given the data).[8] In other words, we want a loss function that is very high when the likelihood is low: so low that the alternatives have a higher probability. Conversely, the loss should be low when the likelihood is higher than the alternatives, and we're not really fixated on driving the probability up to 1.

There's a loss function that behaves that way, and it's called *negative log likelihood* (NLL). It has the expression NLL = - sum(log(out_i[c_i])), where the sum is taken over *N* samples and c_i is the correct class for sample *i*. Let's take a look at figure 7.10, which shows the NLL as a function of predicted probability.

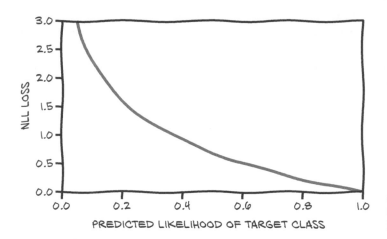

Figure 7.10 **The NLL loss as a function of the predicted probabilities**

---

[8] For a succinct definition of the terminology, refer to David MacKay's *Information Theory, Inference, and Learning Algorithms* (Cambridge University Press, 2003), section 2.3.

The figure shows that when low probabilities are assigned to the data, the NLL grows to infinity, whereas it decreases at a rather shallow rate when probabilities are greater than 0.5. Remember that the NLL takes probabilities as input; so, as the likelihood grows, the other probabilities will necessarily decrease.

Summing up, our loss for classification can be computed as follows. For each sample in the batch:

1 Run the forward pass, and obtain the output values from the last (linear) layer.
2 Compute their softmax, and obtain probabilities.
3 Take the predicted probability corresponding to the correct class (the likelihood of the parameters). Note that we know what the correct class is because it's a supervised problem—it's our ground truth.
4 Compute its logarithm, slap a minus sign in front of it, and add it to the loss.

So, how do we do this in PyTorch? PyTorch has an nn.NLLLoss class. However (gotcha ahead), as opposed to what you might expect, it does not take probabilities but rather takes a tensor of log probabilities as input. It then computes the NLL of our model given the batch of data. There's a good reason behind the input convention: taking the logarithm of a probability is tricky when the probability gets close to zero. The workaround is to use nn.LogSoftmax instead of nn.Softmax, which takes care to make the calculation numerically stable.

We can now modify our model to use nn.LogSoftmax as the output module:

```
model = nn.Sequential(
            nn.Linear(3072, 512),
            nn.Tanh(),
            nn.Linear(512, 2),
            nn.LogSoftmax(dim=1))
```

Then we instantiate our NLL loss:

```
loss = nn.NLLLoss()
```

The loss takes the output of nn.LogSoftmax for a batch as the first argument and a tensor of class indices (zeros and ones, in our case) as the second argument. We can now test it with our birdie:

```
img, label = cifar2[0]

out = model(img.view(-1).unsqueeze(0))

loss(out, torch.tensor([label]))

tensor(0.6509, grad_fn=<NllLossBackward>)
```

Ending our investigation of losses, we can look at how using cross-entropy loss improves over MSE. In figure 7.11, we see that the cross-entropy loss has some slope when the prediction is off target (in the low-loss corner, the correct class is assigned a predicted probability of 99.97%), while the MSE we dismissed at the beginning saturates much earlier and—crucially—also for very wrong predictions. The underlying reason is that the slope of the MSE is too low to compensate for the flatness of the softmax function for wrong predictions. This is why the MSE for probabilities is not a good fit for classification work.

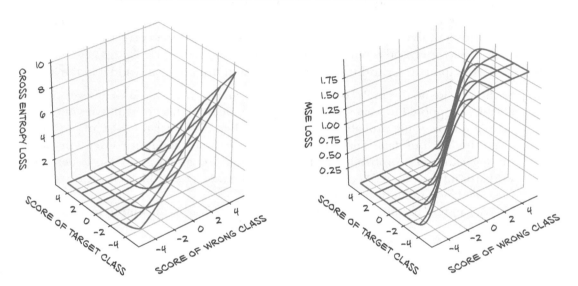

Figure 7.11   The cross entropy (left) and MSE between predicted probabilities and the target probability vector (right) as functions of the predicted scores—that is, before the (log-) softmax

7.2.6   *Training the classifier*

All right! We're ready to bring back the training loop we wrote in chapter 5 and see how it trains (the process is illustrated in figure 7.12):

```
import torch
import torch.nn as nn

model = nn.Sequential(
            nn.Linear(3072, 512),
            nn.Tanh(),
            nn.Linear(512, 2),
            nn.LogSoftmax(dim=1))

learning_rate = 1e-2

optimizer = optim.SGD(model.parameters(), lr=learning_rate)
```

Distinguishing birds from airplanes

```
loss_fn = nn.NLLLoss()

n_epochs = 100

for epoch in range(n_epochs):
    for img, label in cifar2:
        out = model(img.view(-1).unsqueeze(0))
        loss = loss_fn(out, torch.tensor([label]))

        optimizer.zero_grad()
        loss.backward()
        optimizer.step()

    print("Epoch: %d, Loss: %f" % (epoch, float(loss)))
```

Prints the loss for the last image. In the next chapter, we will improve our output to give an average over the entire epoch.

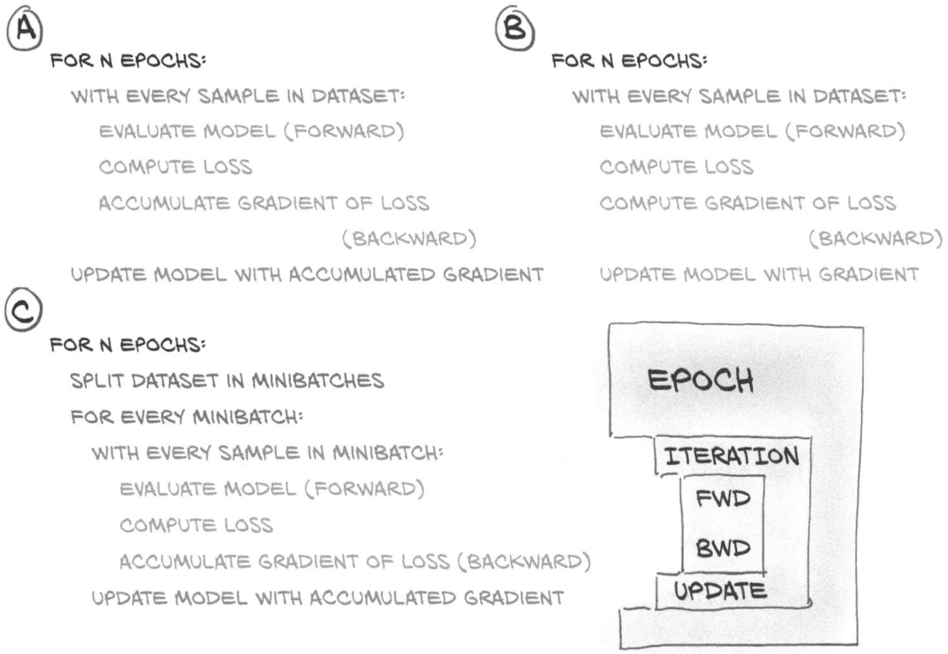

(A)

FOR N EPOCHS:

  WITH EVERY SAMPLE IN DATASET:

    EVALUATE MODEL (FORWARD)

    COMPUTE LOSS

    ACCUMULATE GRADIENT OF LOSS

         (BACKWARD)

  UPDATE MODEL WITH ACCUMULATED GRADIENT

(B)

FOR N EPOCHS:

  WITH EVERY SAMPLE IN DATASET:

    EVALUATE MODEL (FORWARD)

    COMPUTE LOSS

    COMPUTE GRADIENT OF LOSS

         (BACKWARD)

  UPDATE MODEL WITH GRADIENT

(C)

FOR N EPOCHS:

  SPLIT DATASET IN MINIBATCHES

  FOR EVERY MINIBATCH:

    WITH EVERY SAMPLE IN MINIBATCH:

      EVALUATE MODEL (FORWARD)

      COMPUTE LOSS

      ACCUMULATE GRADIENT OF LOSS (BACKWARD)

    UPDATE MODEL WITH ACCUMULATED GRADIENT

EPOCH

ITERATION

FWD

BWD

UPDATE

Figure 7.12 Training loops: (A) averaging updates over the whole dataset; (B) updating the model at each sample; (C) averaging updates over minibatches

Looking more closely, we made a small change to the training loop. In chapter 5, we had just one loop: over the epochs (recall that an epoch ends when all samples in the training set have been evaluated). We figured that evaluating all 10,000 images in a single batch would be too much, so we decided to have an inner loop where we evaluate one sample at a time and backpropagate over that single sample.

While in the first case the gradient is accumulated over all samples before being applied, in this case we apply changes to parameters based on a very partial estimation of the gradient on a single sample. However, what is a good direction for reducing the loss based on one sample might not be a good direction for others. By shuffling samples at each epoch and estimating the gradient on one or (preferably, for stability) a few samples at a time, we are effectively introducing randomness in our gradient descent. Remember SGD? It stands for *stochastic gradient descent*, and this is what the *S* is about: working on small batches (aka minibatches) of shuffled data. It turns out that following gradients estimated over minibatches, which are poorer approximations of gradients estimated across the whole dataset, helps convergence and prevents the optimization process from getting stuck in local minima it encounters along the way. As depicted in figure 7.13, gradients from minibatches are randomly off the ideal trajectory, which is part of the reason why we want to use a reasonably small learning rate. Shuffling the dataset at each epoch helps ensure that the sequence of gradients estimated over minibatches is representative of the gradients computed across the full dataset.

Typically, minibatches are a constant size that we need to set prior to training, just like the learning rate. These are called *hyperparameters*, to distinguish them from the parameters of a model.

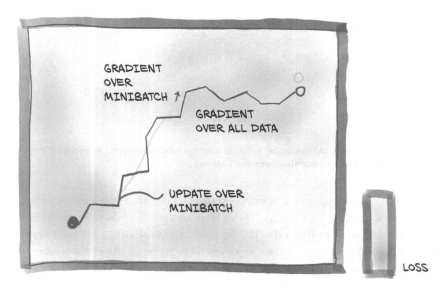

Figure 7.13   Gradient descent averaged over the whole dataset (light path) versus stochastic gradient descent, where the gradient is estimated on randomly picked minibatches

In our training code, we chose minibatches of size 1 by picking one item at a time from the dataset. The `torch.utils.data` module has a class that helps with shuffling and organizing the data in minibatches: `DataLoader`. The job of a data loader is to sample minibatches from a dataset, giving us the flexibility to choose from different sampling strategies. A very common strategy is uniform sampling after shuffling the data at each epoch. Figure 7.14 shows the data loader shuffling the indices it gets from the `Dataset`.

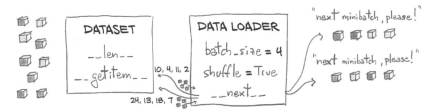

Figure 7.14 A data loader dispensing minibatches by using a dataset to sample individual data items

Let's see how this is done. At a minimum, the `DataLoader` constructor takes a `Dataset` object as input, along with `batch_size` and a `shuffle` Boolean that indicates whether the data needs to be shuffled at the beginning of each epoch:

```
train_loader = torch.utils.data.DataLoader(cifar2, batch_size=64,
                                           shuffle=True)
```

A `DataLoader` can be iterated over, so we can use it directly in the inner loop of our new training code:

```
import torch
import torch.nn as nn

train_loader = torch.utils.data.DataLoader(cifar2, batch_size=64,
                                           shuffle=True)

model = nn.Sequential(
            nn.Linear(3072, 512),
            nn.Tanh(),
            nn.Linear(512, 2),
            nn.LogSoftmax(dim=1))

learning_rate = 1e-2

optimizer = optim.SGD(model.parameters(), lr=learning_rate)

loss_fn = nn.NLLLoss()

n_epochs = 100

for epoch in range(n_epochs):
    for imgs, labels in train_loader:
```

```
batch_size = imgs.shape[0]
outputs = model(imgs.view(batch_size, -1))
loss = loss_fn(outputs, labels)

optimizer.zero_grad()
loss.backward()
optimizer.step()

print("Epoch: %d, Loss: %f" % (epoch, float(loss)))
```

Due to the shuffling, this now prints the loss for a random batch—clearly something we want to improve in chapter 8.

At each inner iteration, `imgs` is a tensor of size $64 \times 3 \times 32 \times 32$—that is, a minibatch of 64 (32×32) RGB images—while `labels` is a tensor of size 64 containing label indices. Let's run our training:

```
Epoch: 0, Loss: 0.523478
Epoch: 1, Loss: 0.391083
Epoch: 2, Loss: 0.407412
Epoch: 3, Loss: 0.364203
...
Epoch: 96, Loss: 0.019537
Epoch: 97, Loss: 0.008973
Epoch: 98, Loss: 0.002607
Epoch: 99, Loss: 0.026200
```

We see that the loss decreases somehow, but we have no idea whether it's low enough. Since our goal here is to correctly assign classes to images, and preferably do that on an independent dataset, we can compute the accuracy of our model on the validation set in terms of the number of correct classifications over the total:

```
val_loader = torch.utils.data.DataLoader(cifar2_val, batch_size=64,
                                          shuffle=False)

correct = 0
total = 0

with torch.no_grad():
    for imgs, labels in val_loader:
        batch_size = imgs.shape[0]
        outputs = model(imgs.view(batch_size, -1))
        _, predicted = torch.max(outputs, dim=1)
        total += labels.shape[0]
        correct += int((predicted == labels).sum())

print("Accuracy: %f", correct / total)

Accuracy: 0.794000
```

Not a great performance, but quite a lot better than random. In our defense, our model was quite a shallow classifier; it's a miracle that it worked at all. It did because our dataset is really simple—a lot of the samples in the two classes likely have systematic differences (such as the color of the background) that help the model tell birds from airplanes, based on a few pixels.

We can certainly add some bling to our model by including more layers, which will increase the model's depth and capacity. One rather arbitrary possibility is

```
model = nn.Sequential(
            nn.Linear(3072, 1024),
            nn.Tanh(),
            nn.Linear(1024, 512),
            nn.Tanh(),
            nn.Linear(512, 128),
            nn.Tanh(),
            nn.Linear(128, 2),
            nn.LogSoftmax(dim=1))
```

Here we are trying to taper the number of features more gently toward the output, in the hope that intermediate layers will do a better job of squeezing information in increasingly shorter intermediate outputs.

The combination of nn.LogSoftmax and nn.NLLLoss is equivalent to using nn.CrossEntropyLoss. This terminology is a particularity of PyTorch, as the nn.NLLoss computes, in fact, the cross entropy but with log probability predictions as inputs where nn.CrossEntropyLoss takes scores (sometimes called *logits*). Technically, nn.NLLLoss is the cross entropy between the Dirac distribution, putting all mass on the target, and the predicted distribution given by the log probability inputs.

To add to the confusion, in information theory, up to normalization by sample size, this cross entropy can be interpreted as a negative log likelihood of the predicted distribution under the target distribution as an outcome. So both losses are the negative log likelihood of the model parameters given the data when our model predicts the (softmax-applied) probabilities. In this book, we won't rely on these details, but don't let the PyTorch naming confuse you when you see the terms used in the literature.

It is quite common to drop the last nn.LogSoftmax layer from the network and use nn.CrossEntropyLoss as a loss. Let us try that:

```
model = nn.Sequential(
            nn.Linear(3072, 1024),
            nn.Tanh(),
            nn.Linear(1024, 512),
            nn.Tanh(),
            nn.Linear(512, 128),
            nn.Tanh(),
            nn.Linear(128, 2))

loss_fn = nn.CrossEntropyLoss()
```

Note that the numbers will be *exactly* the same as with nn.LogSoftmax and nn.NLLLoss. It's just more convenient to do it all in one pass, with the only gotcha being that the output of our model will not be interpretable as probabilities (or log probabilities). We'll need to explicitly pass the output through a softmax to obtain those.

Training this model and evaluating the accuracy on the validation set (0.802000) lets us appreciate that a larger model bought us an increase in accuracy, but not that much. The accuracy on the training set is practically perfect (0.998100). What is this telling us? That we are overfitting our model in both cases. Our fully connected model is finding a way to discriminate birds and airplanes on the training set by memorizing the training set, but performance on the validation set is not all that great, even if we choose a larger model.

PyTorch offers a quick way to determine how many parameters a model has through the `parameters()` method of `nn.Model` (the same method we use to provide the parameters to the optimizer). To find out how many elements are in each tensor instance, we can call the `numel` method. Summing those gives us our total count. Depending on our use case, counting parameters might require us to check whether a parameter has `requires_grad` set to `True`, as well. We might want to differentiate the number of *trainable* parameters from the overall model size. Let's take a look at what we have right now:

```
# In[7]:
numel_list = [p.numel()
              for p in connected_model.parameters()
              if p.requires_grad == True]
sum(numel_list), numel_list

# Out[7]:
(3737474, [3145728, 1024, 524288, 512, 65536, 128, 256, 2])
```

Wow, 3.7 million parameters! Not a small network for such a small input image, is it? Even our first network was pretty large:

```
# In[9]:
numel_list = [p.numel() for p in first_model.parameters()]
sum(numel_list), numel_list

# Out[9]:
(1574402, [1572864, 512, 1024, 2])
```

The number of parameters in our first model is roughly half that in our latest model. Well, from the list of individual parameter sizes, we start having an idea what's responsible: the first module, which has 1.5 million parameters. In our full network, we had 1,024 output features, which led the first linear module to have 3 million parameters. This shouldn't be unexpected: we know that a linear layer computes $y = $ `weight * x + bias`, and if x has length 3,072 (disregarding the batch dimension for simplicity) and y must have length 1,024, then the `weight` tensor needs to be of size $1{,}024 \times 3{,}072$ and the `bias` size must be 1,024. And $1{,}024 * 3{,}072 + 1{,}024 = 3{,}146{,}752$, as we found earlier. We can verify these quantities directly:

```
# In[10]:
linear = nn.Linear(3072, 1024)

linear.weight.shape, linear.bias.shape

# Out[10]:
(torch.Size([1024, 3072]), torch.Size([1024]))
```

What is this telling us? That our neural network won't scale very well with the number of pixels. What if we had a 1,024 × 1,024 RGB image? That's 3.1 million input values. Even abruptly going to 1,024 hidden features (which is not going to work for our classifier), we would have over 3 *billion* parameters. Using 32-bit floats, we're already at 12 GB of RAM, and we haven't even hit the second layer, much less computed and stored the gradients. That's just not going to fit on most present-day GPUs.

7.2.7 *The limits of going fully connected*

Let's reason about what using a linear module on a 1D view of our image entails—figure 7.15 shows what is going on. It's like taking every single input value—that is, every single component in our RGB image—and computing a linear combination of it with all the other values for every output feature. On one hand, we are allowing for the combination of any pixel with every other pixel in the image being potentially relevant for our task. On the other hand, we aren't utilizing the relative position of neighboring or faraway pixels, since we are treating the image as one big vector of numbers.

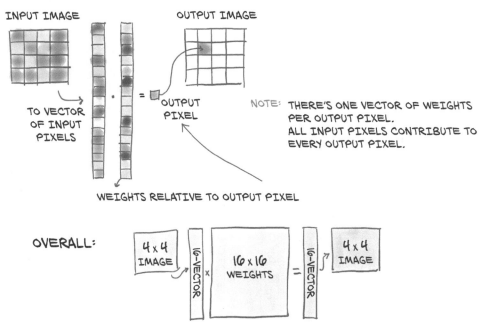

Figure 7.15 Using a fully connected module with an input image: every input pixel is combined with every other to produce each element in the output.

An airplane flying in the sky captured in a 32 × 32 image will be very roughly similar to a dark, cross-like shape on a blue background. A fully connected network as in figure 7.15 would need to learn that when pixel 0,1 is dark, pixel 1,1 is also dark, and so on, that's a good indication of an airplane. This is illustrated in the top half of figure 7.16. However, shift the same airplane by one pixel or more as in the bottom half of the figure, and the relationships between pixels will have to be relearned from scratch: this time, an airplane is likely when pixel 0,2 is dark, pixel 1,2 is dark, and so on. In more technical terms, a fully connected network is not *translation invariant*. This means a network that has been trained to recognize a Spitfire starting at position 4,4 will not be able to recognize the *exact same* Spitfire starting at position 8,8. We would then have to *augment* the dataset—that is, apply random translations to images during training—so the network would have a chance to see Spitfires all over the image, and we would need to do this for every image in the dataset (for the record, we could concatenate a

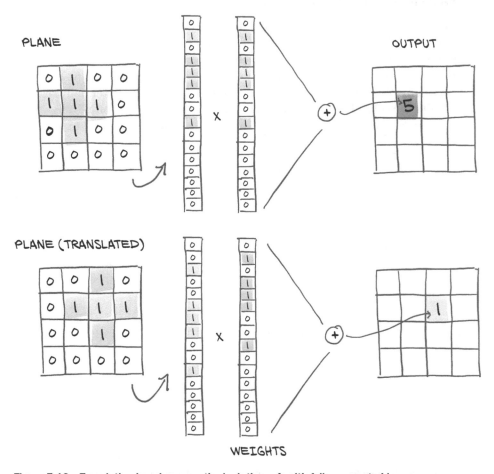

Figure 7.16   Translation invariance, or the lack thereof, with fully connected layers

transform from `torchvision.transforms` to do this transparently). However, this *data augmentation* strategy comes at a cost: the number of hidden features—that is, of parameters—must be large enough to store the information about all of these translated replicas.

So, at the end of this chapter, we have a dataset, a model, and a training loop, and our model learns. However, due to a mismatch between our problem and our network structure, we end up overfitting our training data, rather than learning the generalized features of what we want the model to detect.

We've created a model that allows for relating every pixel to every other pixel in the image, regardless of their spatial arrangement. We have a reasonable assumption that pixels that are closer together are in theory a lot more related, though. This means we are training a classifier that is not translation-invariant, so we're forced to use a lot of capacity for learning translated replicas if we want to hope to do well on the validation set. There has to be a better way, right?

Of course, most such questions in a book like this are rhetorical. The solution to our current set of problems is to change our model to use convolutional layers. We'll cover what that means in the next chapter.

7.3   *Conclusion*

In this chapter, we have solved a simple classification problem from dataset, to model, to minimizing an appropriate loss in a training loop. All of these things will be standard tools for your PyTorch toolbelt, and the skills needed to use them will be useful throughout your PyTorch tenure.

We've also found a severe shortcoming of our model: we have been treating 2D images as 1D data. Also, we do not have a natural way to incorporate the translation invariance of our problem. In the next chapter, you'll learn how to exploit the 2D nature of image data to get much better results.[9]

We could use what we have learned right away to process data without this translation invariance. For example, using it on tabular data or the time-series data we met in chapter 4, we can probably do great things already. To some extent, it would also be possible to use it on text data that is appropriately represented.[10]

7.4   *Exercises*

1   Use `torchvision` to implement random cropping of the data.
   a   How are the resulting images different from the uncropped originals?
   b   What happens when you request the same image a second time?
   c   What is the result of training using randomly cropped images?

---

[9]   The same caveat about translation invariance also applies to purely 1D data: an audio classifier should likely produce the same output even if the sound to be classified starts a tenth of a second earlier or later.

[10]   *Bag-of-words models*, which just average over word embeddings, can be processed with the network design from this chapter. More contemporary models take the positions of the words into account and need more advanced models.

2 Switch loss functions (perhaps MSE).

  a Does the training behavior change?

3 Is it possible to reduce the capacity of the network enough that it stops overfitting?

  a How does the model perform on the validation set when doing so?

7.5   Summary

- Computer vision is one of the most extensive applications of deep learning.
- Several datasets of annotated images are publicly available; many of them can be accessed via `torchvision`.
- `Datasets` and `DataLoaders` provide a simple yet effective abstraction for loading and sampling datasets.
- For a classification task, using the softmax function on the output of a network produces values that satisfy the requirements for being interpreted as probabilities. The ideal loss function for classification in this case is obtained by using the output of softmax as the input of a non-negative log likelihood function. The combination of softmax and such loss is called cross entropy in PyTorch.
- Nothing prevents us from treating images as vectors of pixel values, dealing with them using a fully connected network, just like any other numerical data. However, doing so makes it much harder to take advantage of the spatial relationships in the data.
- Simple models can be created using `nn.Sequential`.

Using convolutions
to generalize

This chapter covers

- Understanding convolution
- Building a convolutional neural network
- Creating custom `nn.Module` subclasses
- The difference between the module and functional APIs
- Design choices for neural networks

In the previous chapter, we built a simple neural network that could fit (or overfit) the data, thanks to the many parameters available for optimization in the linear layers. We had issues with our model, however, in that it was better at memorizing the training set than it was at generalizing properties of birds and airplanes. Based on our model architecture, we've got a guess as to why that's the case. Due to the fully connected setup needed to detect the various possible translations of the bird or airplane in the image, we have both too many parameters (making it easier for the model to memorize the training set) and no position independence (making it harder to generalize). As we discussed in the last chapter, we could augment our training data by using a wide variety of recropped images to try to force generalization, but that won't address the issue of having too many parameters.

There is a better way! It consists of replacing the dense, fully connected affine transformation in our neural network unit with a different linear operation: convolution.

8.1 The case for convolutions

Let's get to the bottom of what convolutions are and how we can use them in our neural networks. Yes, yes, we were in the middle of our quest to tell birds from airplanes, and our friend is still waiting for our solution, but this diversion is worth the extra time spent. We'll develop an intuition for this foundational concept in computer vision and then return to our problem equipped with superpowers.

In this section, we'll see how convolutions deliver locality and translation invariance. We'll do so by taking a close look at the formula defining convolutions and applying it using pen and paper—but don't worry, the gist will be in pictures, not formulas.

We said earlier that taking a 1D view of our input image and multiplying it by an n_output_features × n_input_features weight matrix, as is done in nn.Linear, means for each channel in the image, computing a weighted sum of all the pixels multiplied by a set of weights, one per output feature.

We also said that, if we want to recognize patterns corresponding to objects, like an airplane in the sky, we will likely need to look at how nearby pixels are arranged, and we will be less interested in how pixels that are far from each other appear in combination. Essentially, it doesn't matter if our image of a Spitfire has a tree or cloud or kite in the corner or not.

In order to translate this intuition into mathematical form, we could compute the weighted sum of a pixel with its immediate neighbors, rather than with all other pixels in the image. This would be equivalent to building weight matrices, one per output feature and output pixel location, in which all weights beyond a certain distance from a center pixel are zero. This will still be a weighted sum: that is, a linear operation.

8.1.1 What convolutions do

We identified one more desired property earlier: we would like these localized patterns to have an effect on the output regardless of their location in the image: that is, to be *translation invariant*. To achieve this goal in a matrix applied to the image-as-a-vector we used in chapter 7 would require implementing a rather complicated pattern of weights (don't worry if it is *too* complicated; it'll get better shortly): most of the weight matrix would be zero (for entries corresponding to input pixels too far away from the output pixel to have an influence). For other weights, we would have to find a way to keep entries in sync that correspond to the same relative position of input and output pixels. This means we would need to initialize them to the same values and ensure that all these *tied* weights stayed the same while the network is updated during training. This way, we would ensure that weights operate in neighborhoods to respond to local patterns, and local patterns are identified no matter where they occur in the image.

Of course, this approach is more than impractical. Fortunately, there is a readily available, local, translation-invariant linear operation on the image: a *convolution*. We can come up with a more compact description of a convolution, but what we are going to describe is exactly what we just delineated—only taken from a different angle.

Convolution, or more precisely, *discrete convolution*[1] (there's an analogous continuous version that we won't go into here), is defined for a 2D image as the scalar product of a weight matrix, the *kernel*, with every neighborhood in the input. Consider a 3×3 kernel (in deep learning, we typically use small kernels; we'll see why later on) as a 2D tensor

```
weight = torch.tensor([[w00, w01, w02],
                       [w10, w11, w12],
                       [w20, w21, w22]])
```

and a 1-channel, MxN image:

```
image = torch.tensor([[i00, i01, i02, i03, ..., i0N],
                      [i10, i11, i12, i13, ..., i1N],
                      [i20, i21, i22, i23, ..., i2N],
                      [i30, i31, i32, i33, ..., i3N],
                      ...
                      [iM0, iM1m iM2, iM3, ..., iMN]])
```

We can compute an element of the output image (without bias) as follows:

```
o11 = i11 * w00 + i12 * w01 + i13 * w02 +
      i21 * w10 + i22 * w11 + i23 * w12 +
      i31 * w20 + i32 * w21 + i33 * w22
```

Figure 8.1 shows this computation in action.

That is, we "translate" the kernel on the `i11` location of the input image, and we multiply each weight by the value of the input image at the corresponding location. Thus, the output image is created by translating the kernel on all input locations and performing the weighted sum. For a multichannel image, like our RGB image, the weight matrix would be a $3 \times 3 \times 3$ matrix: one set of weights for every channel, contributing together to the output values.

Note that, just like the elements in the `weight` matrix of `nn.Linear`, the weights in the kernel are not known in advance, but they are initialized randomly and updated through backpropagation. Note also that the same kernel, and thus each weight in the kernel, is reused across the whole image. Thinking back to autograd, this means the use of each weight has a history spanning the entire image. Thus, the derivative of the loss with respect to a convolution weight includes contributions from the entire image.

---

[1] There is a subtle difference between PyTorch's convolution and mathematics' convolution: one argument's sign is flipped. If we were in a pedantic mood, we could call PyTorch's convolutions *discrete cross-correlations*.

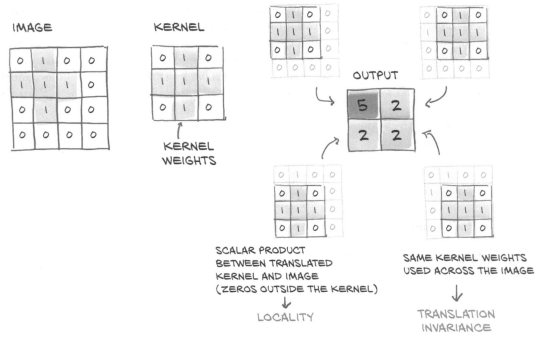

Figure 8.1 Convolution: locality and translation invariance

It's now possible to see the connection to what we were stating earlier: a convolution is equivalent to having multiple linear operations whose weights are zero almost everywhere except around individual pixels and that receive equal updates during training.

Summarizing, by switching to convolutions, we get

- Local operations on neighborhoods
- Translation invariance
- Models with a lot fewer parameters

The key insight underlying the third point is that, with a convolution layer, the number of parameters depends not on the number of pixels in the image, as was the case in our fully connected model, but rather on the size of the convolution kernel (3×3, 5×5, and so on) and on how many convolution filters (or output channels) we decide to use in our model.

8.2 *Convolutions in action*

Well, it looks like we've spent enough time down a rabbit hole! Let's see some PyTorch in action on our birds versus airplanes challenge. The torch.nn module provides convolutions for 1, 2, and 3 dimensions: nn.Conv1d for time series, nn.Conv2d for images, and nn.Conv3d for volumes or videos.

For our CIFAR-10 data, we'll resort to nn.Conv2d. At a minimum, the arguments we provide to nn.Conv2d are the number of input features (or *channels*, since we're dealing with *multichannel* images: that is, more than one value per pixel), the number of output features, and the size of the kernel. For instance, for our first convolutional module, we'll have 3 input features per pixel (the RGB channels) and an arbitrary number of channels in the output—say, 16. The more channels in the output image, the more the capacity of the network. We need the channels to be able to detect many different types of features. Also, because we are randomly initializing them, some of the features we'll get, even after training, will turn out to be useless.[2] Let's stick to a kernel size of 3 × 3.

It is very common to have kernel sizes that are the same in all directions, so PyTorch has a shortcut for this: whenever `kernel_size=3` is specified for a 2D convolution, it means 3 × 3 (provided as a tuple `(3, 3)` in Python). For a 3D convolution, it means 3 × 3 × 3. The CT scans we will see in part 2 of the book have a different voxel (volumetric pixel) resolution in one of the three axes. In such a case, it makes sense to consider kernels that have a different size for the exceptional dimension. But for now, we stick with having the same size of convolutions across all dimensions:

```
# In[11]:
conv = nn.Conv2d(3, 16, kernel_size=3)
conv

# Out[11]:
Conv2d(3, 16, kernel_size=(3, 3), stride=(1, 1))
```

> Instead of the shortcut kernel_size=3, we could equivalently pass in the tuple that we see in the output: kernel_size=(3, 3).

What do we expect to be the shape of the `weight` tensor? The kernel is of size 3 × 3, so we want the weight to consist of 3 × 3 parts. For a single output pixel value, our kernel would consider, say, `in_ch` = 3 input channels, so the weight component for a single output pixel value (and by translation the invariance for the entire output channel) is of shape `in_ch` × 3 × 3. Finally, we have as many of those as we have output channels, here `out_ch` = 16, so the complete weight tensor is `out_ch` × `in_ch` × 3 × 3, in our case 16 × 3 × 3 × 3. The bias will have size 16 (we haven't talked about bias for a while for simplicity, but just as in the linear module case, it's a constant value we add to each channel of the output image). Let's verify our assumptions:

```
# In[12]:
conv.weight.shape, conv.bias.shape

# Out[12]:
(torch.Size([16, 3, 3, 3]), torch.Size([16]))
```

We can see how convolutions are a convenient choice for learning from images. We have smaller models looking for local patterns whose weights are optimized across the entire image.

A 2D convolution pass produces a 2D image as output, whose pixels are a weighted sum over neighborhoods of the input image. In our case, both the kernel weights and

---

[2] This is part of the *lottery ticket hypothesis*: that many kernels will be as useful as losing lottery tickets. See Jonathan Frankle and Michael Carbin, "The Lottery Ticket Hypothesis: Finding Sparse, Trainable Neural Networks," 2019, https://arxiv.org/abs/1803.03635.

the bias conv.weight are initialized randomly, so the output image will not be particularly meaningful. As usual, we need to add the zeroth batch dimension with unsqueeze if we want to call the conv module with one input image, since nn.Conv2d expects a $B \times C \times H \times W$ shaped tensor as input:

```
# In[13]:
img, _ = cifar2[0]
output = conv(img.unsqueeze(0))
img.unsqueeze(0).shape, output.shape

# Out[13]:
(torch.Size([1, 3, 32, 32]), torch.Size([1, 16, 30, 30]))
```

We're curious, so we can display the output, shown in figure 8.2:

```
# In[15]:
plt.imshow(output[0, 0].detach(), cmap='gray')
plt.show()
```

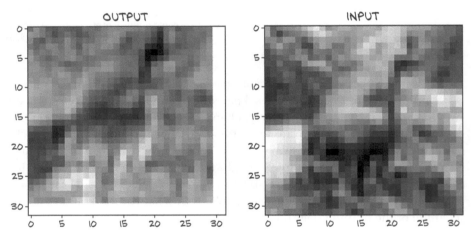

Figure 8.2   Our bird after a random convolution treatment. (We cheated a little with the code to show you the input, too.)

Wait a minute. Let's take a look a the size of output: it's torch.Size([1, 16, 30, 30]). Huh; we lost a few pixels in the process. How did that happen?

8.2.1   *Padding the boundary*

The fact that our output image is smaller than the input is a side effect of deciding what to do at the boundary of the image. Applying a convolution kernel as a weighted sum of pixels in a 3 × 3 neighborhood requires that there are neighbors in all directions. If we are at i00, we only have pixels to the right of and below us. By default, PyTorch will slide the convolution kernel within the input picture, getting width - kernel_width + 1 horizontal and vertical positions. For odd-sized kernels, this results in images that are one-half the convolution kernel's width (in our case, $3//2 = 1$) smaller on each side. This explains why we're missing two pixels in each dimension.

However, PyTorch gives us the possibility of *padding* the image by creating *ghost* pixels around the border that have value zero as far as the convolution is concerned. Figure 8.3 shows padding in action.

In our case, specifying `padding=1` when `kernel_size=3` means i00 has an extra set of neighbors above it and to its left, so that an output of the convolution can be computed even in the corner of our original image.[3] The net result is that the output has now the exact same size as the input:

```
# In[16]:
conv = nn.Conv2d(3, 1, kernel_size=3, padding=1)      <—— Now with padding
output = conv(img.unsqueeze(0))
img.unsqueeze(0).shape, output.shape

# Out[16]:
(torch.Size([1, 3, 32, 32]), torch.Size([1, 1, 32, 32]))
```

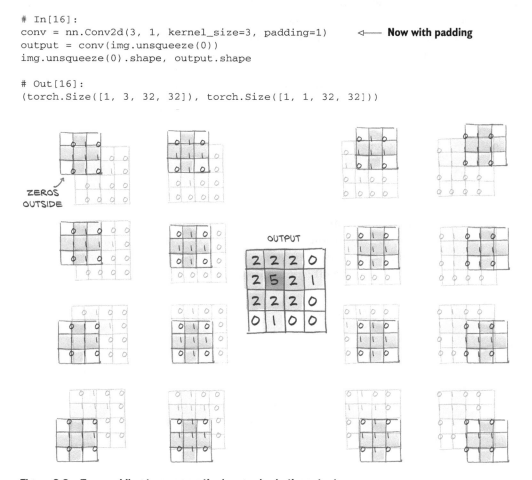

Figure 8.3   Zero padding to preserve the image size in the output

---

[3] For even-sized kernels, we would need to pad by a different number on the left and right (and top and bottom). PyTorch doesn't offer to do this in the convolution itself, but the function `torch.nn.functional.pad` can take care of it. But it's best to stay with odd kernel sizes; even-sized kernels are just odd.

Note that the sizes of weight and bias don't change, regardless of whether padding is used.

There are two main reasons to pad convolutions. First, doing so helps us separate the matters of convolution and changing image sizes, so we have one less thing to remember. And second, when we have more elaborate structures such as skip connections (discussed in section 8.5.3) or the U-Nets we'll cover in part 2, we want the tensors before and after a few convolutions to be of compatible size so that we can add them or take differences.

8.2.2 *Detecting features with convolutions*

We said earlier that weight and bias are parameters that are learned through back-propagation, exactly as it happens for weight and bias in nn.Linear. However, we can play with convolution by setting weights by hand and see what happens.

Let's first zero out bias, just to remove any confounding factors, and then set weights to a constant value so that each pixel in the output gets the mean of its neighbors. For each 3 × 3 neighborhood:

```
# In[17]:
with torch.no_grad():
    conv.bias.zero_()

with torch.no_grad():
    conv.weight.fill_(1.0 / 9.0)
```

We could have gone with conv.weight.one_()—that would result in each pixel in the output being the *sum* of the pixels in the neighborhood. Not a big difference, except that the values in the output image would have been nine times larger.

Anyway, let's see the effect on our CIFAR image:

```
# In[18]:
output = conv(img.unsqueeze(0))
plt.imshow(output[0, 0].detach(), cmap='gray')
plt.show()
```

As we could have predicted, the filter produces a blurred version of the image, as shown in figure 8.4. After all, every pixel of the output is the average of a neighborhood of the input, so pixels in the output are correlated and change more smoothly.

Next, let's try something different. The following kernel may look a bit mysterious at first:

```
# In[19]:
conv = nn.Conv2d(3, 1, kernel_size=3, padding=1)

with torch.no_grad():
    conv.weight[:] = torch.tensor([[-1.0, 0.0, 1.0],
                                   [-1.0, 0.0, 1.0],
                                   [-1.0, 0.0, 1.0]])
    conv.bias.zero_()
```

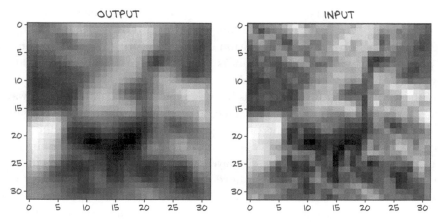

Figure 8.4 Our bird, this time blurred thanks to a constant convolution kernel

Working out the weighted sum for an arbitrary pixel in position 2,2, as we did earlier for the generic convolution kernel, we get

```
o22 = i13 - i11 +
      i23 - i21 +
      i33 - i31
```

which performs the difference of all pixels on the right of i22 minus the pixels on the left of i22. If the kernel is applied on a vertical boundary between two adjacent regions of different intensity, o22 will have a high value. If the kernel is applied on a region of uniform intensity, o22 will be zero. It's an *edge-detection* kernel: the kernel highlights the vertical edge between two horizontally adjacent regions.

Applying the convolution kernel to our image, we see the result shown in figure 8.5. As expected, the convolution kernel enhances the vertical edges. We could build

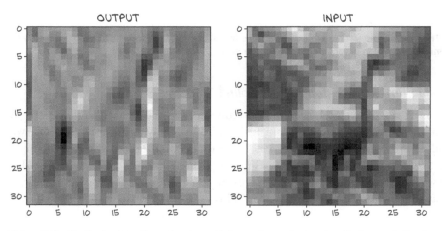

Figure 8.5 Vertical edges throughout our bird, courtesy of a handcrafted convolution kernel

lots more elaborate filters, such as for detecting horizontal or diagonal edges, or cross-like or checkerboard patterns, where "detecting" means the output has a high magnitude. In fact, the job of a computer vision expert has historically been to come up with the most effective combination of filters so that certain features are highlighted in images and objects can be recognized.

With deep learning, we let kernels be estimated from data in whatever way the discrimination is most effective: for instance, in terms of minimizing the negative cross-entropy loss between the output and the ground truth that we introduced in section 7.2.5. From this angle, the job of a convolutional neural network is to estimate the kernel of a set of filter banks in successive layers that will transform a multichannel image into another multichannel image, where different channels correspond to different features (such as one channel for the average, another channel for vertical edges, and so on). Figure 8.6 shows how the training automatically learns the kernels.

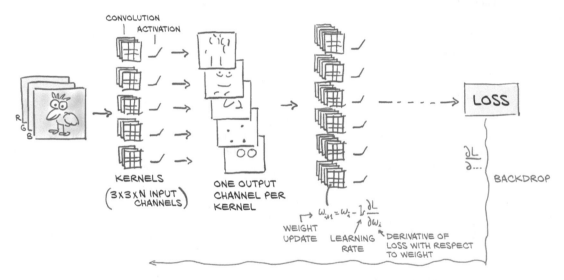

Figure 8.6 The process of learning with convolutions by estimating the gradient at the kernel weights and updating them individually in order to optimize for the loss

8.2.3 *Looking further with depth and pooling*

This is all well and good, but conceptually there's an elephant in the room. We got all excited because by moving from fully connected layers to convolutions, we achieve locality and translation invariance. Then we recommended the use of small kernels, like 3×3, or 5×5: that's peak locality, all right. What about the *big picture*? How do we know that all structures in our images are 3 pixels or 5 pixels wide? Well, we don't, because they aren't. And if they aren't, how are our networks going to be equipped to see those patterns with larger scope? This is something we'll really need if we want to solve our birds versus airplanes problem effectively, since although CIFAR-10 images are small, the objects still have a (wing-)span several pixels across.

One possibility could be to use large convolution kernels. Well, sure, at the limit we could get a 32 × 32 kernel for a 32 × 32 image, but we would converge to the old fully connected, affine transformation and lose all the nice properties of convolution. Another option, which is used in convolutional neural networks, is stacking one convolution after the other and at the same time downsampling the image between successive convolutions.

FROM LARGE TO SMALL: DOWNSAMPLING

Downsampling could in principle occur in different ways. Scaling an image by half is the equivalent of taking four neighboring pixels as input and producing one pixel as output. How we compute the value of the output based on the values of the input is up to us. We could

- *Average the four pixels.* This *average pooling* was a common approach early on but has fallen out of favor somewhat.
- *Take the maximum of the four pixels.* This approach, called *max pooling*, is currently the most commonly used approach, but it has a downside of discarding the other three-quarters of the data.
- *Perform a strided convolution, where only every Nth pixel is calculated.* A 3 × 4 convolution with stride 2 still incorporates input from all pixels from the previous layer. The literature shows promise for this approach, but it has not yet supplanted max pooling.

We will be focusing on max pooling, illustrated in figure 8.7, going forward. The figure shows the most common setup of taking non-overlapping 2 x 2 tiles and taking the maximum over each of them as the new pixel at the reduced scale.

Intuitively, the output images from a convolution layer, especially since they are followed by an activation just like any other linear layer, tend to have a high magnitude

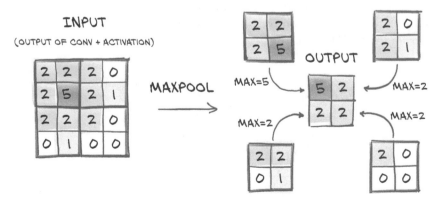

Figure 8.7   Max pooling in detail

where certain features corresponding to the estimated kernel are detected (such as vertical lines). By keeping the highest value in the 2 × 2 neighborhood as the downsampled output, we ensure that the features that are found *survive* the downsampling, at the expense of the weaker responses.

Max pooling is provided by the nn.MaxPool2d module (as with convolution, there are versions for 1D and 3D data). It takes as input the size of the neighborhood over which to operate the pooling operation. If we wish to downsample our image by half, we'll want to use a size of 2. Let's verify that it works as expected directly on our input image:

```
# In[21]:
pool = nn.MaxPool2d(2)
output = pool(img.unsqueeze(0))

img.unsqueeze(0).shape, output.shape

# Out[21]:
(torch.Size([1, 3, 32, 32]), torch.Size([1, 3, 16, 16]))
```

COMBINING CONVOLUTIONS AND DOWNSAMPLING FOR GREAT GOOD

Let's now see how combining convolutions and downsampling can help us recognize larger structures. In figure 8.8, we start by applying a set of 3 × 3 kernels on our 8 × 8 image, obtaining a multichannel output image of the same size. Then we scale down the output image by half, obtaining a 4 × 4 image, and apply another set of 3 × 3 kernels to it. This second set of kernels operates on a 3 × 3 neighborhood of something that has been scaled down by half, so it effectively maps back to 8 × 8 neighborhoods of the input. In addition, the second set of kernels takes the output of the first set of kernels (features like averages, edges, and so on) and extracts additional features on top of those.

So, on one hand, the first set of kernels operates on small neighborhoods on first-order, low-level features, while the second set of kernels effectively operates on wider neighborhoods, producing features that are compositions of the previous features. This is a very powerful mechanism that provides convolutional neural networks with the ability to see into very complex scenes—much more complex than our 32 × 32 images from the CIFAR-10 dataset.

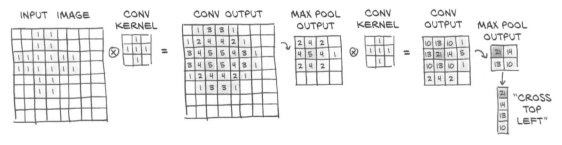

Figure 8.8   **More convolutions by hand, showing the effect of stacking convolutions and downsampling: a large cross is highlighted using two small, cross-shaped kernels and max pooling.**

The receptive field of output pixels

When the second 3 × 3 convolution kernel produces 21 in its conv output in figure 8.8, this is based on the top-left 3 × 3 pixels of the first max pool output. They, in turn, correspond to the 6 × 6 pixels in the top-left corner in the first conv output, which in turn are computed by the first convolution from the top-left 7 × 7 pixels. So the pixel in the second convolution output is influenced by a 7 × 7 input square. The first convolution also uses an implicitly "padded" column and row to produce the output in the corner; otherwise, we would have an 8 × 8 square of input pixels informing a given pixel (away from the boundary) in the second convolution's output. In fancy language, we say that a given output neuron of the 3 × 3-conv, 2 × 2-max-pool, 3 × 3-conv construction has a *receptive field* of 8 × 8.

8.2.4 *Putting it all together for our network*

With these building blocks in our hands, we can now proceed to build our convolutional neural network for detecting birds and airplanes. Let's take our previous fully connected model as a starting point and introduce nn.Conv2d and nn.MaxPool2d as described previously:

```
# In[22]:
model = nn.Sequential(
            nn.Conv2d(3, 16, kernel_size=3, padding=1),
            nn.Tanh(),
            nn.MaxPool2d(2),
            nn.Conv2d(16, 8, kernel_size=3, padding=1),
            nn.Tanh(),
            nn.MaxPool2d(2),
            # ...
            )
```

The first convolution takes us from 3 RGB channels to 16, thereby giving the network a chance to generate 16 independent features that operate to (hopefully) discriminate low-level features of birds and airplanes. Then we apply the Tanh activation function. The resulting 16-channel 32 × 32 image is pooled to a 16-channel 16 × 16 image by the first MaxPool2d. At this point, the downsampled image undergoes another convolution that generates an 8-channel 16 × 16 output. With any luck, this output will consist of higher-level features. Again, we apply a Tanh activation and then pool to an 8-channel 8 × 8 output.

Where does this end? After the input image has been reduced to a set of 8 × 8 features, we expect to be able to output some probabilities from the network that we can feed to our negative log likelihood. However, probabilities are a pair of numbers in a 1D vector (one for airplane, one for bird), but here we're still dealing with multichannel 2D features.

Thinking back to the beginning of this chapter, we already know what we need to do: turn the 8-channel 8 × 8 image into a 1D vector and complete our network with a set of fully connected layers:

```
# In[23]:
model = nn.Sequential(
            nn.Conv2d(3, 16, kernel_size=3, padding=1),
            nn.Tanh(),
            nn.MaxPool2d(2),
            nn.Conv2d(16, 8, kernel_size=3, padding=1),
            nn.Tanh(),
            nn.MaxPool2d(2),
            # ...
            nn.Linear(8 * 8 * 8, 32),           ◁────┐ Warning: Something
            nn.Tanh(),                                │ important is missing here!
            nn.Linear(32, 2))
```

This code gives us a neural network as shown in figure 8.9.

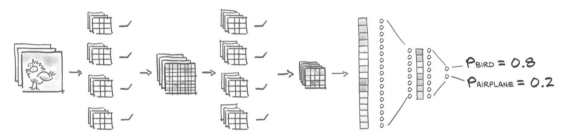

Figure 8.9   Shape of a typical convolutional network, including the one we're building. An image is fed to a series of convolutions and max pooling modules and then straightened into a 1D vector and fed into fully connected modules.

Ignore the "something missing" comment for a minute. Let's first notice that the size of the linear layer is dependent on the expected size of the output of MaxPool2d: 8 × 8 × 8 = 512. Let's count the number of parameters for this small model:

```
# In[24]:
numel_list = [p.numel() for p in model.parameters()]
sum(numel_list), numel_list

# Out[24]:
(18090, [432, 16, 1152, 8, 16384, 32, 64, 2])
```

That's very reasonable for a limited dataset of such small images. In order to increase the capacity of the model, we could increase the number of output channels for the convolution layers (that is, the number of features each convolution layer generates), which would lead the linear layer to increase its size as well.

We put the "Warning" note in the code for a reason. The model has zero chance of running without complaining:

```
# In[25]:
model(img.unsqueeze(0))

# Out[25]:
...
RuntimeError: size mismatch, m1:
➥ [64 x 8], m2: [512 x 32] at c:\...\THTensorMath.cpp:940
```

Admittedly, the error message is a bit obscure, but not too much so. We find references to `linear` in the traceback: looking back at the model, we see that only module that has to have a 512 × 32 tensor is `nn.Linear(512, 32)`, the first linear module after the last convolution block.

What's missing there is the reshaping step from an 8-channel 8 × 8 image to a 512-element, 1D vector (1D if we ignore the batch dimension, that is). This could be achieved by calling `view` on the output of the last `nn.MaxPool2d`, but unfortunately, we don't have any explicit visibility of the output of each module when we use `nn.Sequential`.[4]

8.3 Subclassing nn.Module

At some point in developing neural networks, we will find ourselves in a situation where we want to compute something that the premade modules do not cover. Here, it is something very simple like reshaping,[5]; but in section 8.5.3, we use the same construction to implement residual connections. So in this section, we learn how to make our own `nn.Module` subclasses that we can then use just like the prebuilt ones or `nn.Sequential`.

When we want to build models that do more complex things than just applying one layer after another, we need to leave `nn.Sequential` for something that gives us added flexibility. PyTorch allows us to use any computation in our model by subclassing `nn.Module`.

In order to subclass `nn.Module`, at a minimum we need to define a `forward` function that takes the inputs to the module and returns the output. This is where we define our module's computation. The name `forward` here is reminiscent of a distant past, when modules needed to define both the forward and backward passes we met in section 5.5.1. With PyTorch, if we use standard `torch` operations, autograd will take care of the backward pass automatically; and indeed, an `nn.Module` never comes with a `backward`.

Typically, our computation will use other modules—premade like convolutions or customized. To include these *submodules*, we typically define them in the constructor `__init__` and assign them to `self` for use in the `forward` function. They will, at the same time, hold their parameters throughout the lifetime of our module. Note that you need to call `super().__init__()` before you can do that (or PyTorch will remind you).

---

[4] Not being able to do this kind of operation inside of `nn.Sequential` was an explicit design choice by the PyTorch authors and was left that way for a long time; see the linked comments from @soumith at https://github.com/pytorch/pytorch/issues/2486. Recently, PyTorch gained an `nn.Flatten` layer.

[5] We could have used `nn.Flatten` starting from PyTorch 1.3.

8.3.1   *Our network as an nn.Module*

Let's write our network as a submodule. To do so, we instantiate all the nn.Conv2d, nn.Linear, and so on that we previously passed to nn.Sequential in the constructor, and then use their instances one after another in forward:

```
# In[26]:
class Net(nn.Module):
    def __init__(self):
        super().__init__()
        self.conv1 = nn.Conv2d(3, 16, kernel_size=3, padding=1)
        self.act1 = nn.Tanh()
        self.pool1 = nn.MaxPool2d(2)
        self.conv2 = nn.Conv2d(16, 8, kernel_size=3, padding=1)
        self.act2 = nn.Tanh()
        self.pool2 = nn.MaxPool2d(2)
        self.fc1 = nn.Linear(8 * 8 * 8, 32)
        self.act3 = nn.Tanh()
        self.fc2 = nn.Linear(32, 2)

    def forward(self, x):
        out = self.pool1(self.act1(self.conv1(x)))
        out = self.pool2(self.act2(self.conv2(out)))
        out = out.view(-1, 8 * 8 * 8)
        out = self.act3(self.fc1(out))
        out = self.fc2(out)
        return out
```

This reshape is what we were missing earlier. → `out = out.view(-1, 8 * 8 * 8)`

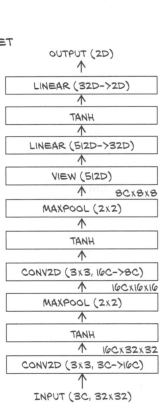

Figure 8.10 Our baseline convolutional network architecture

The Net class is equivalent to the nn.Sequential model we built earlier in terms of submodules; but by writing the forward function explicitly, we can manipulate the output of self.pool3 directly and call view on it to turn it into a $B \times N$ vector. Note that we leave the batch dimension as −1 in the call to view, since in principle we don't know how many samples will be in the batch.

Here we use a subclass of nn.Module to contain our entire model. We could also use subclasses to define new building blocks for more complex networks. Picking up on the diagram style in chapter 6, our network looks like the one shown in figure 8.10. We are making some ad hoc choices about what information to present where.

Recall that the goal of classification networks typically is to compress information in the sense that we start with an image with a sizable number of pixels and compress it into (a vector of probabilities of) classes. Two things about our architecture deserve some commentary with respect to this goal.

First, our goal is reflected by the size of our intermediate values generally shrinking—this is done by reducing the number of channels in the convolutions, by reducing the number of pixels through pooling, and by having an output dimension lower than the input dimension in the linear layers. This is a common trait of classification networks. However, in many popular architectures like the ResNets we saw in chapter 2 and discuss more in section 8.5.3, the reduction is achieved by pooling in the spatial resolution, but the number of channels increases (still resulting in a reduction in size). It seems that our pattern of fast information reduction works well with networks of limited depth and small images; but for deeper networks, the decrease is typically slower.

Second, in one layer, there is not a reduction of output size with regard to input size: the initial convolution. If we consider a single output pixel as a vector of 32 elements (the channels), it is a linear transformation of 27 elements (as a convolution of 3 channels × 3 × 3 kernel size)—only a moderate increase. In ResNet, the initial convolution generates 64 channels from 147 elements (3 channels × 7 × 7 kernel size).[6] So the first layer is exceptional in that it greatly increases the overall dimension (as in channels times pixels) of the data flowing through it, but the mapping for each output pixel considered in isolation still has approximately as many outputs as inputs.[7]

8.3.2 *How PyTorch keeps track of parameters and submodules*

Interestingly, assigning an instance of nn.Module to an attribute in an nn.Module, as we did in the earlier constructor, automatically registers the module as a submodule.

> **NOTE** The submodules must be top-level *attributes*, not buried inside list or dict instances! Otherwise the optimizer will not be able to locate the submodules (and, hence, their parameters). For situations where your model requires a list or dict of submodules, PyTorch provides nn.ModuleList and nn.ModuleDict.

We can call arbitrary methods of an nn.Module subclass. For example, for a model where training is substantially different than its use, say, for prediction, it may make sense to have a predict method. Be aware that calling such methods will be similar to calling forward instead of the module itself—they will be ignorant of hooks, and the JIT does not see the module structure when using them because we are missing the equivalent of the __call__ bits shown in section 6.2.1.

This allows Net to have access to the parameters of its submodules without further action by the user:

---

[6] The dimensions in the pixel-wise linear mapping defined by the first convolution were emphasized by Jeremy Howard in his fast.ai course (https://www.fast.ai).

[7] Outside of and older than deep learning, projecting into high-dimensional space and then doing conceptually simpler (than linear) machine learning is commonly known as the *kernel trick*. The initial increase in the number of channels could be seen as a somewhat similar phenomenon, but striking a different balance between the cleverness of the embedding and the simplicity of the model working on the embedding.

```
# In[27]:
model = Net()

numel_list = [p.numel() for p in model.parameters()]
sum(numel_list), numel_list

# Out[27]:
(18090, [432, 16, 1152, 8, 16384, 32, 64, 2])
```

What happens here is that the `parameters()` call delves into all submodules assigned as attributes in the constructor and recursively calls `parameters()` on them. No matter how nested the submodule, any `nn.Module` can access the list of all child parameters. By accessing their `grad` attribute, which has been populated by `autograd`, the optimizer will know how to change parameters to minimize the loss. We know that story from chapter 5.

We now know how to implement our own modules—and we will need this a lot for part 2. Looking back at the implementation of the `Net` class, and thinking about the utility of registering submodules in the constructor so that we can access their parameters, it appears a bit of a waste that we are also registering submodules that have no parameters, like `nn.Tanh` and `nn.MaxPool2d`. Wouldn't it be easier to call these directly in the `forward` function, just as we called `view`?

8.3.3 *The functional API*

It sure would! And that's why PyTorch has *functional* counterparts for every nn module. By "functional" here we mean "having no internal state"—in other words, "whose output value is solely and fully determined by the value input arguments." Indeed, `torch.nn.functional` provides many functions that work like the modules we find in nn. But instead of working on the input arguments and stored parameters like the module counterparts, they take inputs and parameters as arguments to the function call. For instance, the functional counterpart of `nn.Linear` is `nn.functional.linear`, which is a function that has signature `linear(input, weight, bias=None)`. The `weight` and `bias` parameters are arguments to the function.

Back to our model, it makes sense to keep using nn modules for `nn.Linear` and `nn.Conv2d` so that `Net` will be able to manage their `Parameters` during training. However, we can safely switch to the functional counterparts of pooling and activation, since they have no parameters:

```
# In[28]:
import torch.nn.functional as F

class Net(nn.Module):
    def __init__(self):
        super().__init__()
        self.conv1 = nn.Conv2d(3, 16, kernel_size=3, padding=1)
        self.conv2 = nn.Conv2d(16, 8, kernel_size=3, padding=1)
        self.fc1 = nn.Linear(8 * 8 * 8, 32)
        self.fc2 = nn.Linear(32, 2)
```

```
def forward(self, x):
    out = F.max_pool2d(torch.tanh(self.conv1(x)), 2)
    out = F.max_pool2d(torch.tanh(self.conv2(out)), 2)
    out = out.view(-1, 8 * 8 * 8)
    out = torch.tanh(self.fc1(out))
    out = self.fc2(out)
    return out
```

This is a lot more concise than and fully equivalent to our previous definition of Net in section 8.3.1. Note that it would still make sense to instantiate modules that require several parameters for their initialization in the constructor.

> **TIP** While general-purpose scientific functions like tanh still exist in torch.nn.functional in version 1.0, those entry points are deprecated in favor of functions in the top-level torch namespace. More niche functions like max_pool2d will remain in torch.nn.functional.

Thus, the functional way also sheds light on what the nn.Module API is all about: a Module is a container for state in the forms of Parameters and submodules combined with the instructions to do a forward.

Whether to use the functional or the modular API is a decision based on style and taste. When part of a network is so simple that we want to use nn.Sequential, we're in the modular realm. When we are writing our own forwards, it may be more natural to use the functional interface for things that do not need state in the form of parameters.

In chapter 15, we will briefly touch on quantization. Then stateless bits like activations suddenly become stateful because information about the quantization needs to be captured. This means if we aim to quantize our model, it might be worthwhile to stick with the modular API if we go for non-JITed quantization. There is one style matter that will help you avoid surprises with (originally unforeseen) uses: if you need several applications of stateless modules (like nn.HardTanh or nn.ReLU), it is probably a good idea to have a separate instance for each. Reusing the same module appears to be clever and will give correct results with our standard Python usage here, but tools analyzing your model may trip over it.

So now we can make our own nn.Module if we need to, and we also have the functional API for cases when instantiating and then calling an nn.Module is overkill. This has been the last bit missing to understand how the code organization works in just about any neural network implemented in PyTorch.

Let's double-check that our model runs, and then we'll get to the training loop:

```
# In[29]:
model = Net()
model(img.unsqueeze(0))

# Out[29]:
tensor([[-0.0157,  0.1143]], grad_fn=<AddmmBackward>)
```

We got two numbers! Information flows correctly. We might not realize it right now, but in more complex models, getting the size of the first linear layer right is sometimes a source of frustration. We've heard stories of famous practitioners putting in arbitrary numbers and then relying on error messages from PyTorch to backtrack the correct sizes for their linear layers. Lame, eh? Nah, it's all legit!

8.4   *Training our convnet*

We're now at the point where we can assemble our complete training loop. We already developed the overall structure in chapter 5, and the training loop looks much like the one from chapter 6, but here we will revisit it to add some details like some tracking for accuracy. After we run our model, we will also have an appetite for a little more speed, so we will learn how to run our models fast on a GPU. But first let's look at the training loop.

Recall that the core of our convnet is two nested loops: an outer one over the *epochs* and an inner one of the DataLoader that produces batches from our Dataset. In each loop, we then have to

1 Feed the inputs through the model (the forward pass).
2 Compute the loss (also part of the forward pass).
3 Zero any old gradients.
4 Call loss.backward() to compute the gradients of the loss with respect to all parameters (the backward pass).
5 Have the optimizer take a step in toward lower loss.

Also, we collect and print some information. So here is our training loop, looking almost as it does in the previous chapter—but it is good to remember what each thing is doing:

Uses the datetime module included with Python

Our loop over the epochs, numbered from 1 to n_epochs rather than starting at 0

```
# In[30]:
import datetime

def training_loop(n_epochs, optimizer, model, loss_fn, train_loader):
    for epoch in range(1, n_epochs + 1):
        loss_train = 0.0
        for imgs, labels in train_loader:

            outputs = model(imgs)

            loss = loss_fn(outputs, labels)
            optimizer.zero_grad()

            loss.backward()

            optimizer.step()
```

Feeds a batch through our model ...

Loops over our dataset in the batches the data loader creates for us

After getting rid of the gradients from the last round ...

... and computes the loss we wish to minimize

... performs the backward step. That is, we compute the gradients of all parameters we want the network to learn.

Updates the model

8.4.1 *Measuring accuracy*

In order to have a measure that is more interpretable than the loss, we can take a look at our accuracies on the training and validation datasets. We use the same code as in chapter 7:

```
# In[32]:
train_loader = torch.utils.data.DataLoader(cifar2, batch_size=64,
                                           shuffle=False)
val_loader = torch.utils.data.DataLoader(cifar2_val, batch_size=64,
                                         shuffle=False)

def validate(model, train_loader, val_loader):
    for name, loader in [("train", train_loader), ("val", val_loader)]:
        correct = 0
        total = 0

        with torch.no_grad():
            for imgs, labels in loader:
                outputs = model(imgs)
                _, predicted = torch.max(outputs, dim=1)
                total += labels.shape[0]
                correct += int((predicted == labels).sum())

        print("Accuracy {}: {:.2f}".format(name , correct / total))

validate(model, train_loader, val_loader)

# Out[32]:
Accuracy train: 0.93
Accuracy val: 0.89
```

We do not want gradients here, as we will not want to update the parameters.

Counts the number of examples, so total is increased by the batch size

Gives us the index of the highest value as output

Comparing the predicted class that had the maximum probability and the ground-truth labels, we first get a Boolean array. Taking the sum gives the number of items in the batch where the prediction and ground truth agree.

We cast to a Python `int`—for integer tensors, this is equivalent to using `.item()`, similar to what we did in the training loop.

This is quite a lot better than the fully connected model, which achieved only 79% accuracy. We about halved the number of errors on the validation set. Also, we used far fewer parameters. This is telling us that the model does a better job of generalizing its task of recognizing the subject of images from a new sample, through locality and translation invariance. We could now let it run for more epochs and see what performance we could squeeze out.

8.4.2 *Saving and loading our model*

Since we're satisfied with our model so far, it would be nice to actually save it, right? It's easy to do. Let's save the model to a file:

```
# In[33]:
torch.save(model.state_dict(), data_path + 'birds_vs_airplanes.pt')
```

The birds_vs_airplanes.pt file now contains all the parameters of `model`: that is, weights and biases for the two convolution modules and the two linear modules. So, no structure—just the weights. This means when we deploy the model in production for our friend, we'll need to keep the `model` class handy, create an instance, and then load the parameters back into it:

```
# In[34]:
loaded_model = Net()
loaded_model.load_state_dict(torch.load(data_path
                                + 'birds_vs_airplanes.pt'))
```

> **We will have to make sure we don't change the definition of Net between saving and later loading the model state.**

```
# Out[34]:
<All keys matched successfully>
```

We have also included a pretrained model in our code repository, saved to ../data/p1ch7/birds_vs_airplanes.pt.

8.4.3 Training on the GPU

We have a net and can train it! But it would be good to make it a bit faster. It is no surprise by now that we do so by moving our training onto the GPU. Using the `.to` method we saw in chapter 3, we can move the tensors we get from the data loader to the GPU, after which our computation will automatically take place there. But we also need to move our parameters to the GPU. Happily, `nn.Module` implements a `.to` function that moves all of its parameters to the GPU (or casts the type when you pass a `dtype` argument).

There is a somewhat subtle difference between `Module.to` and `Tensor.to`. `Module.to` is in place: the module instance is modified. But `Tensor.to` is out of place (in some ways computation, just like `Tensor.tanh`), returning a new tensor. One implication is that it is good practice to create the `Optimizer` after moving the parameters to the appropriate device.

It is considered good style to move things to the GPU if one is available. A good pattern is to set the a variable `device` depending on `torch.cuda.is_available`:

```
# In[35]:
device = (torch.device('cuda') if torch.cuda.is_available()
          else torch.device('cpu'))
print(f"Training on device {device}.")
```

Then we can amend the training loop by moving the tensors we get from the data loader to the GPU by using the `Tensor.to` method. Note that the code is exactly like our first version at the beginning of this section except for the two lines moving the inputs to the GPU:

```
# In[36]:
import datetime

def training_loop(n_epochs, optimizer, model, loss_fn, train_loader):
    for epoch in range(1, n_epochs + 1):
        loss_train = 0.0
```

```
for imgs, labels in train_loader:
    imgs = imgs.to(device=device)
    labels = labels.to(device=device)
    outputs = model(imgs)
    loss = loss_fn(outputs, labels)

    optimizer.zero_grad()
    loss.backward()
    optimizer.step()

    loss_train += loss.item()

if epoch == 1 or epoch % 10 == 0:
    print('{} Epoch {}, Training loss {}'.format(
        datetime.datetime.now(), epoch,
        loss_train / len(train_loader)))
```

These two lines that move imgs and labels to the device we are training on are the only difference from our previous version.

The same amendment must be made to the validate function. We can then instantiate our model, move it to device, and run it as before:[8]

```
# In[37]:
train_loader = torch.utils.data.DataLoader(cifar2, batch_size=64,
                                            shuffle=True)

model = Net().to(device=device)
optimizer = optim.SGD(model.parameters(), lr=1e-2)
loss_fn = nn.CrossEntropyLoss()

training_loop(
    n_epochs = 100,
    optimizer = optimizer,
    model = model,
    loss_fn = loss_fn,
    train_loader = train_loader,
)
```

Moves our model (all parameters) to the GPU. If you forget to move either the model or the inputs to the GPU, you will get errors about tensors not being on the same device, because the PyTorch operators do not support mixing GPU and CPU inputs.

```
# Out[37]:
2020-01-16 23:10:35.563216 Epoch 1, Training loss 0.5717791349265227
2020-01-16 23:10:39.730262 Epoch 10, Training loss 0.3285350770137872
2020-01-16 23:10:45.906321 Epoch 20, Training loss 0.29493294959994637
2020-01-16 23:10:52.086905 Epoch 30, Training loss 0.26962305994550134
2020-01-16 23:10:56.551582 Epoch 40, Training loss 0.24709946277794564
2020-01-16 23:11:00.991432 Epoch 50, Training loss 0.22623272664892446
2020-01-16 23:11:05.421524 Epoch 60, Training loss 0.20996672821462534
2020-01-16 23:11:09.951312 Epoch 70, Training loss 0.1934866009719053
2020-01-16 23:11:14.499484 Epoch 80, Training loss 0.1799132404908253
2020-01-16 23:11:19.047609 Epoch 90, Training loss 0.16620008706761774
2020-01-16 23:11:23.590435 Epoch 100, Training loss 0.15667157247662544
```

---

[8] There is a pin_memory option for the data loader that will cause the data loader to use memory pinned to the GPU, with the goal of speeding up transfers. Whether we gain something varies, though, so we will not pursue this here.

Even for our small network here, we do see a sizable increase in speed. The advantage of computing on GPUs is more visible for larger models.

There is a slight complication when loading network weights: PyTorch will attempt to load the weight to the same device it was saved from—that is, weights on the GPU will be restored to the GPU. As we don't know whether we want the same device, we have two options: we could move the network to the CPU before saving it, or move it back after restoring. It is a bit more concise to instruct PyTorch to override the device information when loading weights. This is done by passing the `map_location` keyword argument to `torch.load`:

```
# In[39]:
loaded_model = Net().to(device=device)
loaded_model.load_state_dict(torch.load(data_path
                                + 'birds_vs_airplanes.pt',
                                map_location=device))

# Out[39]:
<All keys matched successfully>
```

8.5 Model design

We built our model as a subclass of `nn.Module`, the de facto standard for all but the simplest models. Then we trained it successfully and saw how to use the GPU to train our models. We've reached the point where we can build a feed-forward convolutional neural network and train it successfully to classify images. The natural question is, what now? What if we are presented with a more complicated problem? Admittedly, our birds versus airplanes dataset wasn't that complicated: the images were very small, and the object under investigation was centered and took up most of the viewport.

If we moved to, say, ImageNet, we would find larger, more complex images, where the right answer would depend on multiple visual clues, often hierarchically organized. For instance, when trying to predict whether a dark brick shape is a remote control or a cell phone, the network could be looking for something like a screen.

Plus images may not be our sole focus in the real world, where we have tabular data, sequences, and text. The promise of neural networks is sufficient flexibility to solve problems on all these kinds of data given the proper architecture (that is, the interconnection of layers or modules) and the proper loss function.

PyTorch ships with a very comprehensive collection of modules and loss functions to implement state-of-the-art architectures ranging from feed-forward components to long short-term memory (LSTM) modules and transformer networks (two very popular architectures for sequential data). Several models are available through PyTorch Hub or as part of `torchvision` and other vertical community efforts.

We'll see a few more advanced architectures in part 2, where we'll walk through an end-to-end problem of analyzing CT scans, but in general, it is beyond the scope of this book to explore variations on neural network architectures. However, we can build on the knowledge we've accumulated thus far to understand how we can implement almost any architecture thanks to the expressivity of PyTorch. The purpose of this section is precisely to provide conceptual tools that will allow us to read the latest research paper and start implementing it in PyTorch—or, since authors often release PyTorch implementations of their papers, to read the implementations without choking on our coffee.

8.5.1   *Adding memory capacity: Width*

Given our feed-forward architecture, there are a couple of dimensions we'd likely want to explore before getting into further complications. The first dimension is the *width* of the network: the number of neurons per layer, or channels per convolution. We can make a model wider very easily in PyTorch. We just specify a larger number of output channels in the first convolution and increase the subsequent layers accordingly, taking care to change the forward function to reflect the fact that we'll now have a longer vector once we switch to fully connected layers:

```
# In[40]:
class NetWidth(nn.Module):
    def __init__(self):
        super().__init__()
        self.conv1 = nn.Conv2d(3, 32, kernel_size=3, padding=1)
        self.conv2 = nn.Conv2d(32, 16, kernel_size=3, padding=1)
        self.fc1 = nn.Linear(16 * 8 * 8, 32)
        self.fc2 = nn.Linear(32, 2)

    def forward(self, x):
        out = F.max_pool2d(torch.tanh(self.conv1(x)), 2)
        out = F.max_pool2d(torch.tanh(self.conv2(out)), 2)
        out = out.view(-1, 16 * 8 * 8)
        out = torch.tanh(self.fc1(out))
        out = self.fc2(out)
        return out
```

If we want to avoid hardcoding numbers in the definition of the model, we can easily pass a parameter to *init* and parameterize the width, taking care to also parameterize the call to view in the forward function:

```
# In[42]:
class NetWidth(nn.Module):
    def __init__(self, n_chans1=32):
        super().__init__()
        self.n_chans1 = n_chans1
        self.conv1 = nn.Conv2d(3, n_chans1, kernel_size=3, padding=1)
        self.conv2 = nn.Conv2d(n_chans1, n_chans1 // 2, kernel_size=3,
                               padding=1)
        self.fc1 = nn.Linear(8 * 8 * n_chans1 // 2, 32)
        self.fc2 = nn.Linear(32, 2)

    def forward(self, x):
        out = F.max_pool2d(torch.tanh(self.conv1(x)), 2)
        out = F.max_pool2d(torch.tanh(self.conv2(out)), 2)
```

```
out = out.view(-1, 8 * 8 * self.n_chans1 // 2)
out = torch.tanh(self.fc1(out))
out = self.fc2(out)
return out
```

The numbers specifying channels and features for each layer are directly related to the number of parameters in a model; all other things being equal, they increase the *capacity* of the model. As we did previously, we can look at how many parameters our model has now:

```
# In[44]:
sum(p.numel() for p in model.parameters())
```

```
# Out[44]:
38386
```

The greater the capacity, the more variability in the inputs the model will be able to manage; but at the same time, the more likely overfitting will be, since the model can use a greater number of parameters to memorize unessential aspects of the input. We already went into ways to combat overfitting, the best being increasing the sample size or, in the absence of new data, augmenting existing data through artificial modifications of the same data.

There are a few more tricks we can play at the model level (without acting on the data) to control overfitting. Let's review the most common ones.

8.5.2 *Helping our model to converge and generalize: Regularization*

Training a model involves two critical steps: optimization, when we need the loss to decrease on the training set; and generalization, when the model has to work not only on the training set but also on data it has not seen before, like the validation set. The mathematical tools aimed at easing these two steps are sometimes subsumed under the label *regularization*.

KEEPING THE PARAMETERS IN CHECK: WEIGHT PENALTIES

The first way to stabilize generalization is to add a regularization term to the loss. This term is crafted so that the weights of the model tend to be small on their own, limiting how much training makes them grow. In other words, it is a penalty on larger weight values. This makes the loss have a smoother topography, and there's relatively less to gain from fitting individual samples.

The most popular regularization terms of this kind are L2 regularization, which is the sum of squares of all weights in the model, and L1 regularization, which is the sum of the absolute values of all weights in the model.[9] Both of them are scaled by a (small) factor, which is a hyperparameter we set prior to training.

---

[9] We'll focus on L2 regularization here. L1 regularization—popularized in the more general statistics literature by its use in Lasso—has the attractive property of resulting in sparse trained weights.

L2 regularization is also referred to as *weight decay*. The reason for this name is that, thinking about SGD and backpropagation, the negative gradient of the L2 regularization term with respect to a parameter w_i is - 2 * lambda * w_i, where lambda is the aforementioned hyperparameter, simply named *weight decay* in PyTorch. So, adding L2 regularization to the loss function is equivalent to decreasing each weight by an amount proportional to its current value during the optimization step (hence, the name *weight decay*). Note that weight decay applies to all parameters of the network, such as biases.

In PyTorch, we could implement regularization pretty easily by adding a term to the loss. After computing the loss, whatever the loss function is, we can iterate the parameters of the model, sum their respective square (for L2) or abs (for L1), and backpropagate:

```
# In[45]:
def training_loop_l2reg(n_epochs, optimizer, model, loss_fn,
                        train_loader):
    for epoch in range(1, n_epochs + 1):
        loss_train = 0.0
        for imgs, labels in train_loader:
            imgs = imgs.to(device=device)
            labels = labels.to(device=device)
            outputs = model(imgs)
            loss = loss_fn(outputs, labels)

            l2_lambda = 0.001                              Replaces pow(2.0)
            l2_norm = sum(p.pow(2.0).sum()                 with abs() for L1
                          for p in model.parameters())  ◁─┘ regularization
            loss = loss + l2_lambda * l2_norm

            optimizer.zero_grad()
            loss.backward()
            optimizer.step()

            loss_train += loss.item()
        if epoch == 1 or epoch % 10 == 0:
            print('{} Epoch {}, Training loss {}'.format(
                datetime.datetime.now(), epoch,
                loss_train / len(train_loader)))
```

However, the SGD optimizer in PyTorch already has a weight_decay parameter that corresponds to 2 * lambda, and it directly performs weight decay during the update as described previously. It is fully equivalent to adding the L2 norm of weights to the loss, without the need for accumulating terms in the loss and involving autograd.

NOT RELYING TOO MUCH ON A SINGLE INPUT: DROPOUT

An effective strategy for combating overfitting was originally proposed in 2014 by Nitish Srivastava and coauthors from Geoff Hinton's group in Toronto, in a paper aptly entitled "Dropout: a Simple Way to Prevent Neural Networks from Overfitting" (http://mng.bz/nPMa). Sounds like pretty much exactly what we're looking for, right? The idea behind dropout is indeed simple: zero out a random fraction of outputs from neurons across the network, where the randomization happens at each training iteration.

This procedure effectively generates slightly different models with different neuron topologies at each iteration, giving neurons in the model less chance to coordinate in the memorization process that happens during overfitting. An alternative point of view is that dropout perturbs the features being generated by the model, exerting an effect that is close to augmentation, but this time throughout the network.

In PyTorch, we can implement dropout in a model by adding an nn.Dropout module between the nonlinear activation function and the linear or convolutional module of the subsequent layer. As an argument, we need to specify the probability with which inputs will be zeroed out. In case of convolutions, we'll use the specialized nn.Dropout2d or nn.Dropout3d, which zero out entire channels of the input:

```
# In[47]:
class NetDropout(nn.Module):
    def __init__(self, n_chans1=32):
        super().__init__()
        self.n_chans1 = n_chans1
        self.conv1 = nn.Conv2d(3, n_chans1, kernel_size=3, padding=1)
        self.conv1_dropout = nn.Dropout2d(p=0.4)
        self.conv2 = nn.Conv2d(n_chans1, n_chans1 // 2, kernel_size=3,
                               padding=1)
        self.conv2_dropout = nn.Dropout2d(p=0.4)
        self.fc1 = nn.Linear(8 * 8 * n_chans1 // 2, 32)
        self.fc2 = nn.Linear(32, 2)

    def forward(self, x):
        out = F.max_pool2d(torch.tanh(self.conv1(x)), 2)
        out = self.conv1_dropout(out)
        out = F.max_pool2d(torch.tanh(self.conv2(out)), 2)
        out = self.conv2_dropout(out)
        out = out.view(-1, 8 * 8 * self.n_chans1 // 2)
        out = torch.tanh(self.fc1(out))
        out = self.fc2(out)
        return out
```

Note that dropout is normally active during training, while during the evaluation of a trained model in production, dropout is bypassed or, equivalently, assigned a probability equal to zero. This is controlled through the train property of the Dropout module. Recall that PyTorch lets us switch between the two modalities by calling

```
model.train()
```

or

```
model.eval()
```

on any nn.Model subclass. The call will be automatically replicated on the submodules so that if Dropout is among them, it will behave accordingly in subsequent forward and backward passes.

KEEPING ACTIVATIONS IN CHECK: BATCH NORMALIZATION

Dropout was all the rage when, in 2015, another seminal paper was published by Sergey Ioffe and Christian Szegedy from Google, entitled "Batch Normalization: Accelerating Deep Network Training by Reducing Internal Covariate Shift" (https://arxiv.org/abs/1502.03167). The paper described a technique that had multiple beneficial effects on training: allowing us to increase the learning rate and make training less dependent on initialization and act as a regularizer, thus representing an alternative to dropout.

The main idea behind batch normalization is to rescale the inputs to the activations of the network so that minibatches have a certain desirable distribution. Recalling the mechanics of learning and the role of nonlinear activation functions, this helps avoid the inputs to activation functions being too far into the saturated portion of the function, thereby killing gradients and slowing training.

In practical terms, batch normalization shifts and scales an intermediate input using the mean and standard deviation collected at that intermediate location over the samples of the minibatch. The regularization effect is a result of the fact that an individual sample and its downstream activations are always seen by the model as shifted and scaled, depending on the statistics across the randomly extracted minibatch. This is in itself a form of *principled* augmentation. The authors of the paper suggest that using batch normalization eliminates or at least alleviates the need for dropout.

Batch normalization in PyTorch is provided through the nn.BatchNorm1D, nn.BatchNorm2d, and nn.BatchNorm3d modules, depending on the dimensionality of the input. Since the aim for batch normalization is to rescale the inputs of the activations, the natural location is after the linear transformation (convolution, in this case) and the activation, as shown here:

```
# In[49]:
class NetBatchNorm(nn.Module):
    def __init__(self, n_chans1=32):
        super().__init__()
        self.n_chans1 = n_chans1
        self.conv1 = nn.Conv2d(3, n_chans1, kernel_size=3, padding=1)
        self.conv1_batchnorm = nn.BatchNorm2d(num_features=n_chans1)
        self.conv2 = nn.Conv2d(n_chans1, n_chans1 // 2, kernel_size=3,
                               padding=1)
        self.conv2_batchnorm = nn.BatchNorm2d(num_features=n_chans1 // 2)
        self.fc1 = nn.Linear(8 * 8 * n_chans1 // 2, 32)
        self.fc2 = nn.Linear(32, 2)

    def forward(self, x):
        out = self.conv1_batchnorm(self.conv1(x))
        out = F.max_pool2d(torch.tanh(out), 2)
```

```
out = self.conv2_batchnorm(self.conv2(out))
out = F.max_pool2d(torch.tanh(out), 2)
out = out.view(-1, 8 * 8 * self.n_chans1 // 2)
out = torch.tanh(self.fc1(out))
out = self.fc2(out)
return out
```

Just as for dropout, batch normalization needs to behave differently during training and inference. In fact, at inference time, we want to avoid having the output for a specific input depend on the statistics of the other inputs we're presenting to the model. As such, we need a way to still normalize, but this time fixing the normalization parameters once and for all.

As minibatches are processed, in addition to estimating the mean and standard deviation for the current minibatch, PyTorch also updates the running estimates for mean and standard deviation that are representative of the whole dataset, as an approximation. This way, when the user specifies

```
model.eval()
```

and the model contains a batch normalization module, the running estimates are frozen and used for normalization. To unfreeze running estimates and return to using the minibatch statistics, we call `model.train()`, just as we did for dropout.

8.5.3 *Going deeper to learn more complex structures: Depth*

Earlier, we talked about width as the first dimension to act on in order to make a model larger and, in a way, more capable. The second fundamental dimension is obviously *depth*. Since this is a deep learning book, depth is something we're supposedly into. After all, deeper models are always better than shallow ones, aren't they? Well, it depends. With depth, the complexity of the function the network is able to approximate generally increases. In regard to computer vision, a shallower network could identify a person's shape in a photo, whereas a deeper network could identify the person, the face on their top half, and the mouth within the face. Depth allows a model to deal with hierarchical information when we need to understand the context in order to say something about some input.

There's another way to think about depth: increasing depth is related to increasing the length of the sequence of operations that the network will be able to perform when processing input. This view—of a deep network that performs sequential operations to carry out a task—is likely fascinating to software developers who are used to thinking about algorithms as sequences of operations like "find the person's boundaries, look for the head on top of the boundaries, look for the mouth within the head."

SKIP CONNECTIONS

Depth comes with some additional challenges, which prevented deep learning models from reaching 20 or more layers until late 2015. Adding depth to a model generally makes training harder to converge. Let's recall backpropagation and think about it in the context of a very deep network. The derivatives of the loss function with respect to the parameters, especially those in early layers, need to be multiplied by a lot of other numbers originating from the chain of derivative operations between the loss and the parameter. Those numbers being multiplied could be small, generating ever-smaller numbers, or large, swallowing smaller numbers due to floating-point approximation. The bottom line is that a long chain of multiplications will tend to make the contribution of the parameter to the gradient *vanish*, leading to ineffective training of that layer since that parameter and others like it won't be properly updated.

In December 2015, Kaiming He and coauthors presented *residual networks* (ResNets), an architecture that uses a simple trick to allow very deep networks to be successfully trained (https://arxiv.org/abs/1512.03385). That work opened the door to networks ranging from tens of layers to 100 layers in depth, surpassing the then state of the art in computer vision benchmark problems. We encountered residual networks when we were playing with pretrained models in chapter 2. The trick we mentioned is the following: using a *skip connection* to short-circuit blocks of layers, as shown in figure 8.11.

A skip connection is nothing but the addition of the input to the output of a block of layers. This is exactly how it is done in PyTorch. Let's add one layer to our simple convolutional model, and let's use ReLU as the activation for a change. The vanilla module with an extra layer looks like this:

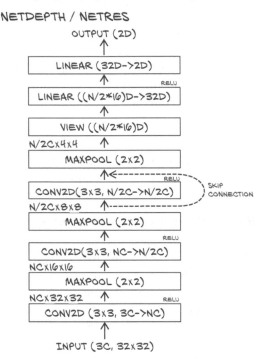

Figure 8.11   The architecture of our network with three convolutional layers. The skip connection is what differentiates `NetRes` from `NetDepth`.

```
# In[51]:
class NetDepth(nn.Module):
    def __init__(self, n_chans1=32):
        super().__init__()
        self.n_chans1 = n_chans1
        self.conv1 = nn.Conv2d(3, n_chans1, kernel_size=3, padding=1)
        self.conv2 = nn.Conv2d(n_chans1, n_chans1 // 2, kernel_size=3,
                               padding=1)
        self.conv3 = nn.Conv2d(n_chans1 // 2, n_chans1 // 2,
                               kernel_size=3, padding=1)
        self.fc1 = nn.Linear(4 * 4 * n_chans1 // 2, 32)
        self.fc2 = nn.Linear(32, 2)
```

```
    def forward(self, x):
        out = F.max_pool2d(torch.relu(self.conv1(x)), 2)
        out = F.max_pool2d(torch.relu(self.conv2(out)), 2)
        out = F.max_pool2d(torch.relu(self.conv3(out)), 2)
        out = out.view(-1, 4 * 4 * self.n_chans1 // 2)
        out = torch.relu(self.fc1(out))
        out = self.fc2(out)
        return out
```

Adding a skip connection a la ResNet to this model amounts to adding the output of the first layer in the forward function to the input of the third layer:

```
# In[53]:
class NetRes(nn.Module):
    def __init__(self, n_chans1=32):
        super().__init__()
        self.n_chans1 = n_chans1
        self.conv1 = nn.Conv2d(3, n_chans1, kernel_size=3, padding=1)
        self.conv2 = nn.Conv2d(n_chans1, n_chans1 // 2, kernel_size=3,
                                  padding=1)
        self.conv3 = nn.Conv2d(n_chans1 // 2, n_chans1 // 2,
                                  kernel_size=3, padding=1)
        self.fc1 = nn.Linear(4 * 4 * n_chans1 // 2, 32)
        self.fc2 = nn.Linear(32, 2)

    def forward(self, x):
        out = F.max_pool2d(torch.relu(self.conv1(x)), 2)
        out = F.max_pool2d(torch.relu(self.conv2(out)), 2)
        out1 = out
        out = F.max_pool2d(torch.relu(self.conv3(out)) + out1, 2)
        out = out.view(-1, 4 * 4 * self.n_chans1 // 2)
        out = torch.relu(self.fc1(out))
        out = self.fc2(out)
        return out
```

In other words, we're using the output of the first activations as inputs to the last, in addition to the standard feed-forward path. This is also referred to as *identity mapping*. So, how does this alleviate the issues with vanishing gradients we were mentioning earlier?

Thinking about backpropagation, we can appreciate that a skip connection, or a sequence of skip connections in a deep network, creates a direct path from the deeper parameters to the loss. This makes their contribution to the gradient of the loss more direct, as partial derivatives of the loss with respect to those parameters have a chance not to be multiplied by a long chain of other operations.

It has been observed that skip connections have a beneficial effect on convergence especially in the initial phases of training. Also, the loss landscape of deep residual networks is a lot smoother than feed-forward networks of the same depth and width.

It is worth noting that skip connections were not new to the world when ResNets came along. Highway networks and U-Net made use of skip connections of one form or another. However, the way ResNets used skip connections enabled models of depths greater than 100 to be amenable to training.

Since the advent of ResNets, other architectures have taken skip connections to the next level. One in particular, DenseNet, proposed to connect each layer with several other layers downstream through skip connections, achieving state-of-the-art results with fewer parameters. By now, we know how to implement something like DenseNets: just arithmetically add earlier intermediate outputs to downstream intermediate outputs.

BUILDING VERY DEEP MODELS IN PYTORCH

We talked about exceeding 100 layers in a convolutional neural network. How can we build that network in PyTorch without losing our minds in the process? The standard strategy is to define a building block, such as a `(Conv2d, ReLU, Conv2d)` + `skip connection` block, and then build the network dynamically in a `for` loop. Let's see it done in practice. We will create the network depicted in figure 8.12.

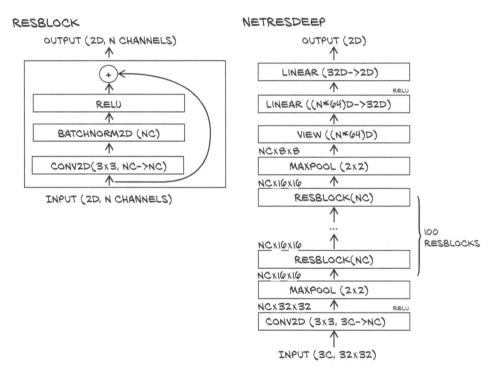

Figure 8.12 Our deep architecture with residual connections. On the left, we define a simplistic residual block. We use it as a building block in our network, as shown on the right.

We first create a module subclass whose sole job is to provide the computation for one *block*—that is, one group of convolutions, activation, and skip connection:

```
# In[55]:
class ResBlock(nn.Module):
    def __init__(self, n_chans):
        super(ResBlock, self).__init__()
        self.conv = nn.Conv2d(n_chans, n_chans, kernel_size=3,
                                padding=1, bias=False)
        self.batch_norm = nn.BatchNorm2d(num_features=n_chans)
        torch.nn.init.kaiming_normal_(self.conv.weight,
                                nonlinearity='relu')
        torch.nn.init.constant_(self.batch_norm.weight, 0.5)
        torch.nn.init.zeros_(self.batch_norm.bias)

    def forward(self, x):
        out = self.conv(x)
        out = self.batch_norm(out)
        out = torch.relu(out)
        return out + x
```

The BatchNorm layer would cancel the effect of bias, so it is customarily left out.

Uses custom initializations . kaiming_normal_ initializes with normal random elements with standard deviation as computed in the ResNet paper. The batch norm is initialized to produce output distributions that initially have 0 mean and 0.5 variance.

Since we're planning to generate a deep model, we are including batch normalization in the block, since this will help prevent gradients from vanishing during training. We'd now like to generate a 100-block network. Does this mean we have to prepare for some serious cutting and pasting? Not at all; we already have the ingredients for imagining how this could look like.

First, in *init*, we create nn.Sequential containing a list of ResBlock instances. nn.Sequential will ensure that the output of one block is used as input to the next. It will also ensure that all the parameters in the block are visible to Net. Then, in forward, we just call the sequential to traverse the 100 blocks and generate the output:

```
# In[56]:
class NetResDeep(nn.Module):
    def __init__(self, n_chans1=32, n_blocks=10):
        super().__init__()
        self.n_chans1 = n_chans1
        self.conv1 = nn.Conv2d(3, n_chans1, kernel_size=3, padding=1)
        self.resblocks = nn.Sequential(
            *(n_blocks * [ResBlock(n_chans=n_chans1)]))
        self.fc1 = nn.Linear(8 * 8 * n_chans1, 32)
        self.fc2 = nn.Linear(32, 2)

    def forward(self, x):
        out = F.max_pool2d(torch.relu(self.conv1(x)), 2)
        out = self.resblocks(out)
        out = F.max_pool2d(out, 2)
        out = out.view(-1, 8 * 8 * self.n_chans1)
        out = torch.relu(self.fc1(out))
        out = self.fc2(out)
        return out
```

In the implementation, we parameterize the actual number of layers, which is important for experimentation and reuse. Also, needless to say, backpropagation will work as expected. Unsurprisingly, the network is quite a bit slower to converge. It is also more fragile in convergence. This is why we used more-detailed initializations and trained our NetRes with a learning rate of 3e − 3 instead of the 1e − 2 we used for the other networks. We trained none of the networks to convergence, but we would not have gotten anywhere without these tweaks.

All this shouldn't encourage us to seek depth on a dataset of 32 × 32 images, but it clearly demonstrates how this can be achieved on more challenging datasets like Image-Net. It also provides the key elements for understanding existing implementations for models like ResNet, for instance, in torchvision.

INITIALIZATION

Let's briefly comment about the earlier initialization. Initialization is one of the important tricks in training neural networks. Unfortunately, for historical reasons, PyTorch has default weight initializations that are not ideal. People are looking at fixing the situation; if progress is made, it can be tracked on GitHub (https://github.com/pytorch/pytorch/issues/18182). In the meantime, we need to fix the weight initialization ourselves. We found that our model did not converge and looked at what people commonly choose as initialization (a smaller variance in weights; and zero mean and unit variance outputs for batch norm), and then we halved the output variance in the batch norm when the network would not converge.

Weight initialization could fill an entire chapter on its own, but we think that would be excessive. In chapter 11, we'll bump into initialization again and use what arguably could be PyTorch defaults without much explanation. Once you've progressed to the point where the details of weight initialization are of specific interest to you—probably not before finishing this book—you might revisit this topic.[10]

8.5.4 *Comparing the designs from this section*

We summarize the effect of each of our design modifications in isolation in figure 8.13. We should not overinterpret any of the specific numbers—our problem setup and experiments are simplistic, and repeating the experiment with different random seeds will probably generate variation at least as large as the differences in validation accuracy. For this demonstration, we left all other things equal, from learning rate to number of epochs to train; in practice, we would try to get the best results by varying those. Also, we would likely want to combine some of the additional design elements.

But a qualitative observation may be in order: as we saw in section 5.5.3, when discussing validatioin and overfitting, The weight decay and dropout regularizations, which have a more rigorous statistical estimation interpretation as regularization than batch norm, have a much narrower gap between the two accuracies. Batch norm, which

---

[10] The seminal paper on the topic is by X. Glorot and Y. Bengio: "Understanding the Difficulty of Training Deep Feedforward Neural Networks" (2010), which introduces PyTorch's *Xavier* initializations (http://mng.bz/vxz7). The ResNet paper we mentioned expands on the topic, too, giving us the Kaiming initializations used earlier. More recently, H. Zhang et al. have tweaked initialization to the point that they do not need batch norm in their experiments with very deep residual networks (https://arxiv.org/abs/1901.09321).

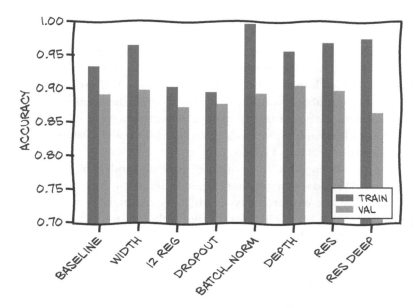

Figure 8.13 The modified networks all perform similarly.

serves more as a convergence helper, lets us train the network to nearly 100% training accuracy, so we interpret the first two as regularization.

8.5.5 It's already outdated

The curse and blessing of a deep learning practitioner is that neural network architectures evolve at a very rapid pace. This is not to say that what we've seen in this chapter is necessarily old school, but a thorough illustration of the latest and greatest architectures is a matter for another book (and they would cease to be the latest and the greatest pretty quickly anyway). The take-home message is that we should make every effort to proficiently translate the math behind a paper into actual PyTorch code, or at least understand the code that others have written with the same intention. In the last few chapters, you have hopefully gathered quite a few of the fundamental skills to translate ideas into implemented models in PyTorch.

8.6 Conclusion

After quite a lot of work, we now have a model that our fictional friend Jane can use to filter images for her blog. All we have to do is take an incoming image, crop and resize it to 32 × 32, and see what the model has to say about it. Admittedly, we have solved only part of the problem, but it was a journey in itself.

We have solved just part of the problem because there are a few interesting unknowns we would still have to face. One is picking out a bird or airplane from a larger image. Creating bounding boxes around objects in an image is something a model like ours can't do.

Another hurdle concerns what happens when Fred the cat walks in front of the camera. Our model will not refrain from giving its opinion about how bird-like the cat is! It will happily output "airplane" or "bird," perhaps with 0.99 probability. This issue of being very confident about samples that are far from the training distribution is called *overgeneralization*. It's one of the main problems when we take a (presumably good) model to production in those cases where we can't really trust the input (which, sadly, is the majority of real-world cases).

In this chapter, we have built reasonable, working models in PyTorch that can learn from images. We did it in a way that helped us build our intuition around convolutional networks. We also explored ways in which we can make our models wider and deeper, while controlling effects like overfitting. Although we still only scratched the surface, we have taken another significant step ahead from the previous chapter. We now have a solid basis for facing the challenges we'll encounter when working on deep learning projects.

Now that we're familiar with PyTorch conventions and common features, we're ready to tackle something bigger. We're going to transition from a mode where each chapter or two presents a small problem, to spending multiple chapters breaking down a bigger, real-world problem. Part 2 uses automatic detection of lung cancer as an ongoing example; we will go from being familiar with the PyTorch API to being able to implement entire projects using PyTorch. We'll start in the next chapter by explaining the problem from a high level, and then we'll get into the details of the data we'll be using.

8.7   *Exercises*

1   Change our model to use a 5 × 5 kernel with `kernel_size=5` passed to the `nn.Conv2d` constructor.
    a   What impact does this change have on the number of parameters in the model?
    b   Does the change improve or degrade overfitting?
    c   Read https://pytorch.org/docs/stable/nn.html#conv2d.
    d   Can you describe what `kernel_size=(1,3)` will do?
    e   How does the model behave with such a kernel?
2   Can you find an image that contains neither a bird nor an airplane, but that the model claims has one or the other with more than 95% confidence?
    a   Can you manually edit a neutral image to make it more airplane-like?
    b   Can you manually edit an airplane image to trick the model into reporting a bird?
    c   Do these tasks get easier with a network with less capacity? More capacity?

8.8 Summary

- Convolution can be used as the linear operation of a feed-forward network dealing with images. Using convolution produces networks with fewer parameters, exploiting locality and featuring translation invariance.

- Stacking multiple convolutions with their activations one after the other, and using max pooling in between, has the effect of applying convolutions to increasingly smaller feature images, thereby effectively accounting for spatial relationships across larger portions of the input image as depth increases.

- Any `nn.Module` subclass can recursively collect and return its and its children's parameters. This technique can be used to count them, feed them into the optimizer, or inspect their values.

- The functional API provides modules that do not depend on storing internal state. It is used for operations that do not hold parameters and, hence, are not trained.

- Once trained, parameters of a model can be saved to disk and loaded back in with one line of code each.

Learning from images in the real world: Early detection of lung cancer

Part 2 is structured differently than part 1; it's almost a book within a book. We'll take a single use case and explore it in depth over the course of several chapters, starting with the basic building blocks we learned in part 1, and building out a more complete project than we've seen so far. Our first attempts are going to be incomplete and inaccurate, and we'll explore how to diagnose those problems and then fix them. We'll also identify various other improvements to our solution, implement them, and measure their impact. In order to train the models we'll develop in part 2, you will need access to a GPU with at least 8 GB of RAM as well as several hundred gigabytes of free disk space to store the training data.

Chapter 9 introduces the project, environment, and data we will consume and the structure of the project we'll implement. Chapter 10 shows how we can turn our data into a PyTorch dataset, and chapters 11 and 12 introduce our classification model: the metrics we need to gauge how well the dataset is training, and implement solutions to problems preventing the model from training well. In chapter 13, we'll shift gears to the beginning of the end-to-end project by creating a segmentation model that produces a heatmap rather than a single classification. That heatmap will be used to generate locations to classify. Finally, in chapter 14, we'll combine our segmentation and classification models to perform a final diagnosis.

Using PyTorch
to fight cancer

This chapter covers

- Breaking a large problem into smaller, easier ones
- Exploring the constraints of an intricate deep learning problem, and deciding on a structure and approach
- Downloading the training data

We have two main goals for this chapter. We'll start by covering the overall plan for part 2 of the book so that we have a solid idea of the larger scope the following individual chapters will be building toward. In chapter 10, we will begin to build out the data-parsing and data-manipulation routines that will produce data to be consumed in chapter 11 while training our first model. In order to do what's needed for those upcoming chapters well, we'll also use this chapter to cover some of the context in which our project will be operating: we'll go over data formats, data sources, and exploring the constraints that our problem domain places on us. Get used to performing these tasks, since you'll have to do them for any serious deep learning project!

9.1 Introduction to the use case

Our goal for this part of the book is to give you the tools to deal with situations where things aren't working, which is a far more common state of affairs than part 1 might have led you to believe. We can't predict every failure case or cover every debugging technique, but hopefully we'll give you enough to not feel stuck when you encounter a new roadblock. Similarly, we want to help you avoid situations with your own projects where you have no idea what you could do next when your projects are under-performing. Instead, we hope your ideas list will be so long that the challenge will be to prioritize!

In order to present these ideas and techniques, we need a context with some nuance and a fair bit of heft to it. We've chosen automatic detection of malignant tumors in the lungs using only a CT scan of a patient's chest as input. We'll be focusing on the technical challenges rather than the human impact, but make no mistake—even from just an engineering perspective, part 2 will require a more serious, structured approach than we needed in part 1 in order to have the project succeed.

> NOTE CT scans are essentially 3D X-rays, represented as a 3D array of single-channel data. We'll cover them in more detail soon.

As you might have guessed, the title of this chapter is more eye-catching, implied hyperbole than anything approaching a serious statement of intent. Let us be precise: our project in this part of the book will take three-dimensional CT scans of human torsos as input and produce as output the location of suspected malignant tumors, if any exist.

Detecting lung cancer early has a huge impact on survival rate, but is difficult to do manually, especially in any comprehensive, whole-population sense. Currently, the work of reviewing the data must be performed by highly trained specialists, requires painstaking attention to detail, and it is dominated by cases where no cancer exists.

Doing that job well is akin to being placed in front of 100 haystacks and being told, "Determine which of these, if any, contain a needle." Searching this way results in the potential for missed warning signs, particularly in the early stages when the hints are more subtle. The human brain just isn't built well for that kind of monotonous work. And that, of course, is where deep learning comes in.

Automating this process is going to give us experience working in an uncooperative environment where we have to do more work from scratch, and there are fewer easy answers to problems that we might run into. Together, we'll get there, though! Once you're finished reading part 2, we think you'll be ready to start working on a real-world, unsolved problem of your own choosing.

We chose this problem of lung tumor detection for a few reasons. The primary reason is that the problem itself is unsolved! This is important, because we want to make it clear that you can use PyTorch to tackle cutting-edge projects effectively. We hope that increases your confidence in PyTorch as a framework, as well as in yourself as a developer. Another nice aspect of this problem space is that while it's unsolved, a lot of teams have been paying attention to it recently and have seen promising results. That means this challenge is probably right at the edge of our collective ability to solve; we won't be wasting our time on a problem that's actually decades away from reasonable solutions. That attention on the problem has also resulted in a lot of high-quality papers and open source projects, which are a great source of inspiration and ideas. This will be a huge help once we conclude part 2 of the book, if you are interested in continuing to improve on the solution we create. We'll provide some links to additional information in chapter 14.

This part of the book will remain focused on the problem of detecting lung tumors, but the skills we'll teach are general. Learning how to investigate, preprocess, and present your data for training is important no matter what project you're working on. While we'll be covering preprocessing in the specific context of lung tumors, the general idea is that *this is what you should be prepared to do* for your project to succeed. Similarly, setting up a training loop, getting the right performance metrics, and tying the project's models together into a final application are all general skills that we'll employ as we go through chapters 9 through 14.

> **NOTE** While the end result of part 2 will work, the output will not be accurate enough to use clinically. We're focusing on using this as a motivating example for *teaching PyTorch*, not on employing every last trick to solve the problem.

9.2 *Preparing for a large-scale project*

This project will build off of the foundational skills learned in part 1. In particular, the content covering model construction from chapter 8 will be directly relevant. Repeated convolutional layers followed by a resolution-reducing downsampling layer will still make up the majority of our model. We will use 3D data as input to our model, however. This is conceptually similar to the 2D image data used in the last few chapters of part 1, but we will not be able to rely on all of the 2D-specific tools available in the PyTorch ecosystem.

The main differences between the work we did with convolutional models in chapter 8 and what we'll do in part 2 are related to how much effort we put into things outside the model itself. In chapter 8, we used a provided, off-the-shelf dataset and did little data manipulation before feeding the data into a model for classification. Almost all of our time and attention were spent building the model itself, whereas now we're not even going to begin designing the first of our two model architectures until chapter 11. That is a direct consequence of having nonstandard data without prebuilt libraries ready to hand us training samples suitable to plug into a model. We'll have to learn about our data and implement quite a bit ourselves.

Even when that's done, this will not end up being a case where we convert the CT to a tensor, feed it into a neural network, and have the answer pop out the other side. As is common for real-world use cases such as this, a workable approach will be more complicated to account for confounding factors such as limited data availability, finite computational resources, and limitations on our ability to design effective models. Please keep that in mind as we build to a high-level explanation of our project architecture.

Speaking of finite computational resources, part 2 will require access to a GPU to achieve reasonable training speeds, preferably one with at least 8 GB of RAM. Trying to train the models we will build on CPU could take weeks![1] If you don't have a GPU handy, we provide pretrained models in chapter 14; the nodule analysis script there can probably be run overnight. While we don't want to tie the book to proprietary services if we don't have to, we should note that at the time of writing, Colaboratory (https://colab.research.google.com) provides free GPU instances that might be of use. PyTorch even comes preinstalled! You will also need to have at least 220 GB of free disk space to store the raw training data, cached data, and trained models.

> **NOTE** Many of the code examples presented in part 2 have complicating details omitted. Rather than clutter the examples with logging, error handling, and edge cases, the text of this book contains only code that expresses the core idea under discussion. Full working code samples can be found on the book's website (www.manning.com/books/deep-learning-with-pytorch) and GitHub (https://github.com/deep-learning-with-pytorch/dlwpt-code).

OK, we've established that this is a hard, multifaceted problem, but what are we going to do about it? Instead of looking at an entire CT scan for signs of tumors or their potential malignancy, we're going to solve a series of simpler problems that will combine to provide the end-to-end result we're interested in. Like a factory assembly line, each step will take raw materials (data) and/or output from previous steps, perform some processing, and hand off the result to the next station down the line. Not every problem needs to be solved this way, but breaking off chunks of the problem to solve in isolation is often a great way to start. Even if it turns out to be the wrong approach for a given project, it's likely we'll have learned enough while working on the individual chunks that we'll have a good idea how to restructure our approach into something successful.

Before we get into the details of how we'll break down our problem, we need to learn some details about the medical domain. While the code listings will tell you *what* we're doing, learning about radiation oncology will explain *why*. Learning about the problem space is crucial, no matter what domain it is. Deep learning is powerful, but it's not magic, and trying to apply it blindly to nontrivial problems will likely fail. Instead, we have to combine insights into the space with intuition about neural network behavior. From there, disciplined experimentation and refinement should give us enough information to close in on a workable solution.

9.3 *What is a CT scan, exactly?*

Before we get too far into the project, we need to take a moment to explain what a CT scan is. We will be using data from CT scans extensively as the main data format for our project, so having a working understanding of the data format's strengths, weaknesses, and fundamental nature will be crucial to utilizing it well. The key point we noted earlier is this: CT scans are essentially 3D X-rays, represented as a 3D array of

---

[1]We presume—we haven't tried it, much less timed it.

single-channel data. As we might recall from chapter 4, this is like a stacked set of gray-scale PNG images.

> **Voxel**
>
> A *voxel* is the 3D equivalent to the familiar two-dimensional pixel. It encloses a volume of space (hence, "volumetric pixel"), rather than an area, and is typically arranged in a 3D grid to represent a field of data. Each of those dimensions will have a measurable distance associated with it. Often, voxels are cubic, but for this chapter, we will be dealing with voxels that are rectangular prisms.

In addition to medical data, we can see similar voxel data in fluid simulations, 3D scene reconstructions from 2D images, light detection and ranging (LIDAR) data for self-driving cars, and many other problem spaces. Those spaces all have their individual quirks and subtleties, and while the APIs that we're going to cover here apply generally, we must also be aware of the nature of the data we're using with those APIs if we want to be effective.

Each voxel of a CT scan has a numeric value that roughly corresponds to the average mass density of the matter contained inside. Most visualizations of that data show high-density material like bones and metal implants as white, low-density air and lung tissue as black, and fat and tissue as various shades of gray. Again, this ends up looking somewhat similar to an X-ray, with some key differences.

The primary difference between CT scans and X-rays is that whereas an X-ray is a projection of 3D intensity (in this case, tissue and bone density) onto a 2D plane, a CT scan retains the third dimension of the data. This allows us to render the data in a variety of ways: for example, as a grayscale solid, which we can see in figure 9.1.

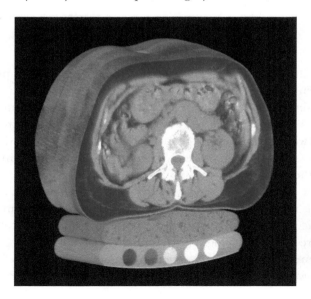

Figure 9.1   A CT scan of a human torso showing, from the top, skin, organs, spine, and patient support bed. Source: http://mng.bz/04r6; Mindways CT Software / CC BY-SA 3.0 (https:// creativecommons.org/licenses/by-sa/ 3.0/deed.en).

NOTE CT scans actually measure radiodensity, which is a function of both mass density and atomic number of the material under examination. For our purposes here, the distinction isn't relevant, since the model will consume and learn from the CT data no matter what the exact units of the input happen to be.

This 3D representation also allows us to "see inside" the subject by hiding tissue types we are not interested in. For example, we can render the data in 3D and restrict visibility to only bone and lung tissue, as in figure 9.2.

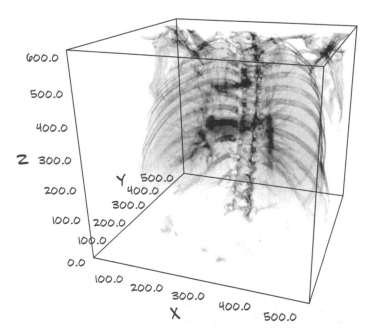

Figure 9.2 A CT scan showing ribs, spine, and lung structures

CT scans are much more difficult to acquire than X-rays, because doing so requires a machine like the one shown in figure 9.3 that typically costs upward of a million dollars new and requires trained staff to operate it. Most hospitals and some well-equipped clinics have a CT scanner, but they aren't nearly as ubiquitous as X-ray machines. This, combined with patient privacy regulations, can make it somewhat difficult to get CT scans unless someone has already done the work of gathering and organizing a collection of them.

Figure 9.3 also shows an example bounding box for the area contained in the CT scan. The bed the patient is resting on moves back and forth, allowing the scanner to image multiple slices of the patient and hence fill the bounding box. The scanner's darker, central ring is where the actual imaging equipment is located.

A final difference between a CT scan and an X-ray is that the data is a digital-only format. *CT* stands for *computed tomography* (https://en.wikipedia.org/wiki/CT_scan#Process).

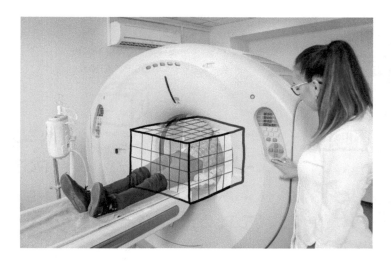

Figure 9.3 A patient
inside a CT scanner, with
the CT scan's bounding
box overlaid. Other than
in stock photos, patients
don't typically wear
street clothes while
in the machine.

The raw output of the scanning process doesn't look particularly meaningful to the human eye and must be properly reinterpreted by a computer into something we can understand. The settings of the CT scanner when the scan is taken can have a large impact on the resulting data.

While this information might not seem particularly relevant, we have actually learned something that is: from figure 9.3, we can see that the way the CT scanner measures distance along the head-to-foot axis is different than the other two axes. The patient actually moves along that axis! This explains (or at least is a strong hint as to) why our voxels might not be cubic, and also ties into how we approach massaging our data in chapter 12. This is a good example of why we need to understand our problem space if we're going to make effective choices about how to solve our problem. When starting to work on your own projects, be sure you do the same investigation into the details of your data.

9.4 The project: An end-to-end detector for lung cancer

Now that we've got our heads wrapped around the basics of CT scans, let's discuss the structure of our project. Most of the bytes on disk will be devoted to storing the CT scans' 3D arrays containing density information, and our models will primarily consume various subslices of those 3D arrays. We're going to use five main steps to go from examining a whole-chest CT scan to giving the patient a lung cancer diagnosis.

Our full, end-to-end solution shown in figure 9.4 will load CT data files to produce a Ct instance that contains the full 3D scan, combine that with a module that performs *segmentation* (flagging voxels of interest), and then group the interesting voxels into small lumps in the search for candidate *nodules*.

The nodule locations are combined back with the CT voxel data to produce nodule candidates, which can then be examined by our nodule classification model to determine whether they are actually nodules in the first place and, eventually, whether

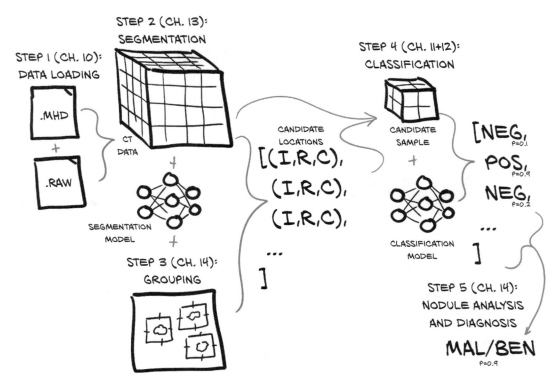

Figure 9.4   The end-to-end process of taking a full-chest CT scan and determining whether the patent has a malignant tumor

> **Nodules**
>
> A mass of tissue made of proliferating cells in the lung is a *tumor*. A tumor can be *benign* or it can be *malignant*, in which case it is also referred to as *cancer*. A small tumor in the lung (just a few millimeters wide) is called a *nodule*. About 40% of lung nodules turn out to be malignant—small cancers. It is very important to catch those as early as possible, and this depends on medical imaging of the kind we are looking at here.

they're malignant. This latter task is particularly difficult because malignancy might not be apparent from CT imaging alone, but we'll see how far we get. Last, each of those individual, per-nodule classifications can then be combined into a whole-patient diagnosis.

In more detail, we will do the following:

1   Load our raw CT scan data into a form that we can use with PyTorch. Putting raw data into a form usable by PyTorch will be the first step in any project you face. The process is somewhat less complicated with 2D image data and simpler still with non-image data.

2   Identify the voxels of potential tumors in the lungs using PyTorch to implement a technique known as *segmentation*. This is roughly akin to producing a heatmap of areas that should be fed into our classifier in step 3. This will allow us to focus on potential tumors inside the lungs and ignore huge swaths of uninteresting anatomy (a person can't have lung cancer in the stomach, for example).

Generally, being able to focus on a single, small task is best while learning. With experience, there are some situations where more complicated model structures can yield superlative results (for example, the GAN game we saw in chapter 2), but designing those from scratch requires extensive mastery of the basic building blocks first. Gotta walk before you run, and all that.

3   Group interesting voxels into lumps: that is, candidate nodules (see figure 9.5 for more information on nodules). Here, we will find the rough center of each hotspot on our heatmap.

Each nodule can be located by the index, row, and column of its center point. We do this to present a simple, constrained problem to the final classifier. Grouping voxels will not involve PyTorch directly, which is why we've pulled this out into a separate step. Often, when working with multistep solutions, there will be non-deep-learning glue steps between the larger, deep-learning-powered portions of the project.

4   Classify candidate nodules as actual nodules or non-nodules using 3D convolution.

This will be similar in concept to the 2D convolution we covered in chapter 8. The features that determine the nature of a tumor from a candidate structure are local to the tumor in question, so this approach should provide a good balance between limiting input data size and excluding relevant information. Making scope-limiting decisions like this can keep each individual task constrained, which can help limit the amount of things to examine when troubleshooting.

5   Diagnose the patient using the combined per-nodule classifications.

Similar to the nodule classifier in the previous step, we will attempt to determine whether the nodule is benign or malignant based on imaging data alone. We will take a simple maximum of the per-tumor malignancy predictions, as only one tumor needs to be malignant for a patient to have cancer. Other projects might want to use different ways of aggregating the per-instance predictions into a file score. Here, we are asking, "Is there anything suspicious?" so maximum is a good fit for aggregation. If we were looking for quantitative information like "the ratio of type A tissue to type B tissue," we might take an appropriate mean instead.

Figure 9.4 only depicts the final path through the system once we've built and trained all of the requisite models. The actual work required to train the relevant models will be detailed as we get closer to implementing each step.

The data we'll use for training provides human-annotated output for both steps 3 and 4. This allows us to treat steps 2 and 3 (identifying voxels and grouping them into nodule candidates) as almost a separate project from step 4 (nodule candidate

On the shoulders of giants

We are *standing on the shoulders of giants* when deciding on this five-step approach. We'll discuss these giants and their work more in chapter 14. There isn't any particular reason why we should know in advance that this project structure will work well for this problem; instead, we're relying on others who have actually implemented similar things and reported success when doing so. Expect to have to experiment to find workable approaches when transitioning to a different domain, but always try to learn from earlier efforts in the space and from those who have worked in similar areas and have discovered things that might transfer well. Go out there, look for what others have done, and use that as a benchmark. At the same time, avoid getting code and running it *blindly*, because you need to fully understand the code you're running in order to use the results to make progress for yourself.

classification). Human experts have annotated the data with nodule locations, so we can work on either steps 2 and 3 or step 4 in whatever order we prefer.

We will first work on step 1 (data loading), and then jump to step 4 before we come back and implement steps 2 and 3, since step 4 (classification) requires an approach similar to what we used in chapter 8, using multiple convolutional and pooling layers to aggregate spatial information before feeding it into a linear classifier. Once we've got a handle on our classification model, we can start working on step 2 (segmentation). Since segmentation is the more complicated topic, we want to tackle it without having to learn both segmentation and the fundamentals of CT scans and malignant tumors at the same time. Instead, we'll explore the cancer-detection space while working on a more familiar classification problem.

This approach of starting in the middle of the problem and working our way out probably seems odd. Starting at step 1 and working our way forward would make more intuitive sense. Being able to carve up the problem and work on steps independently is useful, however, since it can encourage more modular solutions; in addition, it's easier to partition the workload between members of a small team. Also, actual clinical users would likely prefer a system that flags suspicious nodules for review rather than provides a single binary diagnosis. Adapting our modular solution to different use cases will probably be easier than if we'd done a monolithic, from-the-top system.

As we work our way through implementing each step, we'll be going into a fair bit of detail about lung tumors, as well as presenting a lot of fine-grained detail about CT scans. While that might seem off-topic for a book that's focused on PyTorch, we're doing so specifically so that you begin to develop an intuition about the problem space. That's crucial to have, because the space of all possible solutions and approaches is too large to effectively code, train, and evaluate.

If we were working on a different project (say, the one you tackle after finishing this book), we'd still need to do an investigation to understand the data and problem space. Perhaps you're interested in satellite mapping, and your next project needs to consume pictures of our planet taken from orbit. You'd need to ask questions about the wavelengths being collected—do you get only normal RGB, or something more exotic? What about infrared or ultraviolet? In addition, there might be impacts on the images based on time of day, or if the imaged location isn't directly under the satellite, skewing the image. Will the image need correction?

Even if your hypothetical *third* project's data type remains the same, it's probable that the domain you'll be working in will change things, possibly drastically. Processing camera output for self-driving cars still involves 2D images, but the complications and caveats are wildly different. For example, it's much less likely that a mapping satellite will need to worry about the sun shining into the camera, or getting mud on the lens!

We must be able to use our intuition to guide our investigation into potential optimizations and improvements. That's true of deep learning projects in general, and we'll practice using our intuition as we go through part 2. So, let's do that. Take a quick step back, and do a gut check. What does your intuition say about this approach? Does it seem overcomplicated to you?

9.4.1 *Why can't we just throw data at a neural network until it works?*

After reading the last section, we couldn't blame you for thinking, "This is nothing like chapter 8!" You might be wondering why we've got two separate model architectures or why the overall data flow is so complicated. Well, our approach is different from that in chapter 8 for a reason. It's a hard task to automate, and people haven't fully figured it out yet. That difficulty translates to complexity; once we as a society have solved this problem definitively, there will probably be an off-the-shelf library package we can grab to have it Just Work, but we're not there just yet.

Why so difficult, though?

Well, for starters, the majority of a CT scan is fundamentally uninteresting with regard to answering the question, "Does this patient have a malignant tumor?" This makes intuitive sense, since the vast majority of the patient's body will consist of healthy cells. In the cases where there is a malignant tumor, up to 99.9999% of the voxels in the CT still won't be cancer. That ratio is equivalent to a two-pixel blob of incorrectly tinted color somewhere on a high-definition television, or a single misspelled word out of a shelf of novels.

Can you identify the white dot in the three views of figure 9.5 that has been flagged as a nodule?[2]

If you need a hint, the index, row, and column values can be used to help find the relevant blob of dense tissue. Do you think you could figure out the relevant properties of tumors given only images (and that means *only* the images—no index, row, and column information!) like these? What if you were given the entire 3D scan, not just three slices that intersect the interesting part of the scan?

> **NOTE** Don't fret if you can't locate the tumor! We're trying to illustrate just how subtle this data can be—the fact that it is hard to identify visually is the entire point of this example.

---

[2]The series_uid of this sample is 1.3.6.1.4.1.14519.5.2.1.6279.6001.12626457893177825889037 1755354, which can be useful if you'd like to look at it in detail later.

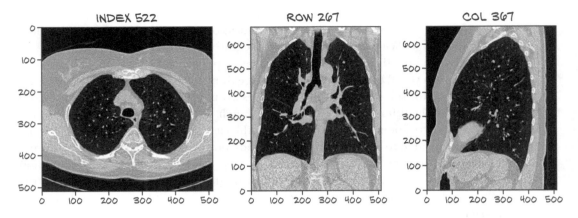

Figure 9.5   A CT scan with approximately 1,000 structures that look like tumors to the untrained eye. Exactly one has been identified as a nodule when reviewed by a human specialist. The rest are normal anatomical structures like blood vessels, lesions, and other non-problematic lumps.

You might have seen elsewhere that end-to-end approaches for detection and classification of objects are very successful in general vision tasks. TorchVision includes end-to-end models like Fast R-CNN/Mask R-CNN, but these are typically trained on hundreds of thousands of images, and those datasets aren't constrained by the number of samples from rare classes. The project architecture we will use has the benefit of working well with a more modest amount of data. So while it's certainly theoretically possible to just throw an arbitrarily large amount of data at a neural network until it learns the specifics of the proverbial lost needle, as well as how to ignore the hay, it's going to be practically prohibitive to collect enough data and wait for a long enough time to train the network properly. That won't be the *best* approach since the results are poor, and most readers won't have access to the compute resources to pull it off at all.

To come up with the best solution, we could investigate proven model designs that can better integrate data in an end-to-end manner.[3] These complicated designs are capable of producing high-quality results, but they're not the *best* because understanding the design decisions behind them requires having mastered fundamental concepts first. That makes these advanced models poor candidates to use while teaching those same fundamentals!

That's not to say that our multistep design is the *best* approach, either, but that's because "best" is only relative to the criteria we chose to evaluate approaches. There are *many* "best" approaches, just as there are many goals we could have in mind as we work on a project. Our self-contained, multistep approach has some disadvantages as well.

Recall the GAN game from chapter 2. There, we had two networks cooperating to produce convincing forgeries of old master artists. The artist would produce a candidate work, and the scholar would critique it, giving the artist feedback on how to

---

[3]For example, Retina U-Net (https://arxiv.org/pdf/1811.08661.pdf) and FishNet (http://mng.bz/K240).

improve. Put in technical terms, the structure of the model allowed gradients to back-propagate from the final classifier (fake or real) to the earliest parts of the project (the artist).

Our approach for solving the problem won't use end-to-end gradient backpropagation to directly optimize for our end goal. Instead, we'll optimize discrete chunks of the problem individually, since our segmentation model and classification model won't be trained in tandem with each other. That might limit the top-end effectiveness of our solution, but we feel that this will make for a much better learning experience.

We feel that being able to focus on a single step at a time allows us to zoom in and concentrate on the smaller number of new skills we're learning. Each of our two models will be focused on performing exactly one task. Similar to a human radiologist as they review slice after slice of CT, the job gets much easier to train for if the scope is well contained. We also want to provide tools that allow for rich manipulation of the data. Being able to zoom in and focus on the detail of a particular location will have a huge impact on overall productivity while training the model compared to having to look at the entire image at once. Our segmentation model is forced to consume the entire image, but we will structure things so that our classification model gets a zoomed-in view of the areas of interest.

Step 3 (grouping) will produce and step 4 (classification) will consume data similar to the image in figure 9.6 containing sequential transverse slices of a tumor. This image is a close-up view of a (potentially malignant, or at least indeterminate) tumor, and it is what we're going to train the step 4 model to identify, and the step 5 model to classify as either benign or malignant. While this lump may seem nondescript to an untrained eye (or untrained convolutional network), identifying the warning signs of malignancy in this sample is at least a far more constrained problem than having to consume the entire CT we saw earlier. Our code for the next chapter will provide routines to produce zoomed-in nodule images like figure 9.6.

We will perform the step 1 data-loading work in chapter 10, and chapters 11 and 12 will focus on solving the problem of classifying these nodules. After that, we'll back up to work on step 2 (using segmentation to find the candidate tumors) in chapter 13, and then we'll close out part 2 of the book in chapter 14 by implementing the end-to-end project with step 3 (grouping) and step 5 (nodule analysis and diagnosis).

NOTE Standard rendering of CTs places the superior at the top of the image (basically, the head goes up), but CTs order their slices such that the first slice is the inferior (toward the feet). So, Matplotlib renders the images upside down unless we take care to flip them. Since that flip doesn't really matter to our model, we won't complicate the code paths between our raw data and the model, but we will add a flip to our rendering code to get the images right-side up. For more information about CT coordinate systems, see section 10.4.

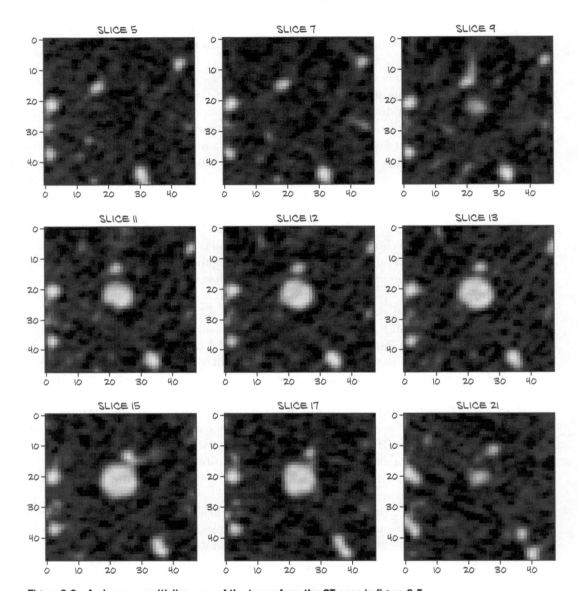

Figure 9.6   A close-up, multislice crop of the tumor from the CT scan in figure 9.5

Let's repeat our high-level overview in figure 9.7.

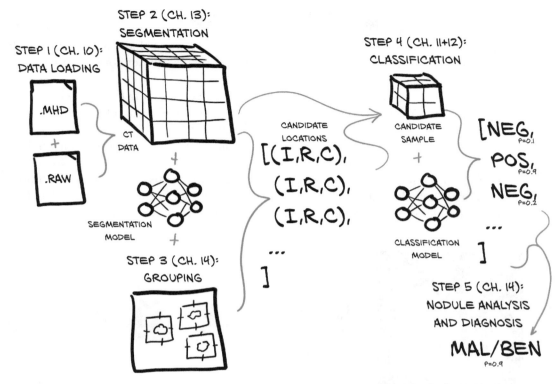

Figure 9.7 The end-to-end process of taking a full-chest CT scan and determining whether the patient has a malignant tumor

9.4.2 What is a nodule?

As we've said, in order to understand our data well enough to use it effectively, we need to learn some specifics about cancer and radiation oncology. One last key thing we need to understand is what a *nodule* is. Simply put, a nodule is any of the myriad lumps and bumps that might appear inside someone's lungs. Some are problematic from a health-of-the-patient perspective; some are not. The precise definition[4] limits the size of a nodule to 3 cm or less, with a larger lump being a *lung mass*; but we're going to use *nodule* interchangeably for all such anatomical structures, since it's a somewhat arbitrary cutoff and we're going to deal with lumps on both sides of 3 cm using the same code paths. A nodule—a small mass in the lung—can turn out to be benign or a malignant tumor (also referred to as *cancer*). From a radiological perspective, a nodule is really similar to other lumps that have a wide variety of causes: infection, inflammation, blood-supply issues, malformed blood vessels, and diseases other than tumors.

---

[4] Eric J. Olson, "Lung nodules: Can they be cancerous?" Mayo Clinic, http://mng.bz/yyge.

The key part is this: the cancers that we are trying to detect will *always* be nodules, either suspended in the very non-dense tissue of the lung or attached to the lung wall. That means we can limit our classifier to only nodules, rather than have it examine all tissue. Being able to restrict the scope of expected inputs will help our classifier learn the task at hand.

This is another example of how the underlying deep learning techniques we'll use are universal, but they can't be applied blindly.[5] We'll need to understand the field we're working in to make choices that will serve us well.

In figure 9.8, we can see a stereotypical example of a malignant nodule. The smallest nodules we'll be concerned with are only a few millimeters across, though the one in figure 9.8 is larger. As we discussed earlier in the chapter, this makes the smallest nodules approximately a million times smaller than the CT scan as a whole. More than half of the nodules detected in patients are not malignant.[6]

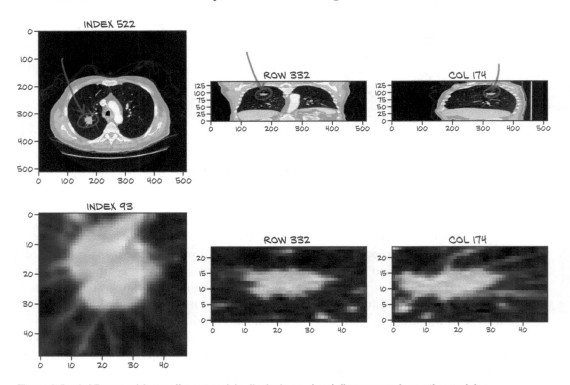

Figure 9.8   A CT scan with a malignant nodule displaying a visual discrepancy from other nodules

---

[5]Not if we want decent results, at least.

[6]According to the National Cancer Institute Dictionary of Cancer Terms: http://mng.bz/jgBP.

9.4.3 *Our data source: The LUNA Grand Challenge*

The CT scans we were just looking at come from the LUNA (LUng Nodule Analysis) Grand Challenge. The LUNA Grand Challenge is the combination of an open dataset with high-quality labels of patient CT scans (many with lung nodules) and a public ranking of classifiers against the data. There is something of a culture of publicly sharing medical datasets for research and analysis; open access to such data allows researchers to use, combine, and perform novel work on this data without having to enter into formal research agreements between institutions (obviously, some data is kept private as well). The goal of the LUNA Grand Challenge is to encourage improvements in nodule detection by making it easy for teams to compete for high positions on the leader board. A project team can test the efficacy of their detection methods against standardized criteria (the dataset provided). To be included in the public ranking, a team must provide a scientific paper describing the project architecture, training methods, and so on. This makes for a great resource to provide further ideas and inspiration for project improvements.

> **NOTE** Many CT scans "in the wild" are incredibly messy, in terms of idiosyncrasies between various scanners and processing programs. For example, some scanners indicate areas of the CT scan that are outside of the scanner's field of view by setting the density of those voxels to something negative. CT scans can also be acquired with a variety of settings on the CT scanner, which can change the resulting image in ways ranging from subtly to wildly different. Although the LUNA data is generally clean, be sure to check your assumptions if you incorporate other data sources.

We will be using the LUNA 2016 dataset. The LUNA site (https://luna16.grand-challenge .org/Description) describes two tracks for the challenge: the first track, "Nodule detection (NDET)," roughly corresponds to our step 1 (segmentation); and the second track, "False positive reduction (FPRED)," is similar to our step 3 (classification). When the site discusses "locations of possible nodules," it is talking about a process similar to what we'll cover in chapter 13.

9.4.4 *Downloading the LUNA data*

Before we go any further into the nuts and bolts of our project, we'll cover how to get the data we'll be using. It's about 60 GB of data compressed, so depending on your internet connection, it might take a while to download. Once uncompressed, it takes up about 120 GB of space; and we'll need another 100 GB or so of cache space to store smaller chunks of data so that we can access it more quickly than reading in the whole CT.[7]

---

[7]The cache space required is per chapter, but once you're done with a chapter, you can delete the cache to free up space.

Navigate to https://luna16.grand-challenge.org/download and either register using email or use the Google OAuth login. Once logged in, you should see two download links to Zenodo data, as well as a link to Academic Torrents. The data should be the same from either.

> **TIP** The luna.grand-challenge.org domain does not have links to the data download page as of this writing. If you are having issues finding the download page, double-check the domain for luna16., not `luna.`, and reenter the URL if needed.

The data we will be using comes in 10 subsets, aptly named `subset0` through `subset9`. Unzip each of them so you have separate subdirectories like code/data-unversioned/part2/luna/subset0, and so on. On Linux, you'll need the `7z` decompression utility (Ubuntu provides this via the `p7zip-full` package). Windows users can get an extractor from the 7-Zip website (www.7-zip.org). Some decompression utilities will not be able to open the archives; make sure you have the full version of the extractor if you get an error.

In addition, you need the candidates.csv and annotations.csv files. We've included these files on the book's website and in the GitHub repository for convenience, so they should already be present in code/data/part2/luna/*.csv. They can also be downloaded from the same location as the data subsets.

> **NOTE** If you do not have easy access to ~220 GB of free disk space, it's possible to run the examples using only 1 or 2 of the 10 subsets of data. The smaller training set will result in the model performing much more poorly, but that's better than not being able to run the examples at all.

Once you have the candidates file and at least one subset downloaded, uncompressed, and put in the correct location, you should be able to start running the examples in this chapter. If you want to jump ahead, you can use the p2ch10_explore_data.ipynb Jupyter Notebook to get started. Otherwise, we'll return to the notebook in more depth later in the chapter. Hopefully your downloads will finish before you start reading the next chapter!

9.5   *Conclusion*

We've made major strides toward finishing our project! You might have the feeling that we haven't accomplished much; after all, we haven't implemented a single line of code yet. But keep in mind that you'll need to do research and preparation as we have here when you tackle projects on your own.

In this chapter, we set out to do two things:

1 Understand the larger context around our lung cancer-detection project
2 Sketch out the direction and structure of our project for part 2

If you still feel that we haven't made real progress, please recognize that mindset as a trap—understanding the space your project is working in is crucial, and the design work we've done will pay off handsomely as we move forward. We'll see those dividends shortly, once we start implementing our data-loading routines in chapter 10.

Since this chapter has been informational only, without any code, we'll skip the exercises for now.

9.6   *Summary*

- Our approach to detecting cancerous nodules will have five rough steps: data loading, segmentation, grouping, classification, and nodule analysis and diagnosis.
- Breaking down our project into smaller, semi-independent subprojects makes teaching each subproject easier. Other approaches might make more sense for future projects with different goals than the ones for this book.
- A CT scan is a 3D array of intensity data with approximately 32 million voxels, which is around a million times larger than the nodules we want to recognize. Focusing the model on a crop of the CT scan relevant to the task at hand will make it easier to get reasonable results from training.
- Understanding our data will make it easier to write processing routines for our data that don't distort or destroy important aspects of the data. The array of CT scan data typically will not have cubic voxels; mapping location information in real-world units to array indexes requires conversion. The intensity of a CT scan corresponds roughly to mass density but uses unique units.
- Identifying the key concepts of a project and making sure they are well represented in our design can be crucial. Most aspects of our project will revolve around nodules, which are small masses in the lungs and can be spotted on a CT along with many other structures that have a similar appearance.
- We are using the LUNA Grand Challenge data to train our model. The LUNA data contains CT scans, as well as human-annotated outputs for classification and grouping. Having high-quality data has a major impact on a project's success.

Combining data sources into a unified dataset

This chapter covers

- Loading and processing raw data files
- Implementing a Python class to represent our data
- Converting our data into a format usable by PyTorch
- Visualizing the training and validation data

Now that we've discussed the high-level goals for part 2, as well as outlined how the data will flow through our system, let's get into specifics of what we're going to do in this chapter. It's time to implement basic data-loading and data-processing routines for our raw data. Basically, every significant project you work on will need something analogous to what we cover here.[1] Figure 10.1 shows the high-level map of our project from chapter 9. We'll focus on step 1, data loading, for the rest of this chapter.

Our goal is to be able to produce a training sample given our inputs of raw CT scan data and a list of annotations for those CTs. This might sound simple, but quite a bit needs to happen before we can load, process, and extract the data we're

---

[1] To the rare researcher who has all of their data well prepared for them in advance: lucky you! The rest of us will be busy writing code for loading and parsing.

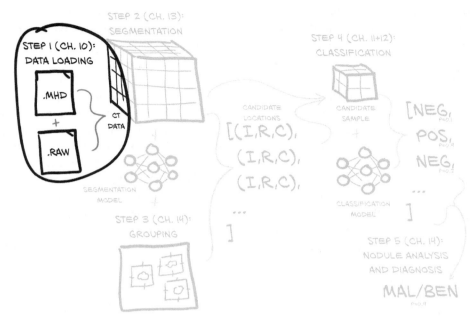

Figure 10.1 Our end-to-end lung cancer detection project, with a focus on this chapter's topic: step 1, data loading

interested in. Figure 10.2 shows what we'll need to do to turn our raw data into a training sample. Luckily, we got a head start on *understanding* our data in the last chapter, but we have more work to do on that front as well.

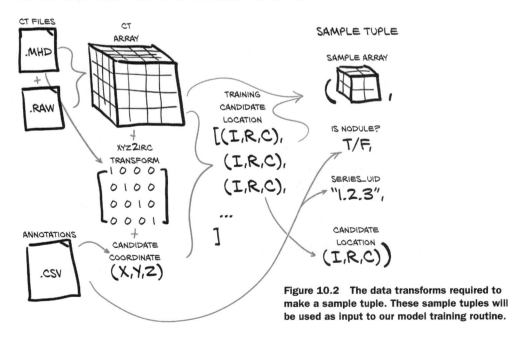

Figure 10.2 The data transforms required to make a sample tuple. These sample tuples will be used as input to our model training routine.

This is a crucial moment, when we begin to transmute the leaden raw data, if not into gold, then at least into the stuff that our neural network will spin *into* gold. We first discussed the mechanics of this transformation in chapter 4.

10.1   *Raw CT data files*

Our CT data comes in two files: a .mhd file containing metadata header information, and a .raw file containing the raw bytes that make up the 3D array. Each file's name starts with a unique identifier called the *series UID* (the name comes from the Digital Imaging and Communications in Medicine [DICOM] nomenclature) for the CT scan in question. For example, for series UID 1.2.3, there would be two files: 1.2.3.mhd and 1.2.3.raw.

Our Ct class will consume those two files and produce the 3D array, as well as the transformation matrix to convert from the patient coordinate system (which we will discuss in more detail in section 10.6) to the index, row, column coordinates needed by the array (these coordinates are shown as (I,R,C) in the figures and are denoted with _irc variable suffixes in the code). Don't sweat the details of all this right now; just remember that we've got some coordinate system conversion to do before we can apply these coordinates to our CT data. We'll explore the details as we need them.

We will also load the annotation data provided by LUNA, which will give us a list of nodule coordinates, each with a malignancy flag, along with the series UID of the relevant CT scan. By combining the nodule coordinate with coordinate system transformation information, we get the index, row, and column of the voxel at the center of our nodule.

Using the (I,R,C) coordinates, we can crop a small 3D slice of our CT data to use as the input to our model. Along with this 3D sample array, we must construct the rest of our training sample tuple, which will have the sample array, nodule status flag, series UID, and the index of this sample in the CT list of nodule candidates. This sample tuple is exactly what PyTorch expects from our Dataset subclass and represents the last section of our bridge from our original raw data to the standard structure of PyTorch tensors.

Limiting or cropping our data so as not to drown our model in noise is important, as is making sure we're not so aggressive that our signal gets cropped out of our input. We want to make sure the range of our data is well behaved, especially after normalization. Clamping our data to remove outliers can be useful, especially if our data is prone to extreme outliers. We can also create handcrafted, algorithmic transformations of our input; this is known as *feature engineering;* and we discussed it briefly in chapter 1. We'll usually want to let the model do most of the heavy lifting; feature engineering has its uses, but we won't use it here in part 2.

10.2   *Parsing LUNA's annotation data*

The first thing we need to do is begin loading our data. When working on a new project, that's often a good place to start. Making sure we know how to work with the raw input is required no matter what, and knowing how our data will look after it loads can help inform the structure of our early experiments. We could try loading individual CT scans, but we think it makes sense to parse the CSV files that LUNA provides, which contain information about the points of interest in each CT scan. As we can see in figure 10.3, we expect to get some coordinate information, an indication of whether the coordinate is a nodule, and a unique identifier for the CT scan. Since there are fewer types of information in the CSV files, and they're easier to parse, we're hoping they will give us some clues about what to look for once we start loading CTs.

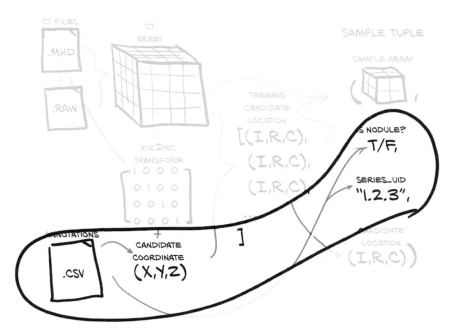

Figure 10.3 The LUNA annotations in candidates.csv contain the CT series, the nodule candidate's position, and a flag indicating if the candidate is actually a nodule or not.

The candidates.csv file contains information about all lumps that potentially look like nodules, whether those lumps are malignant, benign tumors, or something else altogether. We'll use this as the basis for building a complete list of candidates that can then be split into our training and validation datasets. The following Bash shell session shows what the file contains:

```
$ wc -l candidates.csv          ⟵┐ Counts the number
551066 candidates.csv               of lines in the file

$ head data/part2/luna/candidates.csv   ⟵┐ Prints the first few
seriesuid,coordX,coordY,coordZ,class  ⟵     lines of the file
1.3...6860,-56.08,-67.85,-311.92,0
1.3...6860,53.21,-244.41,-245.17,0        The first line of the .csv file
1.3...6860,103.66,-121.8,-286.62,0        defines the column headers.
```

```
1.3...6860,-33.66,-72.75,-308.41,0
...

$ grep ',1$' candidates.csv | wc -l      ◄─┐   Counts the number of lines
1351                                          │   that end with 1, which
                                              └── indicates it is a nodule.
```

NOTE The values in the `seriesuid` column have been elided to better fit the printed page.

So we have 551,000 lines, each with a `seriesuid` (which we'll call `series_uid` in the code), some (X,Y,Z) coordinates, and a `class` column that corresponds to the nodule status (it's a Boolean value: 0 for a candidate that is not an actual nodule, and 1 for a candidate that is a nodule, either malignant or benign). We have 1,351 candidates flagged as actual nodules.

The annotations.csv file contains information about some of the candidates that have been flagged as nodules. We are interested in the `diameter_mm` information in particular:

```
$ wc -l annotations.csv        ◄─┐   This is a different
1187 annotations.csv             │   number than in the
                                 └── candidates.csv file.

$ head data/part2/luna/annotations.csv                    ┐ The last column
seriesuid,coordX,coordY,coordZ,diameter_mm    ◄───────────┘ is also different.
1.3.6...6860,-128.6994211,-175.3192718,-298.3875064,5.651470635
1.3.6...6860,103.7836509,-211.9251487,-227.12125,4.224708481
1.3.6...5208,69.63901724,-140.9445859,876.3744957,5.786347814
1.3.6...0405,-24.0138242,192.1024053,-391.0812764,8.143261683
...
```

We have size information for about 1,200 nodules. This is useful, since we can use it to make sure our training and validation data includes a representative spread of nodule sizes. Without this, it's possible that our validation set could end up with only extreme values, making it seem as though our model is underperforming.

10.2.1 *Training and validation sets*

For any standard supervised learning task (classification is the prototypical example), we'll split our data into training and validation sets. We want to make sure both sets are *representative* of the range of real-world input data we're expecting to see and handle normally. If either set is meaningfully different from our real-world use cases, it's pretty likely that our model will behave differently than we expect—all of the training and statistics we collect won't be predictive once we transfer over to production use! We're not trying to make this an exact science, but you should keep an eye out in future projects for hints that you are training and testing on data that doesn't make sense for your operating environment.

Let's get back to our nodules. We're going to sort them by size and take every *N*th one for our validation set. That should give us the representative spread we're looking for. Unfortunately, the location information provided in annotations.csv doesn't always precisely line up with the coordinates in candidates.csv:

```
$ grep 100225528722236566367866836860 annotations.csv
1.3.6...6860,-128.6994211,-175.3192718,-298.3875064,5.651470635
1.3.6...6860,103.7836509,-211.9251487,-227.12125,4.224708481

$ grep '100225528722236566367866836860.*,1$' candidates.csv
1.3.6...6860,104.16480444,-211.685591018,-227.011363746,1
1.3.6...6860,-128.94,-175.04,-297.87,1
```

These two coordinates are very close to each other.

If we truncate the corresponding coordinates from each file, we end up with (–128.70, –175.32,–298.39) versus (–128.94,–175.04,–297.87). Since the nodule in question has a diameter of 5 mm, both of these points are clearly meant to be the "center" of the nodule, but they don't line up exactly. It would be a perfectly valid response to decide that dealing with this data mismatch isn't worth it, and to ignore the file. We are going to do the legwork to make things line up, though, since real-world datasets are often imperfect this way, and this is a good example of the kind of work you will need to do to assemble data from disparate data sources.

10.2.2 Unifying our annotation and candidate data

Now that we know what our raw data files look like, let's build a `getCandidateInfo-List` function that will stitch it all together. We'll use a named tuple that is defined at the top of the file to hold the information for each nodule.

Listing 10.1 dsets.py:7

```
from collections import namedtuple
# ... line 27
CandidateInfoTuple = namedtuple(
  'CandidateInfoTuple',
  'isNodule_bool, diameter_mm, series_uid, center_xyz',
)
```

These tuples are *not* our training samples, as they're missing the chunks of CT data we need. Instead, these represent a sanitized, cleaned, unified interface to the human-annotated data we're using. It's very important to isolate having to deal with messy data from model training. Otherwise, your training loop can get cluttered quickly, because you have to keep dealing with special cases and other distractions in the middle of code that should be focused on training.

> **TIP** Clearly separate the code that's responsible for data sanitization from the rest of your project. Don't be afraid to rewrite your data once and save it to disk if needed.

Our list of candidate information will have the nodule status (what we're going to be training the model to classify), diameter (useful for getting a good spread in training, since large and small nodules will not have the same features), series (to locate the correct CT scan), and candidate center (to find the candidate in the larger CT). The function that will build a list of these `NoduleInfoTuple` instances starts by using an in-memory caching decorator, followed by getting the list of files present on disk.

Listing 10.2   dsets.py:32

Standard library in-memory caching

requireOnDisk_bool defaults to screening out series from data subsets that aren't in place yet.

```
@functools.lru_cache(1)
def getCandidateInfoList(requireOnDisk_bool=True):
    mhd_list = glob.glob('data-unversioned/part2/luna/subset*/*.mhd')
    presentOnDisk_set = {os.path.split(p)[-1][:-4] for p in mhd_list}
```

Since parsing some of the data files can be slow, we'll cache the results of this function call in memory. This will come in handy later, because we'll be calling this function more often in future chapters. Speeding up our data pipeline by carefully applying in-memory or on-disk caching can result in some pretty impressive gains in training speed. Keep an eye out for these opportunities as you work on your projects.

Earlier we said that we'll support running our training program with less than the full set of training data, due to the long download times and high disk space requirements. The `requireOnDisk_bool` parameter is what makes good on that promise; we're detecting which LUNA series UIDs are actually present and ready to be loaded from disk, and we'll use that information to limit which entries we use from the CSV files we're about to parse. Being able to run a subset of our data through the training loop can be useful to verify that the code is working as intended. Often a model's training results are bad to useless when doing so, but exercising our logging, metrics, model check-pointing, and similar functionality is beneficial.

After we get our candidate information, we want to merge in the diameter information from annotations.csv. First we need to group our annotations by series_uid, as that's the first key we'll use to cross-reference each row from the two files.

Listing 10.3   dsets.py:40, def `getCandidateInfoList`

```
diameter_dict = {}
with open('data/part2/luna/annotations.csv', "r") as f:
  for row in list(csv.reader(f))[1:]:
    series_uid = row[0]
    annotationCenter_xyz = tuple([float(x) for x in row[1:4]])
    annotationDiameter_mm = float(row[4])

    diameter_dict.setdefault(series_uid, []).append(
      (annotationCenter_xyz, annotationDiameter_mm)
    )
```

Now we'll build our full list of candidates using the information in the candidates.csv file.

> **Listing 10.4   dsets.py:51, def `getCandidateInfoList`**

```
candidateInfo_list = []
with open('data/part2/luna/candidates.csv', "r") as f:
  for row in list(csv.reader(f))[1:]:
    series_uid = row[0]

    if series_uid not in presentOnDisk_set and requireOnDisk_bool:
      continue

    isNodule_bool = bool(int(row[4]))
    candidateCenter_xyz = tuple([float(x) for x in row[1:4]])

    candidateDiameter_mm = 0.0
    for annotation_tup in diameter_dict.get(series_uid, []):
      annotationCenter_xyz, annotationDiameter_mm = annotation_tup
      for i in range(3):
        delta_mm = abs(candidateCenter_xyz[i] - annotationCenter_xyz[i])
        if delta_mm > annotationDiameter_mm / 4:
          break
      else:
        candidateDiameter_mm = annotationDiameter_mm
        break

    candidateInfo_list.append(CandidateInfoTuple(
      isNodule_bool,
      candidateDiameter_mm,
      series_uid,
      candidateCenter_xyz,
    ))
```

> If a series_uid isn't present, it's in a subset we don't have on disk, so we should skip it.

> Divides the diameter by 2 to get the radius, and divides the radius by 2 to require that the two nodule center points not be too far apart relative to the size of the nodule. (This results in a bounding-box check, not a true distance check.)

For each of the candidate entries for a given series_uid, we loop through the annotations we collected earlier for the same series_uid and see if the two coordinates are close enough to consider them the same nodule. If they are, great! Now we have diameter information for that nodule. If we don't find a match, that's fine; we'll just treat the nodule as having a 0.0 diameter. Since we're only using this information to get a good spread of nodule sizes in our training and validation sets, having incorrect diameter sizes for some nodules shouldn't be a problem, but we should remember we're doing this in case our assumption here is wrong.

That's a lot of somewhat fiddly code just to merge in our nodule diameter. Unfortunately, having to do this kind of manipulation and fuzzy matching can be fairly common, depending on your raw data. Once we get to this point, however, we just need to sort the data and return it.

Listing 10.5   dsets.py:80, def getCandidateInfoList

```
candidateInfo_list.sort(reverse=True)
return candidateInfo_list
```
← This means we have all of the actual nodule samples starting with the largest first, followed by all of the non-nodule samples (which don't have nodule size information).

The ordering of the tuple members in noduleInfo_list is driven by this sort. We're using this sorting approach to help ensure that when we take a slice of the data, that slice gets a representative chunk of the actual nodules with a good spread of nodule diameters. We'll discuss this more in section 10.5.3.

10.3   *Loading individual CT scans*

Next up, we need to be able to take our CT data from a pile of bits on disk and turn it into a Python object from which we can extract 3D nodule density data. We can see this path from the .mhd and .raw files to Ct objects in figure 10.4. Our nodule annotation information acts like a map to the interesting parts of our raw data. Before we can follow that map to our data of interest, we need to get the data into an addressable form.

> **TIP** Having a large amount of raw data, most of which is uninteresting, is a common situation; look for ways to limit your scope to only the relevant data when working on your own projects.

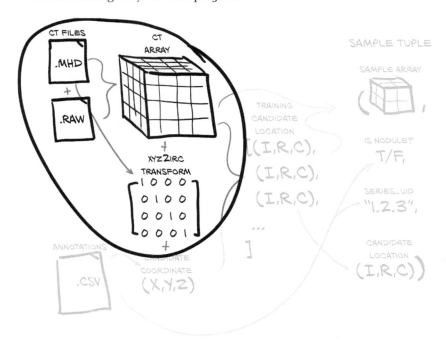

Figure 10.4   Loading a CT scan produces a voxel array and a transformation from patient coordinates to array indices.

The native file format for CT scans is DICOM (www.dicomstandard.org). The first version of the DICOM standard was authored in 1984, and as we might expect from anything computing-related that comes from that time period, it's a bit of a mess (for example, whole sections that are now retired were devoted to the data link layer protocol to use, since Ethernet hadn't won yet).

> **NOTE** We've done the legwork of finding the right library to parse these raw data files, but for other formats you've never heard of, you'll have to find a parser yourself. We recommend taking the time to do so! The Python ecosystem has parsers for just about every file format under the sun, and your time is almost certainly better spent working on the novel parts of your project than writing parsers for esoteric data formats.

Happily, LUNA has converted the data we're going to be using for this chapter into the MetaIO format, which is quite a bit easier to use (https://itk.org/Wiki/MetaIO/Documentation#Quick_Start). Don't worry if you've never heard of the format before! We can treat the format of the data files as a black box and use `SimpleITK` to load them into more familiar NumPy arrays.

Listing 10.6   dsets.py:9

```
import SimpleITK as sitk
# ... line 83
class Ct:
  def __init__(self, series_uid):
    mhd_path = glob.glob(
      'data-unversioned/part2/luna/subset*/{}.mhd'.format(series_uid)
    )[0]

    ct_mhd = sitk.ReadImage(mhd_path)
    ct_a = np.array(sitk.GetArrayFromImage(ct_mhd), dtype=np.float32)
```

> We don't care to track which subset a given series_uid is in, so we wildcard the subset.

> sitk.ReadImage implicitly consumes the .raw file in addition to the passed-in .mhd file.

> Recreates an np.array since we want to convert the value type to np.float3

For real projects, you'll want to understand what types of information are contained in your raw data, but it's perfectly fine to rely on third-party code like `SimpleITK` to parse the bits on disk. Finding the right balance of knowing everything about your inputs versus blindly accepting whatever your data-loading library hands you will probably take some experience. Just remember that we're mostly concerned about *data*, not *bits*. It's the information that matters, not how it's represented.

Being able to uniquely identify a given sample of our data can be useful. For example, clearly communicating which sample is causing a problem or is getting poor classification results can drastically improve our ability to isolate and debug the issue. Depending on the nature of our samples, sometimes that unique identifier is an atom, like a number or a string, and sometimes it's more complicated, like a tuple.

We identify specific CT scans using the *series instance UID* (`series_uid`) assigned when the CT scan was created. DICOM makes heavy use of unique identifiers (UIDs) for individual DICOM files, groups of files, courses of treatment, and so on. These identifiers are similar in concept to UUIDs (https://docs.python.org/3.6/library/uuid.html), but they have a different creation process and are formatted differently. For our purposes, we can treat them as opaque ASCII strings that serve as unique keys to reference the various CT scans. Officially, only the characters 0 through 9 and the period (.) are valid characters in a DICOM UID, but some DICOM files in the wild have been anonymized with routines that replace the UIDs with hexadecimal (0–9 and a–f) or other technically out-of-spec values (these out-of-spec values typically aren't flagged or cleaned by DICOM parsers; as we said before, it's a bit of a mess).

The 10 subsets we discussed earlier have about 90 CT scans each (888 in total), with every CT scan represented as two files: one with a .mhd extension and one with a .raw extension. The data being split between multiple files is hidden behind the `sitk` routines, however, and is not something we need to be directly concerned with.

At this point, `ct_a` is a three-dimensional array. All three dimensions are spatial, and the single intensity channel is implicit. As we saw in chapter 4, in a PyTorch tensor, the channel information is represented as a fourth dimension with size 1.

10.3.1 *Hounsfield Units*

Recall that earlier, we said that we need to understand our *data*, not the *bits* that store it. Here, we have a perfect example of that in action. Without understanding the nuances of our data's values and range, we'll end up feeding values into our model that will hinder its ability to learn what we want it to.

Continuing the __init__ method, we need to do a bit of cleanup on the `ct_a` values. CT scan voxels are expressed in Hounsfield units (HU; https://en.wikipedia.org/wiki/Hounsfield_scale), which are odd units; air is –1,000 HU (close enough to 0 g/cc [grams per cubic centimeter] for our purposes), water is 0 HU (1 g/cc), and bone is at least +1,000 HU (2–3 g/cc).

> **NOTE** HU values are typically stored on disk as signed 12-bit integers (shoved into 16-bit integers), which fits well with the level of precision CT scanners can provide. While this is perhaps interesting, it's not particularly relevant to the project.

Some CT scanners use HU values that correspond to negative densities to indicate that those voxels are outside of the CT scanner's field of view. For our purposes, everything outside of the patient should be air, so we discard that field-of-view information by setting a lower bound of the values to –1,000 HU. Similarly, the exact densities of bones, metal implants, and so on are not relevant to our use case, so we cap density at roughly 2 g/cc (1,000 HU) even though that's not biologically accurate in most cases.

Listing 10.7   dsets.py:96, `Ct.__init__`

```
ct_a.clip(-1000, 1000, ct_a)
```

Values above 0 HU don't scale perfectly with density, but the tumors we're interested in are typically around 1 g/cc (0 HU), so we're going to ignore that HU doesn't map perfectly to common units like g/cc. That's fine, since our model will be trained to consume HU directly.

We want to remove all of these outlier values from our data: they aren't directly relevant to our goal, and having those outliers can make the model's job harder. This can happen in many ways, but a common example is when batch normalization is fed these outlier values and the statistics about how to best normalize the data are skewed. Always be on the lookout for ways to clean your data.

All of the values we've built are now assigned to `self`.

Listing 10.8   dsets.py:98, Ct.__init__

```
self.series_uid = series_uid
self.hu_a = ct_a
```

It's important to know that our data uses the range of −1,000 to +1,000, since in chapter 13 we end up adding channels of information to our samples. If we don't account for the disparity between HU and our additional data, those new channels can easily be overshadowed by the raw HU values. We won't add more channels of data for the classification step of our project, so we don't need to implement special handling right now.

10.4   Locating a nodule using the patient coordinate system

Deep learning models typically need fixed-size inputs,[2] due to having a fixed number of input neurons. We need to be able to produce a fixed-size array containing the candidate so that we can use it as input to our classifier. We'd like to train our model using a crop of the CT scan that has a candidate nicely centered, since then our model doesn't have to learn how to notice nodules tucked away in the corner of the input. By reducing the variation in expected inputs, we make the model's job easier.

10.4.1   The patient coordinate system

Unfortunately, all of the candidate center data we loaded in section 10.2 is expressed in millimeters, not voxels! We can't just plug locations in millimeters into an array index and expect everything to work out the way we want. As we can see in figure 10.5, we need to transform our coordinates from the millimeter-based coordinate system (X,Y,Z) they're expressed in, to the voxel-address-based coordinate system (I,R,C) used to take array slices from our CT scan data. This is a classic example of how it's important to handle units consistently!

As we have mentioned previously, when dealing with CT scans, we refer to the array dimensions as *index, row, and column,* because a separate meaning exists for X, Y, and Z,

---

[2] There are exceptions, but they're not relevant right now.

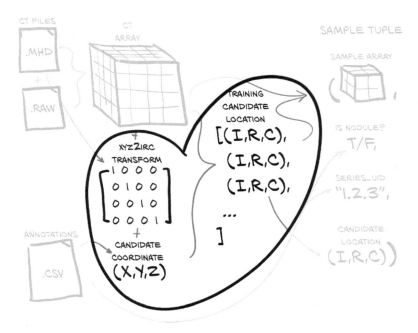

Figure 10.5   Using the transformation information to convert a nodule center coordinate in patient coordinates (X,Y,Z) to an array index (Index,Row,Column).

as illustrated in figure 10.6. The *patient coordinate system* defines positive X to be patient-left (*left*), positive Y to be patient-behind (*posterior*), and positive Z to be toward-patient-head (*superior*). Left-posterior-superior is sometimes abbreviated *LPS*.

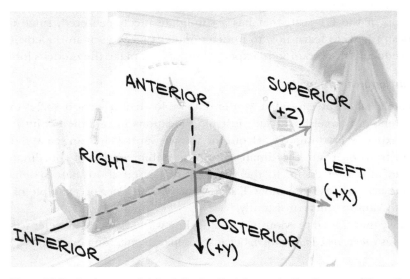

Figure 10.6   Our inappropriately clothed patient demonstrating the axes of the patient coordinate system

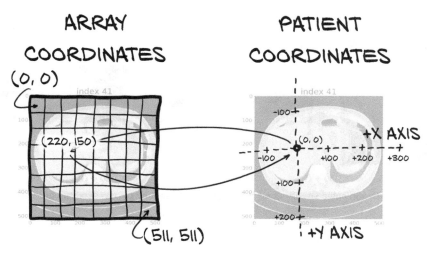

Figure 10.7   Array coordinates and patient coordinates have different origins and scaling.

The patient coordinate system is measured in millimeters and has an arbitrarily positioned origin that does not correspond to the origin of the CT voxel array, as shown in figure 10.7.

The patient coordinate system is often used to specify the locations of interesting anatomy in a way that is independent of any particular scan. The metadata that defines the relationship between the CT array and the patient coordinate system is stored in the header of DICOM files, and that meta-image format preserves the data in its header as well. This metadata allows us to construct the transformation from (X,Y,Z) to (I,R,C) that we saw in figure 10.5. The raw data contains many other fields of similar metadata, but since we don't have a use for them right now, those unneeded fields will be ignored.

10.4.2   *CT scan shape and voxel sizes*

One of the most common variations between CT scans is the size of the voxels; typically, they are not cubes. Instead, they can be 1.125 mm × 1.125 mm × 2.5 mm or similar. Usually the row and column dimensions have voxel sizes that are the same, and the index dimension has a larger value, but other ratios can exist.

When plotted using square pixels, the non-cubic voxels can end up looking somewhat distorted, similar to the distortion near the north and south poles when using a Mercator projection map. That's an imperfect analogy, since in this case the distortion is uniform and linear—the patient looks far more squat or barrel-chested in figure 10.8 than they would in reality. We will need to apply a scaling factor if we want the images to depict realistic proportions.

Knowing these kinds of details can help when trying to interpret our results visually. Without this information, it would be easy to assume that something was wrong with our data loading: we might think the data looked so squat because we were skipping half of

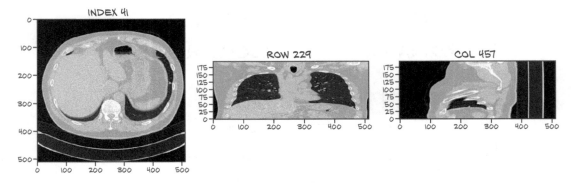

Figure 10.8   A CT scan with non-cubic voxels along the index-axis. Note how compressed the lungs are from top to bottom.

the slices by accident, or something along those lines. It can be easy to waste a lot of time debugging something that's been working all along, and being familiar with your data can help prevent that.

CTs are commonly 512 rows by 512 columns, with the index dimension ranging from around 100 total slices up to perhaps 250 slices (250 slices times 2.5 millimeters is typically enough to contain the anatomical region of interest). This results in a lower bound of approximately 2^{25} voxels, or about 32 million data points. Each CT specifies the voxel size in millimeters as part of the file metadata; for example, we'll call ct_mhd .GetSpacing() in listing 10.10.

10.4.3   *Converting between millimeters and voxel addresses*

We will define some utility code to assist with the conversion between patient coordinates in millimeters (which we will denote in the code with an _xyz suffix on variables and the like) and (I,R,C) array coordinates (which we will denote in code with an _irc suffix).

You might wonder whether the SimpleITK library comes with utility functions to convert these. And indeed, an Image instance does feature two methods—Transform-IndexToPhysicalPoint and TransformPhysicalPointToIndex—to do just that (except shuffling from CRI [column,row,index] IRC). However, we want to be able to do this computation without keeping the Image object around, so we'll perform the math manually here.

Flipping the axes (and potentially a rotation or other transforms) is encoded in a 3 × 3 matrix returned as a tuple from ct_mhd.GetDirections(). To go from voxel indices to coordinates, we need to follow these four steps in order:

1   Flip the coordinates from IRC to CRI, to align with XYZ.
2   Scale the indices with the voxel sizes.
3   Matrix-multiply with the directions matrix, using @ in Python.
4   Add the offset for the origin.

To go back from XYZ to IRC, we need to perform the inverse of each step in the reverse order.

We keep the voxel sizes in named tuples, so we convert these into arrays.

Listing 10.9   util.py:16

Swaps the order while we convert to a NumPy array

```
IrcTuple = collections.namedtuple('IrcTuple', ['index', 'row', 'col'])
XyzTuple = collections.namedtuple('XyzTuple', ['x', 'y', 'z'])

def irc2xyz(coord_irc, origin_xyz, vxSize_xyz, direction_a):
    cri_a = np.array(coord_irc)[::-1]
    origin_a = np.array(origin_xyz)                      The bottom three steps of
    vxSize_a = np.array(vxSize_xyz)                      our plan, all in one line
    coords_xyz = (direction_a @ (cri_a * vxSize_a)) + origin_a
    return XyzTuple(*coords_xyz)

def xyz2irc(coord_xyz, origin_xyz, vxSize_xyz, direction_a):
    origin_a = np.array(origin_xyz)
    vxSize_a = np.array(vxSize_xyz)                      Inverse of the last three steps
    coord_a = np.array(coord_xyz)
    cri_a = ((coord_a - origin_a) @ np.linalg.inv(direction_a)) / vxSize_a
    cri_a = np.round(cri_a)
    return IrcTuple(int(cri_a[2]), int(cri_a[1]), int(cri_a[0]))        Shuffles and
                                                                        converts to
Sneaks in proper rounding                                              integers
before converting to integers
```

The annotations in the listing: "The bottom three steps of our plan, all in one line" points to the `coords_xyz` line. "Inverse of the last three steps" points to the `cri_a = ((coord_a - origin_a)...` line. "Shuffles and converts to integers" points to the `return IrcTuple(...)` line.

Phew. If that was a bit heavy, don't worry. Just remember that we need to convert and use the functions as a black box. The metadata we need to convert from patient coordinates (_xyz) to array coordinates (_irc) is contained in the MetaIO file alongside the CT data itself. We pull the voxel sizing and positioning metadata out of the .mhd file at the same time we get the ct_a.

Listing 10.10   dsets.py:72, class Ct

```
class Ct:
  def __init__(self, series_uid):
    mhd_path = glob.glob('data-
    unversioned/part2/luna/subset*/{}.mhd'.format(series_uid))[0]

                                    Converts the directions to an array, and
        ct_mhd = sitk.ReadImage(mhd_path)    reshapes the nine-element array to its
        # ... line 91                        proper 3 × 3 matrix shape
        self.origin_xyz = XyzTuple(*ct_mhd.GetOrigin())
        self.vxSize_xyz = XyzTuple(*ct_mhd.GetSpacing())
        self.direction_a = np.array(ct_mhd.GetDirection()).reshape(3, 3)
```

These are the inputs we need to pass into our xyz2irc conversion function, in addition to the individual point to covert. With these attributes, our CT object implementation now has all the data needed to convert a candidate center from patient coordinates to array coordinates.

10.4.4 *Extracting a nodule from a CT scan*

As we mentioned in chapter 9, up to 99.9999% of the voxels in a CT scan of a patient with a lung nodule won't be part of the actual nodule (or cancer, for that matter). Again, that ratio is equivalent to a two-pixel blob of incorrectly tinted color somewhere on a high-definition television, or a single misspelled word out of a shelf of novels. Forcing our model to examine such huge swaths of data looking for the hints of the nodules we want it to focus on is going to work about as well as asking you to find a single misspelled word from a set of novels written in a language you don't know![3]

Instead, as we can see in figure 10.9, we will extract an area around each candidate and let the model focus on one candidate at a time. This is akin to letting you read individual paragraphs in that foreign language: still not an easy task, but far less daunting! Looking for ways to reduce the scope of the problem for our model can help, especially in the early stages of a project when we're trying to get our first working implementation up and running.

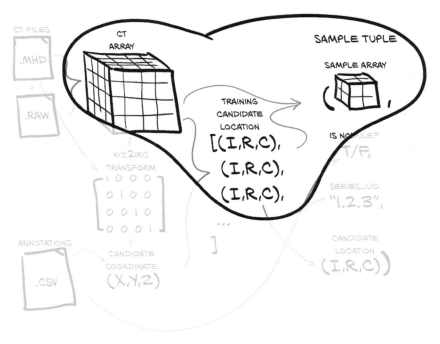

Figure 10.9   Cropping a candidate sample out of the larger CT voxel array using the candidate center's array coordinate information (Index,Row,Column)

---

[3] Have you found a misspelled word in this book yet? ;)

The getRawNodule function takes the center expressed in the patient coordinate system (X,Y,Z), just as it's specified in the LUNA CSV data, as well as a width in voxels. It returns a cubic chunk of CT, as well as the center of the candidate converted to array coordinates.

Listing 10.11 dsets.py:105, `Ct.getRawCandidate`

```
def getRawCandidate(self, center_xyz, width_irc):
  center_irc = xyz2irc(
    center_xyz,
    self.origin_xyz,
    self.vxSize_xyz,
    self.direction_a,
  )

  slice_list = []
  for axis, center_val in enumerate(center_irc):
    start_ndx = int(round(center_val - width_irc[axis]/2))
    end_ndx = int(start_ndx + width_irc[axis])
    slice_list.append(slice(start_ndx, end_ndx))

  ct_chunk = self.hu_a[tuple(slice_list)]

  return ct_chunk, center_irc
```

The actual implementation will need to deal with situations where the combination of center and width puts the edges of the cropped areas outside of the array. But as noted earlier, we will skip complications that obscure the larger intent of the function. The full implementation can be found on the book's website (www.manning.com/ books/deep-learning-with-pytorch?query=pytorch) and in the GitHub repository (https://github.com/deep-learning-with-pytorch/dlwpt-code).

10.5 *A straightforward dataset implementation*

We first saw PyTorch Dataset instances in chapter 7, but this will be the first time we've implemented one ourselves. By subclassing Dataset, we will take our arbitrary data and plug it into the rest of the PyTorch ecosystem. Each Ct instance represents hundreds of different samples that we can use to train our model or validate its effectiveness. Our LunaDataset class will normalize those samples, flattening each CT's nodules into a single collection from which samples can be retrieved without regard for which Ct instance the sample originates from. This flattening is often how we want to process data, although as we'll see in chapter 12, in some situations a simple flattening of the data isn't enough to train a model well.

In terms of implementation, we are going to start with the requirements imposed from subclassing Dataset and work backward. This is different from the datasets we've worked with earlier; there we were using classes provided by external libraries, whereas here we need to implement and instantiate the class ourselves. Once we have done so, we can use it similarly to those earlier examples. Luckily, the implementation of our custom subclass will not be too difficult, as the PyTorch API only requires that any `Dataset` subclasses we want to implement must provide these two functions:

- An implementation of `__len__` that must return a single, constant value after initialization (the value ends up being cached in some use cases)
- The `__getitem__` method, which takes an index and returns a tuple with sample data to be used for training (or validation, as the case may be)

First, let's see what the function signatures and return values of those functions look like.

> **Listing 10.12   dsets.py:176, LunaDataset.__len__**

```
def __len__(self):
  return len(self.candidateInfo_list)

def __getitem__(self, ndx):
  # ... line 200
  return (
    candidate_t,  1((CO10-1))
    pos_t,  1((CO10-2))
    candidateInfo_tup.series_uid,          This is our training sample.
    torch.tensor(center_irc),
  )
```

Our `__len__` implementation is straightforward: we have a list of candidates, each candidate is a sample, and our dataset is as large as the number of samples we have. We don't have to make the implementation as simple as it is here; in later chapters, we'll see this change![4] The only rule is that if `__len__` returns a value of *N*, then `__getitem__` needs to return something valid for all inputs 0 to *N* – 1.

For `__getitem__`, we take `ndx` (typically an integer, given the rule about supporting inputs 0 to *N* – 1) and return the four-item sample tuple as depicted in figure 10.2. Building this tuple is a bit more complicated than getting the length of our dataset, however, so let's take a look.

The first part of this method implies that we need to construct `self.candidateInfo_list` as well as provide the `getCtRawNodule` function.

> **Listing 10.13   dsets.py:179, LunaDataset.__getitem__**

```
def __getitem__(self, ndx):
  candidateInfo_tup = self.candidateInfo_list[ndx]
  width_irc = (32, 48, 48)

  candidate_a, center_irc = getCtRawCandidate(        The return value candidate_a has
    candidateInfo_tup.series_uid,                     shape (32,48,48); the axes are
    candidateInfo_tup.center_xyz,                     depth, height, and width.
    width_irc,
  )
```

---

[4] To something simpler, actually; but the point is, we have options.

We will get to those in a moment in sections 10.5.1 and 10.5.2.

The next thing we need to do in the __getitem__ method is manipulate the data into the proper data types and required array dimensions that will be expected by downstream code.

Listing 10.14 dsets.py:189, LunaDataset.__getitem__

```
candidate_t = torch.from_numpy(candidate_a)
candidate_t = candidate_t.to(torch.float32)          .unsqueeze(0) adds the
candidate_t = candidate_t.unsqueeze(0)    ◀──────┐  'Channel' dimension.
```

Don't worry too much about exactly why we are manipulating dimensionality for now; the next chapter will contain the code that ends up consuming this output and imposing the constraints we're proactively meeting here. This *will* be something you should expect for every custom Dataset you implement. These conversions are a key part of transforming your Wild West data into nice, orderly tensors.

Finally, we need to build our classification tensor.

Listing 10.15 dsets.py:193, LunaDataset.__getitem__

```
pos_t = torch.tensor([
    not candidateInfo_tup.isNodule_bool,
    candidateInfo_tup.isNodule_bool
    ],
    dtype=torch.long,
)
```

This has two elements, one each for our possible candidate classes (nodule or non-nodule; or positive or negative, respectively). We could have a single output for the nodule status, but nn.CrossEntropyLoss expects one output value per class, so that's what we provide here. The exact details of the tensors you construct will change based on the type of project you're working on.

Let's take a look at our final sample tuple (the larger nodule_t output isn't particularly readable, so we elide most of it in the listing).

Listing 10.16 p2ch10_explore_data.ipynb

```
# In[10]:
LunaDataset()[0]

# Out[10]:
(tensor([[[[-899., -903., -825.,  ..., -901., -898., -893.],
          ...,                                                          candidate_t
          [ -92.,  -63.,    4.,  ...,   63.,   70.,   52.]]]]),
cls_t  ──▷ tensor([0, 1]),
         '1.3.6...2879662446442806907337019247886',   ◀── candidate_tup.series_uid (elided)
         tensor([ 91, 360, 341]))
                                            ◀──┐ center_irc
```

Here we see the four items from our __getitem__ return statement.

10.5.1 Caching candidate arrays with the getCtRawCandidate function

In order to get decent performance out of LunaDataset, we'll need to invest in some on-disk caching. This will allow us to avoid having to read an entire CT scan from disk for every sample. Doing so would be prohibitively slow! Make sure you're paying attention to bottlenecks in your project and doing what you can to optimize them once they start slowing you down. We're kind of jumping the gun here since we haven't demonstrated that we need caching here. Without caching, the LunaDataset is easily 50 times slower! We'll revisit this in the chapter's exercises.

The function itself is easy. It's a file-cache-backed (https://pypi.python.org/pypi/diskcache) wrapper around the Ct.getRawCandidate method we saw earlier.

Listing 10.17   dsets.py:139

```
@functools.lru_cache(1, typed=True)
def getCt(series_uid):
  return Ct(series_uid)

@raw_cache.memoize(typed=True)
def getCtRawCandidate(series_uid, center_xyz, width_irc):
  ct = getCt(series_uid)
  ct_chunk, center_irc = ct.getRawCandidate(center_xyz, width_irc)
  return ct_chunk, center_irc
```

We use a few different caching methods here. First, we're caching the getCt return value in memory so that we can repeatedly ask for the same Ct instance without having to reload all of the data from disk. That's a huge speed increase in the case of repeated requests, but we're only keeping one CT in memory, so cache misses will be frequent if we're not careful about access order.

The getCtRawCandidate function that calls getCt *also* has its outputs cached, however; so after our cache is populated, getCt won't ever be called. These values are cached to disk using the Python library diskcache. We'll discuss why we have this specific caching setup in chapter 11. For now, it's enough to know that it's much, much faster to read in 2^{15} float32 values from disk than it is to read in 2^{25} int16 values, convert to float32, and then select a 2^{15} subset. From the second pass through the data forward, I/O times for input should drop to insignificance.

NOTE If the definitions of these functions ever materially change, we will need to remove the cached values from disk. If we don't, the cache will continue to return them, even if now the function will not map the given inputs to the old output. The data is stored in the data-unversioned/cache directory.

10.5.2 *Constructing our dataset in LunaDataset.__init__*

Just about every project will need to separate samples into a training set and a validation set. We are going to do that here by designating every tenth sample, specified by the val_stride parameter, as a member of the validation set. We will also accept an isValSet_bool parameter and use it to determine whether we should keep only the training data, the validation data, or everything.

> **Listing 10.18   dsets.py:149, class LunaDataset**

```
class LunaDataset(Dataset):
  def __init__(self,
         val_stride=0,
         isValSet_bool=None,
         series_uid=None,
      ):
    self.candidateInfo_list = copy.copy(getCandidateInfoList())     ⟵─┐

    if series_uid:                                                     │
      self.candidateInfo_list = [                                      │
        x for x in self.candidateInfo_list if x.series_uid == series_uid
      ]
```

Copies the return value so the cached copy won't be impacted by altering self.candidateInfo_list

If we pass in a truthy series_uid, then the instance will only have nodules from that series. This can be useful for visualization or debugging, by making it easier to look at, for instance, a single problematic CT scan.

10.5.3 *A training/validation split*

We allow for the Dataset to partition out 1/Nth of the data into a subset used for validating the model. How we will handle that subset is based on the value of the isValSet _bool argument.

> **Listing 10.19   dsets.py:162, LunaDataset.__init__**

```
if isValSet_bool:
  assert val_stride > 0, val_stride
  self.candidateInfo_list = self.candidateInfo_list[::val_stride]
  assert self.candidateInfo_list
elif val_stride > 0:
  del self.candidateInfo_list[::val_stride]     ⟵─
  assert self.candidateInfo_list
```

Deletes the validation images (every val_stride-th item in the list) from self.candidateInfo_list. We made a copy earlier so that we don't alter the original list.

This means we can create two Dataset instances and be confident that there is strict segregation between our training data and our validation data. Of course, this depends on there being a consistent sorted order to self.candidateInfo_list, which we ensure by having there be a stable sorted order to the candidate info tuples, and by the getCandidateInfoList function sorting the list before returning it.

The other caveat regarding separation of training and validation data is that, depending on the task at hand, we might need to ensure that data from a single patient is only present either in training or in testing but not both. Here this is not a problem; otherwise, we would have needed to split the list of patients and CT scans before going to the level of nodules.

Let's take a look at the data using p2ch10_explore_data.ipynb:

```
# In[2]:
from p2ch10.dsets import getCandidateInfoList, getCt, LunaDataset
candidateInfo_list = getCandidateInfoList(requireOnDisk_bool=False)
positiveInfo_list = [x for x in candidateInfo_list if x[0]]
diameter_list = [x[1] for x in positiveInfo_list]

# In[4]:
for i in range(0, len(diameter_list), 100):
    print('{:4}  {:4.1f} mm'.format(i, diameter_list[i]))

# Out[4]:
   0   32.3 mm
 100   17.7 mm
 200   13.0 mm
 300   10.0 mm
 400    8.2 mm
 500    7.0 mm
 600    6.3 mm
 700    5.7 mm
 800    5.1 mm
 900    4.7 mm
1000    4.0 mm
1100    0.0 mm
1200    0.0 mm
1300    0.0 mm
```

We have a few very large candidates, starting at 32 mm, but they rapidly drop off to half that size. The bulk of the candidates are in the 4 to 10 mm range, and several hundred don't have size information at all. This looks as expected; you might recall that we had more actual nodules than we had diameter annotations. Quick sanity checks on your data can be very helpful; catching a problem or mistaken assumption early may save hours of effort!

The larger takeaway is that our training and validation splits should have a few properties in order to work well:

- Both sets should include examples of all variations of expected inputs.
- Neither set should have samples that aren't representative of expected inputs *unless* they have a specific purpose like training the model to be robust to outliers.
- The training set shouldn't offer unfair hints about the validation set that wouldn't be true for real-world data (for example, including the same sample in both sets; this is known as a *leak* in the training set).

10.5.4 *Rendering the data*

Again, either use p2ch10_explore_data.ipynb directly or start Jupyter Notebook and enter

```
# In[7]:
%matplotlib inline          ⟵    This magic line sets up the ability for images
from p2ch10.vis import findNoduleSamples, showNodule    to be displayed inline via the notebook.
noduleSample_list = findNoduleSamples()
```

> **TIP** For more information about Jupyter's matplotlib inline magic,[5] please see http://mng.bz/rrmD.

```
# In[8]:
series_uid = positiveSample_list[11][2]
showCandidate(series_uid)
```

This produces images akin to those showing CT and nodule slices earlier in this chapter.

If you're interested, we invite you to edit the implementation of the rendering code in p2ch10/vis.py to match your needs and tastes. The rendering code makes heavy use of Matplotlib (https://matplotlib.org), which is too complex a library for us to attempt to cover here.

Remember that rendering your data is not just about getting nifty-looking pictures. The point is to get an intuitive sense of what your inputs look like. Being able to tell at a glance "This problematic sample is very noisy compared to the rest of my data" or "That's odd, this looks pretty normal" can be useful when investigating issues. Effective rendering also helps foster insights like "Perhaps if I modify things like *so*, I can solve the issue I'm having." That level of familiarity will be necessary as you start tackling harder and harder projects.

> **NOTE** Due to the way each subset has been partitioned, combined with the sorting used when constructing LunaDataset.candidateInfo_list, the ordering of the entries in noduleSample_list is highly dependent on which subsets are present at the time the code is executed. Please remember this when trying to find a particular sample a second time, especially after decompressing more subsets.

10.6 *Conclusion*

In chapter 9, we got our heads wrapped around our data. In this chapter, we got *PyTorch's* head wrapped around our data! By transforming our DICOM-via-meta-image raw data into tensors, we've set the stage to start implementing a model and a training loop, which we'll see in the next chapter.

It's important not to underestimate the impact of the design decisions we've already made: the size of our inputs, the structure of our caching, and how we're partitioning our training and validation sets will all make a difference to the success or

---

5 Their term, not ours!

failure of our overall project. Don't hesitate to revisit these decisions later, especially once you're working on your own projects.

10.7   Exercises

1   Implement a program that iterates through a `LunaDataset` instance, and time how long it takes to do so. In the interest of time, it might make sense to have an option to limit the iterations to the first N=1000 samples.

   a   How long does it take to run the first time?

   b   How long does it take to run the second time?

   c   What does clearing the cache do to the runtime?

   d   What does using the *last* N=1000 samples do to the first/second runtime?

2   Change the `LunaDataset` implementation to randomize the sample list during `__init__`. Clear the cache, and run the modified version. What does that do to the runtime of the first and second runs?

3   Revert the randomization, and comment out the `@functools.lru_cache(1, typed=True)` decorator to getCt. Clear the cache, and run the modified version. How does the runtime change now?

10.8   Summary

- Often, the code required to parse and load raw data is nontrivial. For this project, we implement a `Ct` class that loads data from disk and provides access to cropped regions around points of interest.

- Caching can be useful if the parsing and loading routines are expensive. Keep in mind that some caching can be done in memory, and some is best performed on disk. Each can have its place in a data-loading pipeline.

- PyTorch `Dataset` subclasses are used to convert data from its native form into tensors suitable to pass in to the model. We can use this functionality to integrate our real-world data with PyTorch APIs.

- Subclasses of `Dataset` need to provide implementations for two methods: `__len__` and `__getitem__`. Other helper methods are allowed but not required.

- Splitting our data into a sensible training set and a validation set requires that we make sure no sample is in both sets. We accomplish this here by using a consistent sort order and taking every tenth sample for our validation set.

- Data visualization is important; being able to investigate data visually can provide important clues about errors or problems. We are using Jupyter Notebooks and Matplotlib to render our data.

11

*Training a
classification model
to detect suspected tumors*

This chapter covers

- Using PyTorch `DataLoader`s to load data
- Implementing a model that performs classification on our CT data
- Setting up the basic skeleton for our application
- Logging and displaying metrics

In the previous chapters, we set the stage for our cancer-detection project. We covered medical details of lung cancer, took a look at the main data sources we will use for our project, and transformed our raw CT scans into a PyTorch `Dataset` instance. Now that we have a dataset, we can easily consume our training data. So let's do that!

11.1   *A foundational model and training loop*

We're going to do two main things in this chapter. We'll start by building the nodule classification model and training loop that will be the foundation that the rest of part 2 uses to explore the larger project. To do that, we'll use the `Ct` and `LunaDataset` classes we implemented in chapter 10 to feed `DataLoader` instances. Those instances, in turn, will feed our classification model with data via training and validation loops.

We'll finish the chapter by using the results from running that training loop to introduce one of the hardest challenges in this part of the book: how to get high-quality results from messy, limited data. In later chapters, we'll explore the specific ways in which our data is limited, as well as mitigate those limitations.

Let's recall our high-level roadmap from chapter 9, shown here in figure 11.1. Right now, we'll work on producing a model capable of performing step 4: classification. As a reminder, we will classify candidates as nodules or non-nodules (we'll build another classifier to attempt to tell malignant nodules from benign ones in chapter 14). That means we're going to assign a single, specific label to each sample that we present to the model. In this case, those labels are "nodule" and "non-nodule," since each sample represents a single candidate.

Getting an early end-to-end version of a meaningful part of your project is a great milestone to reach. Having something that works well enough for the results to be evaluated analytically let's you move forward with future changes, confident that you

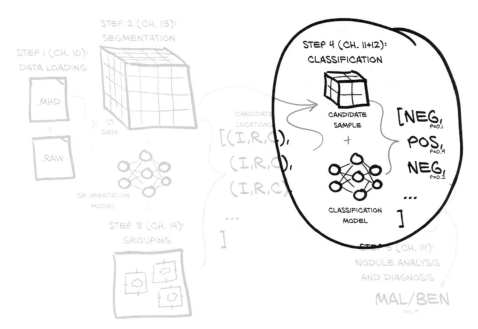

Figure 11.1   Our end-to-end project to detect lung cancer, with a focus on this chapter's topic: step 4, classification

are improving your results with each change—or at least that you're able to set aside any changes and experiments that don't work out! Expect to have to do a lot of experimentation when working on your own projects. Getting the best results will usually require considerable tinkering and tweaking.

But before we can get to the experimental phase, we must lay our foundation. Let's see what our part 2 training loop looks like in figure 11.2: it should seem generally familiar, given that we saw a similar set of core steps in chapter 5. Here we will also use a validation set to evaluate our training progress, as discussed in section 5.5.3.

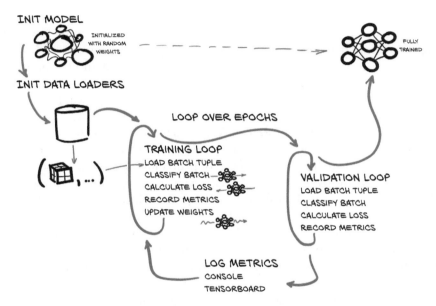

Figure 11.2   The training and validation script we will implement in this chapter

The basic structure of what we're going to implement is as follows:

- Initialize our model and data loading.
- Loop over a semi-arbitrarily chosen number of epochs.
  - Loop over each batch of training data returned by `LunaDataset`.
  - The data-loader worker process loads the relevant batch of data in the background.
  - Pass the batch into our classification model to get results.
  - Calculate our loss based on the difference between our predicted results and our ground-truth data.
  - Record metrics about our model's performance into a temporary data structure.
  - Update the model weights via backpropagation of the error.

- Loop over each batch of validation data (in a manner very similar to the training loop).
- Load the relevant batch of validation data (again, in the background worker process).
- Classify the batch, and compute the loss.
- Record information about how well the model performed on the validation data.
- Print out progress and performance information for this epoch.

As we go through the code for the chapter, keep an eye out for two main differences between the code we're producing here and what we used for a training loop in part 1. First, we'll put more structure around our program, since the project as a whole is quite a bit more complicated than what we did in earlier chapters. Without that extra structure, the code can get messy quickly. And for this project, we will have our main training application use a number of well-contained functions, and we will further separate code for things like our dataset into self-contained Python modules.

Make sure that for your own projects, you match the level of structure and design to the complexity level of your project. Too little structure, and it will become difficult to perform experiments cleanly, troubleshoot problems, or even describe what you're doing! Conversely, too *much* structure means you're wasting time writing infrastructure that you don't need and most likely slowing yourself down by having to conform to it after all that plumbing is in place. Plus it can be tempting to spend time on infrastructure as a procrastination tactic, rather than digging into the hard work of making actual progress on your project. Don't fall into that trap!

The other big difference between this chapter's code and part 1 will be a focus on collecting a variety of metrics about how training is progressing. Being able to accurately determine the impact of changes on training is impossible without having good metrics logging. Without spoiling the next chapter, we'll also see how important it is to collect not just metrics, but the *right metrics for the job*. We'll lay the infrastructure for tracking those metrics in this chapter, and we'll exercise that infrastructure by collecting and displaying the loss and percent of samples correctly classified, both overall and per class. That's enough to get us started, but we'll cover a more realistic set of metrics in chapter 12.

11.2 *The main entry point for our application*

One of the big structural differences from earlier training work we've done in this book is that part 2 wraps our work in a fully fledged command-line application. It will parse command-line arguments, have a full-featured `--help` command, and be easy to run in a wide variety of environments. All this will allow us to easily invoke the training routines from both Jupyter and a Bash shell.[1]

---

[1] Any shell, really, but if you're using a non-Bash shell, you already knew that.

Our application's functionality will be implemented via a class so that we can instantiate the application and pass it around if we feel the need. This can make testing, debugging, or invocation from other Python programs easier. We can invoke the application without needing to spin up a second OS-level process (we won't do explicit unit testing in this book, but the structure we create can be helpful for real projects where that kind of testing is appropriate).

One way to take advantage of being able to invoke our training by either function call or OS-level process is to wrap the function invocations into a Jupyter Notebook so the code can easily be called from either the native CLI or the browser.

Listing 11.1   code/p2_run_everything.ipynb

```
# In[2]:w
def run(app, *argv):
    argv = list(argv)
    argv.insert(0, '--num-workers=4')          We assume you have a four-core, eight-
    log.info("Running: {}({!r}).main()".format(app, argv))    thread CPU. Change the 4 if needed.

    app_cls = importstr(*app.rsplit('.', 1))    This is a slightly cleaner
    app_cls(argv).main()                        call to __import__.

    log.info("Finished: {}.{!r}).main()".format(app, argv))

# In[6]:
run('p2ch11.training.LunaTrainingApp', '--epochs=1')
```

NOTE   The training here assumes that you're on a workstation that has a four-core, eight-thread CPU, 16 GB of RAM, and a GPU with 8 GB of RAM. Reduce `--batch-size` if your GPU has less RAM, and `--num-workers` if you have fewer CPU cores, or less CPU RAM.

Let's get some semistandard boilerplate code out of the way. We'll start at the end of the file with a pretty standard `if main` stanza that instantiates the application object and invokes the `main` method.

Listing 11.2   training.py:386

```
if __name__ == '__main__':
  LunaTrainingApp().main()
```

From there, we can jump back to the top of the file and have a look at the application class and the two functions we just called, `__init__` and `main`. We'll want to be able to accept command-line arguments, so we'll use the standard `argparse` library (https://docs.python.org/3/library/argparse.html) in the application's `__init__` function. Note that we can pass in custom arguments to the initializer, should we wish to do so. The `main` method will be the primary entry point for the core logic of the application.

Listing 11.3   training.py:31, class `LunaTrainingApp`

```
class LunaTrainingApp:
    def __init__(self, sys_argv=None):
        if sys_argv is None:
            sys_argv = sys.argv[1:]

        parser = argparse.ArgumentParser()
        parser.add_argument('--num-workers',
            help='Number of worker processes for background data loading',
            default=8,
            type=int,
        )
        # ... line 63
        self.cli_args = parser.parse_args(sys_argv)
        self.time_str = datetime.datetime.now().strftime('%Y-%m-%d_%H.%M.%S')

        # ... line 137
    def main(self):
        log.info("Starting {}, {}".format(type(self).__name__, self.cli_args))
```

> If the caller doesn't provide arguments, we get them from the command line.

> We'll use the timestamp to help identify training runs.

This structure is pretty general and could be reused for future projects. In particular, parsing arguments in __init__ allows us to configure the application separately from invoking it.

If you check the code for this chapter on the book's website or GitHub, you might notice some extra lines mentioning `TensorBoard`. Ignore those for now; we'll discuss them in detail later in the chapter, in section 11.9.

11.3   *Pretraining setup and initialization*

Before we can begin iterating over each batch in our epoch, some initialization work needs to happen. After all, we can't train a model if we haven't even instantiated one yet! We need to do two main things, as we can see in figure 11.3. The first, as we just mentioned, is to initialize our model and optimizer; and the second is to initialize our `Dataset` and `DataLoader` instances. `LunaDataset` will define the randomized set of samples that will make up our training epoch, and our `DataLoader` instance will perform the work of loading the data out of our dataset and providing it to our application.

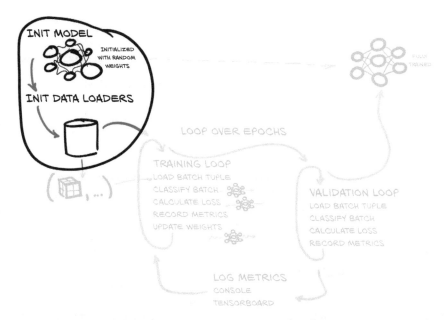

Figure 11.3 The training and validation script we will implement in this chapter, with a focus on the preloop variable initialization

11.3.1 *Initializing the model and optimizer*

For this section, we are treating the details of LunaModel as a black box. In section 11.4, we will detail the internal workings. You are welcome to explore changes to the implementation to better meet our goals for the model, although that's probably best done after finishing at least chapter 12.

Let's see what our starting point looks like.

Listing 11.4 training.py:31, class LunaTrainingApp

```
class LunaTrainingApp:
  def __init__(self, sys_argv=None):
    # ... line 70
    self.use_cuda = torch.cuda.is_available()
    self.device = torch.device("cuda" if self.use_cuda else "cpu")

    self.model = self.initModel()
    self.optimizer = self.initOptimizer()
```

```
    def initModel(self):
      model = LunaModel()
      if self.use_cuda:
        log.info("Using CUDA; {} devices.".format(torch.cuda.device_count()))
        if torch.cuda.device_count() > 1:
          model = nn.DataParallel(model)      ⟵——— Wraps the model
          model = model.to(self.device)    ⟵——┐
        return model                           │  Sends model
                                               │  parameters to the GPU
    def initOptimizer(self):
      return SGD(self.model.parameters(), lr=0.001, momentum=0.99)
```

Detects multiple GPUs ⟶ `if torch.cuda.device_count() > 1:`

If the system used for training has more than one GPU, we will use the nn.DataParallel class to distribute the work between all of the GPUs in the system and then collect and resync parameter updates and so on. This is almost entirely transparent in terms of both the model implementation and the code that uses that model.

> ## DataParallel vs. DistributedDataParallel
>
> In this book, we use DataParallel to handle utilizing multiple GPUs. We chose Data-Parallel because it's a simple drop-in wrapper around our existing models. It is not the best-performing solution for using multiple GPUs, however, and it is limited to working with the hardware available in a single machine.
>
> PyTorch also provides DistributedDataParallel, which is the recommended wrapper class to use when you need to spread work between more than one GPU or machine. Since the proper setup and configuration are nontrivial, and we suspect that the vast majority of our readers won't see any benefit from the complexity, we won't cover DistributedDataParallel in this book. If you wish to learn more, we suggest reading the official documentation: https://pytorch.org/tutorials/intermediate/ddp_tutorial.html.

Assuming that self.use_cuda is true, the call self.model.to(device) moves the model parameters to the GPU, setting up the various convolutions and other calculations to use the GPU for the heavy numerical lifting. It's important to do so before constructing the optimizer, since, otherwise, the optimizer would be left looking at the CPU-based parameter objects rather than those copied to the GPU.

For our optimizer, we'll use basic stochastic gradient descent (SGD; https://pytorch.org/docs/stable/optim.html#torch.optim.SGD) with momentum. We first saw this optimizer in chapter 5. Recall from part 1 that many different optimizers are available in PyTorch; while we won't cover most of them in any detail, the official documentation (https://pytorch.org/docs/stable/optim.html#algorithms) does a good job of linking to the relevant papers.

Using SGD is generally considered a safe place to start when it comes to picking an optimizer; there are some problems that might not work well with SGD, but they're relatively rare. Similarly, a learning rate of 0.001 and a momentum of 0.9 are pretty safe choices. Empirically, SGD with those values has worked reasonably well for a wide range of projects, and it's easy to try a learning rate of 0.01 or 0.0001 if things aren't working well right out of the box.

That's not to say any of those values is the best for our use case, but trying to find better ones is getting ahead of ourselves. Systematically trying different values for learning rate, momentum, network size, and other similar configuration settings is called a *hyperparameter search*. There are other, more glaring issues we need to address first in the coming chapters. Once we address those, we can begin to fine-tune these values. As we mentioned in the section "Testing other optimizers" in chapter 5, there are also other, more exotic optimizers we might choose; but other than perhaps swapping `torch.optim.SGD` for `torch.optim.Adam`, understanding the trade-offs involved is a topic too advanced for this book.

11.3.2 *Care and feeding of data loaders*

The `LunaDataset` class that we built in the last chapter acts as the bridge between whatever Wild West data we have and the somewhat more structured world of tensors that the PyTorch building blocks expect. For example, `torch.nn.Conv3d` (https://pytorch.org/docs/stable/nn.html#conv3d) expects five-dimensional input: (N, C, D, H, W): number of samples, channels per sample, depth, height, and width. Quite different from the native 3D our CT provides!

You may recall the `ct_t.unsqueeze(0)` call in `LunaDataset.__getitem__` from the last chapter; it provides the fourth dimension, a "channel" for our data. Recall from chapter 4 that an RGB image has three channels, one each for red, green, and blue. Astronomical data could have dozens, one each for various slices of the electromagnetic spectrum—gamma rays, X-rays, ultraviolet light, visible light, infrared, microwaves, and/or radio waves. Since CT scans are single-intensity, our channel dimension is only size 1.

Also recall from part 1 that training on single samples at a time is typically an inefficient use of computing resources, because most processing platforms are capable of more parallel calculations than are required by a model to process a single training or validation sample. The solution is to group sample tuples together into a batch tuple, as in figure 11.4, allowing multiple samples to be processed at the same time. The fifth dimension (N) differentiates multiple samples in the same batch.

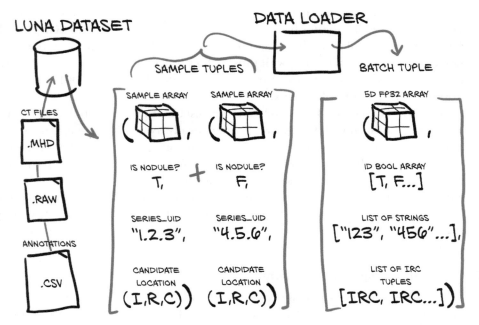

Figure 11.4   Sample tuples being collated into a single batch tuple inside a data loader

Conveniently, we don't have to implement any of this batching: the PyTorch Data-Loader class will handle all of the collation work for us. We've already built the bridge from the CT scans to PyTorch tensors with our LunaDataset class, so all that remains is to plug our dataset into a data loader.

Listing 11.5   training.py:89, `LunaTrainingApp.initTrainDl`

```
def initTrainDl(self):
  train_ds = LunaDataset(        ◁—— Our custom dataset
    val_stride=10,
    isValSet_bool=False,
  )

  batch_size = self.cli_args.batch_size
  if self.use_cuda:
    batch_size *= torch.cuda.device_count()

  train_dl = DataLoader(         ◁—— An off-the-shelf class
    train_ds,
    batch_size=batch_size,              ◁—— Batching is done automatically.
    num_workers=self.cli_args.num_workers,
    pin_memory=self.use_cuda,      ◁┐
  )                                  │ Pinned memory transfers
                                     │ to GPU quickly.
```

```
      return train_dl

# ... line 137
def main(self):
   train_dl = self.initTrainDl()
   val_dl = self.initValDl()                    The validation data loader
                                                is very similar to training.
```

In addition to batching individual samples, data loaders can also provide parallel loading of data by using separate processes and shared memory. All we need to do is specify num_workers=... when instantiating the data loader, and the rest is taken care of behind the scenes. Each worker process produces complete batches as in figure 11.4. This helps make sure hungry GPUs are well fed with data. Our validation_ds and validation_dl instances look similar, except for the obvious isValSet_bool=True.

When we iterate, like for batch_tup in self.train_dl:, we won't have to wait for each Ct to be loaded, samples to be taken and batched, and so on. Instead, we'll get the already loaded batch_tup immediately, and a worker process will be freed up in the background to begin loading another batch to use on a later iteration. Using the data-loading features of PyTorch can help speed up most projects, because we can overlap data loading and processing with GPU calculation.

11.4   *Our first-pass neural network design*

The possible design space for a convolutional neural network capable of detecting tumors is effectively infinite. Luckily, considerable effort has been spent over the past decade or so investigating effective models for image recognition. While these have largely focused on 2D images, the general architecture ideas transfer well to 3D, so there are many tested designs that we can use as a starting point. This helps because although our first network architecture is unlikely to be our best option, right now we are only aiming for "good enough to get us going."

We will base the network design on what we used in chapter 8. We will have to update the model somewhat because our input data is 3D, and we will add some complicating details, but the overall structure shown in figure 11.5 should feel familiar. Similarly, the work we do for this project will be a good base for your future projects, although the further you get from classification or segmentation projects, the more you'll have to adapt this base to fit. Let's dissect this architecture, starting with the four repeated blocks that make up the bulk of the network.

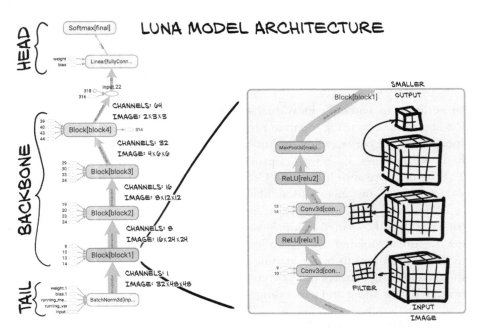

Figure 11.5   The architecture of the `LunaModel` class consisting of a batch-normalization tail, a four-block backbone, and a head comprised of a linear layer followed by softmax

11.4.1   *The core convolutions*

Classification models often have a structure that consists of a tail, a backbone (or body), and a head. The *tail* is the first few layers that process the input to the network. These early layers often have a different structure or organization than the rest of the network, as they must adapt the input to the form expected by the backbone. Here we use a simple batch normalization layer, though often the tail contains convolutional layers as well. Such convolutional layers are often used to aggressively downsample the size of the image; since our image size is already small, we don't need to do that here.

Next, the *backbone* of the network typically contains the bulk of the layers, which are usually arranged in series of *blocks*. Each block has the same (or at least a similar) set of layers, though often the size of the expected input and the number of filters changes from block to block. We will use a block that consists of two 3 × 3 convolutions, each followed by an activation, with a max-pooling operation at the end of the block. We can see this in the expanded view of figure 11.5 labeled `Block[block1]`. Here's what the implementation of the block looks like in code.

Listing 11.6   model.py:67, class `LunaBlock`

```
class LunaBlock(nn.Module):
    def __init__(self, in_channels, conv_channels):
        super().__init__()
```

```
    self.conv1 = nn.Conv3d(
      in_channels, conv_channels, kernel_size=3, padding=1, bias=True,
    )
    self.relu1 = nn.ReLU(inplace=True)   1((CO5-1))
     self.conv2 = nn.Conv3d(
       conv_channels, conv_channels, kernel_size=3, padding=1, bias=True,
    )
    self.relu2 = nn.ReLU(inplace=True)

    self.maxpool = nn.MaxPool3d(2, 2)

  def forward(self, input_batch):
    block_out = self.conv1(input_batch)
    block_out = self.relu1(block_out)
    block_out = self.conv2(block_out)
    block_out = self.relu2(block_out)

    return self.maxpool(block_out)
```

These could be implemented as calls to the functional API instead.

Finally, the *head* of the network takes the output from the backbone and converts it into the desired output form. For convolutional networks, this often involves flattening the intermediate output and passing it to a fully connected layer. For some networks, it makes sense to also include a second fully connected layer, although that is usually more appropriate for classification problems in which the imaged objects have more structure (think about cars versus trucks having wheels, lights, grill, doors, and so on) and for projects with a large number of classes. Since we are only doing binary classification, and we don't seem to need the additional complexity, we have only a single flattening layer.

Using a structure like this can be a good first building block for a convolutional network. There are more complicated designs out there, but for many projects they're overkill in terms of both implementation complexity and computational demands. It's a good idea to start simple and add complexity only when there's a demonstrable need for it.

We can see the convolutions of our block represented in 2D in figure 11.6. Since this is a small portion of a larger image, we ignore padding here. (Note that the ReLU activation function is not shown, as applying it does not change the image sizes.)

Let's walk through the information flow between our input voxels and a single voxel of output. We want to have a strong sense of how our output will respond when the inputs change. It might be a good idea to review chapter 8, particularly sections 8.1 through 8.3, just to make sure you're 100% solid on the basic mechanics of convolutions.

We're using $3 \times 3 \times 3$ convolutions in our block. A single $3 \times 3 \times 3$ convolution has a receptive field of $3 \times 3 \times 3$, which is almost tautological. Twenty-seven voxels are fed in, and one comes out.

It gets interesting when we use two $3 \times 3 \times 3$ convolutions stacked back to back. Stacking convolutional layers allows the final output voxel (or pixel) to be influenced by an input further away than the size of the convolutional kernel suggests. If that output

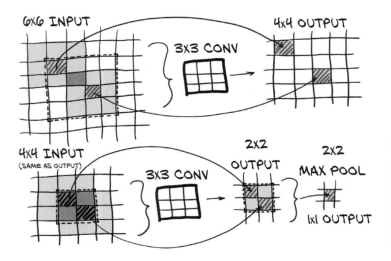

Figure 11.6
The convolutional architecture of a LunaModel block consisting of two 3 × 3 convolutions followed by a max pool. The final pixel has a receptive field of 6 × 6.

voxel is fed into another $3 \times 3 \times 3$ kernel as one of the edge voxels, then some of the inputs to the first layer will be outside of the $3 \times 3 \times 3$ area of input to the second. The final output of those two stacked layers has an *effective receptive field* of $5 \times 5 \times 5$. That means that when taken together, the stacked layers act as similar to a single convolutional layer with a larger size.

Put another way, each $3 \times 3 \times 3$ convolutional layer adds an additional one-voxel-per-edge border to the receptive field. We can see this if we trace the arrows in figure 11.6 backward; our 2×2 output has a receptive field of 4×4, which in turn has a receptive field of 6×6. Two stacked $3 \times 3 \times 3$ layers uses fewer parameters than a full $5 \times 5 \times 5$ convolution would (and so is also faster to compute).

The output of our two stacked convolutions is fed into a $2 \times 2 \times 2$ max pool, which means we're taking a $6 \times 6 \times 6$ effective field, throwing away seven-eighths of the data, and going with the one $5 \times 5 \times 5$ field that produced the largest value.[2] Now, those "discarded" input voxels still have a chance to contribute, since the max pool that's one output voxel over has an overlapping input field, so it's possible they'll influence the final output that way.

Note that while we show the receptive field shrinking with each convolutional layer, we're using *padded* convolutions, which add a virtual one-pixel border around the image. Doing so keeps our input and output image sizes the same.

The nn.ReLU layers are the same as the ones we looked at in chapter 6. Outputs greater than 0.0 will be left unchanged, and outputs less than 0.0 will be clamped to zero.

This block will be repeated multiple times to form our model's backbone.

---

[2] Remember that we're actually working in 3D, despite the 2D figure.

11.4.2 *The full model*

Let's take a look at the full model implementation. We'll skip the block definition, since we just saw that in listing 11.6.

Listing 11.7   model.py:13, class LunaModel

```
class LunaModel(nn.Module):
  def __init__(self, in_channels=1, conv_channels=8):
    super().__init__()

    self.tail_batchnorm = nn.BatchNorm3d(1)     ⟵— Tail

    self.block1 = LunaBlock(in_channels, conv_channels)
    self.block2 = LunaBlock(conv_channels, conv_channels * 2)       ⎫
    self.block3 = LunaBlock(conv_channels * 2, conv_channels * 4)   ⎬ Backbone
    self.block4 = LunaBlock(conv_channels * 4, conv_channels * 8)   ⎭

    self.head_linear = nn.Linear(1152, 2)       ⎫ Head
    self.head_softmax = nn.Softmax(dim=1)        ⎭
```

Here, our tail is relatively simple. We are going to normalize our input using nn.BatchNorm3d, which, as we saw in chapter 8, will shift and scale our input so that it has a mean of 0 and a standard deviation of 1. Thus, the somewhat odd Hounsfield unit (HU) scale that our input is in won't really be visible to the rest of the network. This is a somewhat arbitrary choice; we know what our input units are, and we know the expected values of the relevant tissues, so we could probably implement a fixed normalization scheme pretty easily. It's not clear which approach would be better.[3]

Our backbone is four repeated blocks, with the block implementation pulled out into the separate nn.Module subclass we saw earlier in listing 11.6. Since each block ends with a $2 \times 2 \times 2$ max-pool operation, after 4 layers we will have decreased the resolution of the image 16 times in each dimension. Recall from chapter 10 that our data is returned in chunks that are $32 \times 48 \times 48$, which will become $2 \times 3 \times 3$ by the end of the backbone.

Finally, our tail is just a fully connected layer followed by a call to nn.Softmax. Softmax is a useful function for single-label classification tasks and has a few nice properties: it bounds the output between 0 and 1, it's relatively insensitive to the absolute range of the inputs (only the *relative* values of the inputs matter), and it allows our model to express the degree of certainty it has in an answer.

The function itself is relatively simple. Every value from the input is used to exponentiate e, and the resulting series of values is then divided by the sum of all the results of exponentiation. Here's what it looks like implemented in a simple fashion as a nonoptimized softmax implementation in pure Python:

```
>>> logits = [1, -2, 3]
>>> exp = [e ** x for x in logits]
>>> exp
```

---

[3] Which is why there's an exercise to experiment with both in the next chapter!

```
[2.718, 0.135, 20.086]

>>> softmax = [x / sum(exp) for x in exp]
>>> softmax
[0.118, 0.006, 0.876]
```

Of course, we use the PyTorch version of nn.Softmax for our model, as it natively understands batches and tensors and will perform autograd quickly and as expected.

COMPLICATION: CONVERTING FROM CONVOLUTION TO LINEAR

Continuing on with our model definition, we come to a complication. We can't just feed the output of self.block4 into a fully connected layer, since that output is a per-sample $2 \times 3 \times 3$ image with 64 channels, and fully connected layers expect a 1D vector as input (well, technically they expect a *batch* of 1D vectors, which is a 2D array, but the mismatch remains either way). Let's take a look at the forward method.

Listing 11.8   model.py:50, LunaModel.forward

```
def forward(self, input_batch):
  bn_output = self.tail_batchnorm(input_batch)

  block_out = self.block1(bn_output)
  block_out = self.block2(block_out)
  block_out = self.block3(block_out)
  block_out = self.block4(block_out)

  conv_flat = block_out.view(
    block_out.size(0),        <─── The batch size
    -1,
  )
  linear_output = self.head_linear(conv_flat)

  return linear_output, self.head_softmax(linear_output)
```

Note that before we pass data into a fully connected layer, we must flatten it using the view function. Since that operation is stateless (it has no parameters that govern its behavior), we can simply perform the operation in the forward function. This is somewhat similar to the functional interfaces we discussed in chapter 8. Almost every model that uses convolution and produces classifications, regressions, or other non-image outputs will have a similar component in the head of the network.

For the return value of the forward method, we return both the raw *logits* and the softmax-produced probabilities. We first hinted at logits in section 7.2.6: they are the numerical values produced by the network prior to being normalized into probabilities by the softmax layer. That might sound a bit complicated, but logits are really just the raw input to the softmax layer. They can have any real-valued input, and the softmax will squash them to the range 0–1.

We'll use the logits when we calculate the nn.CrossEntropyLoss during training,[4] and we'll use the probabilities for when we want to actually classify the samples. This kind of slight difference between what's used for training and what's used in production is fairly common, especially when the difference between the two outputs is a simple, stateless function like softmax.

INITIALIZATION

Finally, let's talk about initializing our network's parameters. In order to get well-behaved performance out of our model, the network's weights, biases, and other parameters need to exhibit certain properties. Let's imagine a degenerate case, where all of the network's weights are greater than 1 (and we do not have residual connections). In that case, repeated multiplication by those weights would result in layer outputs that became very large as data flowed through the layers of the network. Similarly, weights less than 1 would cause all layer outputs to become smaller and vanish. Similar considerations apply to the gradients in the backward pass.

Many normalization techniques can be used to keep layer outputs well behaved, but one of the simplest is to just make sure the network's weights are initialized such that intermediate values and gradients become neither unreasonably small nor unreasonably large. As we discussed in chapter 8, PyTorch does not help us as much as it should here, so we need to do some initialization ourselves. We can treat the following _init_weights function as boilerplate, as the exact details aren't particularly important.

Listing 11.9 model.py:30, LunaModel._init_weights

```
def _init_weights(self):
  for m in self.modules():
    if type(m) in {
      nn.Linear,
      nn.Conv3d,
    }:
      nn.init.kaiming_normal_(
        m.weight.data, a=0, mode='fan_out', nonlinearity='relu',
      )
      if m.bias is not None:
        fan_in, fan_out = \
          nn.init._calculate_fan_in_and_fan_out(m.weight.data)
        bound = 1 / math.sqrt(fan_out)
        nn.init.normal_(m.bias, -bound, bound)
```

11.5 *Training and validating the model*

Now it's time to take the various pieces we've been working with and assemble them into something we can actually execute. This training loop should be familiar—we saw loops like figure 11.7 in chapter 5.

---

[4] There are numerical stability benefits for doing so. Propagating gradients accurately through an exponential calculated using 32-bit floating-point numbers can be problematic.

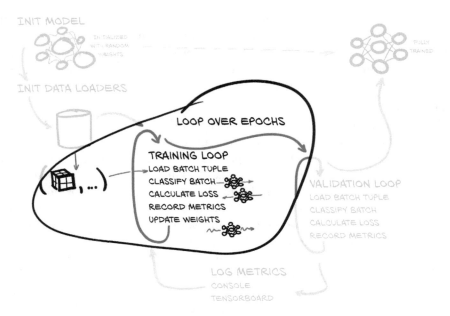

Figure 11.7 The training and validation script we will implement in this chapter, with a focus on the nested loops over each epoch and batches in the epoch

The code is relatively compact (the `doTraining` function is only 12 statements; it's longer here due to line-length limitations).

Listing 11.10   `training.py:137, LunaTrainingApp.main`

```
def main(self):
  # ... line 143
  for epoch_ndx in range(1, self.cli_args.epochs + 1):
    trnMetrics_t = self.doTraining(epoch_ndx, train_dl)
    self.logMetrics(epoch_ndx, 'trn', trnMetrics_t)

# ... line 165
def doTraining(self, epoch_ndx, train_dl):
  self.model.train()
  trnMetrics_g = torch.zeros(          ◁─┐ Initializes an empty
    METRICS_SIZE,                        │ metrics array
    len(train_dl.dataset),
    device=self.device,
  )

  batch_iter = enumerateWithEstimate(   ◁─┐ Sets up our batch looping
    train_dl,                             │ with time estimate
    "E{} Training".format(epoch_ndx),
    start_ndx=train_dl.num_workers,
  )
  for batch_ndx, batch_tup in batch_iter:  ┐ Frees any leftover
    self.optimizer.zero_grad()           ◁─┘ gradient tensors
```

```
loss_var = self.computeBatchLoss(
  batch_ndx,
  batch_tup,
  train_dl.batch_size,
  trnMetrics_g
)
```
⟵ **We'll discuss this method in
detail in the next section.**

```
loss_var.backward()
self.optimizer.step()
```
**Actually updates
the model weights**

```
self.totalTrainingSamples_count += len(train_dl.dataset)
```

```
return trnMetrics_g.to('cpu')
```

The main differences that we see from the training loops in earlier chapters are as follows:

- The trnMetrics_g tensor collects detailed per-class metrics during training. For larger projects like ours, this kind of insight can be very nice to have.
- We don't directly iterate over the train_dl data loader. We use enumerateWith-Estimate to provide an estimated time of completion. This isn't crucial; it's just a stylistic choice.
- The actual loss computation is pushed into the computeBatchLoss method. Again, this isn't strictly necessary, but code reuse is typically a plus.

We'll discuss why we've wrapped enumerate with additional functionality in section 11.7.2; for now, assume it's the same as enumerate(train_dl).

The purpose of the trnMetrics_g tensor is to transport information about how the model is behaving on a per-sample basis from the computeBatchLoss function to the logMetrics function. Let's take a look at computeBatchLoss next. We'll cover logMetrics after we're done with the rest of the main training loop.

11.5.1 *The computeBatchLoss function*

The computeBatchLoss function is called by both the training and validation loops. As the name suggests, it computes the loss over a batch of samples. In addition, the function also computes and records per-sample information about the output the model is producing. This lets us compute things like the percentage of correct answers per class, which allows us to hone in on areas where our model is having difficulty.

Of course, the function's core functionality is around feeding the batch into the model and computing the per-batch loss. We're using CrossEntropyLoss (https://pytorch.org/docs/stable/nn.html#torch.nn.CrossEntropyLoss), just like in chapter 7. Unpacking the batch tuple, moving the tensors to the GPU, and invoking the model should all feel familiar after that earlier training work.

Listing 11.11   training.py:225, .computeBatchLoss

```
def computeBatchLoss(self, batch_ndx, batch_tup, batch_size, metrics_g):
  input_t, label_t, _series_list, _center_list = batch_tup

  input_g = input_t.to(self.device, non_blocking=True)
  label_g = label_t.to(self.device, non_blocking=True)

  logits_g, probability_g = self.model(input_g)
                                                            reduction='none' gives
                                                            the loss per sample.
  loss_func = nn.CrossEntropyLoss(reduction='none')    ◁
  loss_g = loss_func(
    logits_g,                    Index of the one-
    label_g[:,1],            ◁   hot-encoded class
  )
  # ... line 238                 Recombines the loss per
  return loss_g.mean()     ◁     sample into a single value
```

Here we are *not* using the default behavior to get a loss value averaged over the batch. Instead, we get a tensor of loss values, one per sample. This lets us track the individual losses, which means we can aggregate them as we wish (per class, for example). We'll see that in action in just a moment. For now, we'll return the mean of those per-sample losses, which is equivalent to the batch loss. In situations where you don't want to keep statistics per sample, using the loss averaged over the batch is perfectly fine. Whether that's the case is highly dependent on your project and goals.

Once that's done, we've fulfilled our obligations to the calling function in terms of what's required to do backpropagation and weight updates. Before we do that, however, we also want to record our per-sample stats for posterity (and later analysis). We'll use the metrics_g parameter passed in to accomplish this.

Listing 11.12   training.py:26

```
METRICS_LABEL_NDX=0          ◁        These named array indexes are
METRICS_PRED_NDX=1                    declared at module-level scope.
METRICS_LOSS_NDX=2
METRICS_SIZE = 3

  # ... line 225
  def computeBatchLoss(self, batch_ndx, batch_tup, batch_size, metrics_g):
    # ... line 238
    start_ndx = batch_ndx * batch_size
    end_ndx = start_ndx + label_t.size(0)

    metrics_g[METRICS_LABEL_NDX, start_ndx:end_ndx] = \
      label_g[:,1].detach()                                   We use detach since
    metrics_g[METRICS_PRED_NDX, start_ndx:end_ndx] = \        none of our metrics
      probability_g[:,1].detach()                             need to hold on to
    metrics_g[METRICS_LOSS_NDX, start_ndx:end_ndx] = \        gradients.
      loss_g.detach()
                                 Again, this is the loss
    return loss_g.mean()    ◁    over the entire batch.
```

By recording the label, prediction, and loss for each and every training (and later, validation) sample, we have a wealth of detailed information we can use to investigate the behavior of our model. For now, we're going to focus on compiling per-class statistics, but we could easily use this information to find the sample that is classified the most wrongly and start to investigate why. Again, for some projects, this kind of information will be less interesting, but it's good to remember that you have these kinds of options available.

11.5.2 *The validation loop is similar*

The validation loop in figure 11.8 looks very similar to training but is somewhat simplified. The key difference is that validation is read-only. Specifically, the loss value returned is not used, and the weights are not updated.

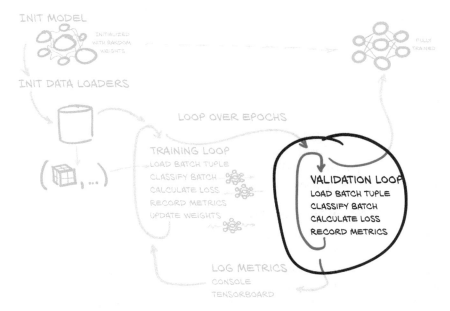

Figure 11.8   The training and validation script we will implement in this chapter, with a focus on the per-epoch validation loop

Nothing about the model should have changed between the start and end of the function call. In addition, it's quite a bit faster due to the `with torch.no_grad()` context manager explicitly informing PyTorch that no gradients need to be computed.

Listing 11.13   training.py:137, `LunaTrainingApp.main`

```
def main(self):
  for epoch_ndx in range(1, self.cli_args.epochs + 1):
    # ... line 157
    valMetrics_t = self.doValidation(epoch_ndx, val_dl)
```

```
        self.logMetrics(epoch_ndx, 'val', valMetrics_t)

# ... line 203
def doValidation(self, epoch_ndx, val_dl):
  with torch.no_grad():
    self.model.eval()                    ⊲── Turns off training-time behavior
    valMetrics_g = torch.zeros(
      METRICS_SIZE,
      len(val_dl.dataset),
      device=self.device,
    )

    batch_iter = enumerateWithEstimate(
      val_dl,
      "E{} Validation ".format(epoch_ndx),
      start_ndx=val_dl.num_workers,
    )
    for batch_ndx, batch_tup in batch_iter:
      self.computeBatchLoss(
        batch_ndx, batch_tup, val_dl.batch_size, valMetrics_g)

  return valMetrics_g.to('cpu')
```

Without needing to update network weights (recall that doing so would violate the entire premise of the validation set; something we never want to do!), we don't need to use the loss returned from computeBatchLoss, nor do we need to reference the optimizer. All that's left inside the loop is the call to computeBatchLoss. Note that we are still collecting metrics in valMetrics_g as a side effect of the call, even though we aren't using the overall per-batch loss returned by computeBatchLoss for anything.

11.6 *Outputting performance metrics*

The last thing we do per epoch is log our performance metrics for this epoch. As shown in figure 11.9, once we've logged metrics, we return to the training loop for the next epoch of training. Logging results and progress as we go is important, since if training goes off the rails ("does not converge" in the parlance of deep learning), we want to notice this is happening and stop spending time training a model that's not working out. In less catastrophic cases, it's good to be able to keep an eye on how your model behaves.

Earlier, we were collecting results in trnMetrics_g and valMetrics_g for logging progress per epoch. Each of these two tensors now contains everything we need to compute our percent correct and average loss per class for our training and validation runs. Doing this per epoch is a common choice, though somewhat arbitrary. In future chapters, we'll see how to manipulate the size of our epochs such that we get feedback about training progress at a reasonable rate.

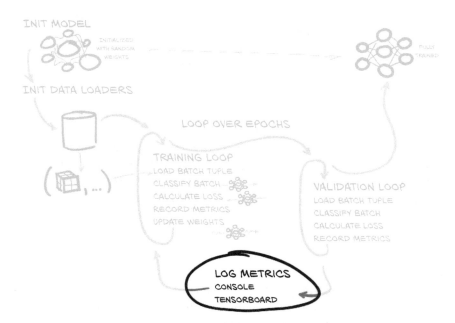

Figure 11.9 **The training and validation script we will implement in this chapter, with a focus on the metrics logging at the end of each epoch**

11.6.1 *The logMetrics function*

Let's talk about the high-level structure of the logMetrics function. The signature looks like this.

Listing 11.14 training.py:251, LunaTrainingApp.logMetrics

```
def logMetrics(
    self,
    epoch_ndx,
    mode_str,
    metrics_t,
    classificationThreshold=0.5,
):
```

We use epoch_ndx purely for display while logging our results. The mode_str argument tells us whether the metrics are for training or validation.

 We consume either trnMetrics_t or valMetrics_t, which is passed in as the metrics _t parameter. Recall that both of those inputs are tensors of floating-point values that we filled with data during computeBatchLoss and then transferred back to the CPU right before we returned them from doTraining and doValidation. Both tensors have three rows and as many columns as we have samples (training samples or validation samples, depending). As a reminder, those three rows correspond to the following constants.

Listing 11.15   training.py:26

```
METRICS_LABEL_NDX=0          ◁┐  These are declared at
METRICS_PRED_NDX=1             │  module-level scope.
METRICS_LOSS_NDX=2
METRICS_SIZE = 3
```

Tensor masking and Boolean indexing

Masked tensors are a common usage pattern that might be opaque if you have not encountered them before. You may be familiar with the NumPy concept called *masked arrays*; tensor and array masks behave the same way.

If you aren't familiar with masked arrays, an excellent page in the NumPy documentation (http://mng.bz/XPra) describes the behavior well. PyTorch purposely uses the same syntax and semantics as NumPy.

CONSTRUCTING MASKS

Next, we're going to construct masks that will let us limit our metrics to only the nodule or non-nodule (aka positive or negative) samples. We will also count the total samples per class, as well as the number of samples we classified correctly.

Listing 11.16   training.py:264, LunaTrainingApp.logMetrics

```
negLabel_mask = metrics_t[METRICS_LABEL_NDX] <= classificationThreshold
negPred_mask = metrics_t[METRICS_PRED_NDX] <= classificationThreshold

posLabel_mask = ~negLabel_mask
posPred_mask = ~negPred_mask
```

While we don't assert it here, we know that all of the values stored in metrics _t[METRICS_LABEL_NDX] belong to the set {0.0, 1.0} since we know that our nodule status labels are simply True or False. By comparing to classificationThreshold, which defaults to 0.5, we get an array of binary values where a True value corresponds to a non-nodule (aka negative) label for the sample in question.

We do a similar comparison to create the negPred_mask, but we must remember that the METRICS_PRED_NDX values are the positive predictions produced by our model and can be any floating-point value between 0.0 and 1.0, inclusive. That doesn't change our comparison, but it does mean the actual value can be close to 0.5. The positive masks are simply the inverse of the negative masks.

> **NOTE** While other projects can utilize similar approaches, it's important to realize that we're taking some shortcuts that are allowed because this is a binary classification problem. If your next project has more than two classes or has samples that belong to multiple classes at the same time, you'll have to use more complicated logic to build similar masks.

Next, we use those masks to compute some per-label statistics and store them in a dictionary, `metrics_dict`.

Listing 11.17   training.py:270, LunaTrainingApp.logMetrics

```
neg_count = int(negLabel_mask.sum())          ◁─┐  Converts to a normal
pos_count = int(posLabel_mask.sum())             │  Python integer

neg_correct = int((negLabel_mask & negPred_mask).sum())
pos_correct = int((posLabel_mask & posPred_mask).sum())

metrics_dict = {}
metrics_dict['loss/all'] = \
  metrics_t[METRICS_LOSS_NDX].mean()
metrics_dict['loss/neg'] = \
  metrics_t[METRICS_LOSS_NDX, negLabel_mask].mean()
metrics_dict['loss/pos'] = \
  metrics_t[METRICS_LOSS_NDX, posLabel_mask].mean()          Avoids integer
                                                             division by
                                                             converting to
metrics_dict['correct/all'] = (pos_correct + neg_correct) \  np.float32
  / np.float32(metrics_t.shape[1]) * 100       ◁─────────
metrics_dict['correct/neg'] = neg_correct / np.float32(neg_count) * 100
metrics_dict['correct/pos'] = pos_correct / np.float32(pos_count) * 100
```

First we compute the average loss over the entire epoch. Since the loss is the single metric that is being minimized during training, we always want to be able to keep track of it. Then we limit the loss averaging to only those samples with a negative label using the `negLabel_mask` we just made. We do the same with the positive loss. Computing a per-class loss like this can be useful if one class is persistently harder to classify than another, since that knowledge can help drive investigation and improvements.

We'll close out the calculations with determining the fraction of samples we classified correctly, as well as the fraction correct from each label. Since we will display these numbers as percentages in a moment, we also multiply the values by 100. Similar to the loss, we can use these numbers to help guide our efforts when making improvements. After the calculations, we then log our results with three calls to `log.info`.

Listing 11.18   training.py:289, LunaTrainingApp.logMetrics

```
log.info(
  ("E{} {:8} {loss/all:.4f} loss, "
    + "{correct/all:-5.1f}% correct, "
  ).format(
    epoch_ndx,
    mode_str,
    **metrics_dict,
  )
)
log.info(
  ("E{} {:8} {loss/neg:.4f} loss, "
    + "{correct/neg:-5.1f}% correct ({neg_correct:} of {neg_count:})"
```

```
    ).format(
      epoch_ndx,
      mode_str + '_neg',
      neg_correct=neg_correct,
      neg_count=neg_count,
      **metrics_dict,
    )
  )
log.info(
  # ... line 319
)
```

> ◁ ── The 'pos' logging is similar
> to the 'neg' logging earlier.

The first log has values computed from all of our samples and is tagged /all, while the negative (non-nodule) and positive (nodule) values are tagged /neg and /pos, respectively. We don't show the third logging statement for positive values here; it's identical to the second except for swapping *neg* for *pos* in all cases.

11.7 *Running the training script*

Now that we've completed the core of the training.py script, we'll actually start running it. This will initialize and train our model and print statistics about how well the training is going. The idea is to get this kicked off to run in the background while we're covering the model implementation in detail. Hopefully we'll have results to look at once we're done.

We're running this script from the main code directory; it should have subdirectories called p2ch11, util, and so on. The python environment used should have all the libraries listed in requirements.txt installed. Once those libraries are ready, we can run:

> ◁ ── This is the command line for Linux/Bash. Windows
> users will probably need to invoke Python
> differently, depending on the install method used.

```
$ python -m p2ch11.training
Starting LunaTrainingApp,
    Namespace(batch_size=256, channels=8, epochs=20, layers=3, num_workers=8)
<p2ch11.dsets.LunaDataset object at 0x7fa53a128710>: 495958 training samples
<p2ch11.dsets.LunaDataset object at 0x7fa537325198>: 55107 validation samples
Epoch 1 of 20, 1938/216 batches of size 256
E1 Training ----/1938, starting
E1 Training   16/1938, done at 2018-02-28 20:52:54, 0:02:57
...
```

As a reminder, we also provide a Jupyter Notebook that contains invocations of the training application.

Listing 11.19   code/p2_run_everything.ipynb

```
# In[5]:
run('p2ch11.prepcache.LunaPrepCacheApp')

# In[6]:
run('p2ch11.training.LunaTrainingApp', '--epochs=1')
```

If the first epoch seems to be taking a very long time (more than 10 or 20 minutes), it might be related to needing to prepare the cached data required by LunaDataset. See section 10.5.1 for details about the caching. The exercises for chapter 10 included writing a script to pre-stuff the cache in an efficient manner. We also provide the prepcache.py file to do the same thing; it can be invoked with `python -m p2ch11 .prepcache`. Since we repeat our dsets.py files per chapter, the caching will need to be repeated for every chapter. This is somewhat space and time inefficient, but it means we can keep the code for each chapter much more well contained. For your future projects, we recommend reusing your cache more heavily.

Once training is underway, we want to make sure we're using the computing resources at hand the way we expect. An easy way to tell if the bottleneck is data loading or computation is to wait a few moments after the script starts to train (look for output like `E1 Training 16/7750, done at...`) and then check both `top` and `nvidia-smi`:

- If the eight Python worker processes are consuming >80% CPU, then the cache probably needs to be prepared (we know this here because the authors have made sure there aren't CPU bottlenecks in this project's implementation; this won't be generally true).
- If `nvidia-smi` reports that `GPU-Util` is >80%, then you're saturating your GPU. We'll discuss some strategies for efficient waiting in section 11.7.2.

The intent is that the GPU is saturated; we want to use as much of that computing power as we can to complete epochs quickly. A single NVIDIA GTX 1080 Ti should complete an epoch in under 15 minutes. Since our model is relatively simple, it doesn't take a lot of CPU preprocessing for the CPU to be the bottleneck. When working with models with greater depth (or more needed calculations in general), processing each batch will take longer, which will increase the amount of CPU processing we can do before the GPU runs out of work before the next batch of input is ready.

11.7.1 Needed data for training

If the number of samples is less than 495,958 for training or 55,107 for validation, it might make sense to do some sanity checking to be sure the full data is present and accounted for. For your future projects, make sure your dataset returns the number of samples that you expect.

First, let's take a look at the basic directory structure of our data-unversioned/part2/luna directory:

```
$ ls -1p data-unversioned/part2/luna/
subset0/
subset1/
...
subset9/
```

Next, let's make sure we have one .mhd file and one .raw file for each series UID

```
$ ls -1p data-unversioned/part2/luna/subset0/
1.3.6.1.4.1.14519.5.2.1.6279.6001.105756658031515062000744821260.mhd
1.3.6.1.4.1.14519.5.2.1.6279.6001.105756658031515062000744821260.raw
1.3.6.1.4.1.14519.5.2.1.6279.6001.108197895896446896160048741492.mhd
1.3.6.1.4.1.14519.5.2.1.6279.6001.108197895896446896160048741492.raw
...
```

and that we have the overall correct number of files:

```
$ ls -1 data-unversioned/part2/luna/subset?/* | wc -1
1776
$ ls -1 data-unversioned/part2/luna/subset0/* | wc -1
178
...
$ ls -1 data-unversioned/part2/luna/subset9/* | wc -1
176
```

If all of these seem right but things still aren't working, ask on Manning LiveBook (https://livebook.manning.com/book/deep-learning-with-pytorch/chapter-11) and hopefully someone can help get things sorted out.

11.7.2 Interlude: The enumerateWithEstimate function

Working with deep learning involves a lot of waiting. We're talking about real-world, sitting around, glancing at the clock on the wall, a watched pot never boils (but you could fry an egg on the GPU), straight up *boredom*.

The only thing worse than sitting and staring at a blinking cursor that hasn't moved for over an hour is flooding your screen with this:

```
2020-01-01 10:00:00,056 INFO training batch 1234
2020-01-01 10:00:00,067 INFO training batch 1235
2020-01-01 10:00:00,077 INFO training batch 1236
2020-01-01 10:00:00,087 INFO training batch 1237
...etc...
```

At least the quietly blinking cursor doesn't blow out your scrollback buffer!

Fundamentally, while doing all this waiting, we want to answer the question "Do I have time to go refill my water glass?" along with follow-up questions about having time to

- Brew a cup of coffee
- Grab dinner
- Grab dinner in Paris[5]

To answer these pressing questions, we're going to use our enumerateWithEstimate function. Usage looks like the following:

---

[5] If getting dinner in France doesn't involve an airport, feel free to substitute "Paris, Texas" to make the joke work; https://en.wikipedia.org/wiki/Paris_(disambiguation).

```
>>> for i, _ in enumerateWithEstimate(list(range(234)), "sleeping"):
...     time.sleep(random.random())
...
11:12:41,892 WARNING sleeping ----/234, starting
11:12:44,542 WARNING sleeping    4/234, done at 2020-01-01 11:15:16, 0:02:35
11:12:46,599 WARNING sleeping    8/234, done at 2020-01-01 11:14:59, 0:02:17
11:12:49,534 WARNING sleeping   16/234, done at 2020-01-01 11:14:33, 0:01:51
11:12:58,219 WARNING sleeping   32/234, done at 2020-01-01 11:14:41, 0:01:59
11:13:15,216 WARNING sleeping   64/234, done at 2020-01-01 11:14:43, 0:02:01
11:13:44,233 WARNING sleeping  128/234, done at 2020-01-01 11:14:35, 0:01:53
11:14:40,083 WARNING sleeping ----/234, done at 2020-01-01 11:14:40
>>>
```

That's 8 lines of output for over 200 iterations lasting about 2 minutes. Even given the wide variance of random.random(), the function had a pretty decent estimate after 16 iterations (in less than 10 seconds). For loop bodies with more constant timing, the estimates stabilize even more quickly.

In terms of behavior, enumerateWithEstimate is almost identical to the standard enumerate (the differences are things like the fact that our function returns a generator, whereas enumerate returns a specialized <enumerate object at 0x…>).

Listing 11.20 util.py:143, def enumerateWithEstimate

```
def enumerateWithEstimate(
    iter,
    desc_str,
    start_ndx=0,
    print_ndx=4,
    backoff=None,
    iter_len=None,
):
  for (current_ndx, item) in enumerate(iter):
    yield (current_ndx, item)
```

However, the side effects (logging, specifically) are what make the function interesting. Rather than get lost in the weeds trying to cover every detail of the implementation, if you're interested, you can consult the function docstring (https://github .com/deep-learning-with-pytorch/dlwpt-code/blob/master/util/util.py#L143) to get information about the function parameters and desk-check the implementation.

Deep learning projects can be very time intensive. Knowing when something is expected to finish means you can use your time until then wisely, and it can also clue you in that something isn't working properly (or an approach is unworkable) if the expected time to completion is much larger than expected.

11.8   *Evaluating the model: Getting 99.7% correct means we're done, right?*

Let's take a look at some (abridged) output from our training script. As a reminder, we've run this with the command line `python -m p2ch11.training`:

```
E1 Training ----/969, starting
...
E1 LunaTrainingApp
E1 trn       2.4576 loss,  99.7% correct
...
E1 val       0.0172 loss,  99.8% correct
...
```

After one epoch of training, both the training and validation set show at least 99.7% correct results. That's an A+! Time for a round of high-fives, or at least a satisfied nod and smile. We just solved cancer! ... Right?

Well, no.

Let's take a closer (less-abridged) look at that epoch 1 output:

```
E1 LunaTrainingApp
E1 trn       2.4576 loss,  99.7% correct,
E1 trn_neg  0.1936 loss,  99.9% correct (494289 of 494743)
E1 trn_pos  924.34 loss,   0.2% correct (3 of 1215)
...
E1 val       0.0172 loss,  99.8% correct,
E1 val_neg  0.0025 loss, 100.0% correct (494743 of 494743)
E1 val_pos  5.9768 loss,   0.0% correct (0 of 1215)
```

On the validation set, we're getting non-nodules 100% correct, but the actual nodules are 100% wrong. The network is just classifying everything as not-a-nodule! The value 99.7% just means only approximately 0.3% of the samples are nodules.

After 10 epochs, the situation is only marginally better:

```
E10 LunaTrainingApp
E10 trn       0.0024 loss,  99.8% correct
E10 trn_neg  0.0000 loss, 100.0% correct
E10 trn_pos  0.9915 loss,   0.0% correct
E10 val       0.0025 loss,  99.7% correct
E10 val_neg  0.0000 loss, 100.0% correct
E10 val_pos  0.9929 loss,   0.0% correct
```

The classification output remains the same—none of the nodule (aka positive) samples are correctly identified. It's interesting that we're starting to see some decrease in the val_pos loss, however, while not seeing a corresponding increase in the val_neg loss. This implies that the network *is* learning something. Unfortunately, it's learning very, very slowly.

Even worse, this particular failure mode is the most dangerous in the real world! We want to avoid the situation where we classify a tumor as an innocuous structure, because that would not facilitate a patient getting the evaluation and eventual treatment they might need. It's important to understand the consequences for misclassification for all your projects, as that can have a large impact on how you design, train, and evaluate your model. We'll discuss this more in the next chapter.

Before we get to that, however, we need to upgrade our tooling to make the results easier to understand. We're sure you love to squint at columns of numbers as much as anyone, but pictures are worth a thousand words. Let's graph some of these metrics.

11.9 Graphing training metrics with TensorBoard

We're going to use a tool called TensorBoard as a quick and easy way to get our training metrics out of our training loop and into some pretty graphs. This will allow us to follow the *trends* of those metrics, rather than only look at the instantaneous values per epoch. It gets much, much easier to know whether a value is an outlier or just the latest in a trend when you're looking at a visual representation.

"Hey, wait," you might be thinking, "isn't TensorBoard part of the TensorFlow project? What's it doing here in my PyTorch book?"

Well, yes, it is part of another deep learning framework, but our philosophy is "use what works." There's no reason to restrict ourselves by not using a tool just because it's bundled with another project we're not using. Both the PyTorch and TensorBoard devs agree, because they collaborated to add official support for TensorBoard into PyTorch. TensorBoard is great, and it's got some easy-to-use PyTorch APIs that let us hook data from just about anywhere into it for quick and easy display. If you stick with deep learning, you'll probably be seeing (and using) a *lot* of TensorBoard.

In fact, if you've been running the chapter examples, you should already have some data on disk ready and waiting to be displayed. Let's see how to run Tensor-Board, and look at what it can show us.

11.9.1 Running TensorBoard

By default, our training script will write metrics data to the runs/ subdirectory. If you list the directory content, you might see something like this during your Bash shell session:

```
$ ls -1A runs/p2ch11/
total 24
drwxrwxr-x 2 elis elis 4096 Sep 15 13:22 2020-01-01_12.55.27-trn-dlwpt/
drwxrwxr-x 2 elis elis 4096 Sep 15 13:22 2020-01-01_12.55.27-val-dlwpt/
drwxrwxr-x 2 elis elis 4096 Sep 15 15:14 2020-01-01_13.31.23-trn-dwlpt/
drwxrwxr-x 2 elis elis 4096 Sep 15 15:14 2020-01-01_13.31.23-val-dwlpt/
```

The single-epoch run from earlier

The more recent 10-epoch training run

To get the `tensorboard` program, install the `tensorflow` (https://pypi.org/project/tensorflow) Python package. Since we're not actually going to use TensorFlow proper, it's fine if you install the default CPU-only package. If you have another version of

TensorBoard installed already, using that is fine too. Either make sure the appropriate directory is on your path, or invoke it with `../path/to/tensorboard --logdir runs/`. It doesn't really matter where you invoke it from, as long as you use the `--logdir` argument to point it at where your data is stored. It's a good idea to segregate your data into separate folders, as TensorBoard can get a bit unwieldy once you get over 10 or 20 experiments. You'll have to decide the best way to do that for each project as you go. Don't be afraid to move data around after the fact if you need to.

Let's start TensorBoard now:

These messages might be different or not present for you; that's fine.

```
$ tensorboard --logdir runs/
2020-01-01 12:13:16.163044: I tensorflow/core/platform/cpu_feature_guard.cc:140]
    Your CPU supports instructions that this TensorFlow binary was not
    compiled to use: AVX2 FMA  1((CO17-2))
TensorBoard 1.14.0 at http://localhost:6006/ (Press CTRL+C to quit)
```

Once that's done, you should be able to point your browser at http://localhost:6006 and see the main dashboard.[6] Figure 11.10 shows us what that looks like.

Figure 11.10   The main TensorBoard UI, showing a paired set of training and validation runs

---

[6] If you're running training on a different computer from your browser, you'll need to replace *localhost* with the appropriate hostname or IP address.

Along the top of the browser window, you should see the orange header. The right side of the header has the typical widgets for settings, a link to the GitHub repository, and the like. We can ignore those for now. The left side of the header has items for the data types we've provided. You should have at least the following:

- Scalars (the default tab)
- Histograms
- Precision-Recall Curves (shown as PR Curves)

You might see Distributions as well as the second UI tab (to the right of Scalars in figure 11.10). We won't use or discuss those here. Make sure you've selected Scalars by clicking it.

On the left is a set of controls for display options, as well as a list of runs that are present. The smoothing option can be useful if you have particularly noisy data; it will calm things down so that you can pick out the overall trend. The original non-smoothed data will still be visible in the background as a faded line in the same color. Figure 11.11 shows this, although it might be difficult to discern when printed in black and white.

Depending on how many times you've run the training script, you might have multiple runs to select from. With too many runs being rendered, the graphs can get overly noisy, so don't hesitate to deselect runs that aren't of interest at the moment.

If you want to permanently remove a run, the data can be deleted from disk while TensorBoard is running. You can do this to get rid of experiments that crashed, had

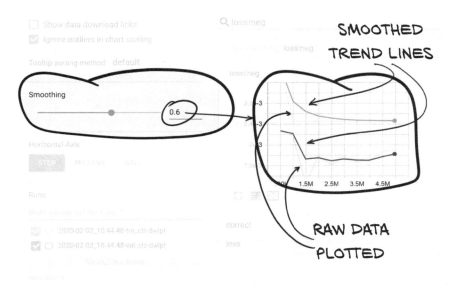

Figure 11.11   The TensorBoard sidebar with Smoothing set to 0.6 and two runs selected for display

bugs, didn't converge, or are so old they're no longer interesting. The number of runs can grow pretty quickly, so it can be helpful to prune it often and to rename runs or move runs that are particularly interesting to a more permanent directory so they don't get deleted by accident. To remove both the `train` and `validation` runs, execute the following (after changing the chapter, date, and time to match the run you want to remove):

```
$ rm -rf runs/p2ch11/2020-01-01_12.02.15_*
```

Keep in mind that removing runs will cause the runs that are later in the list to move up, which will result in them being assigned new colors.

OK, let's get to the point of TensorBoard: the pretty graphs! The main part of the screen should be filled with data from gathering training and validation metrics, as shown in figure 11.12.

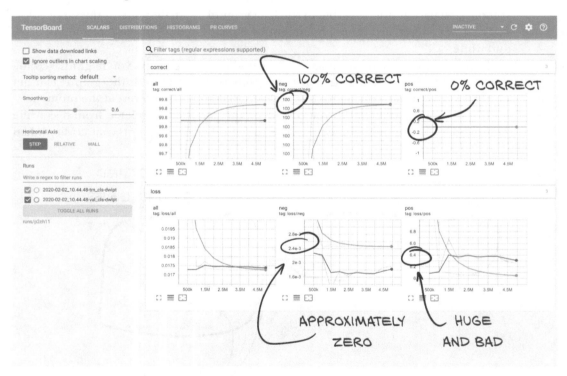

Figure 11.12   The main TensorBoard data display area showing us that our results on actual nodules are downright awful

That's much easier to parse and absorb than `E1 trn_pos 924.34 loss, 0.2% correct (3 of 1215)`! Although we're going to save discussion of what these graphs are telling us for section 11.10, now would be a good time to make sure it's clear what these numbers correspond to from our training program. Take a moment to cross-reference the numbers you get by mousing over the lines with the numbers spit out by training.py during the same training run. You should see a direct correspondence between the Value column of the tooltip and the values printed during training. Once you're comfortable and confident that you understand exactly what TensorBoard is showing you, let's move on and discuss how to get these numbers to appear in the first place.

11.9.2 Adding TensorBoard support to the metrics logging function

We are going to use the `torch.utils.tensorboard` module to write data in a format that TensorBoard will consume. This will allow us to write metrics for this and any other project quickly and easily. TensorBoard supports a mix of NumPy arrays and PyTorch tensors, but since we don't have any reason to put our data into NumPy arrays, we'll use PyTorch tensors exclusively.

The first thing we need do is to create our `SummaryWriter` objects (which we imported from `torch.utils.tensorboard`). The only parameter we're going to pass in is `log_dir`, which we will initialize to something like `runs/p2ch11/2020-01-01_12 .55.27-trn-dlwpt`. We can add a comment argument to our training script to change `dlwpt` to something more informative; use `python -m p2ch11.training --help` for more information.

We create two writers, one each for the training and validation runs. Those writers will be reused for every epoch. When the `SummaryWriter` class gets initialized, it also creates the `log_dir` directories as a side effect. These directories show up in TensorBoard and can clutter the UI with empty runs if the training script crashes before any data gets written, which can be common when you're experimenting with something. To avoid writing too many empty junk runs, we wait to instantiate the `SummaryWriter` objects until we're ready to write data for the first time. This function is called from `logMetrics()`.

Listing 11.21 training.py:127, .initTensorboardWriters

```
def initTensorboardWriters(self):
  if self.trn_writer is None:
    log_dir = os.path.join('runs', self.cli_args.tb_prefix, self.time_str)

    self.trn_writer = SummaryWriter(
      log_dir=log_dir + '-trn_cls-' + self.cli_args.comment)
    self.val_writer = SummaryWriter(
      log_dir=log_dir + '-val_cls-' + self.cli_args.comment)
```

If you recall, the first epoch is kind of a mess, with the early output in the training loop being essentially random. When we save the metrics from that first batch, those random results end up skewing things a bit. Recall from figure 11.11 that TensorBoard has smoothing to remove noise from the trend lines, which helps somewhat.

Another approach could be to skip metrics entirely for the first epoch's training data, although our model trains quickly enough that it's still useful to see the first epoch's results. Feel free to change this behavior as you see fit; the rest of part 2 will continue with this pattern of including the first, noisy training epoch.

> **TIP** If you end up doing a lot of experiments that result in exceptions or killing the training script relatively quickly, you might be left with a number of junk runs cluttering up your runs/ directory. Don't be afraid to clean those out!

WRITING SCALARS TO TENSORBOARD

Writing scalars is straightforward. We can take the `metrics_dict` we've already constructed and pass in each key/value pair to the `writer.add_scalar` method. The `torch.utils.tensorboard.SummaryWriter` class has the `add_scalar` method (http://mng.bz/RAqj) with the following signature.

Listing 11.22   PyTorch torch/utils/tensorboard/writer.py:267

```
def add_scalar(self, tag, scalar_value, global_step=None, walltime=None):
    # ...
```

The `tag` parameter tells TensorBoard which graph we're adding values to, and the `scalar_value` parameter is our data point's Y-axis value. The `global_step` parameter acts as the X-axis value.

Recall that we updated the `totalTrainingSamples_count` variable inside the `doTraining` function. We'll use `totalTrainingSamples_count` as the X-axis of our TensorBoard plots by passing it in as the `global_step` parameter. Here's what that looks like in our code.

Listing 11.23   training.py:323, LunaTrainingApp.logMetrics

```
for key, value in metrics_dict.items():
  writer.add_scalar(key, value, self.totalTrainingSamples_count)
```

Note that the slashes in our key names (such as `'loss/all'`) result in TensorBoard grouping the charts by the substring before the `'/'`.

The documentation suggests that we should be passing in the epoch number as the `global_step` parameter, but that results in some complications. By using the number of training samples presented to the network, we can do things like change the number of samples per epoch and still be able to compare those future graphs to the ones we're creating now. Saying that a model trains in half the number of epochs is meaningless if each epoch takes four times as long! Keep in mind that this might not be standard practice, however; expect to see a variety of values used for the global step.

11.10 Why isn't the model learning to detect nodules?

Our model is clearly learning *something*—the loss trend lines are consistent as epochs increase, and the results are repeatable. There is a disconnect, however, between what the model is learning and what we *want* it to learn. What's going on? Let's use a quick metaphor to illustrate the problem.

Imagine that a professor gives students a final exam consisting of 100 True/False questions. The students have access to previous versions of this professor's tests going back 30 years, and every time there are only *one or two* questions with a True answer. The other 98 or 99 are False, every time.

Assuming that the grades aren't on a curve and instead have a typical scale of 90% correct or better being an A, and so on, it is trivial to get an A+: just mark every question as False! Let's imagine that this year, there is only one True answer. A student like the one on the left in figure 11.13 who mindlessly marked every answer as False would get a 99% on the final but wouldn't really demonstrate that they had learned anything (beyond how to cram from old tests, of course). That's basically what our model is doing right now.

Figure 11.13 A professor giving two students the same grade, despite different levels of knowledge. Question 9 is the only question with an answer of True.

Contrast that with a student like the one on the right who also got 99% of the questions correct, but did so by answering two questions with True. Intuition tells us that the student on the right in figure 11.13 probably has a much better grasp of the material than the all-False student. Finding the one True question while only getting one answer wrong is pretty difficult! Unfortunately, neither our students' grades nor our model's grading scheme reflect this gut feeling.

We have a similar situation, where 99.7% of the answers to "Is this candidate a nodule?" are "Nope." Our model is taking the easy way out and answering False on every question.

Still, if we look back at our model's numbers more closely, the loss on the training and validation sets *is* decreasing! The fact that we're getting any traction at all on the cancer-detection problem should give us hope. It will be the work of the next chapter to realize this potential. We'll start chapter 12 by introducing some new, relevant terminology, and then we'll come up with a better grading scheme that doesn't lend itself to being gamed quite as easily as what we've done so far.

11.11 Conclusion

We've come a long way this chapter—we now have a model and a training loop, and are able to consume the data we produced in the last chapter. Our metrics are being logged to the console as well as graphed visually.

While our results aren't usable yet, we're actually closer than it might seem. In chapter 12, we will improve the metrics we're using to track our progress, and use them to inform the changes we need to make to get our model producing reasonable results.

11.12 Exercises

1 Implement a program that iterates through a `LunaDataset` instance by wrapping it in a `DataLoader` instance, while timing how long it takes to do so. Compare these times to the times from the exercises in chapter 10. Be aware of the state of the cache when running the script.

   a What impact does setting `num_workers=…` to 0, 1, and 2 have?

   b What are the highest values your machine will support for a given combination of `batch_size=…` and `num_workers=…` without running out of memory?

2 Reverse the sort order of `noduleInfo_list`. How does that change the behavior of the model after one epoch of training?

3 Change `logMetrics` to alter the naming scheme of the runs and keys that are used in TensorBoard.

   a Experiment with different forward-slash placement for keys passed in to `writer.add_scalar`.

   b Have both training and validation runs use the same writer, and add the `trn` or `val` string to the name of the key.

   c Customize the naming of the log directory and keys to suit your taste.

11.13 Summary

- Data loaders can be used to load data from arbitrary datasets in multiple processes. This allows otherwise-idle CPU resources to be devoted to preparing data to feed to the GPU.

- Data loaders load multiple samples from a dataset and collate them into a batch. PyTorch models expect to process batches of data, not individual samples.

- Data loaders can be used to manipulate arbitrary datasets by changing the relative frequency of individual samples. This allows for "after-market" tweaks to a dataset, though it might make more sense to change the dataset implementation directly.

- We will use PyTorch's `torch.optim.SGD` (stochastic gradient descent) optimizer with a learning rate of 0.001 and a momentum of 0.99 for the majority of part 2. These values are also reasonable defaults for many deep learning projects.

- Our initial model for classification will be very similar to the model we used in chapter 8. This lets us get started with a model that we have reason to believe will be effective. We can revisit the model design if we think it's the thing preventing our project from performing better.

- The choice of metrics that we monitor during training is important. It is easy to accidentally pick metrics that are misleading about how the model is performing. Using the overall percentage of samples classified correctly is not useful for our data. Chapter 12 will detail how to evaluate and choose better metrics.

- TensorBoard can be used to display a wide range of metrics visually. This makes it much easier to consume certain forms of information (particularly trend data) as they change per epoch of training.

Improving training with metrics and augmentation

This chapter covers

- Defining and computing precision, recall, and true/false positives/negatives
- Using the F1 score versus other quality metrics
- Balancing and augmenting data to reduce overfitting
- Using TensorBoard to graph quality metrics

The close of the last chapter left us in a predicament. While we were able to get the mechanics of our deep learning project in place, none of the results were actually useful; the network simply classified everything as non-nodule! To make matters worse, the results seemed great on the surface, since we were looking at the overall percent of the training and validation sets that were classified correctly. With our data heavily skewed toward negative samples, blindly calling everything negative is a quick and easy way for our model to score well. Too bad doing so makes the model basically useless!

That means we're still focused on the same part of figure 12.1 as we were in chapter 11. But now we're working on getting our classification model working *well* instead of *at all*. This chapter is all about how to measure, quantify, express, and then improve on how well our model is doing its job.

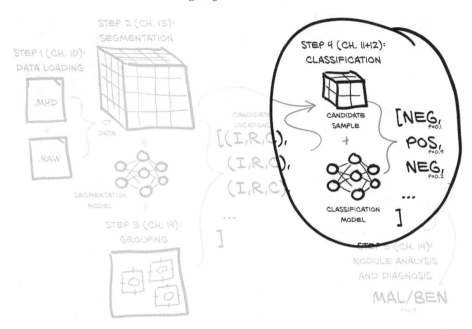

Figure 12.1 Our end-to-end lung cancer detection project, with a focus on this chapter's topic: step 4, classification

12.1 *High-level plan for improvement*

While a bit abstract, figure 12.2 shows us how we are going to approach that broad set of topics.

Let's walk through this somewhat abstract map of the chapter in detail. We will be dealing with the issues we're facing, like excessive focus on a single, narrow metric and the resulting behavior being useless in the general sense. In order to make some of this chapter's concepts a bit more concrete, we'll first employ a metaphor that puts our troubles in more tangible terms: in figure 12.2, (1) Guard Dogs and (2) Birds and Burglars.

After that, we will develop a graphical language to represent some of the core concepts needed to formally discuss the issues with the implementation from the last chapter: (3) Ratios: Recall and Precision. Once we have those concepts solidified, we'll touch on some math using those concepts that will encapsulate a more robust way of grading our model's performance and condensing it into a single number: (4) New Metric: F1 Score. We will implement the formula for those new metrics and look

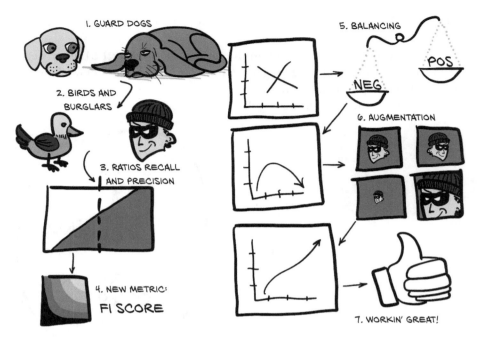

Figure 12.2   The metaphors we'll use to modify the metrics measuring our model to make it magnificent

at the how the resulting values change epoch by epoch during training. Finally, we'll make some much-needed changes to our LunaDataset implementation with an aim at improving our training results: (5) Balancing and (6) Augmentation. Then we will see if those experimental changes have the expected impact on our performance metrics.

By the time we're through with this chapter, our trained model will be performing much better: (7) Workin' Great! While it won't be ready to drop into clinical use just yet, it will be capable of producing results that are clearly better than random. This will mean we have a workable implementation of step 4, nodule candidate classification; and once we're finished, we can begin to think about how to incorporate steps 2 (segmentation) and 3 (grouping) into the project.

12.2   *Good dogs vs. bad guys: False positives and false negatives*

Instead of models and tumors, we're going to consider the two guard dogs in figure 12.3, both fresh out of obedience school. They both want to alert us to burglars—a rare but serious situation that requires prompt attention.

Unfortunately, while both dogs are good dogs, neither is a good *guard* dog. Our terrier (Roxie) barks at just about everything, while our old hound dog (Preston) barks almost exclusively at burglars—but only if he happens to be awake when they arrive.

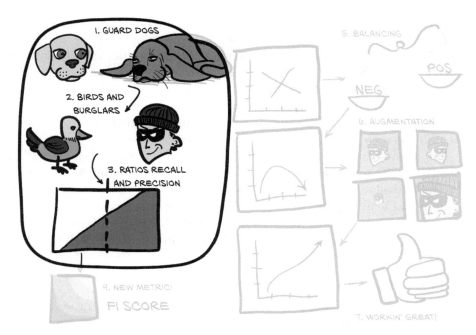

Figure 12.3 The set of topics for this chapter, with a focus on the framing metaphor

Roxie *will* alert us to a burglar just about every time. She will also alert us to fire engines, thunderstorms, helicopters, birds, the mail carrier, squirrels, passersby, and so on. If we follow up on every bark, we'll almost never get robbed (only the sneakiest of sneak-thieves can slip past). Perfect! … Except that being that diligent means we aren't really saving any work by having a guard dog. Instead, we'll be up every couple of hours, flashlight in hand, due to Roxie having smelled a cat, or heard an owl, or seen a late bus wander by. Roxie has a problematic number of false positives.

A *false positive* is an event that is classified as of interest or as a member of the desired class (positive as in "Yes, that's the type of thing I'm interested in knowing about") but that in truth is *not* really of interest. For the nodule-detection problem, it's when an actually uninteresting candidate is flagged as a nodule and, hence, in need of a radiologist's attention. For Roxie, these would be fire engines, thunderstorms, and so on. We will use an image of a cat as the canonical false positive in the next section and the figures that follow throughout the rest of the chapter.

Contrast false positives with *true positives*: items of interest that are classified correctly. These will be represented in the figures by a human burglar.

Meanwhile, if Preston barks, call the police, since that means someone has almost certainly broken in, the house is on fire, or Godzilla is attacking. Preston is a deep sleeper, however, and the sound of an in-progress home invasion isn't likely to rouse him, so we'll still get robbed just about every time someone tries. Again, while it's better than nothing, we're not really ending up with the peace of mind that motivated us to get a dog in the first place. Preston has a problematic number of false negatives.

A *false negative* is an event that is classified as not of interest or not a member of the desired class (negative as in "No, that's not the type of thing I'm interested in knowing about") but that in truth *is* actually of interest. For the nodule-detection problem, it's when a nodule (that is, a potential cancer) goes undetected. For Preston, these would be the robberies that he sleeps through. We'll get a bit creative here and use a picture of a *rodent* burglar for false negatives. They're sneaky!

Contrast false negatives with *true negatives*: uninteresting items that are correctly identified as such. We'll go with a picture of a bird for these.

Just to complete the metaphor, chapter 11's model is basically a cat that refuses to meow at anything that isn't a can of tuna (while stoically ignoring Roxie). Our focus at the end of the last chapter was on the percent correct for the overall training and validation sets. Clearly, that wasn't a great way to grade ourselves, and as we can see from each of our dogs' myopic focus on a single metric—like the number of true positives or true negatives—we need a metric with a broader focus to capture our overall performance.

12.3   *Graphing the positives and negatives*

Let's start developing the visual language we'll use to describe true/false positives/negatives. Please bear with us if our explanation gets repetitive; we want to make sure you develop a solid mental model for the ratios we're going to discuss. Consider figure 12.4, which shows events that might be of interest to one of our guard dogs.

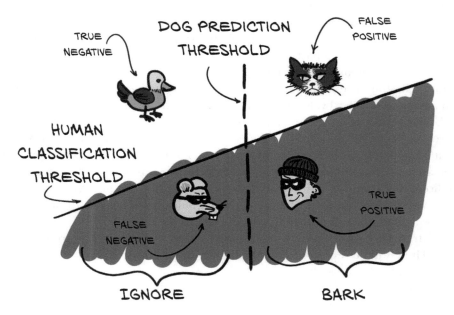

Figure 12.4   Cats, birds, rodents, and robbers make up our four classification quadrants. They are separated by a human label and the dog classification threshold.

We'll use two thresholds in figure 12.4. The first is the human-decided dividing line that separates burglars from harmless animals. In concrete terms, this is the label that is given for each training or validation sample. The second is the dog-determined *classification threshold* that determines whether the dog will bark at something. For a deep learning model, this is the predicted value that the model produces when considering a sample.

The combination of these two thresholds divides our events into quadrants: true/false positives/negatives. We will shade the events of concern with a darker background (what with those bad guys sneaking around in the dark all the time).

Of course, reality is far more complicated. There is no Platonic ideal of a burglar, and no single point relative to the classification threshold at which all burglars will be located. Instead, figure 12.5 shows us that some burglars will be particularly sneaky, and some birds will be particularly annoying. We will also go ahead and enclose our instances in a graph. Our X-axis will remain the bark-worthiness of each event, as determined by one of our guard dogs. We're going to have the Y-axis represent some vague set of qualities that we as humans are able to perceive, but our dogs cannot.

Since our model produces a binary classification, we can think of the prediction threshold as comparing a single-numerical-value output to our classification threshold value. This is why we will require that the classification threshold line to be perfectly vertical in figure 12.5.

Each possible burglar is different, so our guard dogs will need to evaluate many different situations, and that means more opportunities to make mistakes. We can see the clear diagonal line that separates the birds from the burglars, but Preston and Roxie can only perceive the X-axis here: they have a muddled, overlapped set of

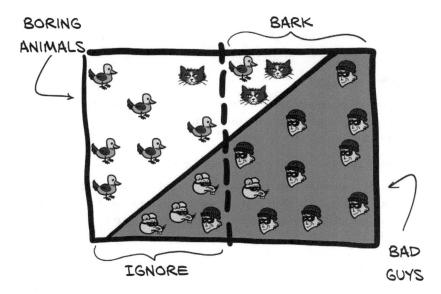

Figure 12.5 Each type of event will have many possible instances that our guard dogs will need to evaluate.

events in the middle of our graph. They must pick a vertical bark-worthiness threshold, which means it's impossible for either one of them to do so perfectly. Sometimes the person hauling your appliances to their van is the repair person you hired to fix your washing machine, and sometimes burglars show up in a van that says "Washing Machine Repair" on the side. Expecting a dog to pick up on those nuances is bound to fail.

The actual input data we're going to use has high dimensionality—we need to consider a ton of CT voxel values, along with more abstract things like candidate size, overall location in the lungs, and so on. The job of our model is to map each of these events and respective properties into this rectangle in such a way that we can separate those positive and negative events cleanly using a single vertical line (our classification threshold). This is done by the nn.Linear layers at the end of our model. The position of the vertical line corresponds exactly to the classificationThreshold_float we saw in section 11.6.1. There, we chose the hardcoded value 0.5 as our threshold.

Note that in reality, the data presented is not two-dimensional; it goes from very-high-dimensional after the second-to-last layer, to one-dimensional (here, our X-axis) at the output—just a single scalar per sample (which is then bisected by the classification threshold). Here, we use the second dimension (the Y-axis) to represent per-sample features that our model cannot see or use: things like age or gender of the patient, location of the nodule candidate in the lung, or even local aspects of the candidate that the model hasn't utilized. It also gives us a convenient way to represent confusion between non-nodule and nodule samples.

The quadrant areas in figure 12.5 and the count of samples contained in each will be the values we use to discuss model performance, since we can use the ratios between these values to construct increasingly complex metrics that we can use to objectively measure how well we are doing. As they say, "the proof is in the proportions."[1] Next, we'll use ratios between these event subsets to start defining better metrics.

12.3.1 *Recall is Roxie's strength*

Recall is basically "Make sure you never miss any interesting events!" Formally, *recall* is the ratio of the true positives to the union of true positives and false negatives. We can see this depicted in figure 12.6.

NOTE In some contexts, recall is referred to as *sensitivity*.

To improve recall, minimize false negatives. In guard dog terms, that means if you're unsure, bark at it, just in case. Don't let any rodent thieves sneak by on your watch!

Roxie accomplishes having an incredibly high recall by pushing her classification threshold all the way to the left, such that it encompasses nearly all of the positive events in figure 12.7. Note how doing so means her recall value is near 1.0, which means 99% of robbers are barked at. Since that's how Roxie defines success, in her mind, she's doing a great job. Never mind the huge expanse of false positives!

---

[1] No one actually says this.

RECALL
IS THE RATIO DETERMINED
BY FALSE NEGATIVES

Figure 12.6 Recall is the ratio of the true positives to the union of true positives and false negatives. High recall minimizes false negatives.

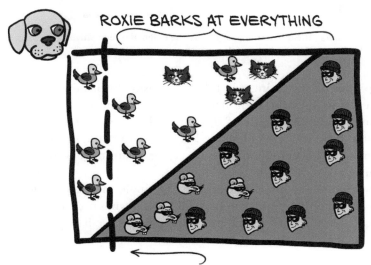

ROXIE BARKS AT EVERYTHING

LOW BARK THRESHOLD, HIGH RECALL

Figure 12.7 Roxie's choice of threshold prioritizes minimizing false negatives. Every last rat is barked at . . . and cats, and most birds.

12.3.2 *Precision is Preston's forte*

Precision is basically "Never bark unless you're sure." To improve precision, minimize false positives. Preston won't bark at something unless he's certain it's a burglar. More formally, *precision* is the ratio of the true positives to the union of true positives and false positives, as shown in figure 12.8.

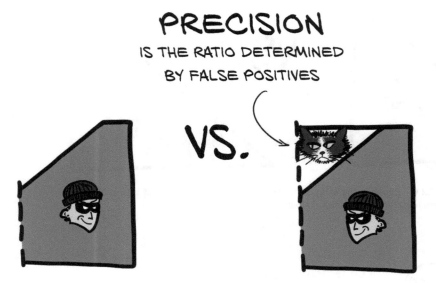

Figure 12.8   Precision is the ratio of the true positives to the union of true positives and false positives. High precision minimizes false positives.

Preston accomplishes having an incredibly high precision by pushing his classification threshold all the way to the right, such that it excludes as many uninteresting, negative events as he can manage (see figure 12.9). This is the opposite of Roxie's approach and means Preston has a precision of nearly 1.0: 99% of the things he barks at are robbers. This also matches his definition of being a good guard dog, even though a large number of events pass undetected.

While neither precision nor recall can be the single metric used to grade our model, they are both useful numbers to have on hand during training. Let's calculate and display these as part of our training program, and then we'll discuss other metrics we can employ.

HIGH BARK THRESHOLD, HIGH PRECISION

PRESTON MOSTLY SLEEPS

Figure 12.9 Preston's choice of threshold prioritizes minimizing false positives. Cats get left alone; only burglars are barked at!

12.3.3 *Implementing precision and recall in logMetrics*

Both precision and recall are valuable metrics to be able to track during training, since they provide important insight into how the model is behaving. If either of them drops to zero (as we saw in chapter 11!), it's likely that our model has started to behave in a degenerate manner. We can use the exact details of the behavior to guide where to investigate and experiment with getting training back on track. We'd like to update the logMetrics function to add precision and recall to the output we see for each epoch, to complement the loss and correctness metrics we already have.

We've been defining precision and recall in terms of "true positives" and the like thus far, so we will continue to do so in the code. It turns out that we are already computing some of the values we need, though we had named them differently.

Listing 12.1 training.py:315, `LunaTrainingApp.logMetrics`

```
neg_count = int(negLabel_mask.sum())
pos_count = int(posLabel_mask.sum())

trueNeg_count = neg_correct = int((negLabel_mask & negPred_mask).sum())
truePos_count = pos_correct = int((posLabel_mask & posPred_mask).sum())

falsePos_count = neg_count - neg_correct
falseNeg_count = pos_count - pos_correct
```

Here, we can see that `neg_correct` is the same thing as `trueNeg_count`! That actually makes sense, since non-nodule is our "negative" value (as in "a negative diagnosis"), and if the classifier gets the prediction correct, then that's a true negative. Similarly, correctly labeled nodule samples are true positives.

We do need to add the variables for our false positive and false negative values. That's straightforward, since we can take the total number of benign labels and subtract the count of the correct ones. What's left is the count of non-nodule samples misclassified as *positive*. Hence, they are false positives. Again, the false negative calculation is of the same form, but uses nodule counts.

With those values, we can compute `precision` and `recall` and store them in `metrics_dict`.

> **Listing 12.2   training.py:333, `LunaTrainingApp.logMetrics`**

```
precision = metrics_dict['pr/precision'] = \
  truePos_count / np.float32(truePos_count + falsePos_count)
recall  = metrics_dict['pr/recall'] = \
  truePos_count / np.float32(truePos_count + falseNeg_count)
```

Note the double assignment: while having separate `precision` and `recall` variables isn't strictly necessary, they improve the readability of the next section. We also extend the logging statement in `logMetrics` to include the new values, but we skip the implementation for now (we'll revisit logging later in the chapter).

12.3.4 *Our ultimate performance metric: The F1 score*

While useful, neither precision nor recall entirely captures what we need in order to be able to evaluate a model. As we've seen with Roxie and Preston, it's possible to game either one individually by manipulating our classification threshold, resulting in a model that scores well on one or the other but does so at the expense of any real-world utility. We need something that combines both of those values in a way that prevents such gamesmanship. As we can see in figure 12.10, it's time to introduce our ultimate metric.

The generally accepted way of combining precision and recall is by using the F1 score (https://en.wikipedia.org/wiki/F1_score). As with other metrics, the F1 score ranges between 0 (a classifier with no real-world predictive power) and 1 (a classifier that has perfect predictions). We will update `logMetrics` to include this as well.

> **Listing 12.3   training.py:338, `LunaTrainingApp.logMetrics`**

```
metrics_dict['pr/f1_score'] = \
  2 * (precision * recall) / (precision + recall)
```

At first glance, this might seem more complicated than we need, and it might not be immediately obvious how the F1 score behaves when trading off precision for recall or

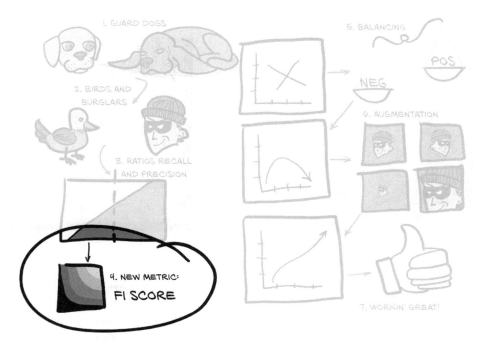

Figure 12.10   The set of topics for this chapter, with a focus on the final F1 score metric

vice versa. This formula has a lot of nice properties, however, and it compares favorably to several other, simpler alternatives that we might consider.

One immediate possibility for a scoring function is to average the values for precision and recall together. Unfortunately, this gives both $avg(p=1.0, r=0.0)$ and $avg(p=0.5, r=0.5)$ the same score of 0.5, and as we discussed earlier, a classifier with either precision or recall of zero is usually worthless. Giving something useless the same nonzero score as something useful disqualifies averaging as a meaningful metric immediately.

Still, let's visually compare averaging and F1 in figure 12.11. A few things stand out. First, we can see a lack of a curve or elbow in the contour lines for averaging. That's what lets our precision or recall skew to one side or the other! There will *never* be a situation where it doesn't make sense to maximize the score by having 100% recall (the Roxie approach) and then eliminate whichever false positives are easy to eliminate. That puts a floor on the addition score of 0.5 right out of the gate! Having a quality metric that is trivial to score at least 50% on doesn't feel right.

> **NOTE** What we are actually doing here is taking the *arithmetic mean* (https://en.wikipedia.org/wiki/Arithmetic_mean) of the precision and recall, both of which are *rates* rather than countable scalar values. Taking the arithmetic mean of rates doesn't typically give meaningful results. The F1 score is another name for the *harmonic mean* (https://en.wikipedia.org/wiki/Harmonic_mean) of the two rates, which is a more appropriate way of combining those kinds of values.

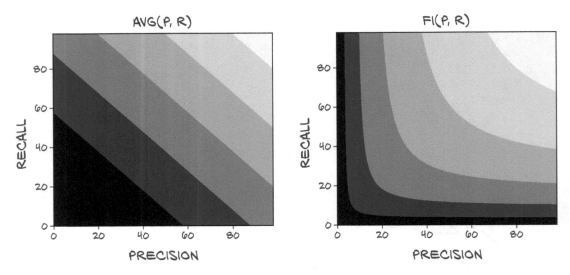

Figure 12.11   Computing the final score with `avg(p, r)`. Lighter values are closer to 1.0.

Contrast that with the F1 score: when recall is high but precision is low, trading off a lot of recall for even a little precision will move the score closer to that balanced sweet spot. There's a nice, deep elbow that is easy to slide into. That encouragement to have balanced precision and recall is what we want from our grading metric.

Let's say we still want a simpler metric, but one that doesn't reward skew at all. In order to correct for the weakness of addition, we might take the minimum of precision and recall (figure 12.12).

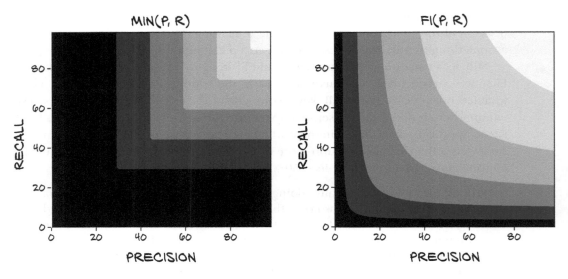

Figure 12.12   Computing the final score with `min(p, r)`

This is nice, because if either value is 0, the score is also 0, and the only way to get a score of 1.0 is to have both values be 1.0. However, it still leaves something to be desired, since making a model change that increased the recall from 0.7 to 0.9 while leaving precision constant at 0.5 wouldn't improve the score at all, nor would dropping recall down to 0.6! Although this metric is certainly penalizing having an imbalance between precision and recall, it isn't capturing a lot of nuance about the two values. As we have seen, it's easy to trade one off for the other simply by moving the classification threshold. We'd like our metric to reflect those trades.

We'll have to accept at least a bit more complexity to better meet our goals. We could multiply the two values together, as in figure 12.13. This approach keeps the nice property that if either value is 0, the score is 0, and a score of 1.0 means both inputs are perfect. It also favors a balanced trade-off between precision and recall at low values, though when it gets closer to perfect results, it becomes more linear. That's not great, since we really need to push both up to have a meaningful improvement at that point.

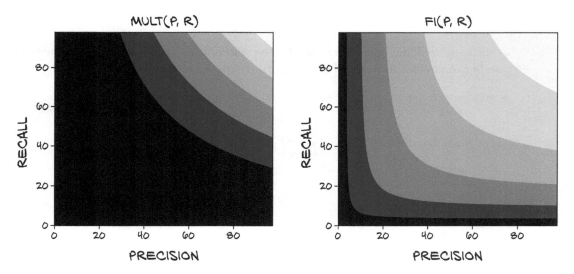

Figure 12.13 Computing the final score with `mult(p, r)`

> **NOTE** Here we're taking the *geometric mean* (https://en.wikipedia.org/wiki/Geometric_mean) of two rates, which also doesn't produce meaningful results.

There's also the issue of having almost the entire quadrant from (0, 0) to (0.5, 0.5) be very close to zero. As we'll see, having a metric that's sensitive to changes in that region is important, especially in the early stages of our model design.

While using multiplication as our scoring function is feasible (it doesn't have any immediate disqualifications the way the previous scoring functions did), we will be using the F1 score to evaluate our classification model's performance going forward.

UPDATING THE LOGGING OUTPUT TO INCLUDE PRECISION, RECALL, AND F1 SCORE

Now that we have our new metrics, adding them to our logging output is pretty straightforward. We'll include precision, recall, and F1 in our main logging statement for each of our training and validation sets.

Listing 12.4 training.py:341, `LunaTrainingApp.logMetrics`

```
log.info(
  ("E{} {:8} {loss/all:.4f} loss, "
    + "{correct/all:-5.1f}% correct, "
    + "{pr/precision:.4f} precision, "        Format string
    + "{pr/recall:.4f} recall, "             updated
    + "{pr/f1_score:.4f} f1 score"
  ).format(
    epoch_ndx,
    mode_str,
    **metrics_dict,
  )
)
```

In addition, we'll include exact values for the count of correctly identified and the total number of samples for each of the negative and positive samples.

Listing 12.5 training.py:353, `LunaTrainingApp.logMetrics`

```
log.info(
  ("E{} {:8} {loss/neg:.4f} loss, "
    + "{correct/neg:-5.1f}% correct ({neg_correct:} of {neg_count:})"
  ).format(
    epoch_ndx,
    mode_str + '_neg',
    neg_correct=neg_correct,
    neg_count=neg_count,
    **metrics_dict,
  )
)
```

The new version of the positive logging statement looks much the same.

12.3.5 *How does our model perform with our new metrics?*

Now that we've implemented our shiny new metrics, let's take them for a spin; we'll discuss the results after we show the results of the Bash shell session. You might want to read ahead while your system does its number crunching; this could take perhaps half an hour, depending on your system.[2] Exactly how long it takes will depend on your system's CPU, GPU, and disk speeds; our system with an SSD and GTX 1080 Ti took about 20 minutes per full epoch:

---

[2] If it's taking longer than that, make sure you've run the `prepcache` script.

```
$ ../.venv/bin/python -m p2ch12.training
Starting LunaTrainingApp...
...
E1 LunaTrainingApp

.../p2ch12/training.py:274: RuntimeWarning:
  invalid value encountered in double_scalars
   metrics_dict['pr/f1_score'] = 2 * (precision * recall) /
  (precision + recall)

E1 trn       0.0025 loss,  99.8% correct, 0.0000 prc, 0.0000 rcl, nan f1
E1 trn_ben   0.0000 loss, 100.0% correct (494735 of 494743)
E1 trn_mal   1.0000 loss,   0.0% correct (0 of 1215)

.../p2ch12/training.py:269: RuntimeWarning:
  invalid value encountered in long_scalars
   precision = metrics_dict['pr/precision'] = truePos_count /
  (truePos_count + falsePos_count)

E1 val       0.0025 loss,  99.8% correct, nan prc, 0.0000 rcl, nan f1
E1 val_ben   0.0000 loss, 100.0% correct (54971 of 54971)
E1 val_mal   1.0000 loss,   0.0% correct (0 of 136)
```

> The exact count and line numbers of these RuntimeWarning lines might be different from run to run.

Bummer. We've got some warnings, and given that some of the values we computed were nan, there's probably a division by zero happening somewhere. Let's see what we can figure out.

First, since *none* of the positive samples in the training set are getting classified as positive, that means both precision and recall are zero, which results in our F1 score calculation dividing by zero. Second, for our validation set, truePos_count and falsePos_count are both zero due to *nothing* being flagged as positive. It follows that the denominator of our precision calculation is also zero; that makes sense, as that's where we're seeing another RuntimeWarning.

A handful of negative training samples are classified as positive (494735 of 494743 are classified as negative, so that leaves 8 samples misclassified). While that might seem odd at first, recall that we are collecting our training results *throughout the epoch*, rather than using the model's end-of-epoch state as we do for the validation results. That means the first batch is literally producing random results. A few of the samples from that first batch being flagged as positive isn't surprising.

> **NOTE** Due to both the random initialization of the network weights and the random ordering of the training samples, individual runs will likely exhibit slightly different behavior. Having exactly reproducible behavior can be desirable but is out of scope for what we're trying to do in part 2 of this book.

Well, that was somewhat painful. Switching to our new metrics resulted in going from A+ to "Zero, if you're lucky"—and if we're not lucky, the score is so bad that *it's not even a number.* Ouch.

That said, in the long run, this is good for us. We've known that our model's performance was garbage since chapter 11. If our metrics told us anything *but* that, it would point to a fundamental flaw in the metrics!

12.4 *What does an ideal dataset look like?*

Before we start crying into our cups over the current sorry state of affairs, let's instead think about what we actually want our model to do. Figure 12.14 says that first we need to balance our data so that our model can train properly. Let's build up the logical steps needed to get us there.

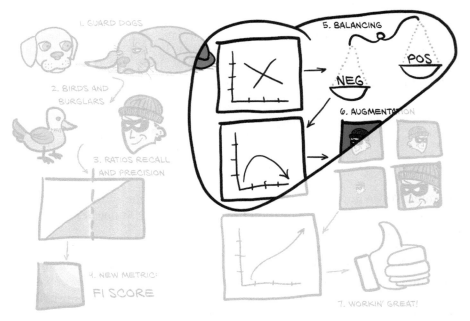

Figure 12.14   The set of topics for this chapter, with a focus on balancing our positive and negative samples

Recall figure 12.5 earlier, and the following discussion of classification thresholds. Getting better results by moving the threshold has limited effectiveness—there's just too much overlap between the positive and negative classes to work with.[3]

Instead, we want to see an image like figure 12.15. Here, our label threshold is nearly vertical. That's what we want, because it means the label threshold and our classification threshold can line up reasonably well. Similarly, most of the samples are concentrated at either end of the diagram. Both of these things require that our data be easily separable and that our model have the capacity to perform that separation. Our model currently has enough capacity, so that's not the issue. Instead, let's take a look at our data.

Recall that our data is wildly imbalanced. There's a 400:1 ratio of positive samples to negative ones. That's *crushingly* imbalanced! Figure 12.16 shows what that looks like. No wonder our "actually nodule" samples are getting lost in the crowd!

---

[3] Keep in mind that these images are just a representation of the classification space and do not represent ground truth.

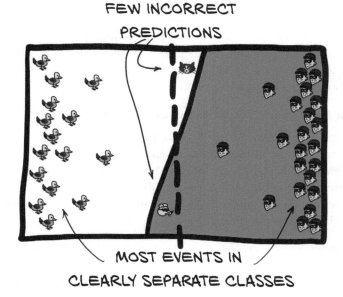

Figure 12.15 A well-trained model can cleanly separate data, making it easy to pick a classification threshold with few trade-offs.

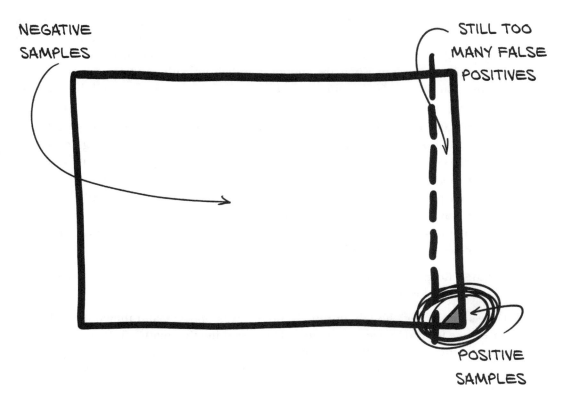

Figure 12.16 An imbalanced dataset that roughly approximates the imbalance in our LUNA classification data

Now, let's be perfectly clear: when we're done, our model will be able to handle this kind of data imbalance just fine. We could probably even train the model all the way there without changing the balancing, assuming we were willing to wait for a gajillion epochs first.[4] But we're busy people with things to do, so rather than cook our GPU until the heat death of the universe, let's try to make our training data look more ideal by changing the class balance we are training with.

12.4.1 *Making the data look less like the actual and more like the "ideal"*

The best thing to do would be to have relatively more positive samples. During the initial epoch of training, when we're going from randomized chaos to something more organized, having so few training samples be positive means they get drowned out.

The method by which this happens is somewhat subtle, however. Recall that since our network weights are initially randomized, the per-sample output of the network is also randomized (but clamped to the range [0-1]).

> **NOTE** Our loss function is nn.CrossEntropyLoss, which technically operates on the raw logits rather than the class probabilities. For our discussion, we'll ignore that distinction and assume the loss and the label-prediction deltas are the same thing.

The predictions numerically close to the correct label do not result in much change to the weights of the network, while predictions that are significantly different from the correct answer are responsible for a much greater change to the weights. Since the output is random when the model is initialized with random weights, we can assume that of our ~500k training samples (495,958, to be exact), we'll have the following approximate groups:

1 250,000 negative samples will be predicted to be negative (0.0 to 0.5) and result in at most a small change to the network weights toward predicting negative.
2 250,000 negative samples will be predicted to be positive (0.5 to 1.0) and result in a large swing toward the network weights predicting negative.
3 500 positive samples will be predicted to be negative and result in a swing toward the network weights predicting positive.
4 500 positive samples will be predicted to be positive and result in almost no change to the network weights.

> **NOTE** Keep in mind that the actual predictions are real numbers between 0.0 and 1.0 inclusive, so these groups won't have strict delineations.

Here's the kicker, though: groups 1 and 4 can be *any size*, and they will continue to have close to zero impact on training. The only thing that matters is that groups 2 and 3 can counteract each other's pull enough to prevent the network from collapsing to a degenerate "only output one thing" state. Since group 2 is 500 times larger than

---

[4] It's not clear if this is actually true, but it's plausible, and the loss *was* getting better . . .

group 3 and we're using a batch size of 32, roughly 500/32 = 15 batches will go by before seeing a single positive sample. That implies that 14 out of 15 training batches will be 100% negative and will only pull all model weights toward predicting negative. That lopsided pull is what produces the degenerate behavior we've been seeing.

Instead, we'd like to have just as many positive samples as negative ones. For the first part of training, then, half of both labels will be classified incorrectly, meaning that groups 2 and 3 should be roughly equal in size. We also want to make sure we present batches with a mix of negative and positive samples. Balance would result in the tug-of-war evening out, and the mixture of classes per batch will give the model a decent chance of learning to discriminate between the two classes. Since our LUNA data has only a small, fixed number of positive samples, we'll have to settle for taking the positive samples that we have and presenting them repeatedly during training.

> ### Discrimination
>
> Here, we define *discrimination* as "the ability to separate two classes from each other." Building and training a model that can tell "actually nodule" candidates from normal anatomical structures is the entire point of what we're doing in part 2.
>
> Some other definitions of discrimination are more problematic. While out of scope for the discussion of our work here, there is a larger issue with models trained from real-world data. If that real-world dataset is collected from sources that have a real-world-discriminatory bias (for example, racial bias in arrest and conviction rates, or anything collected from social media), and that bias is not corrected for during dataset preparation or training, then the resulting model will continue to exhibit the same biases present in the training data. Just as in humans, racism is learned.
>
> This means almost any model trained from internet-at-large data sources will be compromised in some fashion, unless extreme care is taken to scrub those biases from the model. Note that like our goal in part 2, this is considered an unsolved problem.

Recall our professor from chapter 11 who had a final exam with 99 false answers and 1 true answer. The next semester, after being told "You should have a more even balance of true and false answers," the professor decided to add a midterm with 99 true answers and 1 false one. "Problem solved!"

Clearly, the correct approach is to intermix true and false answers in a way that doesn't allow the students to exploit the larger structure of the tests to answer things correctly. Whereas a student would pick up on a pattern like "odd questions are true, even questions are false," the batching system used by PyTorch doesn't allow the model to "notice" or utilize that kind of pattern. Our training dataset will need to be updated to alternate between positive and negative samples, as in figure 12.17.

The unbalanced data is the proverbial needle in the haystack we mentioned at the start of chapter 9. If you had to perform this classification work by hand, you'd probably start to empathize with Preston.

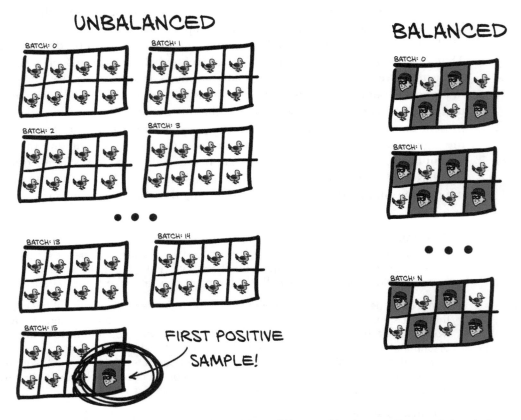

Figure 12.17 Batch after batch of imbalanced data will have nothing but negative events long before the first positive event, while balanced data can alternate every other sample.

We will not be doing any balancing for validation, however. Our model needs to function well in the real world, and the real world is imbalanced (after all, that's where we got the raw data!).

How should we accomplish this balancing? Let's discuss our choices.

SAMPLERS CAN RESHAPE DATASETS

One of the optional arguments to `DataLoader` is `sampler=…` . This allows the data loader to override the iteration order native to the dataset passed in and instead shape, limit, or reemphasize the underlying data as desired. This can be incredibly useful when working with a dataset that isn't under your control. Taking a public dataset and reshaping it to meet your needs is far less work than reimplementing that dataset from scratch.

The downside is that many of the mutations we could accomplish with samplers require that we break encapsulation of the underlying dataset. For example, let's assume we have a dataset like CIFAR-10 (www.cs.toronto.edu/~kriz/cifar.html) that consists of 10 equally weighted classes, and we want to instead have 1 class (say, "airplane") now make up 50% of all of the training images. We could decide to use `WeightedRandomSampler` (http://mng.bz/8plK) and weight each of the "airplane" sample indexes higher, but constructing the `weights` argument requires that we know in advance which indexes are airplanes.

As we discussed, the `Dataset` API only specifies that subclasses provide `__len__` and `__getitem__`, but there is nothing direct we can use to ask "Which samples are airplanes?" We'd either have to load up every sample beforehand to inquire about the class of that sample, or we'd have to break encapsulation and hope the information we need is easily obtained from looking at the internal implementation of the `Dataset` subclass.

Since neither of those options is particularly ideal in cases where we have control over the dataset directly, the code for part 2 implements any needed data shaping inside the `Dataset` subclasses instead of relying on an external sampler.

IMPLEMENTING CLASS BALANCING IN THE DATASET

We are going to directly change our `LunaDataset` to present a balanced, one-to-one ratio of positive and negative samples for training. We will keep separate lists of negative training samples and positive training samples, and alternate returning samples from each of those two lists. This will prevent the degenerate behavior of the model scoring well by simply answering "false" to every sample presented. In addition, the positive and negative classes will be intermixed so that the weight updates are forced to discriminate between the classes.

Let's add a `ratio_int` to `LunaDataset` that will control the label for the *N*th sample as well as keep track of our samples separated by label.

> **Listing 12.6 dsets.py:217, `class LunaDataset`**

```
class LunaDataset(Dataset):
  def __init__(self,
        val_stride=0,
        isValSet_bool=None,
        ratio_int=0,
    ):
    self.ratio_int = ratio_int
    # ... line 228
    self.negative_list = [
      nt for nt in self.candidateInfo_list if not nt.isNodule_bool
    ]
    self.pos_list = [
      nt for nt in self.candidateInfo_list if nt.isNodule_bool
    ]
    # ... line 265

  def shuffleSamples(self):            ◁——— We will call this at the top of each
    if self.ratio_int:                       epoch to randomize the order of
      random.shuffle(self.negative_list)     samples being presented.
      random.shuffle(self.pos_list)
```

With this, we now have dedicated lists for each label. Using these lists, it becomes much easier to return the label we want for a given index into the dataset. In order to make sure we're getting the indexing right, we should sketch out the ordering we want. Let's assume a `ratio_int` of 2, meaning a 2:1 ratio of negative to positive samples. That would mean every third index should be positive:

```
DS Index    0 1 2 3 4 5 6 7 8 9 ...
Label       + - - + - - + - - +
Pos Index   0     1     2     3
Neg Index     0 1   2 3   4 5
```

The relationship between the dataset index and the positive index is simple: divide the dataset index by 3 and then round down. The negative index is slightly more complicated, in that we have to subtract 1 from the dataset index and then subtract the most recent positive index as well.

Implemented in our `LunaDataset` class, that looks like the following.

Listing 12.7 dsets.py:286, LunaDataset.__getitem__

A `ratio_int` of zero means use the native balance.

```python
def __getitem__(self, ndx):
    if self.ratio_int:
        pos_ndx = ndx // (self.ratio_int + 1)

        if ndx % (self.ratio_int + 1):              ◁———  A nonzero remainder
            neg_ndx = ndx - 1 - pos_ndx                   means this should be
            neg_ndx %= len(self.negative_list)            a negative sample.
            candidateInfo_tup = self.negative_list[neg_ndx]   ◁———  Overflow results
        else:                                                       in wraparound.
            pos_ndx %= len(self.pos_list)           ◁———
            candidateInfo_tup = self.pos_list[pos_ndx]
    else:                                                   Returns the Nth sample
        candidateInfo_tup = self.candidateInfo_list[ndx]  ◁———  if not balancing classes
```

That can get a little hairy, but if you desk-check it out, it will make sense. Keep in mind that with a low ratio, we'll run out of positive samples before exhausting the dataset. We take care of that by taking the modulus of `pos_ndx` before indexing into `self.pos_list`. While the same kind of index overflow should never happen with `neg_ndx` due to the large number of negative samples, we do the modulus anyway, just in case we later decide to make a change that might cause it to overflow.

We'll also make a change to our dataset's length. Although this isn't strictly necessary, it's nice to speed up individual epochs. We're going to hardcode our `__len__` to be 200,000.

Listing 12.8 dsets.py:280, LunaDataset.__len__

```
def __len__(self):
  if self.ratio_int:
    return 200000
  else:
    return len(self.candidateInfo_list)
```

We're no longer tied to a specific number of samples, and presenting "a full epoch" doesn't really make sense when we would have to repeat positive samples many, many times to present a balanced training set. By picking 200,000 samples, we reduce the time between starting a training run and seeing results (faster feedback is always nice!), and we give ourselves a nice, clean number of samples per epoch. Feel free to adjust the length of an epoch to meet your needs.

For completeness, we also add a command-line parameter.

Listing 12.9 training.py:31, class LunaTrainingApp

```
class LunaTrainingApp:
  def __init__(self, sys_argv=None):
    # ... line 52
    parser.add_argument('--balanced',
      help="Balance the training data to half positive, half negative.",
      action='store_true',
      default=False,
    )
```

Then we pass that parameter into the LunaDataset constructor.

Listing 12.10 training.py:137, LunaTrainingApp.initTrainDl

```
def initTrainDl(self):
  train_ds = LunaDataset(
    val_stride=10,
    isValSet_bool=False,
    ratio_int=int(self.cli_args.balanced),   ⟵── Here we rely on python's True
  )                                              being convertible to a 1.
```

We're all set. Let's run it!

12.4.2 Contrasting training with a balanced LunaDataset to previous runs

As a reminder, our unbalanced training run had results like these:

```
$ python -m p2ch12.training
...
E1 LunaTrainingApp
E1 trn      0.0185 loss,  99.7% correct, 0.0000 precision, 0.0000 recall,
➥ nan f1 score
```

```
E1 trn_neg   0.0026 loss, 100.0% correct (494717 of 494743)
E1 trn_pos   6.5267 loss,   0.0% correct (0 of 1215)
...
E1 val       0.0173 loss,  99.8% correct, nan precision, 0.0000 recall,
➡ nan f1 score
E1 val_neg   0.0026 loss, 100.0% correct (54971 of 54971)
E1 val_pos   5.9577 loss,   0.0% correct (0 of 136)
```

But when we run with `--balanced`, we see the following:

```
$ python -m p2ch12.training --balanced
...
E1 LunaTrainingApp
E1 trn       0.1734 loss,  92.8% correct, 0.9363 precision, 0.9194 recall,
➡ 0.9277 f1 score
E1 trn_neg   0.1770 loss,  93.7% correct (93741 of 100000)
E1 trn_pos   0.1698 loss,  91.9% correct (91939 of 100000)
...
E1 val       0.0564 loss,  98.4% correct, 0.1102 precision, 0.7941 recall,
➡ 0.1935 f1 score
E1 val_neg   0.0542 loss,  98.4% correct (54099 of 54971)
E1 val_pos   0.9549 loss,  79.4% correct (108 of 136)
```

This seems much better! We've given up about 5% correct answers on the negative samples to gain 86% correct positive answers. We're back into a solid B range again![5]

As in chapter 11, however, this result is deceptive. Since there are 400 times as many negative samples as positive ones, even getting just 1% wrong means we'd be incorrectly classifying negative samples as positive four times more often than there are actually positive samples in total!

Still, this is clearly better than the outright wrong behavior from chapter 11 and much better than a random coin flip. In fact, we've even crossed over into being (almost) legitimately useful in real-world scenarios. Recall our overworked radiologist poring over each and every speck of a CT: well, now we've got something that can do a reasonable job of screening out 95% of the false positives. That's a huge help, since it translates into about a tenfold increase in productivity for the machine-assisted human.

Of course, there's still that pesky issue of the 14% of positive samples that were missed, which we should probably deal with. Perhaps some additional epochs of training would help. Let's see (and again, expect to spend at least 10 minutes per epoch):

```
$ python -m p2ch12.training --balanced --epochs 20
...
E2 LunaTrainingApp
E2 trn       0.0432 loss,  98.7% correct, 0.9866 precision, 0.9879 recall,
➡ 0.9873 f1 score
E2 trn_ben   0.0545 loss,  98.7% correct (98663 of 100000)
E2 trn_mal   0.0318 loss,  98.8% correct (98790 of 100000)
```

---

[5] And remember that this is after only the 200,000 training samples presented, not the 500,000+ of the unbalanced dataset, so we got there in less than half the time.

```
E2 val        0.0603 loss,   98.5% correct, 0.1271 precision, 0.8456 recall,
➥ 0.2209 f1 score
E2 val_ben  0.0584 loss,   98.6% correct (54181 of 54971)
E2 val_mal  0.8471 loss,   84.6% correct (115 of 136)
...
E5 trn        0.0578 loss,   98.3% correct, 0.9839 precision, 0.9823 recall,
➥ 0.9831 f1 score
E5 trn_ben  0.0665 loss,   98.4% correct (98388 of 100000)
E5 trn_mal  0.0490 loss,   98.2% correct (98227 of 100000)
E5 val        0.0361 loss,   99.2% correct, 0.2129 precision, 0.8235 recall,
➥ 0.3384 f1 score
E5 val_ben  0.0336 loss,   99.2% correct (54557 of 54971)
E5 val_mal  1.0515 loss,   82.4% correct (112 of 136)...
...
E10 trn       0.0212 loss,   99.5% correct, 0.9942 precision, 0.9953 recall,
➥ 0.9948 f1 score
E10 trn_ben 0.0281 loss,   99.4% correct (99421 of 100000)
E10 trn_mal 0.0142 loss,   99.5% correct (99530 of 100000)
E10 val       0.0457 loss,   99.3% correct, 0.2171 precision, 0.7647 recall,
➥ 0.3382 f1 score
E10 val_ben 0.0407 loss,   99.3% correct (54596 of 54971)
E10 val_mal 2.0594 loss,   76.5% correct (104 of 136)
...
E20 trn       0.0132 loss,   99.7% correct, 0.9964 precision, 0.9974 recall,
➥ 0.9969 f1 score
E20 trn_ben 0.0186 loss,   99.6% correct (99642 of 100000)
E20 trn_mal 0.0079 loss,   99.7% correct (99736 of 100000)
E20 val       0.0200 loss,   99.7% correct, 0.4780 precision, 0.7206 recall,
➥ 0.5748 f1 score
E20 val_ben 0.0133 loss,   99.8% correct (54864 of 54971)
E20 val_mal 2.7101 loss,   72.1% correct (98 of 136)
```

Ugh. That's a lot of text to scroll past to get to the numbers we're interested in. Let's power through and focus on the val_mal XX.X% correct numbers (or skip ahead to the TensorBoard graph in the next section.) After epoch 2, we were at 87.5%; on epoch 5, we peaked with 92.6%; and then by epoch 20 we dropped down to 86.8%— *below* our second epoch!

> **NOTE** As mentioned earlier, expect each run to have unique behavior due to random initialization of network weights and random selection and ordering of training samples per epoch.

The training set numbers don't seem to be having the same problem. Negative training samples are classified correctly 98.8% of the time, and positive samples are 99.1% correct. What's going on?

12.4.3 *Recognizing the symptoms of overfitting*

What we are seeing are clear signs of overfitting. Let's take a look at the graph of our loss on positive samples, in figure 12.18.

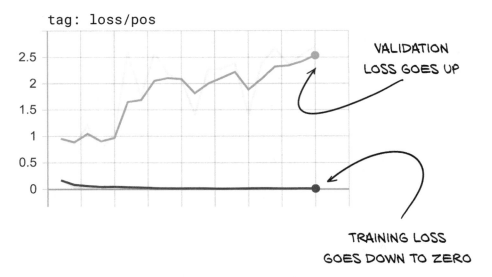

Figure 12.18   Our positive loss showing clear signs of overfitting, as the training loss and validation loss are trending in different directions

Here, we can see that the training loss for our positive samples is nearly zero—each positive training sample gets a nearly perfect prediction. Our validation loss for positive samples is *increasing*, though, and that means our real-world performance is likely getting worse. At this point, it's often best to stop the training script, since the model is no longer improving.

> **TIP**   Generally, if your model's performance is improving on your training set while getting worse on your validation set, the model has started overfitting.

We must take care to examine the right metrics, however, since this trend is only happening on our *positive* loss. If we take a look at our overall loss, everything seems fine! That's because our validation set is not balanced, so the overall loss is dominated by our negative samples. As shown in figure 12.19, we are not seeing the same divergent behavior for our negative samples. Instead, our negative loss looks great! That's because we have 400 times more negative samples, so it's much, much harder for the model to remember individual details. Our positive training set has only 1,215 samples, though. While we repeat those samples multiple times, that doesn't make them harder to memorize. The model is shifting from generalized principles to essentially memorizing quirks of those 1,215 samples and claiming that anything that's not one of those few samples is negative. This includes both negative training samples and everything in our validation set (both positive and negative).

Clearly, some generalization is still going on, since we are classifying about 70% of the positive validation set correctly. We just need to change how we're training the model so that our training set and validation set both trend in the right direction.

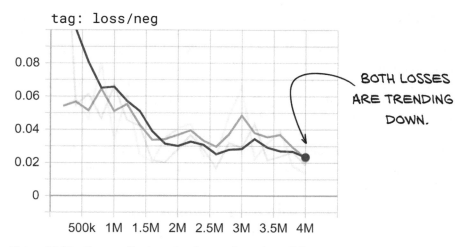

Figure 12.19 Our negative loss showing no signs of overfitting

12.5 Revisiting the problem of overfitting

We touched on the concept of overfitting in chapter 5, and now it's time to take a closer look at how to address this common situation. Our goal with training a model is to teach it to recognize the *general properties* of the classes we are interested in, as expressed in our dataset. Those general properties are present in some or all samples of the class and can be *generalized* and used to predict samples that haven't been trained on. When the model starts to learn *specific properties* of the training set, overfitting occurs, and the model starts to lose the ability to generalize. In case that's a bit too abstract, let's use another analogy.

12.5.1 An overfit face-to-age prediction model

Let's pretend we have a model that takes an image of a human face as input and outputs a predicted age in years. A good model would pick up on age signifiers like wrinkles, gray hair, hairstyle, clothing choices, and similar, and use those to build a general model of what different ages look like. When presented with a new picture, it would consider things like "conservative haircut" and "reading glasses" and "wrinkles" to conclude "around 65 years old."

An overfit model, by contrast, instead remembers specific people by remembering identifying details. "That haircut and those glasses mean it's Frank. He's 62.8 years old"; "Oh, that scar means it's Harry. He's 39.3"; and so on. When shown a new person, the model won't recognize the person and will have absolutely no idea what age to predict.

Even worse, if shown a picture of Frank Jr. (the spittin' image of his dad, at least when he's wearing his glasses!), the model will say, "I think that's Frank. He's 62.8 years old." Never mind that Junior is 25 years younger!

Overfitting is usually due to having too few training samples when compared to the ability of the model to just memorize the answers. The median human can memorize the birthdays of their immediate family but would have to resort to generalizations when predicting the ages of any group larger than a small village.

Our face-to-age model has the capacity to simply memorize the photos of anyone who doesn't look exactly their age. As we discussed in part 1, model capacity is a somewhat abstract concept, but is roughly a function of the number of parameters of the model times how efficiently those parameters are used. When a model has a high capacity relative to the amount of data needed to memorize the hard samples from the training set, it's likely that the model will begin to overfit on those more difficult training samples.

12.6 *Preventing overfitting with data augmentation*

It's time to take our model training from good to great. We need to cover one last step in figure 12.20.

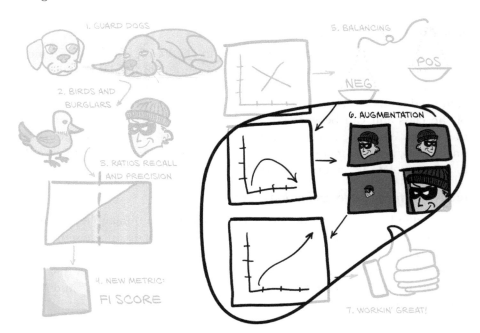

Figure 12.20   The set of topics for this chapter, with a focus on data augmentation

We *augment* a dataset by applying synthetic alterations to individual samples, resulting in a new dataset with an effective size that is larger than the original. The typical goal is for the alterations to result in a synthetic sample that remains representative of the same general class as the source sample, but that cannot be trivially memorized alongside the original. When done properly, this augmentation can increase the training set size beyond what the model is capable of memorizing, resulting in the model being forced to increasingly rely on generalization, which is exactly what we want. Doing so is especially useful when dealing with limited data, as we saw in section 12.4.1.

Of course, not all augmentations are equally useful. Going back to our example of a face-to-age prediction model, we could trivially change the red channel of the four corner pixels of each image to a random value 0–255, which would result in a dataset 4 billion times larger the original. Of course, this wouldn't be particularly useful, since the model can pretty trivially learn to ignore the red dots in the image corners, and the rest of the image remains as easy to memorize as the single, unaugmented original image. Contrast that approach with flipping the image left to right. Doing so would only result in a dataset twice as large as the original, but each image would be quite a bit more useful for training purposes. The general properties of aging are not correlated left to right, so a mirrored image remains representative. Similarly, it's rare for facial pictures to be perfectly symmetrical, so a mirrored version is unlikely to be trivially memorized alongside the original.

12.6.1 *Specific data augmentation techniques*

We are going to implement five specific types of data augmentation. Our implementation will allow us to experiment with any or all of them, individually or in aggregate. The five techniques are as follows:

- Mirroring the image up-down, left-right, and/or front-back
- Shifting the image around by a few voxels
- Scaling the image up or down
- Rotating the image around the head-foot axis
- Adding noise to the image

For each technique, we want to make sure our approach maintains the training sample's representative nature, while being different enough that the sample is useful to train with.

We'll define a function `getCtAugmentedCandidate` that is responsible for taking our standard chunk-of-CT-with-candidate-inside and modifying it. Our main approach will define an affine transformation matrix (http://mng.bz/Edxq) and use it with the PyTorch `affine_grid` (https://pytorch.org/docs/stable/nn.html#affine-grid) and `grid _sample` (https://pytorch.org/docs/stable/nn.html#torch.nn.functional.grid_sample) functions to resample our candidate.

Listing 12.11   dsets.py:149, `def getCtAugmentedCandidate`

```
def getCtAugmentedCandidate(
    augmentation_dict,
    series_uid, center_xyz, width_irc,
    use_cache=True):
  if use_cache:
    ct_chunk, center_irc = \
```

```
    getCtRawCandidate(series_uid, center_xyz, width_irc)
  else:
    ct = getCt(series_uid)
    ct_chunk, center_irc = ct.getRawCandidate(center_xyz, width_irc)

  ct_t = torch.tensor(ct_chunk).unsqueeze(0).unsqueeze(0).to(torch.float32)
```

We first obtain ct_chunk, either from the cache or directly by loading the CT (something that will come in handy once we are creating our own candidate centers), and then convert it to a tensor. Next is the affine grid and sampling code.

Listing 12.12   dsets.py:162, def `getCtAugmentedCandidate`

```
transform_t = torch.eye(4)
# ...                              ⟵┐ Modifications to
# ... line 195                       │ transform_tensor will go here.
affine_t = F.affine_grid(
    transform_t[:3].unsqueeze(0).to(torch.float32),
    ct_t.size(),
    align_corners=False,
)

augmented_chunk = F.grid_sample(
    ct_t,
    affine_t,
    padding_mode='border',
    align_corners=False,
).to('cpu')
# ... line 214
return augmented_chunk[0], center_irc
```

Without anything additional, this function won't do much. Let's see what it takes to add in some actual transforms.

> **NOTE** It's important to structure your data pipeline such that your caching steps happen *before* augmentation! Doing otherwise will result in your data being augmented once and then persisted in that state, which defeats the purpose.

MIRRORING

When mirroring a sample, we keep the pixel values exactly the same and only change the orientation of the image. Since there's no strong correlation between tumor growth and left-right or front-back, we should be able to flip those without changing the representative nature of the sample. The index-axis (referred to as Z in patient coordinates) corresponds to the direction of gravity in an upright human, however, so there's a possibility of a difference in the top and bottom of a tumor. We are going to assume it's fine, since quick visual investigation doesn't show any gross bias. Were we working toward a clinically relevant project, we'd need to confirm that assumption with an expert.

Listing 12.13   dsets.py:165, def getCtAugmentedCandidate

```
for i in range(3):
  if 'flip' in augmentation_dict:
    if random.random() > 0.5:
      transform_t[i,i] *= -1
```

The `grid_sample` function maps the range [−1, 1] to the extents of both the old and new tensors (the rescaling happens implicitly if the sizes are different). This range mapping means that to mirror the data, all we need to do is multiply the relevant element of the transformation matrix by −1.

SHIFTING BY A RANDOM OFFSET

Shifting the nodule candidate around shouldn't make a huge difference, since convolutions are translation independent, though this will make our model more robust to imperfectly centered nodules. What will make a more significant difference is that the offset might not be an integer number of voxels; instead, the data will be resampled using trilinear interpolation, which can introduce some slight blurring. Voxels at the edge of the sample will be repeated, which can be seen as a smeared, streaky section along the border.

Listing 12.14   dsets.py:165, def getCtAugmentedCandidate

```
for i in range(3):
  # ... line 170
  if 'offset' in augmentation_dict:
    offset_float = augmentation_dict['offset']
    random_float = (random.random() * 2 - 1)
    transform_t[i,3] = offset_float * random_float
```

Note that our `'offset'` parameter is the maximum offset expressed in the same scale as the [−1, 1] range the grid sample function expects.

SCALING

Scaling the image slightly is very similar to mirroring and shifting. Doing so can also result in the same repeated edge voxels we just mentioned when discussing shifting the sample.

Listing 12.15   dsets.py:165, def getCtAugmentedCandidate

```
for i in range(3):
  # ... line 175
  if 'scale' in augmentation_dict:
    scale_float = augmentation_dict['scale']
    random_float = (random.random() * 2 - 1)
    transform_t[i,i] *= 1.0 + scale_float * random_float
```

Since `random_float` is converted to be in the range [−1, 1], it doesn't actually matter if we add `scale_float * random_float` to or subtract it from 1.0.

ROTATING

Rotation is the first augmentation technique we're going to use where we have to carefully consider our data to ensure that we don't break our sample with a conversion that causes it to no longer be representative. Recall that our CT slices have uniform spacing along the rows and columns (X- and Y-axes), but in the index (or Z) direction, the voxels are non-cubic. That means we can't treat those axes as interchangeable.

One option is to resample our data so that our resolution along the index-axis is the same as along the other two, but that's not a true solution because the data along that axis would be very blurry and smeared. Even if we interpolate more voxels, the fidelity of the data would remain poor. Instead, we'll treat that axis as special and confine our rotations to the X-Y plane.

Listing 12.16 dsets.py:181, def getCtAugmentedCandidate

```
if 'rotate' in augmentation_dict:
  angle_rad = random.random() * math.pi * 2
  s = math.sin(angle_rad)
  c = math.cos(angle_rad)

  rotation_t = torch.tensor([
    [c, -s, 0, 0],
    [s, c, 0, 0],
    [0, 0, 1, 0],
    [0, 0, 0, 1],
  ])

  transform_t @= rotation_t
```

NOISE

Our final augmentation technique is different from the others in that it is actively destructive to our sample in a way that flipping or rotating the sample is not. If we add too much noise to the sample, it will swamp the real data and make it effectively impossible to classify. While shifting and scaling the sample would do something similar if we used extreme input values, we've chosen values that will only impact the edge of the sample. Noise will have an impact on the entire image.

Listing 12.17 dsets.py:208, def getCtAugmentedCandidate

```
if 'noise' in augmentation_dict:
  noise_t = torch.randn_like(augmented_chunk)
  noise_t *= augmentation_dict['noise']

  augmented_chunk += noise_t
```

The other augmentation types have increased the effective size of our dataset. Noise makes our model's job *harder*. We'll revisit this once we see some training results.

EXAMINING AUGMENTED CANDIDATES

We can see the result of our efforts in figure 12.21. The upper-left image shows an unaugmented positive candidate, and the next five show the effect of each augmentation type in isolation. Finally, the bottom row shows the combined result three times.

Since each __getitem__ call to the augmenting dataset reapplies the augmentations randomly, each image on the bottom row looks different. This also means it's nearly impossible to generate an image exactly like this again! It's also important to

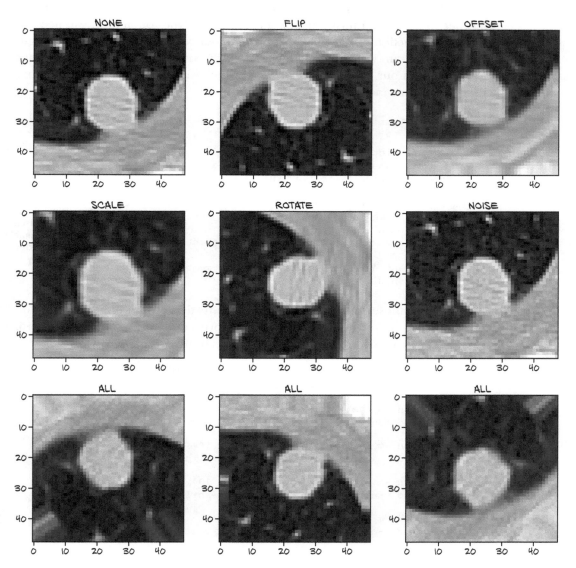

Figure 12.21 Various augmentation types performed on a positive nodule sample

remember that sometimes the `'flip'` augmentation will result in *no* flip. Returning always-flipped images is just as limiting as not flipping in the first place. Now let's see if any of this makes a difference.

12.6.2 *Seeing the improvement from data augmentation*

We are going to train additional models, one per augmentation type discussed in the last section, with an additional model training run that combines all of the augmentation types. Once they're finished, we'll take a look at our numbers in TensorBoard.

   In order to be able to turn our new augmentation types on and off, we need to expose the construction of augmentation_dict to our command-line interface. Arguments to our program will be added by parser.add_argument calls (not shown, but similar to the ones our program already has), which will then be fed into code that actually constructs augmentation_dict.

Listing 12.18   training.py:105, LunaTrainingApp.__init__

```
self.augmentation_dict = {}
if self.cli_args.augmented or self.cli_args.augment_flip:
  self.augmentation_dict['flip'] = True
if self.cli_args.augmented or self.cli_args.augment_offset:
  self.augmentation_dict['offset'] = 0.1
if self.cli_args.augmented or self.cli_args.augment_scale:
  self.augmentation_dict['scale'] = 0.2
if self.cli_args.augmented or self.cli_args.augment_rotate:
  self.augmentation_dict['rotate'] = True
if self.cli_args.augmented or self.cli_args.augment_noise:
  self.augmentation_dict['noise'] = 25.0
```

> These values were empirically chosen to have a reasonable impact, but better values probably exist.

Now that we have those command-line arguments ready, you can either run the following commands or revisit p2_run_everything.ipynb and run cells 8 through 16. Either way you run it, expect these to take a significant time to finish:

```
$ .venv/bin/python -m p2ch12.prepcache
```
> You only need to prep the cache once per chapter.

```
$ .venv/bin/python -m p2ch12.training --epochs 20 \
      --balanced sanity-bal
```
> You might have this run from earlier in the chapter; in that case there's no need to rerun it!

```
$ .venv/bin/python -m p2ch12.training --epochs 10 \
      --balanced --augment-flip    sanity-bal-flip

$ .venv/bin/python -m p2ch12.training --epochs 10 \
      --balanced --augment-shift   sanity-bal-shift

$ .venv/bin/python -m p2ch12.training --epochs 10 \
      --balanced --augment-scale   sanity-bal-scale

$ .venv/bin/python -m p2ch12.training --epochs 10 \
      --balanced --augment-rotate sanity-bal-rotate

$ .venv/bin/python -m p2ch12.training --epochs 10 \
```

```
        --balanced --augment-noise  sanity-bal-noise

$ .venv/bin/python -m p2ch12.training --epochs 20 \
        --balanced --augmented sanity-bal-aug
```

While that's running, we can start TensorBoard. Let's direct it to only show these runs by changing the `logdir` parameter like so: `../path/to/tensorboard --logdir runs/p2ch12`.

Depending on the hardware you have at your disposal, the training might take a long time. Feel free to skip the `flip`, `shift`, and `scale` training jobs and reduce the first and last runs to 11 epochs if you need to move things along more quickly. We chose 20 runs because that helps them stand out from the other runs, but 11 should work as well.

If you let everything run to completion, your TensorBoard should have data like that shown in figure 12.22. We're going to deselect everything except the validation data, to reduce clutter. When you're looking at your data live, you can also change the smoothing value, which can help clarify the trend lines. Take a quick look at the figure, and then we'll go over it in some detail.

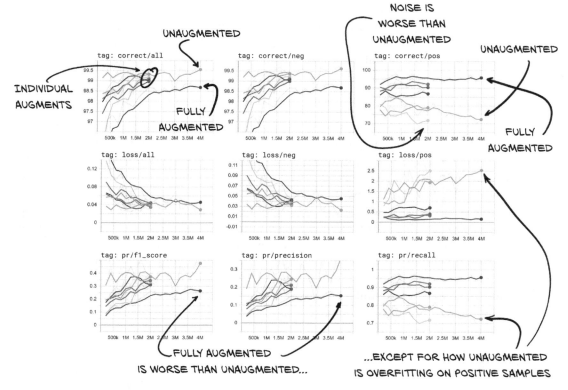

Figure 12.22 Percent correctly classified, loss, F1 score, precision, and recall for the validation set from networks trained with a variety of augmentation schemes

The first thing to notice in the upper-left graph ("tag: correct/all") is that the individual augmentation types are something of a jumble. Our unaugmented and fully augmented runs are on opposite sides of that jumble. That means when combined, our augmentation is more than the sum of its parts. Also of interest is that our fully augmented run gets many more wrong answers. While that's bad generally, if we look at the right column of images (which focus on the positive candidate samples we actually care about—the ones that are really nodules), we see that our fully augmented model is *much* better at finding the positive candidate samples. The recall for the fully augmented model is great! It's also much better at not overfitting. As we saw earlier, our unaugmented model gets worse over time.

One interesting thing to note is that the noise-augmented model is *worse* at identifying nodules than the unaugmented model. This makes sense if we remember that we said noise makes the model's job harder.

Another interesting thing to see in the live data (it's somewhat lost in the jumble here) is that the rotation-augmented model is nearly as good as the fully augmented model when it comes to recall, and it has much better precision. Since our F1 score is precision limited (due to the higher number of negative samples), the rotation-augmented model also has a better F1 score.

We'll stick with the fully augmented model going forward, since our use case requires high recall. The F1 score will still be used to determine which epoch to save as the best. In a real-world project, we might want to devote extra time to investigating whether a different combination of augmentation types and parameter values could yield better results.

12.7   *Conclusion*

We spent a lot of time and energy in this chapter reformulating how we think about our model's performance. It's easy to be misled by poor methods of evaluation, and it's crucial to have a strong intuitive understanding of the factors that feed into evaluating a model well. Once those fundamentals are internalized, it's much easier to spot when we're being led astray.

We've also learned about how to deal with data sources that aren't sufficiently populated. Being able to synthesize representative training samples is incredibly useful. Situations where we have too much training data are rare indeed!

Now that we have a classifier that is performing reasonably, we'll turn our attention to automatically finding candidate nodules to classify. Chapter 13 will start there; then, in chapter 14, we will feed those candidates back into the classifier we developed here and venture into building one more classifier to tell malignant nodules from benign ones.

12.8 Exercises

1 The F1 score can be generalized to support values other than 1.

    a Read https://en.wikipedia.org/wiki/F1_score, and implement F2 and F0.5 scores.

    b Determine which of F1, F2, and F0.5 makes the most sense for this project. Track that value, and compare and contrast it with the F1 score. [6]

2 Implement a `WeightedRandomSampler` approach to balancing the positive and negative training samples for `LunaDataset` with `ratio_int` set to 0.

    a How did you get the required information about the class of each sample?

    b Which approach was easier? Which resulted in more readable code?

3 Experiment with different class-balancing schemes.

    a What ratio results in the best score after two epochs? After 20?

    b What if the ratio is a function of `epoch_ndx`?

4 Experiment with different data augmentation approaches.

    a Can any of the existing approaches be made more aggressive (noise, offset, and so on)?

    b Does the inclusion of noise augmentation help or hinder your training results?

       – Are there other values that change this result?

    c Research data augmentation that other projects have used. Are any applicable here?

       – Implement "mixup" augmentation for positive nodule candidates. Does it help?

5 Change the initial normalization from `nn.BatchNorm` to something custom, and retrain the model.

    a Can you get better results using fixed normalization?

    b What normalization offset and scale make sense?

    c Do nonlinear normalizations like square roots help?

6 What other kinds of data can TensorBoard display besides those we've covered here?

    a Can you have it display information about the weights of your network?

    b What about intermediate results from running your model on a particular sample?

       – Does having the backbone of the model wrapped in an instance of `nn.Sequential` help or hinder this effort?

---

[6] Yep, that's a hint it's not the F1 score!

12.9 Summary

- A binary label and a binary classification threshold combine to partition the dataset into four quadrants: true positives, true negatives, false negatives, and false positives. These four quantities provide the basis for our improved performance metrics.

- Recall is the ability of a model to maximize true positives. Selecting every single item guarantees perfect recall—because all the correct answers are included—but also exhibits poor precision.

- Precision is the ability of a model to minimize false positives. Selecting nothing guarantees perfect precision—because no incorrect answers are included—but also exhibits poor recall.

- The F1 score combines precision and recall into a single metric that describes model performance. We use the F1 score to determine what impact changes to training or the model have on our performance.

- Balancing the training set to have an equal number of positive and negative samples during training can result in the model performing better (defined as having a positive, increasing F1 score).

- Data augmentation takes existing organic data samples and modifies them such that the resulting augmented sample is non-trivially different from the original, but remains representative of samples of the same class. This allows additional training without overfitting in situations where data is limited.

- Common data augmentation strategies include changes in orientation, mirroring, rescaling, shifting by an offset, and adding noise. Depending on the project, other more specific strategies may also be relevant.

Using segmentation to find suspected nodules

This chapter covers

- Segmenting data with a pixel-to-pixel model
- Performing segmentation with U-Net
- Understanding mask prediction using Dice loss
- Evaluating a segmentation model's performance

In the last four chapters, we have accomplished a lot. We've learned about CT scans and lung tumors, datasets and data loaders, and metrics and monitoring. We have also *applied* many of the things we learned in part 1, and we have a working classifier. We are still operating in a somewhat artificial environment, however, since we require hand-annotated nodule candidate information to load into our classifier. We don't have a good way to create that input automatically. Just feeding the entire CT into our model—that is, plugging in overlapping $32 \times 32 \times 32$ patches of data—would result in $31 \times 31 \times 7 = 6{,}727$ patches per CT, or about 10 times the number of annotated samples we have. We'd need to overlap the edges; our classifier expects the nodule candidate to be centered, and even then the inconsistent positioning would probably present issues.

As we explained in chapter 9, our project uses multiple steps to solve the problem of locating possible nodules, identifying them, with an indication of their possible malignancy. This is a common approach among practitioners, while in deep learning research there is a tendency to demonstrate the ability of individual models to solve complex problems in an end-to-end fashion. The multistage project design we use in this book gives us a good excuse to introduce new concepts step by step.

13.1   Adding a second model to our project

In the previous two chapters, we worked on step 4 of our plan shown in figure 13.1: classification. In this chapter, we'll go back not just one but two steps. We need to find a way to tell our classifier where to look. To do this, we are going to take raw CT scans and find everything that might be a nodule.[1] This is the highlighted step 2 in the figure. To find these possible nodules, we have to flag voxels that look like they might be part of a nodule, a process known as *segmentation*. Then, in chapter 14, we will deal with step 3 and provide the bridge by transforming the segmentation masks from this image into location annotations.

By the time we're finished with this chapter, we'll have created a new model with an architecture that can perform per-pixel labeling, or segmentation. The code that

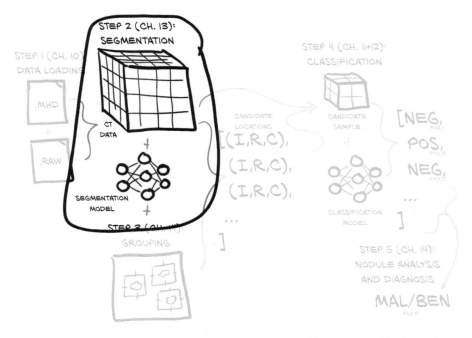

Figure 13.1   Our end-to-end lung cancer detection project, with a focus on this chapter's topic: step 2, segmentation

---

[1] We expect to mark quite a few things that are not nodules; thus, we use the classification step to reduce the number of these.

will accomplish this will be very similar to the code from the last chapter, especially if we focus on the larger structure. All of the changes we're going to make will be smaller and targeted. As we see in figure 13.2, we need to make updates to our model (step 2A in the figure), dataset (2B), and training loop (2C) to account for the new model's inputs, outputs, and other requirements. (Don't worry if you don't recognize each component in each of these steps in step 2 on the right side of the diagram. We'll go through the details when we get to each step.) Finally, we'll examine the results we get when running our new model (step 3 in the figure).

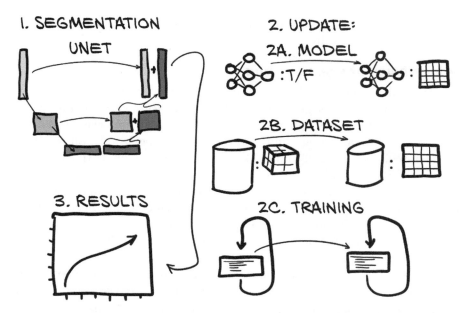

Figure 13.2   The new model architecture for segmentation, along with the model, dataset, and training loop updates we will implement

Breaking down figure 13.2 into steps, our plan for this chapter is as follows:

1. *Segmentation.* First we will learn how segmentation works with a U-Net model, including what the new model components are and what happens to them as we go through the segmentation process. This is step 1 in figure 13.2.
2. *Update.* To implement segmentation, we need to change our existing code base in three main places, shown in the substeps on the right side of figure 13.2.The code will be structurally very similar to what we developed for classification, but will differ in detail:
    a. *Update the model (step 2A).* We will integrate a preexisting U-Net into our segmentation model. Our model in chapter 12 output a simple true/false classification; our model in this chapter will instead output an entire image.

   b *Change the dataset (step 2B).* We need to change our dataset to not only deliver bits of the CT but also provide masks for the nodules. The classification dataset consisted of 3D crops around nodule candidates, but we'll need to collect both full CT slices and 2D crops for segmentation training and validation.

   c *Adapt the training loop (step 2C).* We need to adapt the training loop so we bring in a new loss to optimize. Because we want to display images of our segmentation results in TensorBoard, we'll also do things like saving our model weights to disk.

3 *Results.* Finally, we'll see the fruits of our efforts when we look at the quantitative segmentation results.

13.2 *Various types of segmentation*

To get started, we need to talk about different flavors of segmentation. For this project, we will be using *semantic* segmentation, which is the act of classifying individual pixels in an image using labels just like those we've seen for our classification tasks, for example, "bear," "cat," "dog," and so on. If done properly, this will result in distinct chunks or regions that signify things like "all of these pixels are part of a cat." This takes the form of a label mask or heatmap that identifies areas of interest. We will have a simple binary label: true values will correspond to nodule candidates, and false values mean uninteresting healthy tissue. This partially meets our need to find nodule candidates that we will later feed into our classification network.

Before we get into the details, we should briefly discuss other approaches we could take to finding our nodule candidates. For example, *instance segmentation* labels individual objects of interest with distinct labels. So whereas semantic segmentation would label a picture of two people shaking hands with two labels ("person" and "background"), instance segmentation would have three labels ("person1," "person2," and "background") with a boundary somewhere around the clasped hands. While this could be useful for us to distinguish "nodule1" from "nodule2," we will instead use grouping to identify individual nodules. That approach will work well for us since nodules are unlikely to touch or overlap.

Another approach to these kinds of tasks is *object detection*, which locates an item of interest in an image and puts a bounding box around the item. While both instance segmentation and object detection could be great for our uses, their implementations are somewhat complex, and we don't feel they are the best things for you to learn next. Also, training object-detection models typically requires much more computational resources than our approach requires. If you're feeling up to the challenge, the YOLOv3 paper is a more entertaining read than most deep learning research papers.[2] For us, though, semantic segmentation it is.

---

[2] Joseph Redmon and Ali Farhadi, "YOLOv3: An Incremental Improvement," https://pjreddie.com/media/files/papers/YOLOv3.pdf. Perhaps check it out once you've finished the book.

NOTE As we go through the code examples in this chapter, we're going to rely on you checking the code from GitHub for much of the larger context. We'll be omitting code that's uninteresting or similar to what's come before in earlier chapters, so that we can focus on the crux of the issue at hand.

13.3 Semantic segmentation: Per-pixel classification

Semantic segmentation is used to answer questions of the form "Where is a cat in this picture?" Often, sadly, most pictures of a cat, like figure 13.3, have a lot of non-cat in them; the table or wall in the background, the keyboard the cat is sitting on, that kind of thing. Being able to say "This pixel is part of the cat, and this other pixel is part of the ... requires fundamentally different model output and a different internal structure from the classification models we've worked with thus far. Classification can tell us whether a cat is present, while segmentation will tell us where we can find it.

CLASSIFICATION VS. SEGMENTATION

CAT: YES   CAT: HERE

Figure 13.3 Classification results in one or more binary flags, while segmentation produces a mask or heatmap.

If your project requires differentiating between a near cat and a far cat, or a cat on the left versus a cat on the right, then segmentation is probably the right approach. The image-consuming classification models that we've implemented so far can be thought of as funnels or magnifying glasses that take a large bunch of pixels and focus them down into a single "point" (or, more accurately, a single set of class predictions), as shown in figure 13.4. Classification models provide answers of the form "Yes, this huge pile of pixels has a cat in it, somewhere," or "No, no cats here." This is great when you don't care where the cat is, just that there is (or isn't) one in the image.

Repeated layers of convolution and downsampling mean the model starts by consuming raw pixels to produce specific, detailed detectors for things like texture and color, and then builds up higher-level conceptual feature detectors for parts like eyes

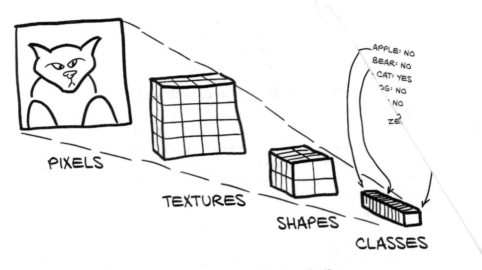

Figure 13.4 **The magnifying glass model structure for classification**

and ears and mouth and nose[3] that finally result in "cat" versus "dog." Due to the increasing receptive field of the convolutions after each downsampling layer, those higher-level detectors can use information from an increasingly large area of the input image.

Unfortunately, since segmentation needs to produce an image-like output, ending up at a single classification-like list of binary-ish flags won't work. As we recall from section 11.4, downsampling is key to increasing the receptive fields of the convolutional layers, and is what helps reduce the array of pixels that make up an image to a single list of classes. Notice figure 13.5, which repeats figure 11.6.

In the figure, our inputs flow from the left to right in the top row and are continued in the bottom row. In order to work out the receptive field—the area influencing the single pixel at bottom right—we can go backward. The max-pool operation has 2×2 inputs producing each final output pixel. The 3×3 conv in the middle of the bottom row looks at one adjacent pixel (including diagonally) in each direction, so the total receptive field of the convolutions that result in the 2 x 2 output is 4 x 4 (with the right "x" characters). The 3×3 convolution in the top row then adds an additional pixel of context in each direction, so the receptive field of the single output pixel at bottom right is a 6×6 field in the input at top left. With the downsampling from the max pool, the receptive field of the next block of convolutions will have double the width, and each additional downsampling will double it again, while shrinking the size of the output.

We'll need a different model architecture if we want our output to be the same size as our input. One simple model to use for segmentation would have repeated convolutional layers without any downsampling. Given appropriate padding, that would result in output the same size as the input (good), but a very limited receptive field

---

[3] ... "head, shoulders, knees, and toes, knees and toes," as my (Eli's) toddlers would sing.

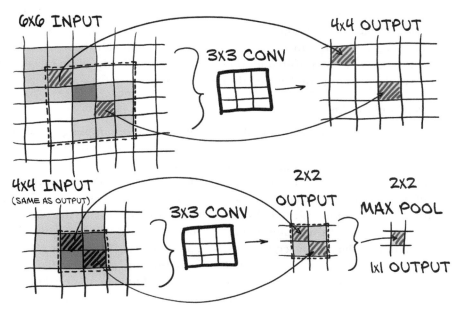

Figure 13.5 The convolutional architecture of a LunaModel block, consisting of two 3 × 3 convolutions followed by a max pool. The final pixel has a 6 × 6 receptive field.

(bad) due to the limited reach based on how much overlap multiple layers of small convolutions will have. The classification model uses each downsampling layer to double the effective reach of the following convolutions; and without that increase in effective field size, each segmented pixel will only be able to consider a very local neighborhood.

> **NOTE** Assuming 3 × 3 convolutions, the receptive field size for a simple model of stacked convolutions is $2 * L + 1$, with L being the number of convolutional layers.

Four layers of 3 × 3 convolutions will have a receptive field of 9 × 9 per output pixel. By inserting a 2 × 2 max pool between the second and third convolutions, and another at the end, we increase the receptive field to …

> **NOTE** See if you can figure out the math yourself; when you're done, check back here.

… 16 × 16. The final series of conv-conv-pool has a receptive field of 6 × 6, but that happens *after* the first max pool, which makes the final effective receptive field 12 × 12 in the original input resolution. The first two conv layers add a total border of 2 pixels around the 12 × 12, for a total of 16 × 16.

So the question remains: how can we improve the receptive field of an output pixel while maintaining a 1:1 ratio of input pixels to output pixels? One common answer is to use a technique called *upsampling*, which takes an image of a given resolution and produces an image of a higher resolution. Upsampling at its simplest just means replacing each pixel with an $N \times N$ block of pixels, each with the same value as the original input pixel. The possibilities only get more complex from there, with options like linear interpolation and learned deconvolution.

13.3.1 The U-Net architecture

Before we end up diving down a rabbit hole of possible upsampling algorithms, let's get back to our goal for the chapter. Per figure 13.6, step 1 is to get familiar with a foundational segmentation algorithm called U-Net.

The U-Net architecture is a design for a neural network that can produce pixel-wise output and that was invented for segmentation. As you can see from the highlight in figure 13.6, a diagram of the U-Net architecture looks a bit like the letter *U*, which explains the origins of the name. We also immediately see that it is quite a bit more complicated than the mostly sequential structure of the classifiers we are familiar with. We'll see a more detailed version of the U-Net architecture shortly, in figure 13.7, and learn exactly what each of those components is doing. Once we understand the model architecture, we can work on training one to solve our segmentation task.

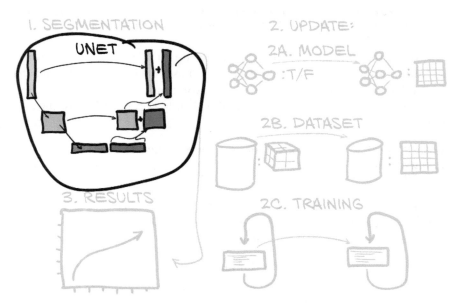

Figure 13.6   The new model architecture for segmentation, that we will be working with

The U-Net architecture shown in figure 13.7 was an early breakthrough for image segmentation. Let's take a look and then walk through the architecture.

In this diagram, the boxes represent intermediate results and the arrows represent operations between them. The U-shape of the architecture comes from the multiple

UNET ARCHITECTURE

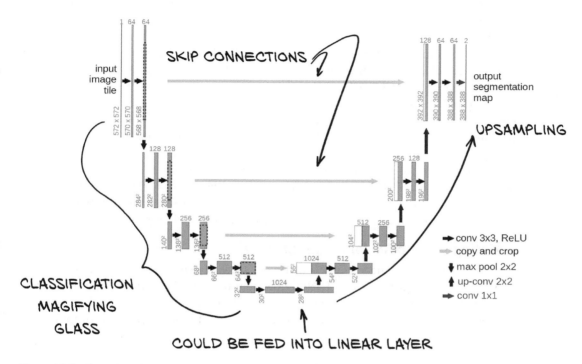

Figure 13.7 From the U-Net paper, with annotations. Source: The base of this figure is courtesy Olaf Ronneberger et al., from the paper "U-Net: Convolutional Networks for Biomedical Image Segmentation," which can be found at https://arxiv.org/abs/1505.04597 and https://lmb.informatik.uni-freiburg.de/people/ronneber/u-net.

resolutions at which the network operates. In the top row is the full resolution (512 × 512 for us), the row below has half that, and so on. The data flows from top left to bottom center through a series of convolutions and downscaling, as we saw in the classifiers and looked at in detail in chapter 8. Then we go up again, using upscaling convolutions to get back to the full resolution. Unlike the original U-Net, we will be padding things so we don't lose pixels off the edges, so our resolution is the same on the left and on the right.

Earlier network designs already had this U-shape, which people attempted to use to address the limited receptive field size of fully convolutional networks. To address this limited field size, they used a design that copied, inverted, and appended the focusing portions of an image-classification network to create a symmetrical model that goes from fine detail to wide receptive field and back to fine detail.

Those earlier network designs had problems converging, however, most likely due to the loss of spatial information during downsampling. Once information reaches a large number of very downscaled images, the exact location of object boundaries gets harder to encode and therefore reconstruct. To address this, the U-Net authors added the skip connections we see at the center of the figure. We first touched on skip connections in chapter 8, although they are employed differently here than in the ResNet architecture. In U-Net, skip connections short-circuit inputs along the downsampling path into the corresponding layers in the upsampling path. These layers receive as input both the upsampled results of the wide receptive field layers from lower in the U as well as the output of the earlier fine detail layers via the "copy and crop" bridge connections. This is the key innovation behind U-Net (which, interestingly, predated ResNet).

All of this means those final detail layers are operating with the best of both worlds. They've got both information about the larger context surrounding the immediate area and fine detail data from the first set of full-resolution layers.

The "conv 1x1" layer at far right, in the head of the network, changes the number of channels from 64 to 2 (the original paper had 2 output channels; we have 1 in our case). This is somewhat akin to the fully connected layer we used in our classification network, but per-pixel, channel-wise: it's a way to convert from the number of filters used in the last upsampling step to the number of output classes needed.

13.4   *Updating the model for segmentation*

It's time to move through step 2A in figure 13.8. We've had enough theory about segmentation and history about U-Net; now we want to update our code, starting with the model. Instead of just outputting a binary classification that gives us a single output of true or false, we integrate a U-Net to get to a model that's capable of outputting a

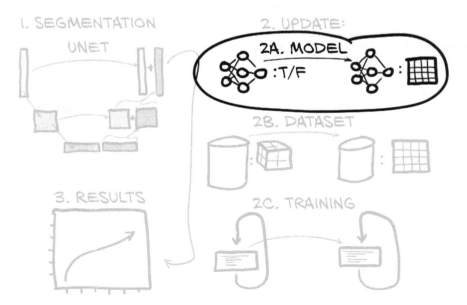

Figure 13.8   The outline of this chapter, with a focus on the changes needed for our segmentation model

probability for every pixel: that is, performing segmentation. Rather than implementing a custom U-Net segmentation model from scratch, we're going to appropriate an existing implementation from an open source repository on GitHub.

The U-Net implementation at https://github.com/jvanvugt/pytorch-unet seems to meet our needs well.[4] It's MIT licensed (copyright 2018 Joris), it's contained in a single file, and it has a number of parameter options for us to tweak. The file is included in our code repository at util/unet.py, along with a link to the original repository and the full text of the license used.

> **NOTE** While it's less of an issue for personal projects, it's important to be aware of the license terms attached to open source software you use for a project. The MIT license is one of the most permissive open source licenses, and it still places requirements on users of MIT licensed code! Also be aware that authors retain copyright even if they publish their work in a public forum (yes, even on GitHub), and if they do not include a license, that does *not* mean the work is in the public domain. Quite the opposite! It means you don't have *any* license to use the code, any more than you'd have the right to wholesale copy a book you borrowed from the library.

We suggest taking some time to inspect the code and, based on the knowledge you have built up until this point, identify the building blocks of the architecture as they are reflected in the code. Can you spot skip connections? A particularly worthy exercise for you is to draw a diagram that shows how the model is laid out, just by looking at the code.

Now that we have found a U-Net implementation that fits the bill, we need to adapt it so that it works well for our needs. In general, it's a good idea to keep an eye out for situations where we can use something off the shelf. It's important to have a sense of what models exist, how they're implemented and trained, and whether any parts can be scavenged and applied to the project we're working on at any given moment. While that broader knowledge is something that comes with time and experience, it's a good idea to start building that toolbox now.

13.4.1 *Adapting an off-the-shelf model to our project*

We will now make some changes to the classic U-Net, justifying them along the way. A useful exercise for you will be to compare results between the *vanilla* model and the one after the tweaks, preferably removing one at a time to see the effect of each change (this is also called an *ablation study* in research circles).

First, we're going to pass the input through batch normalization. This way, we won't have to normalize the data ourselves in the dataset; and, more importantly, we will get normalization statistics (read mean and standard deviation) estimated over individual batches. This means when a batch is *dull* for some reason—that is, when there is nothing to see in all the CT crops fed into the network—it will be scaled more

---

[4] The implementation included here differs from the official paper by using average pooling instead of max pooling to downsample. The most recent version on GitHub has changed to use max pool.

strongly. The fact that samples in batches are picked randomly at every epoch will minimize the chances of a dull sample ending up in an all-dull batch, and hence those dull samples getting overemphasized.

Second, since the output values are unconstrained, we are going to pass the output through an nn.Sigmoid layer to restrict the output to the range [0, 1]. Third, we will reduce the total depth and number of filters we allow our model to use. While this is jumping ahead of ourselves a bit, the capacity of the model using the standard parameters far outstrips our dataset size. This means we're unlikely to find a pretrained model that matches our exact needs. Finally, although this is not a modification, it's important to note that our output is a single channel, with each pixel of output representing the model's estimate of the probability that the pixel in question is part of a nodule.

This wrapping of U-Net can be done rather simply by implementing a model with three attributes: one each for the two features we want to add, and one for the U-Net itself—which we can treat just like any prebuilt module here. We will also pass any keyword arguments we receive into the U-Net constructor.

Listing 13.1   model.py:17, class **UNetWrapper**

kwarg is a dictionary containing all keyword arguments passed to the constructor.

BatchNorm2d wants us to specify the number of input channels, which we take from the keyword argument.

The U-Net: a small thing to include here, but it's really doing all the work.

Just as for the classifier in chapter 11, we use our custom weight initialization. The function is copied over, so we will not show the code again.

```
class UNetWrapper(nn.Module):
    def __init__(self, **kwargs):
        super().__init__()

        self.input_batchnorm = nn.BatchNorm2d(kwargs['in_channels'])
        self.unet = UNet(**kwargs)
        self.final = nn.Sigmoid()

        self._init_weights()
```

The forward method is a similarly straightforward sequence. We could use an instance of nn.Sequential as we saw in chapter 8, but we'll be explicit here for both clarity of code and clarity of stack traces.[5]

Listing 13.2   model.py:50, **UNetWrapper.forward**

```
def forward(self, input_batch):
    bn_output = self.input_batchnorm(input_batch)
    un_output = self.unet(bn_output)
    fn_output = self.final(un_output)
    return fn_output
```

Note that we're using nn.BatchNorm2d here. This is because U-Net is fundamentally a two-dimensional segmentation model. We could adapt the implementation to use 3D

---

[5] In the unlikely event our code throws any exceptions—which it clearly won't, will it?

convolutions, in order to use information across slices. The memory usage of a straight-forward implementation would be considerably greater: that is, we would have to chop up the CT scan. Also, the fact that pixel spacing in the Z direction is much larger than in-plane makes a nodule less likely to be present across many slices. These considerations make a fully 3D approach less attractive for our purposes. Instead, we'll adapt our 3D data to be segmented a slice at a time, providing adjacent slices for context (for example, detecting that a bright lump is indeed a blood vessel gets much easier alongside neighboring slices). Since we're sticking with presenting the data in 2D, we'll use channels to represent the adjacent slices. Our treatment of the third dimension is similar to how we applied a fully connected model to images in chapter 7: the model will have to relearn the adjacency relationships we're throwing away along the axial direction, but that's not difficult for the model to accomplish, especially with the limited number of slices given for context owing to the small size of the target structures.

13.5 *Updating the dataset for segmentation*

Our source data for this chapter remains unchanged: we're consuming CT scans and annotation data about them. But our model expects input and will produce output of a different form than we had previously. As we hint at in step 2B of figure 13.9, our previous dataset produced 3D data, but we need to produce 2D data now.

The original U-Net implementation did not use padded convolutions, which means while the output segmentation map was smaller than the input, every pixel of that output had a fully populated receptive field. None of the input pixels that fed

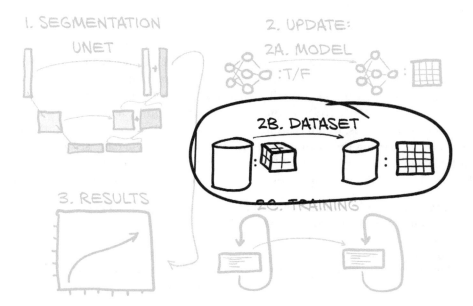

Figure 13.9 The outline of this chapter, with a focus on the changes needed for our segmentation dataset

into the determination of that output pixel were padded, fabricated, or otherwise incomplete. Thus the output of the original U-Net will tile perfectly, so it can be used with images of any size (except at the edges of the input image, where some context will be missing by definition).

There are two problems with us taking the same pixel-perfect approach for our problem. The first is related to the interaction between convolution and downsampling, and the second is related to the nature of our data being three-dimensional.

13.5.1 *U-Net has very specific input size requirements*

The first issue is that the sizes of the input and output patches for U-Net are very specific. In order to have the two-pixel loss per convolution line up evenly before and after downsampling (especially when considering the further convolutional shrinkage at that lower resolution), only certain input sizes will work. The U-Net paper used 572×572 image patches, which resulted in 388×388 output maps. The input images are bigger than our 512×512 CT slices, and the output is quite a bit smaller! That would mean any nodules near the edge of the CT scan slice wouldn't be segmented at all. Although this setup works well when dealing with very large images, it's not ideal for our use case.

We will address this issue by setting the `padding` flag of the U-Net constructor to `True`. This will mean we can use input images of any size, and we will get output of the same size. We may lose some fidelity near the edges of the image, since the receptive field of pixels located there will include regions that have been artificially padded, but that's a compromise we decide to live with.

13.5.2 *U-Net trade-offs for 3D vs. 2D data*

The second issue is that our 3D data doesn't line up exactly with U-Net's 2D expected input. Simply taking our $512 \times 512 \times 128$ image and feeding it into a converted-to-3D U-Net class won't work, because we'll exhaust our GPU memory. Each image is 2^9 by 2^9 by 2^7, with 2^2 bytes per voxel. The first layer of U-Net is 64 channels, or 2^6. That's an exponent of $9 + 9 + 7 + 2 + 6 = 33$, or 8 GB *just for the first convolutional layer*. There are two convolutional layers (16 GB); and then each downsampling halves the resolution but doubles the channels, which is another 2 GB for each layer after the first downsample (remember, halving the resolution results in one-eighth the data, since we're working with 3D data). So we've hit 20 GB before we even get to the second downsample, much less anything on the upsample side of the model or anything dealing with autograd.

> **NOTE** There are a number of clever and innovative ways to get around these problems, and we in no way suggest that this is the only approach that will ever work.[6] We do feel that this approach is one of the simplest that gets the job done to the level we need for our project in this book. We'd rather keep things simple so that we can focus on the fundamental concepts; the clever stuff can come later, once you've mastered the basics.

---

[6] For example, Stanislav Nikolov et al., "Deep Learning to Achieve Clinically Applicable Segmentation of Head and Neck Anatomy for Radiotherapy," https://arxiv.org/pdf/1809.04430.pdf.

As anticipated, instead of trying to do things in 3D, we're going to treat each slice as a 2D segmentation problem and cheat our way around the issue of context in the third dimension by providing neighboring slices as separate channels. Instead of the traditional "red," "green," and "blue" channels that we're familiar with from photographic images, our main channels will be "two slices above," "one slice above," "the slice we're actually segmenting," "one slice below," and so on.

This approach isn't without trade-offs, however. We lose the direct spatial relationship between slices when represented as channels, as all channels will be linearly combined by the convolution kernels with no notion of them being one or two slices away, above or below. We also lose the wider receptive field in the depth dimension that would come from a true 3D segmentation with downsampling. Since CT slices are often thicker than the resolution in rows and columns, we do get a somewhat wider view than it seems at first, and this should be enough, considering that nodules typically span a limited number of slices.

Another aspect to consider, that is relevant for both the current and fully 3D approaches, is that we are now ignoring the exact slice thickness. This is something our model will eventually have to learn to be robust against, by being presented with data with different slice spacings.

In general, there isn't an easy flowchart or rule of thumb that can give canned answers to questions about which trade-offs to make, or whether a given set of compromises compromise too much. Careful experimentation is key, however, and systematically testing hypothesis after hypothesis can help narrow down which changes and approaches are working well for the problem at hand. Although it's tempting to make a flurry of changes while waiting for the last set of results to compute, *resist that impulse.*

That's important enough to repeat: *do not test multiple modifications at the same time.* There is far too high a chance that one of the changes will interact poorly with the other, and you'll be left without solid evidence that either one is worth investigating further. With that said, let's start building out our segmentation dataset.

13.5.3 Building the ground truth data

The first thing we need to address is that we have a mismatch between our human-labeled training data and the actual output we want to get from our model. We have annotated points, but we want a per-voxel mask that indicates whether any given voxel is part of a nodule. We'll have to build that mask ourselves from the data we have and then do some manual checking to make sure the routine that builds the mask is performing well.

Validating these manually constructed heuristics at scale can be difficult. We aren't going to attempt to do anything comprehensive when it comes to making sure each and every nodule is properly handled by our heuristics. If we had more resources, approaches like "collaborate with (or pay) someone to create and/or verify everything by hand" might be an option, but since this isn't a well-funded endeavor, we'll rely on checking a handful of samples and using a very simple "does the output look reasonable?" approach.

To that end, we'll design our approaches and our APIs to make it easy to investigate the intermediate steps that our algorithms are going through. While this might result in slightly clunky function calls returning huge tuples of intermediate values, being able to easily grab results and plot them in a notebook makes the clunk worth it.

BOUNDING BOXES

We are going to begin by converting the nodule locations that we have into bounding boxes that cover the entire nodule (note that we'll only do this for *actual nodules*). If we assume that the nodule locations are roughly centered in the mass, we can trace outward from that point in all three dimensions until we hit low-density voxels, indicating that we've reached normal lung tissue (which is mostly filled with air). Let's follow this algorithm in figure 13.10.

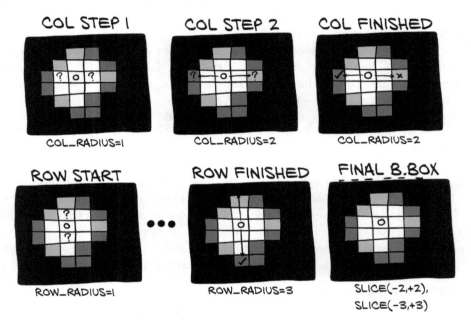

Figure 13.10 An algorithm for finding a bounding box around a lung nodule

We start the origin of our search (O in the figure) at the voxel at the annotated center of our nodule. We then examine the density of the voxels adjacent to our origin on the column axis, marked with a question mark (?). Since both of the examined voxels contain dense tissue, shown here in lighter colors, we continue our search. After incrementing our column search distance to 2, we find that the left voxel has a density below our threshold, and so we stop our search at 2.

Next, we perform the same search in the row direction. Again, we start at the origin, and this time we search up and down. After our search distance becomes 3, we encounter a low-density voxel in both the upper and lower search locations. We only need one to stop our search!

We'll skip showing the search in the third dimension. Our final bounding box is five voxels wide and seven voxels tall. Here's what that looks like in code, for the index direction.

Listing 13.3 dsets.py:131, `Ct.buildAnnotationMask`

```
center_irc = xyz2irc(
  candidateInfo_tup.center_xyz,         ◁─┐ candidateInfo_tup here is the same as
  self.origin_xyz,                         │ we've seen previously: as returned by
  self.vxSize_xyz,                         │ getCandidateInfoList.
  self.direction_a,
)
ci = int(center_irc.index)            ◁─┐ Gets the center voxel
cr = int(center_irc.row)                 │ indices, our starting point
cc = int(center_irc.col)

index_radius = 2
try:                                                              ┐ The search
  while self.hu_a[ci + index_radius, cr, cc] > threshold_hu and \ │ described
      self.hu_a[ci - index_radius, cr, cc] > threshold_hu:    ◁───┘ previously
    index_radius += 1
except IndexError:                    ◁─┐ The safety net for indexing
  index_radius -= 1                      │ beyond the size of the tensor
```

We first grab the center data and then do the search in a `while` loop. As a slight complication, our search might fall off the boundary of our tensor. We are not terribly concerned about that case and are lazy, so we just catch the index exception.[7]

Note that we stop incrementing the very approximate `radius` values *after* the density drops below threshold, so our bounding box should contain a one-voxel border of low-density tissue (at least on one side; since nodules can be adjacent to regions like the lung wall, we have to stop searching in both directions when we hit air on either side). Since we check both `center_index + index_radius` and `center_index - index_radius` against that threshold, that one-voxel boundary will only exist on the edge closest to our nodule location. This is why we need those locations to be relatively centered. Since some nodules are adjacent to the boundary between the lung and denser tissue like muscle or bone, we can't trace each direction independently, as some edges would end up incredibly far away from the actual nodule.

We then repeat the same radius-expansion process with `row_radius` and `col_radius` (this code is omitted for brevity). Once that's done, we can set a box in our bounding-box mask array to `True` (we'll see the definition of `boundingBox_ary` in just a moment; it's not surprising).

OK, let's wrap all this up in a function. We loop over all nodules. For each nodule, we perform the search shown earlier (which we elide from listing 13.4). Then, in a Boolean tensor `boundingBox_a`, we mark the bounding box we found.

---

[7] The bug here is that the wraparound at 0 will go undetected. It does not matter much to us. As an exercise, implement proper bounds checking.

After the loop, we do a bit of cleanup by taking the intersection between the bounding-box mask and the tissue that's denser than our threshold of −700 HU (or 0.3 g/cc). That's going to clip off the corners of our boxes (at least, the ones not embedded in the lung wall), and make it conform to the contours of the nodule a bit better.

Listing 13.4   dsets.py:127, `Ct.buildAnnotationMask`

Starts with an all-False tensor of the same size as the CT

```
def buildAnnotationMask(self, positiveInfo_list, threshold_hu = -700):
    boundingBox_a = np.zeros_like(self.hu_a, dtype=np.bool)

    for candidateInfo_tup in positiveInfo_list:
        # ... line 169
        boundingBox_a[
            ci - index_radius: ci + index_radius + 1,
            cr - row_radius: cr + row_radius + 1,
            cc - col_radius: cc + col_radius + 1] = True

    mask_a = boundingBox_a & (self.hu_a > threshold_hu)

    return mask_a
```

Restricts the mask to voxels above our density threshold

Loops over the nodules. As a reminder that we are only looking at nodules, we call the variable positiveInfo_list.

After we get the nodule radius (the search itself is left out), we mark the bounding box.

Let's take a look at figure 13.11 to see what these masks look like in practice. Additional images in full color can be found in the p2ch13_explore_data.ipynb notebook.

The bottom-right nodule mask demonstrates a limitation of our rectangular bounding-box approach by including a portion of the lung wall. It's certainly something

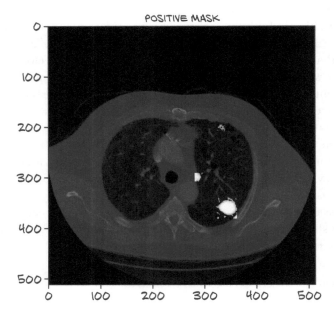

POSITIVE MASK

Figure 13.11   Three nodules from `ct.positive_mask`, highlighted in white

we could fix, but since we're not yet convinced that's the best use of our time and attention, we'll let it remain as is for now.[8] Next, we'll go about adding this mask to our CT class.

CALLING MASK CREATION DURING CT INITIALIZATION

Now that we can take a list of nodule information tuples and turn them into at CT-shaped binary "Is this a nodule?" mask, let's embed those masks into our CT object. First, we'll filter our candidates into a list containing only nodules, and then we'll use that list to build the annotation mask. Finally, we'll collect the set of unique array indexes that have at least one voxel of the nodule mask. We'll use this to shape the data we use for validation.

Listing 13.5 dsets.py:99, Ct.__init__

```
def __init__(self, series_uid):
    # ... line 116
    candidateInfo_list = getCandidateInfoDict()[self.series_uid]

    self.positiveInfo_list = [
        candidate_tup
        for candidate_tup in candidateInfo_list
        if candidate_tup.isNodule_bool
    ]
    self.positive_mask = self.buildAnnotationMask(self.positiveInfo_list)
    self.positive_indexes = (self.positive_mask.sum(axis=(1,2))
                .nonzero()[0].tolist())
```

Filters for nodules → (on `if candidate_tup.isNodule_bool`)

Gives us a 1D vector (over the slices) with the number of voxels flagged in the mask in each slice → (on `self.positive_mask.sum(axis=(1,2))`)

Takes indices of the mask slices that have a nonzero count, which we make into a list → (on `.nonzero()[0].tolist()`)

Keen eyes might have noticed the getCandidateInfoDict function. The definition isn't surprising; it's just a reformulation of the same information as in the getCandidate-InfoList function, but pregrouped by series_uid.

Listing 13.6 dsets.py:87

This can be useful to keep Ct init from being a performance bottleneck. → (on `@functools.lru_cache(1)`)

Takes the list of candidates for the series UID from the dict, defaulting to a fresh, empty list if we cannot find it. Then appends the present candidateInfo_tup to it. → (on `candidateInfo_dict.setdefault(...)`)

```
@functools.lru_cache(1)
def getCandidateInfoDict(requireOnDisk_bool=True):
    candidateInfo_list = getCandidateInfoList(requireOnDisk_bool)
    candidateInfo_dict = {}

    for candidateInfo_tup in candidateInfo_list:
        candidateInfo_dict.setdefault(candidateInfo_tup.series_uid,
                    []).append(candidateInfo_tup)

    return candidateInfo_dict
```

---

[8] Fixing this issue would not do a great deal to teach you about PyTorch.

CACHING CHUNKS OF THE MASK IN ADDITION TO THE CT

In earlier chapters, we cached chunks of CT centered around nodule candidates, since we didn't want to have to read and parse all of a CT's data every time we wanted a small chunk of the CT. We'll want to do the same thing with our new `positive _mask`, so we need to also return it from our `Ct.getRawCandidate` function. This works out to an additional line of code and an edit to the `return` statement.

Listing 13.7   dsets.py:178, `Ct.getRawCandidate`

```
def getRawCandidate(self, center_xyz, width_irc):
    center_irc = xyz2irc(center_xyz, self.origin_xyz, self.vxSize_xyz,
                self.direction_a)

    slice_list = []
    # ... line 203
    ct_chunk = self.hu_a[tuple(slice_list)]
    pos_chunk = self.positive_mask[tuple(slice_list)]        ←—— Newly added

    return ct_chunk, pos_chunk, center_irc     ←—— New value returned here
```

This will, in turn, be cached to disk by the `getCtRawCandidate` function, which opens the CT, gets the specified raw candidate including the nodule mask, and clips the CT values before returning the CT chunk, mask, and center information.

Listing 13.8   dsets.py:212

```
@raw_cache.memoize(typed=True)
def getCtRawCandidate(series_uid, center_xyz, width_irc):
    ct = getCt(series_uid)
    ct_chunk, pos_chunk, center_irc = ct.getRawCandidate(center_xyz,
                            width_irc)
    ct_chunk.clip(-1000, 1000, ct_chunk)
    return ct_chunk, pos_chunk, center_irc
```

The `prepcache` script precomputes and saves all these values for us, helping keep training quick.

CLEANING UP OUR ANNOTATION DATA

Another thing we're going to take care of in this chapter is doing some better screening on our annotation data. It turns out that several of the candidates listed in candidates.csv are present multiple times. To make it even more interesting, those entries are not exact duplicates of one another. Instead, it seems that the original human annotations weren't sufficiently cleaned before being entered in the file. They might be annotations on the same nodule on different slices, which might even have been beneficial for our classifier.

We'll do a bit of a hand wave here and provide a cleaned up annotation.csv file. In order to fully walk through the provenance of this cleaned file, you'll need to know that the LUNA dataset is derived from another dataset called the Lung Image Database

Consortium image collection (LIDC-IDRI)[9] and includes detailed annotation information from multiple radiologists. We've already done the legwork to get the original LIDC annotations, pull out the nodules, dedupe them, and save them to the file /data/part2/luna/annotations_with_malignancy.csv.

With that file, we can update our getCandidateInfoList function to pull our nodules from our new annotations file. First, we loop over the new annotations for the actual nodules. Using the CSV reader,[10] we need to convert the data to the appropriate types before we stick them into our CandidateInfoTuple data structure.

Listing 13.9   dsets.py:43, def getCandidateInfoList

```
candidateInfo_list = []
with open('data/part2/luna/annotations_with_malignancy.csv', "r") as f:
  for row in list(csv.reader(f))[1:]:                    ◄─────   For each line in
    series_uid = row[0]                                           the annotations
    annotationCenter_xyz = tuple([float(x) for x in row[1:4]])    file that
    annotationDiameter_mm = float(row[4])                         represents one
    isMal_bool = {'False': False, 'True': True}[row[5]]           nodule, ...

    candidateInfo_list.append(    ◄─────   ... we add a record to our list.
      CandidateInfoTuple(
        True,                     ◄─────   isNodule_bool
        True,               ◄──
        isMal_bool,              │  hasAnnotation_bool
        annotationDiameter_mm,
        series_uid,
        annotationCenter_xyz,
      )
    )
```

Similarly, we loop over candidates from candidates.csv as before, but this time we only use the non-nodules. As these are not nodules, the nodule-specific information will just be filled with False and 0.

Listing 13.10   dsets.py:62, def getCandidateInfoList

```
with open('data/part2/luna/candidates.csv', "r") as f:   │  For each line in the
  for row in list(csv.reader(f))[1:]:        ◄───────────┘  candidates file ...
    series_uid = row[0]
    # ... line 72                             │  ... but only the non-nodules (we
    if not isNodule_bool:           ◄─────────┘  have the others from earlier) ...
      candidateInfo_list.append(    ◄──
        CandidateInfoTuple(              │  ... we add a candidate record.
```

---

[9] Samuel G. Armato 3rd et al., 2011, "The Lung Image Database Consortium (LIDC) and Image Database Resource Initiative (IDRI): A Completed Reference Database of Lung Nodules on CT Scans," *Medical Physics* 38, no. 2 (2011): 915-31, https://pubmed.ncbi.nlm.nih.gov/21452728/. See also Bruce Vendt, LIDC-IDRI, Cancer Imaging Archive, http://mng.bz/mBO4.

[10] If you do this a lot, the pandas library that just released 1.0 in 2020 is a great tool to make this faster. We stick with the CSV reader included in the standard Python distribution here.

```
              False,      ⟵——— isNodule_bool
              False,    ⟵⎤
isMal_bool ——⟶ False,     ⎦ hasAnnotation_bool
              0.0,
              series_uid,
              candidateCenter_xyz,
          )
      )
```

Other than the addition of the hasAnnotation_bool and isMal_bool flags (which we won't use in this chapter), the new annotations will slot in and be usable just like the old ones.

> **NOTE** You might be wondering why we haven't discussed the LIDC before now. As it turns out, the LIDC has a large amount of tooling that's already been constructed around the underlying dataset, which is specific to the LIDC. You could even get ready-made masks from PyLIDC. That tooling presents a somewhat unrealistic picture of what sort of support a given dataset might have, since the LIDC is anomalously well supported. What we've done with the LUNA data is much more typical and provides for better learning, since we're spending our time manipulating the raw data rather than learning an API that someone else cooked up.

13.5.4 *Implementing Luna2dSegmentationDataset*

Compared to previous chapters, we are going to take a different approach to the training and validation split in this chapter. We will have two classes: one acting as a general base class suitable for validation data, and one subclassing the base for the training set, with randomization and a cropped sample.

While this approach is somewhat more complicated in some ways (the classes aren't perfectly encapsulated, for example), it actually simplifies the logic of selecting randomized training samples and the like. It also becomes extremely clear which code paths impact both training and validation, and which are isolated to training only. Without this, we found that some of the logic can become nested or intertwined in ways that make it hard to follow. This is important because our training data will look significantly different from our validation data!

> **NOTE** Other class arrangements are also viable; we considered having two entirely separate Dataset subclasses, for example. Standard software engineering design principles apply, so try to keep your structure relatively simple, and try to not copy and paste code, but don't invent complicated frameworks to prevent having to duplicate three lines of code.

The data that we produce will be two-dimensional CT slices with multiple channels. The extra channels will hold adjacent slices of CT. Recall figure 4.2, shown here as figure 13.12; we can see that each slice of CT scan can be thought of as a 2D grayscale image.

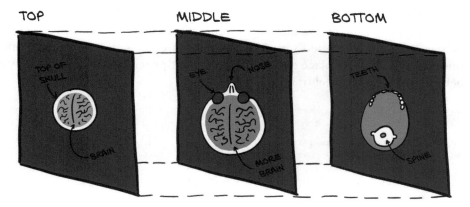

Figure 13.12 Each slice of a CT scan represents a different position in space.

How we combine those slices is up to us. For the input to our classification model, we treated those slices as a 3D array of data and used 3D convolutions to process each sample. For our segmentation model, we are going to instead treat each slice as a single channel, and produce a multichannel 2D image. Doing so will mean that we are treating each slice of CT scan as if it was a color channel of an RGB image, like we saw in figure 4.1, repeated here as figure 13.13. Each input slice of the CT will get stacked together and consumed just like any other 2D image. The channels of our stacked CT image won't correspond to colors, but nothing about 2D convolutions requires the input channels to be colors, so it works out fine.

For validation, we'll need to produce one sample per slice of CT that has an entry in the positive mask, for each validation CT we have. Since different CT scans can have different slice counts,[11] we're going to introduce a new function that caches the

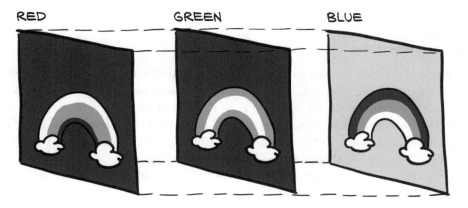

Figure 13.13 Each channel of a photographic image represents a different color.

---

[11] Most CT scanners produce 512 × 512 slices, and we're not going to worry about the ones that do something different.

size of each CT scan and its positive mask to disk. We need this to be able to quickly construct the full size of a validation set without having to load each CT at `Dataset` initialization. We'll continue to use the same caching decorator as before. Populating this data will also take place during the prepcache.py script, which we must run once before we start any model training.

Listing 13.11 dsets.py:220

```
@raw_cache.memoize(typed=True)
def getCtSampleSize(series_uid):
  ct = Ct(series_uid)
  return int(ct.hu_a.shape[0]), ct.positive_indexes
```

The majority of the `Luna2dSegmentationDataset.__init__` method is similar to what we've seen before. We have a new `contextSlices_count` parameter, as well as an `augmentation_dict` similar to what we introduced in chapter 12.

The handling for the flag indicating whether this is meant to be a training or validation set needs to change somewhat. Since we're no longer training on individual nodules, we will have to partition the list of series, taken as a whole, into training and validation sets. This means an entire CT scan, along with all nodule candidates it contains, will be in either the training set or the validation set.

Listing 13.12 dsets.py:242, .__init__

```
if isValSet_bool:
  assert val_stride > 0, val_stride
  self.series_list = self.series_list[::val_stride]    ◁─┐  Starting with a series list
  assert self.series_list                                │  containing all our series, we
elif val_stride > 0:                                     │  keep only every val_stride-th
  del self.series_list[::val_stride]                     │  element, starting with 0.
  assert self.series_list
```
If we are training, we delete every
val_stride-th element instead.

Speaking of validation, we're going to have two different modes we can validate our training with. First, when `fullCt_bool` is `True`, we will use every slice in the CT for our dataset. This will be useful when we're evaluating end-to-end performance, since we need to pretend that we're starting off with no prior information about the CT. We'll use the second mode for validation during training, which is when we're limiting ourselves to only the CT slices that have a positive mask present.

As we now only want certain CT series to be considered, we loop over the series UIDs we want and get the total number of slices and the list of interesting ones.

Listing 13.13 dsets.py:250, .__init__

```
self.sample_list = []
for series_uid in self.series_list:
```

```
index_count, positive_indexes = getCtSampleSize(series_uid)

if self.fullCt_bool:
    self.sample_list += [(series_uid, slice_ndx)
            for slice_ndx in range(index_count)]
else:
    self.sample_list += [(series_uid, slice_ndx)
            for slice_ndx in positive_indexes]
```

⟵ **Here we extend sample_list with every slice of the CT by using range ...**

⟵ **... while here we take only the interesting slices.**

Doing it this way will keep our validation relatively quick and ensure that we're getting complete stats for true positives and false negatives, but we're making the assumption that other slices will have false positive and true negative stats relatively similar to the ones we evaluate during validation.

Once we have the set of series_uid values we'll be using, we can filter our candidateInfo_list to contain only nodule candidates with a series_uid that is included in that set of series. Additionally, we'll create another list that has only the positive candidates so that during training, we can use those as our training samples.

Listing 13.14 dsets.py:261, .__init__

```
self.candidateInfo_list = getCandidateInfoList()          ⟵── This is cached.

series_set = set(self.series_list)                         ⟵─ Makes a set for faster lookup
self.candidateInfo_list = [cit for cit in self.candidateInfo_list
            if cit.series_uid in series_set]               ⟵
                                                           Filters out the candidates
                                                           from series not in our set
self.pos_list = [nt for nt in self.candidateInfo_list
        if nt.isNodule_bool]                               ⟵
                                                           For the data balancing yet to come,
                                                           we want a list of actual nodules.
```

Our __getitem__ implementation will also be a bit fancier by delegating a lot of the logic to a function that makes it easier to retrieve a specific sample. At the core of it, we'd like to retrieve our data in three different forms. First, we have the full slice of the CT, as specified by a series_uid and ct_ndx. Second, we have a cropped area around a nodule, which we'll use for training data (we'll explain in a bit why we're not using full slices). Finally, the DataLoader is going to ask for samples via an integer ndx, and the dataset will need to return the appropriate type based on whether it's training or validation.

The base class or subclass __getitem__ functions will convert from the integer ndx to either the full slice or training crop, as appropriate. As mentioned, our validation set's __getitem__ just calls another function to do the real work. Before that, it wraps the index around into the sample list in order to decouple the epoch size (given by the length of the dataset) from the actual number of samples.

Listing 13.15 dsets.py:281, .__getitem__

The modulo operation does the wrapping.

```
def __getitem__(self, ndx):
    series_uid, slice_ndx = self.sample_list[ndx % len(self.sample_list)]
    return self.getitem_fullSlice(series_uid, slice_ndx)
```

That was easy, but we still need to implement the interesting functionality from the getItem_fullSlice method.

Listing 13.16 dsets.py:285, .getitem_fullSlice

```
def getitem_fullSlice(self, series_uid, slice_ndx):
    ct = getCt(series_uid)                                      Preallocates the output
    ct_t = torch.zeros((self.contextSlices_count * 2 + 1, 512, 512))

    start_ndx = slice_ndx - self.contextSlices_count        When we reach
    end_ndx = slice_ndx + self.contextSlices_count + 1      beyond the bounds of
    for i, context_ndx in enumerate(range(start_ndx, end_ndx)):   the ct_a, we duplicate
        context_ndx = max(context_ndx, 0)                   the first or last slice.
        context_ndx = min(context_ndx, ct.hu_a.shape[0] - 1)
        ct_t[i] = torch.from_numpy(ct.hu_a[context_ndx].astype(np.float32))
    ct_t.clamp_(-1000, 1000)

    pos_t = torch.from_numpy(ct.positive_mask[slice_ndx]).unsqueeze(0)

    return ct_t, pos_t, ct.series_uid, slice_ndx
```

Splitting the functions like this means we can always ask a dataset for a specific slice (or cropped training chunk, which we'll see in the next section) indexed by series UID and position. Only for the integer indexing do we go through __getitem__, which then gets a sample from the (shuffled) list.

Aside from ct_t and pos_t, the rest of the tuple we return is all information that we include for debugging and display. We don't need any of it for training.

13.5.5 *Designing our training and validation data*

Before we get into the implementation for our training dataset, we need to explain why our training data will look different from our validation data. Instead of the full CT slices, we're going to train on 64 × 64 crops around our positive candidates (the actually-a-nodule candidates). These 64 × 64 patches will be taken randomly from a 96 × 96 crop centered on the nodule. We will also include three slices of context in both directions as additional "channels" to our 2D segmentation.

We're doing this to make training more stable, and to converge more quickly. The only reason we know to do this is because we tried to train on whole CT slices, but we found the results unsatisfactory. After some experimentation, we found that the 64 × 64 semirandom crop approach worked well, so we decided to use that for the book.

When you work on your own projects, you'll need to do that kind of experimentation for yourself!

We believe the whole-slice training was unstable essentially due to a class-balancing issue. Since each nodule is so small compared to the whole CT slice, we were right back in a needle-in-a-haystack situation similar to the one we got out of in the last chapter, where our positive samples were swamped by the negatives. In this case, we're talking about pixels rather than nodules, but the concept is the same. By training on crops, we're keeping the number of positive pixels the same and reducing the negative pixel count by several orders of magnitude.

Because our segmentation model is pixel-to-pixel and takes images of arbitrary size, we can get away with training and validating on samples with different dimensions. Validation uses the same convolutions with the same weights, just applied to a larger set of pixels (and so with fewer border pixels to fill in with edge data).

One caveat to this approach is that since our validation set contains orders of magnitude more negative pixels, our model will have a huge false positive rate during validation. There are many more opportunities for our segmentation model to get tricked! It doesn't help that we're going to be pushing for high recall as well. We'll discuss that more in section 13.6.3.

13.5.6 *Implementing TrainingLuna2dSegmentationDataset*

With that out of the way, let's get back to the code. Here's the training set's __getitem__. It looks just like the one for the validation set, except that we now sample from pos_list and call getItem_trainingCrop with the candidate info tuple, since we need the series and the exact center location, not just the slice.

Listing 13.17   dsets.py:320, .__getitem__

```
def __getitem__(self, ndx):
    candidateInfo_tup = self.pos_list[ndx % len(self.pos_list)]
    return self.getitem_trainingCrop(candidateInfo_tup)
```

To implement getItem_trainingCrop, we will use a getCtRawCandidate function similar to the one we used during classification training. Here, we're passing in a different size crop, but the function is unchanged except for now returning an additional array with a crop of the ct.positive_mask as well.

We limit our pos_a to the center slice that we're actually segmenting, and then construct our 64 × 64 random crops of the 96 × 96 we were given by getCtRawCandidate. Once we have those, we return a tuple with the same items as our validation dataset.

Listing 13.18   dsets.py:324, .getitem_trainingCrop

```
def getitem_trainingCrop(self, candidateInfo_tup):
    ct_a, pos_a, center_irc = getCtRawCandidate(      ⟵┐ Gets the candidate with a
        candidateInfo_tup.series_uid,                  │ bit of extra surrounding
        candidateInfo_tup.center_xyz,
```

```
    (7, 96, 96),
)
pos_a = pos_a[3:4]
row_offset = random.randrange(0,32)
col_offset = random.randrange(0,32)
ct_t = torch.from_numpy(ct_a[:, row_offset:row_offset+64,
                col_offset:col_offset+64]).to(torch.float32)
pos_t = torch.from_numpy(pos_a[:, row_offset:row_offset+64,
                col_offset:col_offset+64]).to(torch.long)

slice_ndx = center_irc.index

return ct_t, pos_t, candidateInfo_tup.series_uid, slice_ndx
```

> **Taking a one-element slice keeps the third dimension, which will be the (single) output channel.**

> **With two random numbers between 0 and 31, we crop both CT and mask.**

You might have noticed that data augmentation is missing from our dataset implementation. We're going to handle that a little differently this time around: we'll augment our data on the GPU.

13.5.7 Augmenting on the GPU

One of the key concerns when it comes to training a deep learning model is avoiding bottlenecks in your training pipeline. Well, that's not quite true—there will *always* be a bottleneck.[12] The trick is to make sure the bottleneck is at the resource that's the most expensive or difficult to upgrade, and that your usage of that resource isn't wasteful.

Some common places to see bottlenecks are as follows:

- In the data-loading pipeline, either in raw I/O or in decompressing data once it's in RAM. We addressed this with our diskcache library usage.
- In CPU preprocessing of the loaded data. This is often data normalization or augmentation.
- In the training loop on the GPU. This is typically where we want our bottleneck to be, since total deep learning system costs for GPUs are usually higher than for storage or CPU.
- Less commonly, the bottleneck can sometimes be the *memory bandwidth* between CPU and GPU. This implies that the GPU isn't doing much work compared to the data size that's being sent in.

Since GPUs can be 50 times faster than CPUs when working on tasks that fit GPUs well, it often makes sense to move those tasks to the GPU from the CPU in cases where CPU usage is becoming high. This is especially true if the data gets expanded during this processing; by moving the smaller input to the GPU first, the expanded data is kept local to the GPU, and less memory bandwidth is used.

In our case, we're going to move data augmentation to the GPU. This will keep our CPU usage light, and the GPU will easily be able to accommodate the additional workload. Far better to have the GPU busy with a small bit of extra work than idle waiting for the CPU to struggle through the augmentation process.

---

[12] Otherwise, your model would train instantly!

We'll accomplish this by using a second model, similar to all the other subclasses of nn.Module we've seen so far in this book. The main difference is that we're not interested in backpropagating gradients through the model, and the forward method will be doing decidedly different things. There will be some slight modifications to the actual augmentation routines since we're working with 2D data for this chapter, but otherwise, the augmentation will be very similar to what we saw in chapter 12. The model will consume tensors and produce different tensors, just like the other models we've implemented.

Our model's __init__ takes the same data augmentation arguments—flip, offset, and so on—that we used in the last chapter, and assigns them to self.

Listing 13.19 model.py:56, class SegmentationAugmentation

```
class SegmentationAugmentation(nn.Module):
  def __init__(
      self, flip=None, offset=None, scale=None, rotate=None, noise=None
  ):
    super().__init__()

    self.flip = flip
    self.offset = offset
    # ... line 64
```

Our augmentation forward method takes the input and the label, and calls out to build the transform_t tensor that will then drive our affine_grid and grid_sample calls. Those calls should feel very familiar from chapter 12.

Listing 13.20 model.py:68, SegmentationAugmentation.forward

```
def forward(self, input_g, label_g):
  transform_t = self._build2dTransformMatrix()
  transform_t = transform_t.expand(input_g.shape[0], -1, -1)
  transform_t = transform_t.to(input_g.device, torch.float32)
  affine_t = F.affine_grid(transform_t[:,:2],
      input_g.size(), align_corners=False)

  augmented_input_g = F.grid_sample(input_g,
      affine_t, padding_mode='border',
      align_corners=False)
  augmented_label_g = F.grid_sample(label_g.to(torch.float32),
      affine_t, padding_mode='border',
      align_corners=False)

  if self.noise:
    noise_t = torch.randn_like(augmented_input_g)
    noise_t *= self.noise

    augmented_input_g += noise_t

  return augmented_input_g, augmented_label_g > 0.5
```

Note that we're augmenting 2D data.

The first dimension of the transformation is the batch, but we only want the first two rows of the 3 × 3 matrices per batch item.

We need the same transformation applied to CT and mask, so we use the same grid. Because grid_sample only works with floats, we convert here.

Just before returning, we convert the mask back to Booleans by comparing to 0.5. The interpolation that grid_sample results in fractional values.

Now that we know what we need to do with `transform_t` to get our data out, let's take a look at the `_build2dTransformMatrix` function that actually creates the transformation matrix we use.

Listing 13.21   model.py:90, ._build2dTransformMatrix

```
def _build2dTransformMatrix(self):          Creates a 3 × 3 matrix, but we
  transform_t = torch.eye(3)         ◁─────  will drop the last row later.

  for i in range(2):              ◁────┐ Again, we're augmenting
    if self.flip:                      │ 2D data here.
      if random.random() > 0.5:
        transform_t[i,i] *= -1
# ... line 108
  if self.rotate:
    angle_rad = random.random() * math.pi * 2  ◁─┐ Takes a random angle in radians,
    s = math.sin(angle_rad)                       │ so in the range 0 .. 2{pi}
    c = math.cos(angle_rad)

    rotation_t = torch.tensor([  ◁─┐ Rotation matrix for the 2D rotation by the
      [c, -s, 0],                   │ random angle in the first two dimensions
      [s, c, 0],
      [0, 0, 1]])

    transform_t @= rotation_t    ◁─┐ Applies the rotation to the transformation matrix
                                    │ using the Python matrix multiplication operator
  return transform_t
```

Other than the slight differences to deal with 2D data, our GPU augmentation code looks very similar to our CPU augmentation code. That's great, because it means we're able to write code that doesn't have to care very much about where it runs. The primary difference isn't in the core implementation: it's how we wrapped that implementation into a `nn.Module` subclass. While we've been thinking about models as exclusively a deep learning tool, this shows us that with PyTorch, tensors can be used quite a bit more generally. Keep this in mind when you start your next project—the range of things you can accomplish with a GPU-accelerated tensor is pretty large!

13.6   *Updating the training script for segmentation*

We have a model. We have data. We need to use them, and you won't be surprised when step 2C of figure 13.14 suggests we should train our new model with the new data.

To be more precise about the process of training our model, we will update three things affecting the outcome from the training code we got in chapter 12:

- We need to instantiate the new model (unsurprisingly).
- We will introduce a new loss: the Dice loss.
- We will also look at an optimizer other than the venerable SGD we've used so far. We'll stick with a popular one and use Adam.

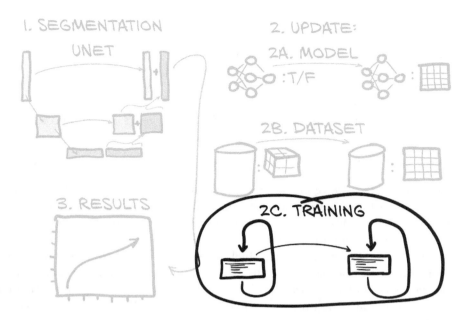

Figure 13.14 The outline of this chapter, with a focus on the changes needed for our training loop

But we will also step up our bookkeeping, by

- Logging images for visual inspection of the segmentation to TensorBoard
- Performing more metrics logging in TensorBoard
- Saving our best model based on the validation

Overall, the training script p2ch13/training.py is even more similar to what we used for classification training in chapter 12 than the adapted code we've seen so far. Any significant changes will be covered here in the text, but be aware that some of the minor tweaks are skipped. For the full story, check the source.

13.6.1 *Initializing our segmentation and augmentation models*

Our `initModel` method is very unsurprising. We are using the `UNetWrapper` class and giving it our configuration parameters—which we will look at in detail shortly. Also, we now have a second model for augmentation. Just like before, we can move the model to the GPU if desired and possibly set up multi-GPU training using `DataParallel`. We skip these administrative tasks here.

Listing 13.22 training.py:133, `.initModel`

```
def initModel(self):
  segmentation_model = UNetWrapper(
    in_channels=7,
```

```
    n_classes=1,
    depth=3,
    wf=4,
    padding=True,
    batch_norm=True,
    up_mode='upconv',
)

augmentation_model = SegmentationAugmentation(**self.augmentation_dict)

# ... line 154
return segmentation_model, augmentation_model
```

For input into UNet, we've got seven input channels: 3 + 3 context slices, and 1 slice that is the focus for what we're actually segmenting. We have one output class indicating whether this voxel is part of a nodule. The `depth` parameter controls how deep the U goes; each downsampling operation adds 1 to the depth. Using `wf=5` means the first layer will have `2**wf == 32` filters, which doubles with each downsampling. We want the convolutions to be padded so that we get an output image the same size as our input. We also want batch normalization inside the network after each activation function, and our upsampling function should be an upconvolution layer, as implemented by `nn.ConvTranspose2d` (see util/unet.py, line 123).

13.6.2 *Using the Adam optimizer*

The Adam optimizer (https://arxiv.org/abs/1412.6980) is an alternative to using SGD when training our models. Adam maintains a separate learning rate for each parameter and automatically updates that learning rate as training progresses. Due to these automatic updates, we typically won't need to specify a non-default learning rate when using Adam, since it will quickly determine a reasonable learning rate by itself.

Here's how we instantiate Adam in code.

> **Listing 13.23   training.py:156, .initOptimizer**

```
def initOptimizer(self):
  return Adam(self.segmentation_model.parameters())
```

It's generally accepted that Adam is a reasonable optimizer to start most projects with.[13] There is often a configuration of stochastic gradient descent with Nesterov momentum that will outperform Adam, but finding the correct hyperparameters to use when initializing SGD for a given project can be difficult and time consuming.

There have been a large number of variations on Adam—AdaMax, RAdam, Ranger, and so on—that each have strengths and weaknesses. Delving into the details of those is outside the scope of this book, but we think that it's important to know that those alternatives exist. We'll use Adam in chapter 13.

---

[13] See http://cs231n.github.io/neural-networks-3.

13.6.3 *Dice loss*

The Sørensen-Dice coefficient (https://en.wikipedia.org/wiki/S%C3%B8rensen%E2 %80%93Dice_coefficient), also known as the *Dice loss*, is a common loss metric for segmentation tasks. One advantage of using Dice loss over a per-pixel cross-entropy loss is that Dice handles the case where only a small portion of the overall image is flagged as positive. As we recall from chapter 11 in section 11.10, unbalanced training data can be problematic when using cross-entropy loss. That's exactly the situation we have here— most of a CT scan isn't a nodule. Luckily, with Dice, that won't pose as much of a problem.

The Sørensen-Dice coefficient is based on the ratio of correctly segmented pixels to the sum of the predicted and actual pixels. Those ratios are laid out in figure 13.15. On the left, we see an illustration of the Dice score. It is twice the joint area (*true positives*, striped) divided by the sum of the entire predicted area and the entire ground-truth marked area (the overlap being counted twice). On the right are two prototypical examples of high agreement/high Dice score and low agreement/low Dice score.

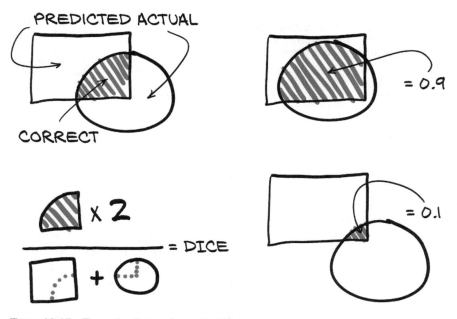

Figure 13.15 The ratios that make up the Dice score

That might sound familiar; it's the same ratio that we saw in chapter 12. We're basically going to be using a per-pixel F1 score!

> **NOTE** This is a per-pixel F1 score *where the "population" is one image's pixels.* Since the population is entirely contained within one training sample, we can use it for training directly. In the classification case, the F1 score is not calculable over a single minibatch, and, hence, we cannot use it for training directly.

Since our `label_g` is effectively a Boolean mask, we can multiply it with our predictions to get our true positives. Note that we aren't treating `prediction_devtensor` as a Boolean here. A loss defined with it wouldn't be differentiable. Instead, we're replacing the number of true positives with the sum of the predicted values for the pixels where the ground truth is 1. This converges to the same thing as the predicted values approach 1, but sometimes the predicted values will be uncertain predictions in the 0.4 to 0.6 range. Those undecided values will contribute roughly the same amount to our gradient updates, no matter which side of 0.5 they happen to fall on. A Dice coefficient utilizing continuous predictions is sometimes referred to as *soft Dice*.

There's one tiny complication. Since we're wanting a loss to minimize, we're going to take our ratio and subtract it from 1. Doing so will invert the slope of our loss function so that in the high-overlap case, our loss is low; and in the low-overlap case, it's high. Here's what that looks like in code.

Listing 13.24   training.py:315, `.diceLoss`

Sums over everything except the batch dimension to get the positively labeled, (softly) positively detected, and (softly) correct positives per batch item

The Dice ratio. To avoid problems when we accidentally have neither predictions nor labels, we add 1 to both numerator and denominator.

```
def diceLoss(self, prediction_g, label_g, epsilon=1):
    diceLabel_g = label_g.sum(dim=[1,2,3])
    dicePrediction_g = prediction_g.sum(dim=[1,2,3])
    diceCorrect_g = (prediction_g * label_g).sum(dim=[1,2,3])

    diceRatio_g = (2 * diceCorrect_g + epsilon) \
        / (dicePrediction_g + diceLabel_g + epsilon)

    return 1 - diceRatio_g
```

To make it a loss, we take 1 – Dice ratio, so lower loss is better.

We're going to update our `computeBatchLoss` function to call `self.diceLoss`. Twice. We'll compute the normal Dice loss for the training sample, as well as for only the pixels included in `label_g`. By multiplying our predictions (which, remember, are floating-point values) times the label (which are effectively Booleans), we'll get pseudo-predictions that got every negative pixel "exactly right" (since all the values for those pixels are multiplied by the false-is-zero values from `label_g`). The only pixels that will generate loss are the false negative pixels (everything that should have been predicted true, but wasn't). This will be helpful, since recall is incredibly important for our overall project; after all, we can't classify tumors properly if we don't detect them in the first place!

Listing 13.25   training.py:282, `.computeBatchLoss`

```
def computeBatchLoss(self, batch_ndx, batch_tup, batch_size, metrics_g,
            classificationThreshold=0.5):
    input_t, label_t, series_list, _slice_ndx_list = batch_tup

    input_g = input_t.to(self.device, non_blocking=True)
    label_g = label_t.to(self.device, non_blocking=True)
```

Transfers to GPU

**Augments as needed if we are training.
In validation, we would skip this.**

```
if self.segmentation_model.training and self.augmentation_dict:
    input_g, label_g = self.augmentation_model(input_g, label_g)

prediction_g = self.segmentation_model(input_g)
```

Runs the segmentation model ...

```
diceLoss_g = self.diceLoss(prediction_g, label_g)
fnLoss_g = self.diceLoss(prediction_g * label_g, label_g)
# ... line 313
return diceLoss_g.mean() + fnLoss_g.mean() * 8
```

... and applies our fine Dice loss

Oops. What is this?

Let's talk a bit about what we're doing with our return statement of `diceLoss_g.mean() + fnLoss_g.mean() * 8`.

LOSS WEIGHTING

In chapter 12, we discussed shaping our dataset so that our classes were not wildly imbalanced. That helped training converge, since the positive and negative samples present in each batch were able to counteract the general pull of the other, and the model had to learn to discriminate between them to improve. We're approximating that same balance here by cropping down our training samples to include fewer non-positive pixels; but it's incredibly important to have high recall, and we need to make sure that as we train, we're providing a loss that reflects that fact.

We are going to have a *weighted loss* that favors one class over the other. What we're saying by multiplying `fnLoss_g` by 8 is that getting the entire population of our positive pixels right is eight times more important than getting the entire population of negative pixels right (nine, if you count the one in `diceLoss_g`). Since the area covered by the positive mask is much, much smaller than the whole 64×64 crop, that also means each individual positive pixel wields that much more influence when it comes to backpropagation.

We're willing to trade away many correctly predicted negative pixels in the general Dice loss to gain one correct pixel in the false negative loss. Since the general Dice loss is a strict superset of the false negative loss, the only correct pixels available to make that trade are ones that start as true negatives (all of the true positive pixels are already included in the false negative loss, so there's no trade to be made).

Since we're willing to sacrifice huge swaths of true negative pixels in the pursuit of having better recall, we should expect a large number of false positives in general.[14] We're doing this because recall is very, very important to our use case, and we'd much rather have some false positives than even a single false negative.

We should note that this approach only works when using the Adam optimizer. When using SGD, the push to overpredict would lead to every pixel coming back as positive. Adam's ability to fine-tune the learning rate means stressing the false negative loss doesn't become overpowering.

---

[14] Roxie would be proud!

COLLECTING METRICS

Since we're going to purposefully skew our numbers for better recall, let's see just how tilted things will be. In our classification computeBatchLoss, we compute various per-sample values that we used for metrics and the like. We also compute similar values for the overall segmentation results. These true positive and other metrics were previously computed in logMetrics, but due to the size of the result data (recall that each single CT slice from the validation set is a quarter-million pixels!), we need to compute these summary stats live in the computeBatchLoss function.

Listing 13.26 training.py:297, .computeBatchLoss

```
start_ndx = batch_ndx * batch_size
end_ndx = start_ndx + input_t.size(0)

with torch.no_grad():
    predictionBool_g = (prediction_g[:, 0:1]
            > classificationThreshold).to(torch.float32)

    tp = (    predictionBool_g *  label_g).sum(dim=[1,2,3])
    fn = ((1 - predictionBool_g) *  label_g).sum(dim=[1,2,3])
    fp = (    predictionBool_g * (~label_g)).sum(dim=[1,2,3])

    metrics_g[METRICS_LOSS_NDX, start_ndx:end_ndx] = diceLoss_g
    metrics_g[METRICS_TP_NDX, start_ndx:end_ndx] = tp
    metrics_g[METRICS_FN_NDX, start_ndx:end_ndx] = fn
    metrics_g[METRICS_FP_NDX, start_ndx:end_ndx] = fp
```

> **We threshold the prediction to get "hard" Dice but convert to float for the later multiplication.**

> **Computing true positives, false positives, and false negatives is similar to what we did when computing the Dice loss.**

> **We store our metrics to a large tensor for future reference. This is per batch item rather than averaged over the batch.**

As we discussed at the beginning of this section, we can compute our true positives and so on by multiplying our prediction (or its negation) and our label (or its negation) together. Since we're not as worried about the exact values of our predictions here (it doesn't really matter if we flag a pixel as 0.6 or 0.9—as long as it's over the threshold, we'll call it part of a nodule candidate), we are going to create predictionBool_g by comparing it to our threshold of 0.5.

13.6.4 Getting images into TensorBoard

One of the nice things about working on segmentation tasks is that the output is easily represented visually. Being able to eyeball our results can be a huge help for determining whether a model is progressing well (but perhaps needs more training), or if it has gone off the rails (so we need to stop wasting our time with further training). There are many ways we could package up our results as images, and many ways we could display them. TensorBoard has great support for this kind of data, and we already have TensorBoard SummaryWriter instances integrated with our training runs, so we're going to use TensorBoard. Let's see what it takes to get everything hooked up.

We'll add a logImages function to our main application class and call it with both our training and validation data loaders. While we are at it, we will make another change to our training loop: we're only going to perform validation and image logging on the first and then every fifth epoch. We do this by checking the epoch number against a new constant, `validation_cadence`.

When training, we're trying to balance a few things:

- Getting a rough idea of how our model is training without having to wait very long
- Spending the bulk of our GPU cycles training, rather than validating
- Making sure we are still performing well on the validation set

The first point means we need to have relatively short epochs so that we get to call `logMetrics` more often. The second, however, means we want to train for a relatively long time before calling `doValidation`. The third means we need to call `doValidation` regularly, rather than once at the end of training or something unworkable like that. By only doing validation on the first and then every fifth epoch, we can meet all of those goals. We get an early signal of training progress, spend the bulk of our time training, and have periodic check-ins with the validation set as we go along.

> **Listing 13.27   training.py:210, `SegmentationTrainingApp.main`**

```
def main(self):
    # ... line 217
    self.validation_cadence = 5
    for epoch_ndx in range(1, self.cli_args.epochs + 1):      <──┐  Our outermost loop,
        # ... line 228                                             over the epochs
        trnMetrics_t = self.doTraining(epoch_ndx, train_dl)
        self.logMetrics(epoch_ndx, 'trn', trnMetrics_t)      <──┘  Logs the (scalar)
                                                                    metrics from training
        if epoch_ndx == 1 or epoch_ndx % self.validation_cadence == 0:   <──┐  after each epoch
            # ... line 239
            self.logImages(epoch_ndx, 'trn', train_dl)
            self.logImages(epoch_ndx, 'val', val_dl)             Only every validation
                                                                 cadence-th interval ...
```

Trains for one epoch → `trnMetrics_t = self.doTraining(epoch_ndx, train_dl)`

... **we validate the model and log images.**

There isn't a single right way to structure our image logging. We are going to grab a handful of CTs from both the training and validation sets. For each CT, we will select 6 evenly spaced slices, end to end, and show both the ground truth and our model's output. We chose 6 slices only because TensorBoard will show 12 images at a time, and we can arrange the browser window to have a row of label images over the model output. Arranging things this way makes it easy to visually compare the two, as we can see in figure 13.16.

Also note the small slider-dot on the `prediction` images. That slider will allow us to view previous versions of the images with the same label (such as val/0_prediction_3, but at an earlier epoch). Being able to see how our segmentation output changes over time can be useful when we're trying to debug something or make tweaks to achieve a specific result. As training progresses, TensorBoard will limit the number of images

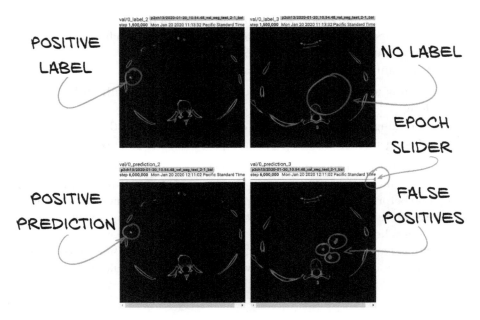

Figure 13.16   Top row: label data for training. Bottom row: output from the segmentation

viewable from the slider to 10, probably to avoid overwhelming the browser with a huge number of images.

The code that produces this output starts by getting 12 series from the pertinent data loader and 6 images from each series.

Listing 13.28   training.py:326, .logImages

```
def logImages(self, epoch_ndx, mode_str, dl):
    self.segmentation_model.eval()              ◁── Sets the model to eval

    images = sorted(dl.dataset.series_list)[:12]  ◁┐ Takes (the same) 12 CTs by
    for series_ndx, series_uid in enumerate(images):  │ bypassing the data loader and using
      ct = getCt(series_uid)                          │ the dataset directly. The series list
                                                      │ might be shuffled, so we sort.
      for slice_ndx in range(6):
        ct_ndx = slice_ndx * (ct.hu_a.shape[0] - 1) // 5     ◁──┐
        sample_tup = dl.dataset.getitem_fullSlice(series_uid, ct_ndx)  │

        ct_t, label_t, series_uid, ct_ndx = sample_tup    Selects six equidistant
                                                          slices throughout the CT
```

After that, we feed `ct_t` it into the model. This looks very much like what we see in `computeBatchLoss`; see p2ch13/training.py for details if desired.

Once we have `prediction_a`, we need to build an `image_a` that will hold RGB values to display. We're using `np.float32` values, which need to be in a range from 0 to 1.

Our approach will cheat a little by adding together various images and masks to get data in the range 0 to 2, and then multiplying the entire array by 0.5 to get it back into the right range.

Listing 13.29 training.py:346, `.logImages`

**CT intensity is assigned to all RGB channels
to provide a grayscale base image.**

```
ct_t[:-1,:,:] /= 2000
ct_t[:-1,:,:] += 0.5

ctSlice_a = ct_t[dl.dataset.contextSlices_count].numpy()

image_a = np.zeros((512, 512, 3), dtype=np.float32)       False positives are flagged as
image_a[:,:,:] = ctSlice_a.reshape((512,512,1))           red and overlaid on the image.
image_a[:,:,0] += prediction_a & (1 - label_a)
image_a[:,:,0] += (1 - prediction_a) & label_a            False negatives
image_a[:,:,1] += ((1 - prediction_a) & label_a) * 0.5    are orange.

image_a[:,:,1] += prediction_a & label_a                  True positives
image_a *= 0.5                                            are green.
image_a.clip(0, 1, image_a)
```

Our goal is to have a grayscale CT at half intensity, overlaid with predicted-nodule (or, more correctly, nodule-candidate) pixels in various colors. We're going to use red for all pixels that are incorrect (false positives *and* false negatives). This will mostly be false positives, which we don't care about too much (since we're focused on recall). `1 - label_a` inverts the label, and that multiplied by the `prediction_a` gives us only the predicted pixels that aren't in a candidate nodule. False negatives get a half-strength mask added to green, which means they will show up as orange (1.0 red and 0.5 green renders as orange in RGB). Every correctly predicted pixel inside a nodule is set to green; since we got those pixels right, no red will be added, and so they will render as pure green.

After that, we renormalize our data to the 0...1 range and clamp it (in case we start displaying augmented data here, which would cause speckles when the noise was outside our expected CT range). All that remains is to save the data to TensorBoard.

Listing 13.30 training.py:361, `.logImages`

```
writer = getattr(self, mode_str + '_writer')
writer.add_image(
  f'{mode_str}/{series_ndx}_prediction_{slice_ndx}',
  image_a,
  self.totalTrainingSamples_count,
  dataformats='HWC',
)
```

This looks very similar to the `writer.add_scalar` calls we've seen before. The `data-formats='HWC'` argument tells TensorBoard that the order of axes in our image has our RGB channels as the third axis. Recall that our network layers often specify outputs that are $B \times C \times H \times W$, and we could put that data directly into TensorBoard as well if we specified `'CHW'`.

We also want to save the ground truth that we're using to train, which will form the top row of our TensorBoard CT slices we saw earlier in figure 13.16. The code for that is similar enough to what we just saw that we'll skip it. Again, check p2ch13/training.py if you want the details.

13.6.5 *Updating our metrics logging*

To give us an idea how we are doing, we compute per-epoch metrics: in particular, true positives, false negatives, and false positives. This is what the following listing does. Nothing here will be particularly surprising.

> **Listing 13.31 training.py:400, .logMetrics**

```
sum_a = metrics_a.sum(axis=1)
allLabel_count = sum_a[METRICS_TP_NDX] + sum_a[METRICS_FN_NDX]
metrics_dict['percent_all/tp'] = \
    sum_a[METRICS_TP_NDX] / (allLabel_count or 1) * 100
metrics_dict['percent_all/fn'] = \
    sum_a[METRICS_FN_NDX] / (allLabel_count or 1) * 100
metrics_dict['percent_all/fp'] = \
    sum_a[METRICS_FP_NDX] / (allLabel_count or 1) * 100    ◁──┐
```

Can be larger than 100% since we're comparing to the total number of pixels labeled as candidate nodules, which is a tiny fraction of each image

We are going to start scoring our models as a way to determine whether a particular training run is the best we've seen so far. In chapter 12, we said we'd be using the F1 score for our model ranking, but our goals are different here. We need to make sure our recall is as high as possible, since we can't classify a potential nodule if we don't find it in the first place!

We will use our recall to determine the "best" model. As long as the F1 score is reasonable for that epoch,[15] we just want to get recall as high as possible. Screening out any false positives will be the responsibility of the classification model.

> **Listing 13.32 training.py:393, .logMetrics**

```
def logMetrics(self, epoch_ndx, mode_str, metrics_t):
  # ... line 453
  score = metrics_dict['pr/recall']

  return score
```

---

[15] And yes, "reasonable" is a bit of a dodge. "Nonzero" is a good starting place, if you'd like something more specific.

When we add similar code to our classification training loop in the next chapter, we'll use the F1 score.

Back in the main training loop, we'll keep track of the best_score we've seen so far in this training run. When we save our model, we'll include a flag that indicates whether this is the best score we've seen so far. Recall from section 13.6.4 that we're only calling the doValidation function for the first and then every fifth epochs. That means we're only going to check for a best score on those epochs. That shouldn't be a problem, but it's something to keep in mind if you need to debug something happening on epoch 7. We do this checking just before we save the images.

Listing 13.33 training.py:210, SegmentationTrainingApp.main

```
def main(self):
  best_score = 0.0
  for epoch_ndx in range(1, self.cli_args.epochs + 1):      ◁——  The epoch-loop
    # if validation is wanted                                      we already saw
    # ... line 233
    valMetrics_t = self.doValidation(epoch_ndx, val_dl)
    score = self.logMetrics(epoch_ndx, 'val', valMetrics_t)       ◁—  Computes the
    best_score = max(score, best_score)                               score. As we saw
                                                                      earlier, we take
    self.saveModel('seg', epoch_ndx, score == best_score)           ◁—  the recall.
```

Now we only need to write saveModel. The third parameter
is whether we want to save it as best model, too.

Let's take a look at how we persist our model to disk.

13.6.6 Saving our model

PyTorch makes it pretty easy to save our model to disk. Under the hood, torch.save uses the standard Python pickle library, which means we could pass our model instance in directly, and it would save properly. That's not considered the ideal way to persist our model, however, since we lose some flexibility.

Instead, we will save only the *parameters* of our model. Doing this allows us to load those parameters into any model that expects parameters of the same shape, even if the class doesn't match the model those parameters were saved under. The save-parameters-only approach allows us to reuse and remix our models in more ways than saving the entire model.

We can get at our model's parameters using the model.state_dict() function.

Listing 13.34 training.py:480, .saveModel

```
def saveModel(self, type_str, epoch_ndx, isBest=False):
  # ... line 496
  model = self.segmentation_model
  if isinstance(model, torch.nn.DataParallel):      ◁——  Gets rid of the DataParallel
    model = model.module                                  wrapper, if it exists
```

```
    state = {
        'sys_argv': sys.argv,
        'time': str(datetime.datetime.now()),
        'model_state': model.state_dict(),        ◁─── The important part
        'model_name': type(model).__name__,
        'optimizer_state' : self.optimizer.state_dict(),   ◁─┐ Preserves momentum,
        'optimizer_name': type(self.optimizer).__name__,     │ and so on
        'epoch': epoch_ndx,
        'totalTrainingSamples_count': self.totalTrainingSamples_count,
    }
    torch.save(state, file_path)
```

We set `file_path` to something like `data-unversioned/part2/models/p2ch13/`
`seg_2019-07-10_02.17.22_ch12.50000.state`. The `.50000.` part is the number of
training samples we've presented to the model so far, while the other parts of the path
are obvious.

> **TIP** By saving the optimizer state as well, we could resume training seamlessly.
> While we don't provide an implementation of this, it could be useful if your access
> to computing resources is likely to be interrupted. Details on loading a model and
> optimizer to restart training can be found in the official documentation
> (https://pytorch.org/tutorials/beginner/saving_loading_models.html).

If the current model has the best score we've seen so far, we save a second copy of
`state` with a .best.state filename. This might get overwritten later by another, higher-
score version of the model. By focusing only on this best file, we can divorce customers of our trained model from the details of how each epoch of training went (assuming, of course, that our score metric is of high quality).

Listing 13.35   training.py:514, `.saveModel`

```
if isBest:
    best_path = os.path.join(
        'data-unversioned', 'part2', 'models',
        self.cli_args.tb_prefix,
        f'{type_str}_{self.time_str}_{self.cli_args.comment}.best.state')
    shutil.copyfile(file_path, best_path)

    log.info("Saved model params to {}".format(best_path))

with open(file_path, 'rb') as f:
    log.info("SHA1: " + hashlib.sha1(f.read()).hexdigest())
```

We also output the SHA1 of the model we just saved. Similar to `sys.argv` and the
timestamp we put into the state dictionary, this can help us debug exactly what model
we're working with if things become confused later (for example, if a file gets
renamed incorrectly).

We will update our classification training script in the next chapter with a similar routine for saving the classification model. In order to diagnose a CT, we'll need to have both models.

13.7 Results

Now that we've made all of our code changes, we've hit the last section in step 3 of figure 13.17. It's time to run `python -m p2ch13.training --epochs 20 --augmented final_seg`. Let's see what our results look like!

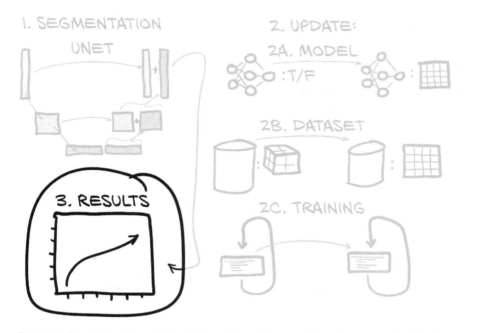

Figure 13.17 The outline of this chapter, with a focus on the results we see from training

Here is what our training metrics look like if we limit ourselves to the epochs we have validation metrics for (we'll be looking at those metrics next, so this will keep it an apples-to-apples comparison):

In these rows, we are particularly interested in the F1 score—it is trending up. Good!	**TPs are trending up, too. Great! And FNs and FPs are trending down.**

```
E1 trn       0.5235 loss, 0.2276 precision, 0.9381 recall, 0.3663 f1 score  ◁─
E1 trn_all   0.5235 loss,  93.8% tp, 6.2% fn,     318.4% fp                  ◁─
...
E5 trn       0.2537 loss, 0.5652 precision, 0.9377 recall, 0.7053 f1 score
E5 trn_all   0.2537 loss,  93.8% tp, 6.2% fn,      72.1% fp                  ◁─
...
E10 trn      0.2335 loss, 0.6011 precision, 0.9459 recall, 0.7351 f1 score
E10 trn_all  0.2335 loss,  94.6% tp, 5.4% fn,      62.8% fp                  ◁─
```

```
...
E15 trn       0.2226 loss, 0.6234 precision, 0.9536 recall, 0.7540 f1 score
E15 trn_all   0.2226 loss,   95.4% tp, <2>  4.6% fn,       57.6% fp
...
E20 trn       0.2149 loss, 0.6368 precision, 0.9584 recall, 0.7652 f1 score
E20 trn_all   0.2149 loss,   95.8% tp, <2>  4.2% fn,       54.7% fp
```

In these rows, we are particularly interested in the F1 score—it is trending up. Good!

TPs are trending up, too. Great! And FNs and FPs are trending down.

Overall, it looks pretty good. True positives and the F1 score are trending up, false positives and negatives are trending down. That's what we want to see! The validation metrics will tell us whether these results are legitimate. Keep in mind that since we're training on 64 × 64 crops, but validating on whole 512 × 512 CT slices, we are almost certainly going to have drastically different TP:FN:FP ratios. Let's see:

The highest TP rate (great). Note that the TP rate is the same as recall. But FPs are 4495%—that sounds like a lot.

```
E1 val        0.9441 loss, 0.0219 precision, 0.8131 recall, 0.0426 f1 score
E1 val_all    0.9441 loss,   81.3% tp,  18.7% fn,    3637.5% fp

E5 val        0.9009 loss, 0.0332 precision, 0.8397 recall, 0.0639 f1 score
E5 val_all    0.9009 loss,   84.0% tp,  16.0% fn,    2443.0% fp

E10 val       0.9518 loss, 0.0184 precision, 0.8423 recall, 0.0360 f1 score
E10 val_all   0.9518 loss,   84.2% tp,  15.8% fn,    4495.0% fp

E15 val       0.8100 loss, 0.0610 precision, 0.7792 recall, 0.1132 f1 score
E15 val_all   0.8100 loss,   77.9% tp,  22.1% fn,    1198.7% fp

E20 val       0.8602 loss, 0.0427 precision, 0.7691 recall, 0.0809 f1 score
E20 val_all   0.8602 loss,   76.9% tp,  23.1% fn,    1723.9% fp
```

Ouch—false positive rates over 4,000%? Yes, actually, that's expected. Our validation slice area is 2^{18} pixels (512 is 2^9), while our training crop is only 2^{12}. That means we're validating on a slice surface that's $2^6 = 64$ times bigger! Having a false positive count that's also 64 times bigger makes sense. Remember that our true positive rate won't have changed meaningfully, since it would all have been included in the 64 × 64 sample we trained on in the first place. This situation also results in very low precision, and, hence, a low F1 score. That's a natural result of how we've structured the training and validation, so it's not a cause for alarm.

What's problematic, however, is our recall (and, hence, our true positive rate). Our recall plateaus between epochs 5 and 10 and then starts to drop. It's pretty obvious that we begin overfitting very quickly, and we can see further evidence of that in figure 13.18—while the training recall keeps trending upward, the validation recall decreases after 3 million samples. This is how we identified overfitting in chapter 5, in particular figure 5.14.

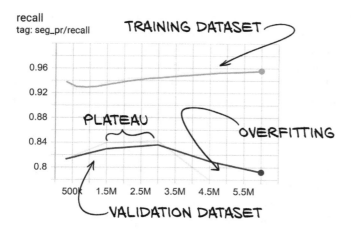

Figure 13.18 The validation set recall, showing signs of overfitting when recall goes down after epoch 10 (3 million samples)

NOTE Always keep in mind that TensorBoard will smooth your data lines by default. The lighter ghost line behind the solid color shows the raw values.

The U-Net architecture has a lot of capacity, and even with our reduced filter and depth counts, it's able to memorize our training set pretty quickly. One upside is that we don't end up needing to train the model for very long!

Recall is our top priority for segmentation, since we'll let issues with precision be handled downstream by the classification models. Reducing those false positives is the entire reason we have those classification models! This skewed situation does mean it is more difficult than we'd like to evaluate our model. We could instead use the F2 score, which weights recall more heavily (or F5, or F10 …), but we'd have to pick an N high enough to almost completely discount precision. We'll skip the intermediates and just score our model by recall, and use our human judgment to make sure a given training run isn't being pathological about it. Since we're training on the Dice loss, rather than directly on recall, it should work out.

This is one of the situations where we are cheating a little, because we (the authors) have already done the training and evaluation for chapter 14, and we know how all of this is going to turn out. There isn't any good way to look at this situation and *know* that the results we're seeing will work. Educated guesses are helpful, but they are no substitute for actually running experiments until something clicks.

As it stands, our results are good enough to use going forward, even if our metrics have some pretty extreme values. We're one step closer to finishing our end-to-end project!

13.8 Conclusion

In this chapter, we've discussed a new way of structuring models for pixel-to-pixel segmentation; introduced U-Net, an off-the-shelf, proven model architecture for those kinds of tasks; and adapted an implementation for our own use. We've also changed our dataset to provide data for our new model's training needs, including small crops for training and a limited set of slices for validation. Our training loop now has the ability to save images to TensorBoard, and we have moved augmentation from the dataset into a separate model that can operate on the GPU. Finally, we looked at our training results and discussed how even though the false positive rate (in particular) looks different from what we might hope, our results will be acceptable given our requirements for them from the larger project. In chapter 14, we will pull together the various models we've written into a cohesive, end-to-end whole.

13.9   Exercises

1   Implement the model-wrapper approach to augmentation (like what we used for segmentation training) for the classification model.

    a   What compromises did you have to make?

    b   What impact did the change have on training speed?

2   Change the segmentation `Dataset` implementation to have a three-way split for training, validation, and test sets.

    a   What fraction of the data did you use for the test set?

    b   Do performance on the test set and the validation set seem consistent with each other?

    c   How badly does training suffer with the smaller training set?

3   Make the model try to segment malignant versus benign in addition to is-nodule status.

    a   How does your metrics reporting need to change? Your image generation?

    b   What kind of results do you see? Is the segmentation good enough to skip the classification step?

4   Can you train the model on a combination of 64 × 64 crops and whole-CT slices?[16]

5   Can you find additional sources of data to use beyond just the LUNA (or LIDC) data?

13.10 Summary

- Segmentation flags individual pixels or voxels for membership in a class. This is in contrast to classification, which operates at the level of the entire image.

- U-Net was a breakthrough model architecture for segmentation tasks.

- Using segmentation followed by classification, we can implement detection with relatively modest data and computation requirements.

- Naive approaches to 3D segmentation can quickly use too much RAM for current-generation GPUs. Carefully limiting the scope of what is presented to the model can help limit RAM usage.

---

[16] Hint: Each sample tuple to be batched together must have the same shape for each corresponding tensor, but the next batch could have different samples with different shapes.

- It is possible to train a segmentation model on image crops while validating on whole-image slices. This flexibility can be important for class balancing.
- Loss weighting is an emphasis on the loss computed from certain classes or subsets of the training data, to encourage the model to focus on the desired results. It can complement class balancing and is a useful tool when trying to tweak model training performance.
- TensorBoard can display 2D images generated during training and will save a history of how those models changed over the training run. This can be used to visually track changes to model output as training progresses.
- Model parameters can be saved to disk and loaded back to reconstitute a model that was saved earlier. The exact model implementation can change as long as there is a 1:1 mapping between old and new parameters.

End-to-end
nodule analysis,
and where to go next

This chapter covers

- Connecting segmentation and classification models
- Fine-tuning a network for a new task
- Adding histograms and other metric types to TensorBoard
- Getting from overfitting to generalizing

Over the past several chapters, we have built a decent number of systems that are important components of our project. We started loading our data, built and improved classifiers for nodule candidates, trained segmentation models to find those candidates, handled the support infrastructure needed to train and evaluate those models, and started saving the results of our training to disk. Now it's time to unify the components we have into a cohesive whole, so that we may realize the full goal of our project: it's time to automatically detect cancer.

14.1 Towards the finish line

We can get a hint of the work remaining by looking at figure 14.1. In step 3 (grouping) we see that we still need to build the bridge between the segmentation model from chapter 13 and the classifier from chapter 12 that will tell us whether what the segmentation network found is, indeed, a nodule. On the right is step 5 (nodule analysis and diagnosis), the last step to the overall goal: seeing whether a nodule is cancer. This is another classification task; but to learn something in the process, we'll take a fresh angle at how to approach it by building on the nodule classifier we already have.

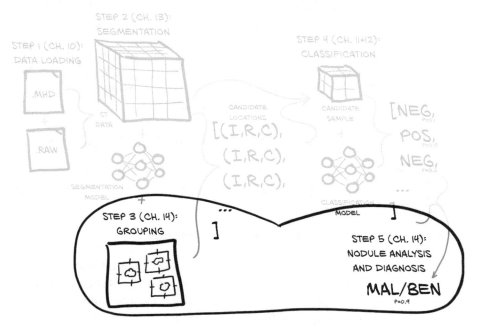

Figure 14.1 Our end-to-end lung cancer detection project, with a focus on this chapter's topics: steps 3 and 5, grouping and nodule analysis

Of course, these brief descriptions and their simplified depiction in figure 14.1 leave out a lot of detail. Let's zoom in a little with figure 14.2 and see what we've got left to accomplish.

As you can see, three important tasks remain. Each item in the following list corresponds to a major line item from figure 14.2:

1 *Generate nodule candidates.* This is step 3 in the overall project. Three tasks go into this step:

   a *Segmentation*—The segmentation model from chapter 13 will predict if a given pixel is of interest: if we suspect it is part of a nodule. This will be done per 2D slice, and every 2D result will be stacked to form a 3D array of voxels containing nodule candidate predictions.

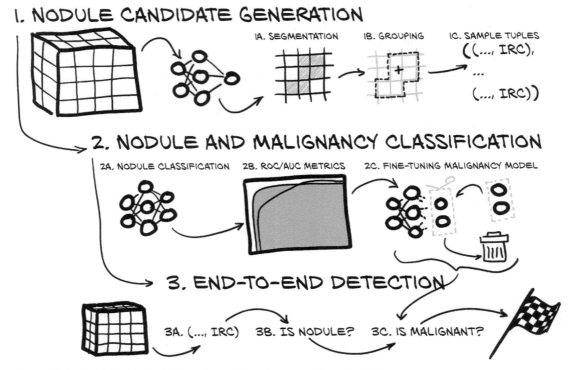

Figure 14.2   A detailed look at the work remaining for our end-to-end project

b   *Grouping*—We will group the voxels into nodule candidates by applying a threshold to the predictions, and then grouping connected regions of flagged voxels.

c   *Constructing sample tuples*—Each identified nodule candidate will be used to construct a sample tuple for classification. In particular, we need to produce the coordinates (index, row, column) of that nodule's center.

Once this is achieved, we will have an application that takes a raw CT scan from a patient and produces a list of detected nodule candidates. Producing such a list is the task in the LUNA challenge. If this project were to be used clinically (and we reemphasize that our project should not be!), this nodule list would be suitable for closer inspection by a doctor.

2   *Classify nodules and malignancy.* We'll take the nodule candidates we just produced and pass them to the candidate classification step we implemented in chapter 12, and then perform malignancy detection on the candidates flagged as nodules:

a   *Nodule classification*—Each nodule candidate from segmentation and grouping will be classified as either nodule or non-nodule. Doing so will allow us to screen out the many normal anatomical structures flagged by our segmentation process.

    b *ROC/AUC metrics*—Before we can start our last classification step, we'll define some new metrics for examining the performance of classification models, as well as establish a baseline metric against which to compare our malignancy classifiers.

    c *Fine-tuning the malignancy model*—Once our new metrics are in place, we will define a model specifically for classifying benign and malignant nodules, train it, and see how it performs. We will do the training by fine-tuning: a process that cuts out some of the weights of an existing model and replaces them with fresh values that we then adapt to our new task.

At that point we will be within arm's reach of our ultimate goal: to classify nodules into benign and malignant classes and then derive a diagnosis from the CT. Again, diagnosing lung cancer in the real world involves much more than staring at a CT scan, so our performing this diagnosis is more an experiment to see how far we can get using deep learning and imaging data alone.

  3 *End-to-end detection.* Finally, we will put all of this together to get to the finish line, combining the components into an end-to-end solution that can look at a CT and answer the question "Are there malignant nodules present in the lungs?"

    a *IRC*—We will segment our CT to get nodule candidate samples to classify.

    b *Determine the nodules*—We will perform nodule classification on the candidate to determine whether it should be fed into the malignancy classifier.

    c *Determine malignancy*—We will perform malignancy classification on the nodules that pass through the nodule classifier to determine whether the patient has cancer.

We've got a lot to do. To the finish line!

> **NOTE** As in the previous chapter, we will discuss the key concepts in detail in the text and leave out the code for repetitive, tedious, or obvious parts. Full details can be found in the book's code repository.

14.2　*Independence of the validation set*

We are in danger of making a subtle but critical mistake, which we need to discuss and avoid: we have a potential leak from the training set to the validation set! For each of the segmentation and classification models, we took care of splitting the data into a training set and an independent validation set by taking every tenth example for validation and the remainder for training.

    However, the split for the classification model was done on the list of nodules, and the split for the segmentation model was done on the list of CT scans. This means we likely have nodules from the segmentation validation set in the training set of the classification model and vice versa. We must avoid that! If left unfixed, this situation could lead to performance figures that would be artificially higher compared to what we would obtain on an independent dataset. This is called a *leak*, and it would invalidate our validation.

To rectify this potential data leak, we need to rework the classification dataset to also work at the CT scan level, just as we did for the segmentation task in chapter 13. Then we need to retrain the classification model with this new dataset. On the bright side, we didn't save our classification model earlier, so we would have to retrain anyway.

Your takeaway from this should be to keep an eye on the end-to-end process when defining the validation set. Probably the easiest way to do this (and the way it is done for most important datasets) is to make the validation split as explicit as possible—for example, by having two separate directories for training and validation—and then stick to this split for your entire project. When you need to redo the split (for example, when you need to add stratification of the dataset split by some criterion), you need to retrain all of your models with the newly split dataset.

So what we did for you was to take LunaDataset from chapters 10–12 and copy over getting the candidate list and splitting it into test and validation datasets from Luna2dSegmentationDataset in chapter 13. As this is very mechanical, and there is not much to learn from the details (you are a dataset pro by now), we won't show the code in detail.

We'll retrain our classification model by rerunning the training for the classifier:[1]

```
$ python3 -m p2ch14.training --num-workers=4 --epochs 100 nodule-nonnodule
```

After 100 epochs, we achieve about 95% accuracy for positive samples and 99% for negative ones. As the validation loss isn't seen to be trending upward again, we could train the model longer to see if things continued to improve.

After 90 epochs, we reach the maximal F1 score and have 99.2% validation accuracy, albeit only 92.8% on the actual nodules. We'll take this model, even though we might also try to trade a bit of overall accuracy for better accuracy on the malignant nodules (in between, the model got 95.4% accuracy on actual nodules for 98.9% total accuracy). This will be good enough for us, and we are ready to bridge the models.

14.3 Bridging CT segmentation and nodule candidate classification

Now that we have a segmentation model saved from chapter 13 and a classification model we just trained in the previous section, figure 14.3, steps 1a, 1b, and 1c show that we're ready to work on writing the code that will convert our segmentation output into sample tuples. We are doing the *grouping*: finding the dashed outline around the highlight of step 1b in figure 14.3. Our input is the *segmentation*: the voxels flagged by the segmentation model in 1a. We want to find 1c, the coordinates of the center of mass of each "lump" of flagged voxels: the index, row, and column of the 1b plus mark is what we need to provide in the list of sample tuples as output.

---

[1] You can also use the p2_run_everything notebook.

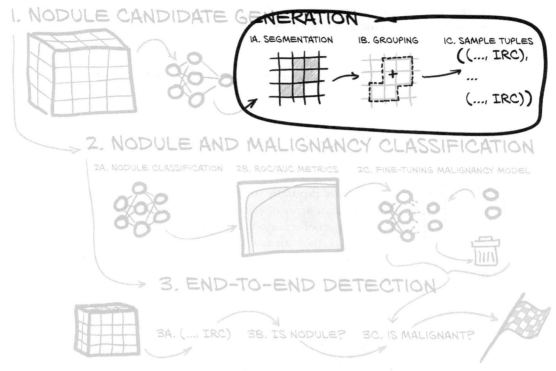

Figure 14.3   Our plan for this chapter, with a focus on grouping segmented voxels into nodule candidates

Running the models will naturally look very similar to how we handled them during training and validation (validation in particular). The difference here is the loop over the CTs. For each CT, we segment *every* slice and then take all the segmented output as the input to grouping. The output from grouping will be fed into a nodule classifier, and the nodules that survive that classification will be fed into a malignancy classifier.

This is accomplished by the following outer loop over the CTs, which for each CT segments, groups, classifies candidates, and provides the classifications for further processing.

Listing 14.1   nodule_analysis.py:324, `NoduleAnalysisApp.main`

Loops over the series UIDs

Gets the CT (step 1 in the big picture)

Runs our segmentation model on it (step 2)

```
for _, series_uid in series_iter:
    ct = getCt(series_uid)
    mask_a = self.segmentCt(ct, series_uid)

    candidateInfo_list = self.groupSegmentationOutput(
        series_uid, ct, mask_a)
    classifications_list = self.classifyCandidates(
        ct, candidateInfo_list)
```

Groups the flagged voxels in the output (step 3)

Runs our nodule classifier on them (step 4)

We'll break down the segmentCt, groupSegmentationOutput, and classifyCandidates methods in the following sections.

14.3.1 *Segmentation*

First up, we are going to perform segmentation on every slice of the entire CT scan. As we need to feed a given patient's CT slice by slice, we build a Dataset that loads a CT with a single series_uid and returns each slice, one per __getitem__ call.

> **NOTE** The segmentation step in particular can take quite a while when executed on the CPU. Even though we gloss over it here, the code will use the GPU if available.

Other than the more expansive input, the main difference is what we do with the output. Recall that the output is an array of per-pixel probabilities (that is, in the range 0...1) that the given pixel is part of a nodule. While iterating over the slices, we collect the slice-wise predictions in a mask array that has the same shape as our CT input. Afterward, we threshold the predictions to get a binary array. We will use a threshold of 0.5, but if we wanted to, we could experiment with thresholding to trade getting more true positives for an increase in false positives.

We also include a small cleanup step using the erosion operation from scipy.ndimage.morphology. It deletes one layer of boundary voxels and only keeps the inner ones—those for which all eight neighboring voxels in the axis direction are also flagged. This makes the flagged area smaller and causes very small components (smaller than $3 \times 3 \times 3$ voxels) to vanish. Put together with the loop over the data loader, which we instruct to feed us all slices from a single CT, we have the following.

Listing 14.2   nodule_analysis.py:384, .segmentCt

We do not need gradients here,
so we don't build the graph.

This array will hold our output: a float array of probability annotations.

We get a data loader that lets us loop over our CT in batches.

```
def segmentCt(self, ct, series_uid):
    with torch.no_grad():
        output_a = np.zeros_like(ct.hu_a, dtype=np.float32)
        seg_dl = self.initSegmentationDl(series_uid)    #
        for input_t, _, _, slice_ndx_list in seg_dl:

            input_g = input_t.to(self.device)
            prediction_g = self.seg_model(input_g)

            for i, slice_ndx in enumerate(slice_ndx_list):
                output_a[slice_ndx] = prediction_g[i].cpu().numpy()

        mask_a = output_a > 0.5
        mask_a = morphology.binary_erosion(mask_a, iterations=1)

    return mask_a
```

... we run the segmentation model ...

After moving the input to the GPU ...

... and copy each element to the output array.

Thresholds the probability outputs to get a binary output, and then applies binary erosion as cleanup

This was easy enough, but now we need to invent the grouping.

14.3.2 *Grouping voxels into nodule candidates*

We are going to use a simple connected-components algorithm for grouping our suspected nodule voxels into chunks to feed into classification. This grouping approach labels connected components, which we will accomplish using `scipy.ndimage` `.measurements.label`. The `label` function will take all nonzero pixels that share an edge with another nonzero pixel and mark them as belonging to the same group. Since our output from the segmentation model has mostly blobs of highly adjacent pixels, this approach matches our data well.

Listing 14.3   nodule_analysis.py:401

**Assigns each voxel the label
of the group it belongs to**

```
def groupSegmentationOutput(self, series_uid,  ct, clean_a):
    candidateLabel_a, candidate_count = measurements.label(clean_a)
    centerIrc_list = measurements.center_of_mass(
        ct.hu_a.clip(-1000, 1000) + 1001,
        labels=candidateLabel_a,
        index=np.arange(1, candidate_count+1),
    )
```

**Gets the center of mass for
each group as index, row,
column coordinates**

The output array `candidateLabel_a` is the same shape as `clean_a`, which we used for input, but it has 0 where the background voxels are, and increasing integer labels 1, 2, …, with one number for each of the connected blobs of voxels making up a nodule candidate. Note that the labels here are *not* the same as labels in a classification sense! These are just saying "This blob of voxels is blob 1, this blob over here is blob 2, and so on."

SciPy also sports a function to get the centers of mass of the nodule candidates: `scipy.ndimage.measurements.center_of_mass`. It takes an array with per-voxel densities, the integer labels from the `label` function we just called, and a list of which of those labels need to have a center calculated. To match the function's expectation that the mass is non-negative, we offset the (clipped) `ct.hu_a` by 1,001. Note that this leads to all flagged voxels carrying some weight, since we clamped the lowest air value to –1,000 HU in the native CT units.

Listing 14.4   nodule_analysis.py:409

```
candidateInfo_list = []
for i, center_irc in enumerate(centerIrc_list):
    center_xyz = irc2xyz(
        center_irc,
        ct.origin_xyz,
        ct.vxSize_xyz,
        ct.direction_a,
    )
```

**Converts the voxel
coordinates to real
patient coordinates**

```
candidateInfo_tup = \
  CandidateInfoTuple(False, False, False, 0.0, series_uid, center_xyz)  ◁──┐
candidateInfo_list.append(candidateInfo_tup)                                │
                                                    Builds our candidate info tuple and
return candidateInfo_list                           appends it to the list of detections │
```

As output, we get a list of three arrays (one each for the index, row, and column) the same length as our candidate_count. We can use this data to populate a list of candidateInfo_tup instances; we have grown attached to this little data structure, so we stick our results into the same kind of list we've been using since chapter 10. As we don't really have suitable data for the first four values (isNodule_bool, hasAnnotation_bool, isMal_bool, and diameter_mm), we insert placeholder values of a suitable type. We then convert our coordinates from voxels to physical coordinates in a loop, creating the list. It might seem a bit silly to move our coordinates away from our array-based index, row, and column, but all of the code that consumes candidateInfo_tup instances expects center_xyz, not center_irc. We'd get wildly wrong results if we tried to swap one for the other!

Yay—we've conquered step 3, getting nodule locations from the voxel-wise detections! We can now crop out the suspected nodules and feed them to our classifier to weed out some more false positives.

14.3.3 *Did we find a nodule? Classification to reduce false positives*

As we started part 2 of this book, we described the job of a radiologist looking through CT scans for signs of cancer thus:

> *Currently, the work of reviewing the data must be performed by highly trained specialists, requires painstaking attention to detail, and it is dominated by cases where no cancer exists.*

> *Doing that job well is akin to being placed in front of 100 haystacks and being told, "Determine which of these, if any, contain a needle."*

We've spent time and energy discussing the proverbial needles; let's discuss the hay for a moment by looking at figure 14.4. Our job, so to speak, is to fork away as much hay as we can from in front of our glassy-eyed radiologist, so that they can refocus their highly trained attention where it can do the most good.

Let's look at how much we are discarding at each step while we perform our end-to-end diagnosis. The arrows in figure 14.4 show the data as it flows from the raw CT voxels through our project to our final malignancy determination. Each arrow that ends with an X indicates a swath of data discarded by the previous step; the arrow pointing to the next step represents the data that survived the culling. Note that the numbers here are *very* approximate.

```
            origin_xyz=ct.origin_xyz,
            vxSize_xyz=ct.vxSize_xyz,
        )
        cls_tup = (prob_nodule, prob_mal, center_xyz, center_irc)
        classifications_list.append(cls_tup)
    return classifications_list
```

This is great! We can now threshold the output probabilities to get a list of things our model thinks are actual nodules. In a practical setting, we would probably want to output them for a radiologist to inspect. Again, we might want to adjust the threshold to err a bit on the safe side: that is, if our threshold was 0.3 instead of 0.5, we would present a few more candidates that turn out not to be nodules, while reducing the risk of missing actual nodules.

Listing 14.6 nodule_analysis.py:333, `NoduleAnalysisApp.main`

If we don't pass run_validation, we print individual information ...

```
┌──▷ if not self.cli_args.run_validation:
        print(f"found nodule candidates in {series_uid}:")
        for prob, prob_mal, center_xyz, center_irc in classifications_list:
            if prob > 0.5:                                        ◁──┐
                s = f"nodule prob {prob:.3f}, "                      │
                if self.malignancy_model:                           │
                    s += f"malignancy prob {prob_mal:.3f}, "        │
                s += f"center xyz {center_xyz}"                     │
                print(s)
```

... for all candidates found by the segmentation where the classifier assigned a nodule probability of 50% or more.

```
    if series_uid in candidateInfo_dict:        ◁──┐
        one_confusion = match_and_score(
          classifications_list, candidateInfo_dict[series_uid]
        )
        all_confusion += one_confusion
        print_confusion(
          series_uid, one_confusion, self.malignancy_model is not None
        )
```

If we have the ground truth data, we compute and print the confusion matrix and also add the current results to the total.

```
print_confusion(
  "Total", all_confusion, self.malignancy_model is not None
)
```

Let's run this for a given CT from the validation set:[3]

```
$ python3.6 -m p2ch14.nodule_analysis 1.3.6.1.4.1.14519.5.2.1.6279.6001
➥ .592821488053137951302246128864
...
found nodule candidates in 1.3.6.1.4.1.14519.5.2.1.6279.6001.5928214880
➥ 53137951302246128864:
```

---

[3] We chose this series specifically because it has a nice mix of results.

This candidate is assigned a 53% probability of being malignant, so it barely makes the probability threshold of 50%. The malignancy classification assigns a very low (3%) probability.

```
nodule prob 0.533, malignancy prob 0.030, center xyz XyzTuple
    (x=-128.857421875, y=-80.349609375, z=-31.300007820129395)
nodule prob 0.754, malignancy prob 0.446, center xyz XyzTuple
    (x=-116.396484375, y=-168.142578125, z=-238.30000233650208)
...
nodule prob 0.974, malignancy prob 0.427, center xyz XyzTuple
    (x=121.494140625, y=-45.798828125, z=-211.3000030517578)
nodule prob 0.700, malignancy prob 0.310, center xyz XyzTuple
    (x=123.759765625, y=-44.666015625, z=-211.3000030517578)
...
```

Detected as a nodule with very high confidence and assigned a 42% probability of malignancy

The script found 16 nodule candidates in total. Since we're using our validation set, we have a full set of annotations and malignancy information for each CT, which we can use to create a confusion matrix with our results. The rows are the truth (as defined by the annotations), and the columns show how our project handled each case:

Prognosis: Complete Miss means the segmentation didn't find a nodule, Filtered Out is the classifier's work, and Predicted Nodules are those it marked as nodules.

Scan ID

1.3.6.1.4.1.14519.5.2.1.6279.6001.592821488053137951302246128864

	Complete Miss	Filtered Out	Pred. Nodule
Non-Nodules		1088	15
Benign	1	0	0
Malignant	0	0	1

The rows contain the ground truth.

The Complete Miss column is when our segmenter did not flag a nodule at all. Since the segmenter was not trying to flag non-nodules, we leave that cell blank. Our segmenter was trained to have high recall, so there are a large number of non-nodules, but our nodule classifier is well equipped to screen those out.

So we found the 1 malignant nodule in this scan, but missed a 17th benign one. In addition, 15 false positive non-nodules made it through the nodule classifier. The filtering by the classifier brought the false positives down from over 1,000! As we saw earlier, 1,088 is about $O(2^{10})$, so that lines up with what we expect. Similarly, 15 is about $O(2^4)$, which isn't far from the $O(2^5)$ we ballparked.

Cool! But what's the larger picture?

14.4 *Quantitative validation*

Now that we have anecdotal evidence that the thing we built might be working on one case, let's take a look at the performance of our model on the entire validation set. Doing so is simple: we run our validation set through the previous prediction and check how many nodules we get, how many we miss, and how many candidates are erroneously identified as nodules.

We run the following, which should take half an hour to an hour when run on the GPU. After coffee (or a full-blown nap), here is what we get:

```
$ python3 -m p2ch14.nodule_analysis --run-validation
```

```
...
Total
                   | Complete Miss |  Filtered Out |  Pred. Nodule
  Non-Nodules  |               |        164893 |          2156
       Benign  |            12 |             3 |            87
    Malignant  |             1 |             6 |            45
```

We detected 132 of the 154 nodules, or 85%. Of the 22 we missed, 13 were not considered candidates by the segmentation, so this would be the obvious starting point for improvements.

About 95% of the detected nodules are false positives. This is of course not great; on the other hand, it's a lot less critical—having to look at 20 nodule candidates to find one nodule will be much easier than looking at the entire CT. We will go into this in more detail in section 14.7.2, but we want to stress that rather than treating these mistakes as a black box, it's a good idea to investigate the misclassified cases and see if they have commonalities. Are there characteristics that differentiate them from the samples that were correctly classified? Can we find anything that could be used to improve our performance?

For now, we're going to accept our numbers as is: not bad, but not perfect. The exact numbers may differ when you run your self-trained model. Toward the end of this chapter, we will provide some pointers to papers and techniques that can help improve these numbers. With inspiration and some experimentation, we are confident that you can achieve better scores than we show here.

14.5 Predicting malignancy

Now that we have implemented the nodule-detection task of the LUNA challenge and can produce our own nodule predictions, we ask ourselves the logical next question: can we distinguish malignant nodules from benign ones? We should say that even with a good system, diagnosing malignancy would probably take a more holistic view of the patient, additional non-CT context, and eventually a biopsy, rather than just looking at single nodules in isolation on a CT scan. As such, this seems to be a task that is likely to be performed by a doctor for some time to come.

14.5.1 Getting malignancy information

The LUNA challenge focuses on nodule detection and does not come with malignancy information. The LIDC-IDRI dataset (http://mng.bz/4A4R) has a superset of the CT scans used for the LUNA dataset and includes additional information about the degree of malignancy of the identified tumors. Conveniently, there is a PyLIDC library that can be installed easily, as follows:

```
$ pip3 install pylidc
```

The `pylicd` library gives us ready access to the additional malignancy information we want. Just like matching the annotations with the candidates by location as we did in chapter 10, we need to associate the annotation information from LIDC with the coordinates of the LUNA candidates.

In the LIDC annotations, the malignancy information is encoded per nodule and diagnosing radiologist (up to four looked at the same nodule) using an ordinal five-value scale from 1 (highly unlikely) through moderately unlikely, indeterminate, and moderately suspicious, and ending with 5 (highly suspicious).[4] These annotations are based on the image alone and subject to assumptions about the patient. To convert the list of numbers to a single Boolean yes/no, we will consider nodules to be malignant when at least two radiologists rated that nodule as "moderately suspicious" or greater. Note that this criterion is somewhat arbitrary; indeed, the literature has many different ways of dealing with this data, including predicting the five steps, using averages, or removing nodules from the dataset where the rating radiologists were uncertain or disagreed.

The technical aspects of combining the data are the same as in chapter 10, so we skip showing the code here (it is in the code repository for this chapter) and will use the extended CSV file. We will use the dataset in a way very similar to what we did for the nodule classifier, except that we now only need to process actual nodules and use whether a given nodule is malignant or not as the label to predict. This is structurally very similar to the balancing we used in chapter 12, but instead of sampling from `pos_list` and `neg_list`, we sample from `mal_list` and `ben_list`. Just as we did for the nodule classifier, we want to keep the training data balanced. We put this into the `MalignancyLunaDataset` class, which subclasses the `LunaDataset` but is otherwise very similar.

For convenience, we create a `dataset` command-line argument in training.py and dynamically use the dataset class specified on the command line. We do this by using Python's `getattr` function. For example, if `self.cli_args.dataset` is the string `MalignancyLunaDataset`, it will get `p2ch14.dsets.MalignancyLunaDataset` and assign this type to `ds_cls`, as we can see here.

> **Listing 14.7 training.py:154, .initTrainDl**

```
ds_cls = getattr(p2ch14.dsets, self.cli_args.dataset)    ←— Dynamic class-name lookup

train_ds = ds_cls(
  val_stride=10,
  isValSet_bool=False,
  ratio_int=1,     ←— Recall that this is the one-to-one balancing of the
)                      training data, here between benign and malignant.
```

14.5.2 *An area under the curve baseline: Classifying by diameter*

It is always good to have a baseline to see what performance is better than nothing. We could go for better than random, but here we can use the diameter as a predictor for malignancy—larger nodules are more likely to be malignant. Step 2b of figure 14.5 hints at a new metric we can use to compare classifiers.

---

[4] See the PyLIDC documentation for full details: http://mng.bz/Qyv6.

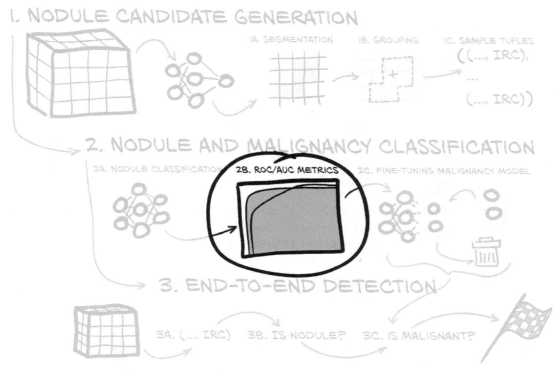

Figure 14.5 The end-to-end project we are implementing in this chapter, with a focus on the ROC graph

We could use the nodule diameter as the sole input to a hypothetical classifier predicting whether a nodule is malignant. It wouldn't be a very good classifier, but it turns out that saying "Everything bigger than this threshold X is malignant" is a better predictor of malignancy than we might expect. Of course, picking the right threshold is key—there's a sweet spot that gets all the huge tumors and none of the tiny specks, and roughly splits the uncertain area that's a jumble of larger benign nodules and smaller malignant ones.

As we might recall from chapter 12, our true positive, false positive, true negative, and false negative counts change based on what threshold value we choose. As we decrease the threshold over which we predict that a nodule is malignant, we will increase the number of true positives, but also the number of false positives. The *false positive rate* (FPR) is FP / (FP + TN), while the *true positive rate* (TPR) is TP / (TP + FN), which you might also remember from chapter 12 as the recall.

Let's set a range for our threshold. The lower bound will be the value at which *all* of our samples are classified as positive, and the upper bound will be the opposite, where all samples are classified as negative. At one extreme, our FPR and TPR will both be zero, since there won't be *any* positives; and at the other, both will be one, since TNs and FNs won't exist (everything is positive!).

No one true way to measure false positives: Precision vs. false positive rate

The FPR here and the precision from chapter 12 are rates (between 0 and 1) that measure things that are not quite opposites. As we discussed, precision is TP / (TP + FP) and measures how many of the samples predicted to be positive will actually be positive. The FPR is FP / (FP + TN) and measures how many of the actually negative samples are predicted to be positive. For heavily imbalanced datasets (like the nodule versus non-nodule classification), our model might achieve a very good FPR (which is closely related to the cross-entropy criterion as a loss) while the precision—and thus the F1 score—is still very poor. A low FPR means we're weeding out a lot of what we're not interested in, but if we are looking for that proverbial needle, we still have mostly hay.

For our nodule data, that's from 3.25 mm (the smallest nodule) to 22.78 mm (the largest). If we pick a threshold value somewhere between those two values, we can then compute FPR(threshold) and TPR(threshold). If we set the FPR value to *X* and TPR to *Y*, we can plot a point that represents that threshold; and if we instead plot the FPR versus TPR for every possible threshold, we get a diagram called the *receiver operating characteristic* (ROC) shown in figure 14.6. The shaded area is the *area under the (ROC) curve*, or AUC. It is between 0 and 1, and higher is better.[5]

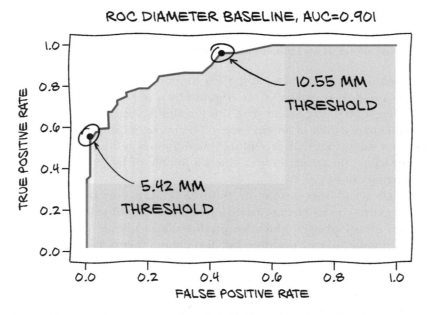

Figure 14.6   **Receiver operating characteristic (ROC) curve for our baseline**

---

[5]   Note that random predictions on a balanced dataset would result in an AUC of 0.5, so that gives us a floor for how good our classifier must be.

Here, we also call out two specific threshold values: diameters of 5.42 mm and 10.55 mm. We chose those two values because they give us somewhat reasonable endpoints for the range of thresholds we might consider, were we to need to pick a single threshold. Anything smaller than 5.42 mm, and we'd only be dropping our TPR. Larger than 10.55 mm, and we'd just be flagging malignant nodules as benign for no gain. The best threshold for this classifier will probably be in the middle somewhere.

How do we actually compute the values shown here? We first grab the candidate info list, filter out the annotated nodules, and get the malignancy label and diameter. For convenience, we also get the number of benign and malignant nodules.

> **Listing 14.8 p2ch14_malben_baseline.ipynb**

Takes the regular dataset and in particular the list of benign and malignant nodules

```
# In[2]:
ds = p2ch14.dsets.MalignantLunaDataset(val_stride=10, isValSet_bool=True)
nodules = ds.ben_list + ds.mal_list
is_mal = torch.tensor([n.isMal_bool for n in nodules])
diam  = torch.tensor([n.diameter_mm for n in nodules])
num_mal = is_mal.sum()
num_ben = len(is_mal) - num_mal
```

Gets lists of malignancy status and diameter

For normalization of the TPR and FPR , we take the number of malignant and benign nodules.

To compute the ROC curve, we need an array of the possible thresholds. We get this from torch.linspace, which takes the two boundary elements. We wish to start at zero predicted positives, so we go from maximal threshold to minimal. This is the 3.25 to 22.78 we already mentioned:

```
# In[3]:
threshold = torch.linspace(diam.max(), diam.min())
```

We then build a two-dimensional tensor in which the rows are per threshold, the columns are per-sample information, and the value is whether this sample is predicted as positive. This Boolean tensor is then filtered by whether the label of the sample is malignant or benign. We sum the rows to count the number of True entries. Dividing by the number of malignant or benign nodules gives us the TPR and FPR—the two coordinates for the ROC curve:

Indexing by None adds a dimension of size 1, just like .unsqueeze(ndx). This gets us a 2D tensor of whether a given nodule (in a column) is classified as malignant for a given diameter (in the row).

```
# In[4]:
predictions = (diam[None] >= threshold[:, None])
tp_diam = (predictions & is_mal[None]).sum(1).float() / num_mal
fp_diam = (predictions & ~is_mal[None]).sum(1).float() / num_ben
```

With the predictions matrix, we can compute the TPRs and FPRs for each diameter by summing over the columns.

To compute the area under this curve, we use numeric integration by the trapezoidal rule (https://en.wikipedia.org/wiki/Trapezoidal_rule), where we multiply the average TPRs (on the Y-axis) between two points by the difference of the two FPRs (on the X-axis)—the area of trapezoids between two points of the graph. Then we sum the area of the trapezoids:

```
# In[5]:
fp_diam_diff =  fp_diam[1:] - fp_diam[:-1]
tp_diam_avg  = (tp_diam[1:] + tp_diam[:-1])/2
auc_diam = (fp_diam_diff * tp_diam_avg).sum()
```

Now, if we run `pyplot.plot(fp_diam, tp_diam, label=f"diameter baseline, AUC={auc_diam:.3f}")` (along with the appropriate figure setup we see in cell 8), we get the plot we saw in figure 14.6.

14.5.3 *Reusing preexisting weights: Fine-tuning*

One way to quickly get results (and often also get by with much less data) is to start not from random initializations but from a network trained on some task with related data. This is called *transfer learning* or, when training only the last few layers, *fine-tuning*. Looking at the highlighted part in figure 14.7, we see that in step 2c, we're going to cut out the last bit of the model and replace it with something new.

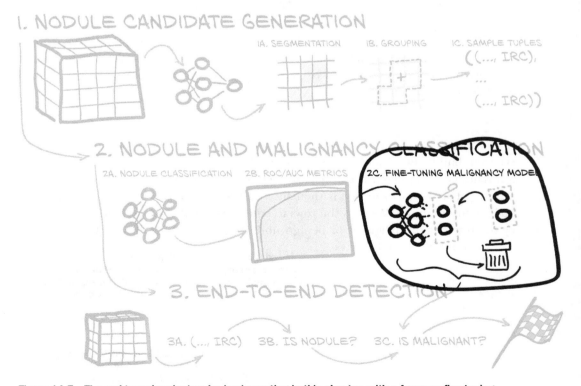

Figure 14.7   The end-to-end project we're implementing in this chapter, with a focus on fine-tuning

Recall from chapter 8 that we could interpret the intermediate values as features extracted from the image—features could be edges or corners that the model detects or indications of any pattern. Before deep learning, it was very common to use hand-crafted features similar to what we briefly experimented with when starting with convolutions. Deep learning has the network derive features useful for the task at hand, such as discrimination between classes, from the data. Now, fine-tuning has us mix the ancient ways (almost a *decade* ago!) of using preexisting features and the new way of using learned features. We treat some (often large) part of the network as a fixed *feature extractor* and only train a relatively small part on top of it.

This generally works very well. Pretrained networks trained on ImageNet as we saw in chapter 2 are very useful as feature extractors for many tasks dealing with natural images—sometimes they also work amazingly for completely different inputs, from paintings or imitations thereof in style transfer to audio spectrograms. There are cases when this strategy works less well. For example, one of the common data augmentation strategies in training models on ImageNet is randomly flipping the images—a dog looking right is the same class as one looking left. As a result, the features between flipped images are very similar. But if we now try to use the pretrained model for a task where left or right matters, we will likely encounter accuracy problems. If we want to identify traffic signs, *turn left here* is quite different than *turn right here*, but a network building on ImageNet-based features will probably make lots of wrong assignments between the two classes.[6]

In our case, we have a network that has been trained on similar data: the nodule classification network. Let's try using that.

For the sake of exposition, we will stay very basic in our fine-tuning approach. In the model architecture in figure 14.8, the two bits of particular interest are highlighted: the last convolutional block and the `head_linear` module. The simplest fine-tuning is to cut out the `head_linear` part—in truth, we are just keeping the random initialization. After we try that, we will also explore a variant where we retrain both `head_linear` and the last convolutional block.

We need to do the following:

- Load the weights of the model we wish to start with, except for the last linear layer, where we want to keep the initialization.
- Disable gradients for the parameters we do not want to train (everything except parameters with names starting with `head`).

When we do fine-tuning training on more than `head_linear`, we still only reset `head _linear` to random, because we believe the previous feature-extraction layers might

---

[6] You can try it yourself with the venerable German Traffic Sign Recognition Benchmark dataset at http://mng.bz/XPZ9.

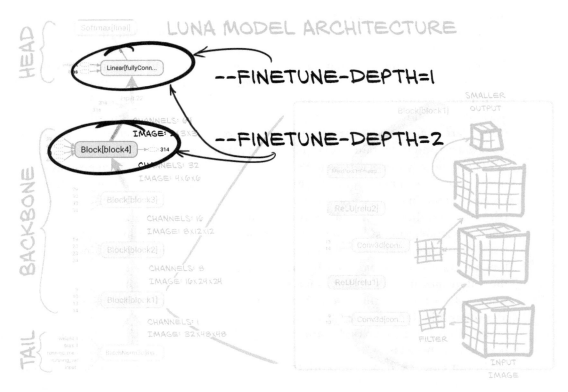

Figure 14.8   The model architecture from chapter 11, with the depth-1 and depth-2 weights highlighted

not be ideal for our problem, but we expect them to be a reasonable starting point. This is easy: we add some loading code into our model setup.

Listing 14.9   training.py:124, .initModel

Filters out top-level modules that have parameters (as opposed to the final activation)

```
d = torch.load(self.cli_args.finetune, map_location='cpu')
model_blocks = [
    n for n, subm in model.named_children()
    if len(list(subm.parameters())) > 0
]
finetune_blocks = model_blocks[-self.cli_args.finetune_depth:]
model.load_state_dict(
    {
        k: v for k,v in d['model_state'].items()
        if k.split('.')[0] not in model_blocks[-1]
    },
```

Takes the last finetune_depth blocks. The default (if fine-tuning) is 1.

Filters out the last block (the final linear part) and does not load it. Starting from a fully initialized model would have us begin with (almost) all nodules labeled as malignant, because that output means "nodule" in the classifier we start from.

```
        strict=False,
    )
    for n, p in model.named_parameters():
        if n.split('.')[0] not in finetune_blocks:
            p.requires_grad_(False)
```

◁── **Passing strict=False lets us load only some weights of the module (with the filtered ones missing).**

◁── **For all but finetune_blocks, we do not want gradients.**

We're set! We can train only the head by running this:

```
python3 -m p2ch14.training \
    --malignant \
    --dataset MalignantLunaDataset \
    --finetune data/part2/models/cls_2020-02-06_14.16.55_final-nodule-
    nonnodule.best.state \
    --epochs 40 \
    malben-finetune
```

Let's run our model on the validation set and get the ROC curve, shown in figure 14.9. It's a lot better than random, but given that we're not outperforming the baseline, we need to see what is holding us back.

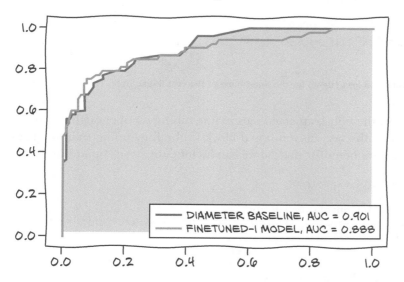

Figure 14.9 ROC curve for our fine-tuned model with a retrained final linear layer. Not too bad, but not quite as good as the baseline.

Figure 14.10 shows the TensorBoard graphs for our training. Looking at the validation loss, we see that while the AUC slowly increases and the loss decreases, even the training loss seems to plateau at a somewhat high level (say, 0.3) instead of trending toward zero. We could run a longer training to check whether it is just very slow; but comparing this to the loss progression discussed in chapter 5—in particular, figure 5.14—we can see our loss value has not flatlined as badly as case A in the figure, but our problem with losses stagnating is qualitatively similar. Back then, case A indicated that we did not have enough capacity, so we should consider the following three possible causes:

- Features (the output of the last convolution) obtained by training the network on nodule versus non-nodule classification are not useful for malignancy detection.
- The capacity of the head—the only part we are training—is not large enough.
- The network might have too little capacity overall.

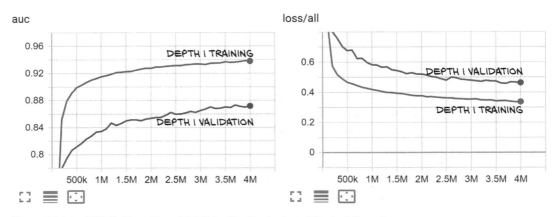

Figure 14.10 AUC (left) and loss (right) for the fine-tuning of the last linear layer

If training only the fully connected part in fine-tuning is not enough, the next thing to try is to include the last convolutional block in the fine-tuning training. Happily, we introduced a parameter for that, so we can include the `block4` part into our training:

```
python3 -m p2ch14.training \
    --malignant \
    --dataset MalignantLunaDataset \
    --finetune data/part2/models/cls_2020-02-06_14.16.55_final-nodule-
nonnodule.best.state \
    --finetune-depth 2 \        ◁─┐ This CLI
    --epochs 10 \                 │ parameter is new.
    malben-finetune-twolayer
```

Once done, we can check our new best model against the baseline. Figure 14.11 looks more reasonable! We flag about 75% of the malignant nodules with almost no false positives. This is clearly better than the 65% the diameter baseline can give us. Trying to push beyond 75%, our model's performance falls back to the baseline. When we go back to the classification problem, we will want to pick a point on the ROC curve to balance true positives versus false positives.

We are roughly on par with the baseline, and we will be content with that. In section 14.7, we hint at the many things that you can explore to improve these results, but that didn't fit in this book.

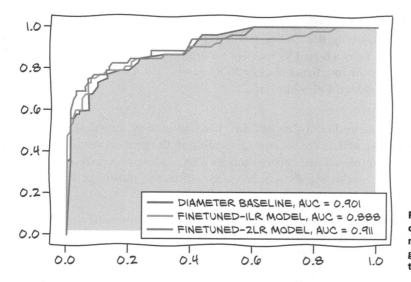

Figure 14.11 ROC curve for our modified model. Now we're getting really close to the baseline.

Looking at the loss curves in figure 14.12, we see that our model is now overfitting very early; thus the next step would be to check into further regularization methods. We will leave that for you.

There are more refined methods of fine-tuning. Some advocate gradually unfreeze the layers, starting from the top. Others propose to train the later layers with the usual learning rate and use a smaller rate for the lower layers. PyTorch does natively support using different optimization parameters like learning rates, weight decay, and momentum for different parameters by separating them in several *parameter groups* that are just that: lists of parameters with separate hyperparameters (https://pytorc .org/docs/stable/optim.html#per-parameter-options).

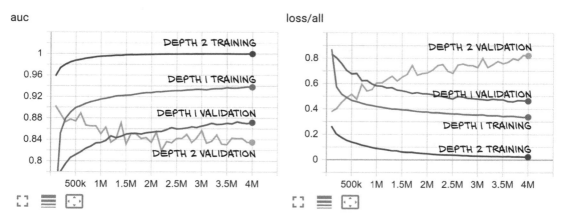

Figure 14.12 AUC (left) and loss (right) for the fine-tuning of the last convolutional block and the fully connected layer

14.5.4 *More output in TensorBoard*

While we are retraining the model, it might be worth looking at a few more outputs we could add to TensorBoard to see how we are doing. For histograms, TensorBoard has a premade recording function. For ROC curves, it does not, so we have an opportunity to meet the Matplotlib interface.

HISTOGRAMS

We can take the predicted probabilities for malignancy and make a histogram of them. Actually, we make two: one for (according to the ground truth) benign and one for malignant nodules. These histograms give us a fine-grained view into the outputs of the model and let us see if there are large clusters of output probabilities that are completely wrong.

> **NOTE** In general, shaping the data you display is an important part of getting quality information from the data. If you have many extremely confident correct classifications, you might want to exclude the leftmost bin. Getting the right things onscreen will typically require some iteration of careful thought and experimentation. Don't hesitate to tweak what you're showing, but also take care to remember if you change the definition of a particular metric without changing the name. It can be easy to compare apples to oranges unless you're disciplined about naming schemes or removing now-invalid runs of data.

We first create some space in the tensor `metrics_t` holding our data. Recall that we defined the indices somewhere near the top.

Listing 14.10   training.py:31

```
METRICS_LABEL_NDX=0
METRICS_PRED_NDX=1
METRICS_PRED_P_NDX=2          ◁──┐  Our new index, carrying the prediction probabilities
METRICS_LOSS_NDX=3               │  (rather than prethresholded predictions)
METRICS_SIZE = 4
```

Once that's done, we can call `writer.add_histogram` with a label, the data, and the `global_step` counter set to our number of training samples presented; this is similar to the scalar call earlier. We also pass in `bins` set to a fixed scale.

Listing 14.11   training.py:496, .logMetrics

```
bins = np.linspace(0, 1)

writer.add_histogram(
  'label_neg',
  metrics_t[METRICS_PRED_P_NDX, negLabel_mask],
  self.totalTrainingSamples_count,
  bins=bins
)
writer.add_histogram(
  'label_pos',
```

```
    metrics_t[METRICS_PRED_P_NDX, posLabel_mask],
    self.totalTrainingSamples_count,
    bins=bins
)
```

Now we can take a look at our prediction distribution for benign samples and how it evolves over each epoch. We want to examine two main features of the histograms in figure 14.13. As we would expect if our network is learning anything, in the top row of benign samples and non-nodules, there is a mountain on the left where the network is very confident that what it sees is not malignant. Similarly, there is a mountain on the right for the malignant samples.

But looking closer, we see the capacity problem of fine-tuning only one layer. Focusing on the top-left series of histograms, we see the mass to the left is somewhat spread out and does not seem to reduce much. There is even a small peak round 1.0, and quite a bit of probability mass is spread out across the entire range. This reflects the loss that didn't want to decrease below 0.3.

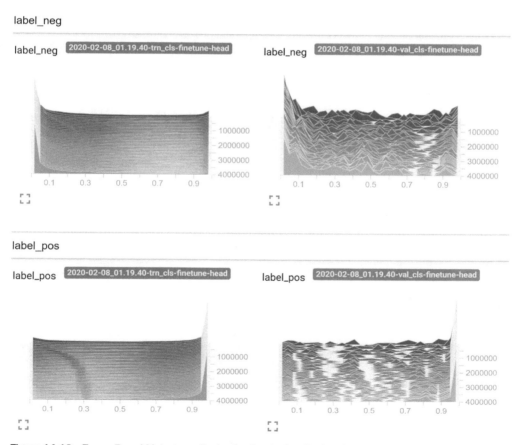

Figure 14.13   TensorBoard histogram display for fine-tuning the head only

Given this observation on the training loss, we would not have to look further, but let's pretend for a moment that we do. In the validation results on the right side, it appears that the probability mass away from the "correct" side is larger for the non-malignant samples in the top-right diagram than for the malignant ones in the bottom-right diagram. So the network gets non-malignant samples wrong more often than malignant ones. This might have us look into rebalancing the data to show more non-malignant samples. But again, this is when we pretend there was nothing wrong with the training on the left side. We typically want to fix training first!

For comparison, let's take a look at the same graph for our depth 2 fine-tuning (figure 14.14). On the training side (the left two diagrams), we have very sharp peaks at the correct answer and not much else. This reflects that training works well.

On the validation side, we now see that the most pronounced artifact is the little peak at 0 predicted probability for malignancy in the bottom-right histogram. So our systematic problem is that we're misclassifying malignant samples as non-malignant. (This is the reverse of what we had earlier!) This is the overfitting we saw with two-layer

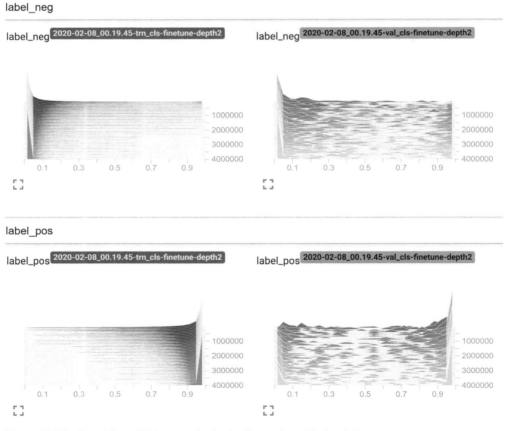

Figure 14.14   TensorBoard histogram display for fine-tuning with depth 2

fine-tuning. It probably would be good to pull up a few images of that type to see what's happening.

ROC AND OTHER CURVES IN TENSORBOARD

As mentioned earlier, TensorBoard does not natively support drawing ROC curves. We can, however, use the ability to export any graph from Matplotlib. The data preparation looks just like in section 14.5.2: we use the data that we also plotted in the histogram to compute the TPR and FPR—tpr and fpr, respectively. We again plot our data, but this time we keep track of `pyplot.figure` and pass it to the `SummaryWriter` method `add_figure`.

Listing 14.12 training.py:482, `.logMetrics`

Sets up a new Matplotlib figure. We usually don't need it because it is implicitly done in Matplotlib, but here we do.

Uses arbitrary pyplot functions

Adds our figure to TensorBoard

```
fig = pyplot.figure()
pyplot.plot(fpr, tpr)
writer.add_figure('roc', fig, self.totalTrainingSamples_count)
```

Because this is given to TensorBoard as an image, it appears under that heading. We didn't draw the comparison curve or anything else, so as not to distract you from the actual function call, but we could use any Matplotlib facilities here. In figure 14.15, we see again that the depth-2 fine-tuning (left) overfits, while the head-only fine-tuning (right) does not.

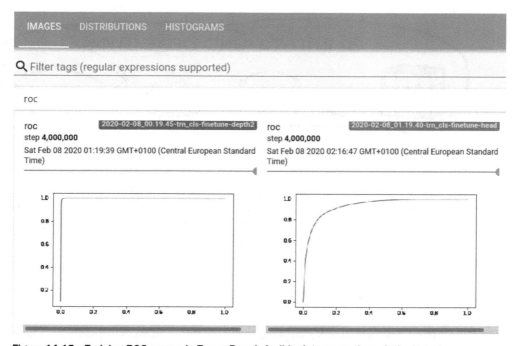

Figure 14.15   Training ROC curves in TensorBoard. A slider lets us go through the iterations.

14.6   *What we see when we diagnose*

Following along with steps 3a, 3b, and 3c in figure 14.16, we now need to run the full pipeline from the step 3a segmentation on the left to the step 3c malignancy model on the right. The good news is that almost all of our code is in place already! We just need to stitch it together: the moment has come to actually write and run our end-to-end diagnosis script.

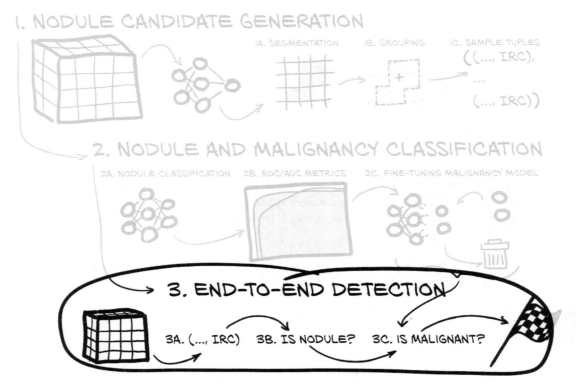

Figure 14.16   The end-to-end project we are implementing in this chapter, with a focus on end-to-end detection

We saw our first hints at handling the malignancy model back in the code in section 14.3.3. If we pass an argument --malignancy-path to the nodule_analysis call, it runs the malignancy model found at this path and outputs the information. This works for both a single scan and the --run-validation variant.

Be warned that the script will probably take a while to finish; even just the 89 CTs in the validation set took about 25 minutes.[7]

---

[7] Most of the delay is from SciPy's processing of the connected components. At the time of writing, we are not aware of an accelerated implementation.

Let's see what we get:

```
Total
              | Complete Miss | Filtered Out | Pred. Benign | Pred. Malignant
 Non-Nodules  |               |       164893  |         1593  |             563
     Benign   |           12  |            3  |           70  |              17
  Malignant   |            1  |            6  |            9  |              36
```

Not too bad! We detect about 85% of the nodules and correctly flag about 70% of the malignant ones, end to end.[8] While we have a lot of false positives, it would seem that having 16 of them per true nodule reduces what needs to be looked at (well, if it were not for the 30% false negatives). As we already warned in chapter 9, this isn't at the level where you could collect millions of funding for your medical AI startup,[9] but it's a pretty reasonable starting point. In general, we should be pretty happy that we're getting results that are clearly meaningful; and of course our *real* goal has been to study deep learning along the way.

We might next choose to look at the nodules that are actually misclassified. Keep in mind that for our task at hand, even the radiologists who annotated the dataset differed in opinion. We might stratify our validation set by how clearly they identified a nodule as malignant.

14.6.1 Training, validation, and test sets

There is one caveat that we must mention. While we didn't explicitly train our model on the validation set, although we ran this risk at the beginning of the chapter, we did *choose* the epoch of training to use based on the model's performance on the validation set. That's a bit of a data leak, too. In fact, we should expect our real-world performance to be slightly worse than this, as it's unlikely that whatever model performs best on our validation set will perform equally well on every other unseen set of data (on average, at least).

For this reason, practitioners often split data into *three* sets:

- A *training set*, exactly as we've done here
- A *validation set*, used to determine which epoch of evolution of the model to consider "best"
- A *test set*, used to actually predict performance for the model (as chosen by the validation set) on unseen, real-world data

Adding a third set would have led us to pull another nontrivial chunk of our training data, which would have been somewhat painful, given how badly we had to fight overfitting already. It would also have complicated the presentation, so we purposely left it out. Were this a project with the resources to get more data and an imperative to build the best possible system to use in the wild, we'd have to make a different decision here and actively seek more data to use as an independent test set.

---

[8] Recall that our earlier "75% with almost no false positives" ROC number was looking at malignancy classification in isolation. Here we are filtering out seven malignant nodules before we even get to the malignancy classifier.

[9] If it were, we'd have done that instead of writing this book!

The general message is that there are subtle ways for bias to creep into our models. We should use extra care to control information leakage at every step of the way and verify its absence using independent data as much as possible. The price to pay for taking shortcuts is failing egregiously at a later stage, at the worst possible time: when we're closer to production.

14.7   *What next? Additional sources of inspiration (and data)*

Further improvements will be difficult to measure at this point. Our classification validation set contains 154 nodules, and our nodule classification model is typically getting at least 150 of them right, with most of the variance coming from epoch-by-epoch training changes. Even if we were to make a significant improvement to our model, we don't have enough fidelity in our validation set to tell whether that change is an improvement for certain! This is also very pronounced in the benign versus malignant classification, where the validation loss zigzags a lot. If we reduced our validation stride from 10 to 5, the size of our validation set would double, at the cost of one-ninth of our training data. That might be worth it if we wanted to try other improvements. Of course, we would also need to address the question of a test set, which would take away from our already limited training data.

We would also want to take a good look at the cases where the network does not perform as well as we'd like, to see if we can identify any pattern. But beyond that, let's talk briefly about some general ways we could improve our project. In a way, this section is like section 8.5 in chapter 8. We will endeavor to fill you with ideas to try; don't worry if you don't understand each in detail.[10]

14.7.1   *Preventing overfitting: Better regularization*

Reflecting on what we did throughout part 2, in each of the three problems—the classifiers in chapter 11 and section 14.5, as well as the segmentation in chapter 13—we had overfitting models. Overfitting in the first case was catastrophic; we dealt with it by balancing the data and augmentation in chapter 12. This balancing of the data to prevent overfitting has also been the main motivation to train the U-Net on crops around nodules and candidates rather than full slices. For the remaining overfitting, we bailed out, stopping training early when the overfitting started to affect our validation results. This means preventing or reducing overfitting would be a great way to improve our results.

This pattern—get a model that overfits, and then work to reduce that overfitting—can really can be seen as a recipe.[11] So this two-step process should be used when we want to improve on the state we have achieved now.

---

[10] At least one of the authors would love to write an entire book on the topics touched on in this section.

[11] See also Andrej Karparthy's blog post "A Recipe for Training Neural Networks" at https://karpathy.github .io/2019/04/25/recipe for a more elaborate recipe.

CLASSIC REGULARIZATION AND AUGMENTATION

You might have noticed that we did not even use all the regularization techniques from chapter 8. For example, dropout would be an easy thing to try.

While we have some augmentation in place, we could go further. One relatively powerful augmentation method we did not attempt to employ is elastic deformations, where we put "digital crumples" into the inputs.[12] This makes for much more variability than rotation and flipping alone and would seem to be applicable to our tasks as well.

MORE ABSTRACT AUGMENTATION

So far, our augmentation has been geometrically inspired—we transformed our input to more or less look like something plausible we might see. It turns out that we need not limit ourselves to that type of augmentation.

Recall from chapter 8 that mathematically, the cross-entropy loss we have been using is a measure of the discrepancy between two probability distributions—that of the predictions and the distribution that puts all probability mass on the label and can be represented by the one-hot vector for the label. If overconfidence is a problem for our network, one simple thing we could try is not using the one-hot distribution but rather putting a small probability mass on the "wrong" classes.[13] This is called *label smoothing*.

We can also mess with inputs and labels at the same time. A very general and also easy-to-apply augmentation technique for doing this has been proposed under the name of *mixup*:[14] the authors propose to randomly interpolate both inputs and labels. Interestingly, with a linearity assumption for the loss (which is satisfied by binary cross entropy), this is equivalent to just manipulating the inputs with a weight drawn from an appropriately adapted distribution.[15] Clearly, we don't expect blended inputs to occur when working on real data, but it seems that this mixing encourages stability of the predictions and is very effective.

BEYOND A SINGLE BEST MODEL: ENSEMBLING

One perspective we could have on the problem of overfitting is that our model is capable of working the way we want if we knew the right parameters, but we don't actually know them.[16] If we followed this intuition, we might try to come up with several sets of parameters (that is, several models), hoping that the weaknesses of each might compensate for the other. This technique of evaluating several models and combining the output is called *ensembling*. Simply put, we train several models and then, in order to predict, run all of them and average the predictions. When each individual model overfits (or we have taken a snapshot of the model just before we started to see the overfitting), it seems plausible that the models might start to make bad predictions on different inputs, rather than always overfit the same sample first.

---

[12] You can find a recipe (albeit aimed at TensorFlow) at http://mng.bz/Md5Q.

[13] You can use nn.KLDivLoss loss for this.

[14] Hongyi Zhang et al., "mixup: Beyond Empirical Risk Minimization," https://arxiv.org/abs/1710.09412.

[15] See Ferenc Huszár's post at http://mng.bz/aRJj/; he also provides PyTorch code.

[16] We might expand that to be outright Bayesian, but we'll just go with this bit of intuition.

In ensembling, we typically use completely separate training runs or even varying model structures. But if we were to make it particularly simple, we could take several snapshots of the model from a single training run—preferably shortly before the end or before we start to observe overfitting. We might try to build an ensemble of these snapshots, but as they will still be somewhat close to each other, we could instead average them. This is the core idea of *stochastic weight averaging*.[17] We need to exercise some care when doing so: for example, when our models use batch normalization, we might want to adjust the statistics, but we can likely get a small accuracy boost even without that.

GENERALIZING WHAT WE ASK THE NETWORK TO LEARN

We could also look at *multitask learning*, where we require a model to learn additional outputs beyond the ones we will then evaluate,[18] which has a proven track record of improving results. We could try to train on nodule versus non-nodule and benign versus malignant at the same time. Actually, the data source for the malignancy data provides additional labeling we could use as additional tasks; see the next section. This idea is closely related to the transfer-learning concept we looked at earlier, but here we would typically train both tasks in parallel rather than first doing one and then trying to move to the next.

If we do not have additional tasks but rather have a stash of additional unlabeled data, we can look into *semi-supervised learning*. An approach that was recently proposed and looks very effective is unsupervised data augmentation.[19] Here we train our model as usual on the data. On the unlabeled data, we make a prediction on an unaugmented sample. We then take that prediction as the target for this sample and train the model to predict that target on the augmented sample as well. In other words, we don't know if the prediction is correct, but we ask the network to produce consistent outputs whether we augment or not.

When we run out of tasks of genuine interest but do not have additional data, we may look at making things up. Making up data is somewhat difficult (although people sometimes use GANs similar to the ones we briefly saw in chapter 2, with some success), so we instead make up tasks. This is when we enter the realm of *self-supervised learning*; the tasks are often called *pretext tasks*. A very popular crop of pretext tasks apply some sort of corruption to some of the inputs. Then we can train a network to reconstruct the original (for example, using a U-Net-like architecture) or train a classifier to detect real from corrupted data while sharing large parts of the model (such as the convolutional layers).

This is still dependent on us coming up with a way to corrupt our inputs. If we don't have such a method in mind and aren't getting the results we want, there are

---

[17] Pavel Izmailov and Andrew Gordon Wilson present an introduction with PyTorch code at http://mng.bz/gywe.

[18] See Sebastian Ruder, "An Overview of Multi-Task Learning in Deep Neural Networks," https://arxiv.org/abs/1706.05098; but this is also a key idea in many areas.

[19] Q. Xie et al., "Unsupervised Data Augmentation for Consistency Training," https://arxiv.org/abs/1904.12848.

other ways to do self-supervised learning. A very generic task would be if the features the model learns are good enough to let the model discriminate between different samples of our dataset. This is called *contrastive learning*.

To make things more concrete, consider the following: we take the extracted features from the current image and a largish number K of other images. This is our *key* set of features. Now we set up a classification pretext task as follows: given the features of the current image, the *query*, to which of the $K + 1$ *key* features does it belong? This might seem trivial at first, but even if there is perfect agreement between the query features and the key features for the correct class, training on this task encourages the feature of the query to be maximally dissimilar from those of the K other images (in terms of being assigned low probability in the classifier output). Of course, there are many details to fill in; we recommend (somewhat arbitrarily) looking at momentum contrast.[20]

14.7.2 *Refined training data*

We could improve our training data in a few ways. We mentioned earlier that the malignancy classification is actually based on a more nuanced categorization by several radiologists. An easy way to use the data we discarded by making it into the dichotomy "malignant or not?" would be to use the five classes. The radiologists' assessments could then be used as a smoothed label: we could one-hot-encode each one and then average over the assessments of a given nodule. So if four radiologists look at a nodule and two call it "indeterminate," one calls that same nodule "moderately suspicious," and the fourth labels it "highly suspicious," we would train on the cross entropy between the model output and the target probability distribution given by the vector `0 0 0.5 0.25 0.25`. This would be similar to the label smoothing we mentioned earlier, but in a smarter, problem-specific way. We would, however, have to find a new way of evaluating these models, as we lose the simple accuracy, ROC, and AUC notions we have in binary classification.

Another way to use multiple assessments would be to train a number of models instead of one, each trained on the annotations given by an individual radiologist. At inference we would then ensemble the models by, for example, averaging their output probabilities.

In the direction of multiple tasks mentioned earlier, we could again go back to the PyLIDC-provided annotation data, where other classifications are provided for each annotation (subtlety, internal structure, calcification, sphericity, margin definedness, lobulation, spiculation, and texture (https://pylidc.github.io/annotation.html). We might have to learn a lot more about nodules, first, though.

In the segmentation, we could try to see whether the masks provided by PyLIDC work better than those we generated ourselves. Since the LIDC data has annotations from multiple radiologists, it would be possible to group nodules into "high agreement" and "low agreement" groups. It might be interesting to see if that corresponds

---

[20] K. He et al., "Momentum Contrast for Unsupervised Visual Representation Learning," https://arxiv.org/abs/1911.05722.

to "easy" and "hard" to classify nodules in terms of seeing whether our classifier gets almost all easy ones right and only has trouble on the ones that were more ambiguous to the human experts. Or we could approach the problem from the other side, by defining how difficult nodules are to detect in terms of our model performance: "easy" (correctly classified after an epoch or two of training), "medium" (eventually gotten right), and "hard" (persistently misclassified) buckets.

Beyond readily available data, one thing that would probably make sense is to further partition the nodules by malignancy type. Getting a professional to examine our training data in more detail and flag each nodule with a cancer type, and then forcing the model to report that type, could result in more efficient training. The cost to contract out that work is prohibitive for hobby projects, but paying might make sense in commercial contexts.

Especially difficult cases could also be subject to a limited repeat review by human experts to check for errors. Again, that would require a budget but is certainly within reason for serious endeavors.

14.7.3 *Competition results and research papers*

Our goal in part 2 was to present a self-contained path from problem to solution, and we did that. But the particular problem of finding and classifying lung nodules has been worked on before; so if you want to dig deeper, you can also see what other people have done.

DATA SCIENCE BOWL 2017

While we have limited the scope of part 2 to the CT scans in the LUNA dataset, there is also a wealth of information available from Data Science Bowl 2017 (www.kaggle .com/c/data-science-bowl-2017), hosted by Kaggle (www.kaggle.com). The data itself is no longer available, but there are many accounts of people describing what worked for them and what did not. For example, some of the Data Science Bowl (DSB) finalists reported that the detailed malignancy level (1...5) information from LIDC was useful during training.

Two highlights you could look at are these:[21]

- Second-place solution write-up by Daniel Hammack and Julian de Wit: http:// mng.bz/Md48
- Ninth-place solution write-up by Team Deep Breath: http://mng.bz/aRAX

NOTE Many of the newer techniques we hinted at previously were not yet available to the DSB participants. The three years between the 2017 DSB and this book going to print are an eternity in deep learning!

One idea for a more legitimate test set would be to use the DSB dataset instead of reusing our validation set. Unfortunately, the DSB stopped sharing the raw data, so unless you happen to have access to an old copy, you would need another data source.

---

[21] Thanks to the Internet Archive for saving them from redesigns.

LUNA PAPERS

The LUNA Grand Challenge has collected several results (https://luna16.grand-challenge.org/Results) that show quite a bit of promise. While not all of the papers provided include enough detail to reproduce the results, many do contain enough information to improve our project. You could review some of the papers and attempt to replicate approaches that seem interesting.

14.8 *Conclusion*

This chapter concludes part 2 and delivers on the promise we made back in chapter 9: we now have a working, end-to-end system that attempts to diagnose lung cancer from CT scans. Looking back at where we started, we've come a long way and, hopefully, learned a lot. We trained a model to do something interesting and difficult using publicly available data. The key question is, "Will this be good for anything in the real world?" with the follow-up question, "Is this ready for production?" The definition of *production* critically depends on the *intended use*, so if we're wondering whether our algorithm can replace an expert radiologist, this is definitely not the case. We'd argue that this can represent version 0.1 of a tool that could in the future support a radiologist during clinical routine: for instance, by providing a second opinion about something that could have gone unnoticed.

Such a tool would require clearance by regulatory bodies of competence (like the Food and Drug Administration in the United States) in order for it to be employed outside of research contexts. Something we would certainly be missing is an extensive, curated dataset to further train and, even more importantly, validate our work. Individual cases would need to be evaluated by multiple experts in the context of a research protocol; and a proper representation of a wide spectrum of situations, from common presentations to corner cases, would be mandatory.

All these cases, from pure research use to clinical validation to clinical use, would require us to execute our model in an environment amenable to be scaled up. Needless to say, this comes with its own set of challenges, both technical and in terms of process. We'll discuss some of the technical challenges in chapter 15.

14.8.1 *Behind the curtain*

As we close out the modeling in part 2, we want to pull back the curtain a bit and give you a glimpse at the unvarnished truth of working on deep learning projects. Fundamentally, this book has presented a skewed take on things: a curated set of obstacles and opportunities; a well-tended garden path through the larger wilds of deep learning. We think this semi-organic series of challenges (especially in part 2) makes for a better book, and we hope a better learning experience. It does not, however, make for a more *realistic* experience.

In all likelihood, the vast majority of your experiments will not work out. Not every idea will be a discovery, and not every change will be a breakthrough. Deep learning is fiddly. Deep learning is fickle. And remember that deep learning is literally pushing at the forefront of human knowledge; it's a frontier that we are exploring and mapping further every day, *right now*. It's an exciting time to be in the field, but as with most fieldwork, you're going to get some mud on your boots.

In the spirit of transparency, here are some things that we tried, that we tripped over, that didn't work, or that at least didn't work well enough to bother keeping:

- Using `HardTanh` instead of `Softmax` for the classification network (it was simpler to explain, but it didn't actually work well).
- Trying to fix the issues caused by `HardTanh` by making the classification network more complicated (skip connections, and so on).
- Poor weight initialization causing training to be unstable, particularly for segmentation.
- Training on full CT slices for segmentation.
- Loss weighting for segmentation with SGD. It didn't work, and Adam was needed for it to be useful.
- True 3D segmentation of CT scans. It didn't work for us, but then DeepMind went and did it anyway.[22] This was before we moved to cropping to nodules, and we ran out of memory, so you might try again based on the current setup.
- Misunderstanding the meaning of the `class` column from the LUNA data, which caused some rewrites partway through authoring the book.
- Accidentally leaving in an "I want results quickly" hack that threw away 80% of the candidate nodules found by the segmentation module, causing the results to look atrocious until we figured out what was going on (that cost an entire weekend!).
- A host of different optimizers, loss functions, and model architectures.
- Balancing the training data in various ways.

There are certainly more that we've forgotten. A lot of things went wrong before they went right! Please learn from our mistakes.

We might also add that for many things in this text, we just picked an approach; we emphatically *do not* imply that other approaches are inferior (many of them are probably better!). Additionally, coding style and project design typically differ a lot between people. In machine learning, it is very common for people to do a lot of programming in Jupyter Notebooks. Notebooks are a great tool to try things quickly, but they come with their own caveats: for example, around how to keep track of what you did. Finally, instead of using the caching mechanism we used with `prepcache`, we could have had a separate preprocessing step that wrote out the data as serialized tensors. Each of these approaches seems to be a matter of taste; even among the three authors, any one of us would do things slightly differently.[23] It is always good to try things and find which one works best for you while remaining flexible when cooperating with your peers.

---

[22] Stanislav Nikolov et al., "Deep Learning to Achieve Clinically Applicable Segmentation of Head and Neck Anatomy for Radiotherapy," https://arxiv.org/pdf/1809.04430.pdf

[23] Oh, the discussions we've had!

14.9 Exercises

1 Implement a test set for classification, or reuse the test set from chapter 13's exercises. Use the validation set to pick the best epochs while training, but use the test set to evaluate the end-to-end project. How well does performance on the validation set line up with performance on the test set?

2 Can you train a single model that is able to do three-way classification, distinguishing among non-nodules, benign modules, and malignant nodules in one pass?

   a What class-balancing split works best for training?

   b How does this single-pass model perform, compared to the two-pass approach we are using in the book?

3 We trained our classifier on annotations, but expect it to perform on the output of our segmentation. Use the segmentation model to build a list of non-nodules to use during training instead of the non-nodules provided.

   a Does the classification model performance improve when trained on this new set?

   b Can you characterize what kinds of nodule candidates see the biggest changes with the newly trained model?

4 The padded convolutions we use result in less than full context near the edges of the image. Compute the loss for segmented pixels near the edges of the CT scan slice, versus those in the interior. Is there a measurable difference between the two?

5 Try running the classifier on the entire CT by using overlapping $32 \times 48 \times 48$ patches. How does this compare to the segmentation approach?

14.10 Summary

- An unambiguous split between training and validation (and test) sets is crucial. Here, splitting by patient is much less prone to getting things wrong. This is even more true when you have several models in your pipeline.

- Getting from pixel-wise marks to nodules can be achieved using very traditional image processing. We don't want to look down on the classics, but value these tools and use them where appropriate.

- Our diagnosis script performs both segmentation and classification. This allows us to diagnose a CT that we have not seen before, though our current `Dataset` implementation is not configured to accept `series_uids` from sources other than LUNA.

- Fine-tuning is a great way to fit a model while using a minimum of training data. Make sure the pretrained model has features relevant to your task, and make sure that you retrain a portion of the network with enough capacity.

- TensorBoard allows us to write out many different types of diagrams that help us determine what's going on. But this is not a replacement for looking at data on which our model works particularly badly.
- Successful training seems to involve an overfitting network at some stage, and which we then regularize. We might as well take that as a recipe; and we should probably learn more about regularization.
- Training neural networks is about trying things, seeing what goes wrong, and improving on it. There usually isn't a magic bullet.
- Kaggle is an excellent source of project ideas for deep learning. Many new datasets have cash prizes for the top performers, and older contests have examples that can be used as starting points for further experimentation.

Part 3

Deployment

In part 3, we'll look at how to get our models to the point where they can be used. We saw how to build models in the previous parts: part 1 introduced the building and training of models, and part 2 thoroughly covered an example from start to finish, so the hard work is done.

But no model is useful until you can actually use it. So, now we need to put the models out there and apply them to the tasks they are designed to solve. This part is closer to part 1 in spirit, because it introduces a lot of PyTorch components. As before, we'll focus on applications and tasks we wish to solve rather than just looking at PyTorch for its own sake.

In part 3's single chapter, we'll take a tour of the PyTorch deployment landscape as of early 2020. We'll get to know and use the PyTorch just-in-time compiler (JIT) to export models for use in third-party applications to the C++ API for mobile support.

Deploying to production

This chapter covers

- Options for deploying PyTorch models
- Working with the PyTorch JIT
- Deploying a model server and exporting models
- Running exported and natively implemented models from C++
- Running models on mobile

In part 1 of this book, we learned a lot about models; and part 2 left us with a detailed path for creating good models for a particular problem. Now that we have these great models, we need to take them where they can be useful. Maintaining infrastructure for executing inference of deep learning models at scale can be impactful from an architectural as well as cost standpoint. While PyTorch started off as a framework focused on research, beginning with the 1.0 release, a set of production-oriented features were added that today make PyTorch an ideal end-to-end platform from research to large-scale production.

445

What deploying to production means will vary with the use case:

- Perhaps the most natural deployment for the models we developed in part 2 would be to set up a network service providing access to our models. We'll do this in two versions using lightweight Python web frameworks: Flask (http:// flask.pocoo.org) and Sanic (https://sanicframework.org). The first is arguably one of the most popular of these frameworks, and the latter is similar in spirit but takes advantage of Python's new async/await support for asynchronous operations for efficiency.

- We can export our model to a well-standardized format that allows us to ship it using optimized model processors, specialized hardware, or cloud services. For PyTorch models, the Open Neural Network Exchange (ONNX) format fills this role.

- We may wish to integrate our models into larger applications. For this it would be handy if we were not limited to Python. Thus we will explore using PyTorch models from C++ with the idea that this also is a stepping-stone to any language.

- Finally, for some things like the image zebraification we saw in chapter 2, it may be nice to run our model on mobile devices. While it is unlikely that you will have a CT module for your mobile, other medical applications like do-it-yourself skin screenings may be more natural, and the user might prefer running on the device versus having their skin sent to a cloud service. Luckily for us, PyTorch has gained mobile support recently, and we will explore that.

As we learn how to implement these use cases, we will use the classifier from chapter 14 as our first example for serving, and then switch to the zebraification model for the other bits of deployment.

15.1 *Serving PyTorch models*

We'll begin with what it takes to put our model on a server. Staying true to our hands-on approach, we'll start with the simplest possible server. Once we have something basic that works, we'll take look at its shortfalls and take a stab at resolving them. Finally, we'll look at what is, at the time of writing, the future. Let's get something that listens on the network.[1]

15.1.1 *Our model behind a Flask server*

Flask is one of the most widely used Python modules. It can be installed using `pip`:[2]

```
pip install Flask
```

---

[1] To play it safe, do not do this on an untrusted network.
[2] Or `pip3` for Python3. You also might want to run it from a Python virtual environment.

The API can be created by decorating functions.

Listing 15.1   flask_hello_world.py:1

```
from flask import Flask
app = Flask(__name__)

@app.route("/hello")
def hello():
  return "Hello World!"

if __name__ == '__main__':
  app.run(host='0.0.0.0', port=8000)
```

When started, the application will run at port 8000 and expose one route, /hello, that returns the "Hello World" string. At this point, we can augment our Flask server by loading a previously saved model and exposing it through a POST route. We will use the nodule classifier from chapter 14 as an example.

We'll use Flask's (somewhat curiously imported) request to get our data. More precisely, request.files contains a dictionary of file objects indexed by field names. We'll use JSON to parse the input, and we'll return a JSON string using flask's jsonify helper.

Instead of /hello, we will now expose a /predict route that takes a binary blob (the pixel content of the series) and the related metadata (a JSON object containing a dictionary with shape as a key) as input files provided with a POST request and returns a JSON response with the predicted diagnosis. More precisely, our server takes one sample (rather than a batch) and returns the probability that it is malignant.

In order to get to the data, we first need to decode the JSON to binary, which we can then decode into a one-dimensional array with numpy.frombuffer. We'll convert this to a tensor with torch.from_numpy and view its actual shape.

The actual handling of the model is just like in chapter 14: we'll instantiate Luna-Model from chapter 14, load the weights we got from our training, and put the model in eval mode. As we are not training anything, we'll tell PyTorch that we will not want gradients when running the model by running in a with torch.no_grad() block.

Listing 15.2   flask_server.py:1

```
import numpy as np
import sys
import os
import torch
from flask import Flask, request, jsonify
import json

from p2ch13.model_cls import LunaModel

app = Flask(__name__)                    ◁─── Sets up our model, loads
                                              the weights, and moves
model = LunaModel()                           to evaluation mode
```

```
model.load_state_dict(torch.load(sys.argv[1],
                    map_location='cpu')['model_state'])
model.eval()

def run_inference(in_tensor):
  with torch.no_grad():                              ◄─────  No autograd for us.
    # LunaModel takes a batch and outputs a tuple (scores, probs)
    out_tensor = model(in_tensor.unsqueeze(0))[1].squeeze(0)
  probs = out_tensor.tolist()
  out = {'prob_malignant': probs[1]}
  return out                                         We expect a form submission
                                                     (HTTP POST) at the "/predict"
@app.route("/predict", methods=["POST"])  ◄───┘      endpoint.
def predict():
  meta = json.load(request.files['meta'])   ◄───┐    Our request will have
  blob = request.files['blob'].read()            │    one file called meta.
  in_tensor = torch.from_numpy(np.frombuffer(
    blob, dtype=np.float32))                 ◄───┐    Converts our data from
  in_tensor = in_tensor.view(*meta['shape'])       │    binary blob to torch
  out = run_inference(in_tensor)
  return jsonify(out)              ◄───────┐    Encodes our response
                                           │    content as JSON
if __name__ == '__main__':
  app.run(host='0.0.0.0', port=8000)
  print (sys.argv[1])
```

Run the server as follows:

```
python3 -m p3ch15.flask_server
➥ data/part2/models/cls_2019-10-19_15.48.24_final_cls.best.state
```

We prepared a trivial client at cls_client.py that sends a single example. From the code directory, you can run it as

```
python3 p3ch15/cls_client.py
```

It should tell you that the nodule is very unlikely to be malignant. Clearly, our server takes inputs, runs them through our model, and returns the outputs. So are we done? Not quite. Let's look at what could be better in the next section.

15.1.2 *What we want from deployment*

Let's collect some things we desire for serving models.[3] First, we want to support *modern protocols and their features*. Old-school HTTP is deeply serial, which means when a client wants to send several requests in the same connection, the next requests will only be sent after the previous request has been answered. Not very efficient if you want to send a batch of things. We will partially deliver here—our upgrade to Sanic certainly moves us to a framework that has the ambition to be very efficient.

---

[3] One of the earliest public talks discussing the inadequacy of Flask serving for PyTorch models is Christian Perone's "PyTorch under the Hood," http://mng.bz/xWdW.

When using GPUs, it is often much more efficient to *batch requests* than to process them one by one or fire them in parallel. So next, we have the task of collecting requests from several connections, assembling them into a batch to run on the GPU, and then getting the results back to the respective requesters. This sounds elaborate and (again, when we write this) seems not to be done very often in simple tutorials. That is reason enough for us to do it properly here! Note, though, that until latency induced by the duration of a model run is an issue (in that waiting for our own run is OK; but waiting for the batch that's running when the request arrives to finish, and then waiting for our run to give results, is prohibitive), there is little reason to run multiple batches on one GPU at a given time. Increasing the maximum batch size will generally be more efficient.

We want to serve several things *in parallel*. Even with asynchronous serving, we need our model to run efficiently on a second thread—this means we want to escape the (in)famous Python global interpreter lock (GIL) with our model.

We also want to do as *little copying* as possible. Both from a memory-consumption and a time perspective, copying things over and over is bad. Many HTTP things are encoded in Base64 (a format restricted to 6 bits per byte to encode binary in more or less alphanumeric strings), and—say, for images—decoding that to binary and then again to a tensor and then to the batch is clearly relatively expensive. We will partially deliver on this—we'll use streaming PUT requests to not allocate Base64 strings and to avoid growing strings by successively appending to them (which is terrible for performance for strings as much as tensors). We say we do not deliver completely because we are not truly minimizing the copying, though.

The last desirable thing for serving is *safety*. Ideally, we would have safe decoding. We want to guard against both overflows and resource exhaustion. Once we have a fixed-size input tensor, we should be mostly good, as it is hard to crash PyTorch starting from fixed-sized inputs. The stretch to get there, decoding images and the like, is likely more of a headache, and we make no guarantees. Internet security is a large enough field that we will not cover it at all. We should note that neural networks are known to be susceptible to manipulation of the inputs to generate desired but wrong or unforeseen outputs (known as *adversarial examples*), but this isn't extremely pertinent to our application, so we'll skip it here.

Enough talk. Let's improve on our server.

15.1.3 *Request batching*

Our second example server will use the Sanic framework (installed via the Python package of the same name). This will give us the ability to serve many requests in parallel using asynchronous processing, so we'll tick that off our list. While we are at it, we will also implement request batching.

Asynchronous programming can sound scary, and it usually comes with lots of terminology. But what we are doing here is just allowing functions to non-blockingly wait for results of computations or events.[4]

---

[4] Fancy people call these asynchronous function *generators* or sometimes, more loosely, *coroutines*: https://en.wikipedia.org/wiki/Coroutine.

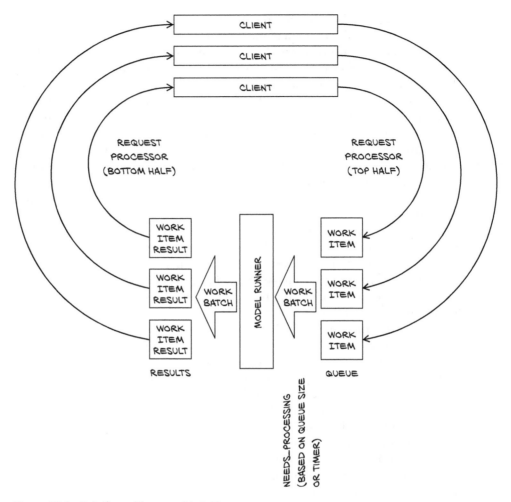

Figure 15.1 Dataflow with request batching

In order to do request batching, we have to decouple the request handling from running the model. Figure 15.1 shows the flow of the data.

At the top of figure 15.1 are the clients, making requests. One by one, these go through the top half of the request processor. They cause work items to be enqueued with the request information. When a full batch has been queued or the oldest request has waited for a specified maximum time, a model runner takes a batch from the queue, processes it, and attaches the result to the work items. These are then processed one by one by the bottom half of the request processor.

IMPLEMENTATION

We implement this by writing two functions. The model runner function starts at the beginning and runs forever. Whenever we need to run the model, it assembles a batch of inputs, runs the model in a second thread (so other things can happen), and returns the result.

The request processor then decodes the request, enqueues inputs, waits for the processing to be completed, and returns the output with the results. In order to appreciate what *asynchronous* means here, think of the model runner as a wastepaper basket. All the figures we scribble for this chapter can be quickly disposed of to the right of the desk. But every once in a while—either because the basket is full or when it is time to clean up in the evening—we need to take all the collected paper out to the trash can. Similarly, we enqueue new requests, trigger processing if needed, and wait for the results before sending them out as the answer to the request. Figure 15.2 shows our two functions in the blocks we execute uninterrupted before handing back to the event loop.

A slight complication relative to this picture is that we have two occasions when we need to process events: if we have accumulated a full batch, we start right away; and when the oldest request reaches the maximum wait time, we also want to run. We solve this by setting a timer for the latter.[5]

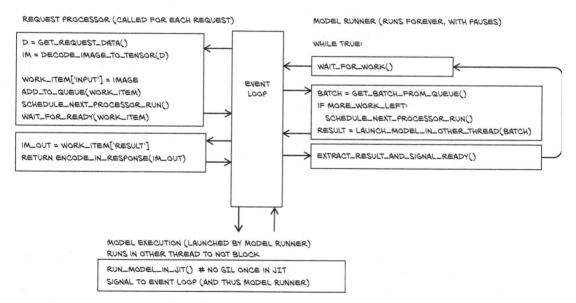

Figure 15.2 Our asynchronous server consists of three blocks: request processor, model runner, and model execution. These blocks are a bit like functions, but the first two will yield to the event loop in between.

---

[5] An alternative might be to forgo the timer and just run whenever the queue is not empty. This would potentially run smaller "first" batches, but the overall performance impact might not be so large for most applications.

All our interesting code is in a `ModelRunner` class, as shown in the following listing.

Listing 15.3   request_batching_server.py:32, ModelRunner

```
class ModelRunner:
    def __init__(self, model_name):
        self.model_name = model_name
        self.queue = []                 ⟵── The queue
        self.queue_lock = None

        self.model = get_pretrained_model(self.model_name,
                             map_location=device)    ⟵
        self.needs_processing = None

        self.needs_processing_timer = None   ⟵── Finally, the timer
```

This will become our lock. → `self.queue_lock = None`

Our signal to run the model → `self.needs_processing = None`

Loads and instantiates the model. This is the (only) thing we will need to change for switching to the JIT. For now, we import the CycleGAN (with the slight modification of standardizing to 0..1 input and output) from p3ch15/cyclegan.py.

`ModelRunner` first loads our model and takes care of some administrative things. In addition to the model, we also need a few other ingredients. We enter our requests into a `queue`. This is a just a Python list in which we add work items at the back and remove them in the front.

When we modify the `queue`, we want to prevent other tasks from changing the queue out from under us. To this effect, we introduce a `queue_lock` that will be an `asyncio.Lock` provided by the `asyncio` module. As all `asyncio` objects we use here need to know the event loop, which is only available after we initialize the application, we temporarily set it to `None` in the instantiation. While locking like this may not be strictly necessary because our methods do not hand back to the event loop while holding the lock, and operations on the queue are atomic thanks to the GIL, it does explicitly encode our underlying assumption. If we had multiple workers, we would need to look at locking. One caveat: Python's async locks are not threadsafe. (Sigh.)

`ModelRunner` waits when it has nothing to do. We need to signal it from `Request-Processor` that it should stop slacking off and get to work. This is done via an `asyncio.Event` called `needs_processing`. `ModelRunner` uses the `wait()` method to wait for the `needs_processing` event. The `RequestProcessor` then uses `set()` to signal, and `ModelRunner` wakes up and `clear()`s the event.

Finally, we need a timer to guarantee a maximal wait time. This timer is created when we need it by using `app.loop.call_at`. It sets the `needs_processing` event; we just reserve a slot now. So actually, sometimes the event will be set directly because a batch is complete or when the timer goes off. When we process a batch before the timer goes off, we will clear it so we don't do too much work.

FROM REQUEST TO QUEUE

Next we need to be able to enqueue requests, the core of the first part of `Request-Processor` in figure 15.2 (without the decoding and reencoding). We do this in our first async method, `process_input`.

Listing 15.4 request_batching_server.py:54

```
async def process_input(self, input):
    our_task = {"done_event": asyncio.Event(loop=app.loop),       Sets up the
                "input": input,                                    task data
                "time": app.loop.time()}
    async with self.queue_lock:                     With the lock, we
        if len(self.queue) >= MAX_QUEUE_SIZE:       add our task and ...
            raise HandlingError("I'm too busy", code=503)
        self.queue.append(our_task)                      ... schedule processing.
        self.schedule_processing_if_needed()             Processing will set
                                                         needs_processing if we have a
                                                         full batch. If we don't and no
    await our_task["done_event"].wait()                  timer is set, it will set one to
    return our_task["output"]                            when the max wait time is up.
```

**Waits (and hands back to the loop using
await) for the processing to finish**

We set up a little Python dictionary to hold our task's information: the `input` of course, the `time` it was queued, and a `done_event` to be set when the task has been processed. The processing adds an `output`.

Holding the queue lock (conveniently done in an `async with` block), we add our task to the queue and schedule processing if needed. As a precaution, we error out if the queue has become too large. Then all we have to do is wait for our task to be processed, and return it.

NOTE It is important to use the loop time (typically a monotonic clock), which may be different from the `time.time()`. Otherwise, we might end up with events scheduled for processing before they have been queued, or no processing at all.

This is all we need for the request processing (except decoding and encoding).

RUNNING BATCHES FROM THE QUEUE

Next, let's look at the `model_runner` function on the right side of figure 15.2, which does the model invocation.

Listing 15.5 request_batching_server.py:71, .run_model

```
async def model_runner(self):
    self.queue_lock = asyncio.Lock(loop=app.loop)
    self.needs_processing = asyncio.Event(loop=app.loop)
    while True:
        await self.needs_processing.wait()        Waits until there is something to do
        self.needs_processing.clear()
        if self.needs_processing_timer is not None:    Cancels the timer if it is set
            self.needs_processing_timer.cancel()
            self.needs_processing_timer = None
        async with self.queue_lock:                     Grabs a batch and schedules
            # ... line 87                                the running of the next batch,
            to_process = self.queue[:MAX_BATCH_SIZE]     if needed
            del self.queue[:len(to_process)]
```

```
    self.schedule_processing_if_needed()
batch = torch.stack([t["input"] for t in to_process], dim=0)
# we could delete inputs here...

result = await app.loop.run_in_executor(
    None, functools.partial(self.run_model, batch)
)
for t, r in zip(to_process, result):
    t["output"] = r
    t["done_event"].set()
del to_process
```

Runs the model in a separate thread, moving data to the device and then handing over to the model. We continue processing after it is done.

Adds the results to the work-item and sets the ready event

As indicated in figure 15.2, model_runner does some setup and then infinitely loops (but yields to the event loop in between). It is invoked when the app is instantiated, so it can set up queue_lock and the needs_processing event we discussed earlier. Then it goes into the loop, await-ing the needs_processing event.

When an event comes, first we check whether a time is set and, if so, clear it, because we'll be processing things now. Then model_runner grabs a batch from the queue and, if needed, schedules the processing of the next batch. It assembles the batch from the individual tasks and launches a new thread that evaluates the model using asyncio's app.loop.run_in_executor. Finally, it adds the outputs to the tasks and sets done_event.

And that's basically it. The web framework—roughly looking like Flask with async and await sprinkled in—needs a little wrapper. And we need to start the model_runner function on the event loop. As mentioned earlier, locking the queue really is not necessary if we do not have multiple runners taking from the queue and potentially interrupting each other, but knowing our code will be adapted to other projects, we stay on the safe side of losing requests.

We start our server with

```
python3 -m p3ch15.request_batching_server data/p1ch2/horse2zebra_0.4.0.pth
```

Now we can test by uploading the image data/p1ch2/horse.jpg and saving the result:

```
curl -T data/p1ch2/horse.jpg
➥ http://localhost:8000/image --output /tmp/res.jpg
```

Note that this server does get a few things right—it batches requests for the GPU and runs asynchronously—but we still use the Python mode, so the GIL hampers running our model in parallel to the request serving in the main thread. It will not be safe for potentially hostile environments like the internet. In particular, the decoding of request data seems neither optimal in speed nor completely safe.

In general, it would be nicer if we could have decoding where we pass the request stream to a function along with a preallocated memory chunk, and the function decodes the image from the stream to us. But we do not know of a library that does things this way.

15.2 Exporting models

So far, we have used PyTorch from the Python interpreter. But this is not always desirable: the GIL is still potentially blocking our improved web server. Or we might want to run on embedded systems where Python is too expensive or unavailable. This is when we export our model. There are several ways in which we can play this. We might go away from PyTorch entirely and move to more specialized frameworks. Or we might stay within the PyTorch ecosystem and use the JIT, a *just in time* compiler for a PyTorch-centric subset of Python. Even when we then run the JITed model in Python, we might be after two of its advantages: sometimes the JIT enables nifty optimizations, or—as in the case of our web server—we just want to escape the GIL, which JITed models do. Finally (but we take some time to get there), we might run our model under libtorch, the C++ library PyTorch offers, or with the derived Torch Mobile.

15.2.1 Interoperability beyond PyTorch with ONNX

Sometimes we want to leave the PyTorch ecosystem with our model in hand—for example, to run on embedded hardware with a specialized model deployment pipeline. For this purpose, Open Neural Network Exchange provides an interoperational format for neural networks and machine learning models (https://onnx.ai). Once exported, the model can be executed using any ONNX-compatible runtime, such as ONNX Runtime,[6] provided that the operations in use in our model are supported by the ONNX standard and the target runtime. It is, for example, quite a bit faster on the Raspberry Pi than running PyTorch directly. Beyond traditional hardware, a lot of specialized AI accelerator hardware supports ONNX (https://onnx.ai/supported-tools .html#deployModel).

In a way, a deep learning model is a program with a very specific instruction set, made of granular operations like matrix multiplication, convolution, relu, tanh, and so on. As such, if we can serialize the computation, we can reexecute it in another runtime that understands its low-level operations. ONNX is a standardization of a format describing those operations and their parameters.

Most of the modern deep learning frameworks support serialization of their computations to ONNX, and some of them can load an ONNX file and execute it (although this is not the case for PyTorch). Some low-footprint ("edge") devices accept an ONNX files as input and generate low-level instructions for the specific device. And some cloud computing providers now make it possible to upload an ONNX file and see it exposed through a REST endpoint.

In order to export a model to ONNX, we need to run a model with a dummy input: the values of the input tensors don't really matter; what matters is that they are the correct shape and type. By invoking the torch.onnx.export function, PyTorch

---

[6] The code lives at https://github.com/microsoft/onnxruntime, but be sure to read the privacy statement! Currently, building ONNX Runtime yourself will get you a package that does not send things to the mothership.

will *trace* the computations performed by the model and serialize them into an ONNX file with the provided name:

```
torch.onnx.export(seg_model, dummy_input, "seg_model.onnx")
```

The resulting ONNX file can now be run in a runtime, compiled to an edge device, or uploaded to a cloud service. It can be used from Python after installing `onnxruntime` or `onnxruntime-gpu` and getting a `batch` as a NumPy array.

Listing 15.6   onnx_example.py

```
import onnxruntime

sess = onnxruntime.InferenceSession("seg_model.onnx")  ◁─
input_name = sess.get_inputs()[0].name
pred_onnx, = sess.run(None, {input_name: batch})
```

The ONNX runtime API uses sessions to define models and then calls the run method with a set of named inputs. This is a somewhat typical setup when dealing with computations defined in static graphs.

Not all TorchScript operators can be represented as standardized ONNX operators. If we export operations foreign to ONNX, we will get errors about unknown `aten` operators when we try to use the runtime.

15.2.2 *PyTorch's own export: Tracing*

When interoperability is not the key, but we need to escape the Python GIL or otherwise export our network, we can use PyTorch's own representation, called the *Torch-Script graph*. We will see what that is and how the JIT that generates it works in the next section. But let's give it a spin right here and now.

The simplest way to make a TorchScript model is to trace it. This looks exactly like ONNX exporting. This isn't surprising, because that is what the ONNX model uses under the hood, too. Here we just feed dummy inputs into the model using the `torch.jit.trace` function. We import `UNetWrapper` from chapter 13, load the trained parameters, and put the model into evaluation mode.

Before we trace the model, there is one additional caveat: none of the parameters should require gradients, because using the `torch.no_grad()` context manager is strictly a runtime switch. Even if we trace the model within `no_grad` but then run it outside, PyTorch will record gradients. If we take a peek ahead at figure 15.4, we see why: after the model has been traced, we ask PyTorch to execute it. But the traced model will have parameters requiring gradients when executing the recorded operations, and they will make everything require gradients. To escape that, we would have to run the traced model in a `torch.no_grad` context. To spare us this—from experience, it is easy to forget and then be surprised by the lack of performance—we loop through the model parameters and set all of them to not require gradients.

But then all we need to do is call `torch.jit.trace`.[7]

Listing 15.7 trace_example.py

```
import torch
from p2ch13.model_seg import UNetWrapper

seg_dict = torch.load('data-unversioned/part2/models/p2ch13/seg_2019-10-20_15
➥ .57.21_none.best.state', map_location='cpu')
seg_model = UNetWrapper(in_channels=8, n_classes=1, depth=4, wf=3,
➥ padding=True, batch_norm=True, up_mode='upconv')
seg_model.load_state_dict(seg_dict['model_state'])
seg_model.eval()
for p in seg_model.parameters():         ⊲──┐ Sets the parameters to
    p.requires_grad_(False)                  │ not require gradients

dummy_input = torch.randn(1, 8, 512, 512)
traced_seg_model = torch.jit.trace(seg_model, dummy_input)   ⊲── The tracing
```

The tracing gives us a warning:

```
TracerWarning: Converting a tensor to a Python index might cause the trace
to be incorrect. We can't record the data flow of Python values, so this
value will be treated as a constant in the future. This means the trace
might not generalize to other inputs!
    return layer[:, :, diff_y:(diff_y + target_size[0]), diff_x:(diff_x +
➥ target_size[1])]
```

This stems from the cropping we do in U-Net, but as long as we only ever plan to feed images of size 512×512 into the model, we will be OK. In the next section, we'll take a closer look at what causes the warning and how to get around the limitation it highlights if we need to. It will also be important when we want to convert models that are more complex than convolutional networks and U-Nets to TorchScript.

We can save the traced model

```
torch.jit.save(traced_seg_model, 'traced_seg_model.pt')
```

and load it back without needed anything but the saved file, and then we can call it:

```
loaded_model = torch.jit.load('traced_seg_model.pt')
prediction = loaded_model(batch)
```

The PyTorch JIT will keep the model's state from when we saved it: that we had put it into evaluation mode and that our parameters do not require gradients. If we had not taken care of it beforehand, we would need to use `with torch.no_grad():` in the execution.

---

[7] Strictly speaking, this traces the model as a function. Recently, PyTorch gained the ability to preserve more of the module structure using `torch.jit.trace_module`, but for us, the plain tracing is sufficient.

TIP You can run the JITed and exported PyTorch model without keeping the source. However, we always want to establish a workflow where we automatically go from source model to installed JITed model for deployment. If we do not, we will find ourselves in a situation where we would like to tweak something with the model but have lost the ability to modify and regenerate. Always keep the source, Luke!

15.2.3 *Our server with a traced model*

Now is a good time to iterate our web server to what is, in this case, our final version. We can export the traced CycleGAN model as follows:

```
python3 p3ch15/cyclegan.py data/p1ch2/horse2zebra_0.4.0.pth
➥ data/p3ch15/traced_zebra_model.pt
```

Now we just need to replace the call to `get_pretrained_model` with `torch.jit.load` in our server (and drop the now-unnecessary `import` of `get_pretrained_model`). This also means our model runs independent of the GIL—and this is what we wanted our server to achieve here. For your convenience, we have put the small modifications in request_batching_jit_server.py. We can run it with the traced model file path as a command-line argument.

Now that we have had a taste of what the JIT can do for us, let's dive into the details!

15.3 *Interacting with the PyTorch JIT*

Debuting in PyTorch 1.0, the PyTorch JIT is at the center of quite a few recent innovations around PyTorch, not least of which is providing a rich set of deployment options.

15.3.1 *What to expect from moving beyond classic Python/PyTorch*

Quite often, Python is said to lack speed. While there is some truth to this, the tensor operations we use in PyTorch usually are in themselves large enough that the Python slowness between them is not a large issue. For small devices like smartphones, the memory overhead that Python brings might be more important. So keep in mind that frequently, the speedup gained by taking Python out of the computation is 10% or less.

Another immediate speedup from not running the model in Python only appears in multithreaded environments, but then it can be significant: because the intermediates are not Python objects, the computation is not affected by the menace of all Python parallelization, the GIL. This is what we had in mind earlier and realized when we used a traced model in our server.

Moving from the classic PyTorch way of executing one operation before looking at the next does give PyTorch a holistic view of the calculation: that is, it can consider the calculation in its entirety. This opens the door to crucial optimizations and higher-level transformations. Some of those apply mostly to inference, while others can also provide a significant speedup in training.

Let's use a quick example to give you a taste of why looking at several operations at once can be beneficial. When PyTorch runs a sequence of operations on the GPU, it calls a subprogram (*kernel*, in CUDA parlance) for each of them. Every kernel reads the input from GPU memory, computes the result, and then stores the result. Thus most of the time is typically spent not computing things, but reading from and writing to memory. This can be improved on by reading only once, computing several operations, and then writing at the very end. This is precisely what the PyTorch JIT fuser does. To give you an idea of how this works, figure 15.3 shows the pointwise computation taking place in long short-term memory (LSTM; https://en.wikipedia.org/wiki/Long_short-term_memory) cell, a popular building block for recurrent networks.

The details of figure 15.3 are not important to us here, but there are 5 inputs at the top, 2 outputs at the bottom, and 7 intermediate results represented as rounded indices. By computing all of this in one go in a single CUDA function and keeping the intermediates in registers, the JIT reduces the number of memory reads from 12 to 5 and the number of writes from 9 to 2. These are the large gains the JIT gets us; it can reduce the time to train an LSTM network by a factor of four. This seemingly simple

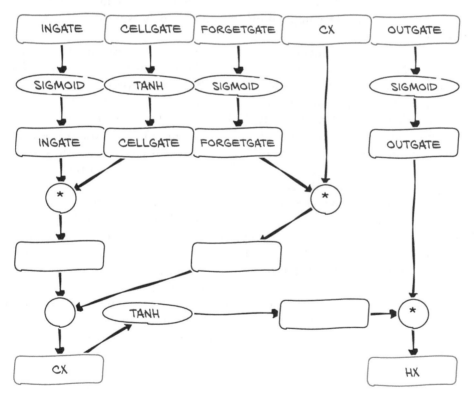

Figure 15.3 LSTM cell pointwise operations. From five inputs at the top, this block computes two outputs at the bottom. The boxes in between are intermediate results that vanilla PyTorch will store in memory but the JIT fuser will just keep in registers.

trick allows PyTorch to significantly narrow the gap between the speed of LSTM and generalized LSTM cells flexibly defined in PyTorch and the rigid but highly optimized LSTM implementation provided by libraries like cuDNN.

In summary, the speedup from using the JIT to escape Python is more modest than we might naively expect when we have been told that Python is awfully slow, but avoiding the GIL is a significant win for multithreaded applications. The large speedups in JITed models come from special optimizations that the JIT enables but that are more elaborate than just avoiding Python overhead.

15.3.2 *The dual nature of PyTorch as interface and backend*

To understand how moving beyond Python works, it is beneficial to mentally separate PyTorch into several parts. We saw a first glimpse of this in section 1.4. Our PyTorch torch.nn modules—which we first saw in chapter 6 and which have been our main tool for modeling ever since—hold the parameters of our network and are implemented using the functional interface: functions taking and returning tensors. These are implemented as a C++ extension, handed over to the C++-level autograd-enabled layer. (This then hands the actual computation to an internal library called ATen, performing the computation or relying on backends to do so, but this is not important.)

Given that the C++ functions are already there, the PyTorch developers made them into an official API. This is the nucleus of LibTorch, which allows us to write C++ tensor operations that look almost like their Python counterparts. As the torch.nn modules are Python-only by nature, the C++ API mirrors them in a namespace torch::nn that is designed to look a lot like the Python part but is independent.

This would allow us to redo in C++ what we did in Python. But that is not what we want: we want to *export* the model. Happily, there is another interface to the same functions provided by PyTorch: the PyTorch JIT. The PyTorch JIT provides a "symbolic" representation of the computation. This representation is the *TorchScript intermediate representation* (TorchScript IR, or sometimes just TorchScript). We mentioned TorchScript in section 15.2.2 when discussing delayed computation. In the following sections, we will see how to get this representation of our Python models and how they can be saved, loaded, and executed. Similar to what we discussed for the regular PyTorch API, the PyTorch JIT functions to load, inspect, and execute TorchScript modules can also be accessed both from Python and from C++.

In summary, we have four ways of calling PyTorch functions, illustrated in figure 15.4: from both C++ and Python, we can either call functions directly or have the JIT as an intermediary. All of these eventually call the C++ LibTorch functions and from there ATen and the computational backend.

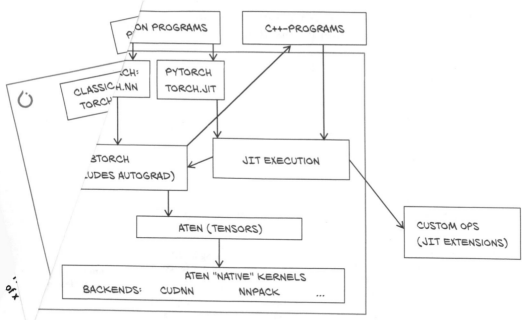

4 **Many ways of calling into PyTorch**

.3.3 TorchScript

TorchScript is at the center of the deployment options envisioned by PyTorch. As such, it is worth taking a close look at how it works.

There are two straightforward ways to create a TorchScript model: tracing and scripting. We will look at each of them in the following sections. At a very high level, the two work as follows:

- In *tracing*, which we used in in section 15.2.2, we execute our usual PyTorch model using sample (random) inputs. The PyTorch JIT has hooks (in the C++ autograd interface) for every function that allows it to record the computation. In a way, it is like saying "Watch how I compute the outputs—now you can do the same." Given that the JIT only comes into play when PyTorch functions (and also nn.Modules) are called, you can run any Python code while tracing but the JIT will only notice those bits (and notably be ignorant of control flow). When we use tensor shapes—usually a tuple of integers—the JIT tries to follc what's going on but may have to give up. This is what gave us the warning wh tracing the U-Net.

- In *scripting*, the PyTorch JIT looks at the actual Python code of our computa and compiles it into the TorchScript IR. This means that, while we can be that every aspect of our program is captured by the JIT, we are restrict those parts understood by the compiler. This is like saying "I am telling yor to do it—now you do the same." Sounds like programming, really.

We can also print the scripted graph, which is closer to the internal representation of TorchScript:

```
# In[5]:
xprint(scripted_fn.graph)
# end::cell_5_code[]

# tag::cell_5_output[]
# Out[5]:
graph(%x.1 : Tensor):
  %10 : bool = prim::Constant[value=1]()
  %2 : int = prim::Constant[value=0]()
  %5 : int = prim::Constant[value=1]()
  %y.1 : Tensor = aten::select(%x.1, %2, %2)
  %7 : int = aten::size(%x.1, %2)
  %9 : int = aten::__range_length(%5, %7, %5)
  %y : Tensor = prim::Loop(%9, %10, %y.1)
    block0(%11 : int, %y.6 : Tensor):
      %i.1 : int = aten::__derive_index(%11, %5, %5)
      %18 : Tensor = aten::select(%x.1, %2, %i.1)
      %y.3 : Tensor = aten::add(%y.6, %18, %5)
      -> (%10, %y.3)
  return (%y)
```

Seems a lot more verbose than we need ← (points to %10 line)

The first assignment of y ← (points to %y.1 line)

Constructing the range is recognizable after we see the code. ← (points to %9 line)

Our for loop returns the value (y) it calculates. → (points to %y line)

Body of the for loop: selects a slice, and adds to y ← (points to %i.1 / %18 / %y.3 lines)

In practice, you would most often use `torch.jit.script` in the form of a decorator:

```
@torch.jit.script
def myfn(x):
    ...
```

You could also do this with a custom `trace` decorator taking care of the inputs, but this has not caught on.

Although TorchScript (the language) looks like a subset of Python, there are fundamental differences. If we look very closely, we see that PyTorch has added type specifications to the code. This hints at an important difference: TorchScript is statically typed—every value (variable) in the program has one and only one type. Also, the types are limited to those for which the TorchScript IR has a representation. Within the program, the JIT will usually infer the type automatically, but we need to annotate any non-tensor arguments of scripted functions with their types. This is in stark contrast to Python, where we can assign anything to any variable.

So far, we've traced functions to get scripted functions. But we graduated from just using functions in chapter 5 to using modules a long time ago. Sure enough, we can also trace or script models. These will then behave roughly like the modules we know and love. For both tracing and scripting, we pass an instance of `Module` to `torch.jit.trace` (with sample inputs) or `torch.jit.script` (without sample inputs), respectively. This will give us the `forward` method we are used to. If we want to expose other methods (this only works in `scripting`) to be called from the outside, we decorate them with `@torch.jit.export` in the class definition.

When we said that the JITed modules work like they did in Python, this includes the fact that we can use them for training, too. On the flip side, this means we need to set them up for inference (for example, using the `torch.no_grad()` context) just like our traditional models, to make them do the right thing.

With algorithmically relatively simple models—like the CycleGAN, classification models and U-Net-based segmentation—we can just trace the model as we did earlier. For more complex models, a nifty property is that we can use scripted or traced functions from other scripted or traced code, and that we can use scripted or traced submodules when constructing and tracing or scripting a module. We can also trace functions by calling `nn.Models`, but then we need to set all parameters to not require gradients, as the parameters will be constants for the traced model.

As we have seen tracing already, let's look at a practical example of scripting in more detail.

15.3.4 *Scripting the gaps of traceability*

In more complex models, such as those from the Fast R-CNN family for detection or recurrent networks used in natural language processing, the bits with control flow like `for` loops need to be scripted. Similarly, if we needed the flexibility, we would find the code bit the tracer warned about.

Listing 15.8 From utils/unet.py

```
class UNetUpBlock(nn.Module):
    ...
    def center_crop(self, layer, target_size):
        _, _, layer_height, layer_width = layer.size()
        diff_y = (layer_height - target_size[0]) // 2
        diff_x = (layer_width - target_size[1]) // 2
        return layer[:, :, diff_y:(diff_y + target_size[0]),
        diff_x:(diff_x + target_size[1])]                        ◁──┐  The tracer warns here.

    def forward(self, x, bridge):
        ...
        crop1 = self.center_crop(bridge, up.shape[2:])
    ...
```

What happens is that the JIT magically replaces the shape tuple `up.shape` with a 1D integer tensor with the same information. Now the slicing `[2:]` and the calculation of `diff_x` and `diff_y` are all traceable tensor operations. However, that does not save us, because the slicing then wants Python `int`s; and there, the reach of the JIT ends, giving us the warning.

But we can solve this issue in a straightforward way: we script `center_crop`. We slightly change the cut between caller and callee by passing `up` to the scripted `center _crop` and extracting the sizes there. Other than that, all we need is to add the `@torch.jit.script` decorator. The result is the following code, which makes the U-Net model traceable without warnings.

Listing 15.9   Rewritten excerpt from utils/unet.py

```
@torch.jit.script
def center_crop(layer, target):                    ◄─┐  Changes the signature, taking
    _, _, layer_height, layer_width = layer.size()   │  target instead of target_size
    _, _, target_height, target_width = target.size()  ◄─┐
    diff_y = (layer_height - target_height) // 2          │  Gets the sizes within
    diff_x = (layer_width - target_width]) // 2           │  the scripted part
    return layer[:, :, diff_y:(diff_y + target_height),
➥    diff_x:(diff_x + target_width)]              ◄─┐
                                                      │  The indexing uses the
class UNetUpBlock(nn.Module):                         │  size values we got.
    ...

    def forward(self, x, bridge):
        ...                                      ┌─  We adapt our call to pass
        crop1 = center_crop(bridge, up)      ◄──┘   up rather than the size.
    ...
```

Another option we could choose—but that we will not use here—would be to move unscriptable things into custom operators implemented in C++. The TorchVision library does that for some specialty operations in Mask R-CNN models.

15.4   LibTorch: PyTorch in C++

We have seen various way to export our models, but so far, we have used Python. We'll now look at how we can forgo Python and work with C++ directly.

Let's go back to the horse-to-zebra CycleGAN example. We will now take the JITed model from section 15.2.3 and run it from a C++ program.

15.4.1   Running JITed models from C++

The hardest part about deploying PyTorch vision models in C++ is choosing an image library to choose the data.[8] Here, we go with the very lightweight library CImg (http://cimg.eu). If you are very familiar with OpenCV, you can adapt the code to use that instead; we just felt that CImg is easiest for our exposition.

Running a JITed model is very simple. We'll first show the image handling; it is not really what we are after, so we will do this very quickly.[9]

Listing 15.10   cyclegan_jit.cpp

```
#include "torch/script.h"          ◄─┐  Includes the PyTorch script header
#define cimg_use_jpeg                 │  and CImg with native JPEG support
#include "CImg.h"
using namespace cimg_library;
int main(int argc, char **argv) {   ┌─  Loads and decodes the
  CImg<float> image(argv[2]);     ◄─┘   image into a float array
```

---

[8] But TorchVision may develop a convenience function for loading images.

[9] The code works with PyTorch 1.4 and, hopefully, above. In PyTorch versions before 1.3 you needed `data` in place of `data_ptr`.

```
image = image.resize(227, 227);                           ◄─── Resizes to a smaller size
// ...here we need to produce an output tensor from input
CImg<float> out_img(output.data_ptr<float>(), output.size(2),          ◄──┐
                    output.size(3), 1, output.size(1));                    │
out_img.save(argv[3]);    ◄──┐                                             │
return 0;                    │      The method data_ptr<float>() gives us a pointer
}                    Saves the image │    to the tensor storage. With it and the shape
                                       information, we can construct the output image.
```

For the PyTorch side, we include a C++ header torch/script.h. Then we need to set up and include the CImg library. In the main function, we load an image from a file given on the command line and resize it (in CImg). So we now have a 227 × 227 image in the CImg<float> variable image. At the end of the program, we'll create an out_img of the same type from our (1, 3, 277, 277)-shaped tensor and save it.

Don't worry about these bits. They are not the PyTorch C++ we want to learn, so we can just take them as is.

The actual computation is straightforward, too. We need to make an input tensor from the image, load our model, and run the input tensor through it.

> **Listing 15.11 cyclegan_jit.cpp**

Puts the image data into a tensor
```
auto input_ = torch::tensor(                            Reshapes and rescales
    torch::ArrayRef<float>(image.data(), image.size()));  to move from CImg
auto input = input_.reshape({1, 3, image.height(),        conventions to
               image.width()}).div_(255);    ◄───────────┘ PyTorch's

auto module = torch::jit::load(argv[1]);    ◄───────────  Loads the JITed model
                                                          or function from a file
std::vector<torch::jit::IValue> inputs;    ◄───────
inputs.push_back(input);
auto output_ = module.forward(inputs).toTensor();    Packs the input into a (one-
                                                     element) vector of IValues
auto output = output_.contiguous().mul_(255);    ◄─┐
                                                   │
Calls the module and extracts the result tensor. For   Makes sure our result
efficiency, the ownership is moved, so if we held on    is contiguous
to the IValue, it would be empty afterward.
```

Recall from chapter 3 that PyTorch keeps the values of a tensor in a large chunk of memory in a particular order. So does CImg, and we can get a pointer to this memory chunk (as a float array) using image.data() and the number of elements using image.size(). With these two, we can create a somewhat smarter reference: a torch::ArrayRef (which is just shorthand for pointer plus size; PyTorch uses those at the C++ level for data but also for returning sizes without copying). Then we can just parse that into the torch::tensor constructor, just as we would with a list.

> **TIP** Sometimes you might want to use the similar-working torch::from_blob instead of torch::tensor. The difference is that tensor will copy the data. If you do not want copying, you can use from_blob, but then you need to take care that the underpinning memory is available during the lifetime of the tensor.

Our tensor is only 1D, so we need to reshape it. Conveniently, CImg uses the same ordering as PyTorch (channel, rows, columns). If not, we would need to adapt the reshaping and permute the axes as we did in chapter 4. As CImg uses a range of 0...255 and we made our model to use 0...1, we divide here and multiply later. This could, of course, be absorbed into the model, but we wanted to reuse our traced model.

> **A common pitfall to avoid: pre- and postprocessing**
>
> When switching from one library to another, it is easy to forget to check that the conversion steps are compatible. They are non-obvious unless we look up the memory layout and scaling convention of PyTorch and the image processing library we use. If we forget, we will be disappointed by not getting the results we anticipate.
>
> Here, the model would go wild because it gets extremely large inputs. However, in the end, the output convention of our model is to give RGB values in the 0..1 range. If we used this directly with CImg, the result would look all black.
>
> Other frameworks have other conventions: for example OpenCV likes to store images as BGR instead of RGB, requiring us to flip the channel dimension. We always want to make sure the input we feed to the model in the deployment is the same as what we fed into it in Python.

Loading the traced model is very straightforward using `torch::jit::load`. Next, we have to deal with an abstraction PyTorch introduces to bridge between Python and C++: we need to wrap our input in an `IValue` (or several `IValue`s), the *generic* data type for any value. A function in the JIT is passed a vector of `IValue`s, so we declare that and then `push_back` our input tensor. This will automatically wrap our tensor into an `IValue`. We feed this vector of `IValue`s to the forward and get a single one back. We can then unpack the tensor in the resulting `IValue` with `.toTensor`.

Here we see a bit about `IValue`s: they have a type (here, `Tensor`), but they could also be holding `int64_t`s or `double`s or a list of tensors. For example, if we had multiple outputs, we would get an `IValue` holding a list of tensors, which ultimately stems from the Python calling conventions. When we unpack a tensor from an `IValue` using `.toTensor`, the `IValue` transfers ownership (becomes invalid). But let's not worry about it; we got a tensor back. Because sometimes the model may return non-contiguous data (with gaps in the storage from chapter 3), but `CImg` reasonably requires us to provide it with a contiguous block, we call `contiguous`. It is important that we assign this contiguous tensor to a variable that is in scope until we are done working with the underlying memory. Just like in Python, PyTorch will free memory if it sees that no tensors are using it anymore.

So let's compile this! On Debian or Ubuntu, you need to install `cimg-dev`, `libjpeg-dev`, and `libx11-dev` to use `CImg`.

You can download a C++ library of PyTorch from the PyTorch page. But given that we already have PyTorch installed,[10] we might as well use that; it comes with all we need for C++. We need to know where our PyTorch installation lives, so open Python and check `torch.__file__`, which may say /usr/local/lib/python3.7/dist-packages/torch/__init__.py. This means the CMake files we need are in /usr/local/lib/python3.7/dist-packages/torch/share/cmake/.

While using CMake seems like overkill for a single source file project, linking to PyTorch is a bit complex; so we just use the following as a boilerplate CMake file.[11]

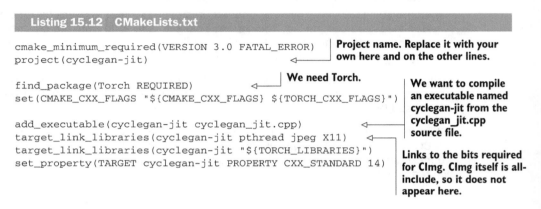

Listing 15.12   CMakeLists.txt

```
cmake_minimum_required(VERSION 3.0 FATAL_ERROR)
project(cyclegan-jit)

find_package(Torch REQUIRED)
set(CMAKE_CXX_FLAGS "${CMAKE_CXX_FLAGS} ${TORCH_CXX_FLAGS}")

add_executable(cyclegan-jit cyclegan_jit.cpp)
target_link_libraries(cyclegan-jit pthread jpeg X11)
target_link_libraries(cyclegan-jit "${TORCH_LIBRARIES}")
set_property(TARGET cyclegan-jit PROPERTY CXX_STANDARD 14)
```

Project name. Replace it with your own here and on the other lines.

We need Torch.

We want to compile an executable named cyclegan-jit from the cyclegan_jit.cpp source file.

Links to the bits required for CImg. CImg itself is all-include, so it does not appear here.

It is best to make a build directory as a subdirectory of where the source code resides and then in it run CMake as[12] `CMAKE_PREFIX_PATH=/usr/local/lib/python3.7/dist-packages/torch/share/cmake/ cmake ..` and finally `make`. This will build the `cyclegan-jit` program, which we can then run as follows:

```
./cyclegan-jit ../traced_zebra_model.pt  ../../data/p1ch2/horse.jpg /tmp/z.jpg
```

We just ran our PyTorch model without Python. Awesome! If you want to ship your application, you likely want to copy the libraries from /usr/local/lib/python3.7/dist-packages/torch/lib into where your executable is, so that they will always be found.

15.4.2 C++ from the start: The C++ API

The C++ modular API is intended to feel a lot like the Python one. To get a taste, we will translate the CycleGAN generator into a model natively defined in C++, but without the JIT. We do, however, need the pretrained weights, so we'll save a traced version of the model (and here it is important to trace not a function but the model).

---

[10] We hope you have not been slacking off about trying out things you read.

[11] The code directory has a bit longer version to work around Windows issues.

[12] You might have to replace the path with where your PyTorch or LibTorch installation is located. Note that the C++ library can be more picky than the Python one in terms of compatibility: If you are using a CUDA-enabled library, you need to have the matching CUDA headers installed. If you get cryptic error messages about "Caffe2 using CUDA," you need to install a CPU-only version of the library, but CMake found a CUDA-enabled one.

We'll start with some administrative details: includes and namespaces.

Listing 15.13   cyclegan_cpp_api.cpp

```
#include <torch/torch.h>        ◁┐  Imports the one-stop
#define cimg_use_jpeg              │  torch/torch.h header and CImg
#include <CImg.h>
using torch::Tensor;    ◁┐  Spelling out torch::Tensor can be tedious, so
                          │  we import the name into the main namespace.
```

When we look at the source code in the file, we find that `ConvTransposed2d` is ad hoc defined, when ideally it should be taken from the standard library. The issue here is that the C++ modular API is still under development; and with PyTorch 1.4, the pre-made `ConvTranspose2d` module cannot be used in `Sequential` because it takes an optional second argument.[13] Usually we could just leave `Sequential`—as we did for Python—but we want our model to have the same structure as the Python CycleGAN generator from chapter 2.

Next, let's look at the residual block.

Listing 15.14   Residual block in cyclegan_cpp_api.cpp

```
struct ResNetBlock : torch::nn::Module {
  torch::nn::Sequential conv_block;
  ResNetBlock(int64_t dim)           ┐  Initializes Sequential,
      : conv_block(          ◁───────┘  including its submodules
            torch::nn::ReflectionPad2d(1),
            torch::nn::Conv2d(torch::nn::Conv2dOptions(dim, dim, 3)),
            torch::nn::InstanceNorm2d(
            torch::nn::InstanceNorm2dOptions(dim)),
            torch::nn::ReLU(/*inplace=*/true),
        torch::nn::ReflectionPad2d(1),
            torch::nn::Conv2d(torch::nn::Conv2dOptions(dim, dim, 3)),
            torch::nn::InstanceNorm2d(
            torch::nn::InstanceNorm2dOptions(dim))) {
    register_module("conv_block", conv_block);   ◁┐  Always remember to register
  }                                                │  the modules you assign, or
                                                   │  bad things will happen!
  Tensor forward(const Tensor &inp) {
    return inp + conv_block->forward(inp);   ◁┐  As might be expected, our forward
  }                                            │  function is pretty simple.
};
```

Just as we would in Python, we register a subclass of `torch::nn::Module`. Our residual block has a sequential `conv_block` submodule.

And just as we did in Python, we need to initialize our submodules, notably `Sequential`. We do so using the C++ initialization statement. This is similar to how we

---

[13] This is a great improvement over PyTorch 1.3, where we needed to implement custom modules for ReLU, InstanceNorm2d, and others.

construct submodules in Python in the __init__ constructor. Unlike Python, C++ does not have the introspection and hooking capabilities that enable redirection of __setattr__ to combine assignment to a member and registration.

Since the lack of keyword arguments makes the parameter specification awkward with default arguments, modules (like tensor factory functions) typically take an options argument. Optional keyword arguments in Python correspond to methods of the options object that we can chain. For example, the Python module nn.Conv2d(in_channels, out_channels, kernel_size, stride=2, padding=1) that we need to convert translates to torch::nn::Conv2d(torch::nn::Conv2dOptions (in_channels, out_channels, kernel_size).stride(2).padding(1)). This is a bit more tedious, but you're reading this because you love C++ and aren't deterred by the hoops it makes you jump through.

We should always take care that registration and assignment to members is in sync, or things will not work as expected: for example, loading and updating parameters during training will happen to the registered module, but the actual module being called is a member. This synchronization was done behind the scenes by the Python nn.Module class, but it is not automatic in C++. Failing to do so will cause us many headaches.

In contrast to what we did (and should!) in Python, we need to call m->forward(…) for our modules. Some modules can also be called directly, but for Sequential, this is not currently the case.

A final comment on calling conventions is in order: depending on whether you modify tensors provided to functions,[14] tensor arguments should always be passed as const Tensor& for tensors that are left unchanged or Tensor if they are changed. Tensors should be returned as Tensor. Wrong argument types like non-const references (Tensor&) will lead to unparsable compiler errors.

In the main generator class, we'll follow a typical pattern in the C++ API more closely by naming our class ResNetGeneratorImpl and promoting it to a torch module ResNetGenerator using the TORCH_MODULE macro. The background is that we want to mostly handle modules as references or shared pointers. The wrapped class accomplishes this.

Listing 15.15 `ResNetGenerator` in cyclegan_cpp_api.cpp

```
                                          Adds modules to the Sequential container in the
                                          constructor. This allows us to add a variable
                                          number of modules in a for loop.
struct ResNetGeneratorImpl : torch::nn::Module {
  torch::nn::Sequential model;
  ResNetGeneratorImpl(int64_t input_nc = 3, int64_t output_nc = 3,
                      int64_t ngf = 64, int64_t n_blocks = 9) {
    TORCH_CHECK(n_blocks >= 0);
    model->push_back(torch::nn::ReflectionPad2d(3));     <—
```

---

[14] This is a bit blurry because you can create a new tensor sharing memory with an input and modify it in place, but it's best to avoid that if possible.

```
      ...
         model->push_back(torch::nn::Conv2d(
```
Spares us from reproducing some tedious things
```
           torch::nn::Conv2dOptions(ngf * mult, ngf * mult * 2, 3)
              .stride(2)
              .padding(1)));        ◄──── An example of Options in action
      ...
      register_module("model", model);
   }
   Tensor forward(const Tensor &inp) { return model->forward(inp); }
};
TORCH_MODULE(ResNetGenerator);    ◄──┐ Creates a wrapper ResNetGenerator around our
                                     │ ResNetGeneratorImpl class. As archaic as it seems,
                                     │ the matching names are important here.
```

That's it—we've defined the perfect C++ analogue of the Python `ResNetGenerator` model. Now we only need a `main` function to load parameters and run our model. Loading the image with CImg and converting from image to tensor and tensor back to image are the same as in the previous section. To include some variation, we'll display the image instead of writing it to disk.

Listing 15.16   cyclegan_cpp_api.cpp `main`

```
ResNetGenerator model;  ◄──── Instantiates our model
   ...
   torch::load(model, argv[1]);  ◄──┐ Loads the
   ...                              │ parameters
   cimg_library::CImg<float> image(argv[2]);
   image.resize(400, 400);
   auto input_ =
      torch::tensor(torch::ArrayRef<float>(image.data(), image.size()));
   auto input = input_.reshape({1, 3, image.height(), image.width()});
   torch::NoGradGuard no_grad;    ◄────

   model->eval();    ◄──┐ As in Python, eval mode is turned on (for our
                        │ model, it would not be strictly relevant).

   auto output = model->forward(input);    ◄──┐ Again, we call
   ...                                         │ forward rather
   cimg_library::CImg<float> out_img(output.data_ptr<float>(),  │ than the model.
                  output.size(3), output.size(2),
                  1, output.size(1));
   cimg_library::CImgDisplay disp(out_img, "See a C++ API zebra!");  ◄──┐
   while (!disp.is_closed()) {                                          │
     disp.wait();           Displaying the image, we need to wait for a key │
   }                        rather than immediately exiting our program. │
```

Declaring a guard variable is the equivalent of the torch.no_grad() context. You can put it in a { ... } block if you need to limit how long you turn off gradients.

The interesting changes are in how we create and run the model. Just as expected, we instantiate the model by declaring a variable of the model type. We load the model using `torch::load` (here it is important that we wrapped the model). While this looks very familiar to PyTorch practitioners, note that it will work on JIT-saved files rather than Python-serialized state dictionaries.

When running the model, we need the equivalent of `with torch.no_grad():`. This is provided by instantiating a variable of type `NoGradGuard` and keeping it in scope for as long as we do not want gradients. Just like in Python, we set the model into evaluation mode calling `model->eval()`. This time around, we call `model->forward` with our input tensor and get a tensor as a result—no JIT is involved, so we do not need `IValue` packing and unpacking.

Phew. Writing this in C++ was a lot of work for the Python fans that we are. We are glad that we only promised to do inference here, but of course LibTorch also offers optimizers, data loaders, and much more. The main reason to use the API is, of course, when you want to create models and neither the JIT nor Python is a good fit.

For your convenience, CMakeLists.txt contains also the instructions for building `cyclegan-cpp-api`, so building is just like in the previous section.

We can run the program as

```
./cyclegan_cpp_api ../traced_zebra_model.pt ../../data/p1ch2/horse.jpg
```

But we knew what the model would be doing, didn't we?

15.5 *Going mobile*

As the last variant of deploying a model, we will consider deployment to mobile devices. When we want to bring our models to mobile, we are typically looking at Android and/or iOS. Here, we'll focus on Android.

The C++ parts of PyTorch—LibTorch—can be compiled for Android, and we could access that from an app written in Java using the Android Java Native Interface (JNI). But we really only need a handful of functions from PyTorch—loading a JITed model, making inputs into tensors and `IValues`, running them through the model, and getting results back. To save us the trouble of using the JNI, the PyTorch developers wrapped these functions into a small library called PyTorch Mobile.

The stock way of developing apps in Android is to use the Android Studio IDE, and we will be using it, too. But this means there are a few dozen files of administrativa—which also happen to change from one Android version to the next. As such, we focus on the bits that turn one of the Android Studio templates (Java App with Empty Activity) into an app that takes a picture, runs it through our zebra-CycleGAN, and displays the result. Sticking with the theme of the book, we will be efficient with the Android bits (and they can be painful compared with writing PyTorch code) in the example app.

To infuse life into the template, we need to do three things. First, we need to define a UI. To keep things as simple as we can, we have two elements: a `TextView` named `headline` that we can click to take and transform a picture; and an `ImageView` to show our picture, which we call `image_view`. We will leave the picture-taking to the camera app (which you would likely avoid doing in an app for a smoother user experience), because dealing with the camera directly would blur our focus on deploying PyTorch models.[15]

---

[15] We are very proud of the topical metaphor.

Then, we need to include PyTorch as a dependency. This is done by editing our app's build.gradle file and adding `pytorch_android` and `pytorch_android_torchvision`.

Listing 15.17 Additions to build.gradle

```
dependencies {      ⟵┤ The dependencies section is very likely        The pytorch_android
    ...               │ already there. If not, add it at the bottom.   library gets the core things
    implementation 'org.pytorch:pytorch_android:1.4.0'  ⟵┘            mentioned in the text.

    implementation 'org.pytorch:pytorch_android_torchvision:1.4.0'    ⟵
}
```
> The helper library pytorch_android_torchvision—perhaps a bit immodestly named when compared to its larger TorchVision sibling—contains a few utilities to convert bitmap objects to tensors, but at the time of writing not much more.

We need to add our traced model as an asset.

Finally, we can get to the meat of our shiny app: the Java class derived from activity that contains our main code. We'll just discuss an excerpt here. It starts with imports and model setup.

Listing 15.18 MainActivity.java part 1

```
...
import org.pytorch.IValue;      ⟵── Don't you love imports?
import org.pytorch.Module;
import org.pytorch.Tensor;
import org.pytorch.torchvision.TensorImageUtils;
...
public class MainActivity extends AppCompatActivity {
    private org.pytorch.Module model;              ⟵── Holds our JITed model

    @Override
    protected void onCreate(Bundle savedInstanceState) {
        ...
        try {                          ⟵─┤ In Java we have to catch the exceptions.
            model = Module.load(assetFilePath(this, "traced_zebra_model.pt"));  ⟵
        } catch (IOException e) {
            Log.e("Zebraify", "Error reading assets", e);   Loads the module from a file
            finish();
        }
        ...
    }
    ...
}
```

We need some imports from the `org.pytorch` namespace. In the typical style that is a hallmark of Java, we import `IValue`, `Module`, and `Tensor`, which do what we might expect; and the class `org.pytorch.torchvision.TensorImageUtils`, which holds utility functions to convert between tensors and images.

First, of course, we need to declare a variable holding our model. Then, when our app is started—in `onCreate` of our activity—we'll load the module using the `Model.load` method from the location given as an argument. There is a slight complication though: apps' data is provided by the supplier as *assets* that are not easily accessible from the filesystem. For this reason, a utility method called `assetFilePath` (taken from the PyTorch Android examples) copies the asset to a location in the filesystem. Finally, in Java, we need to catch exceptions that our code throws, unless we want to (and are able to) declare the method we are coding as throwing them in turn.

When we get an image from the camera app using Android's `Intent` mechanism, we need to run it through our model and display it. This happens in the `onActivityResult` event handler.

Listing 15.19   MainActivity.java, part 2

Performs normalization, but the default is images in the range of 0…1 so we do not need to transform: that is, have 0 shift and a scaling divisor of 1.

Gets a tensor from a bitmap, combining steps like TorchVision's ToTensor (converting to a float tensor with entries between 0 and 1) and Normalize

```
@Override
protected void onActivityResult(int requestCode, int resultCode,
                                Intent data) {
    if (requestCode == REQUEST_IMAGE_CAPTURE &&
        resultCode == RESULT_OK) {
        Bitmap bitmap = (Bitmap) data.getExtras().get("data");

        final float[] means = {0.0f, 0.0f, 0.0f};
        final float[] stds = {1.0f, 1.0f, 1.0f};

        final Tensor inputTensor = TensorImageUtils.bitmapToFloat32Tensor(
            bitmap, means, stds);

        final Tensor outputTensor = model.forward(
            IValue.from(inputTensor)).toTensor();
        Bitmap output_bitmap = tensorToBitmap(outputTensor, means, stds,
            Bitmap.Config.RGB_565);
        image_view.setImageBitmap(output_bitmap);
    }
}
```

This is executed when the camera app takes a picture.

This looks almost like what we did in C++.

tensorToBitmap is our own invention.

Converting the bitmap we get from Android to a tensor is handled by the `TensorImageUtils.bitmapToFloat32Tensor` function (static method), which takes two float arrays, `means` and `stds`, in addition to `bitmap`. Here we specify the mean and standard deviation of our input data (set), which will then be mapped to have zero mean and unit standard deviation just like TorchVision's `Normalize` transform. Android already gives us the images in the 0..1 range that we need to feed into our model, so we specify mean 0 and standard deviation 1 to prevent the normalization from changing our image.

Around the actual call to `model.forward`, we then do the same `IValue` wrapping and unwrapping dance that we did when using the JIT in C++, except that our `forward` takes a single `IValue` rather than a vector of them. Finally, we need to get back to a bitmap. Here PyTorch will not help us, so we need to define our own `tensorToBitmap` (and submit the pull request to PyTorch). We spare you the details here, as they are tedious and full of copying (from the tensor to a `float[]` array to a `int[]` array containing ARGB values to the bitmap), but it is as it is. It is designed to be the inverse of `bitmapToFloat32Tensor`.

And that's all we need to do to get PyTorch into Android. Using the minimal additions to the code we left out here to request a picture, we have a `Zebraify` Android app that looks like in what we see in figure 15.5. Well done![16]

We should note that we end up with a full version of PyTorch with all ops on Android. This will, in general, also include operations you will not need for a given task, leading to the question of whether we could save some space by leaving them out. It turns out that starting with PyTorch 1.4, you can build a customized version of the PyTorch library that includes only the operations you need (see https://pytorch.org/mobile/android/#custom-build).

Figure 15.5   Our CycleGAN zebra app

15.5.1   Improving efficiency: Model design and quantization

If we want to explore mobile in more detail, our next step is to try to make our models faster. When we wish to reduce the memory and compute footprint of our models, the first thing to look at is streamlining the model itself: that is, computing the same or very similar mappings from inputs to outputs with fewer parameters and operations. This is often called *distillation*. The details of distillation vary—sometimes we try to shrink each weight by eliminating small or irrelevant weights;[17] in other examples, we combine several layers of a net into one (DistilBERT) or even train a fully different, simpler model to reproduce the larger model's outputs (OpenNMT's original CTranslate). We mention this because these modifications are likely to be the first step in getting models to run faster.

Another approach to is to reduce the footprint of each parameter and operation: instead of expending the usual 32-bit per parameter in the form of a float, we convert our model to work with integers (a typical choice is 8-bit). This is *quantization*.[18]

---

[16] At the time of writing, PyTorch Mobile is still relatively young, and you may hit rough edges. On Pytorch 1.3, the colors were off on an actual 32-bit ARM phone while working in the emulator. The reason is likely a bug in one of the computational backend functions that are only used on ARM. With PyTorch 1.4 and a newer phone (64-bit ARM), it seemed to work better.

[17] Examples include the Lottery Ticket Hypothesis and WaveRNN.

[18] In contrast to quantization, (partially) moving to 16-bit floating-point for training is usually called *reduced* or (if some bits stay 32-bit) *mixed-precision* training.

PyTorch does offer quantized tensors for this purpose. They are exposed as a set of scalar types similar to `torch.float`, `torch.double`, and `torch.long` (compare section 3.5). The most common quantized tensor scalar types are `torch.quint8` and `torch.qint8`, representing numbers as unsigned and signed 8-bit integers, respectively. PyTorch uses a separate scalar type here in order to use the dispatch mechanism we briefly looked at in section 3.11.

It might seem surprising that using 8-bit integers instead of 32-bit floating-points works at all; and typically there is a slight degradation in results, but not much. Two things seem to contribute: if we consider rounding errors as essentially random, and convolutions and linear layers as weighted averages, we may expect rounding errors to typically cancel.[19] This allows reducing the relative precision from more than 20 bits in 32-bit floating-points to the 7 bits that signed integers offer. The other thing quantization does (in contrast to training with 16-bit floating-points) is move from floating-point to fixed precision (per tensor or channel). This means the largest values are resolved to 7-bit precision, and values that are one-eighth of the largest values to only $7 - 3 = 4$ bits. But if things like L1 regularization (briefly mentioned in chapter 8) work, we might hope similar effects allow us to afford less precision to the smaller values in our weights when quantizing. In many cases, they do.

Quantization debuted with PyTorch 1.3 and is still a bit rough in terms of supported operations in PyTorch 1.4. It is rapidly maturing, though, and we recommend checking it out if you are serious about computationally efficient deployment.

15.6 *Emerging technology: Enterprise serving of PyTorch models*

We may ask ourselves whether all the deployment aspects discussed so far should involve as much coding as they do. Sure, it is common enough for someone to code all that. As of early 2020, while we are busy with the finishing touches to the book, we have great expectations for the near future; but at the same time, we feel that the deployment landscape will significantly change by the summer.

Currently, RedisAI (https://github.com/RedisAI/redisai-py), which one of the authors is involved with, is waiting to apply Redis goodness to our models. PyTorch has just experimentally released TorchServe (after this book is finalized, see https://pytorch.org/blog/pytorch-library-updates-new-model-serving-library/#torchserve-experimental).

Similarly, MLflow (https://mlflow.org) is building out more and more support, and Cortex (https://cortex.dev) wants us to use it to deploy models. For the more specific task of information retrieval, there also is EuclidesDB (https://euclidesdb.readthedocs.io/en/latest) to do AI-based feature databases.

Exciting times, but unfortunately, they do not sync with our writing schedule. We hope to have more to tell in the second edition (or a second book)!

---

[19] Fancy people would refer to the Central Limit Theorem here. And indeed, we must take care that the independence (in the statistical sense) of rounding errors is preserved. For example, we usually want zero (a prominent output of ReLU) to be exactly representable. Otherwise, all the zeros would be changed by the exact same quantity in rounding, leading to errors adding up rather than canceling.

15.7 Conclusion

This concludes our short tour of how to get our models out to where we want to apply them. While the ready-made Torch serving is not quite there yet as we write this, when it arrives you will likely want to export your models through the JIT—so you'll be glad we went through it here. In the meantime, you now know how to deploy your model to a network service, in a C++ application, or on mobile. We look forward to seeing what you will build!

Hopefully we've also delivered on the promise of this book: a working knowledge of deep learning basics, and a level of comfort with the PyTorch library. We hope you've enjoyed reading as much as we've enjoyed writing.[20]

15.8 Exercises

As we close out *Deep Learning with PyTorch*, we have one final exercise for you:

1 Pick a project that sounds exciting to you. Kaggle is a great place to start looking. Dive in.

You have acquired the skills and learned the tools you need to succeed. We can't wait to hear what you do next; drop us a line on the book's forum and let us know!

15.9 Summary

- We can serve PyTorch models by wrapping them in a Python web server framework such as Flask.
- By using JITed models, we can avoid the GIL even when calling them from Python, which is a good idea for serving.
- Request batching and asynchronous processing helps use resources efficiently, in particular when inference is on the GPU.
- To export models beyond PyTorch, ONNX is a great format. ONNX Runtime provides a backend for many purposes, including the Raspberry Pi.
- The JIT allows you to export and run arbitrary PyTorch code in C++ or on mobile with little effort.
- Tracing is the easiest way to get JITed models; you might need to use scripting for some particularly dynamic parts.
- There also is good support for C++ (and an increasing number of other languages) for running models both JITed and natively.
- PyTorch Mobile lets us easily integrate JITed models into Android or iOS apps.
- For mobile deployments, we want to streamline the model architecture and quantize models if possible.
- A few deployment frameworks are emerging, but a standard isn't quite visible yet.

---

[20] More, actually; writing books is hard!

index